Pace
University
New York · Westchester

PACE PLAZA
NEW YORK

The Sonata in the Baroque Era

VI SONATAS or SOLOS
Three for a VIOLIN & Three for a FLUTE
with a Thorough Bass for ye Harpsychord
Most humbly Dedicated
TO THE RIGHT HONOURABLE
CHARLES EARL of MANCHESTER
Viscount Mandevil Baron Kimbolton
and LORD LIEUTENANT of the
county of HUNTINGDON
by ye Author Godfry Finger

London Printed for & Sold by John Walsh. Servant to his Majesty at the Harp and Hautboy in Katherine Street
near Somerset House in the Strand

THE SONATA
IN THE
BAROQUE ERA

THIRD EDITION

By WILLIAM S. NEWMAN

The Norton Library
W · W · NORTON & COMPANY · INC ·
NEW YORK

To My Father

W. W. Norton & Company, Inc. is the publisher of current
or forthcoming books on music by Putnam Aldrich, William Austin,
Anthony Baines, Philip Bate, Sol Berkowitz, Friedrich Blume, How-
ard Boatwright, Nadia Boulanger, Paul Brainerd, Nathan Broder,
Manfred Bukofzer, John Castellini, John Clough, Doda Conrad,
Aaron Copland, Hans David, Paul Des Marais, Otto Erich Deutsch,
Frederick Dorian, Alfred Einstein, Gabriel Fontrier, Harold Gleason,
Richard Franko Goldman, Noah Greenberg, Donald Jay Grout,
James Haar, F. L. Harrison, Daniel Heartz, Richard Hoppin, John
Horton, Edgar Hunt, A. J. B. Hutchings, Charles Ives, Roger
Kamien, Hermann Keller, Leo Kraft, Stanley Krebs, Paul Henry
Lang, Lyndesay G. Langwill, Jens Peter Larsen, Jan LaRue, Maurice
Lieberman, Irving Lowens, Joseph Machlis, Carol McClintock,
Alfred Mann, W. T. Marrocco, Arthur Mendel, William J. Mitchell,
Douglas Moore, Joel Newman, John F. Ohl, Carl Parrish, Vincent
Persichetti, Marc Pincherle, Walter Piston, Gustave Reese, Alexander
Ringer, Curt Sachs, Denis Stevens, Robert Stevenson, Oliver Strunk,
Francis Toye, Bruno Walter, J. T. Westrup, Emanuel Winternitz,
Walter Wiora, and Percy Young.

SBN   393   00622   0

PRINTED IN THE UNITED STATES OF AMERICA

1 2 3 4 5 6 7 8 9 0

Preface
to the First Edition

In this book Chapter 1 is devoted to most of those questions that are usually explored, if with less to-do, in a preface—in particular, questions of scope, meaning, purpose, rationale, and method. There remain only two other matters of an introductory nature to bring up. These, having less place in the main body of the text, are the reason for this Preface.

One matter concerns a minor fact of editorial policy. The reader needs to be cautioned that the spelling and punctuation, though not necessarily the capitalization, of titles and other direct quotations are retained here as they were found in the "best" (usually the earliest) sources available to me. Once a start is made toward "correcting" or modernizing such spelling and punctuation there is no place to draw the line. Instead, one grand *SIC* must be offered here, to be applied ad libitum throughout the book. To be sure, that *sic* could be a carte blanche for carelessness on the author's part. And allowance must always be made, in any case, for the inevitable human errors, especially in a study so filled with fussy details. But the reader may want to check back for himself before condemning such eye-stoppers as "Opera primo," "violadigambicae," or alternatives like "Folia" and "Follia."

When a choice must be made between present-day word forms and spellings, arbitrary decisions are often necessary. That I have preferred the spelling "Georg Friedrich Handel," or "Milan" on the one hand and "Torino" on the other, or Della Corte for one name and Laurencie (rather than La Laurencie) for another can only be explained by my decision to follow certain standard reference works and not others in such matters.

The other, more important matter to bring up is the valued help that has come to this project from many quarters and many persons. In the first place, it would have been impossible to examine much of the more obscure music without the scarce editions, the microfilms, and the scores prepared from separate parts that individual scholars have generously lent to me. For this sort of help I am especially indebted to the late Dr. Alfred Einstein, who sent to me all the instrumental volumes from the priceless collection of 16th-, 17th-, and 18th-century music that he himself copied and scored (see EINSTEIN-SCORESm in the Bibliography) ; to Professor Ross Lee Finney at the University of Michigan, who permitted me to use the scores he made of Italian sonatas in ANTH. ROSTm and in various single publications by Castello, Uccellini, Legrenzi, Cazzati, and Fontana; to Professor William Klenz at Duke University, who made available to me his extensive microfilm collection of 17th-century instrumental music by Bolognese and Modenese composers, and in particular the sonatas by G. M. Bononcini that he has scored; to Professor Henry G. Mishkin at Amherst College, who lent to me his sonatas by Cazzati and Borri that he has scored, and a copy of VATIELLI-MAESTRIm; to Professor James Monroe at Northeast Louisiana State College, who scored all Del Buono's known sonatas; to Mrs. Jane Sumpter Hall, who scored over 40 sonatas by Vivaldi; to Mr. Lee Bostian at the University of North Carolina, who has let me use the scores of Boyce's sonatas that he has prepared; to Professor Herbert Fred at the University of North Carolina, who has let me use his microfilms and editions of sonatas by Pepusch; to Professor Beekman C. Cannon at Yale University, who has furnished reproductions of keyboard sonatas by Mattheson; to Messrs. James Haar and Philip Nelson, who, while studying abroad, helped me to secure sonatas by Marcello; and to Marc Pincherle of Paris, who provided me with a microfilm of the draft of Ecorcheville's unfinished sonata history.

Others have contributed importantly by giving their time and experience to general consultations about the broad problems of sonata history and to authoritative advice on more specific problems such as difficult translations, questions of etymology, single areas of research, and selected chapters in the draft of this book. Some of these persons I have been able to recognize at appropriate places in the text. But without attempting to enumerate here the many and varied contributions they have made I should like especially to express my gratitude to the following: the late Arthur Shepherd, Professor Emeritus at Western Reserve University; Professor Glen Haydon, Chairman of the Department of Music at the University of North Carolina; Dr. George Sherman Dickinson, Professor Emeritus of Vassar College; Professor David D. Boyden, Chairman of the Department of Music at the University of California in Berkeley; Dr. Wolf Franck of New York City; Professor

Paul Lang at Columbia University; Professor Gustave Reese at New York University; Dr. Otto Kinkeldey, Professor Emeritus of Cornell University; Mrs. Helen Bullock at the National Trust for Historic Presentation in Washington; Professor Willis Gates at Willamette University; Professor Willi Apel at Indiana University; Dr. J. M. Coopersmith at the Library of Congress; Professors George S. Lane, Edgar Alden, Joel Carter, and Wilton Mason, and Mr. Edgar Vom Lehn, at the University of North Carolina; Professor Denis Stevens, currently at McGill University in Montreal; Dr. Eduard Reeser in Bilthoven, Holland; Professor Thurston Dart at Jesus College in Cambridge, England; Claudio Sartori in Milan; Ottavio Tiby in Palermo; and Santiago Kastner in Lisbon.

A book of this sort ordinarily depends on assistance from many libraries—many more, in fact, than can be listed here. But I should like in particular to convey my sincere thanks to the more-than-willing staffs of certain institutions that I have periodically bombarded with "urgent" correspondence, or where I have camped for unconscionable periods of frenetic activity in the "stacks." These institutions include the Library of Congress in Washington (with special thanks to the Reference Librarians in the Music Division, Richard Hill and William Lichtenwanger), the Boston Public Library, the New York Public Library, the University of North Carolina libraries (where the staff at the Reference Desk and the music librarians Keith Mixter and Robert Gould have continually responded with efforts well beyond the normal call of duty), the British Museum in London, the Bibliothèque nationale in Paris, and the Biblioteca "G. B. Martini" in Bologna.

Furthermore, I am glad of this opportunity to restate my appreciation of several grants over the last dozen years that have subsidized the research done on this book and the publication of it. These grants include two from the Carnegie Research Foundation, one from the Ford Foundation, two from the University (of North Carolina) Research Council, and a "Kenan Leave" from the University of North Carolina. With this acknowledgment should also go my sincere thanks to the staff of the University of North Carolina Press, who have co-operated so fully and cordially in the present project.

I am grateful, too, to the several firms who have permitted direct quotations from books and music that they publish. These are acknowledged specifically where they occur in the text.

Finally, I find myself least able to put in words the gratitude I feel most deeply of all. I shall have to content myself with the observation that the young lady who had taken no more than a single music appreciation course when we married has become not an assistant in this project but a full partner as in everything else. W.S.N., Chapel Hill, 1959

ABBREVIATIONS

The abbreviations used in this book include some that are standard in most research writing and others that are meant to be self-explanatory to readers at home in Baroque music. In any case, there should be no special problem. Bibliographic references are shortened and set off by small capitals, followed by a lower-case "m" when the item is primarily a music score. These references are assembled and amplified in the one alphabetic sequence of the Bibliography at the end. Abbreviated references to instrumental scorings and groupings are explained in the early pages of Chapter 5.

THE REVISED EDITION

I have taken advantage of the opportunity provided by this revised edition to correct some details, clarify some others, and, mainly, call attention to nearly three hundred new studies, editions, private communications, and other pertinent bits of information that have been published or otherwise made known to me since the first printing in early 1959. The new information is inserted here primarily in additional notes, which are keyed into the margins of the pages and appear in an Addenda beginning on page 393.

The new names of more than passing interest in the new notes have been added to the Index. But the new publications and dissertation titles have not been given short titles or added to the Bibliography unless they are cited at least twice.

The new information derives not only from newly published research, including such aids, already widely consulted, as the *British Union Catalogue*, MGG (up to letter "T" as of this writing), and Ricordi's four-volume *Enciclopedia della musica*, but it also derives from detailed reviews, letters, and other valued advice, especially that of Jan LaRue, Wiley Hitchcock, Ingmar Bengtsson, Peter Evans, Jack Westrup, Franklin B. Zimmerman, Robert Preston, G. Jean Shaw, and Anne Kish—to all of whom and to the others who have helped, my grateful thanks! W.S.N., March 1966

THE PAPERBACK EDITION

I have taken advantage of this paperback edition to incorporate further revisions and updating in both the text proper and the Addenda starting on page 393. The Addenda are consolidated into one paginal sequence. W.S.N., August 1971

Contents

Music Examples

Chapter 1

Introduction, Confession, and Apologia

Some Problems of Sonata History

The Sonata in the Baroque Era is the first volume in a projected "History of the Sonata Idea" or, more exactly, a history of what the word "sonata" has meant and how it has been used from its first appearance as an instrumental title in the 16th century to its continuing application in today's musical concepts. The decision to start with the separate publication of this volume was based on several factors. Between the Baroque and Classic sonata concepts there is a clear break—clearer, in fact, than there is between the Classic and Romantic, or even the Romantic and Modern concepts. But doing the Baroque separately was more than a matter of writing an introductory *Das Rheingold* in order to explain the rest of the tetralogy. On a purely quantitative as well as a qualitative basis the sonata in the Baroque Era proves to make a very respectable showing alongside the sonata of any other era. To these factors may be added the manifest need for a separate, comprehensive survey of the Baroque sonata, with its own special traits, literature, and research problems. And finally, there is the practical consideration of length. The present volume is already larger and more detailed than many a publisher would deem practical. Yet only at that level of detail has it been possible to take in the most significant research on the subject and to disclose other aspects not previously explored. Indeed, while the reader may look askance at such detail, the author laments having to pare his subject to the bone!

To clarify further the what and the why of our subject it may help to retrace a few crucial turns along the unexpectedly tortuous path the present project has had to take over some 20 years. This much autobiography, as against the more impersonal style in the main body of the book, will perhaps be excused as the most expedient way to introduce the sonata's chief problems. Certainly, every initiated researcher knows how his path can be made tortuous not merely by the usual conflicts between such extracurricular projects and one's regular duties, but by all those false starts, dead ends, and other expendable efforts, all the flailing about and confusion that are likely to delay any new project. These are delays hard to avoid, at least until the first and perhaps the biggest problem of all is solved, which is to discover what *is* the problem. Only then can one begin to decide how his subject will be defined, delimited, and organized, and by what tools of research and analysis it can best be brought under control.

My interest in the sonata began, quite as would be expected, with the playing and composing of sonatas. Both experiences are there to thank for some inside views of sonata problems, early as well as recent. They have been responsible, too, for the development of a comprehensive sonata library that has provided much of the source material for the present study.[1] My actual beginning on the path to a sonata history was, as also might be expected, an academic dissertation.[2] From its start the intention had been ultimately to extend it into a much more inclusive study. But a completed dissertation, all nicely typed and bound, is something better left alone. More often than not it becomes a Pandora's box of new problems the moment one attempts to re-examine or extend its findings. No sooner had I resumed work in the field than disturbing questions began to arise, especially in the historical introduction to my main topic, the present-day sonata. For one thing, I was becoming increasingly aware[3] of fallacies in the "evolutionary" approach, an approach nowhere more labored than in sonata historiography, although it can be valid enough within any one phase of development. Repeatedly the first object of existing studies on early sonatas turned out to be not an exposition of the music on its own terms but an evaluation of it based on the extent to which it anticipated the eventual "sonata-allegro" form. Such an evaluation came to seem more and more irrelevant to me, whether as a criterion for an earlier era or even as a criterion for the Classic Era itself, when that form was supposed to reign supreme.

It was this first postdoctoral change of direction that was explored in my earliest publications concerned with the sonata. In one study I concluded that the concept of "sonata-allegro" form as we read it in our 19th- and 20th-century textbooks did not become a fully conscious one until well after the chief composers and theorists of the Classic Era had lived.[4] In another study and a related edition of sonatas the con-

---

1. Cf. NEWMAN-COLLECTOR.   2. NEWMAN-TREND.
3. Thanks partly to ALLEN-PHILOSOPHIES.   4. -THEORISTS.

clusion was reached that doubtful applications of this concept had led to doubtful evaluations of the sonatas by J. S. Bach's best known sons;[5] and in another edition the object was to bring back to light some worthy sonatas apparently blocked from view by preoccupations with the same concept.[6]

The successive shifts of view and direction that followed during the next several years largely grew out of attempts to work with this problem in some more positive way—that is, to find a more flexible approach to sonata form or, rather, sonata forms.   I valued a suggestion from Paul Lang to the effect that musical textures might provide basic clues to Classic and other forms, one result being a study of the "accompanied clavier sonata" as a missing link between Baroque and Classic chamber music.[7]   An effort to penetrate the dynamic nature of sonata forms led to a study of climax as a structural determinant.[8]   And an effort to consider musical form as a generative process—that is, as the structural result of tendencies inherent in its primary ideas—seemed to yield a more fluid approach to form analysis.[9]

During those years of exploration two abortive drafts of the projected history were started, one before and one after World War II. Their failure to reach completion must be charged to problems of definition and organization that still precluded a satisfactory approach to the subject.   About all that it has been possible to salvage from the drafts are a few studies on individual composers,[10] including attempts to make some order out of the bibliographic chaos that confronts most research behind the scenes of Baroque music.   The writing of the present book was finally started only after views diametrically opposite those I originally held were reached on several of the sonata's most basic problems.   To summarize these views comes within the province of the next section in this chapter.

The Scope of This Study

How complete was my reversal of certain views on the sonata— inherited views, they might be called—is illustrated by the one point of contrast most basic to the scope of this study.   In the first draft I set out to write *the history of a single principle, by whatever terms it might be called;* here my aim has been *the history of a single term, by whatever principles it might be governed.*   The former course almost inescapably requires an "evolutionary" approach; *the present course is a semantic*

5. -BACH and -BACHm (with preface).
6. -THIRTEENm.   7. -ACCOMPANIED.
8. -CLIMAX.   9. -GENERATIVE.
10. -DEL BUONO; -ALBINONI; -MARCELLO; -RAVENSCROFT.

approach. To trace the rise (and fall?) of a single principle tends to focus all sonata history on a single peak. Then, no other development has validity except as it leads to or from the consummate masterpieces of Beethoven, or Mozart, or Brahms, or any other composer regarded as exemplifying this peak. The peak tends to become the standard of measure for all else; the basis for selecting just those composers and examples that illustrate "evolutionary" and "devolutionary" trends, even when one composer's work may not have been known to the next; the incentive for discovering causal relationships, however far-fetched or labored; and the occasion for hunting melodic resemblances[11] or devising lettered schemes[12] that will show the "progress" of form. On the other hand, to trace the developing meaning of a term permits each composer to be taken at his own word. To be sure, in this way will be included many a piece called "sonata" that the proponent of any one "sonata principle," viewing it only with hindsight, must reject as invalid. But now it is the sonatas that are allowed to determine the trends, and not the trends the sonatas, as it were.

Immediately, the idea of a semantic approach is bound to raise two questions. First, was the word "sonata" used consistently enough in the Baroque Era, especially in the 17th century, to have any real significance? Second, is there anything more than the word itself to give continuity to nearly four centuries of "sonata" history? The answer to both questions is a qualified "yes." Taking the first question first, the word "sonata" did make its first appearances merely as the general term for any music to be played on instruments rather than sung by voices. But, as will be seen in the next chapter, it quickly acquired meanings at least no more vague than "sinfonia," "canzona," or other instrumental titles of the period. In fact, almost from the start theorists attempted to distinguish it from other types, and composers revealed individual if not general distinctions, each in his own works. By the second half of the 17th century the word's application, at least in Italy, was already fairly clear and consistent. One of the most fascinating aspects of sonata history is the way "sonata" took on more and more definite shape and meaning during that century. Modern writers have tended to overstate this word's vagueness at the time. That fact and their apparent predilection for anything called "sonata"—perhaps by association with favorite masterpieces of later centuries—even seems to have caused the title to be used in numerous modern editions over pieces not so called.[13] With these considerations in mind, the reader will

11. E.g., cf. SEIFFERT-KLAVIERMUSIK, *passim.*
12. E.g., cf. BOSQUET-ORIGINE.
13. E.g., the "sonatas" reprinted in SCHERING-BEISPIELEm, no. 182, RIEMANN-

perhaps understand in succeeding chapters what might otherwise seem to be undue attention to such matters.

As to the second question, whether there is anything more than the word itself to unify nearly four centuries of sonata history, the fact must be acknowledged at once that there is virtually no known instrumental form that has not been included under that title at one time or another. Furthermore, there is a vast gulf in kind as well as degree between, say, a little organ "Suonata" by Banchieri in 1605 and the recent *III. Sonate für Klavier* by Hindemith. Yet an over-all unity does exist, one that others have argued for, too (among them, Jules Écorcheville, who left an incomplete draft of a sonata history dated 1897[14]). Although no valid over-all definition can be formulated around any one, or even any several form principles, it is possible to list six basic traits that have prevailed throughout at least the main currents of sonata history. Thus, first, the sonata has always been an instrumental piece, aside from a rare example here and there with one or more voice parts. Second, it has been largely if not quite so consistently limited to solo or chamber music—that is, music for from one to about four players. Third, it has usually comprised a cycle of several contrasting movements, some notable one-movement exceptions notwithstanding. Fourth, it has consisted primarily of "absolute" music, again in spite of some notable exceptions. Fifth, it has characteristically embodied the broadest structural principles and, hence, has provided the most extended designs in "absolute" music. And sixth, the sonata has generally served an aesthetic or diversional rather than a utilitarian purpose, even in the Baroque Era (as discussed in chap. 3).

Most of the exceptions to these six traits did occur in the Baroque Era, while "sonata" was crystallizing into a first tangible concept (recalling one of our reasons for giving a separate volume to the Baroque sonata). One may also note that one or more of the same traits have characterized other instrumental forms from time to time, too, chiefly as these forms crossed paths with the sonata. But to no other form have they applied over so long a period or so generally. Now, if one over-all definition be attempted, something like the following will result: Primarily, *the sonata is a solo or chamber instrumental cycle of aesthetic or diversional purpose, consisting of several contrasting movements that are based on relatively extended designs in "absolute" music.*

Such a definition may still seem rather general. But it is no more

---

BEISPIELEm, no. 99, and Ex. 13 in BUKOFZER-BAROQUE, p. 53, were all originally called "Symphonia" or "Sinfonia."

14. P. 4 ff. in the typed MS, now in the library of Marc Pincherle, who has very kindly provided a copy on microfilm.

so than the definitions one would have to give for allied, concurrent forms like the concerto or symphony if their over-all histories were likewise to be included. In at least one sense the historian who preferred to trace a single sonata principle would have to be still more general. He would feel obliged to include the symphony, concerto, string quartet, or any other type whenever it revealed this principle. Yet writers on the latter types—to which, by the way, they have devoted several over-all accounts of a sort scarcely attempted as yet on the sonata—have not felt obliged, conversely, to include the sonata per se in their discussions. Of course, even in our semantic approach other forms must be taken into consideration, but only as they came into contact with the sonata during particular moments in its history.

In summary, then, the scope of this study is defined by the range of meanings and uses that "sonata" underwent as a musical title in the Baroque Era. The Baroque Era itself, usually fixed at about 1600 to 1750, is loosely defined for our purposes by the thorough-bass practice. But that convenient delimitation does have to be regarded as a loose one. At the start of the era, thorough bass was perhaps the most conspicuous stylistic innovation, yet hardly touched one of the main categories of the sonata. This was the category classified here as "multivoice." At the end of the era thorough bass still had many years to go as the prevailing practice, yet internal signs of its eventual deterioration were already present. Chiefly, it was becoming increasingly static or tending more and more to outline chords, thus co-operating in the slower harmonic rhythm, more homophonic texture, broader tonal plateaus, and more regular phrases that were to be identified rather with the coming Classic style. The celebrated violinists Pugnani and Nardini were among numerous composers still writing sonatas with thorough bass in the later 18th century, but they are not included in this volume because their thorough basses are mere vestiges of a tradition and fail to conceal the markedly Classic traits in their music. However, many other composers in the decades immediately after 1750 have had to be placed within or beyond the Baroque Era much more arbitrarily or, at any rate, subjectively, depending chiefly on whether their sonatas seem to be following or leading the way.

Naturally, thorough-bass practice applied not at all, or only remotely, to sonatas for keyboard instruments, for one or more unaccompanied solo instruments, or for plucked stringed instruments. However, these sonatas were not the most prevalent Baroque types. The keyboard sonata in particular, although the object of much historical interest, had only a scattered existence up to about 1740. When it did rather abruptly come into its own with such names as Alberti and C. P. E. Bach, it marked one start on pre-Classic trends. Hence, most of the composers of keyboard sonatas first published around 1740 are saved for the next volume in this history, even including such borderline notables as D. Scarlatti and Platti (junior? cf. p. 265), but not including composers of more distinctly Baroque sonatas like Martini and Arne.

Geographically the Baroque Era is limited for our purposes to activities in Italy, Germany, England, and France—that order being the chronological one by which the sonata originated and spread—and to occasional activities in other countries to the north and east. Needless to say, as viewed here the endings of the Baroque Era in the several countries were not necessarily coterminous.

The Method of Approach

The way in which the present book is divided into two parts represents another distinct change from the previous two drafts, in which I had planned to include everything under one chronological order by countries. Now, in Part I the general nature of the Baroque sonata is explored, after which in Part II the specific production of individual composers is surveyed, chronologically by regions and by schools (if any). To explore the nature of the sonata a different facet is considered in each of the next few chapters. Thus, Chapter 2 begins with the word itself, Chapter 3 discusses the sonata's place in Baroque society, and so on, Part I being concluded with the consideration of structure in Chapter 6. In these five chapters are abstracted those larger trends that can only be discovered, documented, and developed by the more detailed evidence of Part II. One price that must be paid for a many-sided approach of this sort is a certain amount of repetition. But that repetition has been kept to a minimum and what remains may well prove to be more welcome than not in a book of this length.

In Part II the chronological divisions within each region are based on the idea of early, middle, and late phases of the Baroque Era. The actual divisions made here are similar to but not identical with the ones developed in Bukofzer's *Music in the Baroque Era*. For our purposes they might better be defined as before, during, and after Corelli's highly influential career in Rome. That definition would apply in the main regardless of the region and although there was little "before" in England and none in France. The grouping of composers by regions is based here on the place of residence at the time the sonatas were composed rather than the nationality of birth or even the locale of early training when there is a difference. Hence we meet Farina in Dresden,

Geminiani in London, Locatelli in Amsterdam, and so on (the Italians being the ones who emigrated most). To the extent that influences can actually be demonstrated, and aside from unanswerable questions of environment versus heredity, a composer is generally more significant to history by virtue of the influence he exercises than that which he receives. Even this basis of classification leaves us with a number of composers too obscure to be placed with certainty and others who moved around so much that only their birthplace can be used anyway.

As suggested earlier, one aim in discussing the question of Baroque sonata form, all-important to this study, has been to view the structural problems dynamically—in action, so to speak. The how and why of this aim are given further consideration at the start of Chapter 6. We need note here only that in that chapter the over-all cycles and the single-movement forms are treated as separate problems, though not unrelated ones. In the same chapter, Corelli's sonatas are necessarily the first point of reference by virtue of their unprecedented influence and success. In such an instance—that is, in the immediately perceivable rise and fall of a particular genre—there is perhaps the best justification for taking an "evolutionary" approach, at least in a limited sense. It is illuminating to start with Corelli and compare what led directly up to and what led away from him.

Since Chapter 6 considers Baroque sonata form in general, the later chapters, in which the composers are discussed one by one, consider only individual distinctions and variants in the handling of styles and forms. Actually, the first problem that the single composers usually pose is that of clarifying what sonatas each wrote and published, and what ones are now available. Until this problem is dealt with, the music is hard to see in proper perspective. In order to get at the problem, considerable bibliographic detail has frequently been included, perhaps more than some readers will be expecting but usually not without a fascination of its own for students in the field.

The treatment of subject matter in this book is intended to be comprehensive and objective. To implement comprehensive treatment, standard reference works have been combed,[15] in particular with the object of including every composer of demonstrable significance to the sonata in the Baroque Era. The "demonstrable significance" pertains to priority or other historical distinction in any main trend of the sonata; to conspicuous success, as shown by the number and geographical spread of contemporary publications, re-editions, or MSS in which the

15. Including EITNER-QL, GROVE, MGG, BRITISH PRINTED, BIBLIOTHÈQUE NATIONALE, CAT. BOLOGNA, the PUBBLICAZIONI series, HAAS-ESTENSISCHEN, and SARTORI-BIBLI-OGRAFIA.

composer's sonatas are found; to acknowledgement of his influence by colleagues, pupils, and contemporary writers; and to recent interest in the composer, especially that resulting in special studies and modern editions of his sonatas. Experience has shown how easy it is to overlook a "significant" name. But the book does include at least every such name encountered in its preparation, along with a few more not so significant.

The Status of Sonata Research

The substance of this last section in our first chapter is that no general, over-all history of the sonata has been written, but that the time has certainly been made ripe for one by the abundant studies and editions of recent decades. Under the headings of general histories, special studies, bibliographic aids, modern editions, and contemporary sources the current status of sonata research may be summarized here.

More than a century ago, in 1845, Imanuel Faisst began the first historical sketch of the keyboard sonata with the statement, "To our knowledge the historical development of the sonata has still never been presented in full, nor even in part."[16] Before him, in 1837, there had been only C. F. Becker's article on Kuhnau as the "first" composer of keyboard sonatas, prefaced by a few historical findings. But also since Faisst there has been surprisingly little in the way of a general history. In fact, up to the time of this writing there has still been no comprehensive account of what has certainly yielded some of the grandest and most favored concepts in the art of music. Faisst's own study, a doctoral dissertation of about 80 pages, goes as far as C. P. E. Bach. It represents fine spadework, but its concentration on Kuhnau, D. Scarlatti, and C. P. E. Bach planted the very misleading idea still prevalent that these were three main figures in a single chronological line leading directly to "sonata form."[17]

After Faisst, C. H. H. Parry wrote an account that does not stop with C. P. E. Bach or the keyboard sonata, but does suffer from the fact that it is a highly "evolutionary," selective survey. It is the 30-page article that appeared under "Sonata" in the first edition of *Grove's Dictionary* (1878-89) and, for that matter, still appears almost intact in the new fifth edition. Passing over shorter, less consequential articles by Selmar Bagge, Robert Eitner, Hugo Goldschmidt, A. Schüz, and others, we come to the first complete book on the sonata, by J. S. Shed-

---

16. In the present discussion the author's name will be a sufficient clue to the pertinent listing in the Bibliography except where indirect references have had to be added.
17. Cf. NEWMAN-THIRTEEN, p. 1.

lock (1895). Though a pioneer work and one limited to the piano
sonata except for a few preliminaries, Shedlock's book remains the
single best start toward a general view of the sonata. Otto Klauwell's
sonata history of 1899 is based largely on Shedlock's and the more
specialized publications of Wasielewski. Since this book appeared there
have been published only some compilations of lectures for laymen (as by
Michel in 1907, Gáscue in 1910, and Refoulé in 1922), a book by
Blanche Selva (1913) that is derived almost verbatim from the historically shaky but musically stimulating descriptions in Vincent d'Indy's
Cours de composition musicale, and a little book by Eugène Borrel that
appeared in 1951.

The situation with respect to special studies directly bearing on the
sonata is quite the opposite. The concluding Bibliography should give
some idea of the literally hundreds of contributions of this sort that have
appeared in ever increasing number since Wasielewski, Riemann, Seiffert, Sandberger,[18] and a few others led the way. These occur as
dissertations or other separate monographs, articles in journals and
scholarly collections, prefaces to the bigger editions of old music, and
so on. Merely to name a few representative types, there have been
excellent studies on individual composers, like Koole's on Locatelli; on
single genres, like Meyer's on the German "multivoice" sonata in the
17th century; on activities in a particular locale, like Vatielli's on those
in Bologna; or on music for a single instrument, like Laurencie's on the
violin in France. Exceptionally, one study alone—for example, that of
Laurencie just noted or Torrefranca's on the Italian keyboard sonata
of the 18th century—virtually completes and resolves the needed research in a whole area of sonata history. On the other hand, one must
acknowledge that there are still many serious gaps in sonata research.
Aside from the greatest figures, less has been covered in Italy and England than Germany or France. Even so great a sonata composer as
F. M. Veracini—one of the most significant of the Baroque Era, in my
opinion—remains almost untouched either in studies or editions. Others
are not much better off when only very inferior books exist about them,
as about Legrenzi, since these books may have been just enough to
discourage further research.

From the researcher's standpoint the least usable portions of the
special studies often prove to be the sections devoted to music analysis.
These sections are frequently illuminating and much to be valued by the
general reader, but to the researcher they are likely to be too personal,
too slanted toward a particular theory or goal, to be transferable. He

18. DTBm, I.

can hardly go very far without having the score at hand for his own inspection, in any case. But what he is less likely to have at hand and probably needs most is the factual information surrounding the music, especially the exact bibliographic information about what, where, and when. In this regard, a few extremely helpful bibliographies that include or consist mainly of sonatas have appeared in recent years, and more are on the way. Representative of the best of them are Sartori's on Italian instrumental music printed up to 1700, Smith's on Walsh publications up to 1720, Johansson's on French publishers' catalogs, and Hoffman-Erbrecht's on Haffner's plate numbers. Preceding these more specialized bibliographies there had appeared the valuable catalogs of some of the great libraries housing large collections of sonatas, especially the British Museum,[19] the Bibliothèque nationale, the Hausbibliothek in Berlin, and the University libraries in former Breslau.[20] Further catalogs important to the sonata include Robert Haas's of the Este collection in Vienna, the *Pubblicazioni* series of the libraries in numerous Italian cities, Åke Davidsson's of the University library in Uppsala,[21] and those of the magnificent private libraries collected by Werner Wolffheim and Paul Hirsch. One only hopes that the enormous deposits of sonatas in certain other libraries for which only partial listings now exist, especially those in Washington and Berlin, will eventually be recorded in the international and union catalogs currently in progress. Needless to say, the new, fifth edition of *Grove's Dictionary* and the appearance of *Die Musik in Geschichte und Gegenwart* (available to this study through Vol. V) have added much bibliographic (and biographic) information, in spite of some errors that still persist and some valuable sources that are overlooked. At the same time, Eitner's *Quellen-Lexikon* certainly remains a basic reference work not soon to be discarded.

The matter of having scores available is made especially important by the fact that the researcher must otherwise do his own scoring of the separate parts in which all but "solo" pieces were usually published in the 17th and 18th centuries. Obviously, only a relatively limited amount of such scoring can be done in a project so large as this one. The music world will long be indebted to Alfred Einstein for the many MS volumes of vocal and instrumental scores from those centuries that he prepared, not seldom from unique copies that may no longer exist.[22] Fortunately, the publication of modern editions has greatly increased and improved,

19. The new *British-Union Catalogue* was not yet available for this study.
20. BOHN-MUSIKDRUCKWERKE.
21. CAT. UPSALA.
22. Cf. EINSTEIN-SCORESm in the Bibliography.

along with the special studies such as are noted. It is no longer necessary to depend almost exclusively on the helpful yet relatively few examples scored by Wasielewski and Torchi. But it was such pioneers who led the way here, too, with their collections of examples, their initial volumes in the big *Denkmäler* and *Gesamtausgaben* sets, and their practical editions of individual pieces. These editions have been continued, for the most part, and supplemented by such valuable series to the sonata as *Collegium musicum, Nagels Musik-Archiv, Hortus musicus, Organum,* and *Hausmusik*. Austro-German music is easily the best represented in all these sources.

Finally, contemporary sources are mentioned last only because their yield has been relatively small in so far as they are known to this study. Occasional nuggets of information do appear in definitions by theorists, incidental comments found in other writings, and the lavish prefaces by the composers themselves. But in those very aspects of the sonata about which one would expect the most information, especially performance practices of the time, many interesting questions remain largely unanswered. This fact will be most evident in the next few chapters, which treat of the meaning and uses of the Baroque sonata and depend almost entirely on contemporary sources.

Part I

The Nature of the Baroque Sonata

Chapter 2

The Meaning of "Sonata"

Origins and First Uses of the Word

There is much of interest and significance to our subject in the semantic approach—that is, in how the word "sonata" itself developed. This word is but one of the many musical terms introduced primarily by way of the Italian language, often as feminine past participles. *Sonata* comes from *sonare,* to sound, as *toccata* comes from *toccare,* to touch, or *cantata* from *cantare,* to sing, or *ballata* from *ballare,* to dance.[1] An Italian title like the following that Banchieri used in 1607 is a veritable mine of incipient musical terms: *Ecclesiastiche Sinfonie dette canzoni in aria francese, a quatro voci, per sonare, et cantare, et sopra un basso seguente concertare entro l'organo.* In particular, this title provides one of the countless instances in which *sonare* is opposed to *cantare*—that is, "to play and to sing," or the idea of instrumental versus vocal performance. One might go on to say that in this opposition, distinction, or option the musical term "sonata" was born. Even after "sonata" appeared, the opposition continued to be emphasized by terms like "canzon da sonar" (known since 1572[2]). Those rare, subsequent sonatas that did use voices—such as one each, to be mentioned later, by G. Gabrieli, Monteverdi, and Kindermann—must be regarded merely as sports in the main historical trend.

Of course, the same opposition can be found in equivalent terms of other than Italian nations. Waelrant's and Laet's *Jardin musiqual* of 1556 contains pieces "propices tant a la voix comme aux instruments," while Byrd's *Psalms, Songs and Sonnets* of 1611 are "Fit for Voyces or Viols."[3] But uses of *sonare* and its cognates in specific instrumental

1. More on the etymology and earliest uses of the word "sonata" is given in NEWMAN-ORIGINS. D'Indy's typically schematic attempt to relate *sonare* in particular to the sound of a bow ("produire un son à l'aide d'un archet," -COURS, II, Part 1, 106) has neither etymological nor historical defense.
2. ISTITUZIONIim, II (Benvenuti), xlvi ff.
3. Cf. BRITISH PRINTED, I, 207 and 732.

connotations may be traced back still further, to medieval treatises.[4] Actually, among precedents in several countries, it is in the form of the French cognate "sonnade" that the earliest use occurs of "sonata" as a noun. "Orpheus fera ses sonnades" is a phrase from a Renaissance mystery play dated 1486.[5] Couperin must have had such an ancestry in mind when, in 1724, he patriotically insisted on preserving the spelling "sonade" (cf. p. 357). In our survey we shall find numerous other forms of the noun, among them "sonetta" (Kindermann) or "sonnetto,"[6] "sonatella" (Furchheim) or "sonatille" (Chédeville), and the frequent diminutive "sonatina" (from as early as 1669 by Kelz) or even "sonatino" (D. Becker).

5a

"Sonada" or "sonado" to mean not merely instrumental performance but a piece for instruments was already used in 1535 to distinguish some of the lute-tablature dances in El Maestro by the Spaniard Luis Milan.[7] "Sonata" as an actual title is first known in a Venetian publication of 1561. This is another Intabolatura di liuto, the Book 1 by the blind Italian lutist Giacomo Gorzanis.[8] The "Sonata per liuto" in question consists of a binary "Pass'e mezo" in C meter, followed by its free elaboration as a "Padoano" in 6/8 meter. With this example and numerous less specific examples in Fabritio Caroso's celebrated dance treatise of 1581, Il Ballarino, there begins a rapidly growing literature of sonatas in Italian lute tablatures. To be sure, these first uses had nothing more than the generic meaning of "soundpiece." But, as remarked elsewhere,[9] the "gradual semantic process had to start somewhere and ultimately with some 'first,' however innocent and simple." Concurrently, there is to be noted a more limited German literature of "field and court" sonatas for one or more trumpets.[10] These elaborate prototypes of our relatively simple, modern bugle calls and related brass fanfares are solo and ensemble pieces that were intended for processions, ceremonies, and other festive occasions. They were compiled in two main MSS around the turn of the 17th century. Most of the titles have some further qualification, often the name of a source song (e.g., "Sonnada: den shmide Knecht").[11] A possible clue to the origins of this term "sonnada" lies in the fact that it and "signal," another title found

7a

4. Cf. NEWMAN-ORIGINS, p. 32 ff.   5. Cf. WECKERLIN-NOUVEAU, p. 382.
6. Cf. PINCHERLE-CORELLI, p. 128.
7. Cf. SCHRADE-MILANm, pp. 65, 70, 71, 73, 75, et passim.
8. Information originally received from Mr. Gustave Reese of New York University (cf. -RENAISSANCE, p. 520). Mod. eds., transcribed: CHILESOTTI-MELODIAm, p. 17; DELLA CORTEm, no. 57. Cf., also, Giuseppe Radole, "Giacomo Gorzanis 'Leutonista et cittadino della magnifica città di Trieste,'" in KONGRESS 1956 (Vienna), pp. 525-30.
9. NEWMAN-EARLIEST, p. 201.
10. Mod. ed.: EDMRm, VII (Schünemann, with preface, facsimiles, and pictures). Cf. HENDERSON, p. 8 ff.
11. EDMRm, VII, 47.

in these pieces, and the English word "sennet" were all used in the same sense, although whether they all derive from the same root is debatable.[12]

But by this time it is already possible to find most of the important firsts that are known in the mainstream of sonata history. A few of these may be listed in advance here. G. Gabrieli led the way in 1597 with his polychoir sonatas. Banchieri published little organ pieces in 1605 to which he applied the title of "sonata." And G. P. Cima used the same title in 1610 for the first known "solo" (S/bass) as well as the first known "trio" (SS/bass) sonatas. A little later, but within the same half century, Fantini published the first sonatas for two high, unaccompanied instruments, in his trumpet method of 1638; Del Buono published the first solo sonatas to specify a stringed keyboard instrument (harpsichord, 1641); and G. A. Bertoli published the first sonatas for solo bassoon and *b. c.* (1645). Biber composed the first sonata for unaccompanied violin that is known, in about 1664, and Pachelbel the first for violin and realized keyboard, probably in the 1690's. Not until the mid 1680's were the first sonatas for cello and *b. c.* composed (D. Gabrielli), nor until 1688 did the first ones known for the ancestral viola da gamba and *b. c.* appear (Schenk). Flute sonatas came still later (among them, those by J. B. Loeillet from 1712) and only as the German or transverse flute became popular. Mattheson composed the first known sonata for two keyboard instruments, about 1705, but the first duet sonatas at one keyboard would take us beyond this volume and into the early Classic Era (cf. p. 261).

Confusions with Other Terms

The origins and growth of the Baroque sonata were phenomena inseparable from the rise of independent instrumental music in the Baroque Era. Gradually the sonata became identified more particularly with Baroque chamber music. But on the way it brushed or temporarily merged with nearly every main instrumental type of the time. Which other types it touched most can best be realized by noting those terms with which the word "sonata" was most often confused or even equated at different stages of the Baroque Era. The confusion was not necessarily on the composer's part, for, as we shall see in the later chapters, he usually had some fairly tangible distinction in mind. But this distinction may or may not have harmonized with the one ultimately established in history. Furthermore, one is surprised to discover that only just after the converging terms became confused to the point of synonymity did

12. Information from Professor G. S. Lane at the University of North Carolina. Cf. APEL-DICTIONARY, pp. 672 and 692; also, LaRue in MQ, XLV (1959), 262.

they seem abruptly to go their own ways. Such is true, for example, of three of the terms most closely allied with sonata at different times—of "canzona" and "sonata," about 1650; or "sinfonia" and "sonata," and "concerto" and "sonata," about 1700.[13]

A confusion of terms arises when one term appears in the over-all title of a collection and the other over one or more of the individual pieces. Thus, S. Bernardi used the term "Canzoni" in the over-all title of his Op. 5 (1613) and "Sonata" as the individual title over several of the pieces. Further confusion results when specific and generic uses are mixed, as in a German keyboard anthology of 1673 entitled *Toccate, canzoni, et altre sonate,* which actually contains no piece separately called "sonata."[14] An equation of terms occurs when the same piece is called by different titles in the separate parts. Thus, the twentieth piece, *a 4,* in S. Rossi's Book 1 (1607) has "Sonata" over all the parts but that for the tenor instrument, which is marked "Sinfonia." A "Sonata" by Stradella for a "concerto grosso" and a "concertino" appears so in one MS and merely as "Sinfonia" in another (cf. p. 132). Of course, there are also those literal equations resulting from juxtaposed terms such as "Sinfonia, Sonata" (Clérambault), "Lessons or Sonatas" (Arne), "Sonata overo Toccata" (Uccellini), or merely "Sachen oder Sonaten" (J. M. Nicolai). Many more examples of such ambiguities are met in later chapters of this book.

Some of the terms confused or equated with "sonata" may be considered now, before we come to the question of how the Baroque theorists defined the sonata in their writings. The canzona or *canzon francese* first appeared not later than about 1520,[15] as an Italian instrumental transcription of a French or Flemish chanson. It was cultivated especially in the keyboard and the ensemble music of Italy and Germany, with original compositions gradually replacing the transcriptions. After its main flowering and its decline around the middle of the 17th century, it survived chiefly as an occasional name for the fugal (often the second) movement in ensemble sonatas (by Young and Purcell, for example). In 1687 G. Strozzi was even able to emphasize that *canzon francese* was no longer the proper term for the sonata (cf. p. 161).

The sinfonia appeared throughout much of the 17th century in two general types, aside from its confusion with the sonata. It occurred as a short orchestral introduction to both sacred and dramatic choral works; and it occurred along with more specific dance types as a short dance of

15a

13. Cf. VATIELLI-BOLOGNA, p. 202 ff.

14. Cf. NEWMAN-EARLIEST, p. 205; cf., also, F. W. Riedel, "Eine unbekannte Quelle zu Johann Kaspar Kerlls Musik für Tasteninstrumente," DMF, XIII (1960), 310-14.

15. Cf. JEPPESEN-ORGELMUSIK, p. 56. The two chief studies are KNAPP and CROCKER.

almost any sort, usually in binary design with repeats. By the end of the 17th century it led to a third type and an ancestor of the Classic symphony. This was the Italian opera overture in three movements, F(ast)-S(low)-F.[16]

"Concerto" appeared in the early Baroque Era as a term for vocal music that did have instrumental support, and persisted in this sense especially in German music. From about 1680, primarily in Bologna, it developed during its confusion with the sonata into the concerto grosso and solo concerto that became so important in later Baroque instrumental music.[17] But for at least 60 years the word "concerto," or "concertato," or "concertante" had already been used adjectively to describe the style or process of competitive interchanges between participants in a group. The *stile concertante* was early linked with the *stile moderno* (as by D. Castello).[18]

Other terms were more locally and temporarily confused or equated with "sonata." In 18th-century England, for example, "sonata" often came to be reserved for the trio setting, while "solo" was preferred for the S/bass setting and "lesson" for the keyboard setting. Yet "solo" and "lesson" were almost invariably reconverted to "sonata" in the reprints so frequently and promptly issued by E. Roger, the Italian-minded publisher in Amsterdam. "Solo" in the same sense is also a term preferred by Quantz, whose fairly precise terminology included "trio" and "quadro" for the SS/- and SSS/bass settings. Hence he has almost nothing to write about the "sonata" per se.[19] In Italian (and later in Spanish) keyboard music, whether organ or cembalo, the terms "toccata" and "sonata" were often interchanged (as in the MSS of Pasquini). Since the Italian "sonata da camera" was most often a suite of dances, the frequent equation of "suite" and "sonata" in France, or even "chamber ayres" and "sonata" in England, is understandable enough. The actual intermixture of suite and sonata must be deferred for discussion as more of an internal structural problem. But it is worth adding that after 1700 and as the word "sonata" acquired an increasingly definite meaning the suffixes "da chiesa" and "da camera" tended to disappear. Then, as in Bach's music, "sonata" alone became the term sufficient to designate the continuing church type, while some other term such as "suite" or "partita" was now applied to the court type.

16. Cf. HEUSS-SINFONIEN; LIVINGSTON, a valuable study of the Italian overture from A. Scarlatti to Mozart, including numerous works in score.
17. SCHERING-INSTRUMENTALKONZERT is still the main study.
18. Cf. BUKOFZER-BAROQUE, pp. 20 ff. and 222 ff.
19. Cf. QUANTZ-FACSIMILE, p. 302 ff.

Definitions by Contemporary Theorists (Praetorius, Brossard, Mattheson, Scheibe)

Further light can be turned on the meaning of the word "sonata" in the Baroque Era by consulting the dozen or so definitions written by the most renowned of the contemporary theorists. As in the Classic and later eras, we shall find that most Baroque theorists trailed actual practice by a considerable margin, both in time and substance.[20] On the other hand, a few were remarkably up-to-date in their observations. In these Baroque definitions the sonata is always identified as an instrumental type, of course, and it is defined at least as often as an introductory piece as it is as an independent piece. Musical form in the sense of particular structural plans is scarcely mentioned until the end of the era, except to call attention to fugal or dance movements. But two general concepts do come to the fore. One is that of the sonata as pure musical fantasy, subject only to the whims and good taste of the composer. The other concept, expressed after 1700, centers on the distinction between the *sonata da chiesa* and the *sonata da camera*. Originally, "sonata" connoted fantasy much as did the titles "capriccio," or "toccata," or "preludio," or "fantasia" itself.[21] Any independent instrumental music that could not depend either on a dance type or a vocal text for its design was bound to depend on the composer's fantasy. Banchieri inscribed one piece "Sinfonia d'Istromenti senza voci" in 1607,[22] and over a century later Jacques Aubert still asked royal permission to publish some "Sonates, sans paroles" (cf. p. 374).

Our theorists, most of whom were Germans and lived in the 18th century, may be cited in one chronological, international order.[23] In this way not only the continuity but the dependence of the later writers on their predecessors will be evident. The fact should be noted that few of these writers were themselves interested in composing sonatas. The first to write about the sonata was the German composer, pupil of G. Gabrieli, and scholar Michael Praetorius (1571-1621). Among his significant comments on contemporary forms in Italy, France, England, and Germany, in the third volume of *Syntagma musicum* (1618-19), he makes this remarkably early and oft-quoted distinction between the sonata and the canzona.[24]

20. Cf. NEWMAN-THEORISTS.
21. Cf. REIMANN-FANTASIA, pp. 260 and 274.
22. Cf. SCHERING-BEISPIELEm, no. 151.
23. Several of these theorists were originally cited in BECKER-HAUSMUSIK, p. 33 ff.
24. -SYNTAGMA, III, 24 (actually 22). All translations are new in the present book unless otherwise acknowledged.

The "sonata à sonando" is so named because it is performed as the canzonas are, not with human voices but solely by instruments. Very lovely [examples] of that sort are to be found in the "Canzonibus" and "Symphoniis" of Giovanni Gabrieli and other authors. In my opinion, however, the distinction [between sonata and canzona] lies in this: The sonatas are made to be grave and imposing in the manner of the motet, whereas the canzonas have many black notes running briskly, gayly, and rapidly through them.

Since this distinction does not always follow in the actual music of Gabrieli, not to mention that of his contemporaries, various scholars of the 19th and 20th centuries have attempted to amplify it. Winterfeld saw the distinction as one between changing sections of block harmonic masses in the sonata as against more definitely melodic and figurated sections in the canzona.[25] Wasielewski agreed with Winterfeld as to the melodic character of the canzona but felt Praetorius' effort to relate the sonata to the motet was too vague.[26] More recently, Heuss argued that the distinction was basically one of function, the sonata's purpose being sacred and the canzona's secular.[27] And Pannain found inconsistencies in all these, concluding that both terms were still too new (in 1619) to permit accurate definitions.[28] In the present study, Praetorius' definition does seem to have at least partial validity (cf. p. 100 ff.).   28a

Elsewhere in the same volume Praetorius referred to a type of sonata for wind instruments, used for dining and dancing and made up of an even- and a triple-metered dance.[29] This seems to relate to what we met earlier as the German "field and court" sonata.

In *Harmonie universelle* (1636-37) the Frenchman Marin Mersenne did not mention the sonata, nor did the Englishman Christopher Simpson in the original edition of *The Division Violist* (1659). But in *Musurgia universalis* (1650) another German, Athanasius Kircher, did give it at least passing mention. The mention comes, curiously, under the heading "De Symphonia Clavicymbalo apta." Certain Italianate compositions in preludial style are listed, including "toccatas, sonatas, [and] ricercatas." But the illustrative, 10-page "Phantasia" that follows proves to be a four-voice, severely polyphonic piece on the cantus firmus "Ut, re, mi, fa, sol, la," much in the style of the Italian organ sonatas of the 17th century.[30]

Not until the end of the 17th century is there a third theorist to quote, still another German. Daniel Speer wrote in his *Vierfaches musicalisches Kleeblatt* (1697), "The *sonata* is like the *sinfonia,* but ought to be played

25. WINTERFELD, II, 106 ff.
26. -XVII, p. 13 ff.
27. -ORFEO, p. 217 ff.
28. -PIANISTICA, p. 45 ff.
29. -SYNTAGMA, III, 171.
30. Cf. KIRCHER-MUSURGIA, I, 465 ff.; NEWMAN-EARLIEST, p. 208. A similar, longer statement, from KIRCHER-MUSURGIA, VII, p. 585, is translated in CROCKER, p. 12.

more slowly and gravely."[31]   Here was another distinction that would be difficult to prove.

In 1701 Tomáš Baltazar Janovka, Bohemian author of one of the earliest music dictionaries, added a somewhat different kind of information in a definition marred by imperfect Latin:[32]

> Sonada or Sonata is a grave and imposing musical work for any sort of instruments (meaning [those played] together as well as separately). Some years ago such works were performed in a solemn manner during the Mass after the Epistle. But already I digress, since they smack of the fantasy style (which is discussed under the word Style) and their use [in church?] has altogether ended.

Janovka was to be but the first of numerous authors who for more than two centuries have made premature announcements of the perdurable sonata's end.

32a   In the same year, in another pioneer music dictionary, a Frenchman in Strasbourg whom we do meet again (p. 362 ff.), Sebastien de Brossard, provided much the fullest, most explicit, and most up-to-date definition we have found thus far.   This definition was enlarged and slightly but significantly modernized by a paragraph appended in the third edition (Amsterdam, ca. 1710), the edition to be quoted here.[33] The definition takes up successively the spelling and origins of the word, the fantasy idea, the distinction between church and court types, and the sonata as found in Corelli's works.   Brossard starts by calling "suonata" the more common Italian spelling and "sonate" the French spelling (and a feminine noun).   He explains the opposition to "cantata," then continues:

> Sonatas are ordinarily extended pieces, *Fantasias,* or *Preludes,* etc., *varied* by all sorts of emotions and styles, by rare or unusual chords, by simple or double Fugues, etc., etc., all purely according to the fantasy of the Composer, who, being restricted by none but the general rules of Counterpoint, not by any fixed meter or particular rhythmic pattern, devotes his efforts to the inspiration of his talent, changes the rhythm and the scale as he sees fit, etc. (See *Phantasia* or *Fantasia* [which adds nothing].)   One finds [sonatas] in 1, 2, 3, 4, 5, 6, 7, and 8 Parts, but ordinarily they are for *Violin alone* or for *two* different *Violins* with a *Basso continuo* for the Clavecin, and often a more *figurated bass* for the *Viola da gamba,* the *Bassoon,* etc.   Thus there is an infinity of styles, but the Italians reduce them ordinarily to two types.
>
> The first comprises the Sonatas *da chiesa*—that is, proper for the church—, which begin usually with a *grave* and *majestic* movement, suited to the dignity and sanctity of the place; after which comes some sort of gay and animated fugue, etc.   Those are what are rightly known as *Sonatas.*

31. -KLEEBLATT, p. 286.   32. -THESAURUM, p. 119.
33. BROSSARD, p. 139 ff.

The second type comprises the *Sonatas* called *da Camera*—that is, proper at Court [Chambre]. These are actually suites of several little pieces suitable for dancing and composed in the same Scale or Key. Such Sonatas begin ordinarily with a *Prelude,* or little *Sonata,* which serves as a preparation for all the other [pieces]. Next come the *Allemande,* the *Pavane,* the *Courante,* and other dances or serious Airs; then come the *Gigues,* the *Passacailles,* the *Gavottes,* the *Menuets,* the *Chaconnes,* and other gay Airs; and all that composed in the same Key or Scale and played consecutively comprises a Sonata *da camera.*

[Added in the third edition:] The Sonata generally contains a series of 4, 5, or 6 movements, most often in one key, although one finds some [sonatas] that change the key in one or two movements of the work; but [then] one returns to the original key and writes at least one movement in it before the end. The Sonata *da Chiesa* differs from that called *da Camera,* or *Balletti* [*sic*] in that the movements of the *da chiesa* [sonata] are Adagios or Largos, etc., mixed with fugues that provide the Allegros; whereas the movements of the *da Camera* [sonata] consist, after the Adagio [type], of the airs of a regularized [i.e., nonfree] type of movement, such as an Allemande, a Courante, a Saraband, and a gigue; or perhaps after a Prelude, an Allemande, an Adagio, a Gavotte, a bourée, or a Minuet. For models see the works of Corelli.

Brossard's article has been quoted almost in full because it served as the accurate basis for most of the definitions that followed in the 18th century and because it can serve here, similarly, as a mid-Baroque point of reference. The additions and changes to be found in later 18th-century authors are largely concerned with details. Brossard also defined "Suonatina," as "a Little Sonata, intended as a *Prelude* or introduction to some major work."[34]

The German scholar and composer Johann Mattheson provided a variety of brief but noteworthy statements about the sonata that add up to a general definition. These occur in several of his treatises published between 1713 and 1739. They concern the sonata as orchestral, violin, and keyboard types, and as a vehicle for the emotions. In 1713, in a paragraph on the "Symphonie" as a free instrumental composition, he identified this type as an "overture" when it precedes a dramatic work and a "sonata" when it precedes a church work.[35] In 1717 he further qualified this type of sonata with the adjective "starke," the equivalent of *forte* in music, to mean orchestral scoring with more than one player to a part.[36]

In 1713, on the subject of the sonata itself, Mattheson also wrote:[37]

34. *Ibid.,* p. 140.   35. -ORCHESTRE, p. 171 ff.
36. -BESCHÜTZTE, p. 129; cf. ROWEN, p. 120 ff. (a valuable dissertation on styles and concepts of chamber music, especially in the early 18th century).
37. -ORCHESTRE, p. 175.

The sonata is a kind of instrumental, especially a violin, piece, which consists of alternating adagio and allegro [sections]. By now it is beginning to be dated and to be largely replaced and superseded by the newer so-called concertos and suites. Yet, at the same time, it is being revived afresh as a fully realized ["vollstimmigen"] keyboard [piece], although it takes a man to compose as well as to execute such show pieces.

As given here the last clause in particular is a free translation of a very idiomatic passage in German.[38] Mattheson may have had his own original but isolated keyboard sonata of 1713 in mind (cf. p. 290). This is a work in the "stylo phantastico," to use the term Kircher and Janovka had used, and that Mattheson himself used in 1740 with reference to a sonata by Kaspar Förster.[39] He may also have been thinking of Kuhnau's keyboard sonatas, written some 20 years earlier, and the defense of the keyboard's use and style with which Kuhnau prefaced them (cf. p. 240). Furthermore, Mattheson could have had in mind an early experience he did not relate until 1739, of hearing Corelli's sonatas played in Holland on the organ alone,[40] presumably with the upper part or parts on one or two manuals and the *b. c.* on the pedal keyboard.[41]

Additional light on Mattheson's remarks about the keyboard sonata is shed by a statement he published in 1737 and slightly revised in 1739 (the version quoted here).[42] First comes a paragraph on the expressive range of the sonata that might be taken for a forerunner of the later 18th-century *Affektenlehre*:

The sonata [is] for several violins or for certain solo instruments such as the transverse flute. Its object is primarily adaptability or suitability, since a certain complaisance must prevail in the sonata that will accommodate it to everyone and by which each hearer is satisfied. A melancholiac will discover something doleful and pitiful in the varied aspects of the sonata, a pleasure-seeker something pretty, a choleric person something impassioned, etc. Such a purpose must the composer also bear in mind in his adagio, andante, presto, etc. In this way the task will succeed.

For several years sonatas have been written for keyboard with good reception. So far these have still not [struck] the right style ["Gestalt"], and tend to be more affected than affecting—that is, they aim more at moving the fingers than the heart. Yet astonishment over exceptional dexterity is [itself] also one kind of emotional response, which gives birth to envy; although one must add that its own mother is ignorance.

38. ". . . wiewohl ein Mann so wohl zu der Composition, als Execution solcher Hand-Sachen gehöret."
39. -EHRENPFORTE, p. 21; cf. ROWEN, p. 10 ff.
40. -CAPELLMEISTER, p. 91. Mattheson was in Amsterdam in 1704 (cf. CANNON-MATTHESON, p. 29).
41. Cf. NEWMAN-EARLIEST, pp. 203, 204, and 205.
42. -KERN, p. 124 and -CAPELLMEISTER, p. 233 ff., respectively; cf. NEWMAN-EARLIEST, p. 203.

There is little new in the paragraph on the sonata that appeared in the posthumous, third edition (1721) of the second part of Friedrich Erhard Niedt's *Musicalische Handleitung*.[43] Two types are distinguished, both actually introductory. One is the sonata (long) or sonatina (short) that, like a "Praeludio," precedes a vocal work. And the other is the more independent sonata followed by a suite of dances. In the incomplete third volume (1717), on the subject of composing church music Niedt wrote,[44] "At the start I ordinarily write a sonata, yet not one filled with such foolish caprices as would make one want to dance, but rather, as said before, in a wholly modest manner and directly based on the text of the time and occasion."

In 1732 Johann Gottfried Walther's *Musikalisches Lexikon* appeared, with the following brief definition,[45] one obviously derived from Mattheson's main statement of 1713 and in turn just as obviously repeated in many a German source right up to the present *Deutsches Wörterbuch*. The sonata "is a grave and ingenious piece scored for instruments, especially violins, and consisting of alternating *Adagio* and *Allegro* [sections]." Five years later, in a condensed music dictionary, Walther added the type, "almost like a *Symphonia* or *Praeludium*," that introduces a vocal work, and even restated the essence of Praetorius' distinction between the sonata and the canzona, a century after the fact.[46]

The first information of any consequence on the structural aspects of the Baroque sonata occurs in Johann Adolph Scheibe's *Critischer musikus,* a revision published in 1745 of a periodical that had appeared irregularly from 1737-40. Scheibe begins with a main description of the "trio" sonata, followed by further traits peculiar to the sonata *a 4* ("Quadro"), *a 5,* and *a 6,* as well as the "solo" (S/bass) type.[47] Under "Trio" he cites both Telemann and [J. G.?] Graun as models. He notes the usual choices for a like or mixed pair of high instruments; the need for good ideas and interest in all three parts, although the bass is not required to participate in the ideas; and the desirability of "fugal" [imitative?] treatment with no one part predominant. The usual order of movements is stated to be S-F-S-F (the church type), unless the first movement is omitted as in the concerto. The first movement is preferably pleasing and agreeable in character, although a more stimulating and earnest type is acceptable, too. The three parts may start together but the treatment must still be "fugal." The main idea can be played by only one upper part (at a time?) but the other may repeat it or state

46a

43. NIEDT, II, 106.   44. *Ibid.,* III, 39.
45. WALTHER-LEXIKON, p. 571.
46. Quoted in BECKER-HAUSMUSIK, p. 34.
47. -CRITISCHER, p. 675 ff. (No. 74, Jan. 20, 1740).

something of a different character. If not a complete fugue the first fast movement must be at least fugal in treatment except during cadences. A good main idea (subject?), solid counterpoint, and interesting subordinate details are essential. The second slow movement is preferably more serious than the first and in a different meter. But there is leeway here, even to the point of a capricious melody. Finally, the second fast movement must be different from and livelier than the first fast movement, but still contain "fugal" treatment. Much melody in the upper parts is desirable.

Scheibe added little except instrumentation in his discussion of the other settings. Since he regarded the sonata as of less consequence than the symphony, concerto, or overture,[48] it is not surprising to find a more detailed discussion of the symphony's movements (in the order F-S-F), especially the tonal and thematic plan of the first movement.[49] When we come to Quantz as a composer we shall find in his *Versuch* of 1752 similar but more detailed and specific descriptions of the "trio," "quadro," and "solo" sonata than Scheibe gives (cf. p. 278 below). Discussions of the sonata occurred more and more frequently in the succeeding decades. For our purposes, of course, they ceased to be contemporary definitions. But as far as the actual structure is concerned, the later theorists add surprisingly little, anyway, for they were usually quite out of touch with, or at least unconcerned about, changes in their own immediate times. Marpurg largely repeated Mattheson and Walther in 1762,[50] still identifying the keyboard sonata with the toccata. Rousseau largely repeated Brossard in 1768,[51] exclusive of his essay on current taste that followed. He still identified suite with sonata.[52]

Other Contemporary Views

In the selected definitions that have just been quoted, the more formal, theoretical concepts of the Baroque sonata are summarized. These concepts may be supplemented by somewhat more incidental and informal clues that also occur in contemporary writings or in the scores themselves, and sometimes have a more practical significance. Thus, a concept of the sonata as a vehicle for bizarre stunts is demonstrable in a number of collections with odd titles, strange technical effects, or scoring peculiarities that are more in the nature of stunts than music. Most of these collections come from the 17th century and are the work of Germans or of Italians in Germany. We shall meet, for example, the echo effects, double-stops, *scordatura* and "altre curiose & moderne

48. *Ibid.*, p. 675.   49. *Ibid.*, p. 628 ff.
50. -CLAVIERSTÜCKE, p. 5 ff.   51. -DICTIONNAIRE, II, 217 ff.
52. *Ibid.*, II, 225 ff.

inventioni" in Biagio Marini's Op. 8 (1629), written while he was in Bavaria; and Kindermann's "Giardino corrupto" (maze), an SS/bass sonata in which the second violin part must be discovered within the first according to a series of directions.

The bizarre might be regarded as but one facet, however exaggerated, of that more general concept—the sonata as fantasy in instrumental music. Another facet, sometimes related to the bizarre, was the programmatic, represented by a small but influential group of sonatas. Best known are the sonatas with barnyard and other sounds that the Italian Farina composed while in Dresden, and, of course, the "Biblical Sonatas" that Kuhnau published at the end of the century. In France some programmatic sonatas were composed, too—especially those by Couperin, around 1725. But the programmatic writing by Kuhnau and Couperin was mostly confined to picturesque inscriptions and to musical symbols well integrated in the musical structure. Not infrequently the word "modern," as in "stile moderno," appears in the titles of sonata collections or single sonatas (e.g., Castello, Justinus). This association goes back to some of the earliest and most distinctive style marks of the Baroque Era—the S/- or SS/bass polarity; the chordal harmony and dissonance; the advance of major-minor tonality; the *stile concitato,* even in instrumental music; the *stile concertante,* mentioned earlier; and the new, more idiomatic instrumental writing.[53]

Besides the basic associations of the sonata with church and court, which underlie our next chapter (on the sonata's place in Baroque society), there were still two other associations of sufficient occurrence to be generalized here. One was the rather frequent presence of the sonata in those Baroque collections that, for want of a better term, might be called intellectual tours de force. Bach's *Musical Offering* is naturally the best known example. But we shall meet several other examples, such as G. B. Vitali's *Artificii musicali* (1689), in which the sonata makes up more if not all of the contents. The sonatas in these collections, often abounding in contrapuntal feats, may border on the academic. Yet in spite of such synonyms as "lessons" the Baroque word "sonata" seldom had the pedagogic connotation that the late-Classic and Romantic types were often to have. The other association was that of the late Baroque *sonata da camera* with arrangements of successful numbers from current theatrical pieces. We shall see, for example, that some sonatas by Handel and the only known sonatas that can be confirmed as Steffani's are of this sort.[54]

53. Cf. BUKOFZER-BAROQUE, p. 9 ff.
54. Many other listings occur throughout SMITH-WALSH.

Along with these associations that show up in the music itself, certain Baroque attitudes toward the sonata crop up time and again in contemporary writings. These attitudes center around the relative importance of the sonata in the whole scheme of music and around its place in the national rivalries and exchanges that figured so vitally in Baroque culture. As for the sonata's relative importance, only a cursory look at landmarks like Bonnet's history and Brossard's dictionary, the satires of Kuhnau and Marcello, the treatises of Mattheson and Niedt, or the periodicals of Addison and of Scheibe suffices to show how greatly church and dramatic music dominated nearly all musical interests.[55] An interesting sidelight on this point is the sizable number of composers important to church and dramatic music—for instance, Gluck, Boyce, and Jommelli—who are represented by but a single set of sonatas. Sometimes this set was merely the easiest and surest road to an "opera prima" in print, and sometimes it was only a matter of paying token respects to the form. To be sure, the whole field of instrumental music was but a poor second to that of vocal music. Moreover, it was only gradually recognized as something quite separated from vocal music.[56] However, these facts do not mean that the sonata was inconsequential in any absolute sense. Telemann, one of the most prolific and versatile of all Baroque composers, made clear that he valued church music above all other music,[57] yet wrote perhaps 200 sonatas not primarily identified with the church.

As for the sonata's relative importance within the field of instrumental music, any authoritative statement would have to take region, quality, and quantity into consideration. We have seen that Mattheson thought the sonata was being superseded by the concerto and suite and that Scheibe rated it below the symphony, concerto, and overture in importance. If true in other countries, as seems reasonable, these statements do not hold for Italy, the unquestioned birthplace of the sonata and the home of Legrenzi, Corelli, Vivaldi, Veracini, Tartini, and not a few other composers who gave the sonata at least an equal position among the categories of their works.

The mention of national differences brings us, finally, to the rivalries, borrowings, and amalgamations among nations, which figure conspicuously in the history of the Baroque sonata from the end of the 17th century. As we shall see, earlier in that century the Italian sonata, along with the violin itself, had been carried by Italian violinists first into Germany, then after the mid century into England. Its reception in

55. Cf. STRUNK-READINGS, *passim.*
56. Cf. ROWEN, p. 2 ff.
57. Cf. KAHL-SELBSTBIOGRAPHIEN, p. 222.

both countries seems to have been generally good,[58] its superiority at the time could hardly come into question, and it met little appreciable resistance. In some instances it remained purely Italian in style, thriving concurrently but independently. In others it already fused with indigenous instrumental forms. But at the end of the century the Italian sonata, meaning in particular the unprecedentedly successful sonatas of Corelli, spread with such renewed force to these and other countries and pushed aside all opposition so completely, at least for the moment, that real resistance to it was bound to develop. Such resistance did develop, especially in France, where the whole force of the late importation struck all at once. Furthermore, this was just the time in France when the celebrated polemics were beginning to appear in the quarrel between the ancients and moderns, with their lively side issues of French versus Italian music.[59]

The rival claims for French and Italian music chiefly concerned opera, of course. But when we come to the sonata in France we shall find that it was drawn into the arguments, too, even to the point of provoking "sonates françaises" (Senallié). Undoubtedly the new resistance to [59a] Italian music was responsible for a number of derogatory remarks about the sonata both in France and in England, where the quarrel was carried on, too. Best known was the quip reportedly made by Fontenelle—in effect, "Sonata, what good are you?" (cf. p. 353). In 1715 and earlier Bonnet spoke of the "fair sex" as being bored by a quarter hour of Italian sonatas.[60] In 1734 Mondonville implied, somewhat as Mattheson had, that exhaustion of the sonata was resulting from a surfeit of this "genre," presumably meaning the Italian sonata.[61] A fundamental ob- [61a] jection to instrumental music in itself underlay the Abbé Pluche's remarks of 1732 that "sonatas are to music what mottled paper is to a painting," and that "sonatas are not much pleasure for the public."[62] Revealing references are also to be found in general literature, such as some citations given under "Sonata" in the Oxford *New English Dictionary* (IX, Part 1, 421). One is a line from Farquhar's *Inconstant* (1703, II, ii), "I see you have a singing face; a heavy dull sonata face."

Actually and quite understandably, the sonata composers themselves seldom shared the hostile attitude toward the sonata of Italy, or of other countries, for that matter. They seemed to be much more interested in appropriating the different styles and forms. As early as the 1680's

58. Cf. the quotation from Aber in MEYER, p. 58.
59. Cf. STRUNK-READINGS, p. 491; ROLLAND-ESSAYS, p. 52 ff.
60. BOURDELOT & BONNET 1715, p. 438.   61. Cf. LAURENCIE, I, 380.
62. Cf. LAURENCIE, III, 192 ff., along with other pertinent comments of considerable interest.

G. B. Vitali and other Italians were introducing the minuet and other French dances in their sonatas. Quite apart from the mere slavish imitators of Corelli—and there were many—the Frenchman Senallié was a true Italophile in his sonatas. Georg Muffat, who could boast close contacts with Pasquini, Corelli, and Lully, was this and a true Francophile, too. In fact, he was one of the first among several advocates of an internationally "mixed style" in his sonatas. One thinks immediately of Couperin and his *Goûts réünis* (cf. p. 356 ff.) ; or Quantz and his *vermischter Geschmack;*[63] or Telemann, who even included Polish traits among his national styles. Telemann, by the way, joined Mattheson, Scheibe and those other patriots who strove to restore a loss of national self-confidence in the then German attitude toward her own share in the arts.[64] Although this attitude kept reappearing for another century in the French and Italian titles that Germans often preferred to their own language, Quantz felt his "mixed style" could well be called the "German style."[65] This style he saw not merely as the happy medium between, but the ideal fusion of, the main French and Italian musical traits—of French unity to the point of monotony as against Italian diversity to the point of confusion; of French dance types as against Italian forms derived from instrumental idioms; of brilliant, spirited French content as against tender, cantabile Italian content, inclining more, since Vivaldi and Tartini, toward boldness and even eccentricity; of specific ornamentation and articulation, precisely written out in the French scores as against improvised ornamentation and a subjective interpretation of the Italian music (depending on the performer's theory training), especially in the slow movements; and of diversional music for amateurs on the part of the French as against music for connoisseurs on the part of the Italians.[66]

63. Cf. QUANTZ-FACSIMILE, p. 332 ff.; SCHÄFKE, p. 214 ff.
64. Cf. ROLLAND-ESSAYS, p. 59 ff.   65. -FACSIMILE, p. 332 ff.
66. *Ibid.,* p. 308 ff.; cf. SCHÄFKE, p. 215 ff.

Chapter 3

The Uses of the Sonata

Three Main Functions

The problem of how the sonata figured in Baroque society is an intriguing and significant one. It obviously deserves a separate chapter in the present study. Yet this is of necessity one of our shortest chapters. If the general uses of the sonata are clear enough, the plain fact must be granted that specific information is wanting so far except for odd bits turned up here and there. One must remember that the whole question of music in society—in other words, a sociological approach to music—is still relatively new and unexplored.[1]

The broad functions of music were frequently outlined in Baroque writings. Pietro della Valle gave nearly a complete list of them in 1640:[2] music in the church, at the theater ("alle scene"), or on the street and music during processionals, masquerades, serenades, banquets, or funerals. In the preface to his concerti grossi of 1701, Georg Muffat reduced these functions by implication to the three that were most often stated in the Baroque Era—music to enhance worship in the church, to heighten dramatic tensions in the theater, and to provide entertainment in court.[3] His exact words are not these but include interesting stylistic qualifications:[4]

These concertos, suited neither to the church (because of the ballet airs and airs of other sorts which they include) nor for dancing (because of other interwoven conceits, now slow and serious, now gay and nimble, and composed only for the express refreshment of the ear), may be performed most appropriately in connection with entertainments given by great princes and

1. General discussions with regard to the Baroque Era do appear in such books as MELLERS-COUPERIN, chaps. 2-4; LANG-WESTERN, pp. 407 ff. and 444 ff.; and BUKOFZER-BAROQUE, chap. 12.
2. SOLERTI-ORIGINI, p. 174 ff.
3. Cf. ROWEN, p. 5.
4. As translated in STRUNK-READINGS, p. 449 (by kind permission of W. W. Norton & Company, Inc.).

lords, for receptions of distinguished guests, and at state banquets, serenades, and assemblies of musical amateurs and virtuosi.

Mattheson wrote at length on the *Kirchen-, Theatralischen-,* and *Kammer-Styl,*[5] but had little to say regarding specific functions of the sonata.

In Church and at Court

These categories naturally bring to mind the universally recognized distinction between *sonata da chiesa* and *sonata da camera,* one that we have already met in the Baroque definitions of the sonata. But this is a distinction that throws less light on functions than might be expected, since it is beset by inconsistencies and contradictions from start to finish. The church-court distinction can be found first in the titles of vocal music, at least by implication—for example, in Viadana's *Cento Concerti ecclesiastici* of 1602 and G. Valentini's *Musiche di camera* of 1621. In 1637 Merula was probably the first to bring the two terms together in a single sonata title, *Canzoni, overo sonate concertate per chiesa, e camera.* However, the intention here was not a distinction between types but simply an indication that all the music in this collection was suitable for either use. An actual distinction of types is first revealed in 1655 in Biagio Marini's *Diverse generi di sonate, da Chiesa, e da Camera,* Op. 22. Yet no sooner does that distinction appear than an overlapping of the types begins.

An unequivocal distinction between church and court sonatas such as Brossard seems to have intended (cf. p. 24 ff.) can be found only rarely—for instance, in the two types as Bassani composed them. The overlapping may occur in both the styles and the titles or inscriptions that are assumed to be appropriate to the two different functions. Often, as we shall see later, the church sonata does have a weightier, more serious character, chiefly as the result of a richer, sometimes a more polyphonic texture, and of more developed forms. Also, it is more likely to call for the organ rather than the harpsichord as a realizing instrument; to exist with multiple parts, suggesting an orchestral rather than a chamber performance (one to a part); to include one movement outside the home key; and to have tempo rather than dance or programmatic titles. But one can expect to find at least one later movement of the church sonata that is a dance in everything but the title, and at least an introductory movement in the court sonata that is a free rather than a dance type, including a tempo rather than a dance title. Not infrequently an actual dance title heads one or more movements of a church sonata (e.g., the "Giga" in Corelli's Son. 5, Op. 5).

5. -CAPELLMEISTER, chap. 10.

This last, of course, was a direct violation of church conventions, when the sonata really was music for church use. Contemporary papal bulls expressly forbade instrumental dances in the church,[6] although the Protestant Praetorius, writing nearly a century earlier, had regarded the pavane and galliard as appropriate for church use,[7] apparently because of their more earnest character in Germany. But as for our attempt to define functions, such contradictions in the later Baroque Era cannot have much bearing, anyway. Under a composer like Abaco or Vivaldi the two types achieved an almost total fusion, even to the use of combined dance and tempo titles by the latter (e.g., "Sarabanda Adagio"). If the fact has any further significance, the priest Vivaldi, like the priest Bonporti, or the earlier Venetian church organists such as Legrenzi, seems to have had no qualms about strong leanings toward dance or operatic influences in his sonatas.[8]

A further confusion of functions is found in the term "da camera." That term did originally mean, in effect, "for use at court."[9] But it quickly took on the two wider, not mutually exclusive meanings of nonchurch or secular, and diversional or chamber in our modern musical sense. Moreover, the association of *sonata da camera* with suite of dances was only a typical, not an invariable fact. Occasional statements that actually refer to the dancing of dances in *sonate da camera* can be found, chiefly from the 17th century.[10] But there are *sonate da camera* that consist only of programme pieces (Blavet), or arrangements of opera tunes (Steffani), or even of movements limited entirely to standard church types and without any dance titles (A. M. Veracini). There is actually a distinction implied between *sonata da camera* and dance music in such a title as G. M. Bononcini's *Sonate da camera, e da ballo,* Op. 2 (1667). In short, in that same search for functions, what we are most likely to find in either the church or the court type, especially after 1700, is diversional chamber music pure and simple. Whether it happened to serve for use in church or at court becomes a relatively incidental matter. In any case, for our purposes the distinction itself tended to disappear after 1700. As we have seen, the term *sonata da camera* eventually gave way to *balletto da camera* or some other term, the "da chiesa" suffix being dropped meanwhile from the supposed church type. In other words, the music that survived under the name "sonata" was that primarily derived in style and forms from the older

6. Cf. DTÖM, LXXXV (Schenk), ix.
7. -SYNTAGMA, III, 190.
8. Cf. SCHLOSSBERG, p. 35 ff.
9. Cf. WALTHER-LEXIKON, p. 130 ("Cammer-Music") ; ROWEN, p. 6 ff.
10. E.g., cf. SARTORI-BIBLIOGRAFIA, item 1681d.

church sonata, and in function from the older court sonata, in so far as either source can be delimited.

Some Specific Church Uses

It is when we attempt to go into the specific functions that only random notes can be offered. Exactly how and under what circumstances was the sonata used in the church, at court, or in the theater? Curiously, the best information is that on the lesser branches of the sonata such as the one-movement introductory and organ types—or perhaps not so curiously, since these were the branches most likely to be composed for some purpose more specialized than diversion per se. In the previous chapter certain functions were identified with the miscellaneous progenitors that were called "sonatas"—actual dancing in the lute sonatas and fanfare or signal music in the German field and court sonatas. Aside from these earliest instances, the functions first specified pertain to the church and in particular to the Roman Catholic liturgy.

Some of G. Gabrieli's instrumental pieces were designated for use in the Offertory of the Mass.[11] Some of Banchieri's short organ "sonatas" already carried inscriptions such as "Alla Levatione" or "Graduale,"[12] while further clues of the same sort can be found in the similarly purposed if more developed pieces of Frescobaldi's *Fiori musicali* (1635)—"Avanti la Messa della Domenica," "Dopo l'Epistola," "Dopo il Credo," "post il Comunio," "Dopo il Postcomunio," and so on—although Frescobaldi did not happen to use the title "sonata." In Vienna and in Salzburg relatively short sonatas in SS/bass and other settings were played in connection with the Gradual and Epistle as late as Mozart's so-called "Epistle sonatas." Whether these were usually played before, after (as Frescobaldi and Janovka had stated), or (softly) during the Epistle, or even in place of the sung "Gradual," is not clear.[13]

13a

Outside of the Mass the sonata appears to have been played often in church in connection with Vespers.[14] An early example was Monteverdi's "Sonata sopra Sancta Maria" of 1610 (with a sung chant). When Mattheson heard Corelli's ("trio"?) sonatas played on the organ alone in Holland, they came at the end of the Vespers service.[15] Further uses of the sonata in church included Biber's "Rosary Sonatas," devoted to the 15 Mysteries (cf. p. 217), and that short orchestral, introductory type, also called "overture" or "sinfonia." This last we shall meet

11. WASIELEWSKI-XVII, p. 50.   12. Cf. FROTSCHER, p. 220 ff.
13. The question is discussed with regard to Salzburg, including information from C. A. Rosenthal, in TANGEMAN-MOZART, p. 589 ff.
14. Cf. LIESS-TRIO, p. 13 ff.   15. -CAPELLMEISTER, p. 91.

especially as the opening and sometimes as an interlude in many German sacred cantatas by the predecessors and contemporaries of Bach as well as Bach himself. As will be recalled, it is prominent in most of the German definitions quoted in the previous chapter.

Some Specific Secular Uses

With regard to the place of the sonata in court life or other high society, specific information is even more scanty. Only rare hints can be gleaned from excellent sources in which one might hope to find much more—for example, Sartori's rich *Bibliografia,* with its complete transcription of the effusive dedications and notes "to the gentle reader" that accompany so many Baroque publications; Strunk's selection and translation of various contemporary writings and reports; Lafontaine's and Senn's compilations of court records pertaining to music from London and Innsbruck, respectively; Kahl's collection of autobiographies by 18th-century musicians; or Cucüel's monograph on chamber music at the celebrated musical soirées of La Pouplinière. One reason so little can be found is the simple fact, made obvious again in these sources, that independent instrumental music was generally of so much less consequence to the major court activities than church or dramatic music.

At the great courts one or more members of the sovereign family were usually active musicians themselves. Naturally the professional musicians attached to the court were expected to instruct these members as part of their duties, one consequence being the composition and dedication of sets of relatively easy sonatas for this pedagogic purpose. Thus, Buonamente wrote to Duke Cesare Gonzaga of Mantua in 1627 that he was sending "a new solo violin sonata that I hope Your Highness will be pleased to play without ornamentation ["schietta"], and for the convenience of the young desiring to adorn it with *passaggi* I have made it not too difficult."[16]

Probably the best known example of the sonata's use by court members is provided in the accounts by Burney and others of the regular, routinized musical evenings that Frederick the Great held for many years in Berlin and Potsdam (cf. p. 299 ff.). On these formal occasions the King played little other than his own many concertos and sonatas or those of his teacher Quantz. The famous Twenty-four Violins under Louis XIV and Louis XV and the copy of this group that Charles II assembled in London produced many a sonata composer and doubtless many a performance of the sonatas, too. This is no more than one as-

---

16. The complete letter is printed in NETTL-BUONAMENTE, p. 529, along with parts of other pertinent letters, p. 541 ff.

sumes to be true of any of the main instrumental groups at the larger courts.

With regard to other diversionary uses of the sonata, Albinoni, Marcello, and Bonporti were all self-styled dilettantes from noble families who apparently wrote their sonatas primarily for the recreational enjoyment of their friends and themselves. The same may be said for Weckmann and other middle-class composers in the Hamburg Collegium musicum or J. F. Fasch and his friends in the Leipzig Collegium musicum. We shall find, further, that sonatas were definitely among the staples in the musical fare offered at some of the early public concerts in Europe—the Abendmusik concerts for which Buxtehude composed in Lübeck, the Concerts spirituels in Paris, and various private concerts sponsored in and around London. Sonatas were used on lighter occasions, too, as one might well guess from such titles as *Les galanteries amusantes, sonates à deux musettes* by N. Chédeville (1739). They figured in some of the German *Tafelmusik* and French *Musique de table* collections (in effect, dinner music),[17] and were often played in the coffee houses of Leipzig,[18] or in English ale houses and public gardens according to both Hawkins and Burney (cf. pp. 318 and 330). Niedt's delightful, satirical description of a chamber music rehearsal at which a sonata, evidently in "trio" setting, was rehearsed suggests that the use of the sonata was by no means confined to the solemn atmosphere of the church.[19]

Burney also speaks of the sonatas of Boyce as being used for "act-tunes." This incidental reference is one of the very few such references found here to an actual use of the sonata in the theater, that third main category of Baroque music functions. To judge from the rarity of introductory sonatas in early opera (e.g., in Cesti's *Il pomo d'oro*, 1667[20]) or such an incident as Legrenzi's creation of an opera sinfonia out of elements from several of his own sonatas,[21] the immediate relation of the sonata and theater music was an inconsequential one.

17. Cf. CUCÜEL, p. 381 ff.   18. Cf. ROWEN, p. 8.
19. STRUNK-READINGS, p. 456.
20. Its "Sonata" is printed in reduced score in SCHERING-BEISPIELEM, no. 202.
21. Cf. SCHLOSSBERG, p. 57 ff.

Chapter 4

The Spread of the Baroque Sonata

Regions, Schools, and Leaders

The spread of the sonata throughout the Baroque Era from isolated, sporadic firsts to a standard, international commodity makes a fascinating story in itself. Primarily the story is that of Italy's growing influence on the music of the three other main regions or nations of Europe—Austro-Germany, England, and France.[1] How soon the sonata spread to each of these depended as much on a receptive attitude toward the new Italian styles as on certain other important considerations, including regional political conditions, the existence and enterprise of publishers, the native cultivation of chamber music, the presence of immigrant or itinerant musicians from Italy (especially violinists), and the acceptance of the violin family (itself largely an importation from Italy) in place of the older viol family.

In Italy the sonata proper began around the turn of the 17th century and flourished chiefly in the northern provinces of Piedmont, Lombardy, Venetia, and Emilia—Italy at the time, of course, being nothing but a conglomeration of independent states. It spread first to some of the many similarly independent regions in Austria and Germany, no later than the second decade of the 17th century. Chiefly responsible for this initial expansion were such early Italians on foreign duty as Giovanni Valentini, B. Marini, Farina, and Buonamente. Other Italians were made known through the intercourse of great families and the remarkable enterprise of the early Venetian publishers. Not until the end of the Thirty Years' War (1648) did native Germans and Austrians take an appreciable interest in the sonata, and then only by adding the strong imprint of their own orchestral suite and other indigenous influences. Like the English and French after them, they seldom exerted a reciprocal

1. Cf. the map of Italian musicians abroad from ca. 1675-1750 in LANG-WESTERN after p. 464.

influence on the Italian sonata, since they went to Italy much less often except as students, and since their compositions were much less likely to reach the Italians.

The sonata spread to England immediately after the Restoration (1660). This time the way was paved by such virtuosos on the violin as the Italian Matteis and the German or Swedish Baltzar, and by the influence of Louis XIV's Twenty-four Violins. Again indigenous traits were incorporated, especially the English ensemble fantasia. Some idea of the resistance to these trends may be read in a statement made by John Playford in the first edition of his *Introduction to the Skill of Musick* (1654) :[2]

> But musick in this Age (like other Arts and Sciences) is in low esteem with the generality of People. Our late and Solemn Musick, both Vocal and Instrumental, is now justled out of Esteem by the new Corents and Jigs of Foreigners, to the Grief of all sober and judicious Understanders of that formerly solid and good Musick.

Yet how quickly this resistance was overcome may be realized from the nearly contrary statement made by Purcell less than 30 years later, as quoted in Chapter 13 (p. 307).

Finally, around the end of the 17th century, the sonata reached France. It had been delayed not until the resolution of any political upheaval but until the resistance against such cultural foreignisms in this absolute monarchy gave way at least partially to the pro-Italian arguments in the quarrel of the ancients and moderns (cf. p. 353 ff.), and more particularly to the overwhelming successes of Corelli's sonatas. As will be seen later, the French composers were the one group that never did fully lose their identity in Italian styles.

The sonata reached a very few other countries during the Baroque Era, too, but chiefly as these countries—mainly Bohemia, Poland, Holland, Denmark, and Sweden—came into the sphere of our four main regions. As the Baroque Era ended, the "sonata" (under that name) was just taking root in Spain and Portugal. However, it has seemed more appropriate in this study to defer any further mention of Iberian developments, including the keyboard music of Carlos Seixas, the Portuguese contemporary of Domenico Scarlatti, until our discussion of pre-Classic trends. The sonata did not reach outlying and younger countries like the United States until the Classic Era,[3] but it is interesting to find that some of the most popular collections of Baroque sonatas were

---

2. P. 132 in PLAYFORD (16th edition used here).
3. The keyboard sonatas of Reinagle were the first favorites, with Pleyel's second in popularity (cf. SONNECK, *passim*).

among those brought back to this country by Jefferson (cf. p. 336). Up to about 1805 the only example of Corelli's sonatas published here was, as would be expected, "Corellis Gavot" from Sonata 10 of Op. 5 (in *The Compleat Tutor for the Fife,* Philadelphia, *ca.* 1805).[4]

The sonata was, above all, a product of the greatest music centers, every one of which has been the subject of one or more special studies of concern here. Each of these centers was identified with at least one main establishment. Usually there was an orchestra at that establishment, among whose directors and members there were likely to be composers of sonatas. The post of church organist also proved to be a fertile breeding ground for sonata composers. All that was needed in either activity was one dominating figure in this field—some person outstanding in composition, performance, and/or teaching—and a school of sonata composers was almost certain to follow. In Venice, the first great center of concern here, the establishment was, of course, the church of St. Mark, with its two important organ posts of long standing[5] and its orchestras of exceptional size and make-up for the 17th century.[6] G. Gabrieli at the start of the century and Legrenzi at the end may both be named as the heads of Venetian schools of sonata composers. Even Albinoni, Vivaldi, and Marcello, who entered upon more diverse activities in the early 18th century, all seem to have come under the direct influence of Legrenzi in one way or another.[7]

Similarly, Bologna was the center, the chapel of San Petronio with its fine orchestra was the establishment, and Cazzati was the founder of another such school in the late 17th century—in fact, the most productive school in Italy during the Baroque Era.[8] At the same time, Modena, where the principal court of the powerful Este family was located, became the center for still another group of sonata composers.[9] Founded largely by Uccellini, this group had close ties with the Bolognese school, especially through G. B. Vitali.

Vienna, the main seat of the imperial court, was naturally a main Austro-German center for the sonata during much of the Baroque Era, the more so as it had strong ties around 1700 with the Estense court in Modena.[10] But its chief contributors to the sonata, Schmelzer and Fux, were less important as such than Biber and Muffat at the archducal court in Salzburg.[11] In Germany, significant schools of sonata composers were

4. Cf. SONNECK & UPTON, p. 85 (also, p. 244).
5. Cf. WINTERFELD, I, 197 ff. 6. Cf. HAAS-AUFFÜHRUNGSPRAXIS, p. 167.
7. Cf. GIAZOTTO-ALBINONI, p. 67 ff. 8. Cf. VATIELLI-BOLOGNA.
9. Cf. SCHENK-MODENESE; PANCALDI & RONCAGLIA.
10. Cf. HAAS-ESTENSISCHEN; NETTL-WIENER; LIESS-WIENER.
11. Cf. SCHNEIDER-SALZBURG.

fostered at the electoral courts in Munich (including Abaco)[12] and Dresden (including J. J. Walther, Westhoff, and Quantz),[13] and at Frederick the Great's court in Berlin (including himself, the Graun brothers, and Quantz in his later years).[14] But in the very active center of Hamburg the sonata composers were brought together mostly to fill positions as church organist, town musician (*Ratsmusikus*) in one of several civic organizations, or member of Keiser's opera entourage. Among these composers were Weckmann, Becker, Mattheson, and both Handel and Telemann at different stages of their careers.[15] From the standpoint of sonata composers, Leipzig was primarily a center of church organ posts and civic groups, too (including Pezel, Reiche, Kuhnau, and Telemann in his earlier years).[16]

As centralized monarchies, England and France naturally had their chief cultural centers in London and Paris, where their governments were located.[17] The large majority of English and French composers to be met in our later chapters were connected in one way or another with their respective royal courts in these centers. Thus, both Purcell and Couperin were organists in the royal service. Also, as noted earlier, numerous sonata composers came from the Twenty-four Violins of Louis XIV and XV and the groups modeled after this one by Charles II and his successors.

While these passing mentions are given to some main figures of sonata history, three great predecessors should be named, in whose spheres much of the earlier sonata writing was done—Monteverdi in Mantua and Venice, Schütz (pupil of G. Gabrieli) in Dresden, and Lully in Paris. Except for Monteverdi's unusual "Sonata sopra Sancta Maria" these men were not themselves composers of sonatas. But among associates, students, and members of the orchestras each conducted are many of the first names we shall meet in Italy, Germany, and France. Other important composers will be named from time to time—for example, Frescobaldi, Froberger, and Rameau—who were influential in other ways, yet showed no inclination to join the growing numbers of sonata composers.

Among the sonata composers themselves, the man who exerted far and away the most influence was Corelli in Rome (cf. p. 155 ff.). Through his personal reputation as teacher and violinist and through the remarkable number of reprints that his five sets of sonatas had al-

---

12. Cf. Sandberger's preface in DTBM, I.
13. Cf. FÜRSTENAU, II.   14. Cf. SPITTA-FRIEDRICH.
15. Cf. MGG, V, 1389 ff. (Stephenson).
16. Cf. SCHERING-LEIPZIG, II.
17. Cf. LAFONTAINE and BRENET-CONCERTS, respectively.

ready undergone when he died in 1713, Corelli standardized and inter-
nationalized the Italian sonata almost singlehandedly.[18]   That fact runs
like a theme through the later chapters of this book.   In every main
region we shall meet composers who copied his styles and forms
slavishly, including not a few, from Albinoni on, who deliberately began
one of their "solo" sonatas in the unusual manner of his first "solo"
sonata (Op. 5) or ended the set with variations on the Folia tune.   We
shall find among his actual pupils (out of the legion who claimed this
magic distinction[19]) some of our main names, such as Somis in Torino,
Locatelli in Amsterdam, Mascitti in Paris, Geminiani in London, and
perhaps Muffat in Salzburg.   We shall also come to numerous sets of
sonatas that honored Corelli's music, among them *Dissertazioni del Sigr.
Francesco Veracini sopra l'Opera Quinta del Corelli;* Couperin's two
"Apothéose" sonatas, in both of which Corelli has a main share in the
programmatic content; and Telemann's *Corellisirende Sonaten.*   Roger
North summed up the English view about 1728 that seemed to be
characteristic everywhere:[20]

> The other circumstance I hinted ["Wch. concurred to convert the English
> musick Intirely over from the french to the Italian tast," besides "the coming
> over of old Nicholai Mateis"] was the numerous traine of yong travellers of
> the best quallity & estates, that about this time went over into Italy &
> resided at Rome and venice, where they heard ye best musick and learnt of
> the best masters and as they went out with a favour derived from old Nichola,
> they came home confirmed in ye love of the Itallian manner, & some con-
> tracted no little skill & proved exqui[si]te performers; then came over
> Corellys first consort [i.e., ensemble music] that cleared ye ground of all
> other sorts of musick whatsoever; by degrees the rest of his consorts & at
> last ye conciertos came, all wch. are to ye musitians like ye bread of life.

Mattheson and Quantz were among other near contemporaries who
wrote of Corelli's international influence,[21] as did Hawkins and Burney
a generation later.[22]

The Publication of Sonatas

This section might well start with the words by which Roger North
continued the statement just quoted:[23]

> And to name the rest of ye forreign consorts of ye Itallian style, that by
> means of Monsr. Estienne Rogers in Holland and other printers in England,

18. Cf. PINCHERLE-CORELLI, p. 113 ff.   19. Cf. PINCHERLE-CORELLI, p. 115.
    20. -GRAMARIAN, p. 37.   Cf. Purcell's similar remarks on p. 307 of the present
study.
    21. MATTHESON-CAPELLMEISTER, p. 91; QUANTZ-FACSIMILE, pp. 308 and 309.
    22. HAWKINS, IV, 308 ff.; BURNEY-HISTORY, II, 437 ff.
    23. -GRAMARIAN, p. 37 ff.

came more or less into vogue, would be of small Importance to this designe; and now thro ye art of graving etching & printing, musick is come to great perfection, being thereby strongly propagated, much more than when all passed in MSS. wch. were not onely hard to get, but often slovenly wrote.

The spread of the sonata did indeed depend on the enterprise of certain publishers in some of the main centers of the sonata. A fine composer like Zelenka in Dresden remained obscure largely because King Friedrich August I wanted to keep his music for himself and expressly forbade either its publication or circulation for copying (cf. p. 274). Among the most active publishers in different generations of the Baroque Era were Gardano, Amadino, Magni, Vincenti, and Sala in Venice, Monti in Bologna, Roger and Le Cène in Amsterdam, Walsh in London, and Le Clerc and Boivin in Paris. These publishers served not only local composers but others far away. Thus, Buonamente and B. Marini sent their music back to Vincenti and to Gardano to be published while they were in Austria and Germany, respectively, where less publishing was done. More surprising is the alacrity with which both Roger and Walsh discovered and reprinted new Italian works when they themselves did not issue them first. Indeed, both had editions of Corelli's Op. 5 on the market in 1700, the very year it first appeared in Rome.[24] These publishers had begun business only a few years earlier. Roger, the publisher cited in North's words, was often first to get an Italian 25a publication, with Walsh soon copying him (sometimes literally).[25] It is remarkable, too, how widely dispersed the Baroque sonata publications were, again chiefly the Italian ones. The great Estense library in Vienna noted earlier, the various Breslau (Wroclaw) libraries, the Bodleian Library, and the Royal University Library in Uppsala are partial evidence of this dispersal and of the cultural exchanges that help to explain it.[26]

The financing of these publications would make an interesting subject for a special study. The publishers were first of all men of the business world. Naturally they were most likely to undertake works by composers already well established or reprintings of works of proven success. The latter were all too often examples of those piracies or plagiarisms that were common in a day that did not yet know adequate copyright protection (as will be seen when we come to Corelli, Ravenscroft, and Eccles, among others).[27] Not seldom the composer himself was

24. Cf. PINCHERLE-CORELLI, p. 168.
25. Cf. SMITH-WALSH, p. xvi ff.; PINCHERLE-VIVALDI, I, 294 ff.
26. Cf. SARTORI-BIBLIOGRAFIA; HAAS-ESTENSISCHEN; BOHN-MUSIKDRUCKWERKE; CAT. UPSALA.
27. Cf. Vincenti's bold-faced, naïvely rationalized confession in his dedication to Buonamente's Book 5; also, Leoni's typical complaint, in supposedly subtle sup-

able and preferred to undertake and sell his own publications (as did Locatelli). Usually this arrangement had to be accomplished in conjunction with some publisher, although the latter's name may not have appeared on the title page. Most often the publication was financed by the sovereign, an ecclesiastic, or other high-stationed official in whose service the composer worked or whose favor he sought. The effusive, fawning, and even servile dedications that characteristically headed each publication were at once requests and thanks for such help.[28]   A moderate, not extreme, sample may be found in Purcell's first set of "trio" sonatas (1683) :

To his Sacred Majty.

May it please yor. Majty.
I had not assum'd the confidence of laying ye following Compositions at your Sacred feet; but that as they are the immediate Results of your Majesties Royall favour and benignity to me (which have made me what I am) So, I am constrain'd to hope, I may presume, amongst Others of your Majesties over-oblig'd and altogether undeserving Subjects, that your Majty. will with your accustom'd Clemency, Vouchsafe to Pardon the best Endeavours of Yor. Majesties

Most Humble
and most Obedient
Subject and Servant

One should insert here that the tone becomes much franker (though still apologetic) and the information becomes more pertinent to the music when the composer adds a note "to the gentle reader," as is often the case. Naturally, the composer had one eye on the spread and acceptance of his music when he gave individual dedicatory titles to the separate pieces or even the separate movements. Used chiefly prior to 1675, these titles honored associates, superiors, teachers, friends, distinguished contemporaries, and so on—for example, "Il Monteverde [,] Balletto . . . " in Marini's Op. 1 (although we shall usually find the article and name feminized, to agree with "sonata," "canzona," "sinfonia," and the majority of other form types).

The sonata constituted an appreciable part of most publishers' output in the Baroque Era, as one can readily see by glancing through the catalogs of any of the great libraries of music.[29] It did not come close in quantity to songs and opera arrangements, but was certainly the most published of the more serious instrumental forms. It was ahead, for ex-

port of his own reputation, that his music was being copied by others, badly and without acknowledgement (SARTORI-BIBLIOGRAFIA, pp. 332 ff. and 415, respectively).
  28. Cf. LAURENCIE, I, 262.
  29. BRITISH PRINTED and BIBLIOTHÈQUE NATIONALE give two of the most cosmopolitan views.

ample, of the Baroque concerto, sinfonia, and overture. Of course, the
latter types meant more of an investment for the publisher, especially if
such an exceptional convenience as a printed full score were to be included.[30] In the later Baroque Era the printing of sonatas seldom meant
the printing of more than three parts. Since *concertante* versions of the
b. c. had almost disappeared, there were only the two upper parts in the
"trio" sonata plus the one *b. c.* part for both the harpsichordist and for the
cellist looking over the harpsichordist's left shoulder. Full scores of
"trio" sonatas were almost never printed.[31] But full scores were the preferred, almost invariable method of publishing S/bass sonatas until the
accompanied clavier sonata appeared. At best the printing of music was
still a clumsy process. In printed Italian instrumental parts of the 17th
century, which are generally harder to read clearly than the contemporary
MSS, only flags could be used for short note values, not beams. Printed
German parts in the same period often have the beams, but a third beam
usually had to be inked in when 32d-notes were intended, just as the lower
note in double-stops had to be inked in or even added in a separate staff
(cf. pp. 210 and 218). But while such problems are cited, the many Baroque editions of sonatas that exhibit outstanding engraving skills in both
the notation and designs should not pass unnoticed. Two of the most
striking and artistically attractive are ANTH. BOLOGNAm III (*ca.* 1700;
cf. pp. 140 and 414) and the original edition of D. Scarlatti's *Essercizi*
32a   (*ca.* 1739).[32]

Quantitative Aspects

The reference a few sentences previously to the sonata's quantitative
importance suggests another fruitful subject for a special study and a kind
of approach that would probably be rewarding in many other aspects of
music history, too. For example, what was an average number of copies
printed in an edition of sonatas? One guesses a small number, to judge
from the scarcity of copies that have survived in most instances. A very
large edition published by subscription, such as Walsh's edition of
Boyce's "trio" sonatas in 1747, might reach 600 copies.[33]

Again, what was the ratio of sonatas published to sonatas left in MS?
Any answer to this question would have to depend, of course, on the
period, locale, and composer. Curiously, in the present study no MS
sonatas composed in Italy before the middle of the 17th century have

30. Cf. CARSE-XVIII, p. 113 ff.
31. Cf. p. 102 for a rare, early example (1611).
32. Cf. KIRKPATRICK-SCARLATTI, ills. 32-34; WOLFFHEIM, I, Tafelband 23 and 27;
SMITH-WALSH, plates 6, 8, and 19.
33. Cf. SMITH-WALSH, p. xiv ff.: ". . . two or three hundred copies was a good
edition, even for composers as important as Handel."

turned up except ones that also appeared in print. The same cannot be said for any other period or region during the Baroque Era. Thus, substantial quantities of German MS sonatas were reported in 1649 and again in 1662.[34] No fewer than 577 MS sonatas were listed in an account of losses from a Bamberg or Rudolstadt chapel fire in 1735.[35] These included 62 *a 2-13* by Erlebach alone (cf. p. 242). In later chapters, other, similar MS deposits will be noted in all four main regions of the sonata. Surely at least as many sonatas were left in MS as were published.

35a

Viewed in its entirety, the sheer quantity of Baroque sonatas must astonish anyone who explores the field. We shall meet not a few highly prolific, usually facile composers whose total output ran into the hundreds of sonatas, whether largely published, as by Pepusch, Boismortier, and Fesch, or more than half in MSS, as by Telemann, Colombi, and Tartini. At least 7,500 sonatas can be credited to the approximately 300 composers given special attention in this book (including about 105 active in Italy, 90 in Germany, 45 in England, 40 in France, and 20 in other countries). How many more, signed or anonymous, were written by men too obscure even to be named here, including some long since effaced by time?[36] Sonata for sonata, the Baroque composers seem to have been quite as productive as the composers of later eras, in an absolute as well as a relative sense.

Sets of Sonatas

Of course, the Baroque composers generally wrote shorter, less pretentious sonatas than the later composers wrote. And they were encouraged to write in quantity both by the continuing, practical uses for their sonatas and by the custom of publishing them in sets. Nearly all of their published sonatas appeared in these sets of from 3 to 12 sonatas, or many more on occasion, a custom that gradually gave way to the publication of single sonatas during the later Classic and early Romantic Eras. Most of the few Baroque sonatas published singly appear in anthologies or as separate issues in music periodicals.[37] We have these Baroque anthologies and periodicals to thank,[38] by the way, for many a sonata not found elsewhere and for one clue as to which composers were favorites at the time. The earliest anthology con-

---

34. Cf. MEYER, pp. 58 and 113.   35. Cf. MEYER, p. 113 ff.

36. Mr. Denis Stevens, writing to me about a MS thematic index made of the sonatas listed in STEVENS-BODLEIAN, is probably not so wide of the mark as he meant to be when he adds, "My index has about 4,000 themes; I suppose there must be another 96,000 somewhere else!"

37. Cf. SMITH-WALSH, items 257 etc., and pp. 149-151.

38. Listed under ANTH. in the Bibliography.

sisting only of sonatas was a collection of 12 "trio" sonatas published by Monti in Bologna (ANTH. SILVANIm; cf. p. 138). An unusual 17th-century anthology was the French MS of some 150 German and Italian "trio" sonatas referred to here as ANTH. ROSTm (cf. p. 363). More single sonatas appeared in MSS—mostly works written for special occasions, separate copies made by other composers, or merely pieces not yet collected into a set and given an opus or "Libro" number for publication. One composer, Krieger, made a special point of publishing each sonata of a set as a separate piece so that performers would not have to be burdened with the carrying of so much music at any one time (cf. p. 236).

With further regard to individual sets of sonatas, the earliest sonatas appeared merely as adjuncts to sacred or secular vocal collections (as by G. Gabrieli and Turini, respectively) or as part of the miscellany that made up many instrumental collections of the earlier 17th century (B. Marini). Such collections often had as many as 100 pieces in them (Fantini, Del Buono). Only a slight reduction in number and variety is seen in the collections that brought sonatas, canzonas, sinfonias, and dances together (Staden). But before the mid century there are also numerous more concentrated collections in which the sonata is combined with only one instrumental type, especially the canzona (Buonamente). Furthermore, "Sonate" was already the main term in the titles of two collections published in 1608 with vocal music as an adjunct (Gussago and Pico) ; and sonatas were the sole content, for the first time, of a collection published in 1621 (Castello). (As we shall see in the next chapter, on scoring, some precedent for nearly every aspect of the Baroque sonata can be found in its earliest years.) Contrary to the quantitative trend of scoring types, the earliest collection made up entirely of "trio" sonatas (SS/- or SSB/bass) seems not to have appeared before 1655 (Legrenzi), not until after the first collections made up entirely of "solo" sonatas (Bertoli's for bassoon and *b. c.* in 1645 and Leoni's for violin and *b. c.* in 1652).

As these collections were reduced to sets usually of 6 to 12 sonatas in the same scoring, an over-all organization of the sets themselves became evident, crystallizing somewhat as did the structure of the separate sonatas. In fact, one may infer that the frequent writing of sonatas a whole set at a time was undoubtedly one factor in the development of structural stereotypes from even before the time of Corelli, especially in the works of prolific, busy composers like the Modenese. For one thing, a designated function—church, court, and so on—gave a certain over-all continuity to a set of sonatas. Very common was the practice of designating half of the sonatas in a set "da chiesa" and the other half "da camera." When the church and court sonatas (or suites, or *balletti*) were alternated in the set, then the church type may actually have been intended as an introduction to each suite of dances that followed, as was certainly true in Reinken's *Hortus musicus.* Sometimes the set had a programmatic unity—for instance, Biber's "Rosary Sonatas" or Kuhnau's "Biblical Sonatas." Kuhnau, Buxtehude, and Fux were among those who wrote sets of seven sonatas, one on or for each day of the week.

Although no set of Baroque sonatas can be cited with the over-all, symmetrical plan and "center piece" that Hans David finds in Bach's *Musical Offering* (cf. p. 273), many of the sets do have some organizational principle beyond the extrinsic relationships just noted. Typical is the cumulative effect implied when something special is made of the final sonata, often a brilliant group of variations, to top off the set, as it were. Best known is "Follia," the group of variations that comprises Sonata 12 in Corelli's Op. 5. Sets that have a variety of scorings almost always progress from those *a 2* to those *a 3, a 4,* and so on. Sets in which the sonatas are written in the successive major and minor keys in the circle of 5ths (rarely beyond four sharps or flats) or according to some other plan are frequently found, too (Purcell, Martini). In at least one instance (Del Buono) all the sonatas of a set are written around one and the same melody. This melody serves as a *cantus firmus* rather than as a subject (as in Bach's *Art of Fugue*). At first, a published set of court sonatas usually meant an assortment of dances or other pieces grouped merely by types, from which the performer could make up his own suites to fit the need and occasion. Thus, Legrenzi's Op. 4 (1656), after opening with several complete (introductory?) sonatas, still follows with six *correnti* in a row, six *balletti,* three *sarabande,* and three *alemande.* But by the 1670's composers were more inclined to do their own grouping, at least on a small scale as G. M. Bononcini did in his Op. 9 (1675).[39]

39. Cf. SARTORI-BIBLIOGRAFIA, items 1682f and 1675b, respectively.

Chapter 5

Instruments and Settings

Trends

Primarily, the Baroque sonata was chamber music for strings, especially for members of the violin family. But, as this chapter should show, that generalization calls for a good many qualifications and clarifications. Chamber music can hardly be limited here to our modern understanding of precisely one player to a part, or of a particular instrument for each part, or even of an exact number of parts. In fact, only exceptionally was Baroque chamber music set within these limits. In the first place, it depended on somewhat different textural principles growing out of the prevailing use of thorough bass (or *b. c.* for *basso continuo*); and, in the second place, it provided flexibility in the choice of instruments, the styles of performance, and even the "realization" or elaboration of certain parts, depending on individual taste and the practical circumstances of any one performance.

With considerable hesitation and for want of a better term, "melo/bass" has been coined here to designate that general opposition of melody and *b. c.* parts so characteristic of Baroque scoring. It concerns what Bukofzer has called "the polarity . . . between harmonic support and a new type of melody dependent on such support."[1] Under the larger heading "Das Generalbasszeitalter" Riemann stretched "Monodie" into an inclusive but self-contradictory term for this polarity, whether the voice is represented or not and regardless of how many melody parts there might be.[2] All these terms attempt to pin down the same trait, actually the one most nearly consistent trait among the widely different styles of over 150 years that we commonly lump under "Baroque Era."

In short, what we have is a distinctive musical texture in search of a name, a texture that lies somewhere between the familiar but loosely delimited types called "homophony" and "polyphony." Agazzari showed

1. -BAROQUE, p. 11.   2. -MUSIKGESCHICHTE, II, Part 2.

himself already to be fully aware of this "melo/bass" opposition at the start of the Baroque Era, in his essay *Del sonare sopra il basso* (Rome, 1607). He spoke of two classes of instruments:

Like a foundation are those [instruments] that guide and support the entire body [*il corpo*] of voices and instruments of the so-called *Concerto* [ensemble]. These are the organ, cembalo, etc.; and, correspondingly, when there are [but] a few [parts in all] and [when there are] solo voices, [the foundation instruments are] the lute, theorbo, harp, etc. Like an ornamentation are those [instruments] that gaily and contrapuntally render the harmony more agreeable and sonorous—that is, the lute, theorbo, harp, *lirone* [lira da gamba], cittern [related to the lute and guitar], *spinetta* [square type of cembalo or harpsichord], *chittarina* [small lute?], violin, pandora [type of lute], and others of the sort.[3]

Agazzari's distinction is confusing in one sense. Except for the violin his instruments of ornamentation are not the melody instruments that actually were to predominate in Baroque music. At the same time, the polarity that he implies must be recognized throughout the Baroque Era as not necessarily that of bass and soprano (as Bukofzer has implied) but more broadly that of the harmonic support furnished by the "foundation" of *il corpo* versus any ornamenting or melodizing instruments in whatever range they may lie. The same instrument might have either function on occasion. When it carried the melody or shared in its exchanges, both it and the part it played generally came to be described by the adjective *concertante*.

Melo/bass sonatas are not, of course, the only kinds we shall meet in the Baroque Era. There is a substantial literature still based on the Renaissance principle of several melodic parts that are equally active throughout the range of the music. "Multivoice" is the general adjective preferred here for this style. "Polyphonic" would be too severe a term for the frequently relaxed textures to be found in such sonatas, which include orchestral and even polychoir music. There are also the relatively infrequent keyboard sonatas, the lute and guitar sonatas, and a very few unaccompanied violin or viola da gamba sonatas to be cited as types that are generally, though not always, excluded from melo/bass scorings.

Falling within the prevailing melo/bass category, the "trio" setting of two soprano instruments and *b. c.* (with or without an added *concertante* part that elaborates the *b. c.*) may be regarded as the most characteristic and numerous setting not only of the Baroque sonata but of all Baroque instrumental music, not to mention considerable vocal

3. Translated from the reprint in KINKELDEY, p. 216 ff. The entire essay is translated in STRUNK-READINGS, p. 424 ff., including a few terms interpreted slightly differently from the above. Cf., also, ARNOLD, pp. 67-74; Gloria Rose, "Agazzari and the Improvising Orchestra," JAMS, XVIII (1965), 382-93.

music. But the broad trend throughout the era was from many to few parts—from multivoice to "trio" to "solo" settings, the last being mostly that melo/bass type for one soprano instrument and *b. c.* (again, with or without a *concertante* bass part). In other words, between the early multivoice and late "solo" predominance the "trio" sonata marked a "classic" peak, a peak that coincided with the advent of both Corelli and the Stradivari violin. The end of the Baroque sonata is defined at least in part by the breakdown of the melo/bass principle, the deterioration of *b. c.* practice, and the invasion of that new pre-Classic phenomenon, the accompanied clavier sonata.[4]

As is well known, and as our need to coin new terms suggests, the Baroque titles are no sure clue to either the number of separate parts or the number of players intended. Quite apart from the performance question of one or more players to a part, which seems to have depended largely on the time and place, melo/bass titles in particular often fail to reveal whether the *b. c.* is included in the indicated number of parts and in what range each part lies. Thus, we shall find, in the numerous examples to be cited here, some "Sonate a due" that mean one solo soprano (instrument) and *b. c.*; others that mean one solo soprano plus one solo or *concertante* bass and *b. c.*; others that mean two sopranos and *b. c.*; others that mean two sopranos plus a *concertante* bass and *b. c.*; and still others that mean various pairings of instruments without any separate accompaniment at all.[5] Purcell's sonatas "of III parts" and those "in Four Parts" have identical settings (SSB/bass); Corelli's *Sonate à tre* of the church type have four parts while those of the court type have three, and so on, and so on. Perhaps a generalization might be made to the effect that the title indicates the number of *concertante* or melody parts, while the addition of a *b. c.* part can be assumed. But, as is already obvious, at best this can only be a loose generalization.

In the present study melo/bass settings are frequently indicated by a flexible system of abbreviations in order to specify exactly what parts are intended without circumlocutions otherwise unavoidable. These abbreviations—for example, SS/bass or SSB/bass—are intended to be self-explanatory. But it still may be well to confirm that on the left, or "melo," or *concertante* side of the melo/bass polarity "S," "A," "T," and "B" are used, as usual, for the main "voice" ranges; while on the right side, after the dividing slant, "bass" is used to mean *b. c.* and anything else that might share in *il corpo*. Occasionally such alterna-

---

4. Cf. NEWMAN-ACCOMPANIED.
5. Several such titles are given in MISHKIN, p. 92 ff.

tives as "solo/bass" and "duo/bass" suffice or are all that can be determined about sonatas not available to this study. Such terms as "S alone" and "SS alone" are used for solos, duets, and so on that literally have no accompaniment, *b. c.* or otherwise. But quotation marks are used in "solo" sonata and "trio" sonata, as the general and familiar terms for S/- or SB/- and SS/- or SSB/bass settings, respectively, in order to remind the reader that these terms do not indicate accurately the number of the parts or the participants. Actually, "trio sonata" is a term used only in modern times, the nearest Baroque term being "trio," "sonate en trio," or "sonata a tre" (abbreviated then and here as *a 3,* etc.).

The Instruments

Closely allied with the progress of the Baroque sonata were the histories of the various instruments that played it. Agazzari had a little more to say about instruments, including a preference for strings over winds in ensembles that was still voiced by A. Scarlatti when Quantz visited him in 1725.[6] But M. Praetorius, who soon expanded Agazzari's ideas while discussing *"Omnivoca* [chordal] or fundamental instruments" as against *"Univoca* or ornamental instruments,"[7] seems to have allowed the winds that nearly equal position that they were in fact to hold as far as several types of the Baroque sonata were concerned. The actual instruments most used to play solo, melody, or *concertante* parts, however one describes them, were the violin, throughout the era; the *Zink* or *cornetto,* often interchangeable with the violin up to the later 17th century; the transverse flute and, to a lesser extent, the oboe, similarly interchangeable with the violin from about 1700; the trumpet, in certain special branches of the sonata; and the viola da gamba, cello, and bassoon, each both in *concertante* elaborations of the *b. c.* and in actual solos with accompaniment. The instruments most used to play and realize the figured *b. c.* part—that is, the instruments "da corpo," to use the term as it actually appears in titles[8]—were the organ; the harpsichord or its variants; the *chitarrone;* the theorbo; the lute; the guitar; the harp; and the viola da gamba, cello, bassoon, and trombone among monophonic types that played only the *b. c.* line.[9]

Most of these main instruments need to be remarked individually in so far as their uses in the Baroque sonata are concerned. At the head

6. Cf. STRUNK-READINGS, p. 425; KAHL-SELBSTBIOGRAPHIEN, p. 135 ff.
7. Cf. ROWEN, p. 15 ff.
8. E.g., cf. SARTORI-BIBLIOGRAFIA, item 1607c.
9. FORTUNE-CONTINUO is a pertinent discussion of these instruments in Italian monodies of the early 17th century.

must be the violin, which was used as a solo instrument as early as Cima's sonatas of 1610. The violin may be said to have made its debut, reached a first peak in both construction and technical exploitation, spread from Italy to other, originally less receptive lands, and attracted some of the first great instrumental virtuosos, all primarily as a vehicle of the sonata.[10] From the tremolo and "altre curiose & moderne inventioni" of B. Marini to the comprehensive pyrotechnics of Locatelli, Veracini, Tartini, and Leclair a whole century before Paganini, there were few resources of the violin that we shall not be meeting in the Baroque sonata. Much of this technical treatment was introduced in variation movements, which afforded ideal opportunities for imaginative decoration and display.

Near the start of the era some experimental uses of the violin already revealed many of its extreme possibilities, often by way of out-and-out stunts (Farina). After these first random trials the majority at least of the Italians seem to have dropped back to a more gradual and idiomatic development of the instrument. Even Corelli did not exceed an extended third position, although in his "solo" sonatas the polyphony in double-stops, the implied bowing, and some twisting passagework can still present a real challenge on occasion. Meanwhile the Germans and Austrians extended the techniques of double-stops (J. J. Walther) and *scordatura* (Biber) to levels never surpassed. Influences of 17th-century violin playing in Germany are clearly present in Bach's unaccompanied solo violin sonatas. Among curious stages in the development of the violin sonata are the general reluctance to make any extensive use of the G string during most of the 17th century and the frequent persistence of the old first-line G clef in France, up to at least 1725, as a conscious symbol of resistance to the new Italianisms (Couperin).

Among other instruments of the violin family the alto viola was used chiefly as a filler part when it was specified at all in Baroque sonatas. The cello had a more distinctive development, somewhat later than the violin's. *B. c.* parts were already designated for "violoncino" early in the era (Fontana, Cavalli), but *concertante* parts and "solo" cello sonatas did not appear until further technical advances in Bologna about the time of Corelli's first publications (Gabrielli).[11] Fine examples by Vivaldi and lesser men like Jacchini, L. Taglietti, or Boni were followed late in the era by veritable schools of the cello sonata in Paris and

10. Cf. STRAETEN-FIDDLE, chaps. 1 and 2.
11. VATIELLI-BOLOGNA, p. 121 ff., is a study of origins; cf. also STRAETEN-VIOLONCELLO, chaps. 9-12, 15, and 17.

London. The "violone" often specified in *b. c.* parts seems to have meant the cello or an instrument between the cello and double bass in size.[12]   12a

As the violin was on the way in during the sonata's first great flowering, so the viola da gamba (in the *basse de viole* size), our chief representative of the viol family, was on the way out. This last was a gentle-sounding instrument, usually with flat back, gut frets, curved-out bow, six strings, and a but slightly arched bridge that favored chordal and polyphonic playing.[13] Like the cello, it was often associated with the *b. c.* part. But it was more often specified as a *concertante* elaboration of the *b. c.* than was the cello, especially in both SB/- and SSB/bass settings. Chiefly outside of Italy and around the middle of the era a limited but distinctive literature of sonatas for viola da gamba, whether as a solo or a *concertante* ensemble instrument, was created by one of the last generations of interested composers (Schenk, Kühnel, Buxtehude, Erlebach).[14] A near kiss of death for the instrument was Le Blanc's celebrated essay (1740), which argued for it in preference to the newer violin and cello.[15]

Various forms of the guitar in Italy and Spain, and of the lute especially in Germany, were used as the solo instrument in a considerable number of sonatas, although much music in this class has yet to be explored. The guitar sonatas of Italians like Granata, Marchetti, and Pasqualini were characteristically light and capricious. On the other hand, the lute sonatas of such Germans as Reussner and Weiss, though associated with the suite, have considerable textural weight, expressive depth, and structural development. Among various kinds of archlutes used on the *b. c.* part the chief, as we have seen, were the *chitarrone* and the theorbo.[16]

Among wind instruments the *cornetto* or *Zink* was the leading treble type when the sonata appeared. This was a narrow, slightly curved tube of wood with cupped mouthpiece at the end, six holes, and a thumb hole.[17] Reportedly it had a clear, sweet, singing tone capable of wide dynamic range if not quite the ring of the trumpet. That it was made interchangeable with the violin in so many 17th-century "trio" and "solo" sonatas is evidence enough of the technical agility that could be achieved on it. The *cornetto* was still specified as an alternative to the violin in Cazzati's S/bass sonatas, Op. 55 (1670). When it was used, its partner on the *b. c.* line was usually the trombone.

12. Cf. SACHS-INSTRUMENTS, p. 363.   13. Cf. SACHS-INSTRUMENTS, p. 347 ff.
14. EINSTEIN-GAMBA is a basic study of the German literature; cf. also STRAETEN-VIOLONCELLO, chaps. 3-7, *passim.*
15. Cf. LE BLANC.
16. Cf. SACHS-INSTRUMENTS, p. 370 ff.
17. Cf. BAINES, p. 259 ff. and plate 20.

By contrast, the natural trumpet or *clarin,* as the ideal instrument for ceremonial and military occasions, and the sonata, as the ideal concert music, met halfway in such bypaths of sonata history as the Bolognese "trumpet sonatas" (actually closer to the concerto grosso; cf. p. 141 ff.) and the *Turmsonaten* of Pezel and Reiche. The German "field and court" sonatas around the turn of the 17th century and the celebrated trumpet method of Fantini (1638) confirm that trumpet playing was

18a   already well developed when the sonata was still in its infancy.[18] The then usual name *clarin* derived from the high, clear (*clarino*) register achieved by skillful control of the highest harmonics.

The flute as a soprano instrument became most important to the sonata early in the 18th century as the modern "conical" German, transverse, or cross type replaced the end-blown recorder, also called *flûte douce* or *flûte à bec*.[19] The celebrated Hotteterre family, makers of wind instruments, and flute virtuosos like Quantz in Germany, Dothel in Italy, Blavet and Naudot in France, and Loeillet in England had much

19a   to do with the popularity of this instrument. Roger, Walsh, and Le Clerc seem to have been especially interested in publishing flute sonatas, often giving priority to the flute when it was interchangeable with violin, or adding it to the title when violin alone was named in the original title. The oboe's use in the Baroque sonata was somewhat less conspicious but otherwise paralleled that of the flute in time and manner.[20]

The bassoon was already assigned to play short but difficult solo passages in Castello's *Sonate concertate* of 1621 and to serve as the even more virtuosic solo instrument in Bertoli's sonatas of 1645. Thereafter its use to play the *b. c.* line or a *concertante* elaboration was considerable, whether specified or added ad libitum. But further "solo" sonatas for

20a   bassoon, such as those of Galliard, were not numerous.

Keyboard instruments served primarily to realize the *b. c.* in the Baroque sonata. But they were also used as solo instruments in certain

20b   lesser branches of the sonata. As we have already seen, beginning with Banchieri in 1605 polyphonic one-movement organ "sonatas" were composed throughout the era for specific uses in the church liturgy. "Sonatas" for harpsichord alone (or clavicembalo, clavecin, spinet, etc.) were written as early as 1641 (Del Buono) but only appeared in scattered instances (e.g., Kuhnau, Della Ciaja) until the flurry of pre-Classic examples around 1740.[21] As early as 1621 the harpsichord had been

---

18. HENDERSON is a detailed master's thesis on the trumpet in the 17th century. MENKE treats its use especially in Germany around the time of Bach and Handel.
19. Cf. BAINES, p. 290 ff.; KÖLBEL, p. 95 ff.; GIRARD, p. 37 ff.
20. Cf. BAINES, p. 277 ff., including a movement from a sonata for oboe or violin by the Englishman Babell; BECHLER & RAHM, p. 27 ff.
21. Cf. NEWMAN-EARLIEST. KENYON is a limited survey of the harpsichord's

specified as the realizing instrument in Italy (Castello's *Sonate concertate* again), and soon after, it was so named in Germany (Staden, 1643). Mention of the clavichord is rare in Baroque sonatas. The new, young pianoforte was specified, for the first time in any music, in Giustini's sonatas of 1732. Organ and harpsichord were made interchangeable as often in the mid Baroque Era as harpsichord and pianoforte were a century later in the mid Classic Era. After 1700 the occasional sonatas for harpsichord often revealed a freer, thinner, and more brilliant style of writing (Marcello, Durante) that distinguished them more and more from the sonatas for organ.

Among exceptional instruments for which solo sonatas were written may be named the musette or bagpipe and the hurdy-gurdy or vielle in France (e.g., Naudot); the theorbo itself, with *b. c.* support, in Italy;[22] and the musical clock in London (Handel).

Ad Libitum Practices

Remarkable flexibility in Baroque scoring resulted from various optional practices expressly allowed by the composer or simply assumed by the performer according to the need and the occasion. One choice the performer had more often than not was that of the instrument itself. In the early 17th century the decision was frequently left entirely to him in part books that still revealed nothing more specific than the clefs or the words "canto," "alto," and so on (Gussago). When instruments were specified, then and later, the usual alternatives were those we have already noted in both the *concertante* and *b. c.* categories. But exactly what constituted *il corpo* generally remained fairly open, while some-   22a
times the possible *concertante* choices were increased considerably.   T. Vincent's *Six Solos,* Op. 1, are for "Hautboy, German Flute, Violin, or Harpsicord with a Thorough Bass."[23]   The original, Paris edition of *Il Pastor fido* (S/bass), Op. 13, by Vivaldi is typically French in the choice it offers of musette, vielle, flute, oboe, or violin for the solo part. J.-B. Masse wrote unaccompanied duets for two cellos, or two bassoons, or two viols, or even two violins.   23a

The choice often depended on the place. The organ was more likely to be used in church and the harpsichord at court or on other less solemn occasions, quite apart from the character of the music itself. Corelli made that distinction in his church and court sonatas, for example. The *cornetto* was likely to be used when greater volume might be de-

---

use, largely in the Baroque Era.   HARICH/SCHNEIDER is one of several books that throw light on harpsichord playing.

22. Cf. SARTORI-BIBLIOGRAFIA, item 1669b.
23. Cf. BRITISH PRINTED, II, 631.

sired than the violin could achieve. Then, as we have seen, care was usually taken to balance the bass properly, trombones being paired with *cornetti*, or cellos with violins, and so on (Pezel).[24]

A second ad libitum decision that affected the scoring and had to be made in performance was that of how many players would participate. For one thing, would there be more than one person to a part? This familiar question of Baroque performance practices has no clue in any Baroque source quite so helpful as that title from a London publication in the Classic Era, "Twelve Sonatas for Two Violins and a Bass or an Orchestra" (*ca.* 1770; cf. p. 197). But there are varied clues leading to the conclusion that here, too, was a matter decided flexibly by the time and place. J. A. P. Schulz's remark in the early 1770's that multiple performance was appropriate to the "trio" sonata in church and single performance to the "Kammertrio"[25] was anticipated in 1717 by Mattheson's mention of "starke" or orchestrally performed sonatas (cf. p. 25), and probably had been the practice since the first distinctions
25a between church and court types. The existence of multiple parts for sonatas by Bolognese composers at San Petronio is incontrovertible evidence, of course, of multiple performance, although such evidence happens to be surprisingly rare unless, as in this instance, the sonatas are clearly orchestral in their make-up. Similar evidence is provided by the not rare occurrence of "T." and "S." for *tutti* and *soli* in sonatas that clearly relate to the concerto grosso (e.g., by Fux and Muffat). Infrequently the title itself is more explicit. Buxtehude even headed the introduction to a vocal work, *Sonatina forte con molti violini all unisono*.

The actual disposition of the parts could affect the number of players. Thus, as suggested earlier, a "solo" sonata might well mean at least four players—for example, in a SB/bass setting with both a monophonic
25b and a chordal realizing instrument on the *b. c.* part. On the other hand, the number could be reduced, as in B. Marini's SS/bass sonata "per l'Organo è Violino ó Cornetto," Op. 8, in which the second soprano part was played by the organist's right hand; or in Couperin's SS/bass sonatas, which, he said (in *Apothéose de Lulli*), could be played on two clavecins, with one upper part on each and the same *b. c.* for both; or in Buini's S/bass sonatas, which provided the rather frequent option of cembalo performance, with the soprano in the right hand and at least the *b. c.* line in the left.

A more fundamental consideration with regard to the number of

---

24. The extent to which balance came to be considered is frequently reflected in the performance advices in QUANTZ-FACSIMILE, e. g., pp. 210 ff. and 224 ff.
25. SULZER-ALLGEMEINE, IV, 805 (regarding Schulz's authorship, cf. RIEMANN-LEXIKON, 1667).

players was that of options affecting the very texture of the sonatas. The most familiar variable was the improvised realization of the *b. c.*, which might be anything from H. N. Gerber's polyphonic enrichment, as found in Bach's corrected version,[26] to a mere succession of 6th chords, as ridiculed by Marcello.[27] Sometimes the realization itself was made optional (but rarely the *b. c.* line), as Buonamente made clear in a letter of 1627 regarding an SS/bass sonata[28] and as one assumes from such a title as *Six Sonatas or Trios for three Violoncellos or two Violins and a Bass* (Cervetto, *ca.* 1745). With the realization present, it is no wonder that composers and performers sometimes regarded parts in the middle register as optional.[29] G. B. Vitali explained that the SSSATB/-bass settings of his *Varie Sonate,* Op. 11, could be reduced to "il primo Violino solo, e Violone" if desired. Several quasi-quartet settings (SSA/bass) in the literature of the Baroque sonata have optional viola parts (G. M. Bononcini). When these are not used, the kinship with the "trio" sonata becomes more apparent. As examples of other textural options, Buonamente permitted the second soprano to be left out, "a beneplacito," in his SS/bass "sonatas" of Book 5;[30] and Locatelli wrote a "Largo" movement (Son. 12, Op. 2) in which the S/bass setting could be converted, optionally, to SS/BB by making a canon of each part. With this latter change Locatelli also had adjustments in the instrumental balance to recommend (cf. p. 349).

Further insight into optional textural changes may be had by examining the changes already made in many Baroque transcriptions. In some of these the melo/bass setting is merely transplanted to the keyboard—for example, in Geminiani's two collections of harpsichord pieces (1743 and 1762) that he himself made from movements of his S/bass sonatas or in those *Suittes pour le Clavecin* "arranged" from movements of Corelli's sonatas (Amsterdam, *ca.* 1715).[31] Pepusch simply adds to the lengthy title of his edition of Corelli's Opp. 1-4 in score, "they also make compleat Lessons for the Harpsichord." Both Corelli's "trio" and his "solo" sonatas continued to appear in scores as organ or harpsichord publications throughout the 18th century. Evidently very successful in

26. Cf. SPITTA-BACH, III, 388 ff.

27. MARCELLO, p. 89. Of course, the realizations in modern editions vary greatly, too, from overly timid writing in simple four-part style to romanticized elaborations that are nothing short of tasteless anachronisms.

28. Cf. NETTL-BUONAMENTE; also, Cecchino's similar advice in SARTORI-BIBLI-OGRAFIA, item 1628e.

29. Cf. ROWEN, pp. 25 (including a quotation from SULZER-ALLGEMEINE to this effect) and 83 ff. (but read *correnti* for *canzoni* in the reference to Neri).

30. Cf. SARTORI-BIBLIOGRAFIA, item 1629a. But the instruction does not mean, as claimed in MOSER-VIOLINSPIEL, p. 60, that single performance is being requested in place of multiple performance on the solo part.

31. Cf. BRITISH PRINTED, I, 307.

this vein were the Longman & Broderip editions of Opp. 1 and 2 in the 1780's, prepared by Edward Miller, "Mus. D.," with a quasi-scholarly preface on Corelli and with the first fast movements usually repeated in place of the finales.

In such "transcriptions," although the original lines were retained, the resulting texture was actually impoverished by the loss of the improvised *b. c.* realization. The most the keyboard player might add, as in some other keyboard music of the time, would be filler tones in the harmony when the hand stretches and tempo permitted. Inevitably, too, there was a textural loss when the transcription was made "down" to a smaller ensemble, as in the "solo" violin sonatas that John Stanley and Heinichen arranged, each from his own concerti grossi. On the other hand, when the sonatas were transcribed "up" to larger ensembles, as they sometimes were, the texture might well be enriched. Geminiani was also one of those who arranged "solo" into "trio" sonatas (cf. p. 322 ff.).

While ad libitum practices affecting texture are being considered, one should recall the common Baroque practice of improvising ornamental elaborations in melodic lines, especially in the solo lines of slow movements. Ornaments could enrich the texture by making it more active and by filling out or qualifying the harmony. Questions have been raised about the amount and kind of ornamentation that were introduced (as with Corelli's Op. 5), but there is proof enough of the fact of its wide use in the frequent requests not to use it ("come stá") from Buonamente to Veracini. In a few precious instances we have first-hand evidence of the manner in which the ornamenting was done, including Roger's edition of Corelli's Op. 5 with the ornaments of the adagios "composed [?] by Corelli as he played them" (cf. p. 158), Veracini's rewriting (*Dissertazioni*) of Corelli's Op. 5, Geminiani's rewriting of his own "solo" sonatas Op. 1, Tartini's *Trattato delle appogiature,* and Couperin's *Apothéose de Lulli.*

The Settings

From the foregoing discussion the fact becomes obvious that any description of individual settings can only be a generalization of the very flexible performance practices in the Baroque Era. In other words, in the following references to the most standardized settings one must not forget that any number of cross types also grew out of those practices.

Multivoice settings of the sonata were numerous in Italy and Germany throughout the 17th century and were still being composed in the early 18th century. One tends to underestimate their quantitative importance today, chiefly because so few of the larger settings achieved publication and so many of the MSS have not survived. Muffat, Albinoni, and Somis were among later composers who wrote multivoice settings. But these later examples were all orchestral pieces closely related to the concerto grosso. Multivoice sonata settings were few in England and virtually nonexistent in France. The polychoir type of multivoice setting was chiefly an early Venetian product. It appeared first as the main setting in G. Gabrieli's pioneer sonatas but survived in Venice only up to the publications of Neri and Cavalli around the mid 17th century. Thereafter it appeared occasionally outside of Venice, as in the examples by Cazzati while he was still in Bergamo (1654), Strutius in the former Danzig (1658), Schmelzer in Vienna (1662), or J. P. Krieger in Weissenfels (as late as 1717). Other orchestral types of multivoice settings included the so-called "trumpet sonatas," which were especially the product of the Bologna school in the later 17th century; the *Turmsonaten* ("tower" sonatas), played in Leipzig around the mid Baroque Era; and the various other large groupings created for special occasions, mostly before 1700, at the Imperial court in Vienna (Bertali, Ziani) and some of the larger courts in Germany (Albrici, Krieger).

As is well known, the polychoir sonatas of G. Gabrieli derived primarily from the *cori spezzati* occasioned by the two facing choir lofts at St. Mark's church, each with its own organ.[32] His were not only the earliest but some of the most elaborately scored sonatas of this type. We shall see, for example, that one sonata in his posthumous set of 1615 is scored for 22 instruments in 5 choirs of $6 + 4 + 4 + 4 + 4$ parts! Although the parts in that example specify only two of the instruments used—*cornetti* and trombones—and the ranges of the others, we know from further examples that violas (or violins) and rarely flutes were also used in the high and middle ranges, and violas or viols and bassoons in the low ranges. An organ was sometimes used to play at least the *b. c.* line or, what was more usual in early multivoice settings, the *basso seguente,* which was simply the line formed by the lowest notes in any part at any one moment. In addition to various simultaneous combinations of the choirs, antiphony was inherent in the nature of the polychoir setting. Both polyphonic and chordal writing are found. All together, opposition or variety could be achieved through contrasted ranges, textures, instrumental colors, and dynamics (as in the echo effects of Gabrieli's celebrated "Sonata Pian & Forte"). But the contrast was seldom one of different musical ideas. As the 17th

32. Cf. REESE-RENAISSANCE, p. 372 ff.

century advanced, the polychoir setting, like other multivoice settings, approached the melo/bass principle more and more. A frequent cross type, already found in S. Rossi's music, was the sonata *a 4* or *6* in which, for the most part, two SS/- or SSB/bass groupings were treated antiphonally ("in dialogo").

The single-choir multivoice sonatas that were not necessarily identified with orchestra scoring or multiple performance were predominantly in 4 to 8 parts. A typical grouping of six might be indicated simply by the clefs

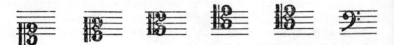

(Gussago). In the interest of balance a homogeneous rather than a heterogeneous instrumentation (the English "whole" versus "broken consort") would seem to have been more likely. Certainly the tendency toward a single family of instruments became greater as the dominance of the violin family became established. Then, with less contrast available through a variety of instrumental colors, more contrast had to be achieved in the structural or internal aspects of the music—for example, by imitations in different ranges, keys centered on different pitch levels, and separate movements in different tempos, styles of figuration, and rhythmic patterns.[33] The single-choir multivoice setting approached the melo/bass principle as the melodic interest became concentrated in the outer parts, probably for the sake of the more telling sonorities and bolder melodic projection that resulted. At the same time the inner parts tended to become the more or less optional fillers (as mentioned previously). A frequent cross type in this instance was the sonata for three or four equal instruments and bass—perhaps four violins, *concertante* bass, and *b. c.,* or even four "viole da gambe ò come piace" (both exemplified by Legrenzi). The exception to the trend toward melo/bass settings was, of course, the fugal or other polyphonic type of sonata, which tended to retain the equal distribution of parts and melodic interest throughout the total pitch range.

Among orchestral settings a representative "trumpet sonata" of the Bolognese school might have two different parts for *concertante* trumpets, for violins, and for violas (in the alto and tenor ranges) ; a cello part ; and *b. c.* parts in triplicate for bass viol, organ, and theorbo (Franceschini).[34] A link with the melo/bass principle here and in most

33. Cf. "La Buscha," Op. 8, by Legrenzi, in DAVISON & APELm, no. 220.
34. Cf. SCHLOSSBERG, pp. 87 ff. and 101 ; VATIELLI-BOLOGNA, p. 214 ff.

"sonatas" that bordered on the new concerto grosso was the typical "trio" setting of the *soli* parts.[35] The *Turmsonaten* of Pezel and Reiche have only five and four different parts, respectively. Two *cornetti* and three trombones (or two violins, two violas, and *violone*) are called for by Pezel and one less *cornetto* by Reiche. As for orchestral sonatas played by special orchestras on special occasions, a sample might be A. Poglietti's *Sonata a 8* for two violins, two *clarini,* four viols, and organ. The orchestra was hardly a standardized organization in the 17th century. A well-known example was the orchestra of 34 instruments under Legrenzi's direction at St. Mark's —8 violins, 11 *violette, 2 viole da braccia,* 2 viole da gamba, 1 *violone,* 4 theorbos, 2 *cornetti,* 1 bassoon, and 3 trombones. But other large groups were assembled in several Austrian and German centers, too,[36] and on occasion in London and Paris. To what extent the full resources of these groups were used, if ever, for the playing of sonatas cannot be answered here except by the general statements already made on multiple performance.

As we have seen, the melo/bass was the most characteristic Baroque setting, especially the "trio" type, which was used in sonatas from 1610 on (Cima, Negri, Rossi). Precedents for the "trio" setting are readily found in a variety of sources—for example, the vocal canzonetta (Banchieri, 1603), the instrumental canzona derived from it (Monteverdi, 1607), and ad libitum practices that reduced larger settings or expanded smaller ones to the "trio" type.[37] An interesting example from 1600 that combines voice and instruments is Cavalieri's "Aria cantata e sonata [i. e., sung and played], al modo antico" for tenor with a pair of flutes or *sordelline* (small bagpipes) above it.[38] The trio setting seems to have provided an ideal meeting point between the older vocal styles and the newer instrumental styles and between the older, stricter polyphony and the new emphasis on accompanied melody.[39] Something of this halfway attitude is reflected in words written by Pietro della Valle in 1640:[40] 39a

To play along with other instruments brings out not so much the artifices

35. Cf. Muffat's own statements on this, as translated in STRUNK-READINGS, p. 450 ff.; also, Rousseau's similar statement with regard to the "Symphonie," noted in LAURENCIE, I, 187.
36. Cf. MEYER, p. 58. Mr. Nathan Broder, Associate Editor of *The Musical Quarterly,* is currently at work on a history of the orchestra. In the meantime only such scattered and brief studies of the orchestra in the 17th century can be cited here as NEF-INSTRUMENTATION, SCHNEIDER-BESETZUNG (with specific and impressive examples), and CARSE-XVII.
37. Cf. ROWEN, p. 21 ff.
38. The piece, appended to   separate from Cavalieri's *Rappresentazione,* is reproduced in SCHERING-BEIS⌐   ᴵ, no. 170.
39. Cf. the statement to this ⌐ ᴵt by Écorcheville in the draft of an incomplete sonata history, quoted in PINCHERLE-CORELLI, p. 41.
40. As reprinted in SOLERTI-ORIGINI, p. 159.

of counterpoint as the graces of the art; because, if the performer is good
he need not try so much to display his own art as to accommodate himself
to all the others. . . . Those who sing and play well must bide their time in
a group and take pleasure in the charm of the imitations rather than the
more subtle artifices of counterpoint.

In discussing "Composition of Three Parts" Purcell summed up his
view of the "trio" sonata setting (*ca.* 1695) :[41]

When you make a *Second Treble* to a Tune, keep it always below the
Upper Part, because it may not spoil the Air. But if you Compose *Sonata's*
there one *Treble* has as much Predominancy as the other; and you are not
tied to such a strict Rule, but one may interfere with the other, as thus:
[followed by six measures in which the upper parts cross freely].

We have seen that Scheibe and Quantz said much the same in 1740 and
1752, respectively (cf. p. 27 ff.), adding that the bass must be an
interesting support but need not share in the melody. In the French
polemics on the supremacy of Italian or French music, Raguenet and
Freneuse even argued the relative merits of the "trio" setting, including
its spacing versus multivoice texture and whether the second high
instrument was actually the equal of the first.[42] As we shall have numerous occasions to observe in the present study, the general trend in
the Baroque Era was from near, if rarely complete, equality of the upper
parts, in both range and melodic activity, to an increasing subordination
of the second part as a filler in a homophonic texture (cf. Exs. 64 and
58, respectively). Within this trend we shall also meet numerous
variants in the handling of the "trio" setting, including canonic conduct
of the upper parts (Uccellini), fugal treatment of all three parts (Ex.
63), free imitation between the upper parts (Ex. 60), wide-ranged
passagework in the upper parts (Ex. 59), chains of suspensions and
resolutions created by the intertwining upper parts against the bass
(especially in slow movements; Ex. 29), note-for-note 3ds and 6ths in
the upper parts (Ex. 21), and simple parallel 3ds (Ex. 39). But we
shall also find that nearly every style of the "trio" setting was already
present or anticipated in some of the earliest examples (S. Rossi).

The logical conclusion in the trend toward relegating the second
upper part to filler material was obsolescence of the figured bass and its
realization. In short, here was one road to the end of the melo/bass
principle. Pertinent to this trend was the quasi-quartet setting (SSA/-
bass) that we have already noted.[43] Another example was the setting

---

41. PLAYFORD, p. 133 ff. Purcell's contribution to Playford's *Introduction* first
appeared in the 12th edition (1694).

42. Cf. ROWEN, p. 37 ff.

43. Cf. "Quatuor" in QUANTZ-FACSIMILE, p. 302.

for violin, viola da gamba, and *b. c.*, which was cultivated especially in Germany and England in the 17th century. When the viola da gamba was actually independent and not merely a *concertante* elaboration of the *b. c.*, the setting often proved to be SA/- or ST/- rather than SB/bass. And when the *b. c.* was played at the keyboard alone, as must have happened often, the result was a true ancestor of the Classic piano trio.

The S/bass and other "solo" settings of the sonata may be regarded as instrumental counterparts of vocal monody. They had common origins not only in this vocal style but in instrumental practices like Diego Ortiz's use (1553) of a viola da gamba to elaborate the descant of a polyphonic vocal texture played on the harpsichord.[44] Originating the same year and in the same collection as the "trio" sonata (Cima's *Concerti ecclesiastici,* 1610), the "solo" sonata was described by the adjective "solo" at least as early as 1627 in a letter written by Buonamente (cf. p. 37) and in 1645 in an actual title (Bertoli). We have also seen that "solo" as a noun became a common English designation in the 18th century for the S/bass sonata. The occasional reduction to an S/bass setting in an inner movement only, as by Buxtehude, brought the sonata close to the concerto grosso again. The sonata for solo instrument with a realized keyboard part, such as was composed chiefly by Bach and composers in his circle, had a tie with the "trio" setting, as in B. Marini's sonata from Op. 8 cited earlier. It also had a bearing on the future accompanied keyboard sonata and on the ultimate, true duo for piano and violin (or other solo instrument).[45]

The unaccompanied solo sonata was another "setting" brought to a peak by Bach. It was even more exclusively his own development, for the only other Baroque examples known here for violin alone are the single sonatas by Biber, Pisendel, and Geminiani (plus a suite by Westhoff). There are a few for viola da gamba alone, too, as by Schenk. 45a The unaccompanied solo setting often attained a remarkably rich, even polyphonic, texture by virtue of multiple stops and chordal bowing across the strings. But it belongs in a separate, "unaccompanied" category, since the melo/bass principle is no longer concerned. With it might be grouped the settings for two or three like instruments without accompaniment. The duet type was especially popular in the 18th century and outside of Italy—for example, Telemann's "6. Sonaten, in 18. melodischen Canons für 2. Trav. oder Viol. ohne Bass" (to use his own wording) or Fesch's sonatas for two cellos alone. 45b

Keyboard, lute, and guitar settings, in which some of the earliest sonatas were composed, are self-sufficient, of course, and might variously

---

44. Cf. EINSTEIN-GAMBA, p. 14 ff.   45. Cf. NEWMAN-ACCOMPANIED.

be placed in the multivoice or melo/bass categories. Their very variety of textures was one of their chief distinctions, although one tends to associate strict polyphony more with the organ, *freistimmig* writing with the lute and guitar, and the still lighter, more homophonic textures with the keyboard and its suitability to fluent passagework and brilliant display. On this basis organ and harpsichord sonatas from the 18th century are often clearly distinguishable, but not those from the 17th century. Even keyboard sonatas that were not alternative dispositions of S/bass settings sometimes had figures over the bass, implying a melo/bass treatment and an improvised filling out of the characteristically thin two-part texture (Noordt). Sonatas for two keyboard instruments were too rare (Pasquini and Mattheson) to permit generalizations in this chapter.

Chapter 6

The Structure of the Baroque Sonata

An Approach to Baroque Form

This final chapter in Part I, "The Nature of the Baroque Sonata," concerns the basic problem of structure. The object is still to outline only the predominant methods, styles, and trends, leaving the rarer and more special cases to be noted in Part II as we come to the sonatas of individual composers. In all the main aspects of structure the most central point of reference is certainly to be found in the 60 sonatas that make up Corelli's Opp. 1 to 5, first published between 1681 and 1700. These include four sets of 12 "trio" sonatas each—Opp. 1 and 3 of the church type, Opp. 2 and 4 of the court type—plus the one set of "solo" sonatas, Op. 5, of which the first half are church and the second are court types. With Corelli's sonatas in mind we then have a basis for comparing related trends in the sonatas of his strongest, most original contemporaries (including Legrenzi, G. B. Vitali, Biber, Purcell, Kuhnau, and Buxtehude), predecessors (including Rossi, Marini, and Buonamente), and successors (including Vivaldi, F. M. Veracini, Tartini, Couperin, Leclair, Bach, Handel, and Boyce).

Bibliographic information on Corelli's output will be found in Chapter 8, where we treat this composer as an individual contributor to the sonata. In advance of that discussion we may note that his works, so carefully polished and neatly organized, seem to have provided a field day for music statisticians and other analysts seeking objective data.[1] Some data of that sort must be presented in this chapter, too. However, as noted in our introductory chapter, each venture into music analysis must ordinarily be undertaken anew by each researcher. No matter how objective he means to be, the researcher must still adapt his analysis to the needs of his study, to any particular view of history that he may have

1. E.g., PINCHERLE-CORELLI, p. 39 ff.; GATES-CORELLI; STILLINGS.

taken, and to subjective reactions of his own that cannot be denied.[2] The present approach is based on an attempt to observe musical form in action—that is, to see it as a generative process determined by its materials. In this way it and its elements do not have to be classified so much in an absolute sense, by forcing them into abstract molds or pigeonholes, as in a relative sense, by placing them somewhere between the extremes of musical structure. Among various dichotomies by which "all" musical structure can be viewed, the extremes and their generative processes preferred in the present study are those explored elsewhere in some detail under the headings of "motivic play" and "phrase grouping."[3]

Briefly, motivic play is understood here as the process of reiterating a motive (fragmentary idea) by sequence or imitation. The "generative" tendencies within that process, if not within the motive itself, are most likely to produce a polyphonic texture, rapid harmonic rhythm, metric diversity, and constant modulation or tonal flux. The most usual structural result of motivic play is a monothematic cursive form.[4] By diametric contrast, phrase grouping is understood as the process of opposing, apposing, or otherwise juxtaposing similar or dissimilar phrases (complete ideas), whether in simple question-answer or more complex and extended relationships. It tends to "generate" a homophonic texture, slow harmonic rhythm, metric regularity, and broad tonal plateaus. And its most usual structural result is a polythematic, integrated, hierarchic design (units within units). One might make the sweeping generalization that much of the writing in Baroque sonatas comes nearer to motivic play than phrase grouping. But the generalization would also apply that this writing is less likely to attain the two extremes than to fall somewhere between such respectively ideal examples as Prelude in G minor from Bach's *Well-Tempered Clavier* II and "Hornpipe" from Handel's "Water Music."

In the consideration of structural traits that follows, the procedure is to take up the whole cycle first, then the individual movement in its various forms. In both the cycle and the individual movement the traits are discussed one by one, but with an attempt to relate them to the over-all dynamic effect. These traits are less often approached chronologically than from the vantage point of Corelli and his contemporaries, or what

2. Pertinent examples of other personal approaches to Baroque form occur in BOSQUET-ORIGINE; KIRKPATRICK-SCARLATTI, chap. 11.

3. NEWMAN-GENERATIVE; NEWMAN-UNDERSTANDING, chaps. 8-10.

4. ALDEN-MOTIVE is a thoughtful, illuminating investigation into the structural role of the motive. RATZ-FORMENLEHRE and FISCHER-WIENER pay special attention to the motive in Baroque instrumental music.

might be called the classical peak of the Baroque sonata. Then, as already suggested, a basis is provided for comparing earlier and later traits. However, by way of a preview, there is also the need, at this point, at least to summarize these traits chronologically.

Thus, the sonata in the first third or more of the Baroque Era may be said to reflect the fairly new problem of achieving extent in independent instrumental music. Deprived of a supporting text, composers still resorted to successive points of imitation in the prevailing manner of the vocal motet and instrumental *ricercare*. Or they indulged in sheer fantasy, often by experimenting with instrumental technique and basic musical processes. Or they found a much more tangible prop in the writing of variations on a familiar tune or bass. But all three means were still relatively short-breathed, tending toward multisectional forms rather than the eventual broader cycles of fewer, longer, separate "movements."

These last were only to be made possible through the larger, more compelling organization of tonality and rhythm that obtained during the middle third of the Baroque Era, especially after about 1670. In Corelli's and other sonatas of that period a fine balance of forces is achieved, with all of music's elements conspiring to produce well-proportioned and well-contrasted forms. But the forms and ideas themselves generally remained fluid and hence unclassifiable except for the now standardized order of the whole cycle and for the broader distinctions between our motivic play and phrase grouping within the separate movements.

Further standardizations of the cycle, plus more standardized plans and tangible ideas within the movements, mark trends in the late Baroque sonata. These trends apply whether in sonatas such as Bach's that capped the more conservative, motivic styles or in sonatas such as F. M. Veracini's that introduced newer styles, including regular phrases in balanced groupings and homophonic textures. One can speak quite unequivocally now of a fugue, a rondo, an A-B-A design, or a French overture.

The Cycle as a Whole

It was Corelli who established once and for all that most characteristic cycle of the Baroque sonata, four movements in the order of S(low)-F(ast)-S-F. Nearly all of the earliest sonatas had been only single movements (Banchieri) although many of them were multisectional in the manner of the canzona (e. g., by Merula) or of variations on a familiar melody (Buonamente). Complete single-movement "sonatas" of these last two types survived beyond 1700, the canzona in the liturgical organ sonata, the variations especially in German melo/bass sonatas and in pieces like Corelli's "Follia" that were used to top off an entire set. A cycle of separate movements became more clearly defined as the problem of greater extent was met with increasing success. This process was one not only of breaking apart but of coming together. On the one hand, the multisectional pieces graduated into separate movements as though by a kind of cell division, leading mainly to the church sonata in so far as it can be distinguished from the court type. On the other hand, separate, contrasting dances were combined into effective suites, first at the performer's discretion and later at the composer's (cf. p. 49), leading mainly to the court sonata.

Some indication of how much the sonata's extent was increased throughout the Baroque Era may be had from a comparison of average lengths in terms of measures. (Of course, this basis of comparison affords only a very rough indication, since it does not take into account specific settings, methods of barring, tempos and actual duration, repeat signs, or even the option of deleting some movements that several composers offered.) Corelli's "trio" sonatas of the court type average only about 100 measures, those of the church type about 150, or a half more. His "solo" sonatas maintain about the same ratio but are still longer by another 60 to 70 measures, because they usually have an added quick movement. Taking some other representative examples in approximately chronological order, Rossi's sonatas average about 55 measures, Buonamente's 65, Marini's 85, Uccellini's 90, Legrenzi's 140, G. B. Vitali's 150, Biber's 200, Buxtehude's 250, Vivaldi's from 150 for the "trio" to 200 for the "solo" type, and F. M. Veracini's more than 500. Veracini's sonatas, close in length to the average of Mozart's late quartets, are, significantly enough, among those in which the performer is invited to delete movements at his discretion. Exceptionally long sonatas from the early Baroque Era almost invariably prove to be variations (Rossi, Buonamente) or fantasias too long for their content (as in sonatas of more than 200 measures by Farina).

Even after separate movements were established, their exact demarcation was not always clear. Corelli's sonatas are no exception. An extreme example is the last sonata of his Op. 3, in which the first half-dozen tempo inscriptions and time signatures may or may not have been conceived as defining separate movements. Certainly, no break could be intended between those sections connected by a continuing passage or a tied note. In earlier sonatas one supposes that the characteristic change from quadruple to triple meter and imitative to chordal texture (or vice

Ex. 1. From "Sonata a 4" by Giovanni Battista Riccio (after EINSTEIN-SCORESm, I).

versa) marked a change equivalent, on a smaller scale, to the later break between movements (Ex. 1), although these changes are sometimes bridged by continuing passages or ties, too (e. g., near the end of Marini's Son. 2, Op. 22). Tempo marks—"Allegro," "Adasio," "Presto"—were already used to mark contrasting sections by important pioneers like Castello and Buonamente, while early as 1655 Marini introduced the designations "Prima parte," "Seconda parte," and so on (terms still used by Ziani around the end of the century).[5]   In the late Baroque sonata the demarcation of movements is no longer a problem except as one may wonder whether to regard the occasional French overture as one or two of a sonata's opening movements, or the typically short, slow third movement, ending with its Phrygian cadence, as an independent movement or merely an introduction to the finale. It is even possible to regard some S-F-S-F cycles as being but a pair of French overtures (e.g., Son. 12 in Corelli's Op. 1).

To make a broad generalization about the number of movements in the Baroque sonata, one can say of both the church and court types that four or five movements were most common in Corelli's time and three or four in the late Baroque Era.[6] But from our previous paragraph the difficulty even of generalizing about the earlier sonatas should be obvious. "Multisectional" when applied to them might mean any number from two to a dozen or more sections (e.g., in Neri's and still in Buxtehude's sonatas), however distinct these were intended to be. The early instrumental canzona is often thought of as falling into only three sections, in an A-B-A plan. However, more sections are found quite as often and in a good variety of dispositions, not to mention fugal and other very different kinds of treatment.[7] From the 1670's four- and five-movement cycles began to prevail in the chief Venetian, Bolognese, and Modenese publications of sonatas. All in all, Corelli himself gave

5. More on the establishment of separate movements is in SCHLOSSBERG, p. 21 ff.
6. The table in HAAS-ESTENSISCHEN, p. 16 ff., provides a representative sampling of the number and order of movements in the half century that overlapped the mid and late phases of the era (ca. 1675-1725).
7. Cf. CROCKER, pp. 100 ff. and 138 ff.

preference to four movements, although within his court "trio" sonatas there is an equal proportion in three movements and within the "solo" sonatas of both types there is a greater proportion in five movements. Larger numbers of movements were most likely to occur in programmatic sonatas such as those by Kuhnau and Couperin. Yet there were as many as nine separate movements in Westhoff's "solo" violin sonata of 1682, which has nothing more programmatic than one movement headed "La guerra." Tartini, Fux, G. B. Somis, Gluck, Quantz, Tessarini, Telemann, and several French composers were among those who produced three-movement cycles in the late Baroque Era, especially in "solo" sonatas. Tartini also wrote many "trio" sonatas in only two movements, in the order S-F, thus anticipating the frequent examples of two-movement sonatas in pre-Classic music.

It is also possible to generalize about the order of movements in the Baroque sonata, but again only for the mid and later phases of the era. With first regard to tempos, the order established in the mid Baroque Era, especially in Corelli's church sonatas, was that S-F-S-F sequence already remarked. In spite of some uncertain, chance anticipations early in the 17th century (cf. pp. 112 and 115), this order was not present or approximated to any marked degree until the 1670's.[8] But if it was still varied with some flexibility by Corelli himself, it was observed almost without compromise by all but the most independent of his direct disciples and imitators. The two plans of the three-movement sonata cycle most favored by the later generation of composers were S-F-F and F-S-F. These plans are sometimes explained as S-F-S-F cycles with either slow movement omitted,[9] which explanation seems especially plausible for the S-F-F cycle. The F-S-F cycle is perhaps more readily related to the Italian opera sinfonia or concerto grosso;[10] or even, in Bach's organ sonatas, to a slow movement inserted between a prelude and a fugue.[11]

Other trends were less definite. As one example, the court sonata of Corelli's time often proved to have the same sequence of tempos as the church sonata. As a second example, especially in Venice and Modena an appreciable number of sonatas were written in the five-movement plan of F-S-M(oderate)-S-F, typically with two outer, often similar fugal movements separated by two transitional adagio movements from

8. The uncertainty results from the frequent absence of tempo marks and from ambiguous terms such as "largo" (broad, but not necessarily slow). Even the dance titles are not sure indicators. Thus, the finale of Corelli's Son. 8, Op. 4, is headed "Sarabanda, Allegro."
9. Cf. SCHEIBE-CRITISCHER, p. 676 ff.
10. Cf. EITNER-SONATE, p. 164 ff.
11. Cf. SPITTA-BACH, III, 211.

a central, more homophonic movement in triple meter. But this plan, almost illustrated by Legrenzi's well-known Sonata "La Cornara"[12] (if the opening tempos are assumed correctly), has actually seemed no more predominant in this study than the A-B-A canzona mentioned earlier, out of which it is said to have grown.[13] There was also an appreciable trend, in the later Baroque Era, toward movements in a moderate tempo such as the "Gratioso" types by Boyce and Leclair. However, except for anticipations of the pre-Classic minuet finale (e.g., by A. Scarlatti or Tartini), no order can be generalized around this type.

Perhaps the basic generalization to be made about the order of movements, one that applies not only to plans just noted but to earlier sonatas and to cycles not otherwise generalizable, is the fact that contrast between adjacent movements was recognized as a paramount need. As will be recalled from Chapter 2, some mention of this need entered into nearly every definition quoted from contemporary theorists. It is true that two and even three fast movements can be found side by side not infrequently (e.g., Sons. 6 and 1, respectively, in Corelli's Op. 3). But then a clear contrast is almost certain to exist in the meter, ideas, and styles. Two slow movements in succession are not so frequent (Sons. 6, 9, and 12 in Corelli's Op. 1), while three, such as occur in several of Degli Antoni's expressive sonatas, are rare. Of course, too many slow movements would be more likely to aggravate that crucial problem of any time art, the problem of arranging a work so as best to accommodate "the normal increase and decline of the listener's attention."[14]

An effective solution to the problem of listener's attention is demonstrated as we come to the more specific question of what the standard order of movements meant with regard to types as well as tempos. The S-F-S-F plan of Corelli's church sonatas puts the more weighty, polyphonic movements first, while the attention is freshest, and the more songful or tuneful and homophonic movements last, when the interest might otherwise flag. This progression from fuller to lighter textures and more solemn to gayer moods is enhanced by a typical stepping up of the meter from simple quadruple to simple triple and then to compound duple (Ex. 2). The opening slow movement is usually in 4/4 meter. It is often characterized (in duo- or trio/bass settings) by intertwining upper lines that progress by suspensions and resolutions over a "running" 8th-note bass. Frequently one finds dotted rhythms, so characteristic of

12. WASIELEWSKI-XVIIm, no. 23. Several examples of the F-S-M-S-F plan occur in G. B. Vitali's Op. 5.
13. Cf. SCHLOSSBERG, p. 42 ff.
14. NEWMAN-UNDERSTANDING, p. 126; cf. p. 193 ff.

Ex. 2. From the incipits of the movements in Sonata 2,
Op. 3, by Arcangelo Corelli (after JOACHIM & CHRYSANDERm,
II, 130 ff.).

the opening section of the French overture and much other Baroque
music (e.g., Son. 8 in Corelli's Op. 3). The second movement is also
likely to be in 4/4 meter; and it is most likely to be a loose quasi fugue
if not a fully consistent one. Usually the center of gravity in the church
sonata, this movement probably was the final form in which the more
polyphonic type of canzona survived, still under that name in Purcell's
sonatas. In the late Baroque Era the fugal movement became even
stricter in the hands of a Bach or gave way to a more homophonic allegro
in the hands of a Tartini. The third movement is commonly in 3/2 or
3/4 meter. When it amounts to more than a few measures of tonal
departure or transition, it is often a homophonic quasi saraband. Occasionally it reduces from a "trio" to a "solo" setting, with one upper

part relegated to simple accompaniment or with the two upper parts taking turns, dialogic style, in playing a single line over the *b. c.* (e.g., Sons. 1 and 5, respectively, in Handel's Op. 2). In Abaco's sonatas it is this movement that is regarded by one author as the center of gravity.[15] The finale, coming where the liveliest and surest attention-getter is needed, is characteristically in the compound meter of the French gigue or the triple meter of the Italian *giga* (e.g., Son. 2 in Corelli's Op. 5).

As for the Baroque court sonata (and suite), the venerable S-F pairing of a simple- and a compound-meter dance can be found as far back as the "Pass'e mezo" and "Padoano" in our earliest known sonata (Gorzanis, 1561). The order of dances that was ultimately standardized internationally—allemande, courante, saraband, and gigue—was already employed fairly regularly by D. Becker in 1668 and by Rosenmüller in 1682. However, Corelli still did not use that particular order in any of his court sonatas and treated this type less regularly in any case. The most regular aspect of the order in his sonatas is the opening "Preludio," followed by an "Allemanda" or "Corrente" or by both in either order. Aside from an occasional "Adagio" or "Grave" and, of course, disregarding the two variation sonatas that end Opp. 2 and 5, the remaining movements are any one or more of three dance types—"Sarabanda," "Giga," and "Gavotta."

Among other dances encountered frequently in the court sonatas of Corelli's Italian contemporaries are the *brando, branle, gagliarda,* and *canario,* and a little later the Siciliano and *borea.* To these may be added such dancelike but less specific types as that headed by the general term "ballo" or "balletta," the capriccio, the aria or arietta, the sinfonia, and even the toccata (for violin!).[16] French dances became international favorites by the turn of the 18th century and in the sonatas of Abaco, Heinichen, Krebs, Handel, G. B. Somis, and numerous other later Baroque composers. As early as the 1680's they were already known in Modena, where G. B. Vitali published minuets in Lully's manner in 1685, one year after his *Varie sonate alla francese, & all'Itagliana.* Even earlier, Georg Muffat in Salzburg had included the bourrée, minuet, and rondeau among other French novelties in his sonatas of 1682. Favorite among English dances were the hornpipe (as by Galliard) and "jigg" (Arne).

The fact that the court sonata usually had one or more free movements along with its dances and that the church sonata had one or more quasi dances along with its freer movements recalls the close overlapping of the two types, as was discussed in Chapter 3. These types, which

15. MOSER-VIOLINSPIEL, p. 221.   16. Cf. SARTORI-BIBLIOGRAFIA, 1678c.

were mainly conceived as such by mid Baroque composers, were but rarely differentiated throughout their cycles. Bassani was exceptional, for example, in reserving his short, binary, relatively homophonic designs exclusively for each of the four dances that make up each of his court sonatas, Op. 1, as against the freer, more polyphonic movements and less regular cycles in all his church sonatas. The greatest overlapping of the types came just before the distinction was generally abandoned, after which "da chiesa" was usually dropped from the title of the church type and some other term applied to the court type (as by Bach). During this confusion neither the texture, aesthetic import, choice of instruments (e.g., organ or harpsichord as the realizing instrument), nor even the title is a reliable basis for a distinction. Representative of the most complete fusion are sonatas in the S-F-S-F plan (e.g., Vivaldi's Op. 5, Nos. 2 and 3) in which four tempo titles join with four titles found in the typical suite. Besides the overlapping and actual fusion of the church and court sonata there was the simple juxtaposition of these two types, produced by adding a complete suite of dances to an introductory sonata also complete in itself. This procedure, primarily mid Baroque and German, had been anticipated by the introductory sinfonia and dances in Buonamente's Book V (1629). It was employed by Kelz in 1658 under the heading of "sonata," apparently for the first time, and made popular in the next half century in the works of D. Becker, Rosenmüller, Buxtehude, and others.

We have seen contrast to be the most recognized determinant in the order of movements. Naturally that contrast applied not only to tempos, meters, and styles or forms but to melodic ideas and expressive forces as well. Contrasts of ideas and expression or character are most readily demonstrated in the late Baroque sonatas, for within the separate movements of these the most distinctive, identifiable tunes and the most explicit inscriptions are likely to be found (Ex. 3). With special regard to the expressive contrast, a more pointed illustration from Tartini than Example 3 might have been found in any of the movements over which he quoted various poetic sentiments or phrases in his private code —for example, "The horror of the tempest."[17] From such an illustration, which is but an extension of "affettuoso," "malinconica," "suave," and the many other of those more characterful inscriptions that turn up throughout the era, one might proceed to the actual, detailed programmatic content of Kuhnau's "Biblical Sonatas," Couperin's "apotheosis" sonatas, or even the earlier "battaglia" sonatas by S. Bernardi, Abel, and others. Works of this sort left no doubt as to the expressive meaning

17a

17. Cf. CAPRI, p. 200.

Ex. 3. The incipits from the movements in Sonata 6, Op. 2,
by Giuseppe Tartini (after BACHMANN-VIOLINISTES, p. 334 ff.).

and contrasts between movements that were intended, although they cannot be regarded as belonging in the mainstream of the Baroque sonata.

Of course, since "variety within unity" is the *sine qua non* of any
art form, where there was contrast there had to be repetition (to use
equivalent antitheses more pertinent to music's processes).   That at
least some Baroque composers were fully conscious of the need for an
over-all balance of these forces in their sonata cycles is made evident
enough in several ways.   It is evident, for example, in the kinds of
revisions that G. Muffat made when he republished his multivoice
"sonatas" as "concertos," including changes in the number, order,
length, and structure of the movements, or in the elaborate recasting of
Corelli's Op. 5 that F. M. Veracini dared to make.   To be sure, Veracini
did permit performers to delete one or two movements at their discretion
in the four- or five-movement sonatas of his own Op. 2, saying that two
or three would "suffice to comprise a sonata of just proportions."   But
the sonatas themselves belie his statement, for they show unusual concern with the order and interrelation of the movements, including partial
repetitions of one movement in another, and further interlocking devices
not unlike those found today in the sonatas of Copland, Sessions, Hindemith, and others.   An interlocking of movements also resulted from the
alternation of pairs of dances (as by the Frenchman Aubert).   In
Corelli's sonatas this kind of interrelation had occurred not between
movements but between the alternate slow and fast sections within his
several movements that are multisectional (e.g., I/5,3 [i.e., Op. 1, Son.
5, third movement; this form will be used hereafter] and V/1,1).   As
far back as Rossi we find an obvious concern with the over-all balance
and dynamic curve, as in the instruction that follows two sonatas of his
Book 3, "Repeat the last section, only faster."   From the canzona must

have come the sonatas by Buonamente (e.g., VI/1 and VI/6) and other early composers in which the sections or incipient movements fall into unmistakable A-B-A and rondo plans. Although such plans do not seem to have had a major influence on the later Baroque sonata, we do meet several instances, in the chapters that follow, of sonatas (such as Kuhnau's) in which the performer is invited to round off the whole by repeating the first movement at the end or in which some similar procedure is observed (as by Cazzati, Rosenmüller, Pezel, and G. B. Vitali).

An important but more localized interrelation of the movements in the sonata cycle remains to be noted. This is the use of similar incipits in some or all of the movements, a very common practice throughout the era in all regions of the sonata and in other multisectional or cyclic forms as well (e.g., Frescobaldi's variation *ricercari* or Handel's concerti grossi). We shall even be meeting an example now and then of a sonata cycle in which an entire movement is simply a variation, usually in a different meter, of some previous movement (as by T. A. Vitali). One such example is afforded in our earliest known sonata again, that by Gorzanis. But still holding in this chapter to the mainstream of the sonata, we are concerned now only with successive variants of the original idea, which usually do not exceed the initial two to six measures. The process is more often subtle than obvious, and therefore open to false analysis. One runs the risk of reading similarities where there are none, perhaps by the arbitrary selection of a melodic outline within the many more notes of a florid line. Or, at worst, the similarities he finds may be no more than a negative consequence of limited ideas and resources on the composer's part. But in the experience of this study the relationships exist and were intended more often than has generally been supposed, in Corelli's sonatas quite as much as others'. When the relationship is as clear as it is in Example 2, quoted earlier from Corelli, we can at least be sure the composer had the principle in mind and we can be more confident in our recognition of other examples by him, such as seem to be intended in III/7 and III/10 or V/6 and V/8. An irrefutable example of how subtle the process can be is provided by the various guises of the "Royal Theme" in the "trio" sonata of Bach's *Musical Offering*. A similarly subtle and hardly fortuitous example by F. Francoeur may be seen in Example 80 (p. 373). Whether thematic relationships were intended in Example 3 (partly by inversion?) is more problematical, although Tartini did leave numerous less equivocal examples (including those in both "The Devil's Trill" and "Didone abbandonata").

In the sonatas of Corelli and many of his contemporaries and successors, if one allows for inversion of the original idea (such as was traditional in the second half of a gigue), for the elaboration or pruning of it, for its regrouping in different meters, or for its possible completion by the other upper part in "trio" settings, he soon wonders whether there are any cycles in which the incipits do not interrelate. It is interesting in several instances to find Corelli stating the idea in its simplest form not as an incipit but in the course of the second slow movement and at the end of the final one (e.g., III/2,3; III/4,3; and III/8,4). Sometimes it is the style rather than the actual contour of the original idea that reappears in the succeeding movements. Thus, III/12 by Corelli and VIII/3 by Legrenzi have incipits that seem too distinctively and consistently chordal to result from mere coincidence. Brilliant "solo" violin sonatas of the late Baroque Era, with their rapid, wide-ranging figuration, are most likely to have this kind of relationship if they have any at all.

The consideration of tonality has been kept to the last among factors influencing the Baroque cycle as a whole only because it stands somewhat apart from the others and certainly not because it is any less significant. Since most of the court sonatas and many of the church sonatas have all their movements in the same key, tonality contributed not so much to the order, contrast, or specific interrelations of the movements as to their general unity. A clear majority of all Corelli's sonatas remain entirely in one key so far as the beginning and end of each movement are concerned. Only the six church sonatas in Op. 5 do not support this majority, each one having one movement that starts or stays wholly in another key. When a movement is in another key that movement is almost invariably a slow movement, but not the first or last movement. Furthermore, with but two inconclusive exceptions (II/4,3 and V/5,3) the relative minor is the key chosen for this movement. The exceptions represent Corelli's only minor sonatas that do not stay entirely in the home key.

By comparison, Bach and Handel used the relative key about equally in their major and minor sonatas. It should be noted that Corelli wrote nearly as many sonatas in minor as in major keys, whereas Bach and Handel preferred major in a ratio of roughly two to one, and Tartini and Locatelli[18] in a ratio more nearly three to one. All Baroque composers generally confined their choices of keys in their sonatas to those of fewest accidentals. With equal temperament still not popularized, Heinichen understandably advised in 1728 that the keys of B and A-flat were seldom used, and those of F-sharp and C-sharp never.[19]

18. Cf. KOOLE, p. 237.   19. Cf. LAURENCIE, I, 189.

Vivaldi was one who several times used the subdominant key for his second slow movement (e.g., XIV/1,3). Couperin used either relative key or he changed the mode on the original tonic.

Often the starting key and concluding key are different in movements that depart from the home key, especially transitional slow movements. Thus, the four-measure introductory "Grave" of II/4,3 in E minor by Corelli starts in the dominant minor, ends with the characteristically Baroque Phrygian cadence on the dominant of that key, then leads directly to the longer "Adagio," which also starts in the dominant minor but ends with a Phrygian cadence on the dominant of the home key. In I/3,3 and I/5,3 by the same composer the third movement begins in the relative but ends in the home key. Corelli did not employ the frequent method used by Abaco, Handel, and others of starting in the relative and ending with a Phrygian cadence on the dominant of the home key. Occasionally the first or some other movement may end on the dominant (e.g., III/1,1 by Leclair), but this departure is usually limited to the cadence itself.

These tonally transitional movements and their cadences derive from modal practices that were still strong in the early 17th century and persisted to some extent even past 1700, especially in the music of certain English and French composers. In spite of numerous claims for examples of "clear tonality" early in the 17th century, and in spite of a few examples such as we shall meet in Buonamente's sonatas that do seem remarkably advanced for their time, tonality did not come under general control in the sense of clear major or minor keys until that same decade of the 1670's—not in the sonata nor in other music.[20] One can say broadly that the Mixolydian and especially the Ionian modes led to the major scale, and the Aeolian and especially the Dorian to the minor scale. But before the 1670's the question of key plan that was just considered has much less meaning, if any. Indeed, early in the century, while there prevailed that mood of experimentation identified with the *stile moderno,* the modal and tonal practices were generally too confused and unpredictable to permit any systematic description. To be sure, Rossi shows a clear sense of direction in the separate variations of his variation sonatas, which stay throughout within the same tonal limits. But even these separate variations may be said to vacillate when they are based on tunes like the Romanesca that shift from "major" to "relative minor."

Marini is clearer in his tonal direction, at least to the extent that his

20. BESWICK is a thorough and penetrating study of tonality in the 17th century, with discussions of special interest to the present one in chaps. 5 and 6.

Ex. 4.   From Sonata 2 in Biagio Marini's Op. 22 (after
TORCHIm, VII, 50, but without the realization).

later harmonies often progress by dominants (Ex. 4; cf. Ex. 49, p. 234).
But he allows the dominants to take him out of the "key" more often than
not, whereas one of the distinct signs in the next generation that tonality
is grasped at the structural level is a new conservativeness about leaving
the key at all.   Judged by this last criterion, Legrenzi's apparent 3d
relationships (e.g., VIII/2)—resulting, for instance, when one movement or section ends in major and the next begins on the dominant of
the relative key—must not be regarded as striking new key contrasts
between movements but as vestiges of the greater variety of cadences
possible in modality.   In other words, these cadences bring us again to
the tonally transitional movements.   For the rest, Legrenzi was clearly
on the threshold of unequivocal major and minor tonality.

The Separate Movements

The main object of this last section on the structure of the Baroque
sonata is to consider more fully those standard types of movements that
could only be given passing mention in our discussion of the cycle as a
whole.   To go into these movements as forms means bringing up the
generative processes of motivic play and phrase grouping that were
summarized at the start of the chapter.   For Baroque instrumental
form is better understood as the organized accomplishment of certain
dynamic, cursive processes than as the kind of integrated but static
scheme by which theorists like Marx or Goetschius have been able to
classify every member, phrase, period, part, and section in Mendelssohn's
Songs Without Words.   Put differently, Baroque form, especially in
extended concepts like the sonata, is largely a matter of individual
structural results that are too fluid to be classed according to standardized designs.   In the terms of the present study, the explanation lies in
the fact that this form is based much more on motivic play than on phrase
grouping.   In fact, sections or movements in which motivic play is
virtually the sole process occur frequently throughout the Baroque Era
(e.g., S. Rossi, I/20, entire, 1607; Kuhnau, *Frische Clavier Früchte* /5,2,

1696; Bach, *Sei Solo* for unaccompanied violin/5,1, 1720), whereas phrase grouping as an almost exclusive process is confined largely to movements in the lightest, shortest, and latest sonatas (cf. Ex. 81, p. 378, by Chédeville, 1739).

However, as suggested earlier, the processes that prevail in most Baroque sonata movements are ordinarily not quite such unadulterated examples of motivic play. The extent to which they depart from that extreme toward the opposite extreme of phrase grouping provides what seems to be our best basis for distinguishing their structural results, in so far as any line can be drawn between them. Thus, the fugal movements and other movements based largely on imitation or other polyphonic devices may be placed first, since in them the maximum motivic play is likely to occur. The binary movement with each half repeated may be placed next, a type that is present at every stage of the Baroque sonata. In spite of its over-all sectional plan, this movement ordinarily depends on at least a degree of motivic play for its continuity, and not seldom a very concentrated degree (as in the sonatas of Martini). The movement (or entire sonata) based on the variation principle may be placed next, since the figuration in each variation usually derives from motivic reiteration (as in "Ciacona," which makes up all of II/12 by Corelli). But here the motive changes with each variation or so and becomes secondary to the complete phrase or phrase grouping of the recurring melody. Hence the motivic play does not lead to monothematic structure and can no longer be regarded as a dominant structural influence. Finally, there is the freer or fantasia kind of movement (such as prevails in Biber's sonatas when variations are not under way). In this movement motivic play, phrase grouping, or any cross between these may occur, and in any degree of texture between polyphony and homophony, or in actual monophony. But now the difference is that none of these processes is regularized sufficiently to control the form.

Taking these four broad types of movement in the same order, we may start with the fugal movement. The full-fledged Baroque fugue is viewed here not necessarily in the traditional textbook sense of a tonal and organic A-B-A plan. Rather it is viewed as a series of complete or incomplete expositions of a single subject in several nearly related keys, bridged by modulatory episodes that progress by sequential motivic play on some element of that subject or its attendant counterpoint.[21] This definition is necessarily flexible but can still serve as a basis for comparison along with such allied considerations as the extent and individuality of the subject, the density and quality of the texture, the

21. Cf. APEL-DICTIONARY, p. 285 ff.; NEWMAN-UNDERSTANDING, p. 149 ff.

direction of the tonal course, and the concentration or drive of the form as a whole. Naturally, the most developed fugues as defined here occur in the later Baroque sonatas—for example, the second movements each of Sonata I for violin and realized keyboard by Bach, I/10 by F. M. Veracini, *L'Apothéose de Corelli* by Couperin, II/6 by Handel, and "trio" Sonata in D minor, Op. 4, by Leclair. Such fugues are decidedly more complete, consistent, and concentrated than the average to be found in the mid Baroque sonata. For that matter, we have seen that they are not necessarily representative of their own times, during which the fugue was usually replaced in the more "modern" sonatas, as it had been in the court sonata, with a relatively homophonic type of allegro movement.

· Corelli's fugal movements are more representative of the average. They tend to be less tightly constructed than those just cited because the subject itself may undergo changes (I/6,2) or even disintegrate by gradual fragmentation (V/1,2; I/7,1), the complementary tonic-dominant relationship between subject and answer may be disregarded (III/1,2), other material may compete for attention (III/4,2), and the fugal process itself may be abandoned little by little as both entries and episodes give way to more neutral passages (I/7,1 and V/5,2; cf. the free introduction of extraneous material in many of Handel's vigorous fugues, as in I/13,2). Yet in their very freedom Corelli's fugal movements seem to make more effective chamber music than a stricter fugue might make. At least when governed by his sense of proportion, such movements as III/1,2, V/2,2, or V/4,2 have a rhythmic verve and purposefulness not often surpassed in the experience of this study. Furthermore, there is much appeal in the subjects themselves, especially the extended, distinctive ones like those in I/6,2, I/7,1 (Ex. 5), III/5,2, and V/3,2. Their rhythmic patterns (both thetic and anacrustic),

Ex. 5. From the opening of Sonata 7, Op. 1, by Arcangelo Corelli (after JOACHIM & CHRYSANDERm, I, 40).

provide Corelli's most original ideas, even though some other subjects that he uses are less extended and individual, in the manner of the *soggetto* rather than the *andamento* (V/6,2).

Naturally, Corelli's fine sense of contrapuntal interest has much to do with the success of his fugal movements, too. If his texture is seldom as concentrated as Bach's it nonetheless reveals that delightfully fluent Italian art of suggesting more activity than actually occurs. The explanation lies largely in the shrewd timing of the entries; in the addition of frequent "false" entries on the *tête du sujet;* in at least a gesture toward the standard contrapuntal devices such as a countersubject by inversion (III/2,2) or a double subject in invertible counterpoint (III/4,2); and in relatively slow harmonic rhythm, which associates with counterpoint that is more chordal than linear and helps to account for the fluency. With his separate *concertante* bass part in the church "trio" sonatas, Corelli does let the bass contribute to the fugal texture much of the time, not merely at the starts of new sections and during rests in the upper parts, as was more often true in the Baroque sonata. Yet even in the "solo" sonatas, without the separate part, the *b. c.* line contributes enough that it and the frequent double-stops in the violin often make three real parts (V/2,2). Finally, the compelling tonal course, frequently by dominants, must be mentioned as an important factor in the success of fugal movements such as Corelli's.

To cite the music of an important non-Italian, we may note that Purcell's canzonas or fugal movements are also notable for their distinctive subjects (cf. Ex. 63, p. 306). They are more concentrated than Corelli's as regards both the consistence and persistence of the ideas (first set/4,2). In fact, several of them have ever-recurring subjects, as the ancestral English fantasia usually had. But the over-all tonal course is less compelling, perhaps because of the modal traces that still survive; and the episodes are both fewer and more formalized (as in mss. 19-24, first set/3,2). Buxtehude, important in any case as a direct predecessor of Bach in the writing of fugues, left fully developed examples in his sonatas (e.g., I/1,3). The unusual length of these results partly from their unusually long subject and partly from unusually long episodes that have seemed here to attenuate the tonal plan to the point of monotony. Since its function is largely modulatory, the episode may be said to have acquired significance in the fugue directly proportional to the rise of tonality. When the extent of its use and the degree of its clarity are observed, this special structural agent affords one main basis for evaluating the historical maturity of a fugue.

The monothematic principle in the fugue, not being dependent on tonality, is present earlier. Much as it occurs in several of Frescobaldi's keyboard *ricercari,* so it occurs in several movements of Castello's and Buonamente's ensemble canzonas and sonatas. Probably for the very reason that Buonamente was so prescient tonally, there are also anticipations of the episode in his sonatas. An instance may be seen in VI/2 (Ex. 6; cf. Ex. 15, p. 115), although whether this figure was intended

Ex. 6. From Giovanni Battista Buonamente's "Sonata Seconda à 2," Bk. 6 (after EINSTEIN-SCORESm, II).

as a variant of the "subject" in the manner of the variation *ricercare* or as a momentary digression before returning to the original "subject" is hard to know. It cannot be said actually to bridge two "keys" without overstating the breadth of Buonamente's tonal perspective. In the next chapter are cited the sonatas of other Italians, Neri and Legrenzi in particular, as revealing further important landmarks in the history of the monothematic, tonal fugue with episodes.

After the fugal type of movement there may be considered the type in which motivic play alone is the predominant process, without the broader control of an intermittently recurring subject. This type occurs most commonly in the very prevalent binary design with each half repeated, and at tempos from moderate to very fast. But it can also be found to a lesser extent in a much wider range of examples. At one extreme are undivided movements in a fairly dense polyphonic texture of continuous imitations. At the other are binary designs in a homophonic texture that permits sequentially reiterated motives to group into regular phrases. Our remarks can best follow this path from one extreme to the other.

It may help to introduce these remarks with certain structural aspects of motivic play not previously mentioned here. First is the fact that the recurring motive itself is typically a fragment of about three to seven notes. In Corelli's sonatas it is most often stepwise (I/1,4) or chordal (IV/3,2) and hence of fairly neutral character. But there are other frequently met types of more distinctive character, among them the "fate" motive best known in Beethoven's Fifth Symphony (e.g., VI/Son. 2 *a 3* by Buonamente and VIII/Son. 1 *a 2* by Marini), the dotted short-long-short-long pattern (e.g., Son. 3,1 *a 3* by Handel[22]), and the de-

22. -WERKEm, XXVII, 68.

scending chromatic tetrachord (as throughout Merula's long organ sonata). Second, in persistent motivic play the bass is likely to participate somewhat less regularly than in fugal writing. Even in the S/bass setting it is more likely to furnish a harmonic support while the motive is reiterated by sequence (e.g., V/10,3 by Corelli). Third, with this further mention of sequence, attention may be called to a primary means of continuation in Baroque instrumental music,[23] a means not seldom overdone (cf. Ex. 32 by Vivaldi, p. 171) and scarcely employed to such an extent in any other era. Fourth, the broad organizing principle within which motivic play operates, whether by sequence or imitation, is the tour of nearly related keys. In Baroque tonal music these keys are rarely more than one degree from the tonic key in the circle of fifths. The tour is implemented chiefly by those successions of dominants that produce one modulatory drive-to-the-cadence after another, each new progression veering off at once (Ex. 7).[24] Finally, a frequent method

Ex. 7. From Sonata 2 for organ by Johann Sebastian Bach (after -WERKEM, XV, 13).

of rounding off these motivic forms is to repeat the last measures *piano,* as an echo. At the end of I/3,4 Corelli goes through the original and its echo twice. In V/3,5 only the repetition comes twice, but occurs exceptionally in the tonic minor (Ex. 8), the effect being almost the ghoulish one of Iago's refrains in the drinking song from Verdi's *Otello.*

Examples representative of the wide range of motivic forms may be cited, again mainly in Corelli's sonatas. A type closest to the fugue is

23. MISHKIN-SEQUENCE is a valuable study into this aspect of Baroque form.
24. Cf. the enlightening discussion in BUKOFZER-BAROQUE, p. 359 ff.

Ex. 8.   From Sonata 3, Op. 5, by Arcangelo Corelli (after
JOACHIM & CHRYSANDERm, III, 35).

found in I/2,2, in which a subject is announced at the start, then recurs
only in occasional free alterations and in the course of constant motivic
play on derived elements (III/5,4 and III/6,4).   Many Baroque gigue
or quasi-gigue finales in both undivided and binary designs fall into this
type.   One step removed from this type, in the direction of lighter,
more homophonic texture, is I/1,4 by Corelli.   In this movement the
subject is heard in full only at the start, with the motive's repetitions
recurring more by sequence than imitative exchanges.   An undivided
movement, it is one of many by Corelli and his contemporaries that have
a single repeat sign, at the very end.   Since a repetition of the entire
movement would not affect its form (although it would naturally affect
the balance of the complete cycle), one assumes the sign was meant
merely as an option by which the sonata's total length could be regulated.

In binary designs, especially the shorter dances of the court sonata,
we can find frequent examples of motivic play that groups more or less
into phrases.   One step toward such phrases is illustrated in III/6,1 by
Corelli, where the motivic imitations converge in a cadence every few
measures.   Here the meter still has some of the irregularity of constant
motivic play.   Often the first phrase of a dance is regular but is followed
by overlapping motives that trail off in a more continuous, braidlike
texture (IV/2,2).   At other times the movement divides into phrases
that are all distinguishable, yet hardly regular.   In fact, they are irregular
in an easy, natural way that should have seemed quite ideal to those later
composers like Beethoven who sought to escape "the tyranny of the

barline." Thus, the first half of II/2,2 divides into one phrase of
$3 + 3 + 3$ measures, another phrase of $2 + 2 + 2$ measures, and a
cadential phrase of 7 measures. A more regular construction occurs in
the "Corrente" II/1,3, which divides into two repeated periods, each
with a "question" phrase of $3 + 4$ measures and an "answer" phrase
of $4 + 5$ measures. But only in the very shortest dances is complete
regularity to be found. Both the "Gavotta" that follows this "Corrente"
and the celebrated "Gavotta" V/10,4 consist simply of two "square,"
four-measure phrases with repeat signs.

In any case, Corelli's larger binary designs are generally asymmetrical, with the second half extended by modulations. Sometimes the
first half merely cadences in the tonic key (V/4,5), as was still truer
of dance movements composed earlier in the century. But more often
it reaches the relative or dominant key, from which point the second
half returns by circuitous routes through nearly related keys. In this
way the subdominant side of the tonal balance is maintained (V/3,5).
The thematic organization of the binary design seems to have depended
on how distinctive the ideas themselves were. Corelli's motives being
neutral in character, his binary movements do not necessarily have the
similar, parallel incipits and final cadences in the two halves that became
more and more standard after 1700 (cf. II/2,1 and IV/7,2). Abaco's
court sonatas, for example, do consistently reveal in their binary movements both the more distinctive motives and the parallelism (e.g.,
III/7,4).

The still later sonatas by Vivaldi, F. M. Veracini, Tartini, and
Locatelli, among others, reveal further control of thematic organization.
The importance of the main idea is increased by the clear, regular
phrases, the more homophonic texture, and the slower harmonic rhythm
that now absorb, transform, or transcend the motivic process (Ex. 9).
It is partly this importance that explains the return of the main idea in
the course of the second half of the asymmetrical binary form. Parallelism at this point with the start of the movement seldom lasts more
than a measure or so, because the music now remains in or near the tonic
where the first half had soon departed from it. But there is no denying
at least an incipient A-B-A design in many such movements. Thus,
almost every movement, slow as well as fast, in Vivaldi's outstanding
cello sonatas is a well-balanced example of this design.

The movement (or complete sonata) based on the variation process
may be noted next, although as the relatively obvious, secure principle
that it was, it requires less clarification here. Virtually all sonata
variations were written on recurring melodies or basses. The majority

Ex. 9. The opening of Sonata 2, Op. 2, by Francesco Maria
Veracini (after the original edition of 1744).

of these melodies and basses are a few favorites that appeared in many
kinds and regions of Baroque music and have been the subjects of considerable research. One of the basses was the descending tetrachord or
related line in triple meter most often called "chaconne" and used chiefly
in its minor and chromatic forms (e.g., in V/4,4 by Leclair). The
Romanesca (usually notated in quadruple meter but understood in
triple meter[25]) and the Ruggiero were also used as basses in triple meter,
each in several versions.[26] The Bergamasca, a popular tune in 4/4 meter
from Bergamo,[27] was treated as a descant or soprano tune (cf. Ex. 14,
p. 113). The Folia has been known in many sets of variations over the
past three centuries including V/12 ("Follia") by Corelli. It includes
both a descant melody and a bass, either of which could serve for variations when they were not used together.[28]

The usual length of the Baroque tune and each variation is four
measures. When the constant factor is a recurring bass, each note of
the line ordinarily occupies one whole measure. However, in the later
variations, that note usually undergoes considerable melodic elaboration
of its own in keeping with the motivic play in progress above it. When
the constant factor is a descant tune, the elaboration begins from the first
variation and is likely to become more and more decorative. Originally
this decoration was in the manner of intricate diminutions. Later it
developed into pyrotechnics (as by Tartini, Locatelli, and Leclair) that

25. Cf. BUKOFZER-BAROQUE, pp. 39 ff. and 46 ff.
26. Cf. GOMBOSI-OSTINATO on the Romanesca; EINSTEIN-RUGGIERO and EINSTEIN-
ANCORA.
27. Cf. NETTL-BERGAMASKA.
28. Cf. MOSER-FOLIES; PINCHERLE-CORELLI, p. 74 ff.

Ex. 10. From elaborations of a bass line in Giovanni Battista Buonamente's "Sonata sesta sopra Rugiero" and of a descant tune in his "Sonata nona sopra Questo è quel luoco," both in Bk. IV (after EINSTEIN-SCORESm, II).

clearly anticipate Paganini's dazzling melodic variations. Both processes were already well established in the music of S. Rossi, Buonamente, and other pioneers of the sonata (Ex. 10).

Less often the tune is treated as a roving cantus firmus, as in B. Marini's "Sonata sopra Fuggi dolente core" (XXII/3), in which the tune appears at different times in each of the three *concertante* parts of the SSB/bass setting but undergoes no changes except to accommodate the shifts to triple meter and back. Corelli's "Ciacona" (II/12) and Purcell's Sonata 6 in his posthumous set of 1697 are both complete "trio" sonatas consisting of variations on similar chaconne basses, including the three or four notes that often follow the descending tetrachord. Corelli puts his *ostinato* in G major and treats it more freely by changing its rhythmic position and length, elaborating it, and occasionally departing from it slightly. Purcell's ground is in G minor, lasts five measures each time, and undergoes no changes. Biber's remarkable "Passacaglia" for unaccompanied violin (sixteenth of the "Rosary Sonatas") is based only on the four-note descending minor tetrachord (cf. p. 217). Corelli's "Follia" generally retains both the traditional bass and melody as well as the harmonic progression associated with them. But the composer had no hesitation about making modest departures from any of these wherever the musical or technical interest seemed to require them.[29] In this sonata are some of his most advanced uses of the violin.

Our final type of movement, the fantasia, calls for little further comment since it depends only on free applications and mixtures of the basic processes already described. For example, in one of Corelli's most expressive slow movements in "trio" setting (III/11,1; cf. Ex. 29, p. 159), a relatively homophonic phrase appears first, after which motivic play prevails. The same procedure, emphasized by a change from "Grave" to "Andante," occurs in III/5,1. A characteristic method of progression in the phrases of slow movements in the "trio" setting is that in which the two upper parts create successions of suspensions and resolutions over a "running" bass. In "solo" settings the same process is created by the solo and bass parts alone. Examples 2 and 69 (pp. 74 and 328) illustrate the two processes.

It should be noted that the fantasias are most often slow movements and virtuoso movements of a toccata character (as in every sonata of F. M. Veracini's Op. 2). The rather frequent examples that we shall be meeting in the following chapters of fantasia movements in fast tempos are mostly by composers who were still wrestling with the problems of extent in instrumental music (e.g., Schmelzer and J. J. Walther), as discussed early in this chapter.

29. Cf. PINCHERLE-CORELLI, p. 79 ff.

Part II

The Composers and Their Sonatas

Chapter 7

Italy from 1597 to about 1650

A Summary View

We begin Part II with Baroque composers in Italy, in the country where a sonata idea first took root and ripened. However, Italy was the "country" that Count Metternich could still dismiss as "a geographical expression" in the 19th century. As is well known, throughout the 17th and 18th centuries and until it was finally unified around 1870, Italy was but a political conglomerate of more-or-less independent cities and states. These were identified in some instances with foreign powers, in others with local kingdoms, principalities, duchies, church communities, or elite families stemming from an ancient republican ancestry. Hence the art history of Italy, like the political history, is best surveyed one city or region at a time.

In Chapters 7 to 9 more than 100 Baroque composers are grouped into about 25 Italian cities. Their heavy concentration in northern Italy—in the provinces of Piedmont, Lombardy, Venetia, and Emilia—is suggested on the adjoining map, with surprisingly few names to list in such great musical centers as Rome and Naples. Especially productive of instrumental as well as other music were Bologna and Venice, where certain composers, important posts, active publishers, a significant instrumental tradition, nearness to the great violin makers, and specific needs provided unusual inducements to sonata writing.

The Baroque sonata production in Italy falls into three rather clearly defined periods, from 1597 to about 1650, 1650 to 1700, and 1700 to 1750. The first of these periods is marked by scattered publications, chiefly vocal collections in which sonatas appear as instrumental appendages or instrumental collections in which they are mixed in with a variety of differently titled pieces. The sonatas in this period are naturally innovational and extremely diverse in form. Only to a limited extent do their composers fall into perceivable schools, as in Mantua and Venice. The second period is marked by the rise of more prominent

Italian cities in which Baroque sonatas were composed and/
or published (with the number of composers included in this
survey as being active in each city).

and lasting schools, especially in Venice, Bologna, and Modena. It
culminates in the "classic" church and court sonatas of Corelli and his
contemporaries. The third period extends from the international influence of Corelli to the mid 18th century and the later but more conservative sonatas with *b. c.* It overlaps, by a decade or two, other
Italian sonatas that are saved for a succeeding volume because they are
regarded here as heralds of the Classic era.

By way of previewing the first period chronologically, it is possible to list here, as far as they are known to this study, all Italian composers of collections that first appeared in print before 1651 and contain pieces called sonatas.[1] In parentheses after each composer's name is given the city where he then lived as well as the year and general scoring of his first published "sonatas" (using the scoring terminology mentioned on page 52). For the sake of near completeness Italians are included who, as can be seen, were active abroad at least during the years given here, and who, for that reason, may not turn up again until a later chapter. Not included are three non-Italians to be met later, who published sonatas before 1650, all of them Germans. The city of publication is not given in the list. But Venice (especially with its publishers Gardano and Vincenti) had such a monopoly at this time, including publications by composers abroad, that it is assumed to be the city in the subsequent discussions of this first period unless another city is named.[2]

Italian Composers of Sonatas
Published Before 1651

Giacomo Gorzanis (Trieste, 1561, lute tablature)
Fabritio Caroso (Venice, 1581, lute tablature)
Giovanni Gabrieli (Venice, 1597, polychoir)
Adriano Banchieri (Bologna, 1605, organ)
Salomone Rossi (Mantua, 1607, multivoice)
Cesario Gussago (Brescia, 1608, multivoice and polychoir)
Archangelo Crotti (Ferrara, 1608, multivoice)   2a
Paolo Funghetto (Verona, 1609, multivoice?)
Gian Paolo Cima (Milan, 1610, S/- and SS/bass)
Claudio Monteverdi (Mantua, 1610, multivoice)
Academico Caliginoso (Rome?, 1610?, guitar tablature)
Marc'Antonio Negri (Venice, 1611, SS/bass)
Steffano Bernardi (Verona, 1613, multivoice and polychoir)
Giovanni Battista Riccio (Venice, 1614, multivoice)
Biagio Marini (Venice, 1617, S/- and SSB/bass)
Giovanni Priuli (Vienna, 1618, polychoir)
Francesco Usper (Venice, 1619, polychoir)
Gabriele Usper (Venice, 1619, SSB/- and SSBB/bass)
Innocentio Vivarino (Adria, 1620, S/bass)
Francesco Turini (Brescia, 1621, SS/- and SSB/bass)

1. Two sets of "Sonate a cinque," one ascribed to Giovanni Croce (Venice, 1580) and the other to Andrea Gabrieli (Venice, Angelo Gardano, 1586) in BECKER-TONWERKE, pp. 286 and 287, are certainly lost, if they ever did exist. The "sonatas" ascribed to Ercole Porta (1613) and Pellegrino Possenti (1628) in EITNER-QL are not actually so called. As noted in chap. 4, this study has not turned up MS sonatas composed by Italians in Italy and definitely dated before 1651 that did not also appear in print, although several by Italians in Vienna (Giovanni Valentini, A. Bertali, and G. Arrigoni) certainly originated before then without achieving publication.
2. Cf. EITNER-VINCENTI.

Benedetto Sanseverino (Milan, 1622, guitar tablature)
Tarquinio Merula (Warsaw, 1624, melo/bass)
Nicolo Corradini (Cremona, 1624, melo/bass)
Giovanni Battista Buonamente (Vienna, 1626, SS/bass)
Carlo Farina (Dresden, 1626, solo/- and SS/bass)
Michel'Angelo Grancini (Milan, 1627, multivoice?)
Pietro Milioni (Rome, 1627, guitar tablature)
Tomaso Cecchino (Verona?, 1628, S/- and SS/bass)
Ottaviomaria Grandi (Reggio, 1628, melo/bass, multivoice, and polychoir
Giuseppe Scarani (Venice, 1630, melo/bass)
Giacomo Arrigoni (Vienna, 1635, multivoice)
Guglielmo Lipparino (Bologna, 1635, SB/- and SBB/bass)
Gerolamo Casati (Novara, 1635, melo/bass)
2b Girolamo Fantini ("Francofort" [or Florence?], 1638, S/- and SS alone)
Marco Uccellini (Modena, 1639, melo/bass)
Agostino Trombetti (Bologna, 1639, guitar tablature)
Francesco Corbetta (Bologna, 1639, guitar tablature)
Paolo Zasa (Venice, 1640, melo/bass)
Giovanni Battista Fontana (Venice, 1641 [posthumous], melo/bass)
Gioanpietro Del Buono (Palermo, 1641, cembalo)
Massimiliano Neri (Venice, 1644, multivoice)
Giovanni Antonio Bertoli (Brescia, 1645, B/bass)
Ludovico Monte (Venice, 1645, guitar tablature)
Carlo Calvi (Bologna, 1646, guitar tablature)
Maurizio Cazzati (Bozzolo, 1648, multivoice)
Antonio Ferro (Vienna, 1649, melo/bass and multivoice)
Gaspare Filippi (Vicenza, 1649, melo/bass and multivoice)
Bernardo Gianoncelli (Venice, 1650, lute tablature)

Space would hardly permit such a listing for later Italian composers or, after 1700, for the composers of any country significantly devoted to the sonata. Even this early listing would quickly get out of hand were the numerous reprints and succeeding publications by the same composers to be included. Furthermore, it could no doubt be expanded considerably were Claudio Sartori's invaluable, detailed bibliography of early Italian instrumental publications supplemented to include the stream of lute and guitar collections that had begun well before Gorzanis' first *Intabolatura*.

Venice (Gabrieli, Marini, Fontana, Neri)

First to be noted among these earliest Italian composers should be those working in Venice, where the church of St. Mark had for long been the hub of musical activity and the heart of the Republic. With Andrea and Giovanni Gabrieli, uncle and nephew at St. Mark's, Venice was entering upon its most brilliant century and a half of music. Furthermore, the Venetians in our early group mark the clearest link between Renaissance and Baroque styles.

Giovanni Gabrieli (*ca.* 1555-1612 or 1613), the first and greatest of these, actually marked the consolidation and peak of past trends as well as the start of new ones. The polychoir orchestral dispositions that especially identify his splendrous, stentorian canzonas and sonatas had stemmed, of course, from Willaert and other St. Mark's predecessors. With Gabrieli these dispositions were chiefly new in their application to instruments alone (and, to be sure, in their remarkable craftsmanship). In any case, they did not introduce a long continuing concept of the sonata. Under the heading "sonata," polychoir writing declined in quantity and significance during the next half century in Venice. It persisted a little longer in a few isolated, less directly related flowerings like that of the Bolognese orchestral "trumpet sonata." But in so far as it survived at all in instrumental music its province finally became that of the concerto.

Among his purely instrumental compositions Giovanni Gabrieli left a total of 8 actually called "sonata" (or "sonatta") as against at least 36 called "canzona," not to mention the 2 programmatic "Battaglie" for 8 instruments or the *Intonationi, Ricercari,* and *Toccate* for organ. The sonatas and most of the canzonas occur in two collections by him alone, among some 12 main collections in which he appears alone or in conjunction with his uncle. Two sonatas and 14 canzonas are included with motets and other vocal music in *Sacrae Symphoniae,* published in 1597;[3] and 5 sonatas and 16 canzonas comprise the entire collection *Canzoni e sonate,* published posthumously in 1615.   3a

Of áll Gabrieli's works "Sonata Pian & Forte," in the 1597 set, is the most celebrated, chiefly because both its dynamic markings and its exact designations of orchestral instruments are the earliest now known.[4] It is scored for two four-part choirs, the second being a 5th to an octave lower in range. "Primus Chorus" has a *cornetto* above three trombones, and "Secundus Chorus" a *violino* above three more trombones. "Violino" here means not an early use of the violin but a *viola da braccio,* since the range of its part is d to a'. However, a tenor viola da gamba would be necessary if the whole piece were transposed down a 4th, as the inscription beside the title, "Alla quarta bassa," seems to allow. "Pian" is generally marked when either of the choirs plays alone and "Forte" when the two play together. The other sonata in the 1697 set, "Sonata

3. Mod. ed. of the 16 instrumental pieces in full score: ISTITUZIONIm, II (Benvenuti), with a valuable preface by G. Cesari (especially pp. lxvi ff. and lxxxv ff.).
4. Among separate mod. eds.: DAVISON & APELm, no. 173; SCHERING-BEISPIELEm, no. 148.

Octavi Toni," is scored, in a more polyphonic texture, for two six-part choirs in the same range. Neither the instruments, except for the range of each part, nor the dynamic markings are indicated.

At least in the 1597 set Praetorius' attempt to distinguish between Gabrieli's canzonas and sonatas may be accepted as a reasonable generalization, if not a rule (cf. p. 23). These sonatas do lack "the many black notes" (that is, 8th-note passages) that prevail in most of the canzonas, though much less, for example, in Canzonas 10, 13, and 16. And they are graver in character, especially with their stately, often chromatic, chord progressions in broad harmonic rhythms. To add to Praetorius' statement is the fact that all but two of the canzonas begin with the characteristic pattern of a long note followed by two short notes, whereas only one of the canzonas and all four of the sonatas that could be seen here

Ex. 11. From Giovanni Gabrieli's "Sonatta con tre violini" (after WASIELEWSKI-XVIIm, no. 7).

(including two in the 1615 set) begin with a dotted whole-note followed by a half-note or two quarter-notes.

With one exception, the five sonatas among the *Canzoni e sonate* of 1615 have yet to be scored and made accessible in modern reprints. A good reason may be their massive scoring, which is in even more parts, divided into more choirs, than in the 1597 set. The exception is the well-known "Sonatta con tre violini," last piece in the 1615 set.[5] This piece calls for the smallest instrumental grouping used anywhere by Gabrieli. In it three actual violins continually imitate and cross within the limits of d' to c''' and over a "Basso per L'Organo." The bass, with its optional reinforcement ("Basso se piace"), is indispensable, since it provides a slow-moving support for the harmony or shares in some of the motivic play above it. This polarity of bass and high parts, the consistent motivic play, the broad approaches to tonal cadences, and the interest in an over-all design (A-B-B) were modernisms that placed "Sonatta con tre violini" ahead even of its posthumous date (Ex. 11).

The other four sonatas in the 1615 set are all extreme examples of the polychoir type. Sonata 13 is *a 8*. Sonata 18 is scored for 14 instruments grouped into two 5-part choirs, each with 2 *cornetti* over 3 trombones, plus a third, still lower choir of 4 trombones. Sonata 19 is for 15 instruments divided into 4 choirs, and Sonata 20 is for 22 instruments divided into 5 choirs of $6 + 4 + 4 + 4 + 4$ parts! These last two sonatas specify only some of the instruments (*cornetti* and trombones, again) and fall into several sections with contrasting meters (presumably $4/2$ and $3/1$).[6]

Before the appearance of Gabrieli's last set came two more vocal collections containing sonatas, by obscure composers then active in Venice. One was the collection *Affetti amorosi . . . Libro secondo,* published in 1611 by **Marc'Antonio Negri,**[7] who rose to vice-maestro di cappella at St. Mark's in 1612. This set includes three "sonatas" for

---

5. Among mod. eds.: WASIELEWSKI-XVIIm, no. 7; STRAETEN-FIDDLE, p. 24; HORTUSm, no. 70 (Danckert, with preface).

6. A little information about the 1615 set appears in WINTERFELD, II, 109 and 114; WASIELEWSKI-XVI, pp. 161 and 163, and -XVII, pp. 7 ff. and 16; RIEMANN-MUSIK-GESCHICHTE, II, Part 1, 472 ff. (with examples from Son. 20); and KENTON (including reference to an article by William Yeomans). A dissertation on the set by Mr. L. F. Brown at North Texas State College is reported in progress (JAMS, IX [1956], 208). One of 3 canzonas for 6 instruments in this set, with sections in contrasting meters, is scored in WASIELEWSKI-XVIIm, no. 8. Also as of this writing, an edition of the 1615 set is projected by the American Institute of Musicology in Rome.

7. Listed in full in SARTORI-BIBLIOGRAFIA, which also lists nearly all the other publications before 1701 that are mentioned in this chapter, usually including the complete dedication, preface if any, and contents.

"doi Violini," which are actually very early "trio" (SS/bass) settings, printed in a three-staff, superimposed score at that. But the bass is not mentioned in the title, since it is purely a slow-moving harmonic support. The upper parts move almost entirely in parallel 3ds, aside from an initial imitation or two. Lasting only from one to two dozen measures, the three sonatas are all in quadruple meter.

The other publication before 1615 was that in 1614 of *Il secondo Libro delle divine lodi* by one **Giovanni Battista Riccio,** followed in 1620 by this author's Book 3 under the same title.[8] Both sets consist of sacred vocal compositions plus one multivoice "Sonata a 4" each among several canzonas for two to four instruments. In the 1620 book the canzonas even more than the sonata exhibit such sure traits of the *stile moderno* as the use of *tremolo,* quick alternations of *pian* and *forte,* and sequences of distinctly idiomatic instrumental figures. Evidently by 1620 Riccio already knew two intervening publications in Venice, by Marini and Usper, shortly to be noted. As for instruments, in the 1620 set Riccio specified the usual violins, *cornetti,* and trombones in certain canzonas, but still indicated only four clef ranges for the sonata— mezzo-soprano, alto, tenor, and baritone, plus the *b. c.* that was conventional by this time even when not needed, as it was not in this multivoice distribution (cf. Ex. 1, p. 71).

In 1617 appeared the "opera prima" by a composer considerably more important to the early sonata and to early violin music, **Biagio Marini** (*ca.* 1597-1665). Marini is introduced at this point since he was active in Venice at the time of his first and last publications, which were 38 years apart. But in between these he shifted positions frequently, including important stays in German cities at the time he published his two other extant collections that contain sonatas. To sum up, out of 22 collections of music composed by Marini, according to his opus numbers, 16 are extant. Out of these last the three that are exclusively instrumental, plus one mixed collection, contain a total of 34 melo/bass pieces called "sonata." Probably at least two of the six lost collections contained sonatas, too, since "Libro terzo" appears beside "Opera XXII" in the last collection's title, the one title that mentions only sonatas, yet no Book 1 or Book 2 has been found.[9]

Among the 28 melo/bass "symfonie," canzonas, dances, and other

9a

---

8. EINSTEIN-SCORESm, I, contains all the instrumental pieces from the 1620 set.
    9. EINSTEIN-SCORESm, III, includes all of Marini's Opp. 1, 8, and 22. ISELIN is the chief source, including several reprints and a list of several others (to which the sonata from Op. 8 in SCHERING-BEISPIELEm, no. 183, should be added). In RIEMANN-MUSIKGESCHICHTE, II, Part 2, 145, the example from "a fourth book of canzonas by Marini," dated 1651, is actually by Tarquinio Merula (1637) and not a clue to Marini's missing Op. 17, as Iselin supposes (p. 47).

pieces in *Affetti musicali* (*Musical Emotions*), Op. 1, only three are called "sonata," along with typical dedicatory subtitles.[10]   These three stand apart somewhat from their fellows about as Gabrieli's sonatas do. They are generally slower in pace and more conservative in style and character.   "La Ponte" is an early, rudimentary, 38-measure example of the S/bass type, while "La Foscarina" and "La Aguzzona" qualify as SSB/bass sonatas, since below the two high instruments in each is also a *concertante* version of the *b. c.* "La Foscarina" reveals the first known request for tremolo on stringed instruments (Ex. 12), seven years before Monteverdi's well-known use, although Marini may have learned

Ex. 12. From "La Foscarina, Sonata a 3," Op. 1, by Biagio Marini (after EINSTEIN-SCORESm, III).

it during two years of playing violin under Monteverdi's direction at St. Mark's. (Or might he even have been imitating the techniques of the then celebrated guitarist Academico Caliginoso detto Il Furioso, whose real name was Foscarini?) Surprising in Example 12 is the climax on the *fermata* after several measures of driving 16th-notes and before the complete measure rest that precedes the tremolo. This rest may have had both a dramatic purpose and the practical one for a cembalist on the *b. c.* part, of allowing time to actuate some stop intended by the instruction "metti il tremolo."

There are no so-called sonatas in Marini's 1620 set, Op. 3, which contains the frequently cited "Romanesca" for violin and optional bass.

10. The "sonata" reprinted from this set in SCHERING-BEISPIELEm, no. 182, was actually called "Symfonia" by Marini.

But sonatas soon figured more importantly in his output, for they make up nearly a third of the enormous instrumental collection published in Venice in 1629 as Op. 8 and composed at least three years earlier during his stay in Neuberg, Bavaria. The intriguing title reads, *Sonate, symphonie, canzoni, pass'emezzi, baletti, corenti, gagliarde, & retornelli, a 1. 2. 3. 4. 5. & 6. voci, per ogni sorte d'instrumenti. Un Capriccio per sonar due violini quatro parti. Un ecco per tre violini, & alcune sonate capricciose per sonar due è tre parti con il violino solo, con altre curiose & moderne inventione.* More specifically, out of 68 pieces there are 21 sonatas in an extraordinary variety of melo/bass scorings. Adventure-some variety is, in fact, the clue to the "curiose & moderne inventione" in the title. Least unusual are the opening pieces, 12 sonatas *a 2*. Seven of these are of the SS/bass type, with violins, *cornetti,* or flutes on the melody parts. Two are BB/bass sonatas, with two bassoons or two trombones that sometimes sound in harmony but chiefly result in a single line by merely alternating in the doubling or embellishing of the *b. c.* part. And three are SB/bass sonatas with inscriptions to the effect that either the bass or soprano solo may be omitted, thus leaving only the other and the *b. c.*

More experimental, as their titles suggest, are most of the other sonatas in Op. 8. "Sonata senza cadenza" (SS/bass) successfully meets the challenge of a form with no breaks, not even a rest or a half-cadence for 81 measures. "Sonata . . . per Sonar variato" (S/bass) makes a point of constant style changes throughout an even longer form. "Sonata in Ecco" (SSS/bass) requires the first violin to play "forte," in full view, and two other violins to answer "piano," in quick succession, out of view. "Sonata . . . d'Inventione" (S/bass) introduces Marini's only passage in *scordatura,* although it does happen to play much easier in normal tuning. And "Sonata . . . per Sonar con due corde" (S/bass) contains his most advanced passage in double-stops, plus a near compendium of the expressive terms found at the time—chiefly, *groppo* for a kind of trill, *t.* for *trillo* or tremolo, *affetti* presumably for some variant of tremolo or other ornament, bowing slurs, *tardo, presto, forte,* and *piano.* The *scordatura* and double-stops are the chief Germanisms in Marini's violin writing and appear only in Op. 8. Finally, there is "Sonata per l'Organo è Violino ó Cornetto," which is actually an SS/bass type with the bass and second soprano parts written out for the organist.[11] All in all, the sonatas in this set are at least as extended as, and much more adventuresome than, the canzonas, which include two

---

11. Cf. SCHERING-SOLOSONATE, including reprint, though without the separate part in tenor clef that differs slightly from the 2d soprano part given to the organist.

in the older polychoir style. The sinfonias, as is generally true in 17th-century ensemble music, are distinctly slighter pieces, usually cast in the binary design of the dances.

In 1644, while he was in Düsseldorf, Germany, Marini's *Corona melodica . . .*, Op. 15, was published in Antwerp. This is a sacred vocal collection that includes four SS/bass sonatas. Nothing about their titles recalls the experiments of Op. 8. However, since only the *b. c.* part is extant, further discussion of them is not possible.

To complete this summary of Marini's sonata output, his final collection, Op. 22, must be noted here, although it takes us in style and form as well as date beyond the approximate mid-century limit of our first group of Italian composers. Published in Venice in 1655 after Marini had returned there, *Diversi generi di Sonate, da Chiesa, e da Camera* contains 6 "sonatas" actually so called that must have been thought of as the "church" type. It also contains 19 differently entitled items in the "chamber" or "court" category, including 3 dance cycles and 6 separate dances or dancelike sinfonias.[12] The "sonatas," set in various melo/bass scorings, are the most serious and mature by Marini. In our chapter on structure (p. 71) we had occasion to note their sub-division into movements (marked "Prima parte" and so on), as well as certain other traits of form. Here it is worth noting that now, for Marini, the term "sonata" was no longer a mere license or special occasion to create novelties, that it dominated the over-all title and headed pieces filling almost half the collection in space if not in number, and that it seems to have replaced the canzona as an instrumental concept. Perhaps the most appealing and best known of the six sonatas in Op. 22 is the third, in SSB/bass scoring. It is the one based on the popular tune "Fuggi dolente core," which is still heard today, notably as the "river theme" in Smetana's *Moldau*. Two sonatas in Marini's Op. 8 had also been based on melodies then popular, but scarcely with the expressive force found in this one, especially as regards the handling of the subordinate lines.

All but one of the "sonate da camera" in Op. 22 are SSA/bass settings, with the alto being an optional viola part. "Balletto primo" and "Balletto secondo" come closest to the new identification of *sonata da camera* with suite, since each divides into five separate "parts," including several with separate dance titles.

12. Few other sonata collections of this time have been so well represented in recent reprints. TORCHIm, VII, 19 ff., though careless in many details, contains everything of concern here except Son. 4, which ISELIN reprints. Other mod. eds.: WASIELEWSKI-XVIIm, nos. 21 and 22; RIEMANN-CHAMBERm, III, 81; HORTUSm, no. 129 (Danckert).

The Venetians who published sonatas soon after Marini's first opus had appeared in 1617 are almost as obscure to us now as Negri and Riccio. *Compositioni armoniche,* published by **Francesco Usper** (or Spongia) in 1619, contains 14 vocal motets, a programmatic "Battaglia per cantar e sonar a 8," and 10 instrumental items.[13]   As his onetime teacher Andrea Gabrieli had done, Francesco collaborated in this set with a nephew. His own contribution to the "sonata" was a polychoir example "a 8," with a low choir of four trombones and a high one of two violins and two *cornetti*. In addition, there is the almost invariable *b. c.,* which proves to be nothing but a *seguente* bass in so full a score. The two choirs contrast not only in range but in the *tutti-soli* oppositions that they generate, with even a sense of rondo form, in the manner of the later concerto grosso.[14]

How differently the younger generation was already coming to view the sonata is seen in the two examples contributed by the nephew **Gabriele Usper.** Both are melo/bass types (SSB/bass and SSBB/bass) and both exhibit favorite traits of the *stile moderno,* including tremolo, "pian" and "forte" in quick alternations, bowing slurs, sequences of idiomatic instrumental figures, and even some programmatic effects ("sampogna" for bagpipe and "lirate" for lyre).

Much less a product of the modern style were *Otto Sonate per il violino ò altro simile stromento* by **Innocentio Vivarino,** organist in near-by Adria.[15]   Dated 1620, this group of sonatas did mark the first to consist entirely of the S/bass type, although it was only an appendix to a book of vocal motets in the same scoring. But except for a little more thematic interest in the *b. c.,* Vivarino's sonatas are as rudimentary and conservative as "La Ponte," the only S/bass sonata in Marini's first opus. To be sure, Vivarino justifies their shortness when he tells, in his preface, how pleased he had been to hear his music in the course of sacred dramas, the Mass, Vespers, and "other occasions when there was need of brevity."

By contrast, *Sonate concertate in stilo moderno* is the very title of two "books" by **Dario Castello,** consisting for the first time of nothing but sonatas. Book 1 was published in 1621, 1629, and 1658;[16] and Book 2 in 1629 and 1644. As head of a "Society of Wind Instruments" or of all the instruments, Castello was another composer who evidently worked in the immediate sphere of Monteverdi at St. Mark's. It is unfortunate

13. All but the motets are in EINSTEIN-SCORESm, I.
14. Cf. EINSTEIN-CONCERTO regarding a Sinfonia "a 8" in this set by Francesco (including examples).
15. All 8 are in EINSTEIN-SCORESm, I. Mod. ed. of No. 7: SCHERING-SOLOSONATE, p. 319.
16. The 1658 reprint is listed in STEVENS-BODLEIAN, p. 70.

that none of his sonatas has been made available in modern reprints, for the ones known to this study have much of interest, both historical and musical.[17] These already divide into movements that contrast clearly in style, meter, and tempo (marked "Adagio" or Allegro") and that end, generally, in free climactic passages over a pedal bass in the manner of a cadenza (Ex. 13). At least two of the allegro movements prove to

Ex. 13. From the end of "Sonata Seconda à sopran solo," Bk. 2, by Dario Castello (after a score copied by Ross Lee Finney).

be brief but well-realized, monothematic fugues. Noteworthy, too, are the advanced understanding of the violin's capabilities that Castello reveals and of the bassoon's techniques in virtuosic elaborations of the figured bass, including remarkable solo flights.[18] In a characteristic note "to the gentle readers" that appears in the second edition of Book 1, Castello even makes a point of the difficulties. He says, in short, that they are the consequence of the new style everyone is observing and hopes the players will not give up on the first try.[19]

These traits must account for the introduction of a term that was to appear often in the course of the century, "sonate concertate." (In fact, this term was adopted promptly, in 1630, by a Venetian organist named Giuseppe Scarani as the title for a single publication of sonatas, all melo/bass.) Castello's titles also specify the *clavicembalo* or *spinetta* as an alternative to the organ for the realization of the *b. c.*, which seem to be the first mentions of a stringed keyboard instrument in any sonata title. In the two collections there is a total of 29 sonatas, all in varied

17. Cf. schlossberg, pp. 29 and 31, for short exs. from Bk. 2, and stevens-bodleian, p. 70, for a listing of the only complete set of Bk. 2 that is known.
18. Cf. haas-aufführungspraxis, p. 167, and haas-barock, p. 91, for exs. from Bk. 1.
19. bohn-musikdruckwerke, p. 90. Cf. schering-instrumentalkonzert, p. 10.

melo/bass scorings. Book 2 includes another "ecco" sonata among three sonatas in SSSS/bass settings.

A strong composer and violinist was **Giovanni Battista Fontana,** who died in Padua in 1630 (or 1631?) during one of the terrible waves of plague that devastated all Europe in the 17th century. He is known only for one publication, *Sonate a 1. 2. 3. per il violino, o cornetto, fagotto, chitarone, violoncino* (the first clear mention of the cello in a music title) *o simile altro Istromento*. This publication was brought out in memory of him in 1641 by the maestro di cappella in the Brescian (not Venetian) Church of Santa Maria delle Grazie, where Fontana had served at one time. It contains 18 melo/bass sonatas in the usual variety of settings—6 in S/bass, 3 each in SS/bass and SB/bass, 5 in SSB/bass and one in SSS/bass.[20] The five sonatas known to this study would seem to date from Fontana's last years, if one may judge by their clear division into contrasting sections; their unusually broad, long, and unified forms; their advanced use of the violin; and, especially, their lines extended in cantilena fashion in the sections of 3/2 meter.

Although these sonatas imply a later stage of development than Marini's of 1617, Fontana has been suggested as Marini's probable teacher, since both were born in Brescia.[21] Fontana was certainly the older man. As early as 1608 he had been recognized as an outstanding virtuoso by another Brescian, Cesario Gussago (in the dedication of his *Sonate*). But in 1608 Marini was only 11 and by then Fontana had already left for Venice. Marini may very well have gone to Fontana after he himself got to Venice in 1615 or sooner, but the dominating figure in all Venetian music now seems to have been Monteverdi.

Finally to be mentioned among the Venetians in our first group are two others in Monteverdi's sphere of influence, both organists at St. Mark's. Their names are **Massimiliano Neri** and **Francesco Cavalli** (1602-76). These men left the last Venetian examples of the polychoir sonata (none in more than two choirs or twelve parts), along with multivoice and melo/bass types. Moreover, Neri was probably the last Venetian to publish canzonas and sonatas together (1644) and Cavalli was one of the later Italians to publish sonatas as an adjunct to a vocal collection (1656). Hence, Cavalli is included among the first group although his sole publication of concern here appeared one year after the "Libro primo" by that most important Venetian in the next half century, Giovanni Legrenzi.

20. Mod. eds.: No. 1, DAVISON & APELm, no. 198, and ISELIN, no. 13; No. 3, TORCHIm, VII, 92; Nos. 4 and 8, WASIELEWSKI-XVIIm, nos. 13 and 12.

21. ISELIN, p. 2. The dedicatory titles in Marini's Op. 1 include Monteverdi, the publisher Gardano, and many others of importance to Marini, but Fontana is not among them.

Between 1644 and 1664 Neri left two publications of instrumental music alone and one of motets. *Sonate e canzone a quatro da sonarsi . . . in chiesa, & in camera con alcune correnti . . . opera prima,* dated 1644, contains two multivoice sonatas. These are early examples of our modern string-quartet setting except for the *b. c.,* which amounts to no more than a *seguente* bass here. The collection also contains six canzonas in the same or melo/bass settings, plus six *correnti* flexibly scored so as to permit reduction from four to three or even two parts as desired. From the title alone one cannot be sure what the "chiesa-camera" distinction means. But whatever the interpretation and with only one sonata and one canzona to judge by,[22] no distinction can be established between the sonata and canzona in this instance. One can merely recall that when the two terms did become synonymous, "canzona" as a title was near its end.

In point of fact, Neri's second publication, in 1651, drops this term and contains only "sonatas." There are 15 in all, ranging from melo/bass to polychoir settings, and from 3 to 12 parts plus *b. c.* Again, little is at hand in the way of reprints or special studies. At least one sonata *a 4* is the multivoice type just mentioned; one for two choirs is scored for three flutes, two violins, *violetta,* and *tiorba* or *viola di basso;* and one *a 3* is the SSB/bass type.[23] Still another specifies 12 instruments in 2 choirs—2 *cornetti,* 4 trombones, and a bassoon in the first choir and 2 violins, 2 violas, and *tiorba* or *viola di basso* in the second.

One only hopes that this strong music still survives in the Wroclaw (Breslau) University Library if not in one of the Berlin libraries, or that a copy has been made somewhere, suitable for the detailed study that is needed. The available sonatas reveal music that stands well above the average of its time. As several writers have observed, the fugal allegros in particular are landmarks in the history of the fugue. They have distinctive subjects, genuine episodes, monothematic plans, contrapuntal skill, and a clear grasp of tonality (although several titles still specify church tones).

We are even less well off when it comes to Cavalli's sonatas, notwithstanding the considerable attention that has been paid to his principal contributions, in the field of opera. There are neither studies nor reprints. Six sonatas are included in his collection for voices and instruments, *Musiche sacre* (1656). These appear to repeat the scorings employed five years earlier in Neri's second set. Furthermore, Cavalli's mentions

22. Mod. eds.: Son. 1, RIEMANN-BEISPIELEm, no. 98; "Canzone del terzo tuono" *a 4,* WASIELEWSKI-XVIIm, no. 18.
23. Mod. eds., respectively: WASIELEWSKI-XVIIm, nos. 19 and 20 (fragments only); RIEMANN-MUSIKGESCHICHTE, II, Part 2, 152 (incomplete).

of *tutti, soli,* and *ripieni* in his preface suggest that his polychoir sonatas may have foretokens of the later concerto grosso in them as do the polychoir sonatas by Neri that were cited. Over the separate parts of the individual "sonatas" Cavalli sometimes wrote "sinfonia" or "canzona" without any apparent distinction.

Mantua (Rossi, Buonamente)

Mantua was next to Venice in the importance if not the quantity of its sonata composers during the first half of the 17th century. Unlike Venice, Mantua was ending her greatest period, a glorious century and a half of music and other art under the powerful Gonzaga family. But the two cities had a notable musical bond in Monteverdi, who served some twenty years at the Gonzaga court under Duke Vincenzo I before his appointment in 1613 as maestro di cappella at St. Mark's.

Claudio Monteverdi (1567-1643) himself composed one work with the title "sonata" while he was still in Mantua. This is the well-known "Sonata sopra Sancta Maria ora pro nobis a 8" from the vesper music *Sanctissimae Virgini* published in Venice in 1610.[24] It is interesting to discover that a work of the same title had been published two years earlier in Venice as the 20th item in *Il primo libro de' concerti ecclesiastici* by one Frate Archangelo Crotti from Ferrara.[25] This predecessor is scored for two *cornetti* or violins, one or more trombones, and a *seguente* bass, with the Gregorian litany sung eight times in the soprano range.[26]

26a   Monteverdi's work is remarkably similar, even to the persistent interplay of short, angular motives. His eight instruments perform in pairs, with two *violini da brazzo* and two *cornetti* on top; two trombones (one interchangeable with *viola da brazzo*) in the middle; and a single bass line taken alternately or jointly by a *viola da brazzo* and a *trombone doppio* and reinforced by a *seguente* bass part. Into this busy texture the same *cantus firmus* is woven intermittently, 11 times in all, by one or more voices in the soprano range.

Although Monteverdi's orchestral sonata with its literal *cantus firmus* had a predecessor, it seems not to have had a successor. Novel as was its scoring, it also had much that was stylistically archaic. Yet from among the Mantuan musicians under Monteverdi's direction, after his promotion to maestro di cappella in 1602, there were two other violinists

24. Among mod. eds.: MONTEVERDIm, XIV, 250-273; TORCHIm, IV, 51-72.
25. Information from Mr. Thurston Dart at Jesus College, Cambridge, Eng.; listed in CAT. BOLOGNA, II, 412.
26. ANTIPHONALEm, p. 62*.

in this first "school of violin playing"[27] who may be ranked with Marini and Fontana as pioneers in the main line of the Italian sonata. These were Salomone Rossi and Giovanni Battista Buonamente.

Salomone Rossi (1570?-1630?) published a total of 13 collections of music between 1589 and 1628, all during an even longer period of service at the Gonzaga court. Out of these, four are instrumental "books," first published in 1607, 1608, 1613, and 1622,[28] followed by many reprints. The statistics show an increasing importance given to the sonata in these successive collections, as in Marini's. Rossi entitled only one piece "sonata" out of 27 pieces in Book 1,[29] no pieces out of 35 in Book 2, 6 out of 33 in Book 3, and 13 out of 29, or nearly half, in Book 4. What is more, in the last two books, each reprinted twice by 1642, the sonatas developed significantly in size, definition, and traits of the *stile moderno*.

Books 1 and 2 by Rossi mention only "sinfonie et Gagliarde" in their titles. The one piece individually called "sonata" is a multivoice, fugal movement of but 27 measures, yet about twice the average length of all the other pieces except three multivoice canzonas in the second collection. Otherwise the sonata does not differ from these last or the few multivoice sinfonias. Only the ranges are given for the individual pieces—*canto, alto, tenore, basso* for the sonata. But in the first title are specified "two violas, or two *cornetti,* and a *chittarrone* or other instrument *da corpo* [that is, in the bass group]." Thus, emphasis is placed on the SS/bass or "trio" setting of the majority of the pieces. This instrumental setting was an innovation in 1607, not only here but in the music of Monteverdi, who used the identical scoring for the instrumental ritornelli in his *Scherzi musicali.*[30]

In the last two collections Rossi confined himself exclusively to the SS/bass setting, employing it in all 19 sonatas as well as in the lighter pieces.[31] Even "Sonata a Quattro Violini, e doi Chittarrone," which

---

27. Cf. MOSER-VIOLINSPIEL, p. 52; but Farina, whom we shall meet among composers active in Dresden, and Buonamente should have been included in this "Mantuan violin school."

28. The entire contents of the first three books are in EINSTEIN-SCOREsm, III. For the 1613 date cf. BOHN-MUSIKDRUCKWERKE, p. 341. A detailed study of Rossi's instrumental music is lacking.

29. Item 20; but it is called "sinfonia" in the separate tenor part.

30. More on this in SCHRADE-MONTEVERDI, p. 219 ff. (but on p. 220 "violini" should read "viole").

31. The Rossi "Trio Sonata" of 1607 in BUKOFZER-BAROQUE, p. 53, is actually the 10th "Sinfonia" from Bk. 1. Riemann has provided the only reprints from Bks. 3 and 4, mostly "edited," unfortunately, in accordance with his well-known theories of rhythm and expression: Bk. 3, Son. "detta la Moderna," RIEMANN-TRIOSONATEN, p. 135; Son. "sopra l'Aria della Romanesca," -BEISPIELEm, no. 81; portions of Son. "in dialogo detta la Viena" and Son, "sopra l'Aria di Ruggiero,"

concludes Book 4, proves simply to be the prototype of those sonatas in which two SS/bass groups alternate in polychoir fashion, uniting only at cadences. Rossi showed at once the main techniques of scoring in the SS/bass setting—the motivic play between the upper parts, though rarely including the bass; the chordal, purely homophonic style of all three parts; the successions of suspensions and resolutions as the upper parts work against the bass; and actual monody through alternate solos in the upper parts, as in "Sonata in dialogo" in Book 3. Not until Book 4 are "violini" designated in place of "viole da braccio" on the upper parts. The option of using *cornetti* had not been offered after Book 1. The bass parts have almost no figures, no *concertante* elaborations by other bass instruments, and scarcely any thematic interest except when they state the recurring idea in a set of variations.

The titles in the last two collections differ to the extent of listing "varie Sonate, Sinfonie, Gagliarde, Brandi, e Corrente." The sinfonias remain short and otherwise similar in character to the dances. There are no further canzonas, leaving the sonatas to stand well apart by virtue of their variety and extent. They range from around 30 to well over 100 measures. Much the longest are those based on the variation principle. Rossi was as important a pioneer in this most tangible means of erecting and anchoring the new, abstract instrumental forms as he was in the scorings he used. For the recurring ideas in his variation forms he used some of those popular melodies that turn up repeatedly in 17th-century Italian sonatas. The melodies appear only in the bass in the variation sonatas of the third collection, as in "Sonata sopra l'Aria della Romanesca" or "Sonata sopra l'Aria di Ruggiero." They appear on top in at least some instances in the fourth collection—for example, the sonatas on "la Scatola" and "la Bergamasca" (Ex. 14). Either treatment gives occasion for much livelier and more ornate figuration than can be found in the shorter sonatas, not based on the variation principle.

These last, without such solid form props, fall back mainly, though less predictably, on the familiar sectional contrasts achieved through metric changes. One assumes those changes are often associated with tempo changes as well, such as 3/1 meter and adagio. But it seems risky to assume the changes in terms of later developments, as Hugo Riemann did in his often cited reprint of "Sonata Prima detta la Moderna."[32] In this piece, which has only the typical change to triple meter and back, Riemann suggested tempo marks that would make of it

---

-MUSIKGESCHICHTE, II, Part 2, 87 and 94; Bk. 4, Son. 1, -CHAMBERm, III, 120; fragments from Son. 11 "detta la Scatola," -KOMPOSITIONSLEHRE, I, 136.

32. -TRIOSONATEN, p. 135.

Ex. 14. The Bergamasca tune as used for variation treatment by Salomone Rossi in Sonata 11 "sopra la Bergamasca,"
Bk. 4 (after NETTL-BERGAMASKA, p. 291).

a chance anticipation of the later church sonata with the four-movement
sequence of S(low)-F(ast)-S-F. The only tempo change indicated by
Rossi in his pieces occurs in an instruction that shows a strong feeling
for form and effect. The player is asked to repeat the lively measures
that end both the "Romanesca" and "Ruggiero" sonatas, "ma più presto."
Beyond this, the "Moderna" in the title mentioned previously must be
taken to refer to such rather conservative modernisms as the SS/bass
setting and a few experimental adaptations of it, some decidedly idiomatic violin figurations in the variation sonatas, and occasional terms like
"ecco," "pian," and "forte."

A direct successor to Rossi in both styles and forms was **Giovanni
Battista Buonamente** (?-1643), from whom the only extant works are
four instrumental collections published in 1626, 1629, 1636, and 1637.[33]
Since these are Books 4 to 7, one supposes that three earlier collections,
now lost, may have appeared from about 1615. Buonamente is grouped
among the Mantuans because he seems to have served at the Gonzaga
court until 1622, although from perhaps that year at least through the
time of Books 4 and 5 he served under Emperor Ferdinand II in Vienna,
and at the time of Book 6 he was back in Italy, in Assisi (where he died
seven years later[34]). His first sonata in Book 7 is dedicated to Monteverdi.

34a

The titles of Books 4, 5, and 7 by Buonamente are almost identical
in their wording to Rossi's. Thus, Book 4 has the title, *Varie sonate, sinfonie, gagliarde, corrente, & brandi per sonar con due violini, & un
basso di viola.* In spite of this title Book 5 actually has no pieces individually called "sonata." Book 6, perhaps the latest in order of com-

33. All four collections are in EINSTEIN-SCORESm, II. NETTL-BUONAMENTE is
the only study of consequence. Riemann, again, has provided the main reprints, all
from Bk. 6 and, unfortunately, among the least interesting in that set: Son. 1
a 2 and Son. 1 *a 3*, RIEMANN-CHAMBERm, III, 124 ff.; part of Son. 3 *a 2*, -MUSIK-
GESCHICHTE, II, Part 2, 118.
34. SCHMIDL, Supp., p. 134.

position,[35] is entitled *Sonate, et Canzone*. It differs in many respects
from the other three books. As indicated, it includes no dances but does
include canzonas. Furthermore, it includes no variation sonatas, which
make up 9 of the 20 sonatas in Books 4 and 7, but does include sonatas
that seem more advanced in other respects. For one thing, while the
other sets contain only SS/bass pieces, Book 6 has a considerable variety
of melo/bass types, with from one to four upper parts, and it has both
sonatas and canzonas, *a 5* and *a 6*, that are multivoice. Only in this set
are some of the *b. c.* parts figured beyond an occasional accidental and
some elaborated by a *concertante* bass part. And here the instruments
are more often specified.

Sonatas fill almost half the pages in Books 4, 6, and 7. As was true
of Rossi's, they are decidedly more extended and developed than the
dances and the dancelike sinfonias, but not than the canzonas. How do
Buonamente's sonatas differ from his canzonas? Some distinction
seems to be implied by the fair regularity with which they are alternated
and counterbalanced by scoring types in Book 6, but this is no sharply
drawn distinction. The fact that there are three canzonas of the
SB/bass type but no sonata with only one upper part, or that there are
no variation canzonas, may be a mere accident. More to the point,
probably, is the greater freedom and variety in the scoring and ideas of
many of the sonatas. Where the canzona sticks pretty much to its
stereotyped opening, angular motives, and steady 8th-notes (or longer
values in the sections of triple meter), the sonata has more varied
openings, more lyrical ideas spread over a wider arch (Ex. 15), and
more diverse rhythms, including numerous passages in 32d-notes.

The sonatas explore the scoring possibilities more than do the
canzonas. The alternation of upper parts to achieve antiphonal S/bass
dispositions occurs in "Sonata a doi Violini, & doi Bassi," Book 6,
recalling Rossi's use of the term "dialogo." In this sonata the two bass
parts and added *b. c.* reduce to a single line, as they often did, whether
the two *concertante* parts alternate or coincide as they double the *b. c.*
The opening sonata of Book 7 presents the two upper parts throughout
in strict canon. The first of the two sonatas *a 6* (SSATBB/bass) in
Book 6 is scored for violin, *cornetto,* three trombones and a *liuto tiorbato.*
It differs notably from the one "Canzon a sei" in this set, for it treats
the violin as a solo part in dialogue with an "orchestra" made up of the
other parts, producing a rather remarkable precursor of the solo concerto.

Buonamente used most of the tunes for variations that Rossi used
(including three "Romanesca" sonatas) plus some others. He used the

35. One or more sonatas in Bk. 7 were composed in 1627 (NETTL-BUONAMENTE,
p. 542).

Ex. 15. From Giovanni Battista Buonamente's "Sonata Seconda à 2," Bk. 6 (after EINSTEIN-SCORESM, II).

same few terms for performance and expression, and, as we have seen, the same form titles. But he went beyond Rossi's sonatas in the variety of figuration, especially in the *b. c.* parts, which sometimes join fully in the display passages of the variations (as in the "Ruggiero" sonata, Book 4). And, mainly, Buonamente surpassed Rossi in breadth of ideas and grasp of form. For this reason, his free, non-variation sonatas are not so much shorter than his variation sonatas. Tentative rondo forms are numerous—for example, A-B-A-C-A in "Sonata Quarta" of Book 4, 71 measures in all. A much closer approximation of the later church-sonata sequence than Rossi can supply is found in "Sonata Terza detta la Cavazza," Book 7, including the marks "allegro" and "adasio." Lastly, quite ahead of its time and a clue to his grasp of form is Buonamente's sure feeling for major-minor tonality and the essentials of modulation, at least in short passages (Ex. 16).

Brescia

Brescia was another busy music center that had close ties with Venice in these earliest decades of the sonata. It was not merely a political territory of the Republic but the home of many a musician who later went to Venice, including, as we have seen, both Fontana and Marini; and it was the home of the first fine violin making, by Gasparo da Salò

Ex. 16. From Giovanni Battista Buonamente's "Sonata a
doi Violini, & doi Bassi," Bk. 6 (after EINSTEIN-SCORESm, II).

and his pupils. Three Brescians deserve at least brief mention in our
first group of Italians.

In 1608 the Brescian organist **Cesario Gussago** (*ca.* 1550 to at least
1612) published the first extant collection to give sonatas the main listing
in the title. The interesting title reads, *Sonate a quattro, sei, et otto,
con alcuni concerti a otto, con le sue sinfonie da suonare avanti, & doppò
secondo il placito, & commodo de Sonatori.*[36] In other words, here, for
a change, was a collection in which vocal music was subordinate to the
instrumental sonatas. Gussago's "concerti," true to the word's early
meaning, are vocal-instrumental pieces (with sacred texts), "each with
its [instrumental] sinfonia that can be played before or after [the con-
certo] as desired." Of the 20 sonatas, 14 are multivoice, including 10
a 4 and 4 *a 6;* the other 6 are polychoir, *a 8,* with a high and a low choir
opposed (except for No. 19, with two high choirs). All of these sonatas
are about 45 measures in length. There are no indications of instruments except clef ranges, no added *b. c.* parts or figures, no markings
of any sort, and few changes to triple meter and back. Most interest lies
in the polychoir oppositions, which are achieved by differences in the
phrase lengths and rhythms as well as in the ranges of the two choirs.
Otherwise, the successive points of imitation and tentative sectional
designs make these sonatas quite like the contemporary canzona, which
was then at the peak of its popularity.[37]

Another Brescian organist, **Francesco Turini** (*ca.* 1589-1656), in-

36. All the sonatas are in EINSTEIN-SCORESm, I, plus the first two concertos with
sinfonias, and the third sinfonia.
37. Cf. SARTORI-BIBLIOGRAFIA, especially throughout this same year of 1608.

cluded three melo/bass sonatas and a sinfonia in his *Madrigali . . . Libro primo*. The set was published in 1621 and twice again in 1624, with an additional sonata in one of the reprinted sets (Vincenti). Two of the sonatas, both SSB/bass, are based on variation tunes, treated in the upper parts. One of these, the only Turini sonata presently available,[38] is based on the charming tune "Tanto tempo hormai," which Rossi, Buonamente, Uccellini, and others used for variations, too. Turini's variations are resourceful in their rhythmic changes and abreast of Rossi's in their technical demands. Perhaps Charles Burney, the English historian of the later 18th century, was too harsh in his review of one of Turini's two "free" sonatas.[39] Because Turini's sonatas were the earliest he had found, he troubled to score this one, which he described "as only a single movement, in fugue and imitation throughout." He concluded that the "violin does not appear to have been Turini's instrument," for "each part might have been as well played on one instrument as another."

To Turini, who may have been his teacher, one **Giovanni Antonio Bertoli** dedicated his *Compositioni musicali . . . fatte per sonare col fagotto solo,* published in 1645.[40] This is the earliest known sonata collection to consist only of "solo" sonatas, to use the term "solo" rather than "a due" in the title, and to contain "solo" bassoon pieces. More specifically, it contains nine sonatas for bassoon and *b. c.* or for "various other instruments, and by [the study of] which even the singers can profit." It would take no ordinary singer—for that matter, no ordinary bassoonist—to master the passagework in these sonatas, with a solo range from C to d',[41] intricate rhythms, and extended runs in 32d-notes, both scale- and chordwise. Perhaps Bertoli knew the solo bassoon flights mentioned earlier in Castello's sonatas. At any rate, he also urges the reader not to succumb too readily to the difficulties as they first appear. Charming in Sonata 4 is the refrain of several measures that recurs in the *b. c.* at each of the bassoonist's very necessary breathing spaces.

Other Northern Italian Cities (Merula, Uccellini)

In Milan, where an era of great musical glory had come and gone more than a century before, there lived the composer of the earliest

38. SCHENK-TRIOSONATEM, no. 2.   39. BURNEY-HISTORY, II, 434.
40. "Francesco Turino organista nella Cathedrale di Brescia," as named in this dedication, was surely our "Francesco Turini organista del Duomo di Brescia [until 1656]," as named in his own titles. However, this Bertoli cites in his preface the much better known Antonio Bertali, "Valoroso nel Violino" (cf. p. 206), removing any chance for confusion there. All three men had connections then or earlier with the Imperial courts at Vienna and Prague.
41. BOHN-MUSIKDRUCKWERKE, p. 59.

known sonatas both of the "solo" (S/bass) and of the "trio" (SS/bass) types. This was **Gian Paolo Cima,** who included two of each in his *Concerti ecclesiastici . . . & sei sonate,* published in Milan in 1610.[42] One of the S/bass sonatas specifies violin and bass only, qualifying it as the first known violin solo, too. Its bass part is not figured and actually shares almost equally in the ideas stated by the violin. Both parts reveal enough octave leaps and scales to suggest idiomatic string techniques, more so than in the other S/bass sonata, which adds the option of *cornetto* and trombone. The SS/bass sonata that could be examined here is scored for violin, *cornetto,* and bass. As before, the bass participates in the play of ideas. There are fewer leaps but more of that solid contrapuntal skill for which Cima is remembered in this and other publications. In both sonatas known here, some continuity is achieved by initial ideas that return later, once or more.

In Milan in 1635 were published three melo/bass sonatas interesting for their typical scoring options. These were added to his collection of sacred choral music by **Gerolamo Casati** ("detto Filago") from nearby Novara. The violin and the *violone* are the only instruments specified. No options are offered in "La Santina Suonata à 2" (SB/bass), but "La Maltivoglia Suonata à 3" may be played as an SSB/-, SB/-, or SS/ bass sonata and "La Bentivoglia Suonata à 4" as an SSBB/- or SS/bass sonata. Of course, the purpose of such options was flexibility to meet local needs and resources. Since the bass parts reduce to one line anyway, the only real musical difference in the second sonata would be the loss of one upper part.

Two composers from Verona appear early in our list of "Italian Composers of Sonatas Published Before 1651," though their music has yet to be explored. **Paolo Funghetto** framed his 1609 set of choral vesper music with a "Sonata A 4" at the start and a "Canzon A 4" at the end. Although *b. c.* parts are added, the settings are presumably multivoice. **Tomaso Cecchino** added eight melo/bass sonatas to his 1628 set of Masses and motets. Seven of these, he explains, may be played by violin or *cornetto* with no other bass than the organ, and the eighth similarly but by two violins or violin and *cornetto.*

Between these two dates came the slightly better known sonatas of **Steffano Bernardi** (?-1638), distinguished maestro di cappella at the Verona Cathedral. Among some 17 vocal publications that he left, sacred or secular, four include instrumental pieces and three of these

---

42. Two of the "sei sonate" are separately entitled "Capriccio," with only "strumenti" specified, and are by Gian Paolo's brother Andrea. Mod. eds.: Son. "per Violino, & Violone," BECKMANNm, I, no. 1 (cf. BECKMANN, p. 12 ff.); Son. "per il Violino, Cornetto, & Violone," SCHENK-TRIOSONATEm, no. 1.

four use the title "sonata." But the confusion between "sonata," "canzona," and "sinfonia" seems at first to be more than average, even for this time. *Motetti . . . con alcune canzoni per sonare con ogni sorte di stromenti, con il basso per l'organo,* Op. 5 (1613 and later), contains five pieces individually called "sonata" and a "Sonata sesta in Sinfonia."[43] On the other hand, *Madrigaletti . . . con alcune sonate a tre per due violini overo, cornetti, & un chitarrone, trombone, overo fagotte,* Op. 12 (1621 and later), contains seven "canzonas." However, *Madrigali . . . con alcune sonate accomodate per ogni sorte d'istromenti,* Op. 13 (1624), does contain eight "sonatas."

If only Bernardi's titles over the separate pieces are considered, a more consistent distinction soon becomes apparent. "Sonata" seems to have meant for him the older, more conservative style, in which he excelled. His "sonatas" are all multivoice or polychoir types without exact instrumental designations, whereas the "canzonas" are all SSB/-bass settings with instruments specified. The sonatas in Op. 5 are all scored *a 4,* plus a *seguente* bass with occasional figures. Only in "Sonata sesta in Sinfonia" does a melo/bass scoring result—that is, in the first half, where the two upper parts alternate in phrases marked "solo" while the *b. c.* alone accompanies them. The sonatas in Op. 13 are all scored *a 6* except the last, which is *a 12* and divides into three choirs.[44] A-B-A is the plan of the sonatas in Op. 5. One of the sonatas in Op. 13 is another example of the programmatic "Battaglia" that Giovanni Gabrieli, Francesco Usper, and others had composed before Bernardi.

From Cremona, home of both the Amati and Stradivari families, came a composer of a different sort, **Tarquinio Merula** (*ca.* 1595 to at least 1652[45]), who was active in several cities. Out of some 18 publications by him, five dated from 1624 to 1651 are of most concern here. *Il primo libro de motetti, e sonate concertati* (1624) was composed while he was in Warsaw. It includes two sonatas, both SB/bass, with the usual designation of violin or *cornetto* for the upper part. *Libro secondo de concerti spirituali con alcune sonate* (1628), composed in Cremona, includes two SSB/bass pieces separately entitled "Canzone." *Canzoni, overo sonate concertate per chiesa, e camera* (1637) contains 19 SS/- or SSB/bass pieces separately entitled "Canzon" along with a descriptive or dedicatory name (plus five more with only the other names).[46] *Pegaso . . . salmi motetti, suonate, e letanie* (Venice, 1640)

45a

46a

43. All six pieces are in EINSTEIN-SCOREsm, I.
44. A little information is supplied in POSCH, p. 19 ff.
45. Regarding these dates cf. NEWMAN-EARLIEST, p. 207.
46. Mod. eds.: "La Strada," SCHERING-BEISPIELEM, no. 184; "La Gallina" and "Ruggiero," RIEMANN-CHAMBERm, III, 108; "La Pedrina," RIEMANN-BEISPIELEm,

contains one SB/bass "Canzone." And *Il quarto libro delle canzoni da suonare* (Venice, 1651) contains 29 pieces "à Doi, & à Tre" (SS/-, SB/-, and SSB/bass), of which three are separately called "Sonata," one is called "Sinfonie," and the rest have only dedicatory titles.

Some distinction would seem to be implied by the grouping of titles in this last collection. Yet, though no use of the word "sonata" occurs in three previous books of canzonas (1615, 1639, and before 1649), it becomes obvious that Merula was like Neri around the mid century in simply equating canzona and sonata. He freely made either one a sub-class of the other. Furthermore, the mention of "chiesa" and "camera" in the 1637 set did not yet signify any functional classification of the pieces (as has been suggested elsewhere) but rather their suitability for either or any use, much as Merula had described himself in 1624 as "organista di chiesa, e di camera."

Merula belongs with the chief sonata composers of his day. Although he is another whose music awaits a detailed study, the few canzona-sonatas that have appeared in later reprints[47] are sufficient to reveal an exceptional unity of form, chiefly through prolonged exploitation of but one or two ideas and a strong metric drive. There is also a genial, pert humor in the ideas themselves, which make frequent use of repeated notes and octave skips. Several of the canzona-sonatas in the 1637 set have programmatic titles, among them "La Gallina," based on the clucking of the hen. They are not surprising from the composer of the celebrated comic madrigal "Nominativo hic haec hoc." On the other hand, the "sonatas" in the 1651 set are reportedly more polyphonic and without the metric changes to be found in the other pieces of this set and in the earlier canzonas (usually C, 3/2, C). Perhaps these "sonatas" and those in the three sacred collections reflect a more serious, conservative view of the sonata.

Such is certainly the view reflected in one other piece by Merula, "Sonata cromatica" for keyboard, which is known only in a MS copy of the 18th century.[48] This piece is the first we have met in that special branch of the "sonata," the single fugal organ movement, which can be traced throughout the 17th and 18th centuries. It is outstanding in its time for the extent of its concentration on a single idea, 116 measures in all. This single idea is the descending chromatic tetrachord that was much used in the period.

---

no. 90; portions of three others, RIEMANN-MUSIKGESCHICHTE, II, Part 2, 120 ff. and 145 ff. (not by Marini!).

47. All of Bk. 2 (Canzoni, 1639) is copied in EINSTEIN-SCORESm, III; mod. eds. from this: WASIELEWSKI-XVIIm, nos. 16 and 17; DAVISON & APELm, II, no. 210.

48. CAT. BOLOGNA, IV, 28. Among mod. eds.: TORCHIm, III, 345; TAGLIAPIETRAm, VI, 94.

From an organist and "Professore di Violino" in Reggio, **Ottavio-maria Grandi,** came one of the early collections made up exclusively of sonatas. This only extant collection by him, *Sonate per ogni sorte di Stromenti à 1. 2. 3. 4. & 6. con il basso per l'organo,* Op. 2 (1628), contains 20 relatively short pieces scored progressively in all the most popular settings. Included are two sonatas of the S/bass type, four SS/-, eight SSB/-, four SSBB/bass, one multivoice, and one polychoir. Only the first two and last two sonatas specify instruments (violins and trombones). Grandi's command of violin techniques was apparently more than up to date. Thus, Sonata 1 for violin with *b. c.* makes use of the third position and bowing slurs over entire measures. Furthermore, it employs double-stops in a genuinely contrapuntal passage probably not matched by any other violin music composed in Italy during the first half of the century.[49] Among other scorings, at least one of the SSBB/bass sonatas alternates one *canto-basso* pair with the other in the familiar *dialogo* manner. The multivoice sonata, a clear A-B-A design, presents a *concertante* violin part over a slower moving choir of four trombones.[50] And the final, polychoir sonata sets three violins against three trombones.

Among further men on our list of "Italian Composers of Sonatas Published Before 1651" only five came from Bologna, the same city whose sonata production was to outdistance that of Venice or any other city during the next half century. Of these, four must be passed by for want of information, even including the much published monk Guglielmo Lipparino and the widely popular guitarist Francesco Corbetta. There is left to discuss only **Adriano Banchieri** (1568-1634), a learned and fascinating theorist, organist, and composer, to be sure, but one in whose vast output the sonata figured only incidentally.[51] Five of Banchieri's 10 collections that include instrumental music have one or more "sonatas." Three of these five are the three very different and much republished versions of the celebrated treatise *L'Organo suonarino,* including 13 sonatas in Op. 13 (1605), two in Op. 25 (1611), and 5 in Op. 43 (1622). There are also an SSB/bass variation sonata "sopra l'aria del Gran Duca" in *Messe e motetti concertato,* Op. 42 (Venice, 1620), and three multivoice sonatas, equated with canzonas, in *Il Virtuoso ritrovo academico* (Venice, 1626). Out of all five sets only some of the sonatas in the first version of the treatise are available for examination.[52]   52a

49. Exs. in BECKMANN, Anhang no. 4 (cf. p. 19).
50. Ex. in SCHLOSSBERG, p. 19.   51. Cf. MGG, I, 1206 ff. (Redlich).
52. Five in TORCHIm, III, 354; four of these and three more "edited" in TAGLIAPIETRAm, III, 78 and 81; one and part of another in HAAS-AUFFÜHRUNGS-

Printed in open score, the organ "sonatas" average only about 20 measures in length, remain entirely in 4/2 or 4/4 meter, and fulfill a primarily didactic purpose. Presumably, in Banchieri's later, concerted sonatas and the earlier, similarly unexplored *Canzoni alla francese a quattro* (1596) and *Fantasie overo canzoni alla francese . . . a quattro* (before 1603) the extent, metric variety, and contrapuntal activity are

53a   greater.[53] But the organ sonatas do have musical interests of their own, plus considerable historical interest. To mention the latter first, they are noteworthy in our semantic approach to the early sonata as the first keyboard pieces to receive this title. And they are legitimate firsts in that special branch, the organ sonata, to which we saw Merula contribute. Moreover, they are interesting for their specific instructions regarding organ registrations—for example, "Principale & Ottava" as against "Levasi Ottava" to achieve antiphony in "Terza Suonata in Dialogo"— and for their indicated uses in the liturgy, with respect to the Gradual, Offertory, Communion, and psalm singing.

The organ sonatas are musically interesting as models for improvisation, including four SB/bass types—violin, trombone, and organ *b. c.*— to illustrate organ accompaniment (at the end of Op. 43). Being primarily fugal in construction, they do not have the tempo changes, expressive terms, or dance elements of the secular, thinner-textured organ pieces included in the second version (Op. 25).[54] But they do show the more intellectual side of Banchieri's remarkable command of styles, what with stretto, diminution (in both senses), liturgical themes, and ever-recurring subjects. Their titles, fascinating in themselves, are clues to the main emphasis in each piece. One example is the "dialogo" title quoted earlier. Among other examples, Sonata 1, "fuga plagale," proves to be a monothematic *ricercare* characterized by the hypodorian mode and "tonal" answers a 4th below the final. Sonata 8 "in aria francese" is a symmetrical A-B-A design with a homophonic, marchlike B section. And Sonata 7, "concerto enarmonico," is a chordal piece with curious accidentals that presuppose a special keyboard.

Modena, another city that was to do much for the sonata in the next half century, likewise gives us only one name to consider here, but an important one both for that future development and for violin playing in general. **Marco Uccellini** (*ca.* 1603-80), who was in Modena from 1641 to 1665, left a total of 73 melo/bass string sonatas that are still

PRAXIS, p. 175. Several of the foregoing do reappear in the second or third version, mostly under altered titles.
53. Cf. two fantasias reprinted in WASIELEWSKI-XVIIm, nos. 5 and 6, and a sinfonia "without text" (1607) in SCHERING-BEISPIELEm, no. 151.
54. See "La Battaglia" and "Canzone italiana" in TORCHIm, III, 360.

extant.[55] These occur in four collections, Books (or Opp.) 2-5, published in 1639, 1642, 1645, and 1649.[56] "Sonate" comes first in all four titles but, again near the mid century, is equated with "Canzoni" in Book 5, though only in the title. In Books 2-4 there are also lighter pieces—sinfonias and dances—as there are in three later collections, Books 7-9, which date from 1667 to 1669 but contain no further sonatas, and as there probably were in Books 1 and 6, now lost. In the title of Book 4, "sì da Camera, come da Chiesa" merely means that this is dual purpose music, as with Merula.

During the decade that the four sonata collections spanned, Uccellini showed a decided trend from plural/bass to solo/bass sonatas. Thus, Book 5 consists of twelve S/bass sonatas (the earliest known to be entitled "à violino solo") and but one of the SS/bass type. Perhaps his own growth as a soloist had a bearing on this trend. In any case, his disinterest in either multivoice or polychoir settings and the distribution of his sonatas within the main categories of melo/bass scorings seem representative of the general preferences near the mid century. Disregarding for the moment whether a *concertante* bass is present, 59 per cent of his sonatas are of the "trio" type (SS/-, SSB/-, or SSBB/bass), 38 are of the "solo" type (S/- or SB/bass), and 3 of the SSS/- or SSSB/bass type. "Violino" and "basso" are the only instruments specified other than trombone twice requested as the bass.

Uccellini, as the namesake of the birds (*uccelli*), likened his melodies to their songs in the dedication of Book 4. His melodies do soar in long lines, embellished by diminutions and ornaments and carried through much of the violin's range. They speak well for his ability as a performer, as does his knowledge of the violin's techniques, which has surprised historians of violin playing.[57] Passages that go up to the fifth or sixth position and bowing slurs are frequent. Uccellini also showed the predilection of many a 17th-century composer for introducing novelties into his sonata collections. In the last piece of Book 5, "Tromba sordina per sonare con Violino solo," the trumpet's sound is suggested by *scordatura,* which is seen by one writer as the first of several uses of *scordatura* peculiar to the "Modenese instrumental school."[58] But more particularly, Uccellini developed the canonic treatment of the upper parts in the SS/bass setting, a treatment we first saw in Buona-

55. New biographic information in PANCALDI & RONCAGLIA, V.

56. Mod. eds.: Bk. 4, Nos. 16 and 17 (both SS/bass sonatas) and 5 dance pieces, TORCHIm, VII, 265 (cf. TORCHI, p. 48 ff.); Bk. 5, No. 2 (S/bass), RIEMANN-CHAMBERm, IV, 135; No. 13 (SS/bass), RIEMANN-KOMPOSITIONSLEHRE, II, 386; No. 7 (S/bass), BECKMANNm, I, no. 4.

57. E. g., BECKMANN, p. 25 ff.; MOSER-VIOLINSPIEL, p. 61 ff.

58. SCHENK-MODENESE, pp. 8, 13, and 26.

mente's Book 7. Thus, in Book 3, Sonata 12 "in Canon detta la Tar-
taruca [tortoise] à 3. Violini" is actually an SS/bass setting in which
the third violinist is meant to pick out only the whole-notes from the
first violinist's part, starting over when he has finished. In Book 5 the
last sonata is a similar setting with but one violin part, the second to be
read backwards from the first.

Without the aid of variation techniques Uccellini often extended his
sonatas beyond 100 measures. The explanation lies again in a growing
concept of tonality and in the larger organization of sections, both in the
older canzona designs and the newer tempo divisions. The anticipation
of the church sonata plan becomes rather frequent in his sonatas. A
special trait of Uccellini's style is the persistent treatment of a single
motive while it undergoes minute, almost nervous changes (Ex. 17).
And a favorite melodic line, almost a mannerism, is the roundabout
descent from bb" over a dominant harmony to eb' on the tonic (Ex. 18).

Ex. 17. Some changes in a motive, from Marco Uccellini's
Sonata 8 "a violino e Basso," Bk. 4 (after a score copied by
Ross Lee Finney).

Our only early sonata composer from Florence was **Girolamo Fantini**
(*ca.* 1602 to ?), "trombetta maggiore" in the service of Ferdinand II,
Duke of Tuscany and member of the Medici family. Peerless performer
of his day, Fantini is remembered primarily for bringing the technique
of the relatively simple, natural trumpet to a peak at the time when that
of the new stringed instruments was just being explored. But he is worth
noting for his sonatas, too, which appear in his only publication, *Modo
per imparare a sonare di tromba* (Frankfurt, 1638).[59]

59. FANTINI-FACSIMILEm. Discussed in EICHBORN-FANTINI, with contrary opinions

Ex. 18. From Marco Uccellini's Sonata 4 "a violino solo detta la Hortensia virtuose," Bk. 4 (after a score copied by Ross Lee Finney).

Among some 120 pieces that make up this method, including 100 individually dedicated to 100 important Italian or German families, there are exercises, dances, military pieces, and 26 "sonatas." Since the method is progressive in difficulty, the sonatas progress in size from about 10 to about 70 measures, in range, and in musical import. Only two of them are purely exercises without accompaniment. Of the others, 18 are in S/bass settings (without figures or thematic interest in the *b. c.*) and 6 are unaccompanied duets (the first such "sonatas" known to this study). The "tavola" clearly sets the sonatas apart from the other pieces. The earlier sonatas, with repeated sections, are like the dances, although not identified with particular meters. But the later ones are much longer, more ornamental, and technically more advanced than the dances. Also, they have *f* and *p* signs, and an occasional change to triple meter. Fantini's music has clear metric organization and appealing tunes, some of which were certainly not original with him but were arranged.

Central and Southern Italy

Almost nothing can be reported in the way of sonatas by composers resident in Rome or Naples during the first half century. The greatest instrumental composer of this period, **Girolamo Frescobaldi,** lived mainly in Rome but did not use "sonata" in his titles.[60] There is more of

---

in MGG, III, 1800 ff. (Karstädt) on the performance of the occasional tones not in the natural series. Florence rather than Frankfurt may have been the actual city of publication (SCHMIDL, I, 519).

60. The editor of CLASSICIM, I, no. 12, loosely used the over-all title *Sonate* for an assortment of Frescobaldi pieces.

significance than chance in this fact. Frescobaldi, like Bach a century later, marked the culmination of a past era more than the founding of a new one.[61] Where he came closest to the contemporary sonata he touched on its more conservative aspects. One example is his liturgical organ collection *Fiori musicali* (1635), of which many pieces recall the severe type of organ sonata that we have so far met only in Banchieri and Merula but are about to meet again in an immediate successor to Frescobaldi. The other example is his *Canzoni ad una, due, trè, e quattro voci; accomodate per ogni sorte de stromenti*. This collection appeared in Rome in 1623 and in later altered and expanded editions that figured, it is pertinent to note, among the last collections to consist entirely of ensemble canzonas. Instruments are only rarely specified (as in the two remarkable toccatas for realized *spinettina* or lute, one with violin, that appear only in the 1628 edition). Among the scorings the melo/bass types predominate over the multivoice, in keeping with the times. And both dynamic and tempo contrasts are indicated. But in place of the further modernisms if not downright novelties, the scorings, and the texture of the sonatas by his less skilled contemporaries, Frescobaldi preferred to hold to his wonderfully plastic rhythms and polyphony, distributed equally among all the parts.[62]

The last of the early Italians to be mentioned here is **Gioanpietro Del Buono,** from Palermo in Sicily (where Bartolomeo Montalbano had published his melo/bass and multivoice *Sinfonie* in 1629). This otherwise unknown composer inserted "XIIII. Sonate di cimbalo" as the eighty-third and penultimate item in a large collection of vocal *canoni* and *oblighi* based on the Gregorian Vesper hymn "Ave maris stella" (Palermo, 1641).[63] Admittedly inspired by Francesco Soriano's similarly titled but purely vocal publication based on the same popular hymn (Rome, 1610), Del Buono's collection was one of those tours de force in recherché polyphony that cropped up often in the 17th and 18th centuries and reached their zenith in Bach's *Art of Fugue* and *Musical Offering*. The 14 sonatas, although based on the same hymn and made recherché enough in their own right, were apparently thrown in as a concession to more modern tastes and as a temporary relaxation of the intellectual rigors.

These sonatas have an appreciable, twofold significance. Pertinent again to our semantic approach, they anticipated by half a century any other known pieces for stringed keyboard instrument that bore the

61. Cf. MGG, IV, 912 ff. (Reimann) ; APEL-NEAPOLITAN.
62. Cf. RONGA, p. 224 ff.; MACHABEY-FRESCOBALDI, p. 103 ff.; CROCKER, p. 416 ff. Two canzonas from the 1628 edition are reprinted in RIEMANN-CHAMBERm, I, 27.
63. Cf. NEWMAN-DEL BUONO, with examples.

title "sonata," including those we shall meet presently by Strozzi, Pasquini, Noordt, and Kuhnau. The honor is one that has been contested with surprising enthusiasm if somewhat less reason.[64]   Secondly, Del Buono's sonatas prove to be original, effective keyboard music. Their significance in this respect is enhanced by their appearance at the outset of the period between Frescobaldi and Pasquini, a period that has been viewed as a relatively barren one for Italian keyboard music.[65]

The sonatas are all in four parts, printed in open score. In each the complete hymn or *cantus firmus* is stated once through, most often in whole-notes in the tenor part. Except for their greater freedoms the sonatas resemble the contemporary organ *versetti*. They belong, in fact, in the category of the organ sonata as we have seen it thus far. Even their chromaticism and ingenious, lively figuration do not suffice to distinguish the cembalo (harpsichord) from the organ. Incisive ideas, bold dissonances, intricate rhythms, and long lines also characterize the style. There are tempo contrasts but no metric changes within any one sonata.

65a

64. Cf. NEWMAN-EARLIEST, pp. 201 and 208 ff.
65. Cf. PANNAIN-PIANISTICA, p. 120 ff. The subject is being investigated in a Ph.D. dissertation by Mr. James Monroe in progress at The University of North Carolina at the time of this writing.

Chapter 8

Italy from about 1650 to 1700

Our middle group of Italians continued to write their sonatas chiefly in the northern cities. But contributions now came from Naples, too, and of course from Rome, where Corelli marked the first main peak in sonata history. The number of sonata composers rose sharply during this period, many of them members of clearly defined schools. Although it would no longer be practical to give even passing mention to all of them who are still known, there also would no longer be the same reason for doing so. The diverse sonata concepts of the first half century were fast crystallizing into a more consistent and unified concept that was much the same for one composer as another. By the end of this middle period one can already find a routine or stereotyped sonata.

Venice (Legrenzi, Stradella)

Venice makes the best starting point again, as the main link with the past. To be sure, it was soon to be surpassed in sonata activity by both Bologna and Modena, and even in sonata publishing by Bologna. Yet there were two Venetians in this period, Legrenzi and Stradella, who may be ranked among the leading composers of the 17th century, for their chamber music as well as their important operas and sacred music.

Giovanni Legrenzi (1626-90), another of the many church organists we have met, actually composed only the last of his four extant sonata collections in Venice (Op. 10, 1673). Opp. 2 and 4 had been published while he was still in Bergamo (1655 and 1656), and Op. 8 while he was in Ferrara (1663).[1] But, if one center must be preferred, Venice was the city where nearly all of his publications and republications were issued, where he spent more than half of his adult career, and where he made his chief mark.

1. The listings of three other collections in EITNER-QL (and EITNER-MISCELLANEA, III, 946), SCHLOSSBERG, and SCHMIDL appear to be based on errors. But a post-humous set of dances, Bk. 5, Op. 16 (1691), is confirmed in STEVENS-UNIQUE, p. 410 ff.

The sonatas in all four collections add up to a total of 63, in a good variety of melo/bass and multivoice scorings. By comparison with Uccellini's sonatas (p. 123), the distribution leans even more toward the "trio" type. Disregarding *concertante* basses again, 68 per cent are duo/bass, 13 are solo/bass, 8 are quarto/bass, and the remaining 11 per cent are multivoice. Taking these important collections individually, *Sonate a due, e tre,* Op. 2 (or Book 1), contains 18 sonatas (including one by Giovanni's father)—3 SB/bass, 6 SS/bass, and 9 SSB/bass.[2]   2a
Suonate dà chiesa, e dà camera, correnti, balletti, allemande, e sarabande à tre, Op. 4 (Book 2?), has 12 SSB/bass sonatas plus 18 separate dances.[3] *Sonate a due, trè, cinque, e sei stromenti,* Op. 8 (or Book 3), contains 16 sonatas—3 SB/bass, 3 SS/bass, 4 SSB/bass, 2 SSSSB/-bass, and 4 multivoice (2 a 5 and 2 a 6).[4] And *La Cetra . . . Sonate a*   4a
due tre e quattro stromenti, Op. 10 (or Book 4), contains 17 sonatas—2 SB/bass, 3 SS/bass, 6 SSB/bass, 3 quarto/bass (1 SSSS/bass and 2 for 4 "viole da gambe ò come piace"), and 3 multivoice.[5]   5a

Stringed instruments are specified throughout Legrenzi's sonatas, with bassoon indicated as an optional bass only four times and only in the first three sets. "La Buscha à 6," in Op. 8, divides into two SSB/bass groups, one with the option of *cornetti* and bassoon. These groups are set in opposition through contrapuntal imitations although not the actual antiphony of the older polychoir sonata. In Legrenzi's *concertante* bass parts, two interesting extremes can be found. On the one hand are instances where the *b. c.* not only joins in the more rapid figuration but even outdoes the *concertante* part in this respect, as in "La Bevilaqua à 3," in Op. 8. On the other hand is at least one instance, Sonata 4 *a 2* from Op. 10, in which the *concertante* part is so independent of the *b. c.* as to result in three separate parts much of the time or in a prototype for the later piano trio when the *b. c.* is realized. The writing for all the stringed instruments shows a keen understanding of their idioms, not in virtuoso or stunt passages but in basic scale and arpeggio

2. Mod. eds.: "La Cornara," WASIELEWSKI-XVIIm, no. 23 and elsewhere; "La Torriana," RIEMANN-BEISPIELEm, no. 102 and elsewhere; "La Valvasona," RIEMANN-CHAMBERm, IV, 152; most of "La Savorgnana," RIEMANN-MUSIKGESCHICHTE, II, Part 2, 156; "La Raspona," HORTUSm, no. 31 (Danckert). Unfortunately, FOGACCIA, the recent and only book on Legrenzi, does not supply the long-overdue study of his instrumental music (cf. HITCHCOCK).
3. Full listing, with thematic index, in HAAS-ESTENSISCHEN, p. 52 ff.; more on pp. 13 and 16. Mod. ed.: Son. 1, "La Bernarda," HAUSMUSIKm, no. 74 (Schenk).
4. All 16 in EINSTEIN-SCOREStm, III. Mod. eds.: "La Rosetta" and "La Fugazza," WASIELEWSKI-XVIIm, nos. 30 and 24; "La Buscha," DAVISON & APELm, no. 220; short exs. from the multivoice sonatas, with discussion, SCHLOSSBERG, pp. 43-58.
5. Mod. eds.: the first SB/- and SSSS/bass sonatas, HORTUSm, nos. 84 and 83 (both Fellerer).

figures, leaps across intervening strings, bowing slurs, and lyrical passages in the most effective ranges.

Legrenzi's sonatas may all be classed as church types except for the second group of six sonatas in Op. 4 (1656). In this set the composer made a functional and musical distinction between *chiesa* and *camera,* one year after Marini had made the first such distinction (Op. 22). Legrenzi used merely the word "Sonata" over each of the church types, as was the more common Baroque practice, but he inscribed "Sonata da camera" over each of the pieces in the second group. His court type proves to be only a single movement, evidently intended as the introduction to a suite that could be made up at random, to suit the occasion, from the sets of dance types that followed. In other words, here was the "custom suite," mentioned in a previous chapter (p. 49), which prevailed in Italy before standard suite cycles were established. As discussed earlier, Legrenzi's church sonatas are notable for their usually clear division into several movements, sometimes in the order of F-S-M(oderate)-S-F, with the two outer movements being fugal allegros thematically related. Following close after Marini's precedent again, the movements are variously marked off by double bars, repeat signs, tempo marks, meter changes, and key (though not key-signature) changes. But Marini's terms "Prima parte" and so on are not used, and the divisions are still a matter of conjecture at times.

In Legrenzi's sonatas the fugal craft of Neri, the tonal sureness of Buonamente, and the agile wit of Merula are rolled into one and carried forward. The ideas themselves are given strong individuality by well-defined outlines in pitch and meter (Ex. 19), as Bach and Handel no doubt thought when they borrowed from his fugue subjects.[6] The key

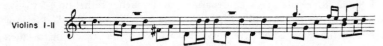

Ex. 19. From the opening of "La Bonacossa à 3" (SSB/bass), Op. 8, by Giovanni Legrenzi (after EINSTEIN-SCOREsm, III).

relationships between movements are daring, especially when the major chord at the end of one movement is followed by the relative minor's dominant harmony at the start of the next (as in "La Pia" from Op. 8). Furthermore, expressive harmonies, sharp dissonances, and long lines in solid contrapuntal textures lend introspective depth to Legrenzi's slow movements. Example 20 quotes in full one of the short, transi-

6. Cf. GROVE, V, 113 ff. (Gehring).

Ex. 20.   From Sonata 3 "à due violini," Op. 10, by Giovanni
Legrenzi (after a score prepared by Ross Lee Finney).

tional slow movements.   The movement begins thus after a strong
cadence in G major at the end of the previous movement.

The important, much romanticized composer **Alessandro Stradella**
(1642?-82) probably belongs among the Venetians by virtue of his
style and such little information as can be found about various places of
residence.   Usually he is identified with Modena, if only because nearly   6a
150 of his MS items (*ca.* 1670-80) are there, in the Biblioteca Estense.
But on this basis alone there would be equal justification here for placing
him in Torino, where even more instrumental MSS, including the only
ones entitled "sonata," are to be found in the Biblioteca nazionale.[7]   7a
And there would be good reason for placing him in Bologna, including
the fact that he wrote the type of "trumpet sonata" that we shall meet
there.   Unfortunately, the information ordinarily to be gleaned from
title pages and dedications is lacking for Stradella, since very little of his
instrumental music was published in his era (or has been since then).

Within the 36 MSS of 27 different instrumental works in Modena
and Torino there is some confusion of title not unusual for the later 17th

7. Cf. PUBBLICAZIONI-MODENA, p. 496, and PUBBLICAZIONI-TORINO, p. 30 ff.   The
Este MSS are surveyed in the valuable study RONCAGLIA-STRADELLA (with examples), and the Torino MSS in GENTILI, p. 357 ff.

century between the words "sonata," "sinfonia," and "concerto." However, as has usually proved true, the confusion was not so much within
the composer's own classifications as in their departure from prevailing
trends that have only become clear through historical perspective.   In
the main, "sonata" seems to have meant to Stradella any of the new
concerto grosso dispositions in which he pioneered so significantly,[8]
"sinfonia" any of the smaller, melo/bass ensembles over which we would
now expect the title "sonata."   "Concerto" he used only in the terms
"concerto grosso" and "concertino" to qualify the scoring.   All together,
five works by Stradella are known under the title "sonata."   Two are
SS/bass types in two Bolognese anthologies of 1680 and about 1700.[9]
But both of these sonatas must have been so called only by their compilers,
since they are apparently two of the eight SS/bass "sinfonias" among
the Modena and Torino MSS.   The other three "sonatas" are MSS in
the Torino library—*Sonata a otto viole con una tromba e basso continuo;
Sonata di viole, cioé per concerto grosso di viole, concertino di due violino
e leuto;* and *Sonata a quattro, due violini e due cornetti, divisi in due
chori, ciascuno col basso* (the *dialogo* setting that we met in the sonatas
of Rossi and others).

Only the last two uses of "sonata" are contradicted in the MSS, for
among the 18 "sinfonias" that comprise all of Stradella's independent
instrumental music in the Modena library are other copies of the same
two works with different titles—for example, *Sinfonia per violini e
bassi a due concertini distinti.*[10]   Aside from this and one other concerto
type of sinfonia, the sinfonias to be found in both libraries are all
melo/bass types (S/-, SB/-, or SS/bass).[11]   These remarkable pieces
should not remain unrecognized while less worthy music of the period
is being brought back to light.   Possibly the mere fact of their less
conventional titles has deterred prospective editors.   At any rate, in all
but the name, here is the Baroque sonata suddenly come of age.   The
large view of tonality based on sequences of strong dominant progressions, the full harmonic vocabulary, and the broad although not consistent
cycle of movements (totaling around 150 measures) all leave little to be
added.   Moreover, far from being a purely academic achievement, this
music stands with some of the best of its time in boldness, sweep,
mastery of form, and quality of ideas.

8. Cf. SCHERING-INSTRUMENTALKONZERT, p. 41 ff.
9. ANTHS. SILVANIm and BOLOGNAm II.
10. RONCAGLIA-STRADELLA, pp. 88 and 91.
11. Mod. eds.: SB/bass sinfonia (no. 2 in Estense Mus. G. 210 [not 209]),
SCHERING-BEISPIELEm, p. 229; two others (Estense Mus. G. 210, no. 3, and F.
1129, no. 7), BARISON-STRADELLAm, with the title "sonata" and disturbing editorial
changes.

Legrenzi's pupil and successor at St. Mark's, **Carlo Francesco Pollarolo** (1653-1722), was apparently the "Pollaroli di Venezia" who contributed the second of the 18 fugal organ pieces in the oft-cited ANTH. ARRESTIm (compiled *ca.* 1695).[12]   Another at St. Mark's, and perhaps a descendant of the Monteverdi circle in Mantua, was **Carlo Grossi.** He is remembered for two "trio" sonatas (SS/- and SSB/bass) that are further examples to appear in a sacred vocal collection (1657).[13] Besides these two, the remaining Venetian to be mentioned here is the obscure opera composer **Giovanni Maria Ruggieri,** who left two sets of *Suonate da camera* in 1689 (SB/bass) and 1690 (SS/bass) and two of *Suonate da chiesa* in 1693 and 1697 (both SSB/bass).   All four sets, Opp. 1-4, were published in Venice.   Each contains ten sonatas.[14] In Op. 1, *Bizzarie armoniche,* the composer begs the performer's indulgence on behalf of the jokes of a dilettante.   One of these *scherzi* is a canonic sonata like the examples by Buonamente and Uccellini, although here the bass player reads the violin part upside down.   Evidently Op. 2, *Scherzi geniali ridotti a regola armonica,* is similar in purpose and character.   The church sonatas in Opp. 3 and 4 are largely based on the S-F-S-F cycle that already had been established in the previous decade by Corelli and his contemporaries.   Those in Op. 3 reveal a firm sense of thematic unity and of tonality, with rather neutral themes and conservative technical requirements.

Bologna (Cazzati, G. B. Vitali, P. Degli Antoni)

That Bologna was the foremost center of the sonata in the later 17th century can be credited largely to the musical chapel of San Petronio, with its small but efficient orchestra, to the Accademia dei Filarmonici (founded in 1666), and to two among several publishers, Monti and Silvani.[15]   The heightened activity began in 1657 with the appointment of Maurizio Cazzati as director of the San Petronio chapel.   Even more significant to the instrumental developments proved to be his pupil, the violinist Giovanni Battista Vitali.   After Cazzati was discharged 14 (or 16?) years later for his feud with Arresti, the chapel continued to thrive under the esteemed church composer Giovanni Paolo Colonna.

---

12. Mod. ed.: TORCHIm, III, 341, from a MS source (cf. NEWMAN-EARLIEST, p. 206 ff.).

13. Cf. MGG, V, 953 ff. (Tagliavini).

14. Op. 2 is known here only through listings in FÉTIS-BU, VII, p. 349, and SCHMIDL, II, 418.   Thematic index of Opp. 3 and 4 in HAAS-ESTENSISCHEN, p. 62 ff. Mod. ed.: Op. 3, entire, HAUSMUSIKm, nos. 64-67, 122, 123, 129, 135, 141, and 142 (all Nowak, with prefaces).

15. Cf. VATIELLI-BOLOGNA, *passim;* MGG, II, 85 ff. (Sartori); MORINI; CHRYSANDER-MUSIKVERLAG.

But by the end of the century financial difficulties caused the dispersion of many of the Bolognese instrumentalists to other centers (especially Florence and Vienna), with a not unbeneficial effect on those centers.[16]

Maurizio Cazzati (*ca.* 1620-77) left nearly 70 collections of music. Out of some 11 made up entirely of instrumental music, 5 are extant, containing a total of 54 melo/bass, multivoice, and polychoir sonatas. *Il secondo libro delle sonate a una, doi, tre, e quattro,* Op. 8, 1648,[17] appeared while Cazzati was at Bozzolo (between Cremona and Mantua). It includes 14 pieces, both melo/bass and multivoice.[18] Typical again of the mid-century equivalence of terms is the fact that three "canzonas" and two "sinfonias" are among the subtitles. Also, in spite of the over-all title, the last piece, "Sonata detta la Vecchia," calls for six instruments, adding a third violin and a trombone to the string-quartet setting of the other four multivoice pieces *a 4* (plus *b. c.*).

Correnti e balletti . . . con alcune sonata a 5. 6. 7. 8., Op. 15 (Book 4), was first published about 1654,[19] while Cazzati was in Bergamo. It is his only set that combines dances and sonatas. The sonata *a 5* is multivoice, while the remaining three sonatas divide into choirs, providing rather rare examples of the polychoir setting outside of Venice and this late.

Suonate a due violini, Op. 18, was first published in 1656 (not 1651), still before Cazzati left Bergamo for Bologna.[20] It presents 12 "trio" or SS/bass sonatas with optional *concertante* bass parts, to which is added a "Capriccio" over a 16-note *basso ostinato.* The latter was typical of the stunt pieces often used to top off a set of sonatas in the 17th century.

Sonate à due, trè, quattro, e cinque, con alcune per Tromba, Op. 35 (Bologna, 1665), is a different sort of collection. Along with six SS/- or SSB/bass sonatas and four in string-quartet setting are three multivoice sonatas *a 5* for trumpet, violin, alto viola, tenor viola, and *violone.* These last introduced a whole literature of sonatas with one or more trumpets, a literature that extended well into the 18th century and is largely preserved today among the MSS of the Archivio di San Pe-

16. Cf. VATIELLI-BOLOGNA, p. 199 ff.

17. "Il primo libro" is missing. Perhaps it was the unknown Op. 4 or was reserved for the 8 *Canzoni a 3,* Op. 2 (1642), which had been given no book number. But the date "1639 or earlier" offered in RIEMANN-TRIOSONATEN, p. 146, is based on an error.

18. Mod. eds.: "La Calva" and "La Pezzola" (both S/- or SB/bass), FINNEY-CAZZATIm; part of "La Lucilla" (SSB/bass), RIEMANN-MUSIKGESCHICHTE, II, Part 2, 148 ff.; exs. of the multivoice sons. from Opp. 8, 15, and 35, with discussion, SCHLOSSBERG, pp. 62-71 and 88-91.

19. Cf. SCHLOSSBERG, p. 101.

20. Mod. eds.: "La Martinenga," HORTUSm, no. 34; portions of "La Varana" and "La Strozza," VATIELLI-BOLOGNA, p. 167 and HEUSS-SINFONIEN, p. 476, respectively.

tronio.[21]   They represent an offshoot of the Baroque sonata concept   21a
most closely related to the concerto grosso,[22] on the one hand, and out-
door festive music, on the other.   Moreover, as such they were intended
for performance by an orchestral rather than a chamber group, a fact
confirmed by the existence of multiple parts for many of the MSS.

Finally, in 1670 Cazzati published twelve *Sonate a due . . . cioè
violino, e violone,* Op. 55.[23]   This set brought the percentage of Cazzati's
"solo" sonatas to 28, behind the favorite "trio" setting at 44 per cent,
but ahead of the multivoice at 22 and, of course, the polychoir at 6
per cent.

That Cazzati made his mark is attested by the number of reprints
several of his publications enjoyed, including three of Op. 18 and two of
Op. 35 (one of each being in Antwerp).   But he seems to have been
important more as a precursor than as an important composer in his
own right.   His music suffers by comparison with Legrenzi's and
Stradella's, whether in the quality of ideas or the breadth of forms.
The instrumental writing is modest for its time, with nothing more
unusual than tremolo by way of special techniques.   In the violin
sonatas of Op. 55 the *cornetto* is still made optional.   The trumpet
sonatas of Op. 35 are homophonic, not polyphonic in the usual manner
of Cazzati's other music or of subsequent Bolognese trumpet sonatas.
Although they confine the trumpet to the D- or A-major scale between
a' and a", Cazzati still felt obliged in his preface to allow the substitu-
tion of a violin if a trumpet player of sufficient training were not at hand.
Among conspicuous traits in his other sonatas are the simple but clearly
tonal harmonies; the concentration of single motives in fairly dense
textures; the variety of movements, although in no set order of tempos;
the use of related ideas in some or all of the movements; and even an
optional return, at the end, to the first two movements ("La Maltese"
in Op. 8).

Cazzati leads us directly to his pupil in counterpoint, **Giovanni
Battista Vitali** (*ca.* 1644-92), a member of the San Petronio orchestra
highly esteemed by his contemporaries both for his violin and cello
playing and for his composing.[24] Vitali left scarcely a fifth as many   24a
publications as his teacher, but these were almost all instrumental, with
as many sets that contained sonatas and even more that enjoyed reprints.   Moreover, he devoted himself almost exclusively to the "trio"

21. Cf. PUBBLICAZIONI-PETRONIO.
22. Cf. SCHERING-INSTRUMENTALKONZERT, p. 27 ff.
23. Cf. MISHKIN, p. 101 ff.   Mod. ed.: Son. 1, DAVISON & APELm, no. 219, and
GIEGLING-SOLOm, no. 4.
24. Cf. Silvani's laudatory preface in SARTORI-BIBLIOGRAFIA, item 1671d; also,
VATIELLI-BOLOGNA, p. 134.

sonata, leaving only 2 out of 38 church sonatas that are "solo" types and 3 that are multivoice. Two of the sonata publications were published while he was in Bologna and four more after he moved to Modena in 1674, where he eventually became maestro di cappella at the Este court.

In his *Correnti, e balletti da camera,* Op. 1 (1666), Vitali made the typical apology expected of the new, young composer for "these weak efforts of mine," promising to try better to meet his public's taste the next time by composing some *Sonate à due violine.* In Op. 2, published the very next year, he kept his word with twelve SS/bass sonatas that, like Op. 1, won enough approval to justify three further editions within 15 years.[25] The request for organ as the *b. c.* instrument and the absence of dance titles suggest that this set was conceived as the church type.

Two years later (1669), in Op. 5, Vitali published twelve more sonatas. This time he ended with three multivoice pieces after nine of the SS/- or SSB/bass type.[26] The multivoice sonatas are exceptional in Bologna at this time for not being trumpet sonatas. Perhaps Vitali would have written that sort had he stayed longer in Bologna.

The lighter, secular tastes at the Este court may explain why he wrote mainly dance music in Modena. However, in Op. 9, published by Heuss in Amsterdam in 1684, he wrote another 12 *Sonate da chiesa a due violini* (SS/bass).[27] These are Vitali's most serious and developed sonatas, averaging about 150 measures in total length as against about 80 in his earlier and 110 in his later sonatas. The last sonata is another example of both the retrograde canonic type ("Sogetto contrario riverso") and of the topping off of a set with something special.

Vitali's only "solo" (S/bass) violin sonatas occur as the final 2 of 60 items in another of those contrapuntal tours de force—in fact, the best known one from the 17th century—*Artificii musicali ne quali si contengono in diverse maniere, contrapunti dopii, inventioni curiose, 28a capritii, e sonate,* Op. 13 (1689).[28] "He deserves not to be called a *Musico,*" his preface begins, "who knows not how to handle the more recondite secrets of the art in whatever style." But this time the sonatas

25. Mod. eds.: Son. 3, WASIELEWSKI-XVIIm, no. 26 (cf. WASIELEWSKI-XVII, p. 61 ff.) ; Son. 6, HAUSMUSIKm, no. 147 ; Son. 1, RIEMANN-CHAMBERm, IV, 146 ; exs. from Sons. 10 and 7, RIEMANN-KOMPOSITIONSLEHRE, II, 16 and 39. Though Vitali is comparatively well represented in modern reprints, a detailed study of his music is still lacking.

26. Mod. eds.: "La Gratiani" (SS/bass) and "Cappricio detto il Molza," WASIELEWSKI-XVIIm, nos. 27 and 28; exs. from the multivoice sonatas, with discussion, SCHLOSSBERG, pp. 71-74 and 81-83.

27. The only specific listing of this publication is in BRITISH PRINTED, 2d Supp., p. 81, the MS of which is Mus. F. 1249 in PUBBLICAZIONI-MODENA, p. 500.

28. Mod. ed.: both sonatas and 5 other pieces, TORCHIm, VII, 179.

themselves do not partake in the intellectual feats nor are they quite on the scale of the huge "Passagallo" in this set.

Last to be cited are two of Vitali's eleven dance collections. In these two the word "sonata" is used as the over-all title, although not as any of the individual titles. One set is *Varie sonate alla francese, & all'Itagliana à sei stromenti,* Op. 11 (1684). The other is *Sonate da camera a trè,* Op. 14, published posthumously by his son Tomaso Antonio Vitali in 1692 in the very month of Vitali's death.[29] The pieces in Op. 11 are only tentatively grouped, whereas those in Op. 14 are clearly grouped in pairs—"Ballo and Giga," "Gavotta" and "Minuet," and so on. Only to this extent are Vitali's *Sonate da camera* actual suites of dances. Although Op. 11 is for six instruments (and *b. c.*), even it might be placed in a melo/bass category (SSSATB/bass), since the five higher parts simply proceed in block chords against the bass. In fact, Vitali advises that the pieces in this set may be played, optionally, with violin alone and bass (SB/bass).

Vitali's dances are outstanding for their fetching tunes, distinct phrases, straightforward homophony, and purposeful, tonal harmony (Ex. 21). These traits carry over to his central, triple-metered move-

Ex. 21. Opening of "Minuet" from *Sonate da camera a trè,* Op. 14, by Giovanni Battista Vitali (after TORCHIM, VII, 203).

ments and gigue-like finales that do not have dance titles. His frequent use of the minuet (from 1685 in Op. 12), probably deriving from Lully in Paris, ranks with Giuseppe Torelli's (Op. 2, 1686) among the earliest in Italian dance groupings.[30]

29. Mod. ed.: 4 separate pieces from Op. 11, and 9 from Op. 14, some in pairs, TORCHIM, VII, 212 ff. and 199 ff.
30. Cf. SCHENK-MODENESE, p. 17 ff. In *Suonate da camera,* Op. 1 (1687),

In the church sonatas Vitali's over-all plan generally borders on the S-F-S-F cycle, although that exact sequence appears only occasionally. The fugal movements are compact, chiefly because they seldom have episodes and because the ideas overlap so much in stretto or other close imitation. The slow movements often describe one long line from start to cadence, kept in motion by a repeated figure in the line itself and by suspensions and resolutions over the underlying harmony. As shown by convincing modulations, the grasp of major and minor tonal relationships is very sure (even including the frequent use of our modern signatures for E major and G minor). Between two or more of the movements there is almost always some sort of thematic tie, however subtle or apparent it may be.

From Vitali as a significant contributor to the "trio" sonata we turn now to one of Bologna's most important creators of the "solo" sonata. **Pietro Degli Antoni** (1648-1720), a charter member of the Accademia dei Filarmonici and self-styled "Concertista di Cornetto e Compositore," left five collections of instrumental music, about as many more of sacred vocal music, and several oratorios. Two of the instrumental collections are made up only of paired or separate dances, Opp. 1 and 3 (1670 and 1671). Two consist entirely of church-like *Sonate a violino solo* (and *b. c*), there being twelve in Op. 4 (1676), and eight in Op. 5 (1686).[31] And one is a volume of *Sonate e versetti . . . per l'organo,* Op. 9 (1712). There is also extant one "trio" sonata that he left. It is No. 5 in Marino Silvano's *Scielta delle Suonate* (Bologna, 1680), which is the first known anthology of sonatas and the first of at least five important sonata anthologies to be published in Bologna up to 1706.[32]

The rather rare term in titles up to now, "a violino solo," is certainly justified in the music of Degli Antoni's Opp. 4 and 5. The *b. c.* shares in the thematic material about as in Vitali's sonatas—that is, little more than to provide an imitation at the start or to fill breathing spots in the solo part. A *concertante* bass part is not included. Especially in the moderate and slow movements Degli Antoni's bass parts are more

listed in STEVENS-UNIQUE, p. 406 ff., Benedetto Vinacese from Castiglione (delle Stiviere) acknowledges the novelty of mixing "Menuetti" with the other dances.

31. For discussions of Opp. 4 and 5, with liberal examples, cf. TORCHI, p. 77 ff.; VATIELLI-BOLOGNA, p. 173 ff.; and, especially, MISHKIN, p. 103 ff. Mod. eds.: 4 unrelated movements from Op. 4 (not 5), VATIELLI-MAESTRIm, II, 15 ff.; Op. 5, Nos. 1, 4, and 6, PAUMGARTNER-DEGLI ANTONIm (with preface).

32. ANTHS. SILVANIm; ARRESTIm; and BOLOGNAm I, II, and III. Add. 31436 in BRITISH MS, III, 260, proves to be a copy of ANTH. SILVANIm (and some of G. B. Vitali's Op. 9), hence does not contain a further SS/bass sonata by Degli Antoni. The two anthologies of 1681 and 1682 listed in STEVENS-UNIQUE, p. 402 ff., which were published in Venice without authors' names, are not reprints of ANTH. SILVANIm or related to each other (information from Mr. Denis Stevens).

likely to make an ideal foil for the longer notes of the solo part out of steady, running quarter-notes or 8th-notes. This bass style (Riemann's *gehende* bass) was to become as important to Baroque texture as the later Alberti bass to Classic texture.

But it is in the solo part that Degli Antoni chiefly distinguished himself, for he was an unexcelled melodist in the noble style of the late 17th century, roughly a decade ahead of his friend Corelli. He was a master of the finely drawn line, whether continuous or broken up into short utterances in the manner of a recitative (Ex. 22). Naturally, an im-

Ex. 22. From Sonata 4, Op. 5, by Pietro Degli Antoni (after the original edition).

portant factor in the affective quality of his lines is the compelling harmony, including such chromatic chords as the Neapolitan 6th and the dominant with flatted 5th. His predilection for the lyrical and affective is also evident both in the preponderance of slow movements (often in cycles that approach the S-F-S-F church plan) and in their variety as distinguished by nicely differentiated terms—"Adagio affettuoso," "Grave," "Aria grave," "Lento," and "Aria posata." All of these traits are to be found to a more moderate degree in Degli Antoni's "trio" sonata. This is a remarkably effective work, yet a simple one in its imitative texture and passage work. Four of its five movements are on the slow side, in the order of "Largo," (Allegro?), "Grave," "Lento," and "Grave." The observation need only be added here that a modern edition of at least a half dozen of Degli Antoni's "solo" sonatas would be a welcome and significant contribution to the violinist's repertoire.

Two further Bolognese composers remembered chiefly for their "solo" sonatas were **Domenico Gabrielli** (*ca.* 1659-90) and his pupil **Giuseppe**

Jacchini(?-1727). Of particular interest, they wrote some of the earliest sonatas for cello.[33] Both played cello in the San Petronio orchestra and both also left several of those Bolognese "trumpet sonatas" for orchestra that Cazzati had pioneered. Gabrielli, who had studied composition with Legrenzi, wrote in most of the current forms but published only a collection of dances in his short lifetime (Op. 1, 1684). It was probably in his remaining six years that he wrote two "Sonate a Violoncello solo con il B. C."[34] and other cello pieces, an SS/bass sonata that appeared posthumously in ANTH. BOLOGNAm II, and the trumpet sonatas.

Jacchini, apparently devoting himself exclusively to instrumental sonatas, published some 50 "solo," "trio" (mostly SSB/- rather than SS/bass), and multivoice (or orchestral) examples in five collections from about 1694 to 1703. Two each in Opp. 1 and 3 are "solo" cello sonatas.[35] There are also his MS trumpet sonatas, as well as one "solo" cello sonata and one "solo" violin sonata in ANTHS. BOLOGNAm II and III, respectively. The latter anthology is, incidentally, an astonishing product of Bolognese music publishing, each sonata being framed by what are certainly among the most extravagant scenic engravings in Baroque music editions (as may be judged from a copy in the Library of Congress). Jacchini used the term "per camera" in the over-all titles of each of his five collections, although except for one "Sarabanda" and two "Aria" titles all the movements in the 13 of his sonatas known to this study have only tempo headings. "Concerti" appears in place of "Sonate" in the over-all titles of Opp. 3 and 4, while both "concerto" and "sinfonia" are equated with "sonata" in the trumpet-sonata titles of Gabrielli, Jacchini, and their contemporaries. This short-lived but total synonymity of terms was reached right at the turn of the century, paralleling that of "sonata" and "canzona" at the previous mid century and immediately preceding the disentanglement and clarification of the terms by most composers.

The cello sonatas of Gabrielli and Jacchini, almost all in S-F-S-F cycles, are remarkably mature for pioneer examples. The basic techniques of the instrument are fully utilized, including sweeping runs, varied bowings, and double notes. What is more, both composers understood how to write melodies that would draw forth those elegiac, sonorous tones peculiar to the best ranges of the cello (Ex. 23).

33. Cf. VATIELLI-BOLOGNA, p. 119 ff., the principal study of this subject, including numerous examples; also, ALBINI-GABRIELLI and STRAETEN-VIOLONCELLO, p. 133 ff.
34. Mus. F. 416 in Biblioteca Estense. Among mod. eds.: SCHOTT CELLOm, nos. 76 and 77 (both Landshoff), with preface.
35. Cf. CAT. BOLOGNA, IV, 118, for Op. 4 (1701) and HAAS-ESTENSISCHEN, p. 49 ff., for Op. 5 (1703), with thematic index. Mod. eds.: two cello sonatas, Op. 1, VATIELLI-MAESTRIm, II, 24 ff.; Son. in G. Op. 5, No. 3 (SS/bass), UPMEYER-JACCHINIm (with preface).

Ex. 23. From the third movement of a "solo" cello sonata,
Op. 1, by Giuseppe Jacchini (after VATIELLI-MAESTRIm, II, 25).

The "trumpet sonatas" by Gabrielli and Jacchini, as well as those by
their fellow Bolognese creators in the same genre—mainly P. Albergati,
G. Aldrovandini, G. P. Colonna, P. Franceschini (Gabrielli's cello
teacher), G. A. Perti, and G. Torelli—are generally scored in five to
nine parts and *b. c.*[36] Typical of this direct ancestor of the concerto   36a
grosso is a "Sonata a 5 con Tromba" by Torelli (*ca.* 1690), with solo
parts for first and second violins, cello, bass viol, and trumpet, plus an
organ *b. c.,* but also plus a *tutti di ripieno* that might include multiple
parts for anything from two violins to a full orchestra.[37]   The one or
more solo trumpets might double the violin parts or stand apart from the
other instruments with imitative figures and brilliant flourishes in passages far more difficult and wide-ranged than Cazzati had written.   In
the solo cello parts, especially Jacchini's, an elaborate obbligato is often
achieved around the *b. c.* line.   The number of movements averages between three and four as against four and five in the Bolognese melo/bass
sonatas.

The most important of these innovators of the concerto grosso, the
violinist **Giuseppe Torelli** (1658-1709), has received considerable attention on that account but almost none for his more intimate, melo/bass
sonatas.[38]   He was another composer who seems to have devoted himself   38a
largely to instrumental music.   In all, it has been possible to locate 54
pieces individually called "sonata," although one must remember that
the same confusion of three terms exists here.   Some 47 per cent are
"trio" or SSSB/bass settings, 32 are multivoice or orchestral, and 21 are
"solo."   These sonatas occur in three kinds of sources, which require
more specific clarification, in view of conflicting records.   Among 8
instrumental collections published between 1686 and 1709 (posthumous),

36. Cf. PUBBLICAZIONI-PETRONIO, p. 138 ff.; SCHLOSSBERG, p. 89 ff. (with examples).
37. No. 1 in Lib. T. 3, Archivio di San Petronio. Cf. VATIELLI-BOLOGNA, p. 233 ff.
38. VATIELLI-BOLOGNA, p. 193 ff. and GIEGLING-TORELLI (with thematic index)
treat mainly his importance to the concerto, including his "trumpet sonatas."
BRENZONI-TORELLI reports recent biographic findings. WASIELEWSKI-XVIIm, no.
34, and HORTUSm, no. 69 (Giegling, with preface), are the only complete "sonatas"
published in recent times (SB/- and B/bass, after MSS in Dresden and Bruchsal).
The first two movements of "Sonata a quattro" (SSAB/bass, after a MS in San
Petronio) are in DELLA CORTEM, no. 93; the work is discussed in GIEGLING-TORELLI,
p. 33 ff.

Op. 1, *Sonate à tre stromenti,* contains 10 SSB/bass sonatas,[39] and Op. 3, *Sinfonie à 2. 3. 4. Istromenti* (1687), contains 2 "solo," 6 "trio," one SSSB/bass and 3 multivoice sonatas.[40] In ANTHS. CORONAm and BOLOGNAm I, II, and III are 3 "solo," and 2 "trio" sonatas. And among over 70 Torelli MSS in Dresden, Bruchsal, Vienna, and mainly San Petronio are 7 "solo," 5 "trio," one SSSB/bass, and 14 multivoice or orchestral types.[41]

41a

A number of other pieces by Torelli might also have been called "sonata" in the senses of the word that then prevailed. He preferred the titles "Concerto da camera" or "Concertino per camera" for the SS/- and S/bass dances grouped into suites in Opp. 2 and 4. And he preferred "sinfonia" for the six SS/bass pieces in the somewhat polyphonic church style, which alternate throughout Op. 5 (1692) with six multivoice concertos intended to be played several to a part according to the composer's own suggestion.[42] But all of his music might be said to have a common denominator in his inclination toward what was rapidly becoming identified as the concerto style. Even in the "trio" sonatas of his Op. 1 there are long solo passages (especially Son. 8). And in several of the subsequent "solo" sonatas the virtuoso displays border on fanfares, as do both some solo and some *concertante* cello passages in the SB/bass MS that Wasielewski published. These traits, plus frequent dynamic and tempo changes, plus surprising harmonic subtlety and depth in slow movements, give Torelli's sonatas an affective quality that brings him closer to Stradella than any of the other Bolognese composers were.

Other notables among Bolognese sonata composers of the time must be mentioned more briefly. The violinist **Pirro Albergati** (1663-1735) left, along with much sacred and dramatic vocal music, a set of dances and two sets of "trio" sonatas, Opp. 3 and 5 (1683 and 1687). Op. 5 is marked "da camera." Although he acknowledged himself to be a "nobile dilettante" and not a professional, his music is described as combining the hymnic quality of Corelli with the virtuosic style of Torelli.[43] **Giovanni Battista Borri** published 12 *Sinfonie à trè,* Op. 1, in 1688, each with the individual title "Sonata." They adhere through-

39. Cf. VATIELLI-BOLOGNA, p. 215 ff. One copy is at the Library of Congress.
40. Cf. VATIELLI-BOLOGNA, p. 218 ff.; SCHLOSSBERG, p. 106, with discussion and examples p. 85 ff. The MS of Op. 3 in the Biblioteca Estense (Mus. F. 1180) has "Sonate" rather than "Sinfonie" in the over-all title.
41. Cf. EITNER-QL, HAAS-ESTENSISCHEN, PUBBLICAZZIONI-PETRONIO, and GIEGLING-TORELLI. Two duplications were eliminated in the foregoing summary, but there may well be others.
42. Cf. GIEGLING-TORELLI, p. 37 ff., and SCHERING-INSTRUMENTALKONZERT, p. 30 ff. Information is lacking about Torelli's *Capricci musicali,* Op. 7.
43. Cf. MGG, I, 287 ff. (Schmitz).

out to the S-F-S-F church plan except for Nos. 7 and 10, in which the first movements undergo frequent tempo changes. **Bartolomeo Bernardi** (?-1732) left 12 "trio" sonatas *da camera,* Op. 1 (1692), that specify *cimbalo* as the *b. c.* instrument and 12 apparently in the church category, Op. 2 (1696), that specify organ. Shortly after he moved to Copenhagen about 1700, he published a third set of 12 sonatas, Op. 3 (Amsterdam). These already reveal influences foreign to Bologna, especially in their much greater technical demands and their average of seven to nine movements.[44] Was it such innovations that brought on the contemporary charge of no unity, melody, or harmony in Bernardi's music?[45]

Before the century drew to a close a number of composers were already writing with skill and assurance in a strongly Corellian manner. One was **Carlo Andrea Mazzolini,** who left six *Sonate per camera à trè,* Op. 1 (1687), and three other sonatas, "trio" and "solo," in ANTHS. CORONAm and BOLOGNAm I and III. Another was **Bartolomeo Girolamo Laurenti** (1644-1726), who left 12 "solo" *Suonate per camera,* Op. 1, in 1691, each consisting of an "Introdutione" and three dances.[46] A further sonata by him of this sort is in ANTH. BOLOGNAm I (no. 5, but not no. 6), while his only "trio" sonata is in ANTH. CORONAm. And a third composer in the Corellian manner was **Giorgio Buoni,** whose Opp. 1 to 3, all published in 1693, consist of 12 church sonatas by himself (Op. 2) along with two sets of "feeble" dances by his students.

Giulio Cesare Arresti (1625-1701) should be mentioned both for his 12 SS/- or SSB/bass sonatas, Op. 4 (1665),[47] and for ANTH. ARRESTIm, which he compiled about 1695 and first published about five years later. The anthology, *Sonate da organo di varii autori,* includes three pieces by him and two each by Colonna and Bartolomeo Monari from Bologna, among the 11 composers represented.[48] Throughout the 18 pieces is 48a a variety of styles from preludial to strictly polyphonic (Ex. 24). Some have sections in contrasting meters and some sound like string music transcribed (e.g., G. B. Bassani, no. 4).

The name of **Giovanni Battista Granata** (? to at least 1684) may be added, too, as the most important of numerous composers for the Spanish guitar, which instrument had all but supplanted the lute in Italy. The last five of his seven known collections, published in tablature in Bologna between 1646 and 1684, contain "sonatas."[49] These are appealing,

44. Cf. MISHKIN, p. 109 ff. Another "solo" sonata is in ANTH. BOLOGNAm I.
45. SCHEIBE-CRITISCHER, p. 759 ff.
46. Mod. ed.: 3 unrelated movements, VATIELLI-MAESTRIm, II, 7 ff.
47. A complete set of parts is listed in STEVENS-BODLEIAN, p. 69.
48. Cf. FROTSCHER, p. 769 ff.
49. Cf. TORCHI, p. 149 ff., with examples; also, CAT. BOLOGNA, IV, 169 ff. A tablature facsimile is given in WOLF-NOTATIONSKUNDE, II, 190-191.

Organ

Ex. 24. From "Sonata VII," by Giovanni Paolo Colonna,
in ANTH. ARRESTIm (after REEDm).

skillful pieces, sometimes colored by the *bizzarrie* and stunts associated
with this music.

Modena (*G. M. Bononcini, Colombi, T. A. Vitali*)

Modena enjoyed one of its most productive periods in music and the
other arts during the later 17th century, while Duke Francesco II
headed the cosmopolitan Este court.   In this city, too, music publishing
thrived, although it was still the Venetian and Bolognese firms that issued
most of the sonata publications to be mentioned here.[50]   Three Modenese
composers in particular stand out for their sonatas—G. M. Bononcini,
G. Colombi, and T. A. Vitali.   These and other Modenese composers
wrote virtually all of their sonatas in "solo" or "trio" settings, an exception being the two SSSSB/bass sonatas (one subtitled "Sinfonia
Piena") in Sisto Reina's sacred choral collection of 1664.   In the secular
activities that predominated at court there was little place for the more
weighty scorings appropriate to the church.

Giovanni Maria Bononcini (1642-78), perhaps a pupil of Uccellini
in Modena (but not trained in Bologna), was the father of Giovanni
Battista and Antonio Bononcini.   He is another 17th-century figure who
has been duly acknowledged by historians, yet has remained largely
unexplored by both researchers and performers.[51]   Among the many
instrumental pieces that make up 9 of his 13 publications, crowded into

50. Cf. SCHENK-MODENESE and RONCAGLIA-COLOMBI (including a list of Modenese
publications in the 17th century).

51. PANCALDI & RONCAGLIA, VII, contains new biographic information.   SCHENK-
MODENESE, p. 12 ff., discusses the music briefly.   A doctoral dissertation on G. M.
Bononcini's life and works is now in process by Professor William Klenz of Duke
University.

but a dozen years before his early death, only two sonatas have appeared in any recent reprints known to this study.[52]   The sonatas, which occur in five of these publications, divide clearly into church and court types. In Opp. 1, 3, 6, 9, and ANTH. SILVANIm there is a total of 34 sonatas not specified as *da chiesa* but assumed to be so simply because Bononcini always added *da camera* when he used "sonata" as the title for dances (although also for one nondance type).   These church sonatas are all in SS/- or SSB/bass settings.   In Opp. 2, 3, and 9 there are dances collectively or individually entitled "sonate da camera."   How many "sonatas" these dances amount to cannot be said, of course, since the grouping of the dances is tentative at most (chiefly by keys and the customary pairings).   The court sonatas are mainly "trio" settings, too, but some also have the optional viola part that was often provided in this period, especially in the dance pieces, and one sonata in Op. 5 is *a 5*.

The fact that Bononcini interested himself in music theory to the extent of publishing a treatise (1673) shows up in Op. 3 (1669), in particular.   Here, besides two pieces called "Sonata da camera a 4" and ". . . a 3," are 10 "Canoni studiosi, et osservati."[53]   These last include four canonic, SS/bass sonatas of the sort we have already met in Uccellini, Cazzati, G. B. Vitali, and earlier composers.   Thus, while the *b. c.* provides the necessary harmonic support, the upper parts engage in a canon at the unison, or at the 3d below in double counterpoint, or in retrograde motion.   In his preface, Bononcini cautions his "benigno lettore" that the counterpoint may not seem exactly in accordance with traditional precepts, but it is so only because his object is entertainment; he has wanted to delight the ear with a variety of "sonatas, *fughe,* and diverse imitations" in what he feels is more vivid harmony.[54]

To judge from about half of the sonatas in Opp. 6 and 9 and the one in ANTH. SILVANIm, which were available in score for this study, skill in part writing is, in fact, the chief strength in G. M. Bononcini's sonatas. Two sonatas (Op. 6, No. 10, in C minor, and Op. 9, No. 1, in A minor) reveal a reserved but considerable depth and development.   Otherwise, the impression is mainly that of competence in the production of fluent agreeable pieces, but not of unusual expressive values in the melody, harmony, or larger rhythmic organization, nor of any special contribution to instrumental scoring or techniques.   (These last, including *scordatura* in Op. 4, are to be found more in his other instrumental music.)   By

52. Op. 1, No. 6, HAUSMUSIKm, no. 130 (Schenk); Op. 6, No. 9, SCHENK-TRIOSONATEm, p. 34.

53. A 12-"voice" canon, not called sonata, is reprinted in SCHERING-BEISPIELEm, no. 219.

54. Cf., also, his preface to Op. 6 in the first edition (SARTORI-BIBLIOGRAFIA, item 1672a).

comparison with Legrenzi's sonatas, which average about 140 measures in total length, Bononcini's average about 95 measures, with both fewer movements and less developed forms. Possibly those lacks, if such they really are, partly explain why this composer's published sonatas did not achieve the reprints that Legrenzi's, Cazzati's, and G. B. Vitali's did.

Another probable pupil of Uccellini and violin teacher of the Duke, **Giuseppe Colombi** (*ca.* 1635-94) seems to have spent his entire life in Modena and to have given it almost entirely to instrumental music.[55] He wrote nearly three times as much as his acknowledged rival G. M. Bononcini wrote, but published not half as much. His opus numbers ran to at least 12 and a further set of *libro* numbers to at least 22, not to mention a variety of separate pieces. Much of this music is still extant in the Biblioteca Estense,[56] though it too remains largely unexplored and unreported. The extant portion is divided about equally between "solo" and "trio" settings, with some 17 collections containing sonatas to about half that many containing separate dances or related pieces. Opp. 1 to 5 are the only published works, dating from 1668 to 1689, with no re-editions. These include 2 sonatas "à 2, 3, e 4 se piace" added to the sinfonias and dances of Op. 1; 12 SS/bass sonatas in Op. 2 (called "Sinfonie" in the over-all title); 12 more in Op. 4, with optional *concertante* bass; and 11 more in Op. 5, marked "da camera," topped off with a final "Giga."

Only the 23 sonatas of Opp. 4 and 5 were available for examination in this study. In their length, forms, and conservative technical range they are similar to those of G. M. Bononcini that were available. Their uniformity of procedure is even greater, to the point of suggesting a formula or stereotype in each set. For example, nearly all of the church sonatas in Op. 4 have three movements in the order of F-S-F, with the first two in quadruple meter and the last in triple. Nearly all of the court sonatas in Op. 5 have an introductory movement and three dances. On the whole, Colombi's sonatas seem a little brighter in quality than Bononcini's. One explanation is the less dense texture, which reveals a more chordal approach to polyphony when it is not actually homophonic. Another is the more tuneful if somewhat discursive melodies that result from repeated, square-cut figures (Ex. 25).

Surprisingly little is known about the son of G. B. Vitali, **Tomaso Antonio Vitali** (*ca.* 1665 to at least 1734),[57] notwithstanding the lasting

55. Recent biographic findings in PANCALDI & RONCAGLIA, VIII. Brief survey of the music in RONCAGLIA-COLOMBI, where a tenuous argument for relating Corelli is advanced.

56. Cf. PUBBLICAZIONI-MODENA.

57. If 1665 is the correct year of birth (from SCHMIDL, II, 672) he was only 10 when he became one of the violinists at the Este court (RONCAGLIA-COLOMBI, p. 36).

Violin I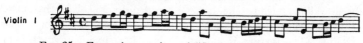

Ex. 25. From the opening of "Sonata Prima," Op. 4, by Giuseppe Colombi.

popularity of the violin *Ciaccona* in G minor (which may or may not be his own composition). Except for this fine piece and a MS concerto,[58] all of his extant works are "trio" and "solo" sonatas. There is a total of 50 sonatas, 48 in 4 published sets of 12 each (1693, 1693, 1695, and 1701), another in ANTH. CORONAm, and a "solo" sonata in MS.[59] Opp. 1 and 2 contain church sonatas with three or four movements mostly in the S-F-S-F sequence.[60] Op. 3 contains court sonatas, each with an introductory movement followed by three or four dances, except Sonata 12, which is a set of variations "sopra l'aria del pass' e mezzo."[61] And Op. 4, *Concerto di Sonate,* contains some church and some court sonatas, plus two that cut across these types. Again the final sonata is a set of variations, this time on the familiar Folia theme that Corelli, Vivaldi, and others used about the same time.[62] There is also, in the opening movement of Sonata 8, one of several instances we shall meet in which the tempo and style changes in the opening movement of Corelli's first "solo" sonata served as a model. Opp. 1-3 are in "trio" setting and Op. 4 is in "solo" setting; interesting from the standpoint of preferred scorings is the fact that Op. 1 originally consisted of "solo" sonatas, to which a second violin part was fitted for publication.[63] A moderately independent *concertante* bass is added to Opp. 1 and 4. In the other sets the *b. c.* joins in the imitations only at focal points in the forms.

T. A. Vitali's sonatas, if they do not seem distinguished by exceptional creative flashes, do come near to the classic ideal around 1700 of purity in line, harmony, and design.[64] Above a steadily moving bass, frequently the running type in 8th-notes, the slower lines describe smooth arches in expressive, *bel canto* style, while the faster thematic material generally consists of those neutral scale and arpeggio figures (especially in Op. 4) that acquire such vigor in the music of Corelli and Vivaldi. The harmony is just that needed to direct the melody within

58. HAAS-ESTENSISCHEN, p. 194.   59. *Ibid.,* p. 115.
60. Mod. eds.: Op. 1, Son. 4, DAVISON & APELm, no. 263; Op. 2, Son. 5, SCHERING-BEISPIELEm, no. 241; another sonata, VATIELLI-MAESTRIm, II, 31.
61. Cf. PERRACHIO-VITALI, with examples. The *Ciaccona* is not in Op. 3, as supposed in MOSER-VIOLINSPIEL, p. 74, nor in any of the other sonatas listed here. See also, DTBm, I (Sandberger), xli.
62. Mod. ed.: Op. 4, entire, SILBERT & PARKER & ROODm.
63. PERRACHIO-VITALI, p. 345.
64. Cf. TORCHI, pp. 91 and 98 ff., including some negative reactions characteristic of that study.

the prevailing tonality (key scheme) and no more. The rhythms are persistent, clearly metric, and often characterized by strong upbeat patterns. The texture is almost always interesting in a contrapuntal sense. In the "trio" sonatas the upper parts vie with each other, inter-cross, or advance by suspensions and resolutions in the ways most associated with that setting (Ex. 26). The sense of proportion in the

Ex. 26. From "Sonata" in G minor by Tomaso Antonio Vitali, Op. 2 (after VATIELLI-MAESTRIM, II, 33).

forms seems well developed. Small sections are often given an echo contrast by *f* and *p* signs. And helping to bind the entire piece are clear thematic ties between two or more movements in most of the sonatas. In fact, the finale in the sonata that Schering reprints is simply a complete variation in compound meter of the opening movement in quadruple meter.

Other Northern Italian Cities

Besides Venice, Bologna, and Modena, there were several other northern Italian cities in which at least one or two sonata composers of some importance were active. Genoa gives us one minor name, **Agostino Guerrieri,** whose only known publication was *Sonate di violino*

a 1. 2. 3. 4. per chiesa, & anco aggionta per camera, Op. 1 (1673).[65]
This set contains 21 church and 3 court sonatas, the latter being two
balletti and a "Partite sopra Ruggiero." The melodic construction and
fugal techniques are reportedly above average. In Novara, near Milan,
the celebrated nun **Isabella Leonarda** published, besides some 19 sacred
vocal collections, 12 *Sonate à 1. 2. 3. 4 istromenti,* Op. 16 (1693).[66]

The Mantuan **Andrea Grossi,** descendant of famed Lodovico Grossi
da Viadana, published 2 sets of 8 dance suites each,[67] one set of 12 sonatas
for 2-5 instruments and *b. c.,* Op. 3 (1682), another of 12 SSB/bass
sonatas, Op. 4 (1685), and one SS/bass sonata in ANTH. SILVANIm.
Op. 4 in particular is stated to reveal outstanding unity, drive, and
craftsmanship.[68] Three multivoice sonatas *a 5* in Op. 3 are trumpet
sonatas, each with three movements in the eventual concerto order of
F-S-F.[69]

A native of Pistoia, **Giovan Pietro Franchi** (?-1731), published an
"Opera Prima" of 12 SSB/bass sonatas (1685) that deserve to be
examined along with his subsequent dramatic and sacred works.[70]

More can be said about two superior composers in Ferrara, G. B.
Mazzaferrata and G. B. Bassani, each of whom served for a time as
maestro di cappella at the important Accademia della Morte. Twelve
SS/bass sonatas with an optional (though really essential) *concertante*
bass, Op. 5, comprise the only known instrumental music by **Giovanni
Battista Mazzaferrata** (?-1691). But they are sufficient to reveal a very
fresh, independent style. It is not surprising that the set was reprinted
three times (not twice) and copied in several MSS after its original
publication in 1674.[71] In each of the sonatas there are four movements
with tempo marks and time signatures that usually contrast, but in no set
order. The last one is exceptional in having four "Allegro" movements,
all in triple or compound meter.

In its style if not its forms Mazzaferrata's music could pass for late
Baroque or even early Classic writing. The chief explanation seems to
lie in chordal rather than linear counterpoint. The ideas themselves are
often chordal in outline, with frequent use of repeated notes. Conse-

65. Cf. CAT. BOLOGNA, IV, 116; TORCHI, p. 63 ff., with exs.; and SCHLOSSBERG.
pp. 45, 49, 53, and 56, with exs. Two of the last church sonatas are actually by
Guerrieri's teacher, A. M. Turati.
66. Cf. SCHMIDL, I, 835.
67. Op. 1 (1678) is listed in STEVENS-UNIQUE, p. 402.
68. TORCHI, pp. 73-74, with examples.
69. Cf. SCHLOSSBERG, pp. 93-95, with exs.
70. MGG, IV, 626 ff. (Sartori).
71. Cf. HAAS-ESTENSISCHEN, pp. 13, 146, and 59 ff. (with thematic index);
TORCHI, p. 91 ff., including several exs. Mod. eds.: Son. 4, WASIELEWSKI-XVIIm,
no. 31; Son. 6, HAUSMUSIKm, no. 148 (Schenk).

quently the harmonic rhythm is slowed, making for a lighter, more fluent texture. The counterpoint to the ideas tends to be a decorative accompaniment more than a competing line. Imitations frequently occur in complementary rhythms between the parts, with a further lightening of the texture. When this texture moves at an allegro tempo in clear two-measure units or pairs of such units, the piquant style of Domenico Scarlatti's or Gaetano Pugnani's allegro writing is anticipated (Ex. 27).

Ex. 27. From finale of "Sonata Decima," Op. 5, by Giovanni Battista Mazzaferrata (after TORCHI, p. 93).

Giovanni Battista Bassani (*ca.*1657-1716) is an interesting composer of dramatic, sacred, and instrumental music—in some ways a rather strange one. But his reputation as an instrumental composer, perhaps exaggerated, has resulted not so much from his style as from Hawkins' and Burney's undocumented reports, over a century later, that he was the violin teacher of Corelli.[72] Aside from Bassani's being four years

72. HAWKINS, IV, 308, and BURNEY-HISTORY, II, 437. The arguments in support of this idea in RINALDI-CORELLI, p. 61 ff., seem very tenuous. PASINI is still the main biographic study. HASELBACH (the dissertation cited as being in progress in MGG, I, 1397 [Engel]) is concerned primarily with Bassani's sacred choral works; it includes a detailed "Werkkatalog" (with some unacknowledged duplications in the sonata listings) but adds little new in its sections on the biography or the instrumental music.

younger than Corelli, there is the question of when these composers might have crossed paths. The one year that Bassani is known to have spent in Bologna (1682-83) came some 12 years after Corelli's 4-year stay in Bologna seems to have ended (1666-70). But more to the point here is the wide difference between their two styles, about as wide as could be in two men working at the same time, in the same medium, and in related environments. However, one must grant that most pairs of composers similarly linked in music history by era and locale—Bach and Handel, Haydn and Mozart, Debussy and Ravel—actually represent styles just as far apart.

In the instrumental category Bassani left only two known collections plus one SS/bass sonata in ANTH. SILVANIm and one organ sonata in ANTH. ARRESTIm. The first collection, *Balletti, correnti, gighe, e sarabande,* Op. 1, contains 12 SS/bass suites with optional second violin, each consisting of 4 dances in the order indicated by the title.[73] In the second of the three editions (1677, 1680, and 1684) of this set the title is preceded appropriately by the term "Suonate da camera."

The other collection was *Sinfonie a due, e trè instrumenti,* Op. 5, in which each of the twelve pieces is called "sonata."[74] In the last two of its four editions (1683, 1688, 1691, and *ca.* 1710) the over-all title is changed to *Sonate da chiesa* and *Suonate.*[75] The setting this time is SS/- or SSB/bass. In further respects these church sonatas show about as sharp a contrast to the court sonatas of Op. 1 as can be found in Bassani's time. Instead of the set plan of four specific dances they have a free one, of four to seven movements in any order of tempos. Instead of the short, straightforward binary designs with each half repeated, they have longer, less tangible forms, some fugal, some loosely sectional. And, as might be expected, instead of a prevailingly homophonic texture they have a texture that is more often polyphonic.

However, it is by comparison with the compact, simple, and purposeful outlines in Corelli's forms that the most characteristic features of Bassani's are revealed. Bassani seems to prefer long lines that unfold without breaks to shorter, separated, balanced phrases. But to produce such lines within relatively narrow limits of pitch and harmony it becomes necessary for him to change direction and turn around single

73. Mod. eds.: one suite, WASIELEWSKI-XVIIm, no. 32 (cf. WASIELEWSKI-XVII, p. 65 ff.) ; "Corrente Nona," VATIELLI-CORELLI, p. 194 ff. Cf., also, TORCHI, p. 87 ff.
74. Mod. eds.: Sons. 1 (not 7) and 8, WASIELEWSKI-XVIIm, nos. 33 and 34; Sons. 2, 6, and 7, TORCHIm, VII, 229 ff.
75. For the last edition see the title photographed in MGG, I, 1396 (disregarding 1683 in the caption). If the neat MS score of Sons. 1-3 in the Library of Congress (ML 96/B343) is actually a holograph as claimed, then its date of 1691 suggests it was part of a new copy made by Bassani for the third edition.

Ex. 28. From Sonata 1 by Giovanni Battista Bassani, in
ANTH. SILVANIm.

tones frequently (Ex. 28). The effect may then be one of preoccupation
with detail, even of poetic rumination in the slow movements (e.g., the
"Adagio" in No. 6), and sometimes of monotony. In spite of telling
ideas, effective use of dissonance, and unquestioned skill in part writing,
the forms tend to be heard more as strings of connected sections than as
integrated wholes.

In Florence two sonata composers of distinction in the service of the
Grand Duchess Vittoria of Tuscany were **Giovanni Battista Gigli,**
who had just come from Modena, and **Antonio Veracini** (*ca.* 1650 to at
least 1696), uncle of the celebrated F. M. Veracini. Along with a few
oratorios and cantatas, one set of 12 *Sonate da chiesa, e da camera à 3
strumenti col basso continuo per l'organo,* Op. 1 (1690), still remains
from Gigli.[76] In accordance with the standard plan of such collections
around 1700, six of these SSB/bass sonatas are serious, four-movement
church types and six are suites of several dances with a slow introduction.

Antonio Veracini is known for little besides his three sets of sonatas,
10 in each, published between 1692 and 1696.[77] Op. 1 contains church
sonatas in "trio" (SSB/bass) setting, not in any fixed order of movements. Opp. 2 and 3 contain "solo" sonatas (S/- and SB/bass, respectively). Although these two collections are marked "da camera,"
at least each of the sonatas in Op. 3 is composed of four movements
without dance titles (although not without dance rhythms) and in the
standard church order, S-F-S-F. Perhaps for that reason Op. 2 reappeared as *Sonate da Chiesa* among reprints of all three opera published
by Estienne Roger in Amsterdam.[78]

76. Brief comments and exs. in TORCHI, p. 85 ff.
77. Mod. eds.: Sons. in C minor, Op. 1, and A minor, Op. 3, WASIELEWSKI-
XVIIm, nos. 37 and 38; same with realized *b. c.,* JENSEN-VIOLINm, Vols. 7415 and
7416.
78. Cf. FÉTIS-BU, VIII, 318; WASIELEWSKI-XVII, p. 77 ff.; BRITISH PRINTED, 2d
Supp., p. 80; HAAS-CAT. 20, no. 557k; and BIBLIOTHÈQUE NATIONALE, VIII, 162, for
pertinent though slightly conflicting listings.

The two sonatas by Veracini that have been republished in modern sources only whet one's appetite for more and for the needed study of them. Especially the one in A minor from Op. 3 reveals all that broad direction and organization that seemed to be secondary in Bassani's musical interests. Both of its slow movements, though quite different in styles, have simple outlines that are defined by progressions to and from only two or three climaxes. In the sonata from Op. 1 the harmony seems a bit circumscribed for the length of the movements. Not only is there a definite limit to the variety of chords but the drive-to-the-cadence becomes something of a formula. Almost invariably this last includes a diminished 3d in the melody that tops a progression from the minor subdominant to the secondary-dominant 7th chord (in third inversion or root position). "Adagio e affett." and "Affett." are the titles of two expressive movements in this sonata, both in the $||:A:||:B:||$ design that could now be found almost as often in church as in court sonatas.

Carlo Antonio (not Ambrogio) **Marini**(*ca.* 1671 to ?) was a violinist in the chapel of Santa Maria Maggiore in Bergamo. He published six sets of sonatas plus one set of four-movement suites and one of solo cantatas between 1687 (when he was only about 16) and 1707 at the latest. Both the composer and his music have yet to be explored. Until someone develops this potential dissertation subject, only certain external facts are available. Of the six sets of sonatas, Opp. 1, 3, 7, and 8 are reported in extant or lost Italian editions, while Opp. 3, 5, 6, and 8 are known in reprints published by Estienne Roger in Amsterdam.[79] There are 72 sonatas in all, twelve in each set, with the last one in Op. 8 being subtitled "Ciacona." The only "solo" (S/bass) set by C. A. Marini is Op. 8. The other sets are all in "trio" (SSB/bass) settings except for 10 multivoice sonatas (all SSAB/bass). These last are the last 4 sonatas of Op. 3 and the last 6 of Op. 6. Four of the 6 sets have church sonatas, mostly but not all with the S-F-S-F plan. Op. 1, *Sonate da camera,* has 12 pairs of dances, and Op. 5, *Sonate alla francese,* is presumably constituted in some like manner.

Similarly unexplored are the sonatas of two violinists in Brescia, the brothers **Giulio** and **Luigi Taglietti** (both born *ca.* 1660).[80] Yet Giulio's

---

79. Cf. HAAS-ESTENSISCHEN, pp. 56, 93, 95, and 71 (not 67), including indices of Opp. 7 and 8; also, FÉTIS-BU, V, 457. The Roger publication numbers (from 106 to 248) cannot be dated except "before 1716" (in spite of DEUTSCH-NUMBERS, p. 19; cf. PINCHERLE-VIVALDI, I, 294 ff.). BRITISH PRINTED, II, 95, lists a "Nouvelle Edition" of Op. 7 published by Mortier in Amsterdam (*ca.* 1730) and "corrigée de Plus de 300 fautes"!

80. The possibility that these two men, both working at the same post as "Maestro,'" were actually one person is a "brother-problem" hinted and dismissed in CAT. BOLOGNA, IV, 150 ff., where the bulk of their music is listed. Could they have been twins?

output was large (if such a fact does not sometimes deter the researcher) and both men made interesting contributions to instrumental music. For example, Giulio developed new violin techniques and figurations,[81] and he deliberately adopted the principle of the *aria da capo,* as can be seen from his title *Pensieri musicali a violino, e violoncello col basso continuo a parte all'uso d'arie cantabili, quali finite si ritorna a capo, e si finisce al mezzo cioè al segno*⌒ (Op. 6, 1707). Luigi added to the early literature of the sonata for cello, which was another instrument that he played. Five of Giulio's 13 publications are sets of sonatas dating from 1695 to 1715. Opp. 1, 5, and 9 are "trio" settings, 7 and 13 are "solo." All are classed as *da camera* except Op. 7. Luigi's Opp. 1, 4, and 5 are extant, dating from 1697 to about 1707. Op. 1 contains "trio" sonatas *da camera,* Op. 4 "solo" sonatas, presumably of the church type, and Op. 5 "trio" *concertini e preludi.* Luigi's cello sonatas, without opus number, are in MS.[82] They include five of the church type, in three to six movements, and five suites in three or four movements.

Rome and Naples (Corelli, Pasquini)

In Rome musical activities under papal control broadened considerably during the 17th century. Among these was the important Congregazione ed Accademia di Santa Cecilia, the instrumental section of which was headed by Corelli from 1700. Also pertinent to our subject was the growth of publishing firms and of opera houses. Yet prior to Corelli only two composers who wrote sonatas in Rome can be mentioned here, plus one who, like Frescobaldi before him, should be mentioned for the fact that he did *not* write them. To be sure, a number of other sonata composers, from Fontana on, had periods of residence in Rome. But it may be significant that those periods generally seem not to have been the ones in which they were stimulated to compose sonatas, whether *da chiesa* or *da camera.*

No information is available on **Giovanni Antonio Leoni** except that contained in a vocal anthology of 1625 to which he contributed and in the only known publication of his own, *Sonate di violine a voce sola,* Book I, Op. 3 (Rome, 1652).[83] This collection takes us back almost to our earliest group of sonata composers. It may, in fact, be cited as the first known collection to be made up entirely of "solo" violin sonatas,

---

81. MOSER-VIOLINSPIEL, p. 77. The disparagement in TORCHI, p. 101 ff., including an example from Giulio's Op. 1, is too characteristic of that survey to be accepted without further checking.

82. HAAS-ESTENSISCHEN, p. 110 ff., with thematic index.

83. Leoni's residence in Rome seems to be confirmed by his dedication to Cardinal Pallotta, almost certainly the Roman Giambattista Pallotta (MORONI, LI, 65), and his indication that both live in the same city.

since, as we saw, neither Vivarino's Book I nor Uccellini's Op. 5 quite qualified for this historical distinction, and Bertoli's "solo" sonatas of 1645 were for bassoon and *b. c.* Leoni's set is a large one, with 31 S/bass sonatas spread over a *partitura* of 188 pages. The sonatas were intended for use in the liturgy, as indicated by the church tone listed for each and by Leoni's own statement that he himself had played such as these for many years in the church. Incidentally, he had more to say, and on a subject that recurs in these Italian prefaces. He was indignant, even sarcastic, about how his sonatas had been played without acknowledgment by others of less high professional standards or had been reproduced in scarcely disguised copies. Hence, at the insistence of his dearest friends, the most eminent professors of music, and others, he has published these new sonatas, etc., etc.

The other Roman to be mentioned prior to Corelli is **Tomaso Marchetti.** A contemporary of G. B. Granata in Bologna, Marchetti was another favored performer on the Spanish guitar. He left one publication, in 1660. It is a guitar method that includes "molte sonate passeggiate" in tablature.[84] The Roman who did *not* write sonatas was Michelangelo Rossi, Frescobaldi pupil and composer of an important set of *Toccate e corrente* for keyboard that first appeared before 1657. About a half century ago questions were first raised as to the authorship of an "Andantino" and "Allegro" attributed to him in numerous "old masters" anthologies for the piano. About a quarter century ago these two pieces turned up as a two-movement sonata (no. 3) in the *Sei sonate per cembalo* that Lorenzo de Rossi published some hundred years after M. Rossi's *Toccate* appeared. Yet they continue, right to this day, to be republished under the older Rossi's name. The matter would hardly deserve this much emphasis if it did not present what seems to be, at least in retrospect, an almost unmatched error in style appraisal, perhaps equalled only by the continued ascription to Frescobaldi of a popular "Toccata" in B minor "arranged" for cello and for orchestra, or by the incredible hoax that must be related when F. W. Rust is met in the Classic Era.

We have come now to **Arcangelo Corelli** (1653-1713), one of the principal names in the over-all history of the sonata.[85] From 1675, perhaps earlier, Corelli lived all or most of his years in Rome. In any

---

84. CAT. BOLOGNA, IV, 171.

85. PINCHERLE-CORELLI remains the standard study of both the man and his music. RINALDI-CORELLI, nearly three times as long in all respects, includes documents, a thematic index, pictures, related topics, and many more music examples and other aids, but falls short in both its historical conclusions and music analysis (cf. PINCHERLE-RINALDI). STILLINGS provides a detailed, style-critical analysis of the music.

case, the present study identifies him with that city because it was in Rome that he composed his six main collections, Opp. 1-6, and it was there that the first publications of all the sonatas occurred, Opp. 1-5 (1681, 1685, 1689, 1694, and 1700). He himself preferred the title "il Bolognese" in Opp. 1-3. This title referred to his four years of training in Bologna, culminating in membership at the Accademia dei Filarmonici in 1670, and perhaps to his chief style derivations (although the Bologna styles in turn had had roots in Roman music[86]). When later he discarded "il Bolognese," mentioning only his birthplace, Fusignano, in Opp. 4-6, he may have been disclosing his prolonged embitterment over the much publicized "quarrel of the fifths" that had started over a

87a   passage in Sonata 3 of Op. 2 (mss. 3-5 of the first "Allemanda").[87]

In Rome Corelli lived a charmed life and one of luxury such as few great composers have known. He figured importantly in the personal lives as well as the exceptional art interests and remarkable society of at least three of the persons of high rank to whom his five sets of sonatas were dedicated. He was a close friend of several other renowned musicians, including Bernardo Pasquini and Alessandro Scarlatti, who were among those that brought him into the exclusive Accademia degli Arcadi in 1706. From almost the moment his Op. 1 appeared, his sonatas enjoyed unparalleled success. In all, they achieved no fewer than 78 reprints during his lifetime (48 in Italy) and another 30 during the next century.[88] Op. 5 alone achieved 43 reprints up to about 1815, including publications in Italy, Holland, England, France, Spain, and Austria. Even before he died Corelli had earned an international reputation in his field, one of pre-eminence that stood unchallenged.

Corelli left only sonatas and concertos.[89] No other category of instrumental music by him is confirmed, nor a single vocal work. Of the chief masters of music we shall meet, not even Domenico Scarlatti and Chopin restricted their variety of mediums and forms so severely. Moreover, one can name several lesser composers but it is hard to think of any other master, unless he be Abaco, who similarly waited until maturity, then neatly issued all his works at fairly regular intervals in just so many sets, with just so many pieces per set. Prior to the 12 concertos in Op. 6, Corelli left 48 "trio" and 12 "solo" sonatas. There are 12 each in

86. Cf. VATIELLI-BOLOGNA, p. 122 ff.

87. Cf. RINALDI-CORELLI, pp. 108 ff. and 429 ff., including the original correspondence.

88. Among several bibliographies of Corelli's editions, cf. SARTORI-"44" and SARTORI-"51"; PINCHERLE-CORELLI, p. 165 ff.; CAT. CORELLIANA.

89. JOACHIM & CHRYSANDERm is the standard "Urtext" edition, based on the first publications and early Dutch ones. Among practical editions of Opp. 1-5 is WOEHLm.

Opp. 1 and 3 of the SSB/bass church type,[90] the same number in Opp. 2 and 4 of the SS/bass court type, and 6 each of the church and court types in Op. 5, which is all S/bass. Two of the final court sonatas are actually sets of variations, "Ciaccona" in Op. 2 and the best known of all Corelli's pieces, "Follia," in Op. 5.

Perhaps the very neatness and finality of this output has worked against the acceptance or study of other works that are ascribed to Corelli, mainly about 15 "solo," 60 "trio," and 3 multivoice sonatas.[91] Some of these, for example, the S/bass sonata in ANTH. BOLOGNAm III, leave little reason to question their authenticity. Others can be ruled out at once, like the "Opera Quarta . . . Nuovamente Ristampata [!]" two years before the genuine Op. 4 first appeared[92] or the 12 "trio" sonatas that the Englishman John Ravenscroft published in Rome in 1695, 9 of which were passed off as Corelli's in a later, posthumous reprint of about 1735.[93] We had occasion in a previous chapter (cf. p. 59) to note some of the interesting arrangements in which Corelli's music appeared, including editions of the S/bass scores as two-hand harpsichord sonatas.

91a

93a

93b

Like other composers who define peaks in history, Corelli marked at once the convergence of past trends in momentarily ideal forms and the branching point for a variety of new trends. Furthermore, he came at the time of other peaks in Baroque music—notably, from his standpoint, those in the *bel canto* style and the art of violin making. But, of course, these facts in themselves do not necessarily make Corelli the "greatest" composer in his field at that time (even assuming such evaluations were possible). In the experience of this study, Legrenzi wrote more intensive, developed, characterful fugues. Stradella and Torelli wrote with a more dramatic, virtuosic sweep in their passage work. Degli Antoni wrote more affective, sensitive lines in his slow movements. And numerous 17th-century composers imposed greater technical requirements, although the fact that Corelli did not exceed the third position on the violin is misleading, for violinists speak with respect of the bowing problems and of the double-stops in the "solo" sonatas.

What Corelli did reveal was a remarkable sense of balance in the concentration and direction of all his musical forces. The very fact that

90. But "da chiesa" in JOACHIM & CHRYSANDERm is added to the original titles.
91. Cf. the list in PINCHERLE-CORELLI, p. 177 ff., to which may be added an SS/bass sonata with trumpet (BRITISH MS, III, 48, Add. 30839, no. 241), and 12 "solo" violin sonatas in a MS formerly owned by Alfred Moffat (HAAS-CAT. 20, no. 190; now Library of Congress M219/C7956).
92. Cf. ARNOLD-CORELLI and SQUIRE-CORELLI.
93. See p. 311 ff. Cf. HAWKINS, IV, 311 and 318; GERBER-LEXIKON, I, 788; PINCHERLE-PIRATERIE, p. 136 ff.; PINCHERLE-CORELLI, p. 180 ff.; NEWMAN-RAVENS-CROFT.

each element is treated in moderation—rhythm, melody, or harmony—helps to explain its efficient co-operation with the other elements toward over-all unity of form. The result was a consolidation of procedures in two fairly definite plans, church and court, that became international patterns to be copied slavishly or altered advisedly through the rest of the Baroque era. Thus, among the 30 church sonatas, the S-F-S-F sequence of movements clearly predominates, being present, too, within the five-movement plans of all six "solo" church sonatas. Among the 30 court sonatas the same sequence is the one most often approximated by the dances and free movements, although these sonatas generally have one less movement than the corresponding church types. The average lengths for the church sonatas are around 150 measures for the "trio" types and 220 for the "solo," while they are about a third less for the corresponding court types. Otherwise, cross influences between the church and court types are numerous, to the point where the main differences aside from the titles are the lighter character and more homophonic texture of the latter.

The music itself in Corelli's sonatas was the point of reference for our discussion of Baroque structure in Chapter 6. There remains only to recall here that his moderation in all things must not be taken to mean a temperament limited to placid and unperturbed expression. "A person who had heard him perform," writes Hawkins,[94] "says that whilst he was playing on the violin it was usual for his countenance to be distorted, his eyes to become as red as fire, and his eyeballs to roll as in agony." Pincherle cautions against attaching too much significance to the Christian name of Arcangelo.[95] The several reports of unhappy experiences that are related may or may not be true, such as Corelli's morbid humiliation after the fiasco in Naples.[96] But there is no mistaking the poignancy and depth of a passage such as quoted in Example 29. Undoubtedly, the long steady notes that seem to describe serene lines in many of the "solo" slow movements (as in the third movement of Op. 5, No. 5) have actually concealed the more impassioned, if not rhapsodic, character that these movements acquire when ornaments and other elaborations are appropriately improvised. This widespread practice by Corelli and his contemporaries is illustrated among other places in an Estienne Roger edition of the six church sonatas in Op. 5, "ou l'on à joint les agréemens des Adagio de cet ouvrage, composez par Mr. A. Corelli comme il les joue."[97] Since the edition dates from about 1710,

94. HAWKINS, IV, 310.   95. PINCHERLE-CORELLI, p. 32 ff.
96. Cf. BURNEY-HISTORY, II, 439 ff.
97. Reproduced in JOACHIM & CHRYSANDERm, III. Cf. PINCHERLE-CORELLI, p. 87 ff., for a concise summary of the problem; also, BRITISH PRINTED, I, 306; QUANTZ-FACSIMILE, p. 151 ff.

Ex. 29.   From Arcangelo Corelli's Sonata 11, Op. 3 (after JOACHIM & CHRYSANDERm, II, 178).

the ornaments certainly represent contemporary practice if not actually Corelli's own composition.   We shall meet some further clues to performance practices associated with his sonatas (and concertos) when we come to his Austrian pupil and contemporary Georg Muffat.

There remain four composers to include in our middle group of Italians, Bernardo Pasquini and Giuseppe Piccini in Rome, and Gregorio Strozzi and Alessandro Scarlatti in Naples.   Pasquini and probably Strozzi were organists.   Both contributed some of the earliest known sonatas for keyboard after the 1641 set by Del Buono.   **Bernardo Pasquini** (1637-1710), much the better known of the two, was brought to light as a sonata composer by the Englishman J. S. Shedlock, whose findings and edition are the main basis for the few further reports that have so far appeared.[98]   The question must be asked at once whether Pasquini's importance to this field has not been overrated.   There is no question of quality.   The keyboard pieces in other categories that Shed-

98a

98. SHEDLOCK-SONATA, p. 71 ff., and SHEDLOCK-PASQUINIm (with preface). Cf. NEWMAN-EARLIEST, p. 209 ff. A doctoral dissertation was reported in progress in 1954 by M. Brooks Haynes at Indiana University, and another in 1955 by W. Heinrich at Berlin Free University.

lock published are clearly of a high order. Rather the question is one of too few pieces, left in a manner perhaps too incomplete for authoritative reconstruction.

The only pieces over which Pasquini himself is known to have put the title "sonata" are the last 12 of 14 pieces "A due Cembali" from the year 1704. These occur in the volume dated 1703-04 among three MS volumes prepared for the use of his nephew.[99] The difficulty lies in the fact that only a figured bass is supplied for each cembalist, perhaps to provide a novel and agreeable kind of training in the art of realization and accompaniment. Played together on one two-manual harpsichord the two basses exchange motives somewhat in the manner of an invention. In fact, one author suggests that such a performance might have been the original intention.[100] However, this possibility seems to be ruled out by the separate set of figures for each bass. Granting that Shedlock's realization of the third sonata, in D minor, is a plausible and ingenious one,[101] one must still agree that an unusual responsibility was left to the performers even for that ad libitum era, let alone today when the impromptu realization of figured basses has become virtually a lost art. Each of the sonatas is in three movements in the same key. Most of them seem to be in a F-S-F sequence, in so far as the tempo can be guessed from the music. However, there are only two tempo indications, both slow, and one appears over a finale.

As far as these pieces go, they may be called the earliest sonatas for two keyboard instruments, and among the earliest keyboard sonatas in more than one movement. But whether they were copies of pieces composed earlier or actually not composed until Pasquini's sixty-seventh year cannot now be ascertained. There were operas and oratorios by him composed as early as 1672. But none of the extant keyboard MSS by him is dated before 1697, nor any of the very few keyboard pieces that were his only publications.

Three of the one-movement organ "sonatas" in ANTH. ARRESTIm (nos. 12 to 14) are credited only to "N. N. di Roma" but are thought to be by Pasquini.[102] They are but a few of the many evidences of Frescobaldi's deep influence on Pasquini. On the other hand, a two-movement "Sonata" in C major that appears in several solo piano

99. BRITISH MS, III, 154, Add. 31501, Vol. i; cf. also pp. 111 and 91. Lists of Pasquini's works occur in REV. DE MUS., II (1920-21), 189 and 236; and SCHMIDL, II, 238, and Supp., p. 595.

100. BONAVENTURA-PASQUINI, p. 104 ff.

101. Two others are realized in BOGHEN-PASQUINIm.

102. Cf. PIRRO-ORGANISTES, p. 1335 ff.; also, BRITISH MS, III, 337. No. 12 is printed in TORCHIm, III, but from a different MS source; cf. NEWMAN-EARLIEST, p. 206.

anthologies was taken from a MS item that actually has no title.[103]

The organist **Giuseppe Piccini** (1640-1726), in Rome from 1666 to ?,[104] is presumably the composer of "Sonata di Cimbalo dell Piccini" that appears in a MS collection of the late 17th century at the Library of Congress (M21/M185, Case). The undated collection is entitled "Toccatas, Sonatas [one], and Suites for the Harpsichord." The inclusion of at least one Englishman (Francis Forcer), at least one Italian active in London (G. B. Draghi), and an occasional English term suggests that the MS was copied by an Englishman. In the sonata in question there are two movements, a free, toccata-like form and a "Canzona." The music is effective and very close to that of Pasquini in its keyboard idiom, tonal limitations, and melodic material. If anything, this obviously early example of the keyboard sonata is more conservative in style. Pasquini is among the composers represented in the volume, but not by a sonata.

Gregorio Strozzi, self-styled "Dottor Napolitano dell'una, e l'altra legge, e Protonotario Apostolico," is known only through two publications. One is Op. 2 (1683), a liturgical collection for voice and *b. c.* that concludes with a "Sonata di Basso solo nel Ten." The other is Op. 3 (1687), a set of *Capricci da sonare cembali, et organi* that includes three sonatas printed in open score on four staffs.[105] The three   105a keyboard sonatas are in three or four movements of contrasting meters and tempos (again, in so far as tempos are marked or self-evident). Otherwise, they have much from the earlier 17th century in them. Thematic relationships exist between at least two movements of each sonata. The rhythms are stiff and the melodies are angular in character. Church tones are specified, pointing to the modality that is still present to a marked degree. And Frescobaldi's influence is again present in the skillful keyboard figuration, in the titles of the other pieces in the 1687 set, and in the structural methods.

Strozzi was not only immersed in the past but, to judge from his dedication and explanations, he was inclined toward academicism and pedantry. Because he was a stickler for precision, he headed his first keyboard sonata, "per Cembali & Organi, à modo Italiano, Con pensiero del secondo tono naturale all' ottava sopra, detta da altri impropriamente Canzona Francese." Presumably the "impropriamente" refers merely

103. BRITISH MS, III, 114, Add. 14,248, no. 24; first printed in WEITZMANN, p. 298.

104. SCHMIDL, II, 274.

105. First reported in APEL-DICTIONARY, 3d printing, p. 828. Cf. NEWMAN-EARLIEST, pp. 206 and 209.

to the fact that what was once called "canzona" is now called "sonata." In any case, older canzona traits are certainly still in evidence.

Finally, **Alessandro Scarlatti** (1659-1725), active in both Naples and Rome, left about eight melo/bass and multivoice sonatas in MSS. These have attracted interest chiefly as sidelights to his much greater importance in opera, cantata, and oratorio. As listed by his chief biographer, E. J. Dent, in GROVE, there are two sonatas (one "doubtful") for one flute, two violins, and *b. c.;* another for two flutes, two violins, and *b. c.;* another for three flutes and *b. c.;* and four "Sonate a quattro" in string-quartet setting, among the first of their kind without *b. c.*[106] The mention of 30 sonatas for keyboard that is made by Eitner, Villanis, and other older writers appears to be based on an error.[107] The ensemble sonatas have struck no writers as being of special consequence, although there is obvious craftsmanship in all of them. Perhaps most interesting are the lively binary minuets that serve as finales in some of them.

106a

106. Various modern reprints are listed in ALTMANN. One of the "Sonate a quattro" is in DAVID-SCARLATTIm and another is in PRALLm, both with prefaces; cf. DENT-QUARTETS (although the priority of these as string quartets is a debatable question, as shown in PINCHERLE-QUARTET and HULL-QUARTET).

107. Cf. EITNER-QL, VIII, 457 and VILLANIS-CLAVECINISTES, p. 803. But there is no such mention in SHEDLOCK-SCARLATTI, DENT-SCARLATTI, or SARTORI-SCARLATTI

Chapter 9

Italy from about 1700 to 1750

We come to the last of our three groups of Baroque composers active in Italy. This group was spread over a larger number of cities. It also showed another slight increase in central and southern Italy, although the sonata production in the northern cities continued to lead by far. Venice and Bologna are the chief centers, again, with Florence and Torino next in importance. But identification of several composers with particular cities is made more arbitrary by their international activities as recital virtuosos.

The influence of Corelli, direct or indirect, and the inevitable mutations in his styles and forms that began even before he died, define the most significant trends of the sonata during the late Baroque Era. In the schools that were founded by his pupils are seen the chief branches of this influence, as one discovers from the various genealogical charts that writers on instrumental music have prepared.[1] Most independent of the Corelli influence were the keyboard sonatas that now appeared in increasing numbers, although still only sporadically.

Out of some 30 Italians included here in this third group, the top fourth in renown (with the notable exception of F. M. Veracini) have been the subject of complete books or extended studies. These are the ones, too, whose sonatas have fared best in modern reprints. The others remain largely hidden in obscurity, at least so far as their sonatas are concerned, even more so than many of their 17th-century predecessors. Since they do not represent the beginnings of any main stream and since their styles and forms are fairly uniform, historical curiosity about these men has not been aroused. Furthermore, full records of their often extensive output are generally lacking, for we have now passed the 1700 limit set by Sartori, Bohn, and other bibliographers.

1. Cf. MOSER-VIOLINSPIEL, p. 574 ff., HOFFMANN-TRIOSONATE, p. 181 ff., BACH-MANN-VIOLINISTES, p. 17, among others.

At best, as we get to the later men in this group it becomes increasingly hard to draw the line between late Baroque and early Classic. Our chief external sign of the Baroque, the presence of a *b. c.* part, becomes less and less of a reliable style indicator. It cannot conceal the slow harmonic rhythm, prevailing homophony, and generally Classic feel of Pugnani's sonatas, for example. After all, this device still figured in earlier works of Haydn and Mozart. Whether a composer proved to be mainly a follower or a leader helps to place him when that fact can be established. Partly on that basis, Domenico Scarlatti, exact contemporary of Bach, is saved here for the Classic Era. In any case, the necessarily hard-and-fast organization of history into eras and of books into chapters and sections must not be taken as a hard-and-fast classification of composers in an art that has and must always exist in a state of flux.

Venice (*Albinoni, Vivaldi, Marcello*)

Venice, continuing into the 18th century as one of most brilliant headquarters and chief crossroads of music,[2] is once more the first city whose sonata activity is considered here. Of eight composers to be mentioned, four are well enough known to musicians—Albinoni, Caldara, B. Marcello, and Tessarini—and one, Vivaldi, was a principal composer of the Baroque Era. Several of these were direct successors, if not actual pupils, of Legrenzi or members of his orchestra at St. Mark's.

Tomaso Albinoni (1671-1741?), like both Alessandro and Benedetto Marcello and a number of other active Venetian musicians, was a self-styled dilettante ("Musico di violino dilettante veneto") from a well-to-do family.[3] Possibly a pupil of Legrenzi, Albinoni published 10 sets of sonatas, sinfonias, concertos, or *balletti* between 1694 and about 1720, including Opp. 1 to 9 and an unnumbered set of five SB/bass sonatas published about 1717 in Amsterdam. He also produced at least 48 operas or other theatrical works during his life, these being his predominant musical activity in his last 20 years. But his renown abroad must be credited to his instrumental music, which was published or republished not only by Sala in Venice but by Roger, Mortier, and Le Cène in Amsterdam, Walsh in London, and Le Clerc in Paris.

Albinoni left at least 55 sonatas that are known today. However, that figure must be qualified by the fact that Sonatas 1 and 2 in the 1717

2. Cf. PINCHERLE-VIVALDI, I, 35 ff.
3. GIAZOTTO-ALBINONI is the main source, including documents, thematic index, and many examples; but preference is given here to the death date, 1741, in PINCHERLE-VIVALDI, I, 228, rather than 1750, and to the dates for Roger and Le Cène editions in DEUTSCH-NUMBERS. Cf. NEWMAN-ALBINONI, with a further discussion of the sonatas.

"solo" set (unnumbered) are largely reissues of Sonatas 1 and 5 in Op. 4, which had evidently been two of his most successful sonatas.[4] From No. 1 of Op. 4 also comes the second movement of Sonata 4 in Op. 6. As to distribution by types, 44 per cent are "trio," 43 are "solo," and 13 are multivoice. There are 12 "trio" (SSB/bass) sonatas in Op. 1 (1694), 6 more that alternate with 6 *balletti* in Op. 8 (*ca.* 1720), and 6 in MS. There are 6 "solo" (S/bass) sonatas in Op. 4 (*ca.* 1704), 12 more (SB/bass) in *Trattenimenti armonici per camera,* Op. 6 (*ca.* 1711), 5 more (S/bass) in the 1717 set, and a MS sonata (S/bass) dedicated to the German violinist Pisendel. And there are 6 sonatas *a 5* (SSATB/bass) that alternate with six concertos in Op. 2 (1700), as well as a Bolognese-type "trumpet sonata" *a 6* in MS.[5]

Albinoni's music suffered harsh criticism at the hands of earlier lexicographers,[6] although they had but little knowledge of it. This criticism might have discouraged any later interest in Albinoni, such as Giazotto's biography or the several reprints, had it not been for the by-ways of Bach scholarship. For Albinoni was another of the Italians, along with Legrenzi, Corelli, and Vivaldi, from whom Bach borrowed some musical ideas. Bach borrowed the subjects and attendant material from the fugal second movements of Sonatas 3 and 8 in Albinoni's Op. 1, using them as the main ideas, respectively, for a clavier fugue in A and two successive versions of a clavier fugue in B minor.[7] Albinoni's fugal movements seem creditable enough, the more so for an "Opera Prima." But—and perhaps this fact influenced the harsh criticism—they can hardly stand alongside Bach's. It is especially instructive to see how Bach supersedes Albinoni's B-minor fugal movement of 36 measures, first with a fugue of 88 measures, then (*ca.* 1709) with a still tighter-knit, more developed and plastic fugue of 112 measures. Bach was also concerned with Albinoni's Op. 6. His correction of a bass realization for Sonata 6 as prepared by his pupil H. N. Gerber is re-printed in full by Spitta.[8]

In his earlier works Albinoni was obviously under the strong in-

8a

4. Mod. ed.: Op. 4, No. 1, MOFFAT-VIOLINm I, no. 12.
5. The Pisendel MS is reported in GIAZOTTO-ALBINONI, p. 241 ff., and the other MSS (overlooked by Giazotto) in HAAS-ESTENSISCHEN, pp. 165 ff. (168) and 137 ff. (with mention of further "trio" sonatas in Dresden MSS that have not been confirmed here).
6. E.g., FÉTIS-BU, I, 54 ff.
7. SCHMIEDER-BWV, no. 950 and nos. 951a and 951 (all marked "Echtheit angezweifelt," without much apparent reason); cf. SPITTA-BACH, I, 425 ff. Mod. eds. of Albinoni's Op. 1: Son. 3, NAGELSm, no. 34 (Upmeyer); Son. 8, second movement, SPITTA-BACH, III, 364; Son. 6, HAUSMUSIKm, no. 111 (Schenk).
8. SPITTA-BACH, III, 388 (cf. II, 293 ff.). Other mod. eds.: Sons. 1 and 11, NAGELSm, no. 9 (Upmeyer); Son. 6 (as a flute sonata), NAGELSm, no. 74 (Schäffler).

fluence of Corelli, who must at least have known about the younger man
through roundabout connections.[9]   Albinoni's 12 church sonatas in Op.
1 were consistently modelled after the S-F-S-F plan standardized by
Corelli's Opp. 1 and 3, with regard both to the individual movement types
and the over-all plan.   They show a similar handling of the "trio"
texture, too, as may be seen by comparing Exs. 29 (p. 159) and 30.
In the first two movements of Sonata 4 in the 1717 "solo" set Albinoni

Ex. 30.   From the opening of Sonata 10, Op. 1, by Tomaso
Albinoni (after the E. Roger edition, *ca.* 1710).

was one of those half dozen or more composers who literally copied the
procedures in the corresponding movements of Corelli's first "solo"
sonata, Op. 5—the tempo changes, the cadenzas, the double-stops, the
arpeggiations, and even the melodic styles.   Here he was clearly trying
to capitalize on his predecessor's success.

On the other hand, there are already the first unmistakable signs in
Albinoni's sonatas of the slow but sure transformation that was to take
place in Corelli's noble style of writing.   These signs appear increasingly
among the stylistic advances that can be noted in each successive publica-

9. Cf. GIAZOTTO-ALBINONI, p. 32.

tion (right up to the remarkably Classic-sounding *Sinfonie a quattro* preserved in MSS of about 1735[10]). Especially in the pathetic slow movements of the 1717 set, including one actually labelled "Patetico," a breakdown is evident in Corelli's extended purposeful lines. Albinoni's lines are disrupted by his preoccupation with intense details—chromaticism, often resulting from the Neapolitan and augmented 6th chords; expressive rests between short rhythmic units; yearning leaps; ornamental minutiae. Example 31 is representative.

Albinoni's form types are sharply contrasted. They define extremes in his musical makeup,[11] alternating with surprising regularity through-

Ex. 31. The third movement (in full) from Sonata 5 in an unnumbered publication by Tomaso Albinoni, *ca.* 1717 (after the original Roger edition).

10. Cf. GIAZOTTO-ALBINONI, p. 259 ff.
11. Cf. GIAZOTTO-ALBINONI, pp. 118 and 297.

out his publications, from one work to the next and even within Opp. 2 and 8, as noted earlier. All the pieces entitled "sonata" are of the church type, in spite of two movements with dance titles and "da camera" in the title of Op. 6. "Da chiesa" was dropped by Albinoni as a qualifying term in all the sonata titles but that of Op. 4, since "balletto" rather than "sonata da camera" was now used for the dance suites.[12] The concertos and *balletti* were the vehicles for Albinoni's more progressive side and the sonatas for his conservative side. Thus, it is in the six sonatas of *Sonate e balletti,* Op. 8, that all the quick movements are three-voice fugues with strict two-voice canons in the upper parts. Yet, occasional solo flights, such as we saw as far back as Castello's *Sonate concertate,* do occur in the multivoice sonatas as well as the concertos of Op. 2.

Another possible pupil of Legrenzi was **Antonio Caldara** (*ca.* 1670-1736). He is placed in Venice, where he lived as cellist well past the dates of his two early sonata publications, although his reputation in music history rests much more on his subsequent successes in opera, oratorio, and cantata at the Imperial court in Vienna.[13] A total of 39 sonatas by Caldara are known. His Op. 1 (1693) consists of 12 SSB/bass sonatas and his Op. 2 (1699) of 11 more, *da camera,* plus a concluding "Chiacona."[14] Among MSS, there are also 8 "solo" (S/bass) violin sonatas[15] and 7 "trio" sonatas (2 SS/bass with 2 *clarini* in the upper parts, and 5 SSB/bass).[16]

The five published "trio" sonatas from Caldara's Op. 1 that have been made available in modern reprints are all in the standard S-F-S-F church plan, whereas the MS "solo" sonatas have variable plans in two to five movements. The two court sonatas available from Op. 2 are suites of dances. On the basis of the modern reprints, Caldara's sonatas seem competently written, not demanding or unusual in their instrumental techniques, abreast of the times in their styles and forms, and blessed with effective ideas in the fast movements though nowhere with

12. Son. 4 and Balletto 4 from Op. 8 are reprinted in HAUSMUSIKm, no. 114 a/b (Schenk); but there is no explicit basis for the editor's assumption that each sonata of this set was meant to be played before its companion *balletto* in the same key.

13. Cf. LUIN for a recent biographic summary.

14. Mod. eds.: Op. 1, Nos. 4 and 6, NAGELSm, nos. 5 and 12 (both Upmeyer; originally misattributed to A. Steffani); Nos. 5 and 9, HAUSMUSIKm, Nos. 59 and 121 (Schenk); No. 7, SCHENK-TRIOSONATEm, no. 4. Op. 2, No. 3, HAUSMUSIKm, no. 85 (Schenk); No. 4, CONTINUOm, UE 10677 (Geiringer).

15. Thematic index in HAAS-ESTENSISCHEN, p. 88 ff. The B-minor and G-minor "trio" sonatas ascribed to Caldara in COLLEGIUMm, no. 44 (Riemann), and RIEMANN-BEISPIELEm, no. 124, respectively, have been shown in SCHENK-NEUAUSGABEN to be Nos. 2 and 3 in John Ravenscroft's Op. 1; but the B-minor sonata is still credited to Caldara in MGG, III, 645 ff. (Paumgartner) along with a MS clavier sonata that does not exist (based on a misreading of EITNER-QL, II, 279).

16. HAAS-ESTENSISCHEN, p. 90.

any striking originality. Interesting, and no doubt a consequence of the changed locale, is the fact that Caldara's "solo" and "trio" sonatas composed after he reached Vienna no longer adhere to the S-F-S-F plan but generally have the F-S-F plan of the Neapolitan opera sinfonia, many of the movements actually being adapted from Caldara's own instrumental overtures.[17]

Probably a third pupil of the aging Legrenzi, precocious enough to have played in his orchestra at St. Mark's, was the front-rank composer and fine violinist **Antonio Vivaldi** (1678-1741).[18] "Il Prête rosso" [18a] (The Redheaded Priest), as his contemporaries knew him, spent the better part of his life teaching violin, directing the orchestra, and composing to order at that most famous of the four girls' foundling *conservatori* in Venice, Seminario musicale dell' Ospitale della Pietà.[19] [19a] His vast output of some 650 known compositions, vocal and instrumental, includes at least 90 operas, oratorios, and cantatas; 454 concertos—the category for which he is most recognized; 23 sinfonias; and 73 pieces actually called "sonata."[20] [20a]

Among the 73 sonatas, 72 per cent are "solo," 25 are "trio," and 3 are multivoice types. This distribution points to the distinct trend in the late Baroque Era toward the "solo" and away from the multivoice type. Vivaldi's sonatas are not exclusively for strings, as virtually all of Corelli's and Albinoni's are (except for organ or cembalo on the *b. c.* part). They are predominantly so or for flute, but also include other melody (or *concertante*) instruments as might be expected of so orchestrally minded a composer. In Vivaldi's lifetime 42 of the sonatas were published in 5 sets, the other 31 being left in MS. The two multivoice pieces called "sonata" are in MS.[21] Though only in SSA/bass settings—i.e., string-quartet settings in which the cello part is figured—they occur among groups of concertos and were presumably so conceived. In any case, most of the MS sonatas so far made available in the new Ricordi edition have distinct traits of the concerto, including F-S-F

17. Cf. LIESS-TRIO, p. 45 ff.
18. The chief studies are PINCHERLE-VIVALDI (with thematic index), concentrated on the life and instrumental music but followed by a condensation, PINCHERLE-VIVALDI/1955, that also takes in the vocal music; RINALDI-VIVALDI (with documents, thematic index and other aids), devoted to the life and all of the works, followed by a revised thematic index, RINALDI-VIVALDI/1945. Pincherle's books have proved more useful and reliable here.
19. Cf. PINCHERLE-OSPITALI; RUDGE; KOLNEDER-PÄDAGOGISCHE.
20. Cf. PINCHERLE-VIVALDI, I, 61 ff., slightly revised by -VIVALDI/1955, p. 53 ff.; but the number of sonatas is two or three less here because of our restriction to works actually so called. The projected complete edition, VIVALDIM, has reached 250 volumes (each a separate work) as of this writing. Cf. PINCHERLE-EDIZIONE; SALTER (including a list of the sonatas and a collation of the first 175 volumes with three thematic indices); KOLNEDER-FRAGE.
21. PINCHERLE-VIVALDI, II, 64.

movement plans, free rondo forms and persistent motoric drive in the fast movements, and cantilena melody over a quasi-ostinato bass in the slow movements. On the other hand, at least a dozen pieces that Vivaldi called "concerto," "sinfonia," "trio," or "solo" might more appropriately have been called "sonata" in keeping with the connotations of this term that were well established by now.[22]

The MSS have not been dated or put into any sure chronological order thus far, although the "solo" violin sonatas composed for Pisendel must not have originated before the latter's study with Vivaldi in Venice (1717). The first editions of the five sonata collections published in Vivaldi's lifetime were spread over a period from about 1701 to 1740, as follows: Op. 1, 1705; Op. 2, 1709; Op. 5, *ca.* 1717; Op. 13, *ca.* 1737; and Op. 14 (?), *ca.* 1740.[23] Opp. 1 and 2 were originally published in Venice, by Sala and Bortoli respectively. Opp. 3-12 were all first published by the firm of Estienne Roger and his relatives in Amsterdam, the same firm that issued so many important sonata collections in this period and one of those fascinatingly complex firms that have turned date seekers into veritable sleuths.[24] The last two sets, Opp. 13 and 14, first appeared in Paris.

Vivaldi's "solo" sonatas include 12 for violin in Op. 2; the first 4, for violin, of the 6 sonatas in Op. 5 (numbered 13 to 18 in continuation of Op. 2) ; 6 in *Il Pastor fido (The Faithful Shepherd)*, Op. 13, with the extraordinary option of musette, vielle, flute, oboe, or violin (an option most often found in late Baroque sonatas published in France, as this set was) ; 6 for cello in Op. 14; 23 in MS for violin; and 2 in MS for cello. Only in 4 of the violin MSS are the settings of the SB/- rather than the S/bass type. In these, the *concertante* bass is often independent enough to make actual trios of the pieces. The "trio" sonatas include 12 in Op. 1, the last 2 in Op. 6, and 4 in MS. All are the SS/bass type or SS alone, with the bass made optional ("anco senza basso se piace") in the MS sonatas.[25]

Even though Vivaldi's sonatas number a third more than Albinoni's they occupy a smaller place, numerically at least, in his total output. Yet they have much of value and deserve more than the passing mentions

22. Cf. SALTER, p. 374, and PINCHERLE-EDIZIONE, p. 135.
23. Cf. PINCHERLE-VIVALDI, I, 53 ff., including the basis for assigning "Op. 14" to the last set; PINCHERLE-VIVALDI/1955, p. 52, for a listing of the original edition of Op. 1, hitherto known to exist but not found; DEUTSCH-NUMBERS, p. 18 ff., for the date of Op. 5 that is preferred here.
24. Cf. PINCHERLE-VIVALDI, p. 293 ff.
25. Among mod. performing eds. of separate opp.: Op. 1, UPMEYER-VIVALDIm; Op. 2, LUCIANI-VIVALDIm, HILLEMANNm; Op. 5, NAGELSm, nos. 162 and 171 (both Upmeyer); Op. 13, HORTUSm, no. 135 (Upmeyer); Op. 14, CHAIGNEAU & RUM-MELm I.

Ex. 32.   From the second movement of Sonata 4, Op. 1, by
Antonio Vivaldi (after the E. Roger edition, *ca.* 1713).

that either of Vivaldi's chief biographers could give them; for Pincherle
and Rinaldi were interested first of all, of course, in his concertos.[26]
Whereas Albinoni's sonatas and concertos represented alternating extremes in his make-up, Vivaldi's were more nearly collateral developments, with more cross influences.   Coming almost a decade later,
Vivaldi's Op. 1 had derived just as clearly as Albinoni's from Corelli's
Op. 5.   It ends with a set of variations on the Folia tune and includes
one of his numerous references ("Preludio" of No. 7) to the celebrated

26. The sonatas are discussed in NEWMAN-ALBINONI.

"Gavotte" in F in Corelli's tenth "solo" sonata—references so numerous in his and other contemporary music, to be sure, that they constitute almost a melodic mannerism of the time.[27] Furthermore, Sonata 2 of Op. 2 belongs, like T. A. Vitali's Op. 4, No .8, and Albinoni's Sonata 4 in his 1717 set, with the sonatas for which the opening movement of Corelli's first solo sonata was the prototype.

But as opposed to Albinoni's sonatas the first four of Vivaldi's five published sets of sonatas may be classified as the court type by virtue of the dance titles in nearly all of the movements, usually joined to a tempo term—for example, "Corrente Presto," "Sarabanda Adagio," or "Giga Allegro." Only Op. 14 falls wholly into the church class, with each sonata based on the S-F-S-F plan. However, Vivaldi's court and church types approach each other more than Albinoni's or even Corelli's. The

Ex. 33. From the "Giga" of Sonata 1, Op. 13, by Antonio Vivaldi (after the original Le Clerc edition).

movements of the church sonatas are often true binary dances without the appropriate titles, while the court movements have much of the polyphonic activity and weight that are exceptional in Corelli's court sonatas. Furthermore, Vivaldi's "trio" and "solo" sonatas are more alike among themselves than the other two men's, both in their over-all plans and their degrees of virtuosity.

The Vivaldi renaissance of the last two decades that has brought a stream of new books, articles, recordings, festivals, and editions seems no more than justified as more and more of his music becomes known. In his sonatas as well as his concertos Vivaldi shows himself to be a universalist, especially by comparison with the more poetic, introspective Albinoni. He was the Schubert rather than the Schumann of his day. Accepting the incomplete evidence that much of his music was written

27. Cf. the allemandes of Vivaldi's Op. 2, Nos. 4 and 10, and the "Giga" of Op. 5, No. 13 (i.e., No. 1).

Ex. 34. From the "Largo" of Sonata 18 (6), Op. 5, by
Antonio Vivaldi (after the original E. Roger edition).

early in the 18th century rather than toward the middle, one must regard
him as a highly original modernist.

He was a master of syntax in late Baroque music, with juxtapositions of melodic elements that are far more subtle rhythmically than can
be found in much Classic phrase grouping.[28] His concentrated reiteration of a single idea is intensive where Corelli's succession of changing
ideas is more extensive, to borrow antitheses used by Bukofzer in comparing Bach and Handel.[29] Here may lie one explanation for the
exceptional and well-known attraction Vivaldi's music held for Bach,
including the sonatas as well as the concertos.[30] On the other hand, in
his chordal polyphony and essential diatonicism he comes closer to
Handel than to Bach. With regard to over-all structures he stands
beside Corelli among the chief composers considered earlier in our
examination of Baroque structures.

All in all, to inject a personal estimate, his sonatas surpass Corelli's
in the boldness of their ideas, rhythmic drive, and unity of form, though
not necessarily in virtuosity nor in pathos. (Representative examples
are Op. 1, No. 8; Op. 2, No. 10; Op. 5, No. 3; and Op. 14, No. 3.)
Citing Wasielewski, Spitta wrote that Vivaldi's "great strength lay in
the treatment of *form;* his ideas are often flat and insignificant, though
occasionally full of fire and expression."[31] It is certainly true that
Vivaldi took a special pleasure in robust, idiomatic passagework for its
own sake, and that many of his ideas prove to be simple scale or
arpeggio figures. There are not a few instances, especially in Op. 1,
when one of the main props of Baroque form, the sequence, is used for
no other purpose than to go up and down the scale (Ex. 32). But when

28. Cf. KOLNEDER-FRÜHSCHAFFEN.   29. BUKOFZER-BAROQUE, p. 347 ff.
30. Cf. PINCHERLE-VIVALDI, p. 247 ff.   31. SPITTA-BACH, I, 411 ff.

the occasion called for it, as often in the lighthearted dances of Op. 13, he could write an out-and-out tune (Ex. 33) or he could spin out an extended, florid line with real depth and considerable variety of rhythm (Ex. 34).

Benedetto Marcello (1686-1739), "Nobile Veneto dilettante di Contrapunto," had many ties with the important sonata composers of his immediate past and present. He was a musical descendant of Legrenzi through Lotti and of both Pasquini and Corelli through Gasparini. He was a member of the Accademia dei Filarmonici in that other main center of the Italian sonata, Bologna, and of the Accademia dei Arcadi in Rome, to which Corelli had belonged. He naturally had many opportunities to know the music of his illustrious senior compatriots, Albinoni and Vivaldi. In particular, Vivaldi's music must have made its mark, if we are only to judge by the longtime acceptance of one or two Marcello concertos as Vivaldi's own in Bach's *16 Konzerte nach A. Vivaldi*.[32] Marcello even had a few lessons with Tartini at the time his older brother Alessandro was studying regularly with the latter.[33] (Alessandro himself, under his Arcadian name of "Eterio Stinfalico," published both solo violin sonatas and concertos,[34] as well as cantatas.) Finally, Benedetto was on close terms with a surprising number of his musical contemporaries throughout Western Europe.

Marcello is recognized mainly for his Psalm settings in *Estro poetico-armonico* and his satire on current musical practices, *Il teatro alla moda*. But he achieved success, too, with his other sacred and dramatic music and with considerable instrumental music. The latter consisted mainly of sonatas and concertos, as did the instrumental music of his fellow Venetians, Albinoni and Vivaldi.

Until the much needed monograph on Marcello's instrumental music is accomplished, the first requisite of any study of the sonatas must be an attempt to bring some order out of the bibliographic chaos that exists in the present literature. With regard to published sonatas, the several confused listings appear to reduce to two, and only two, main collections. Op. 1 is a collection of six sonatas for solo cello and *b. c.* It was presumably composed before 1712 (when Op. 2 appeared) but not published until about 1733, by John Walsh of London, with the characteristic English title of "Solos." This edition was followed in 1735 by a reprint from Le Clerc of Paris, with the title "Sonate."[35] Op. 2 is a collection

32. SCHMIEDER-BWV, nos. 974 and 977 (?).

33. D'ANGELI, p. 10 (the chief biography, with a chapter on the sonatas, p. 169 ff.).

34. Cf. MOSER-VIOLINSPIEL, p. 208 ff.

35. Among mod. eds.: SCHOTT CELLOM, nos. 60 (Sons. 3 and 2), 61 (Sons. 6 and 5), and 64 (Sons. 1 and 4).

of 12 sonatas for solo flute and *b. c.*, first published by Giuseppe Sala of Venice in 1712, then reprinted by Estienne Roger of Amsterdam before 1717 and by John Walsh in 1733.[36]

Walsh began the confusion by interchanging the two opus numbers, a not infrequent habit of his. At the same time he revised the actual Op. 2 for *flûte à bec* so that it could be played on the newly popular German flute, also switching the order of the sonatas and deleting certain movements.[37] Fétis, departing from further errors that had already crept into such earlier dictionaries as Gerber's, compounded the confusion with three new listings that appear to have no basis in fact: *Concerti a cinque,* Op. 1 (Venice: G. Sala, 1701) ; *Sonate di cembalo,* Op. 2 (*"ibid."*) ; and *Sonata a cinque, e flauto solo col basso continuo,* Op. 3 (*"ibid.,* 1712").[38] This last title can only be explained as a hasty *pasticcio* of the concertos, flute sonatas, and *a fiato* (for wind instruments). Unfortunately, Fétis' listings have been accepted by nearly all subsequent lexicographers to this day. Eitner was the notable exception. Reporting "only what I can prove," he prepared a substantial, very different bibliography of Marcello's music, along with the score of most of one flute sonata (Op. 2, No. 10) intended to illustrate weaknesses he found in it.[39] But Eitner did nothing to correct Walsh's opus numbers. To top off the confusion the biographer D'Angeli overlooked Eitner's special study, retained the faulty and conflicting listings of Walsh and Fétis without question, and added some distressingly vague listings of his own, complete with a new set of inconsistencies.[40]

To be sure, with reference to what Fétis called Op. 2, D'Angeli did know a set of 10 cembalo sonatas by Marcello. This set he discusses at some length.[41] Yet, although he refers (without documentation) to its supposed publication, he himself must have seen not this but the holograph of 10 *Suonate per il cembalo* (and two other pieces) at the Biblioteca di S. Marco ("Marciana").[42] Only two keyboard sonatas by Marcello seem to have been published at any time in the 18th century, both posthumously in ANTH. VENIERm, I (nos. 5 and 6).

36. The dates are based on DEUTSCH-NUMBERS, p. 18 ff., and BRITISH PRINTED, II. 88. Among mod. eds.: all 12 sons., 2 vols. (Rome: De Santis, 1964-66).
37. Cf. HAAS-CAT. 20, nos. 438-441.
38. FÉTIS-BU, V, 442.
39. EITNER-MARCELLO and EITNER-QL, VI, 310 ff.
40. D'ANGELI, p. 271 ff. G. Benvenuti did not live to complete the bibliography of Marcello's cembalo and organ works promised in CLASSICIM II, No. 8, p. 245.
41. D'ANGELI, p. 173 ff. For more on the keyboard sonatas cf. NEWMAN-MARCELLO (with thematic index and examples; supplemented as in footnote 43 below).
42. Cf. PUBBLICAZIONI-VENEZIA, p. 366. GAZZETTA ANTOLOGIAm, V, 131 ff., to which he later refers, a Ricordi edition issued more than a century after Marcello's death, contains only movements from Sons. 4, 7, and 12 (as listed in NEWMAN-MARCELLO, p. 31 ff.).

Now, if we are correct in assuming that no earlier or other publication of the keyboard sonatas took place in the 18th century, then it is remarkable how well known the sonatas seem to have become in their day, by way of MS copies. One can only guess that Marcello's widespread circle of friends had a share in making his sonatas so popular. The MSS, especially of three or four favorite sonatas, rest in the libraries of many European cities, the largest number being in Berlin, Paris, Venice, London, Bologna, and Brussels. All together, Marcello may have left as many as 20 different keyboard sonatas. But a thorough survey of the MSS would be more likely to reduce that number through duplications than to increase it. Eitner reported 18 sonatas in one Berlin MS, which has survived in the present Deutsche Staatsbibliothek.[43] At least three of these seem to have been created by subdividing sonatas of four or five movements. In the Bibliothèque nationale in Paris is a careful copy of 12 sonatas plus a thirteenth subtitled "La Ciacona" and 30 short minuets (all in C!).[44] Although not so identified, this copy, like the one in the "Marciana," appears to be a holograph. It reveals the same peculiarities of music notation that can be found in confirmed Marcello holographs as reproduced by D'Angeli.

At this time there is no firm basis for dating the keyboard sonatas short of Marcello's death in 1739. But the decade from about 1710-20 would seem to be the most likely period—that is, from the time of Opp. 1 and 2 to the time when he became almost completely immersed in sacred and dramatic music. There may be some chronological significance in the fact that the sonatas in the Paris and Venice MSS generally show increasing skill and imagination as the volumes progress.

The few keyboard sonatas most copied in Marcello's day are the same few, and the only ones, that have been made generally known in the past 75 years, thanks chiefly to the various "Old Masters" editions.[45] But seldom is any of those sonatas printed intact or complete. Besides the usual 19th-century practice of filling out the texture and "correcting" alleged gaucheries in the harmony, some movements are left out while others are printed as separate pieces, with only the original tempo mark or an added term such as "Toccata" to serve as the title.[46]

46a

The foregoing excursion into bibliographic problems is a luxury that

43. MS 13,550, briefly discussed in SEIFFERT-KLAVIERMUSIK, p. 426 ff.; further mentioned in HOFFMANN/ERBRECHT-KLAVIERMUSIK, p. 63, and in AM, XXXI (1959), pp. 191-96 (with thematic index).

44. BIBLIOTHÈQUE NATIONALE, VI, 179 ff. (with thematic index of first movements).

45. Among "mod." eds.: PAUER-MEISTERm, V; TRÉSORm, XX; RICORDI ARTEm, II; CLASSICIm I, no. 17 (Malipiero), only labelled "Cantate," but bound with two fascicles of pieces for "cembalo od organo"; OESTERLEm, III; TAGLIAPIETRAm, XI.

46. These movements come from Sons. 7-10 and 12 as numbered in the Paris MS.

obviously cannot be indulged often in so broad a survey as this one. It will have to serve here as but a sample, albeit an aggravated one, of all too many similar problems that have beset investigations into sonata history. With regard to the music itself, most of Marcello's sonatas fall into the S-F-S-F plan, the cembalo sonatas being less consistent than the others, with more fast tempos among their three to five movements. They show him to have been a conservative in both styles and forms. Telemann evidently thought so, for in 1731 he dedicated to Marcello not his lighter, newer-type sonatas but his more academic *XX kleine Fugen*. Marcello himself revealed his opposition to newer instrumental styles. Only in the satirical vein of *Il Teatro alla moda* could he endorse the contemporary opera sinfonia, with its closing minuet, gavotte, or gigue; he jested to the effect that this form enabled one to "get around writing fugues, suspensions, or clear-cut themes—which are ancient and outmoded anyway."[47]

The outstanding traits of Marcello's sonatas are, in fact, contrapuntal and harmonic interest (not merely a succession of 6th chords[48]), clear-cut themes, and a remarkably developed sense of phrase balance. Flutists and especially cellists rejoice in the elegant, unsentimental lyricism of his themes. The purity and expressive force of his slow movements belie the rather elementary appearance and few markings of his scores. In these respects, the vocally-minded Marcello came closer to Alessandro Scarlatti than to Domenico, Marcello's almost exact contemporary. To Domenico, who must have known Marcello during the years 1705-08, which he spent in Venice, Marcello came much closer in the matter of keyboard idiom.[49] Many of the faster passages in his cembalo sonatas are certain to bring Domenico to mind when they are played. Since Domenico published nothing until the year of Marcello's death and probably composed most of his music still later, Marcello may even have been the earlier of the two in writing such passages (Ex. 35). Double-notes, hand-crossing, and skips are carried to extremes scarcely surpassed by Domenico Scarlatti, in Sonata 13 of the Paris MS, "La Ciacona." But this piece, with its 110 variations on a four-measure *ostinato,* is otherwise dull, for it also carries to an extreme Marcello's dependence on the Baroque sequence.

Marcello's treatment of the keyboard is actually the most progressive trait of his music. Yet it is particularly his cembalo sonatas that most writers have depreciated as offering nothing new. Even Torrefranca, Italy's most ardent champion of her 18th-century keyboard music, finds

47. MARCELLO, p. 387.
48. Cf. MARCELLO, p. 89.
49. Cf. NEWMAN-MARCELLO, p. 38 ff.

Ex. 35. From Sonatas IX in A and VIII in B-flat by
Benedetto Marcello (after Bibliothèque nationale Vm₇ 5289).

the cembalo sonatas a bit heavy and monotonous.[50]   There is no denying
a certain stodginess, not in their texture but in their structural rhythm.
Without quite the lyrical interest possible to the cello or flute, the
cembalo sonatas sometimes seem excessively symmetrical in their syntax.
But there is also the fact that the early cembalo sonata has been evaluated
disproportionately for its anticipations of Classic "sonata form."   Marcello's keyboard texture, generally in two parts, has a new lightness
about it and a surprising freedom in the treatment of dissonance.[51]   But
in matters of form he happened to belong more in the company of Della

50. TORREFRANCA, p. 56.   Cf. EITNER-SONATE, p. 167, VILLANIS-CLAVECINISTES, p.
808, SEIFFERT-KLAVIERMUSIK, p. 426 ff., GEORGII-KLAVIERMUSIK, p. 45, HOFFMANN/
ERBRECHT-KLAVIERMUSIK, p. 63.
51. Cf. NEWMAN-MARCELLO, p. 36 ff.

Ciaja and Martini than Galuppi and Rutini. The further fact remains that Marcello's cembalo sonatas, so widely known in MSS, were at the font of that steady stream of Italian cembalo sonatas that continued throughout the 18th century.

Prior to Tessarini of the next generation there were no further sonata composers of real importance in Venice. Two minor contemporaries of Vivaldi were **Giorgio Gentili** (*ca.* 1668 to at least 1716?), who published two sets of "trio" sonatas, Opp. 1 and 4, in 1701 and 1707;[52] and **Domenico dalla Bella** of nearby Treviso, who published 12 "trio" sonatas in 1704 and left at least 3 "solo" cello sonatas in MS,[53] very much like Marcello's in both style and quality. A minor contemporary of Tessarini was **Giuseppe Carcano** (1703 to a least 1750), listed chiefly for his operas and oratorios, but also represented by miscellaneous "solo" and "trio" sonatas.[54]

Around 1729, the year of his true Op. 1, **Carlo Tessarini** (1690?-*ca.* 1765) held a post in Venice similar to that of Vivaldi, with whom he may have studied.[55] Thereafter, he concertized and moved about from one Italian or foreign city to another.[56] His very numerous collections of melo/bass music, first published between 1729 and about 1750, and his important treatise on performance practices (*Grammatica di musica,* 1741?) deserve more attention than they have had. But until this attention is paid in the form of a special study, any report must be curtailed, for the bibliographic records are even more confused than Marcello's, with even less basis for sifting them.[57] At least two sets of 12 "solo" violin sonatas, Opp. 1 and 3, and two of 6 "trio" sonatas for violin or flute, Opp. 6 and 9 (?), can be confirmed,[58] plus similar if lighter music under other titles. But the opus numbers can mean little, since of at least 16 that Tessarini used, several were given out two and three times by different publishers in different countries and to different works. No doubt, when the contents are compared, there will be a good many duplications discovered.

The most distinctive qualities of Tessarini's music are ones often to be observed as the Baroque Era drew to a close amidst foretokens of the Classic Era. They are directness, clarity, and balance—as much pronounced at the highest as at the more local levels of the form. Partly

---

52. MGG, IV, 1756 ff. (Giegling).
53. Thematic index of 3 cello sonatas in HAAS-ESTENSISCHEN, p. 20; mod. ed. of the second of these: NAGELSm, no. 83 (Upmeyer).
54. Cf. EITNER-QL, II, 326 ("Carcani, Gioseffo") and SCHÖKEL, p. 49 ff.
55. Cf. MOSER-VIOLINSPIEL, p. 209 ff.; SCHERING-INSTRUMENTALKONZERT, p. 107 ff.
56. On Tessarini in Amsterdam cf. KOOLE, p. 31 ff.
57. As samples, cf. the listings in BRITISH PRINTED, II, 567; BIBLIOTHÈQUE NATIONALE, VIII, 145; SCHMIDL, II, 589; and HAAS-CAT. 20. Cf. KOOLE, p. 32 ff.
58. Cf. ALTMANN for 8 reprints of single sonatas.

responsible are the slower harmonic rhythm and the emphasis on the orbit of primary triads. With regard to designs, the rather loose rondo principle then employed in fast concerto movements becomes a well-defined A-B-A form here; and the concerto's F-S-F cycle of movements becomes a standard plan for both the "solo" and "trio" sonatas of Tessarini. Especially in the "solo" sonatas, the use of the violin shows technical advances to be expected of the mid-century virtuosi, including ranges extending into the seventh position.

Bologna (Martini)

In Bologna's San Petronio, after the financial crisis at the turn of the century had eased, the musical forces regrouped under the direction of G. A. Perti. However, no Bolognese sonata composers appeared in this next half century, with the possible exception of Martini, who could rank beside those best known from the past or beside the main Venetian figures past or present.

A pupil of Perti, **Giuseppe Aldrovandini** (*ca.* 1673-1708) was listed earlier among composers of the Bolognese orchestral "trumpet sonatas." He is also represented by two "solo" violin sonatas in ANTH. BOLOGNAm I,[59] and by 10 "trio" sonatas (Bologna, 1706; Amsterdam later). From **Giuseppe Matteo Alberti** (*ca.* 1685-1751?) we have one set of "solo" violin sonatas, Op. 2 (composed in 1720 and published in 1721),[60] one "trio" sonata in ANTH. CORONAm, and two "trumpet sonatas" in MS. His "solo" sonatas, predominantly in the S-F-S-F sequence, are richly harmonized, full of contrapuntal and technical interest, and blessed with attractive, nicely organized themes (Ex. 36).[61]

Ex. 36. From the start of Sonata 9, "Op. 3" (2!), by Giuseppe Matteo Alberti (after the John Walsh edition *ca.* 1732).

59. Plus another in a MS copy of this anthology (cf. thematic index in HAAS-ESTENSISCHEN, p. 115 ff.). BUSI-MARTINI, p. 130 ff., is still the main source on Aldrovandini.
60. MOSER-VIOLINSPIEL, p. 217 ff., and other sources refer to Op. 3 as though it were another set of 12 "solo" sonatas, but it is merely John Walsh's reprint (1732?) of Op. 2. Similarly, the Walsh edition of Op. 2 (*Sinfonie a quattro*, 1730?) proves actually to be Alberti's Op. 1 (*Concerti*, 1713).
61. Two further examples occur in TORCHI, p. 167 ff.

Gaetano Boni published three sets of sonatas between 1717 and 1741. Op. 1 contains 12 "solo" cello sonatas of the church type. Of these, Sonata 10 in C has been reprinted[62] and proves to have much appeal. One soon realizes that a broad grasp of tonal and structural balance is widespread among our third group of Italian composers. Op. 2 is a set of court sonatas (SB/bass) under the collective title *Divertimenti per camera a violino, violone, cimbalo, flauto, e mandola,* the flute and *mandola* being alternatives for the violin.[63] And Op. 3 is a set of 10 "solo" violin sonatas. Boni also left a volume of 12 sonatas in MS, which are listed as "Sonate da cembalo."[64] However, the MS itself seems to have no title, and these sonatas prove to be for violin and *b. c.* The figured bass would not in itself be conclusive evidence, but the rich figuration in the upper part, including many multiple-stops especially suited to the violin, leaves little doubt.

A set of sonatas, Op. 1 (1720), by **Giuseppe Maria Buini** brings us for the first time to *Suonate per camera da cembalo, ò violino, e violoncello*—that is, keyboard sonatas that might otherwise be played as string sonatas by a violin and a cello on the right- and left-hand parts, respectively.[65] But we may recall the converse in editions of Corelli's S/bass sonatas as harpsichord pieces (p. 59).

Padre Giambattista Martini (1706-84), theorist, historian, bibliophile, teacher of J. C. Bach and Mozart among other later sonata composers, esteemed musical sage of all Europe, and composer of sacred music in the learned Roman manner, is a principal figure in the history of Bolognese music and the last to be considered here.[66] About a tenth of his music is for instruments alone. Of this about a half consists of concertos and sinfonias (smaller ensembles) while the other half consists of sonatas.[67] A very few sonatas are multivoice (including the orchestral "trumpet" type) or "trio" (especially, two flutes and *b. c.*)[68] and a few are of the one-movement, fugal type for organ that traces back to

62. SCHOTT CELLOm, no. 53 (Moffat).

63. This set is apparently the same as the MS of *Divertimenti per camera a violino e basso* listed without opus number in HAAS-ESTENSISCHEN, p. 81 ff. (including thematic index).

64. CAT. BOLOGNA, IV, 34.

65. Thematic index of a MS copy in HAAS-ESTENSISCHEN, p. 84, but without cembalo in the title. Mod. ed.: first movements of Sons. 1, 9, and 10, VATIELLI-MAESTRIm, II, 4 ff. (with Son. 10 in F instead of D, and other changes).

66. BUSI-MARTINI is still the chief biographic source, although unfinished. The keyboard sonatas are discussed in FAISST, p. 51 ff., and HOFFMANN/ERBRECHT-KLAVIERMUSIK, p. 94 ff. (with special regard to the thematic material).

67. The instrumental list in BUSI-MARTINI, p. 498 ff., does not call attention to duplications.

68. Two books of "trio" sonatas sometimes cited (cf. PINCHERLE-CORELLI, p. 121) seem not to have existed.

Banchieri and fulfills specific functions in the liturgy.[69] But the majority
of the sonatas, and the only type published, are mixed cycles of free and
dance movements designated for organ and cembalo.

Two collections of these last are among the surprisingly few publications of Martini's works. The first, containing 12 *Sonate d'intavolatura*
[i.e., not in open but in condensed, keyboard score on two staffs] *per
l'organo e il cembalo* (Op. 2?), was issued in Amsterdam in 1742. The
second, containing six more, was issued in Bologna in 1747.[70] In the
1742 set each of the 12 sonatas is in a different key, as was often the
practice in any instrumental collection of the late Baroque. Each sonata
has five movements, in the order of S-F-S-F-variable. The first three
movements are almost always of the church type, with an arpeggiated
"Preludio," a recherché fugal "Allegro," and a serious "Adagio." The
last two movements are usually dances or dancelike, with the finale
being an aria- or minuet-and-variations in several instances. However,
the church style must be said to prevail not only in the number or order
of movements but in the contrapuntal and intellectual weight of all of
them. Because of the rich counterpoint and frequent stretches that imply
a pedal keyboard, organ would seem to be the preferred instrument,
although the figuration is not without interest to the harpsichordist. By
contrast, the 1747 set has mostly a two-voice texture and only two or
three movements. Organ is specified for Sonatas 1, 3, 5, and cembalo for
the other three.

It is hard to read Martini's sonatas without finding formalism and
conservatism. Formalism is not the inescapable penalty of a scholarly
bent, as is commonly assumed. But one must acknowledge that the
craftsmanship surpasses the imagination in this music. The ideas themselves are usually of a neutral sort, without the necessary leap, dissonance, or rhythm that might lend individuality. And their treatment
at length seems to suffer from the tonal monotony of too narrow a
modulatory range, from a texture too consistently in the three-part
disposition of the Baroque "trio" setting, from uncompromising sequences, and more generally from a lack of daring such as permits the
similarly weighty partitas of Bach to soar effortlessly. It is significant

69. The ensemble sonatas listed in ALTMANN are actually transcriptions of
keyboard sonatas except for SCHROEDER-CELLOm, no. 8, which proves to be by
G. B. Sammartini.
70. Among mod. eds., 1742 set: TRÉSORm, III (with a valuable preface on the
circumstances of the first edition) ; VITALI-MARTINIm; CLEMENTI-HARMONYm, II
and IV (with both sonatas and movements interchanged for no good reason).
1747 set: entire, MITTELDEUTSCHESm, I, Part 5 (Hoffmann-Erbrecht, with preface) ;
Sons. 5, 6, and 2, CLASSICIm I, No. 18 (Lualdi), last fascicle ; Son. 4, OESTERLEm, V,
92. The separate pieces in many "old masters" anthologies appear all to be from
sonatas in the 1742 or 1747 sets.

that the most popular piece by Martini was and is the comparatively thin-textured "Gavotta" in F that ends Sonata 12 (a distant cousin of Corelli's "Gavotte" in F from his tenth "solo" sonata and of Kozeluch's four-hand "Gavotta" in F falsely attributed to both Mozart and Beethoven[71]). Similarly, the shorter sonatas in the 1747 set, with fewer movements, thinner texture, and no fugues, are more likely to appeal to the performer than their predecessors, although one supposes that the 1747 set was something of a concession to pedagogic needs and modern tastes.

71a

Florence (F. M. Veracini)

One name stands out in Florence as a composer of late Baroque sonatas, F. M. Veracini (Nardini being too much later in time and style to be included here). There were some less well-known figures, too. A predecessor of Veracini was the virtuoso violinist, composer, and poet **Giuseppe Valentini** (ca. 1680-ca. 1740), who also held posts in Bologna and Rome. Between 1701 and 1714 several sets of Valentini's "trio" or "solo" sonatas were first published in Amsterdam, Rome, or Bologna, with capricious collective titles such as *Idee per camera* (S/bass), Op. 4; *Villeggiature armoniche a tre,* Op. 5; and *Sonate o allettamenti per camera* (S/bass), Op. 8.[72] The influence and possible instruction of Corelli are suggested by specific references in Valentini's music and one sonata (Op. 5, no. 7) actually called "La Corelli."[73] In Op. 4 Valentini tells us that he provided more than the customary two allegro movements so that the performer could omit those that were too hard![74]

Two minor contemporaries of Veracini were the violinist **Giovanni Piantanida** (1705-ca. 1782), whose *VI. Sonate a tre,* Op. 1, were published in London in 1742; and the flutist **Nicola Dothel,** who published several sets of "solo" and "trio" sonatas for his instrument in London and Paris in the decade from 1755. Both men were met, heard, and praised by Burney in Italy.[75]

Francesco Maria Veracini (1690-1768), pupil of his uncle Antonio Veracini and possibly Corelli, has the distinction (up to this writing)

71. Cf. CUDWORTH-SPURIOSITY, p. 535.

72. For several mod. eds. of single sonatas cf. ALTMANN; but the "cello sonatas" are all arrangements of violin sonatas (cf. Walsh's mistranslation of the original Roger title for Op. 8 [1714] in SMITH-WALSH, item 577). Thematic index of Op. 4 in a MS copy, in HAAS-ESTENSISCHEN, p. 113 ff. It is Op. 8 that was grossly plagiarized by the English violinist Henry Eccles (cf. MOSER-CRIMINALIA, p. 424); although Son. 2 is correctly attributed to Valentini in MOFFAT-VIOLINm II, no. 23, Son. 12 (mixed with part of Son. 1 in Moffat's loose editorial manner; cf. SQUIRE-ECCLES) is wrongly attributed to Eccles in MOFFAT-VIOLINm III, no. 2.

73. MOSER-VIOLINSPIEL, pp. 73 and 79; LAURENCIE, I, 218 ff.

74. Cf. the preface, quoted in CAT. BOLOGNA, IV, 155.

75. BURNEY-FRANCE, pp. 224 and 246.

of being one of the most important violinists and sonata composers of
76a the late Baroque to be neglected by the monographers.[76] Modern editions of his music are hardly sufficient, either. But of short enthusiastic
accounts there is no dearth, past or present. Even Torchi quits the dim
view he had often taken of his earlier countrymen to call Veracini the
Beethoven of the 18th century.[77] And Veracini himself reportedly went
one step further to proclaim "that there was but *one God* and *one
Veracini.*"[78] In the course of his stays in Florence, Venice (and other
Italian cities?), London, Dresden, and Prague, Veracini wrote four
(not two) known sets of 12 sonatas each, plus a few operas, songs, and
unexplored instrumental works in MS, and a lively, highly original
theory treatise.[79]

The sonatas are entirely of the "solo" (S/bass) type. Conspicuous
growth is shown from one set to the next. The first collection, dated
1716 in Venice, was given no opus number, probably because it was not
80a published in Veracini's lifetime.[80] It is designated for violin or flute
and *b. c.* While the sonatas in this set are like so many others in being
of the standard S-F-S-F church type, they clearly mark the debut of a
superior composer, both in the quality of ideas and the grasp of over-all
design.

Veracini's second set, originally published in Amsterdam in about
81a 1720, is labelled Op. 1.[81] Here the sense of form shows up not only in
the separate movements, including clear A-B-A designs, but extends to
the plan of the complete cycles and, in fact, to the organization of the
entire set, almost as in the organization of Bach's *Musical Offering*.
The set begins with six court sonatas in six different minor keys. Each
has a slow, preludial first movement and two or three other free movements or dances. There follow six church sonatas in six different major
keys. Each has five movements, all but the last sonata being in the
order of S-F-F-S-F (assuming "Larghetto" over the second movement
of Son. 7 connotes a fast tempo in this instance, as "Largo" often did in
Italian Baroque music). The last sonata makes a brilliant conclusion
with its final "Capriccio," a free rondo form. In the finale of Sonata 3

76. BÄR-VERACINIm reports that a biography by Bernhard Paumgartner was in
preparation in 1950 and supplies the hitherto unknown death date of Oct. 31, 1768
(Florence).
77. TORCHI, p. 179 ff. Cf., also, MOSER-VIOLINSPIEL, p. 231 ff.
78. Cf. BURNEY-HISTORY, II, 450 ff. and 990.
79. Cf. NALDO.
80. Mod. ed.: Sons. 1, 2, and 3, BÄR-VERACINIm (with preface).
81. This is the E. Roger & Le Cène edition in two books, nos. 488 and 489. It
apparently preceded the Dresden edition of 1721, usually given as the first edition,
by about a year. Among mod. eds.: Sons. 1, 3, 6, 8, 10, and 12, CLASSICIm I, no.
34 (Pizzetti).

the actual title is "Rondo." The theme of this rondo is a good sample of the extent Veracini achieves in his ideas through broad but simple phrase organization, giving them a distinctly Classic feel (Ex. 37). The fugal second movements of the church sonatas are remarkable for the

Ex. 37. From the finale of Sonata 3, Op. 1, by Francesco Maria Veracini (after the E. Roger & Le Cène edition).

contrapuntal activity achieved, much more through double- and triple-stops than the occasional participation of the bass.

Veracini's best-known set is his *Sonate accademiche,* Op. 2, first published "Per l'Autore, a Londra, e a Firenze" in 1744, in a handsome edition that includes a portrait of the author playing the violin.[82] 82a Presumably the sonatas were composed during many previous years of concertizing.[83] This set brings his unusual personality into full play. Its title does not mean sonatas that are formalistic, of course, but rather sonatas suitable to performance in a (music) academy—*morceaux du concours,* so to speak. Departing considerably from Op. 1, the sonatas have all that verve, imagination, and daring that seemed to be lacking in Martini's keyboard sonatas. Op. 2 is also the most virtuosic of Veracini's collections, especially in variation treatments and in nine "Capriccio" movements, some "con due" or "tre Soggetti," that combine the fugal double-stop technique (Ex. 38) with bold sweeping figures of much rhythmic variety.

In Op. 2, again, there is at least a token division into six church and six court sonatas, the former coming first this time. But several of the movements in both types have colorful titles not standard in either type— "Aria Schiavonna [Slavic]," "Ritornello," "Cotillion," "Scozzese

82. Cf. Plate II, Part 3, in BOYDEN-TECHNIQUE, an illuminating discussion of violin playing in this period.
83. The 1711 in "Menuet. 1711," finale of Son. 4, may or may not indicate a year of composition. Mod. eds.: cf. ALTMANN.

Ex. 38. From "Capriccio Terzo, con due Soggetti," third movement of Sonata 2, Op. 2, by Francesco Maria Veracini (after the composer's own edition of 1744).

[Scotch]," "Polonese"—and neither the key distribution nor movement plan are consistent as in Op. 1. Furthermore, in a preface ("Intenzione dell'Autore") significant for its advice on performance practices,[84] Veracini closes with a carefree instruction (perhaps shocking to present-day purists who seek the one right way to restore Baroque music) : "Since each of these sonatas is provided with four or five movements, be advised that such is done for the enrichment and adornment of the collection, and for the greater diversion of amateurs and dilettantes of music. Otherwise, two or three movements of these, selected as one pleases, suffice to comprise a sonata of just proportions." Veracini may have wondered whether performers would accept the greater length of his sonatas, made possible by their broader structural arches. Sonata 1 in this set numbers some 525 measures without repeats, as compared with an average of about 220 in Corelli's longest sonatas (the church types of Op. 5). But, actually, Veracini gave much thought to balance and proportion, a fact evidenced by the interrelated movements in both Opp. 1 and 2. Closely paired movements, as implied by the following titles from Sonata 1 of Op. 2, occur in several instances : "Toccata : Adagio, e come Stá [i.e., without improvised ornamentation]," "Capriccio Primo : Allegro ma non presto," "Allegro," "Epilogo della Toccata : Largo, e Nobile," and "Capriccio Secondo : Allegro, e Brillante." The final sonata in Op. 2 is not simply a "Passagallo," on the descending chromatic tetrachord, but it is this plus a "Capriccio Cromatico con Due Soggetti, e Loro Rovesci veri," and a brilliant, recapitulative "Ciaconna."

The remaining set of 12 "solo" sonatas exists in a MS, apparently not hitherto explored, with the intriguing title *Dissertazioni del Sigr.* 85a *Francesco Veracini sopra l'Opera Quinta del Corelli.*[85] In these sonatas (each called "Dissertazione") Veracini rewrites all 12 sonatas in Corelli's Op. 5 almost as Bach rewrote Albinoni's fugal movements. For the

84. Cf. HARDING-ORIGINS, p. 92 and Plate 23.
85. CAT. BOLOGNA, IV, 157.

student of style and composition techniques the value of the new versions is great, quite apart from their other musical interests. Contrapuntal lines are added, figuration is enriched, ideas are extended and developed, and the bass is made more active, all mostly within Corelli's restriction to the third position. This set is actually but one of several proofs of Corelli's influence on Veracini, which include strong stylistic reminiscences in Veracini's 1716 set and still another imitation, in the first movement of Sonata 1, Op. 2, of the opening movement of Corelli's first solo sonata (cf. p. 171).

Torino (G. B. Somis)

Giovanni Battista Somis (1686-1763) and his younger brother **Lorenzo Giovanni Somis-"Ardy"** (1688-1755) were members of an important musical family in Torino.[86] G. B. Somis was the better known, as an eminent violinist; as a confirmed pupil of Corelli (if not Vivaldi) and a founder of the Piedmontese school of violin playing, which transmitted the Corellian tradition to Pugnani, Giardini, Guignon, Leclair, Chabran, and other of his own pupils; and as a composer of sonatas and concertos. Unlike many of his concertizing colleagues, he left Torino only rarely, including a successful visit to Paris in 1733.[87]

The usual statement that not much is left by which to judge G. B. Somis' music is not quite true. There have been only three sonata reprints that are known here[88] and no special study of the music. But there is considerable material awaiting further investigation. This includes five sets of published "solo" and "trio" sonatas, first issued between about 1717 and 1734, and at least 13 more "solo" sonatas that could be by either G. B. or L. Somis. One of these 13 sonatas is the sixth and last piece printed in ANTH. HANDELm, eight more make up a MS volume in Bologna, and the other four are part of another such volume in Paris.[89] Still other sonatas by G. B. Somis are known to have existed—not only "solo" (viola d'amore, cello, violin), and "trio," but multivoice (a 4 and a 3 "con ripieni").[90] The five published sets by G. B. Somis that are extant include 8 "solo" sonatas in Op. 1 (1722)

86a

90a

---

86. Biographic information in FINO, summarized in SCHMIDL, II, 524 ff.

87. LAURENCIE, I, 100, 274, and 280 quotes two laudatory reports from Paris and another when Quantz visited Torino.

88. Op. 6, No. 10, JONGEN & DEBROUX-SOMISM; Son. in D minor (MS [for viola d'amore?] in the former Königlichen Hausbibliothek of Berlin), EINSTEIN-HISTORYm, no. 32 (with comments); "Adagio and Allegro" (from Op. 1?), JENSEN-VIOLINm, Vol. 7408.

89. CAT. BOLOGNA, IV, 147, and BIBLIOTHÈQUE NATIONALE, VIII, 33 ff. and 64, both sources with thematic index

90. SCHMIDL, II, 524.

and 12 each, "da camera," in Op. 2 (*ca.* 1717),[91] Op. 4 (1726), and Op. 6 (1734). Only one set contains "trio" sonatas. This is Op. 5 (1733), with six *Sonate a tre o sieno trattenimenti per camera.* Opp. 4, 5, and 6 are known only in Paris editions.

Nearly all of G. B. Somis' sonatas have the newer Baroque plan of but three movements, sometimes F-S-F but mostly S-F-F. In spite of the "da camera," few of the movements have dance titles. For the rest, the sonatas do not stand out among the chief examples of the time. For instance, they reveal considerably less advance in all those traits, both musical and technical, that were regarded so highly here in Veracini. The sonatas in Op. 6 are very light. Dedicated to the Earl of Essex, they introduce a number of British tunes (without titles). And there are other novelties, such as the French "Tambourin" at the end of No. 10, with its pedal tone in the cello ("tasto solo") and square eight-measure sections. From Lorenzo Somis are preserved a set of eight "solo" sonatas "da camera," Op. 2 and six *Sonate a tre,* Op. 3 (1725).[92]

A nephew and pupil of G. B. Somis was **Charles Chabran** (*ca.* 1723-?), who carried Somis' teaching from Torino to Paris and London, and in those cities published six "solo" sonatas about 1751 and 1752.[93] A successor to the Somis brothers was **Quirino Gasparini** (?-1778), a pupil of Martini in Bologna, who came to Torino about 1749 and left some "trio" sonatas in MS,[94] as well as three appealing sonatas now available for the cello under his name, but the origin of which is not known to this study.[95]

Other Northern Italian Cities (Tartini)

The Milanese composer and theorist **Giorgio Antoniotto** (*ca.* 1692-1776) published a set of 12 sonatas, Op. 1, in Amsterdam about 1735. The first five are for cello "solo" (T/bass) whereas the last seven are for two cellos, or two violas da gamba, and *b. c.*[96] In the two solo sonatas now available are revealed an advanced knowledge of the cello, some

---

91. Op. 1, which appeared in Rome, has hitherto been taken as his earliest publication. But the Library of Congress has a set of 12 *Sonate da camera* by him that was published by Jeanne Roger of Amsterdam about 1717 (plate no. 456) and is presumably an earlier edition of the set by the same title that Le Cène published about 1725 (BRITISH PRINTED, II, 516). The latter is reportedly a reprint of the Torino edition of 1723 that is marked Op. 2 (SCHMIDL, II, 524). Obviously, further clarification of the bibliography is needed, the more so as another "brother-problem" is involved.

92. Mod. ed.: Son. in G, MOFFAT-VIOLINm II, no. 16.

93. Regarding the given name Charles see GROVE, II, 147 (Straeten). Mod. ed. (under given name of François): Son. 5 in G, ALARD-VIOLINm, no. 26.

94. Cf. CAT. BOLOGNA, IV, 111.

95. Cf. WEIGL, p. 68.

96. EITNER-QL, I, remains the best source. Mod. eds.: cf. WEIGL, p. 55.

skillful counterpoint between the solo and *b. c.* parts, and a melodic pathos achieved mainly by short sighs, yearning leaps, and expressive rests.

The celebrated Modenese composer **Giovanni Battista Bononcini** (1670-*ca.* 1755), son of G. M. Bononcini and an excellent cellist,[97] can only be mentioned in passing here, since the sonata has only a little place in the considerable amount of instrumental music that he left in print. As a title it figures not in the six precocious Bolognese publications of 1685 to 1687, which contain melo/bass or orchestral *trattenimenti* (diversions), and sinfonias; nor in the *Divertimenti da camera* published in London in 1722 both as S/bass pieces and as cembalo arrangements; but only in *XII Sonatas for the Chamber for two Violins and a Bass doubled,* published in London in 1732 (after the period of operatic rivalry between Handel and Bononcini).[98]

In Casalmaggiore, near Cremona, lived **Andrea Zani** (1696-?), among whose numerous instrumental collections were at least three made up of sonatas (*ca.* 1730-*ca.* 1745). There are 12 each in Opp. 3 and 5, and others in Op. 6, plus single "solo" and "trio" sonatas in miscellaneous sources.[99] Op. 5 was published in Vienna, whereas both Opp. 3 and 6 appeared in Paris, where Zani's music was very popular around 1740.[100] His style is described as similar to Vivaldi's, with more strength in the ideas themselves than in their treatment.[101]

Giuseppe Tartini (1692-1770), one of the great composers, violinists, and theorists of the 18th century, stands with Vivaldi and F. M. Veracini among the chief names in our third group of Italian sonata composers.[102] [102a] From 1721 on, except for two years in Prague (1723-25) and an Italian tour in 1740, he served as soloist and orchestra conductor in the St. Antonio Chapel of Padua. There, too, he founded an important school of violin playing that included Nardini and Pugnani (previously a pupil of G. B. Somis) among other renowned students and sonata composers. At perhaps the age of 24 Tartini is said to have heard Veracini play in Venice and to have been much inspired. But the story

97. Cf. HAWKINS, V, 274 ff.; BURNEY-HISTORY, II, 748 ff.

98. The cello "Sonate" in A minor in SCHROEDER-CELLOm, no. 9, is an arrangement of the first cello duet in ANTH. BONONCINIm (and is not from Op. 5 as stated in VATIELLI-BOLOGNA, p. 147). The "Sonates" for keyboard mentioned in MGG, II, 120 ff. (Bollert), should read "suites."

99. Cf. BRITISH PRINTED, II, 715; EITNER-QL. X, 327.

100. Cf. LAURENCIE, II, 6.

101. MGG, II, 1778 (Monterosso).

102. CAPRI is the main source on the man and his music, including a thematic index of the MS sonatas and concertos in the Cappella Antoniana of Padua. A study projected since about 1935 by H. P. Schökel was still listed "in preparation" in 1955. DOUNIAS is a valuable monograph on the concertos, of the sort needed on the sonatas.

has flaws.[103] In any case, Corelli must once more be regarded as the chief influence, especially his Op. 5, which left its clear impress on Tartini's own "solo" sonatas, Op. 1, and became a must for the latter's students and a starting point for his noted bowing study *L'Arte dell'Arco o siano cinquanta variazioni per violino, e sempre collo stesso basso sopra alla più bella Gavotte* [from Sonata 10, again] *del Corelli* (Naples, *ca.* 1750).

As with Veracini, Tartini is remembered only for his instrumental music, which includes sonatas and concertos that have been estimated at as many as 200 each.[104] The biographer Capri erred in supposing that the MSS in the St. Antonio chapel, which make up the single largest deposit of Tartini MSS, fairly well comprehend his total output, including copies of the works that reached publication.[105] Not counting duplications, lost works, and probable misattributions, these MSS include a total of 126 sonatas, of which 82 (65 per cent) are "solo" (S/bass), 40 (32 per cent) are "trio" (SS/bass), and 4 (3 per cent) are multivoice (SSA/bass).[106] That total does include copies of the 12 "trio" sonatas "Printed at the Author's Expence" (Op. 3?, London, 1750). But it can be raised at once to 160 by adding the 9 of the 12 "solo" sonatas published as Op. 1 (Amsterdam, Le Cène, 1734), the 11 of those published as Op. 2 (Rome, Antonius Cleton, 1745), and 14 others that could be confirmed here as not happening to be represented among the St. Antonio MSS.[107] Of the last 14, 12 come from three of still other sets printed in Tartini's lifetime, among them the Boivin edition in Paris of 60 "solo" and 6 "trio" sonatas in nine sets (Opp. 1 to 9, *ca.* 1740-45) ; and there are well over 50 sonatas in other MS deposits, making a total of 200 not at all out of the question.[108] To be sure, as Capri suggests, many printed editions must have been pirated assortments,[109] and many of the MSS must be duplicates.[110] But just

106a

103. Cf. BURNEY-HISTORY, II, 448; DOUNIAS, p. 27 ff.; CAPRI, p. 33 ff.
104. Cf. MOSER-VIOLINSPIEL, p. 250 ff.
105. CAPRI, p. 161 ff.
106. Among mod. eds.: 11 "solo" sonatas not in Opp. 1 or 2, PENTE & ZANONm (cf. CAPRI, pp. 274 ff. and 284) ; 7 of these same plus a Son. in D minor, CLASSICIm I, no. 32 (cf. CAPRI, pp. 297 and 531).
107. Thematic index of all movements in Opp. 1, 2, 5, 6, and 7 in BACHMANN-VIOLINISTES, p. 320 ff.; two further themes, queried in BOYDEN-TARTINI, p. 152, are not in this source. Among mod. eds.: Sons. 1, 3, 4, 5, and 10 from Op. 1 and Son. 12, Op. 2, POLO-TARTINIm; 6 Sons. from Op. 2, LÉONARDm. For others and Op. 3 (?) cf. ALTMANN (including several editions that are much altered).
108. Cf. EITNER-QL, IX, 357 ff.; WOLFFHEIM, I, 276; MEYER & HIRSCH, III, no. 535; HAAS-CAT. 20, nos. 627 ff.
109. Thus the finale in DAVISON & APELm, no. 275, happens to be from an "Op. 3" that is actually a re-edition of Op. 2. But the listing of "Sonatas *a 5 & 6*, Bk. I, Op. 1, 1734" in GROVE, VIII, 312 ff. (Heron & Allen), is merely an error for "Concertos. . . ."
110. CAPRI, pp. 168 and 292.

how many, one could not know until the needed collation of all possible sources is accomplished.[111]

In the discussion of Baroque structures Tartini's sonatas furnished some of our chief examples of changes after Corelli. **These changes in-** clude a reduction in the average number of movements to three in the "solo" sonatas, usually in the order S-F-F that prevailed in Somis' sonatas, and to only two in the "trio" sonatas, usually S-F; a shift to a more homophonic texture and to allegros in binary design rather than fugal form; a growing preference for ternary and larger, free rondo forms; a greater technical range in pitch, speed, variety of figuration, double- and triple-stops, and bowings;[112] and a newly intimate, sensitive expression. Most of these changes can be observed in process even in the ways that Tartini's Op. 2 differs from his Op. 1, especially from the church sonatas in the first half of Op. 1. An external sign is the increased preference for such movement titles as "Andante affettuoso" rather than "Largo" or "Grave."

The intimate style is most in evidence in the freer (later?) "solo" sonatas. The "trio" sonatas have much individuality and charm, too (Ex. 39).[113] But in the "solo" sonatas all else is subordinated to melody —to a refined, poignant, ornamental melody that helps to explain why Tartini would write a *Trattato delle appogiature* (before 1750[114]) or the precise instructions on bowing, shifting, and ornamentation in his famous letter of March 5, 1760, to Signora Maddalena Lombardini.[115] "He doesn't play, he sings on the violin," was a contemporary report of his performance.[116] The romantic lyricism in Tartini's music, with its occasional Slavic folk elements,[117] ties in with his stay in Prague and with the romantic incidents in his life that have made good reading since his own day.[118] His habit of inscribing a Metastasian, Petrarchan, or less poetic sentiment at the start of a new score has lent a programmatic flavor to various works, whether actually intended or not. No small factor in the interest this habit aroused was the mysterious code or cipher that he used. In recent years the code was finally solved by the

---

111. EITNER-QL, IX, 358, lists a thematic index prepared by Alois Fuchs in 1839 (cf. DOUNIAS, p. 235).

112. Cf. MOSER-VIOLINSPIEL, p. 259 ff.

113. The quick dismissal of them as being inferior, in CAPRI, p. 289 ff., seems unwarranted.

114. The Italian edition is lost; the first known publication is the Paris edition of 1771 (not 1782); cf. LAURENCIE, III, 64 ff., and CAPRI, p. 332 ff. Mod. ed. in English: BABITZ-TARTINI (with preface and notes).

115. Burney's standard English translation of 1779 is reproduced in DORING-DUBOURG, XI, 169 ff.

116. Quoted in GROVE, VIII, 314.

117. Cf. CAPRI, p. 205 ff.

118. Cf. DORING-DUBOURG, p. 150 ff.

Ex. 39. From the second movement of Sonata 2, Op. 3 (?), by Giuseppe Tartini (after the London edition of 1750, "Printed at the Author's Expence").

researcher Dounias, who applied techniques not unlike those of the cryptogrammatist in *The Gold Bug* by Poe.[119]

Two of Tartini's most attractive "solo" sonatas, both in G minor, happen to be the two made most popular by their programmatic associations. One, of course, is "The Devil's Trill," a posthumously published work. From 1749 came the published report by the Frenchman Lalande of a dream that Tartini had related to him. In this dream, dated most improbably in 1713, Tartini said he heard the Devil, at the foot of his bed, playing a piece so fantastic that he could but feebly recapture it when he awoke.[120] Whatever their origin, the trills in the finale of the resulting sonata have posed supernatural problems for many a violinist. The other sonata is the tenth in Op. 1, known as "Didone abbandonata" (one of several notable examples in sonata history by the same title). In this instance both the title and the appropriate bits of verse from Metastasio appear to have been added by later editors. So has an additional slow movement in some editions, transposed from Sonata 5 in Op. 1 in order to provide the standard sequence S-F-S-F.

Another musical heir of Corelli, and probably an actual pupil, was the Trent composer, violinist, "gentilhuomo . . . e dilettante di musica," and priest **Francesco Antonio Bonporti** (1672-1749).[121] Bonporti published at least 50 sonatas, 10 each in five of his 11 known instrumental

119. Cf. DOUNIAS, p. 89 ff., and CAPRI, p. 196 ff.
120. Cf. DOUNIAS, p. 164; CAPRI, pp. 276 and 532. DORING-DUBOURG, XI, 111 ff. and 172 ff., gives one of the most garnished accounts.
121. BARBLAN-BONPORTI is the chief source on the man and his music.

sets—Op. 1, 1696; Op. 2, 1698 (not 1703); Op. 4, 1703; Op. 6, 1705; and Op. 7, 1707.[122]   All five sets were originally issued in Venice. All but Op. 1 are marked "da camera." The first four of the sets are of the SSB/bass type, while only Op. 7 is a "solo" (S/bass) set.

But the chief interest in Bonporti has centered in another, still later set of 10 pieces that have the general plan of the court sonata, were reprinted and are sometimes referred to as such, yet bear the title *Invenzioni a violino solo* (S/bass), Op. 10 (1712 or 1713).[123]   Once more the interest has been generated in the bypaths of Bach research, for Inventions 2, 5, 6, and 7 were wrongly included under Bach's name by Alfred Dörffel in volume 45 of the Bach *Werke* (pp. 172-189). But this time the music, the source MS, and even the style have been shown to be not Bach's.[124]

At best, Bonporti's sonatas approach the Handelian majesty in their broad, steady, purposeful flow. The melodic continuity is usually furthered by the continuity of a running (*gehende*) bass so characteristic of late Baroque ensemble music. Bonporti dealt with neutral lines rather than distinctive themes. These lines are much more ornamental and disjunct in the "solo" pieces, especially the *Invenzioni*. Dance titles prevail in the court sonatas, whereas those in the *Invenzioni* are often capricious, such as "Bizaria," "Capricio," "Fantasia," "Scherzo," and "Ecco Adagio."

Another in the highly-stationed, "dilettante" class was the "Cavaliere" **Azzolino Bernardino Della Ciaja** (1671-1744), organist in Siena and Pisa. His importance to our subject is seen in the only instrumental collection among his four publications, that of six *Sonate per cembalo con alcuni saggi, ed altri contrapunti di largo, e grave stile ecclesiastico per grandi organi,* Op. 4 (Rome, 1727).[125]   The organ pieces consist of 18 *ricercari* and a "Pastorale," while each of the cembalo sonatas has four movements in the order of a wholly rhapsodic "Toccata," a resourcefully developed fugal "Canzone," and two shorter, lighter movements marked "Tempo I" and "Tempo II." The last two movements also have specific tempo markings, such as "Lento" and "Allegro," respectively.

There is striking keyboard writing in Della Ciaja's sonatas, in the direct line that had led from Frescobaldi to Pasquini, A. Scarlatti, and

122. Mod. eds., all from Op. 4: Son. 2, HAUSMUSIKm, no. 174 (Schenk); Son. 9, SCHENK-TRIOSONATEm, no. 5; Son. 10, MOFFAT-TRIOm, no. 21.

123. Thematic index in HAAS-ESTENSISCHEN, p. 86 ff.   Among mod. eds.: Sons. 1 to 6, HORTUSm, nos. 44 and 45 (Giegling).

124. WOLFFHEIM-BACHIANA.

125. Cf. TORREFRANCA-DELLA CIAJA; SANDBERGER-KLAVIERMUSIK. New biographic information in SARACINI. Among mod. eds.: Sons. 1-3, BUONAMICI-DELLA CIAJAm.

Zipoli. One finds bold runs, including an early use of an upward glissando;[126] rich ornamentation expressed both in written-out figuration and by signs; difficult passages in octaves, 3ds, or 6ths played by either hand or by both hands in contrary motion; and wide leaps, including abrupt shifts of register that seem to presuppose a two-manual harpsichord. In their frequently subjective quality the toccatas resemble Bach's, what with searching modulations and anguished dissonance, especially that produced by false relations (Ex. 40). Indeed, the

Ex. 40. From the "Toccata" of Sonata 1, Op. 4, by Azzolino Bernardino Della Ciaja (after BUONAMICI-DELLA CIAJAm, but without the added markings).

"brooding" is carried to a point that the French scholar Pirro finds quite intolerable.[127]

The German scholar Sandberger sees significant anticipations of "sonata-allegro" form and of Domenico Scarlatti's keyboard writing in Della Ciaja's lighter movements,[128] which are still in fairly full, three-voice texture. But the anticipations of later form seem negligible in the light of, say, Veracini's and Tartini's handling of separate movements. So does the evidence for a tentative "singing-allegro" style that Torrefranca finds.[129] More to the point, probably, is the "rhythmic impressionism" (plastic freedom of rhythm) that the latter welcomes in Della Ciaja's sonatas, particularly in the toccata movements.

Another keyboardist, **Lodovico Giustini** of Pistoia, is recognized as the composer of the first known, dated music of any sort that specifies

126. MGG, III, 140 ff. (Sartori).
127. -CLAVECINISTES, p. 109 ff.
128. SANDBERGER-KLAVIERMUSIK, p. 24 ff.
129. TORREFRANCA, pp. 377 and 624; TORREFRANCA-DELLA CIAJA.

the use of the pianoforte—only some 23 years, at that, after the first "Gravicembalo col piano e forte" produced by Cristofori in nearby Florence. Published in Florence in 1732, Giustini's sole extant work is entitled *Sonate da cimbalo di piano, e forte detto volgarmente di martelletti*, Op. 1.[130] This music stays within the range of Cristofori's instrument, using every chromatic tone from BB to c''' and hence suggesting a tuning in equal temperament.[131] Not only "piano" and "forte" but "più piano" and "più forte" occur among the dynamic terms. Sometimes the volume seems to be increased merely in the manner known to harpsichordists, by piling on voices (e.g., opening of the first "Giga" in Son. 2, though without dynamic markings). But there are places, such as a stretch of repeated chords marked "più pia." ("Corrente" of Son. 7), that do seem to require a graduation of dynamics possible only on the piano.

Giustini's 12 sonatas are all in four or five movements. Most of the movements have dance as well as tempo titles. Three rondo movements, three minuet finales, and such titles as "Dolce" and "Affettuoso" suggest that the composer was well abreast of the popular tastes in his day. More concrete evidence is found in the clear melodic segments and extensions,[132] the balanced phrase grouping and neat binary designs, the fluent "pianism," and the light texture. Even in two canzona movements— among the infrequent survivors of the venerable type, relegated here, as usual, to the position of fugal second movement—the texture quickly lapses into homophony. The style is closer, of course, to D. Scarlatti's than della Ciaja's. Still, it does not call Scarlatti's idiom so much to mind as does Marcello's, aside from a characteristic clash of the dominant and tonic harmonies superposed (e.g., the "Preludio: Adagio, e arpeggiato nell' acciaccature" of Son. 5).[133] But it is interesting to note that Giustini had a possible connection with both Carlos Seixas of Portugal and Scarlatti through Giovanni de Seixas, who wrote the dedication of Giustini's Op. 1, and through the dedicatee Don Antonio, who was a onetime pupil of Scarlatti in Lisbon.[134] Giustini's style might more 134a accurately be likened to the styles of his contemporaries Loeillet or Platti, although Giustini's is still the lighter of the three.

In any case, Giustini's sonatas are effective over and above their

130. Cf. HARDING-EARLIEST (with examples). Mod. ed., in full: GIUSTINI-FACSIMILEM (with preface). GERBER-LEXIKON, II, 338, mentions Giustini only as the author of "XII Klaviersonaten" published in Amsterdam in 1736. This set is lost, but presumably was a reprint of Op. 1.

131. But the "modulation to G♯ major" quoted from the "Allegro" of Son. 8 in HARDING-EARLIEST, p. 198 ff., is certainly only a passing V in C-sharp minor!

132. Cf. HOFFMANN/ERBRECHT-KLAVIERMUSIK, p. 79 ff.

133. Cf. KIRKPATRICK-SCARLATTI, p. 229 ff.

134. Cf. KASTNER-SEIXAS, p. 82; KIRKPATRICK-SCARLATTI, pp. 72 ff. and 183 ff.

significance to the history of the pianoforte. They deserve a better niche than they have been given in the history of Italian keyboard music. Torrefranca would probably have had much more to say if he had had access to them.[135] But one fears that Giustini's sonatas afford another of the all too many instances in which the music seems to have been penalized for its lack of a "second theme," or a "clear return," or any of those other traditional, alleged foretokens of Classic "sonata form."

Rome and Naples (Durante)

Oddly enough, in Rome, the very city of Corelli, there was no outstanding resident among our third group of sonata composers in Italy. One actual pupil of Corelli can be mentioned, of perhaps many more in Rome that are no longer known. He was the violinist **Giovanni Mossi,** who left three sets of "solo" church and court sonatas (Opp. 1, 3, and 5, ca. 1715-30), along with two sets of concertos. The sonatas are regarded as elegant, lyrical, technically adroit successors to the music of his teacher, which judgment seems to be justified by one sonata that has been reprinted.[136] In Op. 3 is perhaps intended the same option that Buini offered—"Violino e Cello o Cembalo."

The excellent liturgical and dance pieces in Domenico Zipoli's *Sonate d'intavolatura per organo, e cembalo,* Op. 1 (1716), are successors to the music of Frescobaldi and Pasquini.[137] But like Frescobaldi's they are not of direct concern here, since "Sonate" appears only as a generic term in the over-all title, with no further application to the individual pieces.

By contrast to Rome, Naples was the home of several composers of at least minor concern to the sonata in the earlier 18th century, although these men were much better known for their operas and sacred music. Until recently the first of them to come to mind would probably have been the one remembered above all for his *Stabat Mater* and *La Serva padrona,* **Giovanni Battista Pergolesi** (1710-36). In particular, the "trio" sonatas credited to this composer were signaled by Riemann (in his search for Stamitz's background) and succeeding scholars as remarkably early examples of the "singing-allegro" style, of "sonata form," and of a subjectivism identified with the earlier Classical style.[138] But the authentici-

135. Cf. TORREFRANCA, pp. 376 and 380.
136. Cf. MOSER-VIOLINSPIEL, p. 229; RINALDI-CORELLI, p. 320; TORCHI, p. 174 ff. (with examples). Mod. ed.: Son. in C minor, MOFFAT-VIOLINm II, no. 5.
137. Cf. SEIFFERT-KLAVIERMUSIK, p. 410 ff. Mod. eds., almost complete: TRÉSORm, XV; TORCHIm, III, including one piece actually by Durante (cf. PANNAIN-PIANISTICA, p. 156); CLASSICIm, I, vol. 11.
138. E.g., cf. RIEMANN-MUSIKGESCHICHTE, II, Part 3, 120 ff.; FISCHER-1750/1828, pp. 801 ff. and 804 ff.; SAINT/FOIX-PERGOLESI; RADICIOTTI, p. 181 ff. Among mod. eds. of separate items: cf. ALTMANN. DENT-ENSEMBLES, p. 119, makes a special point of "sonata form" found in a vocal trio from the authentic comic opera *Lo fràte 'nnammorato.*

ty of much if not all of Pergolesi's instrumental music, doubted even in the same century by both Hawkins and Burney,[139] has come into serious question since the appearance of Pergolesi's "Opera omnia" in 1940-42[140] (an edition, in the words of Frank Walker, "which, if it cannot challenge comparison with the other *Gesamtausgaben* in matters of scientific method, textual criticism, etc., goes far beyond any of them in one thing—the number of spurious compositions which it includes"[141]).

The majority of the sonatas attributed to Pergolesi may be listed here. Some 30 "trio" sonatas were supposedly written around 1732 for his patron, Prince Colonna of Stigliano. Of the 14 actually known (fascicle 5 in *Opera omnia*), "Twelve Sonatas for Two Violins and a Bass or an Orchestra" were first published about 1770 by Bremner of London, with the inscription, "The Manuscript of these Sonatas were [*sic*] procured by a Curious Gentleman of Fortune during his Travels through Italy." Two more followed in about a year among Bremner's *Periodical Trios*. Six *Sonate per il cembalo* occur in the *Opera omnia* (fascicle 21). In the same volume are three keyboard "Suites" that are actually but three of 16 further keyboard "sonatas" to be found under Pergolesi's name with the typical English collective title *Lessons for the Harpsichord*. These were issued in two sets of eight each by Longman, Lukey, and Company of London in the early 1770's.[142] And the same volume of *Opera omnia* has a "Sonata per organo" and a "Sonata per violino in 'stile di concerto' con accompagamento di due violini viola e basso continuo." Finally, a MS "Sonata di violino e basso" exists in King's College, Cambridge, the second movement of which appears transposed from G to A as the first cembalo "Sonata'" in *Opera omnia*.[143]

It is only possible here to summarize briefly the questions raised about the sonatas in two articles by Walker and by Charles L. Cudworth (on the instrumental works).[144] First of all is the internal evidence. In the present study, "sonata-allegro" form (if it is really indicative of trends) and the "singing-allegro" style do not prove to be so rare in the early 1730's. They can be found in the sonatas of Veracini, Tartini, Abaco, and numerous other contemporaries to be met here. But the *galant* mannerisms that adorn some of the supposed Pergolesi sonatas are definitely in the jargon of a later generation, beyond the idiom of *La Serva padrona,* and hardly the sort of thing that even a genius well ahead of his times might anticipate (Ex. 41). If Pergolesi's authorship in such

144a

139. HAWKINS, V, 375; BURNEY-HISTORY, II, 924.
140. PERGOLESIm.   141. WALKER-PERGOLESI, p. 301.
142. Approximate date based on HUMPHRIES & SMITH, p. 217.
143. CUDWORTH-PERGOLESI, p. 324.
144. WALKER-PERGOLESI and CUDWORTH-PERGOLESI. Cf. also CUDWORTH-RICCIOTTI.

Ex. 41. From the start of Sonata 8 *a 3,* attributed to Giovanni Battista Pergolesi (after the original Bremner edition).

examples were established, then we would be justified in including him among early Classic composers, although merely the run-of-the-mill sort, rather than as a Baroque victim of probable historical errors that can only provide useful sidelights on our subject.

Secondly, the least questionable ascriptions are a few sonatas at the other extreme—that is, so conservative in style (Burney complained of this) that one can hardly believe they could come from the same man, least of all from one who lived only 26 years (Ex. 42). And, as Mr.

Ex. 42. Start of Sonata II from *Eight Lessons for the Harpsichord* (first set), attributed to Giovanni Battisa Pergolesi (after the Longman, Lukey, & Co. edition, London, *ca.* 1780).

Cudworth remarks, "if there is one thing we are sure of in the case of Pergolesi, it is that he died young."

Third, a very few Pergolesi holographs have been confirmed, but none yet that contains instrumental music independent of vocal works, notwithstanding occasional claims to the contrary.[145]

145. Cf. CUDWORTH-PERGOLESI, p. 327.

Fourth, one is therefore led to suppose that since a considerable number of vocal works prove to be spurious (even *Il Maestro di musica*!), an even larger proportion if not all of the instrumental works may well be so. However, so far only one sonata happens to be identifiable as the work of another composer. Sonata 3 among the six keyboard sonatas in the *Opera omnia* proves to be a sonata by Domenico Alberti published only in ANTH. VENIERM II.[146] This particular correction may   146a
help to fan the suspicions but it means less historically, since Alberti, himself another of the many victims in an age of "forgeries and misattributions," is thought to have died only four years after Pergolesi.

Fifth and last, the great interest in Pergolesi that developed right after his death produced no mention of independent instrumental music, aside from a dubious listing in a Breitkopf thematic catalog of MS music,[147] until the publications themselves appeared, and they did not appear for some 35 years. Mr. Cudworth is even able to quote Charles De Brosses's *Lettres* on his Italian tour of 1739 to the effect that Pergolesi was among those who had devoted themselves only to vocal music, instrumental music being the province of the Lombardians.[148] As late as 1783 Forkel wrote a short biography of Pergolesi that makes no mention of instrumental music.[149]

A couple of the 13 *Toccate . . . per cembalo* left in MS by another Neapolitan, Leonardo Leo (1694-1744),[150] have been published from time to time as "sonatas." But by this time the distinction in terms is fairly consistent. "Sonata" as a title for Italian harpsichord music is now reserved almost exclusively for compositions in more than one movement (a fact apparently applicable to D. Scarlatti's works as well as others'[151]). Leo himself seems not to have used the title "sonata" in his few known instrumental works.

By comparison, **Francesco Durante** (1684-1755) did use the title "sonata" when he combined his pieces in pairs—that is, in six *Sonate per cembalo divise in studii e divertimenti* (Naples, ca. 1732).[152] This set, one of the very few publications by the distinguished church composer, teacher, and cembalist, contains the only sonatas known by him

146. No. XV, Part 1, in the thematic index of wörmann-alberti. The tip leading to this identification comes from Ruggero Gerlin by way of cudworth-pergolesi, p. 327.
147. walker-pergolesi, p. 298 ff.
148. cudworth-pergolesi, p. 321.
149. forkel-almanach 1783, p. 109 ff.
150. Cf. pubblicazioni-napoli, p, 612.
151. Cf. kirkpatrick-scarlatti, p. 141.
152. The title is derived only from Durante's dedicatory paragraph. Among mod. eds.: trésorm, I; classicim i, no. 11; paumgartner-durantem (cf. newman-durante).

except for about three left in MS.[153] The 'Studio" that comes first in each pair of movements is a study not only in the digital sense of Domenico Scarlatti's "Essercizi" but in the academic sense of being fugal (twice with the subtitle "Fuga"). It is long, anywhere from about 70 to 120 measures, where the "Divertimento" that follows is only about 20 to 30 measures (although binary repeats permit extensions in three of the divertimentos).

The mention of Durante naturally suggests a further comparison with D. Scarlatti, his co-citizen and almost exact contemporary. It would be hard to believe that the two did not come together as young men for at least a short time, in Naples or perhaps in Rome in the sphere of Pasquini and Zipoli.[154] Scarlatti, whose first publication came only about six years later (London, *ca.* 1738), is just enough over the border in style to be deferred as an early Classic composer. But we may note here that Durante concentrates entirely if not excessively on one idea in each piece,[155] lacking the bubbling imagination with which Scarlatti might have varied it or the sharply contrasted ideas with which he might have opposed it. The texture of the *studii,* varying freely between two and four voices, is generally heavier than Scarlatti's, but not the texture of the two-voice or chordal *divertimenti.* Durante does not go as far in exploiting the keyboard, but does call for deft trills, lively fingerwork, leaps up to three octaves, and rapid hand crossing (all in Studio 6, for example).[156]

153. Cf. PARIBENI; TORREFRANCA, pp. 142, 212, 422.
154. Cf. GROVE, II, 819 (Walker); KIRKPATRICK-SCARLATTI, p. 41 ff. A D-minor "Canzone" in Zipoli's Op. 1 (TORCHIm, III, 380) is actually a toccata by Durante (PANNAIN-PIANISTICA, p. 156).
155. Cf. the discussion of Durante's thematic material in HOFFMANN/ERBRECHT-KLAVIERMUSIK, p. 65 ff.
156. Cf. SEIFFERT-KLAVIERMUSIK, p. 414 ff.

Chapter 10

Austria and Germany from about
1615 to 1650

Chapters 10 to 12 take up sonata activities during the Baroque Era in both Germany and Austria. While the two countries had their separate identities, their citizens both spoke German, bowed at least in theory to one emperor, and enjoyed a fair amount of cultural interchange. Poland and the former Bohemia, Danzig, and Silesia are also included, at this stage in their sadly checkered histories, to the extent of at least one composer each. Within all these areas the geographical classification of the composers is more a matter of broad regions than of a few main cities, as in Italy. Vienna, Dresden, and Hamburg stand out as important centers, of course, but generally the nearly 95 composers to be noted in the three chapters were dispersed rather evenly throughout some 35 regions among as many as 300 sovereign states that made up the empire.

A fuller idea of the Austrian and German regions, centers, and extent of sonata production may be had from the following map. Four geographical regions are distinguished for our purposes, and have been so distinguished by other historians, who also had stylistic differences in mind. Austria and southern Germany were closest to Italian and other Mediterranean influences. Northern Germany was similarly close to English and Scandinavian influences. And central Germany became to some extent a meeting point for these other regions.

Chronologically, our composers active in these four regions may again be divided into three groups. The first is little more than an introductory group, since it consists mostly of Italians who composed or published while at the Imperial court in Vienna between about 1620 and 1650. Not included in this group are the German trumpeters responsible for the "field-and-court sonatas" around the turn of the century, as noted

Map of Germany and Austria. Regions and cities in which
Baroque sonatas were composed and/or published (with the
number of composers included in this survey as being active in
each city).

in an earlier chapter (see p. 18 ff.), nor composers like Paul Peuerl and
J. H. Schein, who made significant contributions to the suite before the
onset of the Thirty Years' War. The second group takes us from some
of the earliest native productions, around 1650 to about 1700, by which
time the native sonata had been converted into the international type
made known by Corelli and his contemporaries. And the third group,
producing from about 1700 to 1750, parallels our Italian third group.

Only this third group can be placed on a par in importance and output with the equivalent group active in Italy. The first group, in the midst of the Thirty Years' War, had little opportunity or occasion to do much more than observe the newly imported sonata. The second group cultivated its largely indigenous brand of sonata, with Italian, English, French, or other national elements grafted to it. Fewer names primarily important to the sonata, a smaller proportion of published sonatas, a lesser place for the sonata among other types of music, and less developed sonatas in themselves are all characteristics applicable to this second group when it is compared with the corresponding group in Italy. On the other hand, thanks to the German propensity for scholarly research, the status of our present information and modern editions is uniformly better for the German and Austrian composers than for the Italian. There were more Frescobaldis in Germany who wrote no sonatas at all—for example the three S's, Schütz, Schein, and Scheidt. But if a German Veracini has been overlooked by the encyclopedists, contributors to periodicals, or *Denkmäler* editors, he is almost certain to have been examined in somebody's dissertation.

Austria (*Giovanni Valentini, Bertali*)

As indicated, our "introductory" group is largely made up of Italians in Vienna. It seems logical, in any case, to start in the southern regions, closest to the Italian centers we have been discussing, although it is astonishing to realize how widely and often these 17th-century musicians travelled, the more so after one reads of such harrowing travel conditions as were reported by Burney and others more than a century later.[1] The Italians to be met now are not ones introduced before. But it is important to recall that a number of sonata composers introduced earlier here, in Italian cities, also had significant periods of residence abroad, during which the influences worked both ways. These include Francesco Turini and Buonamente in Vienna, B. Marini in Neuburg and Düsseldorf, and perhaps Fantini in Frankfurt. When it came to publishing, both categories of Italians generally preferred or felt obliged to send their music back to Venice. With regard to the Germans to be mentioned here, several were trained in Italy, although foreign composers on professional duty in Italy were much less common.

Vienna, one of the world's chief music centers since the end of the 15th century and the reign of Emperor Maximilian I, was to become perhaps the most important center of sonata history by the end of the 18th century. At the Imperial court in the 17th century the marked preference for Italian musicians was gradually modified by the addition of

1. Cf. BURNEY-GERMANY, II, 1 ff. and 17 ff.

increasingly worthy German and native composers, among them Fro-berger, Schmelzer, and Fux. During the Thirty Years' War music for the smaller instrumental ensembles naturally fared better than more elaborate and expensive musical undertakings. But after 1650 opera and oratorio dominated the musical life, exerting their influence as well on instrumental trends.

Our first composer, serving both Ferdinand II and Ferdinand III of the long established Hapsburg family at Graz and Vienna, was the organist **Giovanni Valentini** (?-1649). Valentini came from Venice about 1614, presumably after an intervening period of service at court in Kassel.[2] He is stated to have studied with our first main composer in Italy, Giovanni Gabrieli.[3] Before and after his arrival in Austria, about a dozen sacred and secular vocal collections by him were published in Venice (including one, *Missae quatuor* of 1621, in which he did not hesitate to proclaim the superiority of Italian music). A lost set of *Canzoni per sonar à 4, 5, 6, 8* by him was also published in Venice (before 1621, not 1619).[4] But all of some 11 sonatas by him that are extant are known only in MS.[5]

Valentini's sonatas take us back to the types prevalent in the early 17th century. Seven are multivoice in four or five parts that include the familiar and various combinations of violins, violas, *cornetti,* flutes, trombone, bassoon, and organ bass. Four are SS/bass settings, of which two appear in ANTH. ROSTm. (This last, described further on p. 363 ff., is a remarkable 17th-century MS collection of some 150 instrumental pieces composed before 1688 and consisting mostly of German or Italian sonatas for two violins and *b. c.*[6])

In their own day Valentini's sonatas must have been intended and received as curious experiments, and so they still seem. Essentially they depend for their continuation on variation techniques. The com-poser's method is to create a distinctive, homophonic complex of two or

2. Cf. MEYER, pp. 43, 62 ff., and 92. This study and BECKMANN are two surveys basic to the activities before 1700 as discussed in the present chapter. MEYER includes a valuable bibliography of all types of ensemble music in Germany and of multivoice types in England, the Low Countries, France, Poland, and Scandi-navia. But the aim to include all publications of foreigners resident in Germany and Austria (cf. MEYER, p. 169 ff.) is far from achieved; cf., also, EVANS-DURHAM, p. 210. MEYER-KREMSIER is a further survey of the rich instrumental deposits at the archducal court in the city that is now Kroměříž in Czechoslovakia, at least half of the music being sonatas and many of these by the chief Viennese composers of the Baroque Era.
3. SCHMIDL, II, 639.
4. EITNER-VINCENTI, p. 5; probably the same as the Kassel MS (1613 or earlier) cited in MEYER, p. 63.
5. Cf. MEYER, p. 253, and SCHLOSSBERG, p. 106 ff.
6. Thematic index in BIBLIOTHÈQUE NATIONALE, VIII, 35 ff. Cf. PIRRO-AL-LEMAGNE, p. 922.

more measures, than repeat it indefinitely as a formula, with hardly enough changes in the rhythm and melody to relieve the eventual monotony. Thus, the "Sonata a 5" for two violins, two violas, and *b. c.,* called by Riemann "Enharmonische Sonate,"[7] is based on a two-measure cadence in G minor followed each time by its exact echo, surprisingly enough, a major third higher in B minor.[8] To indicate the echo Valentini used the signs *p, pp,* and even *ppp,* which is their first known use in these graduations. Another "Sonata a 5" begins with its two-measure idea in C, then transposes this to other major or minor keys, including E major next to D minor, and F-sharp minor next to G minor. Occasionally, considerable virtuosity is demanded, although the exact duplication by one instrument of another's part, as in the "Sonata a 4" for violin, *cornettino,* trombone, and bassoon (plus organ bass), belies any idea of idiomatic writing. The SS/bass sonata in ANTH. ROSTm that is subtitled "Aria" proves to be a free set of variations on a free version of the Romanesca tune, in the bass.

An immediate predecessor and a colleague of Valentini in Vienna was **Giovanni Priuli** (?-1629). Probably a native of Venice, too,[9] Priuli similarly published a number of sacred and secular vocal collections there. Among them was *Sacrorum concentum . . . Pars prima* (1618), in which are included two polychoir sonatas in eight instrumental parts (along with ten canzonas in six to eight parts). To judge from Priuli's other successes, these sonatas should be worth exploring.

Likewise unexplored are two sonatas *a 6* and one *a 8* by **Giacomo Arrigoni,** included in his secular vocal collection *Concerti di camera* (Venice, 1635). This composer, probably from the Milan area, was an organist on duty in the Vienna court at least in the later 1630's.[10]

Another who may be added to this same group was the Italian violinist and lutist **Marco Antonio Ferro** (?-1662), who composed 12 *Sonate a due, tre, & quattro* (Venice, 1649) while in Vienna (1642-1658). In this set there are only two melo/bass (SB/bass) sonatas to ten in various multivoice dispositions. But the optional instrumentation that is indicated would seem to convert two of the SAB/bass settings into two more melo/bass types—that is, into the standard "trio" (SSB/bass) setting. Two of the sonatas are for that infrequent combination of four violas and *b. c.* Ferro's sonatas are mostly in four or five movements,

7. Mod. ed.: RIEMANN-CHAMBERm, III, 103.
8. Perhaps it was the shock of this tonal relationship that led Eitner (-QL, X, 24) to suggest Giuseppe Valentini as the true author of these sonatas, a century later!
9. Cf. SARTORI-BIBLIOGRAFIA, item 1626a (preface).
10. SCHMIDL, I, 74, and Supp., p. 42.

with the usual alternation of homophonic adagios and fugal allegros.[11]

Antonio Bertali (or Bartali; 1605-69) was an Italian composer and violinist in Vienna of more renown than any of the four Italians mentioned thus far (cf. p. 117). Born in Verona, where he was a student of Steffano Bernardi,[12] Bertali reached Vienna by 1623 and had already won substantial recognition for his church music by the end of the 1630's. For this and stylistic reasons he is placed in our introductory rather than the second group,[13] although up to at least 1665 he continued to compose dramatic and other music among some 600 works that are mostly now lost. A report of library holdings at the time of Leopold I (Emperor from 1658 to 1705) lists among many other works by Bertali 11 (polychoir?) "Sonate con trombe solenni" in 13 to 18 parts, 17 (multivoice?) "Sonate ordinare per Chiesa à 5 & 6," 10 "Sonate a tre" of which several are for two violins and trombone, and 12 (melo/bass and multivoice?) "Sonate da camera a 3, 5, & 8."[14] However, the sonatas now known by him comprise a somewhat different list. There are perhaps two dozen MS sonatas in a variety of melo/bass and multivoice settings of from one to eight *concertante* parts, including five sonatas in ANTH. ROSTM.[15] And there are two collections credited to Bertali that were published

Ex. 43.   From the opening of Sonata "Taussent Gulden" by Antonio Bertali (after a score prepared by Ross Lee Finney from ANTH. ROSTm, no. 38 [not 37]).

11. Cf. SCHLOSSBERG, pp. 23, 27, 30, 31, and 33 (with examples).
12. SCHMIDL, I, 168. It is also interesting to find "la Merula" as the title of one of his sonatas in ANTH. ROSTM (no. 75).
13. MEYER, p. 114, not having the life dates, puts Bertali in the next generation on the basis of a publication that was actually posthumous.
14. MGG, I, 1798 ff. (Liess).
15. Cf. MEYER, p. 185; BODLEIAN MSS, V, 221; BIBLIOTHÈQUE NATIONALE, III, 35 ff. (with thematic index).

posthumously. *Thesaurus musicus* for three instruments (Dillingen, 1671) can no longer be found. But a copy of *Prothimia suavissima* (Leipzig, 1672), containing 12 sonatas in as many as 8 (not 3 or 4) parts, is in Paris.[16]

As suggested by the early titles, Bertali's sonatas were primarily vehicles for festive, pompous music. Even the sonatas in ANTH. ROSTm, with their relatively simple and more modern settings, often have the character of a fanfare (Ex. 43). These are already made up of a variety of movements contrasting in meter, with tempo changes sometimes indicated. Some striking "key" changes are hinted, too, although the grasp of tonality is still too uncertain to say whether modal cadences were not the basis. Except for brief imitations, homophony prevails. The figuration is limited in variety and pitch range.

Germany (*Farina, Kindermann*)

In Germany proper there were only four men who can be named here for sonatas composed up to 1650, two in the southern and one each in the central and northern regions. The one Italian among them, apart from the less permanent residents mentioned earlier, was the exceptional violinist **Carlo Farina** (*ca.* 1600-*ca.* 1640). Starting like Marini, Rossi, and Buonamente, as one of the Mantuan violinists under Monteverdi, Farina went to Dresden in central Germany in 1625. There he played under and worked closely with the great Heinrich Schütz for four years, after which he can be found only in Danzig in 1637 and perhaps once more in Italy.[17] Five books by Farina, made up variously of 109 separate dances, 5 sinfonias, 2 canzonas, one programmatic piece, and 10 sonatas *a 2-4* were published in Dresden in 1626, 1627, and 1628. Sonatas occur only at the end of Books 1, 4, and 5. They and the few sinfonias and canzonas differ from almost all the other pieces in being in only two or three rather than four parts, including both SS/- and S/bass settings. Thus, only melo/bass sonatas by Farina are known.

Farina is chiefly remembered as an innovator in the realm of violin technique, one who had considerable influence on Vierdanck, J. J. Walther, Westhoff, and other 17th-century Germans. His most novel devices, such as the use of glissando, *col legno,* tremolo, *pizzicato,* or *sul ponticello* to imitate animal and other sounds in pieces like "Capricio stravagante,"[18] are less used in the sonatas. But the latter are often programmatic. Thus, the two SS/bass sonatas called "la Polaca" (Bk.

16. BIBLIOTHÈQUE NATIONALE, III, 36.
17. Cf. MGG, III, 1822 ff. (Hausswald) ; EITNER-QL, III, 388.
18. Mod. ed.: WASIELEWSKI-XVIIm, no. 11 (incomplete) ; cf. BECKMANN, p. 14 ff. (including Farina's important performance advices) and Anhang no. 3.

1) and "la Cingara" (Bk. 4) have characteristic Polish and Hungarian rhythms, respectively, "la Capriola" has long trills with suffixes, and "la desperata," *a 2* (Bk. 5), makes much use of the G string, which was otherwise so seldom used at this time.[19]   As musical forms the sonatas seem less significant.   Melody, harmony, and tonality are all too restricted and repetitious in their treatment to justify the unprecedented lengths of these pieces—some 230 measures in about a dozen sections in "la Polaca"![20]   The structural method is usually the additive one of the motet in which points of imitation are strung together, often with similar incipits as in the variation *ricercare*.

The first German composer whom we know in the mainstream of the Baroque sonata was the Nürnberg organist **Johann Staden** (1581-1634). His sonatas cannot be dated except by his year of death (caused, like G. B. Fontana's in Italy, by the plague).   All of them occur, among "the wealth of MSS he left behind," as 10 of the 70 pieces in the incompletely preserved *Operum musicorum posthumorum . . . Sonat, pavan, canzon, symphonias*, etc. *a 3, 4, 5, 6, 7, 8* (Nürnberg, 1643).[21] Only dances, a few canzonas, and a fantasia are to be found among the instrumental pieces in the 19 sacred and secular collections that had been published during his lifetime.   Unfortunately, no sonata is included in the two volumes of representative pieces by him that have been made available.   But the sonatas are described in the detailed preface and are stated to be very like Staden's sinfonias, eight of which did get into the second of these volumes.[22]

Staden's 10 sonatas include 7 *a 3,* at least some of which are SS/bass types, plus 2 *a 4* and one *a 6* that are multivoice.   Most of the instrumental parts merely specify pitch ranges, but one is marked "Cum Basso ad Organum et Clavicembolo," this use of the cembalo being the first such known in German music.   The similarity of the sonatas and sinfonias tends to be corroborated by one instance in which both terms appear over different instrumental parts of the same piece (No. 31 in the 1643 set).   But the distinct differences between the dances, with their regular meters and binary designs, and the sonatas or sinfonias merely belie a like equation of pavane and sonata that occurs (No. 3).   The canzonas stand somewhat apart, too.   They have the conventional canzona opening and the characteristic A-B-A plan in which two similar

---

19. Cf. MOSER-VIOLINSPIEL, p. 95 ff.

20. As edited in RIEMANN-CHAMBERm, III, 88.   The opening of "la Franzosina" (Bk. 1) is given in BECKMANN, Anhang no. 4.

21. Cf. MEYER, p. 249; but it is the Cantus 3 and Tenor 1 parts that are no longer extant (DTBM, VII, Part 1, xxv).

22. DTBM, VII, Part 1, lxi ff., and VIII, Part 1 (both Schmitz), 122 ff.   Cf. MEYER, p. 60 ff.

fugal sections are separated by a contrasting, sometimes homophonic section. On the other hand, the sonatas and sinfonias are the homophonic, preludial, free types of 10 to 30 measures that often introduced Baroque German vocal works and help to corroborate the fantasy concept that we found to underlie most Baroque definitions of the sonata. Loose rondo forms can be found in some of the sonatas—for instance, A-B-A-C-A (No. 1) or AB-C-AB-D-AB-E (No. 30). In the latter plan the AB combines a chordal section with a section of long notes in triple meter.

Staden's pupil in Nürnberg, the organist **Johann Erasmus Kindermann** (1616-55), was even more prolific in similar categories of publications, but with considerably more emphasis on instrumental music. He, too, is represented in modern editions by two volumes of selected pieces, prefaced by detailed studies.[23]   In the second of these volumes are 8 of the 18 sonatas that can be credited to Kindermann, including 3 of the 10 SS/- and 5 of the 6 S/bass sonatas. The other two, not represented, are an SSS/bass sonata (three violas and *b. c.*) and an unusual sonata for violin, viola, optional alto voice ("Voce alto concertato, se piace"), and *b. c.* Four of the earlier and slightest sonatas are called by the infrequent diminutive, "Sonetta."

In the instrumental domain, besides important sets of church organ music, keyboard suites, and violin music in *scordatura* (lost), Kindermann published six sets of ensemble music. These last include his sonatas. Four of them make up the four books of *Deliciae studiosorum,* published in Nürnberg in 1640, 1642 (two), and 1643, and followed by several reprints. Book 3 is fully extant, but most of the part books for the other three books are now lost. Books 1 and 4 include other composers, especially Frescobaldi and Salomone Rossi. Nearly all of the pieces are in the SS/bass setting for two *cornetti* and trombone or two flutes and bassoon (or alto flute!) with two violins or violas and *b. c.* as optional instruments. The fifth and sixth sets, Kindermann's last known publications, are "Pars prior" and "Pars posterior" of *Canzoni, sonatae,* for one to four violins and *b. c.* (both Nürnberg, 1653).[24]

The sonatas in the last two sets differ strikingly from those in the extant set of 1643. The earlier sonatas are like Staden's in being the short preludial type, with a degree of pomp in their simple affirmation

23. DTBM, XIII (Schreiber) and XXI-XXIV (Schreiber & Wallner). Kindermann could have been in close touch with Biagio Marini in nearby Neuberg, as Wallner suggests (p. xxxi), but he would have been only between the ages of 7 and 11 (cf. ISELIN, p. 3 ff.).

24. The attempt to relate these two sets to the two of M. Neri in 1644 and 1651 in DTBM, XIII, lxxxiv, seems to have no special basis other than a near coincidence of titles.

of key. Occasionally, there are metric changes, in sections too fleeting to be called movements, so that the resulting impression of fantasy is increased. On the other hand, the "solo" sonatas in the two 1653 sets are full-scale, developed pieces in five or six movements. Totalling up to 100 measures, they are on the way to those of the later 17th century. Although the technical demands and the devices such as tremolo are limited, Kindermann wrote these sonatas with an excellent understanding of the violin fingerboard. And it is quite possible that double-stops were actually intended at various points. Like 32d-note beams, they had to be added by hand if they were to appear in German scores of the time. Otherwise they can only be discovered when a comparison with the MS is possible.[25] The straightforward homophony and compelling chromatic harmony in the sonatas have an expressive depth that recalls Heinrich Schütz's choral writing, while the lines have a breadth unusual at the middle of the century (Ex. 44). The movements are effectively

Ex. 44. From the second movement of "Sonata a Violino Solo" from *Canzoni, sonatae II,* No. 2, by Johann Erasmus Kindermann (after DTBm, XXI-XXIV, 79).

juxtaposed through contrasts of meter, style, and tempo (which is frequently indicated).

Kindermann's sonatas generally differ from his canzonas in the same ways that Staden's were seen to differ. In Kindermann's sonatas can also be found some of those stunts so favored in the 17th-century sonata, especially in Germany. Thus, one SS/bass sonata in each of the 1653 sets is marked "vice versa" to indicate the canonic type we have seen in

25. Cf. BECKMANN, pp. 18 ff. and 49.

Uccellini and others—that in which the second violin part is derived by reading the first backwards. Another, in the first of these sets, is called "Giardino corrupto" (maze) because the second violin part is derived by skipping irregularly about the first according to a series of numbered directions! And the third "solo" sonata in the second set makes use of *scordatura* throughout, with the notation transposed accordingly.

Between the sonatas composed by Staden and Kindermann came those published by the last figure to be noted in our early group. **Johann Vierdanck** (*ca*. 1612-46) was in Stralsund in north Germany by 1641, the year of his two instrumental publications. Before then he had served in points as far apart as Copenhagen and Vienna, including an early assignment under Schütz in Dresden. Probably he knew Farina in Dresden and could even have studied with him. In any case, he uses very similar titles and his structural methods recall Farina's. The writing is deliberately more restrained in technical range, with only a few double-stops, but reveals much the same variation-*ricercare* procedures and much the same mechanical sequences.

Vierdanck's only known sonatas are five among the 31 pieces in the "Ander Theil" of his two sets. This set, which he tells us is different from the other with its dances, is entitled *Capricci, Canzoni und Sonaten* for two to five instruments "without and with" *b. c.*[26] One of the sonatas is among 14 pieces without *b. c.*, intended "not for skilled masters but . . . for young musicians." It is the first sonata we have met after Fantini's trumpet duos of 1638 (p. 125) in the sizable literature of unaccompanied duos yet to come.[27] The other four sonatas are of varied melo/bass and multivoice types. According to such miscellaneous information as can be gleaned,[28] one is an SSSS/bass setting with close imitations, another is for three trombones embellished by the sequential diminutions of a *concertante cornetto* part, another falls loosely into the A-B-A-B-A rondo plan, and the last (the final piece of the set) is an SSBBB/bass setting for *cornetti* and trombones, based on a banal student song, "Als ich einmal Lust bekam." This last sonata was exceptional, if not unique, in its way. It alternates each of several *tutti-soli* treatments of some section in the song with a *tutti* statement of the same section in unison, ritornello fashion. The ritornello was probably a facetious gesture on Vierdanck's part.

26. See the composer's foreword in fascimile in MGG, II, 817.
27. Mod. eds.: BECKMANN, Anhang no. 15; HORTUSm, no. 21 (Engel, with preface; but three sonatas, items 27 to 29, are omitted from a list of the contents in the 1641 publication).
28. MEYER. pp. 64, 74, 109, 117, and 119 ff.

Chapter 11

Austria and Germany from about 1650 to 1700

Our second group of sonata composers active in Austria and Germany introduces more than six times as many names as the introductory group, although the number of resident Italians does not increase. Among the names are now such important figures, all natives, as Biber in Vienna, Kuhnau in Leipzig, and Buxtehude in Lübeck. There is a corresponding increase in Austrian and German publishing, too. As with our second group of Italians, it already becomes impossible even to mention all those who are known to have left sonatas. After the Peace of Westphalia (1648) the Empire became more than ever a basis for wide cultural exchanges that extended well beyond its more immediate confines. Thus, the Emperor himself, in Austria, also ruled Bohemia, Belgium, important parts of Italy, and, by the end of the century, Hungary. Other regions were being brought into the Empire's sphere by the heads of the internal sovereignties, especially the King of Prussia and the Elector of Hanover.

Austria (*Young, Schmelzer, Biber, Muffat*)

In Austria under Leopold I the new emphasis on opera and oratorio may have kept the sonata production from growing as fast as that in Germany. As against the four composers in our introductory group there are now few more to mention—seven in all, including three Austrians, three Italians, and one Englishman. First on the list is the Englishman. He is **William Young** (?-1671), a flutist and violinist who published a melo/bass collection of 11 sonatas and 19 dances in Innsbruck (1653) while there in the employ of the Archduke.[1] In MSS by

1. Listed in CAT. UPSALA, II, 155 ff. WHITTAKER-YOUNG is the main source, supplemented by new biographic information in EVANS-DURHAM, p. 221 ff., although this in turn is directly contradicted by considerable new information in

him that are preserved at the Durham Cathedral, there are also at least 5 more sonatas *a 2* or *a 3,* including examples of that frequent 17th-century SB/bass setting of violin, viola da gamba, and *b. c.*[2] Young may have been a refugee from the Commonwealth, since he returned to England with the Restoration (1660).

Young's sonatas of 1653 include 3 of the SSB/-, 7 of the SSSB/-, and one of the SSSSB/bass type. Violins and violas da gamba are specified. Whereas his dances are merely grouped by types in the then usual manner, leaving the players to make suites of their own choosing, each of the sonatas is a well-planned cycle of three to five contrasting movements, with frequent tempo titles rather than dance ones. Especially worth noting is the early appearance of the fugal "canzona" as one of the separate movements of each sonata, usually in a central position but occasionally at the end. We shall meet this use of the canzona again when we come to the sonatas of Purcell, who may well have known Young and his music.

The more homophonic sections in Young's sonatas breathe the spirit of the English catch, with clear metric patterns that resemble Purcell's in their concentration on the bar accent. The more polyphonic sections show the exceptional rhythmic independence of parts that had characterized the Elizabethan madrigal and was still to be found in the English viol fantasias. But even for the home of those two forms Young's dissonance treatment is striking, what with its free resolutions, frequent lack of preparation—the subject in the "Canzona" of Sonata 4 enters several times on a major second—and false relations. The writing for violins suits them well although the pitch range is fairly narrow and the passagework fairly elementary. There is evident none of the German predilection for stunts, either intellectual or technical. Two of the most interesting sonatas are No. 4 in SSSB/- and No. 11 in SSSSB/bass settings. In these, as in the other sonatas, the canzonas, with their bright angular rhythms, tuneful subjects, and imaginatively placed entries, have a special attraction. Nor should the depth of the slower movements be overlooked.

The three Italians to be named in Austria were of minor importance to the sonata as compared with two of the three Austrians, Schmelzer and Biber. One was **Giovanni Antonio Pandolfi Mealli** (from Perugia?), also in Innsbruck and perhaps Young's successor there. He is remembered only for two collections of six "solo" violin sonatas each, "per

<hr>

SENN-INNSBRUCK, p. 262 (including a death date of 1662!). Southgate's mention of 26 sonatas by Young in BRIDGE-PURCELL, p. 12, seems to be an error. Mod. ed.: Sons. 1-11, WHITTAKER-YOUNGM.

2. Cf. MEYER, p. 148; EVANS-DURHAM, p. 211 ff.

chiesa e camera." These are Opp. 3 and 4, both published in Innsbruck in 1660. In one of the church sonatas available to this study (Op. 3, No. 4), both the slow and the fast movements keep the violin going in the free manner of the toccata, over a generally static bass. This was the procedure often used, with more effect and imagination, by Stradella.

Another Italian, this one in Vienna, was the organist **Alessandro Poglietti** (?-1683), best known for his witty, programmatic keyboard music.[3] His sonatas, like virtually all else that he wrote, were left only in MSS. They have yet to be examined. Seven are known, including three SS/bass and four multivoice settings.[4] The largest setting is that 4a of a sonata *a 8* for two violins, two *clarini,* four viols, and organ.

The third Italian active in Austria was a Venetian opera composer in the circle of Cavalli and Cesti, **Pietro Andrea Ziani** (*ca.* 1620-1711 ?).[5] He was in Vienna at least from 1664 to 1667 and again after he had (been?) retired in Naples in 1684, probably right up to the supposed year of his death. His one published sonata collection (Op. 7) appeared in Venice in 1678, shortly after he had left his post as first organist at St. Mark's to go to Naples. Where and when the sonatas had been composed and whether Venice would more properly be the locale in which to place him remain a mystery. But in the reprint published in Freiberg (near Dresden), probably in 1691,[6] Ziani calls himself "maestro di cappella" to the Empress Leonora (the third wife of Leopold I from 1676 to his death in 1705).[7] This reprint adds 6 new sonatas, making 20 in all. In MSS there are also 6 (not 7) multivoice sonatas *a 5* for strings plus another *a 6* for strings with trumpet, in Oxford,[8] and a sonata *a 4* in Vienna.[9] Furthermore, there is a lively fugal organ sonata, subtitled "Capriccio," in ANTH. ARRESTIm.

The ensemble sonatas by Ziani remain to be scored and examined in any detail. Those in the first edition include 4 in "trio" setting and 10 in multivoice settings *a 4-6.* The movements—usually three, in the order of fugal, homophonic, fugal—are still called "Prima Parte," and so on, as they had been called by Biagio Marini in Venice. Elaborate

---

3. Cf. DTÖm, XIII, Part 2 (Botstiber). Further biographic information in KOCZIRZ.
4. DTÖm, XIII, xviii. Cf. a letter by Poglietti given in NETTL-WIENER, p. 174, mentioning the church use of one of his sonatas.
5. Cf. SCHMIDL, II, 730, in which an attempt is made to correct conflicting biographic information. But certain contrary evidence must be preferred, especially that in KRETZSCHMAR-WEITERE and the 1691 title to be mentioned.
6. Cf. SARTORI-BIBLIOGRAFIA, item 1691g. The only known copy of this edition is mistakenly listed under Zeutschner in BIBLIOTHÈQUE NATIONALE, VIII, 217.
7. Yet this title may have meant only an acting post. Cf. KRETZSCHMAR-WEITERE, p. 62.
8. CAT. CHRIST CHURCH, I, 128.
9. SCHLOSSBERG, p. 107.

cadences at the end of each movement tend to make for exceptional breaks from one to the next.[10]

Johann Heinrich Schmelzer (*ca.* 1623-80), hailed in 1660 as "the celebrated and nearly finest *violisten* in all Europe," served as musician at the Imperial court from 1649 and as instrumental composer from 1665 or earlier. In 1673 he was ennobled by the Emperor and in 1679 he followed in the line of the Italians Valentini, Bertali, and G. F. Sances to become "the first German *kaiserlicher Hofkapellmeister*," only to die a few months later from another of those disastrous waves of the plague.[11]   11a His extant published and MS sonatas, totalling around 85 separate pieces, give first place to SS/- or SSB/bass "trio" settings (about 49 per cent) ; second place to multivoice settings, including polychoir (33 per cent) ; and third place to S/- or SB/bass "solo" settings (18 per cent).

Three of Schmelzer's known publications, issued in Nürnberg in 1659 (not 1669), 1662, and 1664, contain sonatas. *Duodena selectarum sonatarum* contains six SS/- and three SB/- and SSB/bass pieces each called "sonata" or "sonatina," with violins, violas da gamba, and organ (*b. c.*) specified. *Sacro-profanus concentus musicus fidium* contains one SS/bass   11b sonata and 12 multivoice types for use in the church, including 2 *a 8* (one of them scored in 2 choirs), 1 *a 7,* 4 *a 6,* 3 *a 5,* and 2 *a 4.* The same strings plus *cornettini,* trumpets, and trombones are specified. *Sonatae unarum fidium* contains 6 S/bass "solo" sonatas, the earliest German publication made up exclusively of this type.[12] Among the sonatas left   12a in MSS in various libraries, 17 in SS/bass and 2 (*a 4*) in multivoice settings are to be found in ANTH. ROSTm ;[13] and 24 melo/bass and multivoice types *a 2-7* are preserved in the Uppsala library. Mention must be   13a made, too, of Schmelzer's use of the title "sonata" or "sonatina" for the initial movement of a suite, as it was often used in the 17th-century German sonata (cf. p. 249). He used it thus from 1672 or earlier in at least a half dozen of the many ballet suites that he wrote for operas given at the Imperial court.[14]

In these suites the scoring is generally orchestral, of course, as it is in some of the MS sonatas and some of the 1662 set. For instance, one

---

10. Cf. SCHLOSSBERG, pp. 43, 45, and 50.
11. NETTL-WIENER, p. 119 ff., a valuable study of this period in Vienna, is the main biographic source, including bibliographic information on the sonata publications and a few of the MSS; see also NETTL-FORGOTTEN, p. 1 ff. MEYER, p. 243 ff., gives a comprehensive list of the sonatas.
12. The complete set is scored in EINSTEIN-SCOREsm, IV. Discussion in BECKMANN, p. 56 ff. Mod. ed.: Son. 3, BECKMANNm, II, no. 6.
13. Thematic index in BIBLIOTHÈQUE NATIONALE, VIII, 23 ff. Mod ed.: No. 10 ("Polnische Sackspfeiffen"), PIRRO-ALLEMAGNE, p. 992.
14. Mod. eds.: DTöm, XXVIII, Part 2 (Nettl), nos. 5, 6, and 13.

introductory "Sonatina" calls for three trumpets, two violins, two violas, *violone,* two timpani, and organ *b. c.*[15]   There is also an introductory "Sonatina" in a MS clavier suite dated 1681 by Schmelzer, being the first use of this term or "sonata" known to this study in German or Austrian keyboard music.[16]   (Previously, Froberger, the great German keyboard master at the Vienna court, had been like his teacher Frescobaldi in not using the word "sonata" as a title.)

Schmelzer's first two sonata publications have not been made available in score.   The third set, the "solo" set of 1664, shows him to be a composer largely dependent on the variation principle for the extension of his instrumental forms.   By this means he is able to exploit the violin's idiom with good understanding although no unusual virtuosity or characteristic German stunts.   But when he occasionally attempts to get along without it he is like some of his Italian predecessors who could write "abstract" instrumental music only in short spans.   Each idea quickly spends itself and reaches for a cadence, to be succeeded by another idea that similarly spends itself.   The result is then a kaleidoscope of meters, tempos, and styles.   Thus, the first "solo" sonata begins with some 40 measures of successively different phrases before the security of a six-measure *ostinato* is attained.   Even during the 70-odd measures of variations that follow there are tempo and meter changes, after which comes another free section similar in style to the opening. Sonatas 2, 3, and 4 are nothing but variations, No. 4 being based on a descending, diatonic tetrachord that recurs throughout in four-measure units of whole-notes.   The same short spans are to be found in Schmelzer's brief introductory orchestral sonatas and in his "trio" sonatas in ANTH. ROSTm.   The latter are mostly programmatic, with effects appropriate to such titles as "Polnische Sackspfeiffen," "Pastorella," and "Lamento."   In all this music the melodic and rhythmic interest seems greater than the harmonic.

With further regard to Schmelzer's special handling of form it is instructive to see the spans lengthen, with correspondingly fewer sections, in two MS sonatas dated 8 and 13 years later, one in SB/bass setting (1672) and the other in SSB/bass setting (1677).[17]   A significant factor in these is Schmelzer's apparent advance in the art of motivic discourse.

Outstanding as a sonata composer and the foremost violinist among the Austrians and Germans of the 17th century, as Burney still acknowledged a century later,[18] was **Heinrich Ignaz Franz Biber** (1644-1704).

15. On the scoring of the orchestral church sonatas see NETTL-WIENER, p. 106 ff.
16. Cf. NETTL-WIENER, p. 147.
17. Uppsala MSS Caps. 58-7 and 58-11, in EINSTEIN-SCORESm, IV.
18. -HISTORY, II, 462.

This virtuoso entered the service of the Archbishop of Salzburg about 1676, after holding a post in Bohemia under the rule of Leopold I. Advancing by rapid stages to the position of Hauptkapellmeister in 1684, he was ennobled in 1690.[19]   A few operas and sacred choral works are known by Biber, but his main output consisted of sonatas and related instrumental music.

About 57 sonatas by Biber can now be cited, of which 25 are "solo" (S/bass), 25 are multivoice, and only 7 are "trio" settings.   These are found in 5 of 7 instrumental collections by him that are known.   Three of the 5 were published between the years 1676 and 1684 and 2 were left in MS.[20]   The total of 57 does not include lost collections nor the use of "sonata" or "sonatina," as Schmelzer and others of the time used it, to mean an introductory movement.   The latter use occurs in some suites of Biber's other two instrumental collections—*Mensa sonora* and *Harmonia artificiosa,* published in 1680 and 1693—and in at least one ballet suite.[21]

Probably the earliest of Biber's sonata collections is that of the 16 "Rosary [or "Mystery"] Sonatas" for solo violin and bass (*ca.* 1674).[22] This is the set for which he is now chiefly remembered, although it is one of his two sonata collections that remained in MSS.   Of the 16 sonatas 15 are devoted to the 15 Mysteries of the Rosary—5 to the joyful, 5 to the sorrowful, and 5 to the glorious Mysteries.   The 16th sonata is a "Passagaglia" for unaccompanied violin solo, the first such sonata setting that we have met here.   It is based on that favorite *ostinato* and fugal subject of the 17th century, the descending tetrachord.   In this instance the four notes are g'-f'-eb'-d', the same with which the song "Einen Engel Gott mir geben" begins.   One must understand that this song of the guardian angel had been specially linked with the Rosary in Salzburg and that the honoring of the Rosary every October was especially emphasized in that city.[23]   Accompanying each sonata in the MS is a picture appropriate to the particular Mystery, much as pictures had occurred beside the successive "scenes" in Froberger's well-known *Lamento* on Ferdinand IV, for clavier.   However, except in rare instances (as in Ex. 45) and contrary to some references to them, these sonatas are not programmatic in the more literal sense of Kuhnau's

19. For biographic and general discussions cf. DTöm, V, Part 2 (Adler), v ff.; NETTL-FORGOTTEN, p. 17 ff. (including some information about the sonatas that is viewed differently here).

20. Cf. the list in MEYER, p. 188 ff.; but two of the publications given are probably only reprints of the 1676 and 1681 sets.

21. Cf. DTöm, V, Part 2, vii ff.   The 1693 date comes from MEYER, p. 189.

22. Among mod. eds. of the entire set: DTöm, XII, Part 2 (Luntz).; REITZm.

23. Cf. SCHMITZ-BIBER; also, BECKMANN, p. 68 ff.

"Biblical Sonatas" 25 years later. At most they are symbolic in the sense that Bach's organ chorale preludes are, being Biber's way, through music alone, of expressing his piety.

In 1676 Biber's 12 *Sonatae tam aris quam aulis servientes,* appropriate "to the altar or the court," were published in Salzburg. These sonatas are variously scored in 5, 6, or 8 parts for 2 trumpets, 2 violins, 4 violas (SATB), and organ or cembalo *b. c.* Hence, they border on the orchestral type, being surpassed in number of instruments only by his MS "Sonata pro Tabula" for 5 flutes, 2 violins, 3 violas, and organ. The sequence S-F-F is said to be well developed,[24] but the sonatas await further study.[25]

A set of 8 more "solo" (S/bass) violin sonatas by Biber was published in Salzburg in 1681 (the year of Corelli's Op. 1 in Rome).[26] Although these include some dances among their movements, they do not fall clearly into either the church or court category. In the last sonata the solo part was originally published on two staffs but meant to be played on one violin as double-stops, "gara di due Violine in uno."

The fourth known sonata collection by Biber is *Fidicinium sacroprofanum* (i.e., for church or court, again), Op. 4, published in Zürich between 1680 and 1684.[27] It contains 12 sonatas, half *a 5* and half *a 4,* described as vigorous, contrapuntally skillful, and diatonic. No dances occur among the 3 to 8 movements that are to be found in each sonata.

Finally, a MS set of six "trio" (SS/bass) sonatas in the library at Wolfenbüttel should be mentioned,[28] although it seems not to have been explored.

In his sonatas Biber reveals definite ties with Schmelzer and may actually have studied with the latter.[29] The instrumentation and kinds of settings by the two men are very similar. Biber's title *Fidicinium sacroprofanum* recalls two of the titles that Schmelzer had used. And Biber has the same free variety as well as the same types of movements, of which the core, both in length and weight, is again the set of variations over an *ostinato* bass. But technically as well as musically Biber surpassed Schmelzer in many ways.

On the technical side, he carried his passages into the seventh position, employed bariolage often, rivalled J. J. Walther in his use of

24. DTÖm, V, Part 2, vii ff.
25. Further mention of orchestral sonatas by Biber occurs in MEYER-KREMSIER.
26. Mod. ed.: DTÖm, V, Part 2.
27. Mod. ed.: Son. 10, in NEF-DEUTSCHEN, p. 63; cf. p. 26 ff.; with the same publication three more sonatas and part of another from this set were originally advertised as being separately available "in manuscript" from the publisher.
28. MEYER, p. 189.
29. Cf. NETTL-WIENER, pp. 122 and 128.

multiple stops, and exploited *scordatura* to a point never since sur-passed.[30] These are all aspects of technique that Schmelzer had de-veloped only slightly, although we have seen that multiple stops and *scordatura* do have a still earlier German and Italian ancestry. When *scordatura* was not used merely as a novelty, it had the chief advantages of technical convenience and new sonorities or effects. Thus, open strings could be "mistuned" to the primary tones in the key of the piece, double-stops could be played by one finger on two adjacent strings, and programmatic effects such as a drone bass could be achieved. It is possible that the device, with its strange-looking transpositions and key signatures, was associated symbolically with "Mystery" in Biber's mind, for it is used in all but the first and last of the "Rosary Sonatas," yet in only two of the "solo" sonatas of 1681 and only occasionally in the "trio" settings of the suites. (In "Rosary Sonata" 11 the *scordatura* is so surprising—e″-a′-d′-g becomes d″-d′-g′-g, respectively!—that the editor of the Austrian *Denkmäler* edition failed to understand it, first arriving at a very unsatisfactory solution and only later issuing a corrected version.[31]) Example 45 includes the instruction "Solo Violone" over the *b. c.* part, meaning that the usual organ or cembalo realization should be omitted at that point so as not to obliterate the imitation of the timpani by the stringed bass (one of the infrequent programmatic effects in these sonatas).

Ex. 45.   From the second movement of Heinrich Ignaz Franz Biber's twelfth "Rosary Sonata" (after DTÖm, XII, Part 2, 59, but without the *b. c.* realization).

Musically, Biber went beyond Schmelzer in nearly everything that then contributed to structural organization. There is greater thematic unity because Biber had greater contrapuntal and harmonic resources by which to keep the theme's reiterations interesting. There is greater over-all unity, too, as the result of greater integration and interrelation-ship of the movements, which include, besides the almost invariable set of variations, dances (even in the "Rosary Sonatas" though not in

30. Cf. MOSER-SKORDATUR.   31. Cf. SCHNEIDER-BIBER.

Fidicinium sacroprofanum), arias, toccata-like sections, and a few polyphonic movements.   Thus, within the eight movements of Sonata 1
from *Fidicinium sacroprofanum* the same "Adagio" recurs four times,
with changes, in rondo fashion as every alternate movement.[32]   There is
also greater rhythmic organization at the phrase level, producing a new
tunefulness and balance, even in the more polyphonic passages (Ex. 46).
All in all, Biber's music has considerable appeal.   The best known "solo"

Ex. 46.   From the fourth movement of Sonata 10 in
Fidicinium sacroprofanum by Heinrich Ignaz Franz Biber
(after NEF-DEUTSCHEN, p. 67).

sonatas would probably figure more on programs if violinists did not
find it so impractical to "mistune" their modern violin strings.

Together, Biber and his almost exact contemporary **Georg Muffat**
(1653-1704) brought music to a peak in Salzburg's rich history. Muffat,
the last name in Austria to figure in our second group, was an organist
in the Archbishop's chapel in Salzburg for 11 years, from 1678 to 1689.[33]
There he composed nearly all the music known by him, although it was
not published until he moved to Passau[34] (not far north, on the German
side of the border), where he became Kapellmeister to the Bishop in
1690.   The chief exceptions were most of the five sonatas we are about
to discuss, which were composed in 1682 during a stay in Rome.[35]   In
all, Muffat left five instrumental collections.   These were all published,
between 1682 and 1701, and contain everything now known by him,
since none of his MSS is extant.[36]   The first publication is the one of

33a

32. NEF-DEUTSCHEN, p. 28.   33. DTÖM, LXXXIX (Schenk), vii.
34. DTÖM, I, Part 2 (Rietsch), vi.   35. DTÖM, XI, Part 2 (Luntz), 105.
36. Cf. MEYER, p. 227.

primary concern here, *Armonico tributo cioé Sonate di camera commodissime a pocchi, ò a molti stromenti* (Salzburg, 1682).[37]   In this set are five multivoice sonatas, all scored for two violins, two violas, and *violone* with cembalo.   The succeeding four collections include the 15 suites for strings in the two sets of the *Florilegium* (1695 and 1698), the toccatas and *versetti* for organ in *Apparatus musico-organisticus* (1690), and the 12 concerti grossi in *Auserlesener . . . Instrumentalmusic* (1701). By 1953 four sets had been made available in the Austrian *Denkmäler* series and the other set (1690) separately.[38]

Muffat's five sonatas in the 1682 set are in five to seven movements that mix church and court types, in spite of the over-all title.   There are slow and fast dances, on the one hand, and there are weighty and light movements of a freer sort that have only tempo inscriptions, on the other hand.   One "Fuga" and one "Passacaglia" occur, both, as might be expected, in the final sonata.   These sonatas have an important bearing on one of Muffat's chief claims to fame, his share in the early concerto grosso.   In his highly informative, quadrilingual foreword to the 1701 set of concerti grossi,[39] which is a much expanded and reworked version of the Italian foreword to the sonatas of 1682,[40] Muffat tells us the sonatas were composed after hearing concerti grossi by Corelli in Rome (some 32 years before Corelli's Op. 6 appeared in print).   That the sonatas themselves were intended as such is further confirmed by Muffat's regular use of "T" and "S" for *tutti* and *soli* passages in nearly every movement including the "Fuga," and by his precise explanation of the "concerto grosso" and "concertino" dispositions, even in the 1682 foreword.   Valuable insight into Corelli's performance practices is gained through Muffat's comments on alternative scorings, including the irreducible minimum of the "trio" setting, the preferred instruments for reinforcing the bass, the choice of soprano instruments, and important matters of tone, dynamics, tempo, texture, repetitions, bowing, pauses, and emotional quality.   Furthermore, a remarkable insight into the growth of a composer is gained by comparing the original five sonatas with Concertos 5, 4, 2, 11, and 10 in the 1701 set, for these five concertos are actually none other than Sonatas 1 to 5, respectively, thoroughly recast. The movements are changed in position and length, or deleted, or

37. Mod. eds.: incomplete, DTöm, XI, Part 2 (including the title pages, dedications, and notes to the "friendly reader" in four languages); complete, DTöm, LXXXIX (with a valuable study of the international influences).

38. The other three sets in DTöm are in I, Part 2, II, Part 2, XI, Part 2, and LXXXIX, respectively; the 1690 set is published by Peters and others.

39. DTöm, XI, Part 2, 8 ff.; English translation in STRUNK-READINGS, p. 449 ff.

40. DTöm, XI, Part 2, 118.

replaced. The harmony and texture are enriched, with correspondingly more figures in the *b. c.* The dances are more fully ornamented. And the syntax is changed into simpler, broader, and more balanced phrases.

Another interesting aspect of Muffat's sonatas concerns his internationally "mixed style," of which he himself makes special mention on more than one occasion.[41] Indeed, what other composer could boast of having studied under Lully, Pasquini, and Corelli? From the French the sonatas derive, for example, the French overture, the rondeau, and such newer dances as the gavotte, bourrée, and minuet (before G. B. Vitali's use of the minuet in Modena). From the Italians they derive the freer, slow, introductory movements, the pathos, the melodic styles, and the figuration or, in Muffat's own words, "certain profound and unusual affects of the Italian manner, various capricious and artful conceits. . . ."[42] And from his own German-Austrian background the sonatas derive their organization into suites, with a "sonata" in one or more sections as the introductory movement and with similar incipits in some of the movements of the same cycle. As for certain concerto traits in these sonatas, such as the interplay of solo passages, precedents existed no more remote than the sonatas that A. Bertali and Schmelzer had composed at the Imperial court.

Muffat's use of "sonata" to mean introductory movement is worth noting, too.[43] In *Florilegium* the quadrilingual titles for the first movements of the suites include "Ouverture" in French, "Exordium" or "Praeludium" in Latin, "Vorspiel" or "Eingang" in German, and "Introduzione" or "Sonata" in Italian. Actually, as we have seen, this meaning of "sonata" was more prevalent in German than Italian usage. Both in Muffat's sonatas of 1682 and in his concertos of 1701, "sonata" is also used as the title of most of the first movements. Thus, in the former we have the use of the term both as an over-all and as an individual movement title. Its use to mean what was later called "concerto" merely brings back the fact that "concerto" still connoted only a style of scoring and playing, as one of the last of the Baroque terms to be identified with a form type.

Muffat's sonatas have none of the technical advances to be found in Biber's. But they do have a convincing directness and clarity of purpose in the faster movements, and they reveal considerable expressive depth in the chromatic harmony of the slower movements, especially those labelled "Grave."

43a

41. E.g., STRUNK-READINGS, pp. 442 ff. and 449.
42. STRUNK-READINGS, p. 449.
43. Cf. his own reference in this sense, STRUNK-READINGS, p. 452.

South Germany

Among some eleven composers to mention from our second group active in south Germany none was as important to the sonata as the three Austrians we have just met. The organist **Philipp Friedrich Boeddeker** (*ca.* 1615-83) was in Strasbourg (then on the German side) in 1651, the year that his *Sacra partitura* was published there and in Frankfurt. In this "solo" collection there are eight sacred songs and two sonatas, one S/- and the other SB/bass (violin, bassoon, and *b. c.;* "sopra 'La Monica' ").[44] The S/bass violin sonata is an effective piece. It has several free sections in contrasting tempos, followed by five variations on an *ostinato* "alla francese." It reveals a firm grasp of tonality, resourceful harmony and figuration, and motivic unity within each section. Boeddeker did not exceed the third position, but used double-stops freely. The other sonata is simply a set of four variations on the binary tune "La Monica," in which the violin repeats the tune while the bassoon makes the variations in rich elaborations of the *b. c.*

Samuel Friedrich Capricornus (or Bockshorn; *ca.* 1629-56), bitter opponent of Boeddeker in Stuttgart and perhaps before either had left Strasbourg,[45] published a set of six SS/- and SSB/bass *Sonaten und Canzonen* (Nürnberg, 1660) plus a lost, posthumous set in which the sonatas were probably introductory movements in suites. He also left two multivoice sonatas in MS.[46] This learned and influential composer acknowledged Valentini and Bertali in Vienna among his models. His sonatas were praised after he died for their instrumental writing and sense of form,[47] but have not been made available in modern times.

Matthias Kelz was in Augsburg in both 1658 and 1669, when he published the four SSB/bass suites totalling 25 pieces in his *Primitiae musicales* and the four suites totalling 51 SB/bass pieces in *Epidigma harmoniae novae,* respectively, as well as three other sets now lost.[48] The first set seems to win the much contested distinction of being the earliest definitely to have an introductory "Sonata" with a suite (cf. p. 249). Before each of the four suites there is a "Sonata" in several sections with such unusual tempo titles as "animosé," "agiliter," "fuso," "acriter," and "nervose." The other extant set contains a "Sonatina capriciosa" in the second suite. Most noteworthy in this set are the

---

44. Cf. EITNER-QL, II, 83 ff.; EITNER-BÖDDECKER (with the composer's interesting foreword on the state of *b. c.* realizations, reprinted in full); BECKMANN, p. 52. Mod. eds.: S/bass son., BECKMANNm, II, no. 4; SB/bass son., ORGANUMm, III, no. 33.
45. Cf. SITTARD, a valuable style study with music examples.
46. Cf. MEYER, p. 194; MGG, II, 818 ff. (Noack).
47. MGG, II, 820.
48. Cf. MEYER, p. 218.

bravura passages—leaps, high ranges, and double-stops—that presumably represent the "Exercitationum" mentioned later in the title.[49]

A better known composer, though not one remembered especially for his sonatas, was the important Munich organist and Hofkapellmeister, **Johann Kaspar Kerll** (1627-93). The only sonatas now known by him are four, all in undated MSS and all of the "trio" type.[50] One is an SS/- and the other three are SSB/bass settings. The SS/bass type is found in ANTH. ROSTm. The most extended of the other three sonatas has been made available in recent times.[51] It consists of an introductory "Adagio," an "Allegro" based consistently on two motives, another "Allegro" in which the first third is given to the *concertante* viola da gamba part before the upper instruments join fugally in the same material, and a concluding, freer and more ornamental movement without a tempo mark. The breadth of forms here seems to justify Mattheson's good report of Kerll's sonatas.[52] Especially interesting is the frequent independence of the viola da gamba part, including instances of contrapuntal interplay with the *b. c.*

Johann Michael Nicolai, who was living in Württemberg in 1669, published a set of 12 SSB/bass sonatas in Augsburg in 1675.[53] The *concertante* bass part is given to bassoon in some of these, and viola da gamba in the others. There are also about a half dozen more sonatas in extant MSS.[54] Four occur in ANTH. ROSTm,[55] including an SB/-, an SS/bass, and two multivoice settings (violin, two violas, and *b. c.*). These four sonatas reveal a composer well worth further study, what with a superior sense of line and form, an artful and concentrated use of motivic play, and a good knowledge of his instruments. They are in several contrasting movements that are clearly interrelated in their thematic material.

Hieronymus Gradenthaller (or Kradenthaller; 1637-1700), organist in Regensburg, may be mentioned for his consistent use of a one-section "Sonata" or "Sonatina" as the introductory movement in numerous suites.[56] The suites were published in the two parts of *Musikalische*

---

49. Cf. PIRRO-ALLEMAGNE, p. 987 ff., and PINCHERLE-VIOLINISTES, p. 30 ff., both with examples (but not from the sonatas).

50. Cf. DTBm, II, Part 2 (Sandberger), lxvii ff.; but there seems to be no reason to doubt the authenticity of the "Sonata modi dorii." The fourth sonata is listed in MEYER, p. 218 ff., and both sources also list an SSB/bass canzona. Three references to keyboard sonatas by Kerll cannot be substantiated, as noted in NEWMAN-EARLIEST, pp. 205, 207, and "Correction."

51. DTBm, II, Part 2, 159.   52. *Ibid.*, p. lxvii.

53. Cf. PIRRO-ALLEMAGNE, p. 1007, and EINSTEIN-GAMBA, p. 54 ff.

54. Cf. MEYER, p. 228 ff.; EVANS-DURHAM, pp. 211 and 222.

55. Thematic index in BIBLIOTHÈQUE NATIONALE, VII, 89; "Nicolaus" on p. 90 is the same Nicolai.

56. Cf. NEF-DEUTSCHEN, p. 19 ff.

Recreation (Regensburg, 1672) for violin and bass, and those of *Deliciarum musicalium* (Nürnberg, 1675 and 1676) in "trio" (SSB/bass) setting.

The celebrated organist, onetime associate of Schmelzer and Kerll in Vienna,[57] and predecessor of Bach, **Johann Pachelbel** (1653-1706) of Nürnberg, can also get but a brief mention here, since his sonatas are relatively few, little known, and outside his primary interests as a composer. Of most significance is his MS "Sonata a Violino solo e Cembalo obligato," undated but probably from the 1690's. This piece is probably the first example of a setting chiefly employed by Bach and a few other Germans; and it was one early ancestor of the "accompanied clavier sonata" that was to be a favorite setting throughout the Classic Era.[58] It has the S-F-S-F sequence of movements. Pachelbel also used a one-section "Sonata" or "Sonatina" as the introductory movement in the six SS/bass suites in *Musikalische Ergötzung* (Nürnberg, 1691).[59] This recently rediscovered collection is probably to be identified with the "7 Sonaten mit zweyen verstimmten Violinen" credited to Pachelbel in J. G. Walther's *Musikalisches Lexikon* of 1732 (p. 458) but long thought to be lost. Except for modest uses of *scordatura* and double-stops Pachelbel's treatment of the violin is conservative.

Sebastian Anton Scherer (1631-1712), organist in Ulm, published 14 SSB/bass sonatas in 1680. These were warmly endorsed by the scholarly musician Sébastien de Brossard, whom Scherer must have known after he moved to Strasbourg in 1684.[60] They are remarkable, among other traits, for the close relationship of incipits in the several movements of each. **Jakob Scheiffelhut** (1647-1709) of Augsburg may be cited here for his well-contrived, six-movement suites of 1684 (SSB/-bass), in each of which a "Sonata" is the introductory movement.[61] By contrast, **Georg Kaspar Wecker** (1632-95), in Nürnberg, may be cited as one who used a multivoice, sometimes orchestral, "Sonata" or "Sonatina" to introduce each of his sacred concertos for voices and instruments (1695).[62] This use, of course, was another way in which the term often appeared in Germany through the time of Bach.

Finally, one Italian may be noted in south Germany, the renowned composer of operas and sacred music **Agostino Steffani** (1654-1728),

57. Cf. DTÖm, VIII, Part 2 (Botstiber), vi.
58. Cf. BECKMANN-PACHELBEL, with examples; NEWMAN-ACCOMPANIED, p. 331 ff.
59. Mod. ed., complete: HORTUSm, nos. 54-56 (Zobeley; nos. 55 and 56 not yet available). For hints of other Pachelbel Sons. cf. SPITTA-BACH, I, 124 ff.
60. Cf. GUILMANT & PIRROm, p. xi ff., with examples; also, EINSTEIN-GAMBA, p. 55.
61. Cf. NEF-SUITE, p. 66, and NEF-DEUTSCHEN, p. 21 ff.
62. Cf. DTBm, VI, Part 1 (Seiffert), 46, 69, and 80.

who spent much of his busy career in Munich. As it happens, the two "trio" sonatas attributed to him and published with high praise some years ago proved to be by Caldara (see p. 168).[63] Now we are left with but six SSB/bass *Sonate da camera*, published by E. Roger of Amsterdam about 1700. These consist of 83 pieces arranged from six operas by Steffani.[64]

Central Germany (Pezel, Krieger, Kühnel, Kuhnau, Erlebach)

There are more than 20 composers to name in central Germany, from our second group, including at least a half dozen of some importance. The first in chronological order was the organist **Georg Arnold,** whose melo/bass *Canzoni, ariae, et sonatae,* for one to four violins and *b. c.,* was published in 1659 in Innsbruck after he had moved from that city to Bamberg.[65] Among the 47 pieces, mostly canzonas *a 2-4,* are two SSSS/bass sonatas.

The second composer to name, and the only Italian in this group, was the organist **Vincenzo Albrici** (1631-96), who came to Dresden from Rome about 1654. Along with Schütz and G. A. Bontempi he was one of the early Hofkapellmeister to the Elector of Saxony, whose court was a major musical center and the home ground of several other sonata composers. One sonata by Albrici is known, in a MS probably dating from the 1650's, and has been made available.[66] It is a melo/bass (SSSSB/bass) setting, though of the orchestral festive type, being scored for two violins, two trumpets, bassoon, and *b. c.* The opposition of trumpets and violins brings concerto grosso techniques to mind. There are two movements, 32 and 63 measures long, in quadruple and triple meter, respectively, both apparently in fast tempos.

Gerhard Diessener, an obscure court musician in Kassel from about 1660 to 1673, is largely the find of the German scholar E. H. Meyer,[67] who does not hesitate to call him "one of the most important masters of instrumental music in the 17th century." Under various spellings, Diessener composed suites with decidedly French traits, keyboard music with English traits, and three sonatas primarily German in their styles. These last Meyer describes as achieving a synthesis of the motoric, motivic style of Weckmann in north Germany, the cantabile style of Rosenmüller in south Germany (whom we shall find here, for

63. Cf. DTBm, XII, Part 2 (Riemann), xviii, for the original ascription of "12 Trio-Sonaten (da chiesa)" to Steffani, still accepted in MEYER, p. 250.
64. DTBm, XII, Part 2, viii.
65. Cf. the full listing in CAT. UPSALA, II, 131.
66. SCHERING-BEISPIELEm, no. 214; cf. SCHERING-INSTRUMENTALKONZERT, p. 12 ff. MEYER, p. 178, lists a "Sonata a 6" that was actually called "Sinfonia."
67. MEYER, p. 99 ff.; MEYER-DIESSENER (with examples); MGG, III, 422 ff.

other reasons, among the north Germans), and subjective features of Diessener's own creation. The sonatas, all in MS, include an SSB/bass type *a 4* and two multivoice types, one in several contrasting sections *a 5* (SSAAB/bass) and the other in one extended, triple-metered movement *a 6* (SSAABB/bass). Not being able to see anything but short fragments, one can only hope this music will be made available, meanwhile accepting Meyer's high evaluations on faith. He particularly refers to "romantic" qualities in the melodic lines, in the advanced harmony for its time, in psychological distinctions between major and minor, and in the "dramatic" contrasts between the movements of the Sonata *a 5*. This sonata, dated 1660, is stated to have the symmetrical sectional plan A-B&C-B'&C'-A'. The "Adagio" A sections are related by similar motives and by their introductory, toccata character. The "Presto" B sections are treated canonically and motivically, and the C sections are expressive "Adagio" contrasts.

The organist **Johann Jakob Loewe** (1628-1703), a pupil of Schütz in Dresden, was in Zeitz at the time his set of 17 *Sonaten, Canzonen und Capriccen* was published (Jena, 1664).[68] All in SS/bass scorings, this set includes four "trio" sonatas. Previously, in 1658 and 1659, Loewe had published two sets of suites. In the first set each introductory movement is called "Synfonia," the oldest such use of this term by a German in an extant score,[69] although Buonamente had so used it some 30 years earlier, in his Book 5 (1629), published while he was serving in Prague and Vienna. It is interesting here to note that in the second set of suites Loewe changed to the title "Sonata" for each introductory movement. There are also three multivoice sonatas in MS by him that are known.[70] The four sonatas of 1664 are relatively simple, short pieces, though not without melodic and motivic interest. All begin in quadruple meter, returning near the end, or sooner in the third, to the original meter but not to the thematic material. Each sonata has an "Adagio" ending.

70a

In Mainz the organist **Philipp Friedrich Buchner** (1614-69) composed two sets totalling 36 sonatas in all. There are 24 *a 2-5* in *Plectrum musicum,* Op. 4 (Frankfurt/M, 1662);[71] and 12 SSB/bass sonatas in *Harmonici instrumentalis,* Op. 5. These sonatas are noteworthy for

68. Full listing in CAT. UPSALA, II, 144. Copied in full in EINSTEIN-SCORESm, IV; cf. EINSTEIN-GAMBA, p. 54.
69. Cf. RIEMANN-SUITE, p. 503 ff., with example.
70. Cf. MEYER, pp. 223 and 111.
71. Cf. the detailed listings in MEYER, p. 192 (with discussion p. 95 ff.) and CAT. UPSALA, II, 134 ff. Mod. ed.: Son. 5 (not Son. 2; SB/bass), EINSTEIN-GAMBA, p. 87 (with discussion p. 54). Further bibliography and music examples cited in MGG, II, 421 ff. (Gottron).

their bold virtuosity and harmony, including considerable chromaticism, and some expressive, cantabile lines that may have been the consequence of Buchner's stay in Venice. But his means of extending his sizable forms seems curiously limited. It consists of little more than successive, brief, sequential "points of imitation." Especially in those sonatas that lack contrasting slow sections the process is undeniably monotonous.

The outstanding lutist **Esaias Reussner** (1636-79), who was in Silesia before moving to Brandenburg in 1674, should be mentioned for his use of a "Sonata" or "Sonatina" as a free introductory movement in various suites. These include two of the 13 he published for lute in 1676, in the first of which the "Sonatina" follows a "Praeludium," and all but Suite 4 of the ten multivoice suites for strings (SAA/bass) published in 1670 as *Musikalische Gesellschaftsergetzung*.[72] The sonata movement is usually in two or three repeated sections and in triple meter.

Daniel Eberlin (*ca.* 1630 to at least 1692), active in Eisenach and Kassel during the 1670's and '80's, published a set of "trio" sonatas (Nürnberg, 1675) that can no longer be found. Its noteworthy title reads, *Trium variantium fidium concordia . . . quos sonatas vocant*.[73] But two other "trio" sonatas still exist, in ANTH. ROSTm.[74] One of these is a long, relatively free work with changing tempos and a variety of passagework, in the manner of a toccata. However, the fact that one passage recurs frequently suggests a rondo interpretation of the form. There is some breadth in the lines and tonal organization.

David Pohle (1624-95), pupil of Schütz in Dresden, left at least 29 multivoice sonatas and perhaps a BB/bass sonata in MSS that probably date from the 1670's, during which years he seems to have been active in Halle, Dresden, and Kassel.[75] These sonatas are in a variety of scorings, mostly for five to eight string parts, with trombone and bassoon specified at least once. The fragments that have been quoted reveal full sonorities, unusually slow harmonic rhythm, and a virtuoso sweep that invite further acquaintance with Pohle's music.

Johann Pezel (1639-94) came to Leipzig as a violinist in 1664, remaining there until 1680. But it was probably his trumpet (*clarin*) playing that soon led this cultured musician to become the most important Stadtpfeiffer in Germany.[76] Largely in the interest of this

72. Cf. RIEMANN-SUITE, pp. 507 ff. and 515 (with reprint of entire first suite of 1676) ; also, KOLETSCHK'A, p. 25 ff.
73. Cf. WALTHER-LEXIKON, p. 221.
74. Mod. ed.: fragments from "La Eminenza" and all of the other sonata in PIRRO-ALLEMAGNE, p. 999 ff.
75. Cf. MOSER-LEXIKON, p. 969 ff.; MEYER, p. 234, with brief comments and examples pp. 102-112 (but the promised monograph has not appeared).
76. Cf. SCHERING-LEIPZIG, p. 271 ff. The techniques and the nature of *clarin* playing around the time of Bach are the main topics in MENKE.

position he published at least 18 instrumental collections between 1669 and 1686, only about a third of which have survived (as well as some sacred vocal music).[77]   Several of these collections belong under the heading of *Turmsonaten*—that is, wind "sonatas" to be played from church or municipal towers at certain hours, especially 10 in the morning and 6 in the evening.   The best known collections are *Hora decima*—i.e., 10 o'clock—(Leipzig, 1670), containing 40 one-movement sonatas for two *cornetti* and three trombones (or, optionally, two violins, two violas, and *violone*); *Musica vespertina*—at 6 p.m.—(Leipzig, 1669), containing 12 suites of 5 to 9 movements for 5 wind or stringed instruments (or fewer, as desired), in which each introductory movement is another, similar one-movement sonata; and *Delitiae musicales* (Frankfurt, 1678), containing six introductory sonatas in six suites for five stringed instruments (SSAAB/bass, with bassoon as an optional *concertante* bass).   Liberal selections from the foregoing are among the *Turmmusiken und Suiten* in the volume of the German *Denkmäler* series that is devoted to Pezel.[78]   There are also 39 introductory sonatinas among the 111 pieces in optional SS/bass settings in *Bicinia* (Leipzig, 1675), and 25 sonatas with titles (one for each letter of his Latin alphabet plus an extra one for C), scored in seven parts for 2 violins, 3 violas, bassoon, and *b.c.,* in *Opus musicum sonatorum*.[79]

Pezel's sonatas are all single movements, usually in three repeated sections totalling around 35 to 70 measures and sometimes approaching the A-B-A plan.   There are occasional metric changes but relatively few tempo marks except for the word "Adagio," to be found often at the start.   In *Hora decima* the 40 sonatas are grouped by keys, but Riemann's attempt to view these groupings as suites[80] lacks sufficient evidence.   The music is more sensitive and developed than one might expect from its special purpose and use.   Of particular interest are the full sonorities, the harmonic resourcefulness, and the persistence of a single idea in the motivic discourse (Ex. 47).

The violinist **Johann Wilhelm Furchheim** (1634-82) published his *Musikalische Tafelbedienung,* a set of multivoice sonatas *a 5,* in Dresden in 1674, and *Auserlesenes Violinen-Exerzitium,* a similar set that includes dances, in Dresden in 1687.[81]   He also left a "trio" sonata and four multivoice sonatas *a 5-7* in MS.   "Sonatella" is actually the title of the

77. Cf. MEYER, p. 232 ff.

78. DDTM, p. 63 (Schering), from which most other mod. eds. have been taken. Another mod. ed.: Sons. 21-40 from *Hora decima,* MÜLLER-PEZELIUSM. The 1669 and 1670 sets are discussed in NEF-DEUTSCHEN, p. 13 ff.

79. Cf. CAT. UPSALA, II, 147 ff.   80. -SUITE, p. 513 ff.

81. MEYER, p. 205, reports both works as lost, but HOFMEISTER, 1936, p. 43, lists a mod. ed. of Sons. 3 and 6 from the 1674 set.

Ex. 47. From Sonata 12 in *Hora decima* by Johann Pezel
(after SCHERING-LEIPZIG, II, 276).

one in seven *concertante* parts (3 violins, 2 violas, bassoon, *violone,*
and *b. c.*), a title that has reappeared occasionally throughout the history
of the sonata. A conspicuous trait of the sonatas is their regular phrase
structure, linked with essentially homophonic textures and expressive
harmonies. The exchanges between instruments in different ranges
qualify only as pseudopolyphony, since they fall into the clearly balanced
phrases and generally coincide with changes in an appropriately slow
harmonic rhythm.[82]

Two minor composers may be mentioned at this point for their use of
sonatas as introductory movements in suites—the Bohemian in Jena,
David Funck (*ca.* 1630 to at least 1690), in his *Stricturae violadigambicae* for four violas da gamba set in string quartet fashion (Leipzig,
1677) ;[83] and **Johann Kaspar Horn** of Dresden, in the fifth installment
of his *Musikalisches Nebenwerk* (SSAAB/bass; Leipzig, 1676).[84]
Horn's sonatinas are in three sections, F-S-F, and can be repeated at
the end of the suite, according to his foreword. It is worth adding that

82. See the examples in MEYER, p. 104 ff.
83. Cf. NEF-SUITE, p. 66.
84. Cf. NEF-SUITE, p. 68 ff., with examples.

his suites of 1672 and 1676 were among the first in Germany (along with D. Becker's of 1668) to incorporate the newer standard sequence of allemande, courante, saraband, and gigue.

The distinction of having written the first independent sonata for keyboard in Germany or Austria (that is, not merely an introductory movement such as Schmelzer's of 1681) should probably go to the organist **Christian Ritter** (*ca.* 1645 to at least 1725), who served variously in Halle, Stockholm, and Dresden. The work in question is a MS "Sonatina für Orgel" in D minor, and the uncertainty of the distinction hinges on the conjectural, undocumented dates that Buchmayer offers—"after 1680" and "1683-88" (while Ritter was Vicekapellmeister and Kammerorganist at the Dresden court).[85]   In any case, the   85a work is a remarkably strong one for a composer now so little known. It also contains surprisingly clear anticipations of Bach's music in the fugal techniques, the bold treatment of dissonance, the supple rhythmic flow, the toccata style and sectional plan, and the purposeful harmony. An opening run leads to a slow, serious chordal section, followed by the central movement or section, which is an equally serious five-voice fugue. The remaining two of the five sections consist of a series of more extended runs that move from the mediant key to the dominant chord, and another serious chordal section by way of a close.   On the lower of the two staffs is a part to be played on the pedal keyboard, clearly marked as such.

The successful violinist, organist, and opera composer **Nikolaus Adam Strungk** (1640-1700) was another who wrote sonatas in Dresden. Unfortunately, his one publication of concern to us is thus far known only through its listing in J. G. Walther's *Musikalisches Lexikon* of 1732. The intriguing title reads, *Musicalische Ubung auf der Violin und Viola dagamba, in etlichen sonaten über die Fest-Gesänge, ingleichen etlichen Ciaconen mit 2 Violinen, bestehend* (Dresden, 1691).   But at some place and point in his career Strungk also left two MS sonatas for strings that do still exist.   One is a multivoice (SSAAB/bass) type in three movements, F-S-F, while the other is a "trio" (SSB/bass) type in four movements.[86]   Both pieces are relatively short, yet reveal considerable power, contrapuntal skill, and breadth of tonal plan.   The slow movements proceed in elegiac, choralelike phrases,[87] while the faster movements are based on imitations that tend to fall into larger rhythmic

85. Cf. BUCHMAYER-RITTER, pp. 374, 375, and the mod. ed. at the end of that article; also, FROTSCHER, p. 563 ff., with listings of other mod. eds.
86. Mod. eds.: Son. *a 6*, HORTUSm, no. 103 (Stein, with preface); Son. *a 3*, ORGANUMm, III, no. 18.
87. Cf. EINSTEIN-CHORAL.

organizations of two or more measures. In the fast movements of the "trio" sonata the three solo instruments take turns in playing quasi cadenzas.

It was perhaps indirectly from Strungk himself, "a notorious brag-gart,"[88] that Walther got his well-known story about the encounter with Corelli.[89]   During a visit to Rome about 1685,[90] Strungk is supposed to have dumbfounded Corelli with his *scordatura* technique. This technique may have been used in Strungk's lost set of 1691, although neither it nor any special virtuosity are to be found in either of the MS sonatas. How-ever, the *bel canto* quality of the latter, along with such specific features as the "Corelli clash" (e.g., measure 25 of the Son. *a 6*) and frequent adroit modulations, suggests that these sonatas may not have been com-posed until after an acquaintance with Corelli's sonatas rather than be-fore the earlier equivocal date of "1665" that appears beside the copyist's initials in the Sonata *a 6*.

Johann Jakob Walther (*ca.* 1650-1717) ranked close to Biber among the foremost German-Austrian violinists of the 17th century. Not quite the same can be said for him as a composer, since the scope and extent of his known works is so much smaller than Biber's and his concepts of the sonata as an over-all form seem somewhat less developed. Walther came to the Dresden court about 1674, apparently after a trip to Italy.[91] In 1676 was published his *Scherzi da violino solo,* with *b. c.* for organ or cembalo and bass viol or lute, containing eight sonatas and four other pieces.[92]   In 1688 his *Hortulus chelicus* appeared, with 28 shorter pieces,[93] only one of which pertains here. This last is the "Aria," No. 14, which is listed in the "Index" with the noteworthy but puzzling title of "Aria in Forma di Sonatina." That both publications were soon re-printed is a sign of success that was then less common in Germany than in Italy.

Walther's sonatas are individual in style and form. They are on a spur rather than a main track of music history. From the first sonata of 1676 there is an increasing freedom, an emancipation from convention and tradition, that is refreshing and spontaneous in effect. Whether these sonatas, averaging a total of 150 measures, are too long to contain such freedom is another question. The slow movements display extended lines built out of many rhythmic combinations and supported by long stationary tones in the bass. Often a long run will be stretched over a single chord (Ex. 48). The fast movements are imitative or even fugal,

88. MOSER-LEXIKON, p. 1247.   89. WALTHER-LEXIKON, p. 583.
90. RINALDI-CORELLI, p. 103 ff.   91. Cf. EDMRm, XVII (Beckmann), vi.
92. Among mod. eds.: complete set, EDMRm, XVII.
93. Copied in full in EINSTEIN-SCOREsm, IV.

Ex. 48. From Sonata 3 in *Scherzi* by Johann Jakob Walther
(after EDMRm, XVII, 20 ff., but without the *b. c.* realization; by
kind permission of Bärenreiter-Verlag).

with the *b. c.* becoming an active participant.   Their continuation depends often on sequences and, perhaps too often, on a rather familiar procedure of 17th-century composers, beginning with B. Marini. This procedure is the use of a modulatory motive that cadences in a new key with
each repetition (Ex. 49). The resulting tonal contrasts are frequently
abrupt, with chromatic surprises.   In such movements a larger organization is occasionally revealed when the constant interchanges of the motive
or subject are relieved by a genuine fugal episode based on a fragment
therefrom (e.g., "Largo" from Son. 3), or when a whole section is set
apart by placing it on a different dynamic terrace (e.g., "Allegro" from
Son. 8).

The many programmatic effects or other "scherzi" that Walther so
clearly derived from Farina and that Adler saw as reason enough for
discounting Walther's importance[94] do not occur in Walther's sonatas.
Nor does Walther apply the term "sonata" to any of his suites. Not so
much as one dance title occurs in the sonatas.   He does include some
very free variation movements, but the only regular set of variations

94. DTÖm, V, Part 2, xi.

Ex. 49. From Sonata 2 in *Scherzi* by Johann Jakob
Walther (after EDMRm, XVII, 17, but without the *b. c.* realization; by kind permission of Bärenreiter-Verlag).

under the heading of sonata is that "Aria in Forma di Sonatina" in the
1688 set. He had used "Aria" for earlier sets of variations without
adding a similar qualification. What did he have in mind in this
instance?

Walther's technical requirements are as great as Biber's, but do not
include *scordatura*. In fact, he decries its use in his foreword to the
1688 set, probably with Biber's "Rosary Sonatas" in mind. The 1688
set also contains some easy pieces, as a concession to young students
after the unmitigated difficulties of the 1676 set. These last include
a peak in the technique of double-, triple-, and quadruple-stops, for which
the 17th-century Germans had shown such a liking; frequent excursions
into the sixth position; rapid shifts of position; wide leaps across the
strings, up to three octaves; tortuous passagework involving fast
harmonic changes; bariolage; a variety of bowings, not usually marked
but made evident by the notes themselves; and several instances of
"harpeggiato" playing.[95] Walther's Italian terms and contrasting move-

95. Cf. BECKMANN, p. 60 ff., and MOSER-VIOLINSPIEL, p. 131 ff., both with
examples.

ments, by the way, are about as far as his early and later Italian visits seem to have influenced his compositions.

One other composer in Dresden from our second group, probably an associate of Walther, was the eminent violinist of Swedish descent **Johann Paul Westhoff** (1656-1705). Westhoff also left only "solo" violin music that is known, including a suite and a sonata published in Paris at the time he played for Louis XIV (1682)[96] and six sonatas published in Dresden in 1694.[97] The 1682 sonata was named "La Guerre" by the delighted Louis XIV, with reference to one of its nine movements, which Westhoff later used again as the finale of Sonata 2 in the 1694 set. All of this music is in S/bass scoring except the suite, which ranks with Biber's sixteenth "Rosary Sonata" (or "Passagaglia") as one of the two earliest and chief precursors of Bach's unaccompanied violin music.

Technically Westhoff was close to Walther, especially in his programmatic effects, which do occur in his sonatas, and his advanced uses of double-stops and bowing techniques. On the other hand, he showed perhaps some Italian influence in the fewer, more clearly defined movements that make up his sonatas, although still in no set plan. As forms these movements are less interesting. They are too long—too long, that is, to depend so much on unimaginative repetitions and sequences.[98] Westhoff used the variation principle, too—not, however, in the popular manner over an *ostinato* but in the sense that one movement often becomes a variant of the previous one.

The important immediate forerunner of Bach and Handel, organist **Johann Philipp Krieger** (1649-1725), was in Weissenfels as Hofkapellmeister from 1680 to his death. Before then, during wide travels, he had enjoyed the diversified instruction of Schütz, Kaspar Förster, Rosenmüller, and Pasquini, among others, and had been ennobled at the early age of 26 by Leopold I during a visit to Vienna.[99] Evidence of Krieger's extraordinary international acquaintance with the chief composers of his time, and of his own prolificity, is found in the detailed record he kept of nearly all the church music he conducted while in Weissenfels.[100] But this record is also evidence that the sonata, at least as church music, figured in only a small part of his activities. From his own music it includes eight sonatas only (dated from 1685 to 1717), out of some 1700

96. Cf. BECKMANN, p. 72 ff.; LAURENCIE, I, 15; PINCHERLE-CORELLI, p. 47.
97. Mod. ed.: Son. 4 (1694) and Suite (1682), BECKMANNm, V, nos. 11 and 13.
98. Cf. BECKMANN, p. 72 ff., with examples in Anhang no. 23; MOSER-VIOLIN-SPIEL, p. 134 ff., with examples.
99. Cf. DDTm, LIII-LIV (Seiffert), x ff., and WAGNER-KRIEGER, p. 147 ff.
100. Published in DDTm, LIII-LIV, xxiv ff. Cf. also, DTBm, XVIII (Seiffert), xxxiii ff.

separate pieces. All eight are now lost. They were orchestral types *a 9-15,* including two or more in polychoir settings. From the music of the many other composers—among them his younger brother Johann, Bertali, Cazzati, Legrenzi, and Rosenmüller are especially prominent—only one sonata was used, an orchestral type *a 13* by Erlebach.

Except for one MS sonata *a 4* (SSAB/bass),[101] the extant sonatas by J. P. Krieger are all of melo/bass types. These include two published sets of 12 each, which appeared in Nürnberg in 1688 and 1693, respectively. The first set, Op. 1, is scored for two violins and *b. c.* The composer explains in his foreword that each sonata was printed separately so that any one sonata could be used on a special occasion, as dinner music for the Prince or diversion in some music group, without the nuisance of having to bring the whole set of parts along or make a copy from them.[102] The second set, Op. 2, is another example of that favored SB/bass setting in the 17th century, violin and viola da gamba (with *b. c.*).[103] There is also a MS "trio" sonata in ANTH. ROSTm.[104]

Krieger's sonatas have not yet received the detailed attention that his church and keyboard music have, neither in special studies nor modern editions. The scoring of Op. 2 probably explains why it has been noticed a little more than Op. 1.[105] Both appeared well after Corelli's fame had spread, but they give no special indication of his influence in spite of Krieger's remarkably catholic tastes. There is certainly no established cycle of movements in either opus. One can only generalize that the principle of contrast operates as usual, and even this statement must be qualified to suit a work like Sonata 3 of Op. 2, in which the last five of the eight movements are all in fast tempos ranging from "poco Allegro" to "Presto." Krieger does create the same solid, purposeful tonality that Corelli creates and reveals somewhat more intensive treatment of motives and fugue subjects. Every movement of Op. 1, No. 3, is a strict canon at the unison, including the final "Ciacconetta." There are also originality in his ideas, skill and imagination in their treatment, and that simple, meaningful, but uncomplicated earnestness in his style—in his lines, rhythms, and harmonies—that one associates with Schütz and his chief successors.

Krieger makes full use of his instruments, especially in the several variation movements such as the "Aria d'Inventione," with "the cembalo

101. Example quoted in MEYER, p. 120.
102. Full listing in DDTm, LIII-LIV, lxx. Mod. ed.: Son. 3, ORGANUMm, III, no. 11.
103. Mod. eds.: Sons. 2 and 3, EITNER-KRIEGERm, pp. 66 and 82; Son. 2, ORGANUMm, III, no. 10; Son. 6, NAGELSm, no. 135 (Osthoff).
104. Opening quoted in BIBLIOTHÈQUE NATIONALE, VI, 48.
105. Cf. EINSTEIN-GAMBA, p. 57 ff.

part to be repeated ten times" (Op. 2, No. 2). But he does not go to extremes nor indulge in any of the stunts of the day. In Op. 2, the viola da gamba most often pairs with the violin in motivic play or in a more homophonic parallelism, although this music is never as purely homophonic as the dances in Krieger's third publication, his *Lustige Feld-Music* (1704). While the two *concertante* instruments are so paired, the *b. c.* (organ or cembalo) provides an independent third part—usually a running bass, or some quasi-*ostinato* pattern, or a mere harmonic support. When the viola da gamba is only a *concertante* elaboration of the *b. c.,* then there are, of course, only two real parts, as is often true in the fugal movements.

A superior composer, associated exclusively with the viola da gamba and similar in his styles to Krieger, was **August Kühnel** (1645-?). Kühnel was in Kassel in 1698 when he published his only known collection, 14 *Sonate o partite ad una o due viole da gamba,* with *b. c.* In this collection Sonatas 1 to 3 and Partitas (suites) 4 to 6 are in BB/bass settings, while Sonatas 7 to 10 and Partitas 11 to 14 are in B/bass settings.[106] But, as the composer tells us in his foreword, the duet sonatas are "so arranged that they can be played without the *basso continuo.*" In other words, in these sonatas an elaboration of the *b. c.* is always to be found in one or the other viola da gamba part. But the solo is always independent of the *b. c.* in the B/bass settings, which practice was generally not the rule in related Italian settings of this and earlier generations. Kühnel's sonatas in this class should be noted as the first for viola da gamba "solo" that are known here after those published by Johann Schenk in Amsterdam in 1688.

Constantly attractive details did not stop Kühnel from keeping the larger outlines of his sonatas in view. The initial slow movement often simply climbs the scale and descends, although taking a fairly devious course. In some of the faster movements of the B/bass sonatas a one-voice fugal outline is suggested by introducing the subject in different ranges of the solo part. There is no set movement plan, but the opening movement may frame the whole sonata by recurring with only moderate changes at the end. The central movement, as in so many German sonatas, is a set of variations. In Sonata 9 there are four movements, the two related, outer ones, a set of nine "Variationen über einen Basso ostinato" in quadruple meter as the second movement, and an "Aria" consisting of four more variations on this same bass converted to triple meter. Sonata 3 is nothing but a set of six variations.

106. Cf. EINSTEIN-GAMBA, pp. 40 and 42 ff. Among mod. eds.: Sons. 1 and 3, EINSTEIN-GAMBA, pp. 64 and 72; Sons. 7, 8, and 9, SCHOTT CELLOm, nos. 69, 78, and 70 (all Döbereiner, with prefaces).

Kühnel was not satisfied with an *ostinato* pattern alone in his variations, but managed to keep an attractive tune going in one or another part. Whatever the theme, it is usually a full binary one with each half repeated. Presumably the repeats were to be done with further embellishments if the player was able to add them. In fact, Kühnel notes in his foreword that he has used only the apostrophe, as a sign for any kind of trill, inviting the "amateur" (to whom much viola da gamba music was addressed[107]) to add "the other *Manieren* as he sees fit, since it is almost impossible to put them on paper."

Like Krieger, Kühnel made full use of his instrument—intricate passages, rapid skips, multiple stops—but did not indulge in the stunts of the time (Ex. 50).

Ex. 50. From the fifth variation of Sonata 3 by August Kühnel (after EINSTEIN-GAMBA, p. 76).

Johann Gottfried Reiche (1667-1734) was the successor to Pezel in Leipzig as Stadtpfeiffer, violinist, trumpeter, and composer of *Turmsonaten*. Much of his music is lost, but his set of *Vier und zwantzig neue Quatricinia* for one *cornett* and three trombones (Leipzig, 1696)

107. EINSTEIN-GAMBA. p. 35 ff.

still survives.[108]   The not surprising difference between Reiche's and
Pezel's sonatas, 25 years apart, is that of increase in span again, at both
the phrase and the over-all levels.   Reiche's sonatas, in four rather than
five instrumental parts, have full-fledged tunes with balanced phrases,
and fugal movements that are developed consistently, at some length
and within a firm orbit of nearly related keys.   They average around
100 measures in length and are in two or three contrasting movements
of no set plan.   Reiche's known prowess in the playing of Bach's high
trumpet parts[109] is not reflected by any unusual difficulties for the
cornett, by then old-fashioned but still specified in his *Neue Quatricinia.*

Our most important name at this time in the musically productive
center of Leipzig was **Johann Kuhnau** (1660-1722).   This composer,
scholar, novelist, and jurist was a pupil of Albrici in Dresden, came to
Leipzig in 1682, was made organist at the Thomaskirche in 1684, and
became cantor at the Thomasschule in 1701, to be succeeded upon his
death by J. S. Bach.[110]   His reputation as a composer rests primarily
on his keyboard music, important chiefly to the early history of the
keyboard sonata as well as to programme music, and on his church
cantatas, most of which happen to have short introductory orchestral
movements called "sonatas."[111]   The keyboard music was all first
published in four sets in the 11 years from 1689 to 1700, followed by
numerous reprints that point to substantial successes.[112]   It includes
14 "Partien" (suites) in the two installments of his *Neüer Clavier
Übung,* the first in 7 major keys (1689) and the second in 7 minor keys
(1692); the Sonata in B flat appended to the second of these sets and
often, although wrongly, hailed as "the first keyboard sonata"; the 7
sonatas in *Frische Clavier Früchte* (1696), which Kuhnau tells us in his
foreword he composed one a day in the space of one week; and the six
programme sonatas that are the celebrated *Biblische Historien* (1700),
composed for organ "or other similar instruments" as well as *clavicembalo.*[113]   In short, aside from the cantata introductions and one single-   113a
movement "Sonatina" that introduces a suite ("Partie IV" in the 1689
set), the known sonatas of Kuhnau consist of the 14 for keyboard of
1692, 1696, and 1700.

108. Biographic information in SCHERING-REICHE.   Among mod. eds.: complete
set, MÜLLER-REICHEM (with preface); cf. ALTMANN.
    109. SCHERING-REICHE, p. 137 ff.
    110. MÜNNICH is the main biographic source.
    111. Cf. DDTm, LVIII-LIX (Schering), 224, 244, and 321.
    112. Cf. GUTMANN-KUHNAU, p. 27 ff.
    113. Among numerous mod. eds.: complete keyboard works, DDTm, IV (Päsler,
with detailed preface and facsimiles of Kuhnau's forewords); the "Six Biblical
Sonatas," STONE-KUHNAUM (with preface, facsimiles, and English translation of
the foreword).   Other reprints are listed in GUTMANN-KUHNAU, p. 29 ff.

Kuhnau's Sonata in B flat of 1692 is the earliest now known in Germany or Austria for a stringed keyboard instrument,[114] although it was preceded by Schmelzer's introductory movement of 1681 and probably by Christian Ritter's organ sonata. Outside of these countries we have already noted the earlier harpsichord sonatas of Del Buono (1641), Strozzi (1687), and Pasquini (if his were actually earlier), and we shall be meeting another such sonata dated about 1690 by the Dutchman Sybrandus van Noordt. But Kuhnau himself implied a certain priority for his Sonata in B flat when he observed in the foreword to the 1692 set, "I have also added a Sonata in B♭ at the end, which should similarly please the [music] lover. After all, why shouldn't one be able to compose such pieces for keyboard as well as for other instruments, the more so as no one [other] instrument has yet challenged the superiority of the keyboard [in completeness of texture]?" More than a century ago, in 1837, the German author Carl Ferdinand Becker took his cue from these remarks, staked out a claim for Teutonic priority in the realm of the keyboard sonata, and led off the long, seldom disputed procession of writers who not only have made more and more of Kuhnau as a key figure in early sonata history but have read into his sonatas a variety of "evolutionary" harbingers of Classic "sonata form."[115] These sonatas do reveal a competent composer with a novel intellectual approach that appealed successfully to the public taste of his day. But they do not reveal an outstanding creator nor a prescient one, and must be said, therefore, to have been emphasized quite out of proportion to either their musical or historical importance.

Kuhnau's announcement of his Sonata in B flat primarily concerns the transplanting of the ensemble sonata to the keyboard.[116] Hence, several authors have pointed to places in this and his subsequent sonatas that happen to be scored in the SS/bass manner.[117] However, such places represent only one among numerous textural dispositions that he uses. To point only to this disposition would be to disregard the very reason that Kuhnau seems to have preferred the keyboard—that is, the textural variety of which it is capable, including great freedom between the outer voices as regards doublings, the addition or subtraction of

---

114. Cf. NEWMAN-EARLIEST, pp. 201 and 205.

115. Cf. BECKER-KLAVIERSONATE; followed in chronological order, among others, by FAISST, p. 10 ff.; GROVE, 1st ed., III, 555 ff. (Parry); BAGGE, p. 204; SHEDLOCK-SONATA, p. 38 ff. (an extended, helpful discussion); KLAUWELL, p. 30 ff.; SEIFFERT-KLAVIERMUSIK, p. 242 ff.; MICHEL, p. 31 ff.; D'INDY-COURS, II, Part 1, 185 ff.; REFOULÉ, p. 25 ff.; and GEORGII-KLAVIERMUSIK, p. 99 ff. Among the few older authors who were already disputing Kuhnau's significance to the sonata may be mentioned SCHÜZ, p. 261, and BIE, p. 92.

116. It is this aspect of his music that is treated in CLERCX-KUHNAU.

117. E.g., cf. GEORGII-KLAVIERMUSIK, p. 100 ff.

voices, and parallelisms.[118]   Thus, in the 1696 set, which shows musical
and technical advances over the 1692 sonata, he writes sometimes in a
purely clavieristic, preludial style (Son. 3, finale) ; or in a heavy chordal
style ("Ciaccona" from Son. 6) ; or in fairly strict fugues, with double
counterpoint (Son. 5, second movement) ; or, except for the outer voices,
in the *freistimmig* or *brisé* style of pseudopolyphony such as is to be
found especially in French lute music of the time (Son. 7, first movement).[119]   It is, in fact, the texture, in all its international styles and
with its rich ornamentation, specified or invited,[120] that provides one of
the most interesting aspects of Kuhnau's sonatas and suites.   As keyboard music they reflect the growing influence in central Germany of the
outstanding keyboard composers in Italy, Austria, and south Germany,
including Pasquini, Froberger, Georg Muffat, Kerll, and Pachelbel.

Kuhnau's sonatas average four or five movements in the 1692 and
1696 sets and three to eight "movements" or scenes in the 1700 set.
The tempos, indicated about half of the time, reveal no set plan other
than contrast.   Indeed, in the foreword to the 1696 set Kuhnau restates
the familiar fantasy concept of the sonata.[121]   But a larger organization
does obtain in some of the sonatas, achieved variously by cyclic relationships of the ideas (Son. 5, 1696) or even a hint of the leitmotiv technique
(Son. 1, 1700), by tonal transitions from the end of one movement to the
start of the next (Son. 1, 1696), or by the recurrence of an opening or
earlier movement at the end (Son. in B flat, 1692; Son. 3, 1700).   A lack
of organization is more often felt within the separate movements.   The
ideas have moderate interest in themselves but generally grow monotonous and stodgy in their many repetitions because the pitch range is so
narrow and because the tonality lacks sufficient direction and range.   Nor
is the vocabulary of harmonies and rhythmic patterns rich enough to
relieve this monotony.

Even the "Biblical Sonatas" show little of the colorful detail that
their programmatic content would seem to demand.   Most often the
programme is conveyed by the general mood, as in the music for Saul's
melancholy (Son. 2) or Jacob's wedding (Son. 3).   The more detailed
effects that do occur now seem incredibly naïve, of course, especially as
they are known to have been done in dead earnest[122] (Ex. 51), not in
the satirical vein of his novel *Der musikalische Quacksalber*.   The best
known examples occur in "Suonata prima: Il Combattimento trà David
e Goliath," including the chromatic progressions to depict the trembling

118. Cf. the 1692 foreword in DDTm, IV, 32; also, p. x ff.
119. Cf. SCHERING-LEIPZIG, II, 429 ff., with examples.
120. Cf. DDTm, IV, xv ff., and STONE-KUHNAUm, p. iv ff.
121. DDTm, IV, 71.   122. Cf. SPITTA-BACH, I, 238 ff.

Ex. 51. From the fifth scene of Johann Kuhnau's "Biblical Sonata" 5, "Gideon, the Savior of Israel" (after DDTm, IV, 167 ff.).

Israelites in prayer, and a sudden run followed by a descending scale to depict the slinging of the stone and the felling of Goliath. In his lengthy, involved, and somewhat capricious foreword, Kuhnau himself indicated some uncertainty as to how and to what extent music can or should convey verbal concepts.[123] There, by the way, he finds precedents for his programme music in that of Froberger and an unnamed "Capell-Meister" who may have been Kerll, among others.[124] Dietrich Becker's *Musikalische Frühlingsfrüchte* (a 3-5, 1668) and R. I. Mayr's *Arion sacer* (a 5, 1678) have also been suggested as precursors of the "Biblical Sonatas."[125] More generally, Kuhnau's "Biblical Sonatas" may be said to bring the contemporary oratorio to the keyboard.[126] But there is no special evidence for singling out Bassani or Rosenmüller as composers whose ensemble sonatas Kuhnau had in mind in adapting his previous, "absolute" sonatas to the keyboard.[127]

The last composer to name in our second group in central Germany is **Philipp Heinrich Erlebach** (1657-1714), who worked up to the position of Hofkapellmeister in Rudolstadt. Erlebach is chiefly remembered for his sacred and dramatic music, but is known to have composed at least 62 sonatas a 2-13.[128] There must have been much use for the sonata in Rudolstadt. In a valuable list, similar to the one J. P. Krieger prepared

---

123. For a modern discussion of representation by musical figures and more subjective aspects of expression in Baroque music cf. HAYDON-EXPRESSION.
124. Cf. SEIFFERT-KLAVIERMUSIK, p. 248.
125. SHEDLOCK-SONATA, p. 43, and NEF-SUITE, p. 66 ff., respectively.
126. Cf. DTöm, LXXXV (Schenk), xi.
127. Cf. DDTm, IV, vi.
128. MEYER, pp. 114 and 199.

in Weissenfels, Erlebach himself catalogued some 305 sonatas *a 1-10* that were in the library around 1700 (cf. also, p. 47).[129]   But extant today from his own music are only his *VI. Sonate a violino e viola da gamba,* published in 1694 in Nürnberg, where he seems to have had some ties,[130] and a few introductory orchestral sonatas in his choral works. Even the 1694 set was lost for a long time and only recently rediscovered, except for Sonata 2, which had been known in separate parts.

In this set of 1694 Erlebach provided an optional, second violin part to be used when no viola da gamba is at hand, thus converting the SB/- to an SS/bass setting.   He also implied that multiple performance of the parts might be desirable, which is not surprising when one recalls that most of his lost sonatas were large multivoice settings.   The first violin part makes use of relatively elementary *scordatura* in Sonatas 3 and 4. The sonatas are remarkable for combining in the seven or eight movements of each almost a complete church and court sonata.   Three movements in the S-F-S tempos and styles of the first three church movements are followed by an allemande, courante, saraband, a variant of this last or a separate set of variations, and a concluding gigue or other movement.

Erlebach's introductory sonatas have the form of the French overture and he shows much French influence in his *VI. Ouvertures . . . nach französicher Art und Manier* (Nürnberg, 1693), although he tells us he had never been in France.[131]   But, significantly, the 1694 set has an Italian title and reveals something of the Corellian or Handelian nobility of line and pace.   None of the whimsicality so characteristic of 17th-century German sonatas is found here.   The opening adagios treat the underlying motive consistently yet creatively, with the larger outlines well in view.   The fugal allegros pursue the subject with a serious, imposing drive.   The second slow movements have an affective quality (as suggested by the marking "Affettuoso" in Sonata 1).   Even the dances, all in binary design, are not without considerable contrapuntal interest.

North Germany (*Weckmann, Becker, Reinken, Rosenmüller, Buxtehude*)

To complete our second group of Germans and Austrians only 11 composers may be noted who were active in north Germany.   Buxtehude and Rosenmüller are the best known of them.   Hamburg, so important to Baroque opera, church, and organ music in Germany, was the main center and the home of lively civic groups of instrumentalists (*Rats-*

---

129. Cf. ᴅᴅᴛm, XLVI-XLVII (Kinkeldey), xxvii.
130. Mod. eds.: Son. 2, ᴇɪɴsᴛᴇɪɴ-ɢᴀᴍʙᴀ, p. 113, and ᴏʀɢᴀɴᴜᴍm, III, no. 5; Sons. 1 and 3, ʜᴏʀᴛᴜsm, nos. 117 and 118 (both Zobeley, with preface).
131. Cf. ᴅᴅᴛm, XLVI-XLVII, xxxvi and xxxvii; ᴄᴀᴛ. ᴜᴘsᴀʟᴀ, II, 137.

musiker), chiefly string players, who were naturally interested in the contemporary sonata.[132]

As early as 1654 the violist **Hans Hake** in Stade (west of Hamburg) published 43 *Pavanen, Sonaten, Arien, Balletten, Brandlen, Couranten und Sarabanden a 2-8*. But this collection is incompletely preserved and the position and function of the sonatas, if they are not merely unattached pieces, has not been clarified.[133] Four years later, in the former Danzig, the organist **Thomas Strutius** (?-1678) published a *Sonata octo Instrument*. Here is another example of the old polychoir type of setting that derived from Venetian practices but persisted longest outside of Italy, in Germany. It is a very extended work, with a movement in even meter followed by one in triple ("altera pars") in the manner of the old pavane and galliard, and with much strict canonic writing.[134]

The organist **Matthias Weckmann** (1619-74) is one of our main sonata composers in Hamburg. A pupil of Schütz in Dresden and of the organist Jakob Praetorius in Hamburg, Weckmann composed in most of the popular forms of the day, including dramatic, sacred, and organ music. The existence of sonatas by him was not realized until comparatively recently.[135] These consist of a MS set of ten multivoice settings *a 4* and *a 3*.[136] Presumably they were composed for the personal diversion of the members in the important Collegium musicum founded in Hamburg in 1660 by Weckmann.[137]

The writer E. H. Meyer singles out Weckmann's sonatas—as opposed to Rosenmüller's with their Italianate unity, cantabile sensuality, and sonority—to illustrate in detail the generally recognized, north German predilection for intellectual and mechanistic or patterned polyphony. This style developed, he says, by way of the English viol fantasias. Gerhard Ilgner echoes this view and extends it. He finds the indirect influences of English virginal music and the organ music of Sweelinck in Weckmann's sonatas. He attributes the mixed scoring of these sonatas and a supposed (but unconfirmed) preference for winds on the composer's part to the nature of the Hamburg Collegium musicum, which is said to have existed primarily for the players themselves rather than for public performances. Also, because of these traits, Ilgner re-

---

132. Cf. MGG, V, 1391 (Stephenson).   133. Cf. NEF-SUITE, p. 72.
134. Cf. MEYER, pp. 64 ff., 69, 81, and 251.
135. There is no mention of them in the comprehensive study published in 1901, SEIFFERT-WECKMANN, which, however, does throw much light on 17th-century instrumental practices in Hamburg.
136. Discussed in MEYER, p. 66 ff., with examples; and in the principal study of Weckmann and his music, ILGNER, pp. 112 ff. and 177. Mod ed., entire: EDMLm, IV (Ilgner), 1 ff.
137. Cf. SEIFFERT-WECKMANN, p. 110 ff.; ILGNER, p. 116.

gards the sonatas as quite different from the other categories of Weckmann's music, much of it composed in Dresden. Such attempts to delimit styles on a geographical basis often prove to be dogmatic. Even in the present sonata history, which groups composers primarily on a geographical rather than a nationalistic basis, some surprising contradictions of styles must be acknowledged in almost every main center of the sonata. But it should be added that, whatever their origin, the indicated traits in Weckmann's sonatas do appear without question.

Eight of these sonatas are SSAB/- and two are SSA/bass settings. The two high parts specify violin, one always interchangeable with *cornettino*. The alto part specifies viola da gamba or trombone, and the *concertante* bass specifies bassoon or *bombardo* (bass shawm). Two to five movements in each sonata are made apparent by changes of meter and style, and by some tempo and dynamic markings. Dances play no part in this music. The most frequent plan is one of two even-metered movements separated by a movement in 3/2 meter. In three of the sonatas the performers are asked to repeat the first movement at the end, giving a closed form to the whole. The structural procedure most encountered in the separate movements, of whatever meter or tempo, is that of the old motet based on successive points of imitation, except that an extended passage by one instrument usually precedes the imitations. In the typically angular motives, the scales, the repeated notes, and the trills, there are evidences of good instrumental writing, though this writing is without that extra margin of technical invention that associates with virtuosity. There is a breadth of pace and line about much of the music, but with its persistent modal traits it still lacks the unifying force of a clear tonal organization.

Two associates of Weckmann in Hamburg should be mentioned here for their use of the sonata as an introductory movement—**Christoph Bernhard** (1627-92), in a sacred choral work;[138] and the violinist **Samuel Peter von Sidon,** in a suite.[139] A third associate, of more importance to the sonata, was the capable violinist and organist **Dietrich Becker** (1623-79).[140] Becker left a total of 30 separate or introductory sonatas *a 2-5* in his three instrumental collections that were published (all in Hamburg) out of four that are extant.[141] *Musicalische Frühlingsfrüchte* (1668) contains nine sonatas in melo/bass and multivoice settings

138. Mod. ed.: DDTm, VI (Seiffert), 142. WALTHER-LEXIKON, p. 89, refers to printed sonatas by him, now lost.
139. Mod. ed.: ORGANUMm, III, no. 23; cf. EITNER-QL, IX, 162.
140. Cf. MGG, I, 1483 ff. (Fock), with further references.
141. Cf. MEYER, p. 186 ff., but "Erster Theil" should be dated 1674 and "Ander Theil," 1679.

a 3-5.[142]   The *Erster . . .* and *Ander Theil zweystimmiger Sonaten und Suiten* (1674 and 1679) contain 9 and 12 SS/- or SB/bass sonatas, respectively (sometimes called "Sonatino" in the latter set).[143]

When one sonata is followed by another in Becker's collections it would seem to be conceived as a separate piece, without any question. But when it is followed by a suite of dances in any of the three sets it may or may not have been intended as an introductory movement. Usually this question is decided by the fact that the sonata and the following suite of dances are in the same key. But doubt arises from Becker's system of numbering each sonata and dance separately in one series from the start to the end of the collection. In any case, each separately numbered sonata is not a single movement, like each separately numbered dance, but a complete cycle averaging five or six movements that contrast, as usual, in tempo, meter, and style. Incidentally, most of the suites are already complete examples of the classic cycle—allemande, courante, saraband, and gigue. Moreover, Becker's 1668 set seems to have marked the first use of the gigue in an ensemble sonata, coming in the same year as the separate gigues that are often cited in G. B. Vitali's Op. 4.[144]

Becker's sonatas are fairly elementary in scope, harmonic vocabulary, and technical range. They are often like Weckmann's in their structural method, but differ in having simpler, firmer tonal outlines; more flowing, distinctive ideas, with less sense of patterns; more consistent treatment of one motive; and a degree of virtuosity. The last trait shows up especially, as might be expected, in occasional variation movements over an *ostinato* (e.g., Son. 46 in the 1674 set) and in solo passages specifically marked "solo" in any of the *concertante* parts (e.g., Son. 26 in the same set).

Johann Theile (1646-1724), organist and violist, held many German posts during his lifetime, including service under Schütz's direction in Weissenfels. He is placed here in Hamburg, where his first instrumental collection was published in 1683. Unfortunately, this collection, containing suites with introductory sonatas, and his 50 *Novae Sonatae* and other pieces, Op. 2 (Leipzig, 1699), are both lost. There are extant only about six MS sonatas *a 3-5*, none of which has been made available in a modern edition.[145]   Four of these MS sonatas come from a counter-

---

142. Listed in CAT. UPSALA, II, 133. Briefly discussed in NEF-SUITE, p. 64 ff.; MOSER-VIOLINSPIEL, p. 108 ff. Mod. eds.: Sons. *a 3* in G, *a 4* in E minor, and *a 5* in G minor, RABSCHm; Son. *a 3* in G, FOCK-TRIOSONATENm, p. 13.

143. The entire *Erster Theil* is in EINSTEIN-SCORESm, IV; mod. ed.: Son. 46 (only) for violin, viola da gamba, and *b. c.*, EINSTEIN-GAMBA, p. 95.

144. E.g., DANCKERT-GIGUE, p. 52 ff.

145. Cf. MEYER, p. 252 ff.; also, p. 75 ff. and 126, with short examples.

point treatise and help explain why Theile's contemporaries called him the "Vater der Kontrapunktisten."[146]   They make much use of double, triple, and quadruple counterpoint, as did the sonatas from Op. 2, according to its detailed title.[147]   E. H. Meyer also calls attention to the symmetrical arrangements of movements.   For example, he cites a sonata *a 3* with "drey doppelt verkehrten Subjectis" in which the plan is A-B-C-B'-C'(contrary motion)-B"-A, B and its variants being short transitional adagios.[148]

The last of these composers in Hamburg (before we come to Keiser, Telemann, and Handel in our third group) was the outstanding organist **Johann Adam Reinken** (1623-1722), who had come from Alsace and The Netherlands and was to die a near centenarian.[149]   Reinken's known sonatas are the six, each followed by a suite, that make up his *Hortus musicus* (Hamburg, 1688), in SSB/bass setting for strings.[150]   Like his organ music, Reinken's sonatas have attracted special attention because of Bach's interest in them.   In fact, Bach arranged two keyboard sonatas, in A minor and C major, out of Sonata 1 and part of Sonata 3, and a separate keyboard fugue in B-flat major out of the first "Allegro" in Sonata 2.[151]   As with Bach's interest in Albinoni, the "arrangements" include not only rescoring, refinement, and enrichment of the music but expansions of it through means highly illuminating to the art of composition.[152]

Reinken numbered his separate sonata cycles and dances, as Becker did, in one series for the entire set.[153]   But this time there are no separate sonatas without dances.   Each sonata cycle is followed by its allemande, courante, saraband, and gigue.   Furthermore, there is not only the uniformity of key to interrelate the sonata and the dances but the fact of unmistakable relationships in some or all of the incipits.   As with Erlebach and Becker, Reinken brings about not the typical fusion of church and court sonata to be found elsewhere around the turn of the century, but rather the literal juxtaposition of these two types, a fact he himself suggests in his dedication.[154]   Preceding the standard dance

146. RIEMANN-LEXIKON, p. 1833.   147. Cf. WALTHER-LEXIKON, p. 603.
148. MEYER, p. 75.
149. Cf. STAHL-REINKEN; PIRRO-REINKEN, p. 251 ff.
150. The date derives from GÖHLER, II, 69, but is also given elsewhere as 1686 or 1687.   Mod. eds.: entire set (including facsimile of cover, dedication, foreword, etc.), VNMM, XIII (Reimsdijk, with preface); Son. 1 and suite, SPITTA-BACH, III, 366.
151. SCHMIEDER-BWV, nos. 965, 966, and 954, respectively.
152. Cf. SPITTA-BACH, I, 429 ff., and SPITTA-AUFSÄTZE, p. 113 ff.; VNMM, XIII, iii ff.; KELLER-REINKEN.
153. Hence, Sons. 6 and 11, so numbered in BACH-WERKEM, XLII, 50 and 42, are actually the second and third sonatas in the set.
154. Cf. SPITTA-AUFSÄTZE, p. 113 ff.

cycle is the sequence of S-F-S within each of the sonatas. The first slow movement is sustained, imitative, and not unlike the opening movement in Corelli's church sonatas. The first fast movement is fugal, but without episodes to relieve the constant entries. (Episodes are among the additions in Bach's transcriptions.) The third movement has the freedom, tempo changes, and virtuosity of the toccata.

It is not hard to understand the appeal that Reinken's sonatas had for Bach. They have strength, originality, and structural perspective. The texture is kept constantly in motion through the skillful use of complementary rhythms. Although the lines suffer from an excess of those mechanical zigzag patterns associated with north German organ music, these patterns are convincingly organized and directed into overall peaks and valleys of the forms.

Clamor Heinrich Abel, perhaps active in Hannover and Braunschweig by 1656,[155] was a grandfather of the better known Karl Friedrich Abel, whom we shall meet among Classic sonata composers in England as one of the last important virtuosos on the viola da gamba. Presumably C. H. Abel played this instrument himself, since on occasion (1677) his use of it calls for *scordatura*. Besides three melo/bass sonatas known in MS, he left three collections of 162 pieces *a 4,* published in Frankfurt/M in 1674, 1676, and 1677, and all republished together in Braunschweig in 1687. These pieces include dances, introductory sonatas, and even an early German example of the programmatic "Sonata-Battaglia" (1676).[156] The latter may be identical with the sonata labelled "Bataille" that is one of the two SS/bass sonatas by C. H. Abel in ANTH. ROSTm.[157] Thus far, Abel's music has not been studied or made available.

The name of **Johann Rosenmüller** (*ca.* 1619-84) appears often in accounts of 17th-century German music, for both his instrumental and sacred choral works. This composer and organist trained in Leipzig, fled in 1655 to Hamburg and on to Venice to escape prosecution for an unknown legal offense, remained in that leading center of the Italian sonata until 1674, then returned to Wolfenbüttel for his last 10 years. His instrumental publications include two sets of dances issued while he was still in Leipzig (1645 and 1654), a set of 11 *Sonate da camera a 5* (or, optionally, SS/bass) issued while he was in Venice (1667, but known only in the Nürnberg reprint of 1670), and the set most pertinent

155. RIEMANN-LEXIKON, p. 3, gives 1665, but a MS by this Abel, dated 1656, is reported in Hannover. In any case, 1665 could not have been the year of birth, as in GROVE, I, 7 (Redlich) and MGG, I, 25 (Redlich); nor is this Abel likely to have been an associate of J. S. Bach at Köthen, as in GROVE.

156. Cf. MEYER, p. 176.

157. Thematic index in BIBLIOTHÈQUE NATIONALE, I, 3.

here, 12 *Sonate à 2. 3. 4 è 5 stromenti, da arco & altri,* issued in 1682, two years before he died.[158] He also left at least four sonatas in MSS 158a that are still known, of which three are in ANTH. ROSTm.[159]

Rosenmüller's 1667 set was hailed some years ago as the pioneer example of the German suite introduced by a free movement.[160] But we have seen this claim to priority contradicted by numerous examples that began nearly 40 years earlier with Buonamente (while he was in Germany) and included Kelz and possibly Hake among the earliest composers to call this movement "sonata."[161] Actually, Rosenmüller used "sonata" only in the over-all title, preferring to call each of the individual introductory pieces "Sinfonia." There probably was no need, and perhaps too little reason, for the writer Karl Nef to argue at length for the tracing of these pieces to the Venetian opera sinfonia.[162] As we have also seen, both the sonata and sinfonia, as well as the style and form traits associated with them, had an independent existence older, more fruitful, and more developed than that of the opera overture up to the period in question. Rosenmüller's sinfonias are cycles of several contrasting movements, usually related by similar incipits and partially integrated by the exact repetition of an inner movement (always the important one in triple meter) at the end. Homophony and broad melodic lines prevail.

Rosenmüller's sonatas of 1682 are scored variously in SS/-, SB/-, SSB/-, SSAB/-, and SSAAB/bass settings for violins, violas, and *b. c.*, with wind options implied in the title. They represent his most developed and expressive instrumental music. These are the sonatas that Meyer regarded as quite the opposites of Weckmann's in the characteristically north German style (see p. 244).[163] They are outwardly similar to the sinfonias of the 1667 set, including the similar incipits and sometimes a return at the end to an inner movement. But they also show that greater economy of material, sense of direction, and breadth that may be attributed as much to the composer's own growth as to the general trends of the century. In the device of repeating the final cadence of a move-

---

158. NEF has done the main studies of Rosenmüller's instrumental music, especially -DEUTSCHEN, pp. 2 ff. and 23 ff., -SUITE, p. 62 ff., and the preface in DDTm, XVIII (mod. ed. of the 1670 set). Among other mod. eds., at least 5 sonatas from the 1682 set have been published separately (cf. ALTMANN), including Nos. 1 and 2 in SS/bass setting, NAGELSm, nos. 29 and 30 (both Saffe, with prefaces).

159. Thematic index in BIBLIOTHÈQUE NATIONALE, VII, 177 ff. Cf. also, MEYER, p. 239.

160. E.g., RIEMANN-TRIOSONATEN, p. 148.

161. Cf. NEF-SUITE, p. 61 ff.

162. Cf. DDTm, XVIII, v ff., after the lead of HEUSS-SINFONIEN. A first objection to this theory, though on somewhat chauvinistic grounds, is voiced in MENNICKE, p. 31 ff.

163. Cf. MEYER, pp. 78-86, with examples.

Ex. 52. From "Prestissimo" in Johann Rosenmüller's Sonata 1, 1682 (after NAGELsm, no. 29, p. 8, but without the editorial additions).

ment as an echo Rosenmüller tends to confirm a sense of balance in the form (Ex. 52), although he does not attain the perspective and sure purpose to be found in Corelli, either in the separate movements or the complete cycle.

The number of movements in these sonatas of 1682 varies from 3 to 12. Although the 1667 set had lacked the gigue used by Becker in 1668 to complete the newly standard cycle of dances, giguelike finales without the title occur in some of Rosenmüller's sonatas of 1682. With regard to texture, even the quasi-fugal movements are relatively homophonic, for the harmonic rhythm is usually very slow and such counterpoint as there is is mostly of the harmonic, decorative sort. There are many original details and much superior writing in the melodic lines, the rhythm, and the harmony—original often to the point of subjective fantasy. Both Mattheson and Scheibe still expressed high praise for Rosenmüller more than a half century after his death.[164]

Finally, in our second group of Austrians and Germans we come to the major composer, organist, and predecessor of Bach, **Dietrich**

164. MATTHESON-EHRENPFORTE, pp. 148 and 357; SCHEIBE-CRITISCHER, p. 651.

Buxtehude (*ca.* 1637-1707). Now thought to have descended from a German family active in Denmark,[165] Buxtehude came to Lübeck about 1667. Apparently without ever leaving that city after he arrived, he soon won a high international reputation as organist at the Marienkirche and especially as composer for the well-known, spiritual Abendmusik concerts, sponsored from about the time of his birth by the Lübeck merchants' group.[166] Above all, Buxtehude wrote sacred and secular keyboard music and sacred vocal music. But he also composed at least three sets of melo/bass sonatas that were published in Lübeck (1684) and Hamburg (Opp. 1 and 2 in 1696),[167] at least eight others now known in MSS,[168] and a few short, introductory orchestral sonatas in cantatas and other vocal works (when the title "sinfonia" is not preferred, without distinction in this sense).[169]

The first published set of 1684 is lost. Its date and title are of interest nonetheless. The date confirms Friedrich Blume's speculation that Buxtehude had composed some of his sonatas before the two sets of 1696 were published,[170] apparently within the period between 1678-87, when Pirro says Buxtehude did most of his composing for the Abendmusik concerts.[171] Buxtehude himself seemed to imply in the dedication of his first 1696 set that he was offering his sonatas at a time when musical activities had waned in Lübeck.[172] On the other hand, the title of the 1684 set would seem partially to contradict Blume's suggestion that Buxtehude's sonatas were intended for use primarily in the Liturgy, as at Communion,[173] for it contains the words "appropriate for church and *Tafel-music.*" Also, one can find the word "Gigue" over the finale of Sonata 3 in Op. 2, and cembalo rather than organ specified as the realizing instrument in both Opp. 1 and 2. And there is the fact that in place of its present "Allegro" finale, Sonata 4 of Op. 1 was originally followed by a complete standard suite known in a MS version that appears to be more rudimentary and therefore earlier.[174]

Perhaps some of Buxtehude's sonatas extant only in MSS are identical with sonatas in the lost set of 1684.[175] Like the latter, most of them

---

165. MGG, II, 548 ff. (Blume).

166. MGG, II, 552 and 557 ff.; I, 32 (Stahl).

167. The 1684 set is reported in GÖHLER, II, 12, a reliable source. Why are the two sets of 1696 labelled Opp. 1 and 2?

168. Cf. MEYER, p. 193 (but with errors).

169. Regarding this introductory type cf. PIRRO-BUXTEHUDE, p. 479, and MGG, II, 564 and 567; among mod. eds.: DDTm, XIV (Seiffert), 1, 15, 39, 57; FOCK-TRIO-SONATENm, p. 1.

170. MGG, II, 564.   171. PIRRO-BUXTEHUDE, p. 438.

172. Cf. PIRRO-BUXTEHUDE, p. 453.   173. MGG, II, 552.

174. Cf. PIRRO-BUXTEHUDE, pp. 445 ff. and 455.

175. The sonatas are discussed subjectively, with some reservations, in PIRRO-BUXTEHUDE, p. 438 ff., and objectively in STAHL-BUXTEHUDE, p. 39 ff., and

are in SS/- or SSB/bass settings, whereas all of the 14 sonatas of Opp. 1 and 2 are in SB/bass settings. The essentially homophonic introductory sonatas in his vocal works are scored not only in multivoice settings, in the usual manner of his contemporaries and of his father-in-law and immediate predecessor Franz Tunder,[176] but in melo/bass settings, presumably with multiple performance intended.[177] Thus, one such piece has the noteworthy title, *Sonatina forte con molti violini all unisono*.

The viola da gamba is Buxtehude's preferred *concertante* bass instrument. An unusual scoring is that of the MS Sonata in D for viola da gamba and *violone* (in cello range), the latter being variously a duplication or *concertante* version of the *b. c.*, or a third, completely independent line. In this sonata and three others (Op. 2, No. 5, and the SSB/bass MSS in F and C), each of the *concertante* instruments is given an entire inner movement in which to play a solo with the *b. c.*, all the instruments playing together only in the outer movements. Not often does the *b. c.* share in the thematic material. The writing for the instruments is effective. On occasion the passagework, the double- or triple-stops, the more ornamental figuration, and the quasi cadenzas presuppose a fairly brilliant technique (e.g., Op. 1, No. 6; Op. 2, Nos. 3 and 5; MS sonatas in G, F, and A minor [SSB/bass], and A minor [SB/bass]).

There is an average of 5 to 8 movements in Buxtehude's sonatas, with extremes of 3 and 13. Their order is based on contrast, the outer movements being fast more often than not. Otherwise there is no set plan. Although Buxtehude significantly changed from German to Italian titles for his sonata collections, the plan of Corelli's church sonatas seems not to have reached or influenced him, nor reached any other north German, for that matter. Nearest to the Italian sonata in style are his short, transitional slow movements, which recall Legrenzi's as much as any other composer's. These movements provide the only sense of key change in the cycles and often attain considerable subjective depth in both harmony and line (Ex. 53). The other movements consist chiefly of fugal allegros, variations on *ostinato* basses, dance types—mostly in

EINSTEIN-GAMBA, pp. 50 ff. and 58 ff. A thorough discussion is wanting. Opp. 1 and 2 and six of the MS sonatas (including three never published—the early version of Op. 1, No. 4; Son. in A minor, SB/bass; and Son. in G, SSB/bass) are copied in EINSTEIN-SCOREsm, IV. Among mod. eds.: Opp. 1 and 2 complete, Sons. in C (SSB/bass) and D (SSB/bass), and the Suite originally intended for Op. 1, No. 4, all in DDTm, XI (Stiehl, with preface, but see EINSTEIN-GAMBA, p. 50, for the corrected title); MS Son. in F (SSB/bass), EINSTEIN-GAMBA, p. 103; cf. also, ALTMANN.

176. Cf. DDTm, III (Seiffert), 22 and 57; BROWN-BACH, p. 2 ff.
177. Cf. BROWN-BACH, p. 4 ff.

Ex. 53. From Sonata 7 of Op. 1 by Dietrich Buxtehude (after DDTm, XI, 74).

gigue style—without the titles, and free movements in recitative style.

In nearly all these movements there is a curious mixture of sure craftsmanship and diffuse structures.   Fantasy, sometimes of a very original sort, is the dominant element throughout some of the sonatas (e.g., Op. 1, No. 6).   Frequently, even in a fugal allegro that seems to be driving steadily ahead, Buxtehude will allow the tension to become dissipated by loose fantasy before the end or by a deceptive cadence leading into the slow movement (e.g., the finale of the SB/bass MS sonata in A minor and the "Allegro" of Son. 1 in Op. 1).   How emotionally such passages were intended to be played is hard to say.   There are no graduated dynamics indicated, but one does find hints in the terms "Con discretione" (Op. 1, No. 6) and "Concitato" (Op. 2, No. 5).

In all of the faster movements there is much calculated, patterned writing, using sequences of zigzag or other involute figures in the manner associated with north German organ music.   Not seldom the figure simply persists on the same pitch level, for its instrumental effect and the sonorities of echo dynamics (Ex. 54).   Variations on *ostinato* basses naturally provide an abundance of such figures.   This German form type that we have met so often in this period occurs in almost every one of Buxtehude's sonatas, sometimes making up nearly all of the sonata (e.g., the SB/bass MS in A minor and Op. 2, No. 2).   As always, it provides the most stable kind of form.   A short and exceptionally attractive example is the "Violino Solo" in Sonata 5 of Op. 1, in which the melody as well as the bass is a constant in the variation treatment.

Here, amidst sonatas that are generally conservative in their styles and forms, the balanced period structure is conspicuously modern.

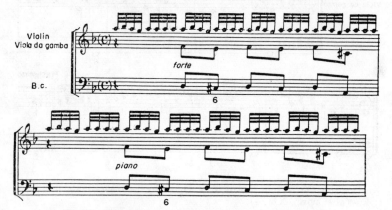

Ex. 54. From an unmarked movement in Sonata 6 of Op. 1 by Dietrich Buxtehude (after DDTm, XI, 62).

Chapter 12

Austria and Germany from about 1700 to 1750

Our third group of composers in Austria and Germany lived in a period of constant political turmoil and readjustment. The Wars of Spanish, Polish, and Austrian Succession were waged and decided none too happily, Frederick the Great came into power (1740), and meanwhile Germany became more than ever a system of little, independent monarchies. At the same time, the West was brought to the start of a new intellectual fermentation that was to culminate in the next half century in the writings of Lessing, Goethe, and Schiller, and to exert a profound influence on the arts in general.

The 35 composers to be noted in this group happen to number about a fourth fewer than those in the second group. But they include two of the greatest Baroque figures, Bach and Handel, and several others, like Fux, Telemann, and Mattheson, of much importance. Yet none of these main composers devoted himself wholly or even principally to the sonata as did Corelli, Veracini, and Tartini in Italy. Among all 35 names only four are those of Italian-born musicians who were living abroad, chief of whom was Abaco in Munich.

Austria (Fux)

A half century before Vienna was to become the supreme center of the Classic sonata there were but two composers active in that city who deserve mention here, such had become the all-prevailing interest in opera and sacred choral music. Even these two gave to the sonata only a lesser part of their attention. One was **Johann Joseph Fux** (*ca.* 1660-1741), generally regarded as the most important Baroque musician in Vienna, and the other was Porpora. Fux probably spent some time in Italy, perhaps in Corelli's sphere, and may have studied with any of his own predecessors right in Vienna, although he cannot be placed there definitely until 1696.[1] From 1698 on he served successively under three avid music lovers at the Imperial court—Leopold I, Joseph I, and Karl VI—becoming Hofkapellmeister (after M. A. Ziani) from 1715 until his death. His main contributions were his church music and his celebrated counterpoint treatise, still highly valued today. In his own day his oratorios and operas came next in importance, and only after these his instrumental music.

Apparently Fux left about 52 ensemble and keyboard sonatas, although a definitive list of his complete works is still lacking.[2] A supposed publication of 36 of his "trio" sonatas in Amsterdam (without any further information) is no longer to be found.[3] Otherwise the sonatas were all left in MSS that generally cannot be dated with any certainty.[4] Not a few of these sonatas have one or more movements that are used in more than one sonata or are transcribed from some other work by Fux, such as an opera or oratorio overture. One complete sonata, K. 351.2, proves to be merely a copy of Corelli's Op. 1, No. 5.[5] In one MS seven of the sonatas also exist in what are assumed to be Fux's own transcriptions for organ or cembalo, along with other pieces that should give him a niche in the history of Viennese keyboard music.[6]

Fux's sonatas were supposedly (though not unequivocally) intended for liturgical use,[7] most probably before, during, or after the Gradual and certain of the Divine Offices.[8] They were evidently performed in the frequent church manner with more than one player to a part—as "starke Sonaten," to use the contemporary term of Mattheson[9] and other Germans—for they exist with multiple MS parts. Thus, in the prevailing setting, SSB/bass, are usually found two first and two second violin parts, a *concertante* bassoon part, and organ *b. c.* reinforced by cello.[10] On occasion further winds probably replaced or reinforced these instru-

---

1. Biographic information from MGG, IV (Liess), 1159 ff.
2. Cf. KÖCHEL-FUX, Beilage X, items 320, 338-351, 360-397, and 398-403. Adler (DTÖm, IX, Part 2, vii) mentions 51. The total of 43 in MGG, IV, 1164 and 1166, is an attempt to eliminate duplications and transcriptions; see also, LIESS-FUX, pp. 75, 76, and 78. LIESS-TRIO is a monograph on 37 of these sonatas in certain Vienna MSS (cf. p. 13), including scores of 11 representative movements and shorter examples. Among other mod. eds.: 3 other movements, LIESS-WIENER, p. 210 ff.; 2 Sons. *a 4* and *a 3*, DTÖm, IX, Part 2 (Adler); about 6 more sons. in separate issues, cf. MGG, IV, 1174.
3. Cf. MGG, IV, 1164, and LIESS-WIENER, p. 106.
4. Cf. LIESS-TRIO, p. 14 ff., and DTÖm, LXXXV (Schenk), ix ff.
5. MGG, IV, 1166. The "K." refers to the numbered catalog of works in KÖCHEL-FUX.
6. Mod. ed. of all 7 sons. and other keyboard pieces: DTÖm, LXXXV (Schenk, with preface).
7. KÖCHEL-FUX, p. 58.
8. Cf. DTÖm, LXXXV, viii ff.
9. MATTHESON-BESCHÜTZTE, p. 129.
10. Cf. LIESS-TRIO, p. 15.

ments.[11]   There are also a few sonatas in which Fux seems to be following Georg Muffat by prescribing *tutti* and *soli,* although his interest is evidently limited to the quantitative contrasts rather than any further style or form traits of the concerto grosso.[12]   The writing for the instruments makes no special demands and only rarely exhibits any display for its own sake unless it be the profusion of *agréments* to be found in the keyboard transcriptions.   The latter are fairly literal arrangements, often in trio setting.   Although playable enough, they are not especially idiomatic.

The majority of Fux's sonatas are in three movements, often F-S-F in the frequent order of the Italian opera sinfonia and concerto grosso.[13] Two writers on Fux differ widely on the extent to which these movements interrelate in the whole sonata.   Andreas Liess regards them generally as quite haphazardly brought together,[14] Erich Schenk, as closely united by numerous ties (with special reference to the keyboard transcriptions).[15] At the much broader level on which the present survey must be made, these relationships, including the usual contrasts and some similarity of incipits, seem average, not more nor less.   As might be expected from the author of *Gradus ad Parnassum,* strict fugues or fugal movements outrank the other movements in both importance and quantity.[16]   The subjects are extended, plastic, and distinctive, sometimes undergoing changes during the fugue; expositions and episodes are skillfully alternated; and a clear if somewhat conservative tonal plan is defined by the internal cadences in nearly related keys.   The non-fugal movements include the elegant slow type, usually in triple meter with a saraband pattern.[17]   This type is tonally transitional and freer in texture, though still more polyphonic than the corresponding movements of Corelli or Vivaldi. Other non-fugal movements include variations on *ostinato* basses that themselves are often varied, one such movement being an imaginative "Passagaglia" (the same spelling Biber had used).[18]   In one sonata all three movements are strict canons for two violas da gamba over an independent *b. c.*[19]

The music of this "Austrian Palestrina" is notably conservative for its time,[20] the sonatas belonging back in the period of Leopold I (d. 1705) if not earlier.   The effect, if any, of the sonatas on future trends must have been the negative one of stemming the tide of the newer Italian

11. Cf. DTÖm, IX, Part 2, vi.
12. Cf. LIESS-TRIO, p. 82 ff. and Beilage 9b.
13. Cf. LIESS-TRIO, p. 42 ff.   14. LIESS-TRIO, p. 44 ff.
15. DDTm, LXXXV, xii ff.   16. Cf. LIESS-TRIO, p. 47 ff.
17. Cf. LIESS-TRIO, p. 69 ff.
18. Cf. LIESS-TRIO, p. 77 ff. and Beilage 8.
19. Mod. ed.: HORTUSM, no. 30 (Wolff).
20. Cf. MGG, IV, 1167 ff.

styles. However, writers on Fux have seen more positive contributions in certain Styrian dance rhythms, including those of the *Ländler* and minuet, that he passed on to Wagenseil, Gottlieb Muffat, and others of his pupils or followers. But such rhythms are certainly less evident in his sonatas than in his orchestral suites or other secular instrumental music.[21] The same writers have also recognized motivic treatment in the development sections of Classic symphonies that points back to Fux's fugal techniques, and they have recalled the influence of *Gradus ad Parnassum* long after Beethoven lived, although surprising disparities have been noted between Fux the theorist and Fux the composer.[22]

The distinguished opera composer, singing teacher, and rival of Handel, **Nicola Antonio Porpora** (1686-1766), lived mainly in Naples and Venice, but it is his stays in London from 1733 to 1736 and especially in Vienna from 1752 to 1758 that concern us here.[23] In London in 1736 were published his six *Sinfonie da camera a tre istromenti*, Op. 2, reprinted about four years later by the ever-alert John Walsh as *Six Sonatas for two Violins with a Thorough Bass*, Op. 2.[24] In Vienna in 1754 appeared his *Sonate XII di violino, e basso*, also reprinted, but not until about 1800.[25] Other sonatas by Porpora, both "trio" and "solo," have been reported,[26] including a fine sonata for cello and *b. c.* left in MS.[27] But no comparison of the various MSS and editions has been made, nor any detailed study of the sonatas, for that matter.

Porpora's sonatas are mostly in four movements, in the S-F-S-F sequence, and only occasionally in three movements. Dance titles are not used, even in the court sonatas. These last seem to differ chiefly in their somewhat shorter movements and lighter texture, there being less fugal writing, too. Using those traits as the criteria, one may include among court sonatas not only the six in Op. 2 but the last six of the 1754 set as well as the cello sonata. Fairly strict fugues occur as the second movements of the first six sonatas in the 1754 set. These are the six fugues "or rather Fugatos" that Clementi arranged for organ or piano.[28]

21. Cf. DTÖm, IX, v ff.; RIETSCH-FUX; LIESS-TRIO, p. 73 and Beispiele 29; MGG, IV, 1171 ff.
22. Cf. LIESS-TRIO, p. 33 ff. (with examples).
23. Dates from GROVE, VI, 876 ff. (Walker).
24. Among mod. eds.: Sons. 1-4, LACCETTIm; Son. 4, COLLEGIUMm, no. 23; Son. 6, HAUSMUSIKm, no. 136.
25. Cf. BRITISH PRINTED, II, 294, and HAAS-CAT. 20, no. 509. Among mod. eds.: Sons. 5, 7, 8, and 10, CLASSICIm I, no. 25; cf. also, ALTMANN, p. 241.
26. E.g., cf. EITNER-QL, VIII, 23, and HAAS-CAT. 20, no. 511.
27. Cf. BRITISH MS, III, 249; STRAETEN-VIOLONCELLO, pp. 375 and 377. Mod. ed.: SCHOTT CELLOm, no. 2 (Piatti); this last is not merely an arrangement of a violin sonata, as assumed in WEIGL, p. 100.
28. CLEMENTI-HARMONYm, I, 38 ff. Are they also the same as the keyboard arrangements of sonatas listed in EITNER-QL, VIII, 23?

The fugues and the braidlike texture that still prevails in the non-fugal movements make Porpora's sonatas conservative in the way that Fux's were. They reveal even more breadth in their purposeful drive to and from a few main peaks, especially the 1754 sonatas, which rank among the finer "solo" sonatas of the time. But clear phrase grouping in a predominantly homophonic texture is not yet employed. However, if Fux's influence is actually to be found in Porpora's music, it did not extend to the technical idiom. Porpora's "solo" writing is much more advanced, with frequent passagework, double-stops, especially in the fugues, and rather rich ornamentation.

South Germany (Pez, Abaco)

Besides Abaco the chief of eight composers in south Germany to be named here was **Johann Christoph Pez** (1664-1716). A probable pupil of J. K. Kerll, Pez was a singer and violinist active successively in Munich, Bonn, Munich, and Stuttgart.[29] Possibly he got to London, too, if eight somewhat duplicative listings by John Walsh between 1704 and 1712 can be taken as a clue.[30] One such listing, that of Sonata 3, Op. 1, in ANTH. HARMONIAM (1707), places Pez among "Six most Eminent Authors," along with Torelli, Purcell, Bassani, Pepusch, and Albinoni.[31] Spread over a period from about 1690 to 1712, the bracketing dates of Pez's sonatas overlap the sonata production of our second and third groups. The chief extant collection is Op. 1, weightily entitled *Duplex genius sive gallo-italus instrumentorum concentus 12 constans Symphoniis.* Containing 12 SSB/bass cycles separately headed "Sonata," this collection was published in Augsburg in 1696 while Pez was in Bonn and reprinted at least twice.[32] But it probably was composed before he left Munich in 1694 and shortly after a visit to Rome in 1689, where, to judge by certain traits of his style, he may have been admitted to the circle of Corelli and Pasquini.[33]

Whereas Pez's Op. 1 seems to be a church collection in so far as it contains frequent fugues and prefers tempo to dance titles, his later collections indicate an increasing interest in lighter court music, especially dances of French origin. These later collections include two for two flutes and *b. c.,* the first being *Sonate da Camera or Chamber Musick*

---

29. Cf. the copious biographic, bibliographic, and analytic details in the preface to DTBm, XXVII-XXVIII (Wallner).

30. Cf. SMITH-WALSH, nos. 150a, 157, 231, 242, 257, 258, 295, and 420.

31. SMITH-WALSH, no. 257.

32. SMITH-WALSH, no. 420, appears to be a third reprint, *ca.* 1712, in addition to the two cited in DTBm, XXVII-XXVIII, xlv.

33. Cf. DTBm, XXVII-XXVIII, xxvi and xlv. Sons. 4, 5, 7, 8, 10, and 12 are reprinted in this volume.

Consisting of Several Sutes of Overtures and Aires and the second being lost.[34] A sample of these is to be seen in a D-minor sonata re-published in 1934 from a MS in Rostock.[34] It begins with a French overture called "Sinfonia" and follows with a "Bourrée," "Aria," "Menuet (alternativement)," "Aria," and "Gigue." Other sonatas published separately or known only in MS include several that border on the solo or group concerto.[36]

The sonatas in Pez's Op. 1 average from four to seven movements in no set plan. Within many of the separate movements, especially the opening ones, there are often further tempo changes. The "gallo-italus" in the title suggests something of the internationalism we found in Georg Muffat. Wallner,[37] perhaps a bit too categorically, compartments the national traits. Italian in style, she says, are the multi-movement cycles, the toccata-like opening movements with their runs and tempo changes, and the hymnic and short, transitional slow movements. French in style are the regular rhythmic patterns, the tunes in the faster movements, the ornamentation, and the pastoral character of certain movements. But, she adds patriotically, although Pez's own country was not acknowledged in the title, German are the frequent fugal movements, including double and triple fugues, and the expressive depths that he attains.

In Stuttgart, where Pez spent his last years, **Reinhard Keiser** (1674-1739) served at court between 1719 and 1721.[38] Since three sonatas for flute, violin, and cembalo (*b. c.*) by Keiser are known through MSS in Rostock dated 1720,[39] Keiser is here placed in Stuttgart, although he is known primarily, of course, as the north German who developed opera significantly in Hamburg. All three sonatas have the S-F-S-F church plan, with suggestions of such dances as the siciliano, saraband, or minuet in the third movements. In general, the classic model of Corelli's sonatas is called to mind, although without quite the pathos and extent of line in the slow movements. To the faster movements, with their tunefulness, vivacious rhythms, and sure tonality, one is tempted to relate the contemporary opera ensemble. Imitative but not recherché writing prevails in all the movements. A harmonic peculiarity in nearly every movement is the sometimes abrupt reference to the subdominant chord of the subdominant key, occasionally with the effect of false relations.

34. Cf. SMITH-WALSH, nos. 231 and 241.
35. NAGELsm, no. 111 (Woehl). For a mod. ed. of another such sonata, cf. ALTMANN, p. 189.
36. Cf. DTBm, XXVII-XXVIII, xlviii ff.; also, MEYER, p. 230 ff. (with errors).
37. DTBm, XXVII-XXVIII, xlvii ff.
38. Cf. the main biographic source, VOIGT, p. 186 ff.
39. Among mod. eds.: NAGELsm, nos. 68, 114, and 132 (all Schenk, with prefaces).

The only other late Baroque name to mention in Stuttgart is that of the important composer of operas **Niccolo Jommelli** (1714-74). This Italian, who lived there from 1753-68, published at least one set of six SS/bass sonatas (London, *ca.* 1760)[40] and left a three-movement sonata in MS for four hands at one keyboard[41] that, even without an exact date, must be recognized as one of the earliest contributions to this subsequent branch of the sonata.[42] Like the duet sonata the "trio" sonatas are also in three movements. Their plan is consistently S-F-minuet. Further-more, in spite of the *b. c.*, they are on the border between Baroque and Classic styles in their generally slow harmonic rhythm, homophonic texture, and clearly phrased melodies. A modern edition and study of representative sonatas by Jommelli should have both historical and musi-cal significance.

The violinist and cellist **Evaristo Felice dall' Abaco** (1675-1742) has already been cited as the chief Italian among our third group in Germany and Austria. Born in Verona, where Torelli was active before going to Bologna in 1685, Abaco served in Modena from 1696 to 1701, during which time he may well have come under T. A. Vitali's influence.[43] Thereafter, from 1704 until his death, Abaco served with increasing honor and distinction at the electoral court of Munich. Perhaps he arrived in time to know Pez. But the years between 1705 and 1715, when all three of his known sonata collections were published, he actually spent in Brussels, Paris, and other French cities, following Maximilian II in exile after the decisive battle of Blenheim (1704). Like Corelli, Abaco was exceptional among important sonata composers in leaving nothing but instrumental sonatas and concertos—in fact, exactly six sets of twelve cycles each, again.

All of Abaco's 36 sonatas have been reprinted in modern sources.[44] Opp. 1 and 4 are violin "solo" (S/bass) sonatas, first published in Brussels (*ca.* 1705) and Amsterdam (*ca.* 1715), respectively.[45] In the original, unpunctuated title of Op. 1 the probable significance of "a Violino é VioC overo Clavicembalo solo" was simply that the usual keyboard realization could be employed without the usual cello rein-

40. Cf. EITNER-QL, V, 299.

41. Listed in CAT. BRUXELLES, II, no. 6094.

42. Cf. SAINT/FOIX, I, 429; GANZER & KUSCHE, p. 149; KING-PIANO, p. 167; NEWMAN-EARLIEST, p. 204.

43. DTBm, I (Sandberger), includes a detailed, pathbreaking study of Abaco, his music, and his musical environment, briefly supplemented in DTBm, IX (also Sand-berger), and partially summarized in MGG, I, 10 ff. (Fellerer). Further biographic facts appear in BRENZONI-ABACO.

44. All of Opp. 1 and 4, and all but Sons. 4, 5, 7, and 9 of Op. 3 are in DTBm, I and IX. Among other mod. eds.: Op. 3, Sons. 4, 5, 9, COLLEGIUMm, nos. 41-43 (Riemann); Son. 7, RIEMANN-ABACOm.

45. See DTBm, I, xxxi ff., for full titles, dedications, and bases for dating.

forcement of the bass line, at the performer's discretion.[46]   On the other
hand, the full participation of the bass in the thematic material, the many
rapid notes in this bass—generally too rapid to allow for the chordal
filler sometimes inserted by the clavierist's left hand or even by the
cellist—and the total absence of *b. c.* figures in Op. 1 do allow for the
different conjecture that here were more sonatas scored optionally for
high and low strings or the right and left hands at the keyboard. (E.g.,
recall Buini's sonatas, p. 181.)   In Op. 4 the two-part writing is
similar, but the bass is figured and there is no mention of *clavicembalo*
in the title.   Only Abaco's Op. 3 (Paris, *ca.* 1714) contains "trio"
(SS/bass) rather than "solo" sonatas.   In these the two violin parts are
still about equal in range and importance.

Of the 36 sonatas 30 are classed by the composer as court sonatas,
with only the opening 6 of Op. 3 as church types.   Actually, most of
Abaco's sonatas illustrate very clearly the synthesis of church and court
types that prevailed around the turn of the century.   There are nondance
types in nearly all the court sonatas, and dance types, without the titles,
often in binary design, in each of the six church "trio" sonatas.   To be
sure, some of the court movements that have only tempo inscriptions are
dances, too.   Thus, in Op. 1, the finales of Sonatas 4 and 10 are like a
courante and a gigue, respectively.   But the only two dance types that
are named in Op. 1 are the "Giga" and the "Ciaconna."   In the court
sonatas of Op. 3 further dance types are to be found, including the
allemande, saraband, and gavotte.   And in Op. 4, although the gavotte
does not reappear, several other French dances are introduced, among
them the rondeau (Ex. 55) and passepied.   These last Abaco may have
heard in Modena, where French importations were much in favor.[47]

The majority of Abaco's sonatas are in four movements, and most
of these are in the standard order of S-F-S-F.   In many of the sonatas
the second slow movement is in the relative key, often ending with a
Phrygian cadence on the dominant.   Less often the movements are
interrelated by similar incipits (e.g., Op. 1, No. 7).   The practice of
topping off a set with something special in the final sonata is evident in
the variations on *ostinato* basses that dominate Sonata 12 in both Opp.
1 and 4.   Besides such movements and the dances, there are hymnic
adagios of the Corelli type, imitative movements or loose fugues, and
binary designs (e.g., the opening movement of Son. 6, Op. 3) in which
some "evolution"-minded writers have seen incipient "sonata form."[48]

46. Cf. DTBm, I, xxxv ff.
47. Cf. p. 137; also, DTBm, I, xxxix ff.
48. E.g., RIEMANN-KOMPOSITIONSLEHRE, I, 427 ff.; MENNICKE, p. 54 ff.

Ex. 55. From the third movement of Sonata 7, Op. 3, by Evaristo Felice dall' Abaco (after DTBM, IX, 73, but without the editor's realization).

Such accidental designs are belied by the generally conservative nature of Abaco's music—its polyphonic texture, motivic treatment, fast harmonic rhythm, and relatively neutral ideas. This music is representative of the Baroque sonata at its classic peak of clarity and sureness of design. Perhaps its most progressive aspects are the regular, balanced phrases of the French dances and an occasional new affectiveness that shows up chiefly in greater preoccupation with details (Ex. 56). Both of these traits tend to divide Opp. 3 and, especially, 4 from Op. 1. But with respect to the depth, pathos, and large view of design that distinguish Abaco's sonatas, his Op. 1 was already a remarkably mature work.

The other composers in south Germany can only be given brief mention. The organist **Justinus à Desponsatione B. M. V.** was a Carmelite friar in Abensberg in 1723 when he published *Musicalische Arbeith und Kurtz-weil*. Appended to this composition treatise (pp. 120 ff.) is a piece headed "Cembalo, Sonata, Alla moderna," one of the infrequent examples of its class from Germany in the early 18th century. The sonata is a one-movement piece of 61 measures, with simple but idiomatic writing and with figures over the bass to indicate a filling out of the texture in three passages that are assumed to be, or are marked, "Adagio." One section in 6/4 meter is marked "Allegro."[49]

Probably while in Württemberg **Johann Daniel Hardt** (1696 to at

49. There is a brief but somewhat misleading description of this piece in SEIFFERT-KLAVIERMUSIK, p. 331.

Ex. 56. From the opening of Sonata 1, Op. 4, by Evaristo Felice dall' Abaco (after DTBm, IX, 55, but without the editor's realization).

least 1755) wrote a set of six sonatas for his instrument, viola da gamba, and *b. c.*, left in MS, and he wrote the four-movement keyboard sonata that appeared in 1760 in ANTH. HAFFNERm (VII, Part 1).[50] The former have been described as "not particularly interesting,"[51] but the tunefulness and effective proportions of the keyboard sonata can be vouched for here. However, this piece is already in the *galant* style.

Between at least 1718 and 1752 the virtuoso violinist **Sebastian Bodinus** was active in the region of Baden, including Württemberg. Born in Altenburg (Saxony), Bodinus (Bodini?) may have been of Italian origin.[52] During his service in Baden he published at least nine collections of sonatas, including at least six in installments under the title *Musicalische Divertiments*. None can be dated except by circumstantial evidence.[53] At least 60 sonatas are contained in these collections, in a variety of settings for string or wind instruments from S/- to SSS/bass. One sonata, with the plan S-F-S (a "Siciliana" finale), for two violins or oboes and *b. c.*, has been made available.[54] It confirms the editor's praise of Bodinus, for it reveals strength in the lines and harmony, and logic in the forms. A. Moser also has high praise for this composer,

50. Cf. EITNER-QL, V, 22; MGG, V, 1505 (Pauls). Although Hardt is supposed to have retired in 1755, the Haffner edition of 1760 still has him at the Württemberg court.
51. STRAETEN-VIOLONCELLO, p. 81 ff.
52. Cf. SCHMIDL, I, 204, and Supp., p. 106.
53. Cf. EITNER-QL, II, 82; FISCHER-BODINUSm (with preface).
54. Son. 1 in E flat, from the "zweiter Teil" of *Musicalische Divertiments* (1727 or 1728), FISCHER-BODINUSm.

especially his exploits in range and technique.[55]   Further editions and
a detailed study are clearly in order.

Last to be named in the Württemberg area, the Venetian oboist,
violinist, cellist, and tenor **Giovanni Platti** (*ca.* 1700-62) served in
Würzburg from at least 1722 until his death.[56]   If only in deference to
Torrefranca's championship of this composer as a forerunner of Mozart
and Beethoven,[57] Platti has been saved for that substantial group of
"pre-Classic" composers whose publications gave such an impetus to
the keyboard sonata around 1740 (cf. p. 330).   But it now appears possible that the controversial cembalo sonatas, the pieces in which Torrefranca was primarily interested, were not the work of this Platti but of
a son, Giovanni Benedetto Platti, whose supposed birth about 1720
would place him in the next era in any case.[58]   Hence in Platti senior
we would be left with a name to be included here mainly to help keep
the record straight.   Among some 80 works of various types credited
to Platti senior in the "Wiesentheid library," not one is for cembalo.[59]
Presumably the 12 four-movement church sonatas for cello and *b. c.*
that Torrefranca brought to light more recently, with no abatement of
his enthusiasm,[60] are by this Platti (as well as four sonata-like *Ricercati*
for cello and *b. c.* published recently[61]).   Those sonatas exist in two MSS
dated from 1725 or earlier.   None of them has been made available yet.
Until more information is forthcoming it seems best to list Platti senior
as the possible composer of interesting sonatas and to save further discussion until the supposed son comes up in a succeeding volume.   61a

Central Germany (*J. S. Bach, Quantz, J. F. Fasch*)

As with our second group, the third had its largest representation in
central Germany.   Among some 20 names, the first in time and importance was that of the Thuringian **Johann Sebastian Bach** (1685-
1750).   The pre-eminence of Bach's music as marking the confluence
and culmination of past trends and the font of not a few new ones is
apparent within his sonatas as well as his total output.   We have already
met specific precedents or actual sources for his sonatas and other
music in the works of such main predecessors as Legrenzi, Corelli,
Albinoni, Marcello, and Vivaldi in Italy; Biber in Austria; and J. J.
Walther, Krieger, Kühnel, Kuhnau, Reinken, Rosenmüller, Buxtehude,

---

55. MOSER-VIOLINSPIEL, p. 329 ff.
56. Cf. TORREFRANCA, pp. 443 ff. and 778 ff.
57. Cf. NEWMAN-THIRTEENm, p. 4 ff.
58. HOFFMANN/ERBRECHT-KLAVIERMUSIK, p. 82.
59. *Ibid.*
60. TORREFRANCA-RICOGNIZIONI (with 23 short examples).
61. HORTUSm, nos. 87 and 88 (Zobeley, with preface).

and Abaco, among many others, in Germany. There were still other predecessors whom we have yet to meet in this survey by countries and regions, including Telemann in north Germany, Purcell in London, and Couperin in Paris. With such a broad background Bach quite naturally wrote sonatas in all the main scoring types that have become familiar here, whether orchestral, "trio," "solo," or keyboard (both stringed and organ). Furthermore, he contributed significantly to three variants of the "solo" type that had made but rare, isolated appearances before him. One was the unaccompanied sonata, another the sonata with a realized keyboard part instead of the usual *b. c.*, and the third the organ sonata in a complete cycle of movements. In these ways, as with his contributions to the keyboard concerto, Bach was an innovator as well as a conservative in sonata history.

Out of nearly 1,100 items more or less confirmed by Schmieder[62] as original compositions, arrangements, or direct transcriptions by Bach, about half are instrumental, but only about 45, or 4 per cent, are sonatas. Of course, quite apart from fussy questions of authenticity and original titles (e.g., "sonata" or "trio"?) this figure can hardly have any precise meaning, since Schmieder's separate items vary in the extreme from the shortest prelude to the whole Mass in B Minor. A partial corroboration is found in the fact that about three per cent of the pages of score in the Bach-Gesellschaft edition are devoted to sonatas, including different versions of the same works but not including four other sonatas discovered in more recent years. Unfortunately, even this figure is made very uncertain by the different amount of vertical space that different scorings require and by such further considerations as the relation of tempo to length. Hence, in this little statistical digression we are forced to the less methodical but more practical observation that modern Bach appreciation has shown an interest in at least certain of his sonatas quite out of proportion to their quantitative position. To support such an observation one might cite, for example, the full sonata listings in current record catalogs.

With regard to the distribution of Bach's sonatas by scoring types, it is surprising to find the largest percentage in the then unusual category of solo with realized keyboard, or over a third of the total of about 45 sonatas. It is equally surprising to find that fewer than a tenth are of that favorite Baroque type, the "trio" sonata. The other types also represent only from an eighth to a tenth of the total each. Whatever the scoring, it should be noted that Bach, above all a composer for the church, had almost exclusively the church plan and character in mind

62. SCHMIEDER-BWV.

when he used the title "sonata." With the possible exception of the unaccompanied flute piece (SCHMIEDER-BWV, no. 1013), the original title of which cannot be confirmed, his sets of dances are called by him not "sonate da camera" but "Partita" or "Suite" or some other title that does not use the word "sonata."

Only one of Bach's sonatas was published during his lifetime, that in *Musicalisches Opfer* (1747). Most of the chamber sonatas are thought to have been composed during his Köthen period (1717-23), where his activities centered around the instruments of the orchestra rather than the choir or the organ. But there are also sonatas as early as 1703 or 1704 and as late as 1747.

In the vast literature on Bach and his music the general question of what the sonata meant to him, especially in relation to his times, has had comparatively little attention.[63] Of special articles on the individual groups of sonatas the chief contributions are those on the unaccompanied violin sonatas.[64] As might be expected, there has been considerable interest in finding anticipations of "sonata form" in Bach's music, whether in the sonatas or other works. Thus, K. A. Rosenthal finds in several categories of his music a tendency toward ternary structure either by evolution of the binary dance design or compression of the loose rondo structure in fast concerto movements.[65] Attention has often been called to varying degrees of "sonata form" in such works as the opening movements of the "Italian Concerto," the third "English Suite," and Sonata 3 for organ, or Preludes 5, 14, and 24 in *The Well-Tempered Clavier* II and the Prelude to the "St. Anne's Fugue" for organ. Although it may be true that "there is nothing new under the sun or in Bach's music," the view hardly needs to be restated in this history that the essence of the Classic sonata lies primarily in a new approach to texture, harmonic rhythm, metric organization, and tonal plan rather than in the often accidental, external features of any one design. In these respects, more often than not Bach was conservative in his day. Polyphony, fast harmonic rhythm, relatively free meter, and constant tonal flux were still essential traits of his style.[66]

By way of more specific information we may take note of Bach's

63. BROWN-BACH is a careful, detailed master's thesis on this question, of considerable help to the present survey. HAUSSWALD-BACHZEIT is a brief discussion, with emphasis on the scoring types.

64. The starting points for each discussion are still, of course, SPITTA-BACH and the prefaces in BACH-WERKEM. Mod. eds. and further references are given under the respective listings in SCHMIEDER-BWV. At the time of this writing no sonatas had yet appeared in the new Bärenreiter edition of Bach begun in 1954.

65. ROSENTHAL-BACH.

66. Cf. TOVEY-BACHm. IA, vi.

sonatas by scoring types. Four of them are introductory movements
to cantatas composed between 1704 and 1725.[67] Stemming from the
similarly purposed sonatas by Buxtehude, Tunder, Kuhnau, and many
another German, these are short pieces of a generally festive character
for variously comprised orchestras. The earliest (SCHMIEDER-BWV, no.
15) is in the S-F plan of the French overture. The second (SCHMIEDER-
BWV, no. 106) is the familiar, undulatory "Sonatina" to *Gottes Zeit ist
die allerbeste Zeit* (or "Actus tragicus"). The third (SCHMIEDER-BWV,
no. 182) is like a concerto grosso,[68] with solo exchanges between a flute
and violin over a simple harmonic support by strings and *b. c.* And the
fourth example (SCHMIEDER-BWV, no. 31) is the longest and most fully
scored, beginning and ending somewhat in the manner of a fanfare.
Bach left about three times as many introductory sinfonias as sonatas.
Although an absolute distinction cannot be drawn, the sinfonias are
generally more developed, unified, flowing, and intimate, with more
homogeneous scoring for fewer instruments.[69]

Some six sonatas for stringed keyboard instruments are attributed to
Bach, dating from about 1703 to 1720.[70] The only sonata originally
composed for keyboard is the five-movement one in D (SCHMIEDER-BWV,
no. 963). Like Bach's better known Capriccio in B flat, this relatively
inconsequential sonata was created in Arnstadt in 1704 and shows the
unmistakable influence of Kuhnau's keyboard sonatas.[71] The only
source is a MS copy with the title "Sonata clamat in D♯ et Fuga in
H moll," suggesting that "sonata" had an introductory connotation here,
too. The last movement, bearing the faulty inscription, "Thema all'
Imitatio Gallina Cucca," develops motives clearly identifiable with the
hen and the cuckoo.[72] Another of Bach's keyboard sonatas, this one
in D minor (SCHMIEDER-BWV, no. 964), is assumed to be his own transcription of his unaccompanied violin sonata in A minor (SCHMIEDER-
BWV, no. 1003).[73] And at least three transcriptions from two movements of his first and third unaccompanied violin sonatas (SCHMIEDER-
BWV, nos. 1001 and 1005) are assumed to be his own arrangements for
lute, harp, and keyboard, respectively (SCHMIEDER-BWV, nos. 539, 1000,

---

67. SCHMIEDER-BWV, nos. 15, 31, 106, and 182; in no. 15 the introduction has no
title but is almost identical with the interludial "Sonata" that is the eighth movement.

68. As suggested editorially in BACH-WERKEm, XXXVII, 23.

69. Almost the opposite distinction seems to be implied in SPITTA-BACH, I, 293.

70. Cf. KELLER-BACH, pp. 58 ff., 101 ff., 105 ff.

71. Cf. SPITTA-BACH, I, 243 ff.

72. Cf. KELLER-BACH, p. 58 ff.; GEIRINGER-BACH, p. 260 ff. The MS title and
this inscription were omitted in BACH-WERKEm, XXXVI, 19 ff.

73. There seems to be no special justification for the "Echtheit angezweifelt"
that still appears beside each keyboard sonata except no. 963 in SCHMIEDER-BWV.

and 968).[74]   The keys are changed in these transcriptions largely to suit the range and technical convenience of the chosen instrument.[75]   Two other keyboard transcriptions are the ones noted earlier (p. 247) as Bach's arrangements (SCHMIEDER-BWV, nos. 965 and 966) of the first and part (minus lost movements?) of the third sonatas in Reinken's *Hortus musicus*.   Only a measure-by-measure analysis can show the ingenuity with which the texture of the originals has been filled out and enriched, both contrapuntally and harmonically, to make these six transcriptions.[76]   Furthermore, much new material has been added to extend the sections of the Reinken originals.   76a

Probably the most played of Bach's sonatas are the first, third, and fifth of his *Sei Solo a violino senza basso accompagnato* (SCHMIEDER-BWV, nos. 1001, 1003, and 1005), dated 1720 in the original holograph.[77] Along with his partitas or suites written variously for unaccompanied violin, or cello, or viola pomposa, or flute, they mark an unquestioned peak in the distinguished but limited literature of this sort.[78]   There had been but few predecessors, among them the pieces by Biber and Westhoff mentioned earlier.   Since Bach's time his "solo" music—his only music so defined in the titles he himself gave—has gradually become the *sine qua non* of the finished violinist, cellist, or flutist, alongside *The Well-Tempered Clavier* for the clavierist, the organ sonatas for the organist, and the several other "bibles" that he left.   The violin sonatas pose severe technical problems as well as musical ones, especially those of fingering, intonation, and bowing such as would naturally be heightened by the remarkable polyphonic and chordal writing.[79]   That some musicians have regarded this music as too much for violin alone may be implied in Schumann's and other editions that have appeared with keyboard accompaniment added.[80]   In all three sonatas, as in a majority,

74. For a more doubtful item in this category see SCHMIEDER-BWV, no. 967 (a movement in A minor).   A supposed keyboard sonata known only as portions of a cantata (SCHMIEDER-BWV, no. 35; cf. BROWN-BACH, p. 28 ff.) is actually a fragment of a keyboard concerto in D minor (SCHMIEDER-BWV, no. 1059) related to this cantata.

75. Cf. SHANET-BACH.

76. Cf. the superimposed examples in KELLER-BACH, p. 102 ff.; see, also, KELLER-REINKEN.   An earlier discussion of interest on the first Reinken transcription, although not so recognized, is in COMBARIEU-SYMPHONIE, p. 459 ff.

77. Cf. BACH-FACSIMILEm.   On the early spread and popularity of this collection see MOSER-BACH, p. 22 ff., and ALTMANN-BACH.

78. An extended historical survey of unaccompanied violin music is provided in GATES-SOLO, including a section on Bach's contribution, p. 96 ff.   On the latter, three detailed studies, among others, are MOSER-BACH (primarily historical), PULVER-BACH (primarily pedagogic), and HAUSSWALD-STILISTIK (primarily style-critical).

79. Cf. SCHWEITZER-GEIGENBOGEN and GEIRINGER-BACH, p. 280, among numerous discussions of the type of bow used for this music.

80. Cf. ALTMANN-BACH, p. 206 ff.

Ex. 57.   From Sonata *2* for unaccompanied violin by Johann Sebastian Bach (after BACH-FACSIMILEm).

but not all, of Bach's sonatas, the S-F-S-F church sequence of movements prevails, although the dance title "Siciliano" appears over the second slow movement of Sonata 1.   Very subtle relationships of incipits can be found throughout the three sonatas.   The expressive reaches and structural logic of this music, as much in the freer as in the strictly fugal or the dancelike movements, must be attributed to a wealth of melodic, harmonic, contrapuntal, and rhythmic resources, and to a skill in their manipulation quite beyond compare in the Baroque Era (Ex. 57).

Less well known and less significant musically are Bach's few S/bass sonatas, including three each for transverse flute and *b. c.* (SCHMIEDER-

BWV, nos. 1033-1035) and for violin and *b. c.* (SCHMIEDER-BWV, nos. 1021, 1023, and 1024). One of the latter, in G (SCHMIEDER-BWV, no. 1021), was discovered in 1928, in an unquestioned autograph;[81] another, a partially weak, stylistically improbable work in C minor (SCHMIEDER-BWV, no. 1024), is identified as Bach's only uncertainly in the pioneer but badly overedited anthology of Baroque sonatas done before 1867 by Ferdinand David.[82] All of these sonatas are thought to have been composed in the Köthen period.[83] The four-movement church plan again predominates, but dances occur here and there as later movements, including the minuetto, siciliano, allemande, and gigue.

The three remaining groups of Bach's sonatas are those for organ, for solo with realized keyboard, and for two soloists with *b. c.* They differ, of course, in the number of players required, but do have in common their uniformly strict writing in three parts—that is, the traditional SS/bass setting, with a bass that supports much more often than it shares the thematic material. Bass figuring occurs consistently only in the literal "trios," and not in the organ sonatas at all. The six organ sonatas (SCHMIEDER-BWV, nos. 525-530) were probably composed shortly after Bach moved to Leipzig, for his eldest son, W. F. Bach.[84] Because they were originally designated "à 2 Clav. e Pedal" there has been some controversy as to the instrument originally intended,[85] but none as to what they should be played on today. Spitta aptly speaks of them as successfully crowning Bach's long attempt to insert a contrasting (slow) movement in the prelude-and-fugue plan.[86] They do stand apart in their consistent F-S-F sequence (the "Adagio" of Son. 4 being only a short introduction to the first movement). Thus, the order but not the types of the three movements often found in the Italian concerto grosso is reproduced in these masterly, extended, and somewhat austere sonatas. In this survey we have already met numerous examples of the one-movement, fugal type of organ "sonata," especially by Italian composers. But the point should be emphasized that Bach was here con-

81. Cf. BLUME-VIOLINSONATE and MT, LXX (1929), 788 ff.; mod. ed.: NBGm, XXX, Part 1 (Blume and Busch). But cf., also, p. 119 in the Kritischer Bericht, VI¹, of the *Neue Bach Ausgabe*.

82. -VIOLINSPIELm, II, 28. Its authenticity has lately been reasserted on bibliographic and internal (chiefly melodic) grounds in LEYDEN, then seriously challenged again in SIEGELE.

83. Cf. SCHMIEDER-BWV, p. 577.

84. Certain of the movements were arranged from earlier works and certain others were used in later works (cf. SCHMIEDER-BWV, p. 410).

85. E.g., cf. SPITTA-BACH, III, 211 ff.; SCHWEITZER-BACH, I, 278 ff.; HANDSCHIN-PEDALKLAVIER, pp. 418 and 425; APEL-DICTIONARY, p. 562; and FROTSCHER, p. 899. SCHRAMMEK, a valuable recent study of organ sonatas, both historical and analytic, summarizes strong arguments for the organ and not the "Pedalklavier" on p. 12.

86. SPITTA-BACH, III, 211.

tributing some of the earliest complete cycles for organ in the more general Baroque meaning of the term "sonata." Such sonatas were still even less common than those for stringed keyboard instruments. Only the slighter examples by Strozzi and Christian Ritter can be cited as predecessors.

Bach's 14 sonatas with realized keyboard include 5 for violin that are of unquestioned authenticity and are heard fairly often (SCHMIEDER-BWV, nos. 1014-1018) and 3 that are little known and cannot be confirmed, at least in this setting (SCHMIEDER-BWV, nos. 1019, 1020, and 1022); 3 for transverse flute (SCHMIEDER-BWV, nos. 1030-1032); and 3 for viola da gamba (SCHMIEDER-BWV, nos. 1027-1029).[87] This is a setting that we shall have occasion to recall later as one ancestor of the accompanied clavier sonata in the Classic Era. It, too, was developed by Bach with very little precedent, chiefly isolated examples (not all sonatas) such as Biagio Marini, Frescobaldi, and especially Pachelbel had left. Interesting are Bach's numerous short passages in which the bass is figured while the clavierist's right hand has rests (e.g., Son. 5, second movement). These and other evidences seem to imply the presence of a second, accompanying keyboard instrument and even a cello or other reinforcing bass, at least during those passages.[88] Bach's sonatas of this type are again mostly in the four-movement church plan, although the F-S-F sequence occurs in three of the sonatas among other variants. A siciliano is found twice, including the familiar one in G minor in the E-flat flute sonata (SCHMIEDER-BWV, no. 1031).

Finally, there are five "trio" sonatas, all in the church plan, that have been attributed to Bach. One, for two violins and b. c. in D minor (SCHMIEDER-BWV, no. 1036), may have been a youthful work but, even so, its inflexible part writing, devoid of any real polyphonic interest, and its inexpressive lines raise serious questions of authenticity.[89] Another for flute, violin, and b. c. in G major (SCHMIEDER-BWV, no. 1038), may date from Bach's Weimar period. It is like the Sonata in F for violin and realized keyboard (SCHMIEDER-BWV, no. 1022) in being constructed over much the same bass as the one in that recently discovered Sonata in G for violin and b. c. (SCHMIEDER-BWV, no 1021). However, SCHMIEDER-BWV, no. 1038, may not be authentic in this version (if only because it would be Bach's sole use of violin *scordatura*).[90] A third

87. Numerous variants, transcriptions, and derivations are cited in the specific listings of SCHMIEDER-BWV. Regarding no. 1022 cf. MACKERNESS. No. 1020 is regarded as a flute sonata in NAGELSm, no. 77 (Balet). A helpful discussion of these sonatas occurs in SCHWEITZER-BACH, I, 394 ff.

88. Cf. BACH-WERKEM, IX (Rust), xvi ff.

89. Among mod. eds.: NAGELSm, no. 49 (Keller).

90. Cf. BACH-WERKEM, IX, xxiv; BLUME-VIOLINSONATE; MACKERNESS.

"trio" sonata is that for two violins and *b. c.* in C (SCHMIEDER-BWV, no. 1037). This is a rather densely polyphonic work that was accepted as Bach's until several copies were noted in the name of Bach's pupil J. T. Goldberg, leaving the authorship in favor of the latter.[91] A fourth "trio" sonata, for two flutes and *b. c.* in G (SCHMIEDER-BWV, no. 1039), is accepted as authentic but raises the question, always pertinent here, of whether Bach chose to call it "Sonata" or "Trio." About all that can be confirmed is that he did call the transcription "Sonata" that he later made for viola da gamba and realized keyboard (SCHMIEDER-BWV, no. 1027). The last in this group is also the last of Bach's sonatas and one of his finest, the "Sonata a 3" for transverse flute, violin, and *b. c.* in his *Musical Offering.* Hans David has provided an unusually detailed analysis of this work in conjunction with his recent edition and study of the entire set.[92] He argues cleverly and convincingly to the effect that the *Musical Offering* was one of those Baroque collections conceived according to an over-all, symmetrical plan.[93] Within the 13 pieces or 5 divisions of this plan the single sonata becomes the "center piece." In fact, David finds the very center of the collection to be the very center, or second movement, of the sonata, itself a symmetrical fugal allegro with a new subject and with the well-known "Royal Theme" as its countersubject.

At the very active Dresden court, four lesser-known German composers of sonatas may be named along with such distinguished foreigners as F. M. Veracini (in Dresden from 1717 to 1722), Lotti, and later, Porpora. The Germans were contemporaries of Bach, probably known to him when he visited Dresden in 1717 if not otherwise, and close to him in style. One was **Johann David Heinichen** (1683-1729), who had trained in Leipzig under Kuhnau, practiced law, published the first edition of his celebrated thorough-bass treatise (1711), and given six years to opera in Italy before he came to Dresden at the age of 34. Like his many other compositions Heinichen's 25 known sonatas were left, and have largely remained, in MSS, without dates.[94] Eight of them are in S/bass settings, with flute, oboe, or violin as the solo instrument.

91. Cf. DÜRR-GOLDBERG; SCHMIEDER-BWV, p. 578 (with further references).
92. DAVID-OFFERINGm and DAVID-OFFERING (especially p. 111 ff.).
93. DAVID-OFFERING, p. 34 ff.
94. HAUSSWALD-HEINICHEN is the chief source, including numerous examples and a full list of the sonatas (mostly with thematic index) p. 155 ff. The thematic index of all Heinichen's works in SEIBEL (the main biographic source) is somewhat less complete for the sonatas (p. 88 ff.). Mod. eds.: Son. for flute and harpsichord, cf. GROVE, IV, 140 (Blom); keyboard reduction of "Larghetto" from Son. in F (SSAAAA/bass), SCHMID-SÄCHSISCHENm, no. 9. See, also, ALTMANN, p. 82, for a "Trio" in mod. ed.

One is a three-movement cembalo sonata in F, with "Concerto" crossed off the title, in a score copied posthumously (1731). Since the concerto was Heinichen's main instrumental contribution, this version may well have been a reduction of such an orchestral piece. In two other instances similar changes of title occur. The largest number of sonatas, 13, are "trio" types, with various pairings of flute, oboe, violin, and viola d'amore in the upper parts.[95] And 3 sonatas are for fuller combinations bordering on the orchestra and the concerto grosso.

The number of Heinichen's sonata movements varies from two to seven, with four in the majority, as usual in the S-F-S-F order.[96] There are also some sonatas with the newer, F-S-F sequence of three movements. Although Italian influences predominate, one sonata, for *concertante* bassoon and cello *b. c.,* has three movements called "Aria," "Menuet," and "L'autre" in the French manner (as in Heinichen's several suites). Otherwise, dance titles are infrequent in the sonatas. The forms in the separate movements when not actually fugal are generally motivic and cursive.[97] Heinichen also left some introductory, one-movement sonatas in vocal works.[98] In the few available examples of Heinichen's instrumental music the superior craftsmanship and melodic invention become evident at once.[99] His polyphonic talents were considerable. He himself called attention (in the 1728 edition of *General-Bass,* p. 935) to a (lost) canonic "Sonata à 6. Violini," in which only two parts were used, each with signs for the canonic entries of two more of the violins. One hopes at least a representative selection of his sonatas will eventually be published.

A second capable composer in Dresden was the Bohemian **Jan Dismas Zelenka** (1679-1745), who was brought to the Dresden court in 1710. There he stayed to become Heinichen's assistant and successor except for a period of study under Fux in Vienna and Lotti in Venice.[100] By an express proprietary ruling of King Friedrich August I, his music could be neither copied nor published,[101] which stipulation may be a clue to the obscurity of his colleagues' music in Dresden as well as his own. Today Sonatas 1 and 6 have been made available out of six *Sonate a due hautbois et basson* (or corresponding strings) that he wrote in 1723 among numerous other works for the coronation ceremonies of Karl VI

95. Five others in this same category are called "Trio."
96. Cf. HAUSSWALD-HEINICHEN, pp. 60 and 64.
97. Cf. HAUSSWALD-HEINICHEN, pp. 74 ff. and 82 ff.
98. Cf. HAUSSWALD-HEINICHEN, p. 61; SEIBEL, p. 48.
99. Cf. the concerto grosso in EDMRM, XI (Komma), 56.
100. A pioneer biographic source is FÜRSTENAU, II, 71 ff. Cf. also, GROVE, IX, 406 ff. (Černušák) ; HAUSSWALD-ZELENKA, p. 243 ff.
101. Cf. HORTUSM, no. 126 (Schoenbaum), p. 3.

in Prague.[102]   As their editor suggests, these are indeed sonatas by a   102a
neglected master.   Recalling the contrapuntal resources and melodic
pathos of both Fux and Lotti, they extend broad, supple themes into
large, majestically paced forms.   Thus, the fugue that comprises the
second movement of the usual church plan in Sonata 1 lasts 136 measures
within the comparatively narrow range of D to b″, yet manages to present
a simple, purposeful outline defined by its clear alternation of expositions
and episodes and by its compelling tonal excursion around nearly related
keys.   In the finale of this same sonata the bright dancelike rhythmic
pattern with its syncopations and its juxtaposition of duolet and triplet
is regarded as distinctly Slavic in character by the editor (Ex. 58).[103]
The texture becomes still richer in the last three sonatas as the scoring
changes from SS/- to SSB/bass.   Especially in the last one are traits
of the concerto grosso to be found (including frequent "tutti," "solo,"
"forte," and "piano" indications).

Ex. 58.   Finale from Sonata 1 by Jan Dismas Zelenka (after
HORTUSm, no. 126, but without the editor's realization; by kind
permission of Bärenreiter-Verlag).

The outstanding violinist **Johann Georg Pisendel** (1687-1755), a
pupil of Torelli, Vivaldi, and Heinichen (theory) among others,[104] is
our third contemporary of Bach to be found in Dresden.   There he was
active from 1712 when he was not on tour.[105]   Albinoni, Vivaldi, and
Telemann were among important musicians who dedicated compositions
to Pisendel.[106]   The two works known by him of concern to this survey
are his unaccompanied violin sonata[107] and his sonata for violin with

102. HORTUSm, nos. 126 and 132 (both Schoenbaum).   Bibliographic details and
discussion of all six sonatas in HAUSSWALD-ZELENKA, pp. 248, 251 ff., 254 ff., and
261, with a recent dissertation cited on p. 243.   Cf. the listing in WOLFFHEIM, II,
no. 1159.
      103. Cf. HAUSSWALD-ZELENKA, p. 257 ff.
      104. But not Corelli (cf. PINCHERLE-CORELLI, p. 114).
      105. Cf. HILLER-LEBENSBESCHREIBUNGEN, p. 188 ff.; FÜRSTENAU, II, 84 ff.;
MOSER-VIOLINSPIEL, p. 316 ff.
      106. For Albinoni, cf. GIAZOTTO-ALBINONI, p. 240 and Tavole ix and xi.
      107. Cf. STUDENY, p. 44 ff.; GATES-SOLO, pp. 78 ff. and 282 ff. (photograph of
Studeny reprint).   Mod. eds.: STUDENY-PISENDELm; HORTUSm, no. 91 (Hausswald).

108a   unfigured *b. c.*,[108] both left in undated MSS. Since both works are close to Bach's music, not only in style but in the one new and one usual setting, there has been speculation whether Pisendel's sonatas might have inspired or been inspired by the corresponding types of Bach.[109] The impression gained in the present survey is that Pisendel's sonatas are strong works that show a marked relation to Bach's but reveal slightly later style traits. In fact, the unaccompanied sonata in particular borders on the *empfindsam* style with its fantasy of rhythm, melody, and modulation; its relaxation of texture—there are no imitative movements, much less fugues; its tendency toward phrase and period structures; and distinct hints, in the ornaments and cadences, of both Friedemann and Emanuel Bach (whom Pisendel must have known in the 1730's and '40's[110]). Both sonatas are in three movements, S-F-F. The unaccompanied sonata ends with a "Giga" that has a variation or double, while the other ends with a charming gigue-like "Scherzando" in 3/4 (i.e., 9/8) meter.

Our fourth composer at the Dresden court was the unexcelled German lutist **Sylvius Leopold Weiss** (1686-1750),[111] the last among the more important lutists to appear in the present survey. Between 1706 and at least 1731 Weiss left some 60 cycles of dances and freer movements for lute. Over three fifths are called sonatas ("Sonate" or "Suonata") and the rest "Partie" or some variant. The terms are applied without distinction, this use of "sonata" to mean the suite itself being relatively infrequent in Germany during the late Baroque Era. Most of Weiss's music is found in two large MS collections in tablature, one in Dresden and one in London.[112] The lute called for by Weiss had as many as 24 strings including courses (both unison and octave), and was tuned according to the "nouveau ton" of Denis Gaultier that had become almost universal. The dances of the cycles usually include not only the standard four that were the core of the classic Baroque suite but numerous others, mostly of French origin. In Weiss's music lies much of the depth, solidity, and breadth that we found in Zelenka's. In these respects, in its extensive use of sequence, and in the character of its motivic play it resembles Bach's lute music (especially SCHMIEDER-

108. Mod. ed.: SCHOTT ANTIQUAm, no. 4162 (Hausswald).
109. Cf. MOSER-VIOLINSPIEL, pp. 140 and 317, as against SPITTA-BACH, II, 71.
110. Cf. SPITTA-BACH, III, 227.
111. The main biographic sources are VOLKMANN and NEEMANN-WEISS II (with lists of MSS and contents, pp. 178 ff. and 185 ff.).
112. Among mod. eds.: 6 sonatas from the Dresden collection (cf. NEEMANN-WEISS I, p. 399 ff., for detailed contents and another sonata), EDMRm, XII (Neemann, with preface), 41 ff. The entire London MS (contents in BRITISH MS, III, 72 ff.) is transcribed as an Appendix to a valuable historical and style-critical orientation in the unpublished dissertation MASON-WEISS.

BWV, nos. 995-997). In technical requirements it is more advanced, whereas in melodic invention, harmonic richness and subtlety, and structural logic it understandably does not attain the peaks that Bach's music does.

While we are naming composers of sonatas in Dresden we may take note of four others who flourished up to a generation after Bach's time—who, in fact, stretched the usual limits now given for the Baroque Era, stylistic as well as temporal. One of these was the renowned flutist **Johann Joachim Quantz** (1697-1773). Quantz was connected with the Dresden court during wide travels and until he moved permanently in 1741 to Berlin as the highly paid and specially privileged teacher of Frederick the Great. Quantz paid much attention to the "mixed" and *galant* styles and to other harbingers of the Classic Era in both his celebrated flute treatise (1752) and in his autobiography (1754).[113] Yet, in these writings, in his close ties with Zelenka, Heinichen, Pisendel, Weiss, Vivaldi, Fux, and Lotti, and in his own compositions the orientation remained mainly toward the Baroque. The known compositions consist mainly of sonatas, S/- or SS/bass and SS or SSS alone, concertos, and a few vocal works.[114] Among numerous other listings, only the six sonatas for flute and *b. c.*, Op. 1 (Dresden, 1734), and six flute *Duetti,* Op. 2 (Berlin, 1759), can be confirmed as publications of instrumental music unquestionably by Quantz.[115] The interest in Quantz as aesthetician, writer on performance practices, and flutist has not extended sufficiently to include the needed bibliographic disentanglement of several hundred more sonatas and concertos that were kept from publication, again by royal order.[116]   116a

To be sure, a stereotype must have resulted from composing to suit Frederick the Great's reportedly narrow tastes.[117] The movements eventually settled into the S-F-F plan we have seen in the sonatas of G. B. Somis, Tartini, and other Italians. What these movements con-

113. E.g., cf. QUANTZ-FACSIMILE, chap. XVIII, section 82 ff.; NETTL-FORGOTTEN, p. 294 ff.; SCHÄFKE, p. 217 ff.
114. Cf. EITNER-QL, VIII, 98 ff.
115. Cf. his own disavowal, in NETTL-FORGOTTEN, p. 317, of an earlier Dutch publication of sonatas under his name. Among mod. eds. of "solo" flute or violin sonatas: 7 sons., FISCHER & WITTENBECHERm; Son. in E minor, SCHREITER-QUANTZm.
116. Cf. BURNEY-GERMANY, II, 152 and 160; CAT. HAUSBIBLIOTHEK, items 4193 ff., including references to a MS thematic index (items 1574 and 1575) and to the similarity of several sonatas to concertos (item 4321). The apparent keyboard sonata mentioned in EITNER-QL, VIII, 98, is not recognized in STILZ, p. 117. Among mod. eds.: SS/bass sons. in C and D, HORTUSm, no. 60 (Birke), and ORGANUMm, III, respectively; Son. for 3 flutes alone, NAGELSm, no. 116 (Doflein); cf. also, ALTMANN.
117. Cf. BURNEY-GERMANY, II, 152 ff. and 156 ff.; MGG, IV, 959 (Becker).

sisted of, Quantz largely tells us himself in describing the ideal "solo" and the ideal "quatuor," or a sonata with three *concertante* instruments and a bass part.[118] (Only this broad use of "sonata" and one other are to be found among the forms that he classifies in his *Versuch*.) Thus, after lamenting the weak state to which the "solo" had fallen and the scarcity of composers able to write both the "solo" and the ensemble types (partly to impress the King with Quantz's own excellence?), he says the opening "Adagio" "must" be songful, suitable to a display of the performer's expressive and perceptive abilities, a mixture of tenderness and some intellectual interest, built on an appropriate and practical bass, not too repetitious in its restatement of ideas at the same or different pitch levels, intensified as necessary by dissonances, and not too long. The first "Allegro" "requires" a fluent, well-knit, somewhat serious tune; satisfactory unity of thought; brilliant passages well related to the tune; a good plan for the repetition of the material; an effective ending of the first section (in binary design) that will be equally effective as an ending when transposed (to the tonic) at the end of the final section; a shorter first than final section; a recurrence of the brilliant passages in the final part; and a naturally set bass that imparts life to the whole. And the "second Allegro" may be lively and fast, or moderate and tuneful, whichever will contrast to the previous "Allegro," variety being essential throughout the "solo." In the "quatuor" emphasis is placed, of course, on the *concertante* and imitative writing. Needless to say, however Quantz may be charged with composing from a mold, and an outmoded one at that, his mastery of the less weighty compositional techniques is not open to question.

Johann Adolf Hasse (1699-1783), the highly successful composer of operas and church music, was connected with the Dresden court for thirty years from 1733, following an initial stay in 1731.[119] However, he spent so much time elsewhere, especially in what might be called his first country, Italy, that he seems to have led a double life. Hasse's instrumental music is still in need of a clear bibliographic organization. Besides the sinfonias,[120] only the keyboard sonatas have been collated and listed.[121] In all, 17 keyboard sonatas are now known, dating from about 1730 to 1758. These include, among others, 4 that are extant out of 8 in a MS "fatte per la Real Delfina di Francia" as a token of thanks during a visit to Paris in 1750, one each in ANTHS. VENIERm, II, and

---

118. QUANTZ-FACSIMILE, p. 302 ff.
119. MGG, V, 1771 (Abert), includes recent findings.
120. Thematic index in MENNICKE, p. 491 ff.
121. Thematic index in HOFFMANN/ERBRECHT-KLAVIERMUSIK, p. 139 ff., with discussion, p. 101 ff.

WELCKERm, and 6 published by Walsh in London as Op. 7 in 1758.[122]
Among the confusing, overlapping editions and MSS of ensemble sonatas
there can be cited at least the publications of 6 SS/- and 12 S/bass
sonatas in various London, Paris, and Amsterdam editions,[123] generally   123a
with the choice of violin or flute in the solo parts. Hasse's sonatas vary
between two and four movements, with the church plan of four predominating in the ensemble types and any order of three, mostly fast
movements in the keyboard sonatas. The finale is frequently a minuet.
The strong points of these sonatas seem to be their smooth Italianate
melody, nicely molded and refined, and their fluency, resulting from a
relatively light texture and regular rhythmic organization.   Hasse's
melodic writing undoubtedly reflects his writing for the voice.   His
skill at the cembalo is similarly reflected in the good writing for keyboard.   The total effect is pleasing, however, rather than forceful or
original, partly owing to the simple, neutral harmony and general
absence of polyphonic depth. Hasse, who in any case was a little slow
to master the basic techniques of composition, was not especially celebrated for his instrumental music in his day.[124]

Georg Gebel junior (1709-53), who began his career as a prodigy at
the keyboard, served at the Dresden court from 1735 to 1747, after
which he moved to Rudolstadt. The MSS of four SS/- and two
S/bass sonatas originally credited to his father and teacher, Georg Gebel
senior,[125] are now credited to the son by virtue of their somewhat later
style.[126]   In both of the two "trio" sonatas that have been made available three movements are found (F-S-F and S-F-F). These are exceptionally attractive works. Their lines are songful, with a more
straightforward, less ornate cantilena than Hasse's lines reveal. The
harmonic and contrapuntal interest is greater, too. Broad relationships
govern the forms. Thus, the first quick movement of the "trio" sonata
in F makes four major landmarks out of the four different upward
leaps by which each of the two violin parts enters in the first and second
halves.

Johann Gottlieb Goldberg (1727-56), supposedly a pupil of J. S.
Bach at the time the latter wrote the "Goldberg Variations" for him,

122. For mod. eds. of several Hasse sonatas in various categories cf. MGG, V,
1787.
    123. Cf. MGG, V, 1778; BRITISH PRINTED, I, 602 ff.; FÜRSTENAU, II, 378.
    124. Cf. GROVE, IV, 129 and 130 (Marshall); and the general estimate in
MENNICKE, p. 327 ff., including that author's characteristic depreciation of opera's
influence on instrumental music. Somewhat opposing views appear in STUDENY,
p. 60 ff., and NAGELSm, no. 159 (Frotscher), p. 2.
    125. EITNER-QL, IV, 186.
    126. Cf. Seiffert's preface in ORGANUMm, III, nos. 12 and 13 (the only mod.
eds.) ; and MGG, IV, 1524 ff. (Wolff).

divided his short life between Dresden, Leipzig, and the former Danzig before becoming the successor to Gebel in Rudolstadt.[127] The relatively few works that he left[128] include four extant "trio" sonatas in MS, two more that are now lost, a multivoice sonata in string-quartet setting (SSAB/bass),[129] and a keyboard sonata that probably was lost in World War II.[130] One of the extant "trio" sonatas is the one in C mentioned earlier here as formerly credited to Bach (SCHMIEDER-BWV, no. 1037),[131] and also found in Goldberg's name as a sonata for violin with realized keyboard.[132] Both this sonata and the "quartet" are works in the four-movement church plan that do bear striking resemblances to Bach's, especially in their full, polyphonic texture and melodic richness.

Leaving the main center of Dresden we may digress long enough to call attention to the only Polish composer to be mentioned here, who was active in nearby Poland. Among the few MS works extant by the Benedictine friar **Stanislaw Sylvester Szarzyński** (sometime between 1650 and 1720) is a "trio" sonata (SS/bass) dated 1706.[133] In seven movements, it is an expressive, melodious work similar in general style to other sonatas discussed in this section. The last movement is a repetition of the first, while the fourth and sixth movements are dances with hints of folk material.

Next may be noted a fellow pupil of Handel under F. W. Zachau in Halle, the organist **Gottfried Kirchhoff** (1685-1746). An eight-movement keyboard "sonata" in E and a six-movement keyboard "Sonatina" in F by Kirchhoff occur in a Hannover MS.[134] The first movement of the latter, called "Aria" and considerably decorated, appears (without the composer's name) in Leopold Mozart's *Notenbuch für Wolfgang,* along with still another keyboard "Sonatina," this one in five (not four) movements.[135] From this fact one assumes that Kirchhoff's reputation must have been considerably greater than it is now. In all three works the writing for keyboard is convenient without being especially idiomatic.

127. Biographic information in DADDER and MGG, V, 478 ff. (Dadder & Dürr).
128. Thematic index in DÜRR-GOLDBERG, p. 54 ff.
129. Mod. ed.: LOTHAR-GOLDBERGm.
130. Cf. DÜRR-GOLDBERG, p. 55; HOFFMANN/ERBRECHT-KLAVIERMUSIK, p. 100.
131. Cf. DÜRR-GOLDBERG (including a keen style analysis); published in BACH-WERKEm, IX, 231.
132. DADDER, p. 69.
133. Cf. GROVE, VIII, 263 (Halski), with references including a mod. ed. done in Warsaw in 1928 by A. E. Chybiński (with preface). Further information is in the unsigned pamphlet, p. 10 ff., that accompanies the Vanguard recording VRS-6017, "Four Centuries of Polish Music."
134. Cf. WERNER-HANNOVER, p. 451 ff. Mod. ed. of 3 movements from each cycle: NAGELSm, no. 3 (Werner, with preface). MOSER-LEXIKON, p. 615, also lists 12 sons. for violin and b. c. by Kirchhoff, not otherwise confirmed here.
135. Mod. ed.: ABERT-LEOPOLDm, p. 28.

The broad, elegant lines of the slower movements are, in fact, somewhat unusual for keyboard. There is a Handelian distinction in these lines, in the occasionally chromatic harmony, and in the strong sense of form. Comparable to Leopold Mozart's recognition of Kirchhoff was J. S. Bach's inclusion of a suite by **Gottfried Heinrich Stöltzel** (1690-1749) in the "*Klavierbuchlein* für Friedemann Bach." After the then usual trip to Italy made by so many German composers, Stöltzel settled in Gotha in 1719, becoming active mainly in church music and opera. But at least five sonatas that have appeared in modern editions reveal an able instrumental composer, too.[136] Best known is the "Enharmonische Claviersonate," as it was called in a posthumous edition of 1761 (ANTH. MARPURGm, I, no. 14). That edition is the only extant source, although the sonata was probably composed about 1740.[137] The other known sonatas are in SSB/bass settings, with typical choices of violins, oboes, or flutes in the upper parts and bassoon or cello for the *concertante* bass.[138] In the keyboard sonata some actual enharmony is found, and used, of course, with considerably more purpose and variety than it had been more than a century earlier in the so-called "Enharmonische Sonate" of Giovanni Valentini. But, as in the "trio" sonatas, direct harmonic chromaticism is the more conspicuous trait. The keyboard sonata is in the newer S-F-F plan, whereas the "trio" sonatas generally favor the older four-movement church plan. For the rest, Stöltzel's sonatas show a competent grasp of materials, a conservative approach to texture and melodic styles, a certain monotony of range within their rather long movements, and no exceptional identifications with Kuhnau's or Bach's music such as have been suggested.[139]

Johann Graff (?-1745), oboist, violinist, and father of six musically active sons, served in Rudolstadt from about 1722.[140] A set of six sonatas by him for violin and *b. c.*, Op. 1, was published in Bamberg in 1718 and another set, Op. 2, in Rudolstadt in 1723. Only Sonata in D, Op. 1, No. 3, has been made available.[141] In its four movements, cast in the standard church plan, a fine knowledge of the violin is disclosed. The lines of the slow movements sing and undergo considerable orna-

---

136. A dissertation on his instrumental music is cited in GROVE, VIII, 101 (Straeten). In KAHL-SELBSTBIOGRAPHIEN, p. 345, Stöltzel says that many instrumental pieces by him were composed and performed before he reached Gotha.
137. Mod. ed.: BÖHME-STÖLTZELm, with preface; the finale had been published in WEITZMANN, p. 338.
138. Among mod. eds.: Son. in F minor, NAGELSm, no. 133 (Osthoff); Son. in C, COLLEGIUMm, no. 72 (Frotscher); cf. ALTMANN.
139. E.g., cf. SEIFFERT-KLAVIERMUSIK, p. 370 ff.; KAHL-SELBSTBIOGRAPHIEN, p. 183 ff.
140. MGG, V, 668 ff. (Scharnagl and Haase).
141. ORGANUMm, III, no. 3.

mentation. In the faster movements there are many sections of idiomatic passagework, including advanced double-stops, although only few sections that are polyphonic.

Johann Adam Birckenstock (1687-1733), in Kassel from 1709, was a co-student of Pisendel and an excellent violinist. He was another composer of "solo" (S/bass) sonatas. His Op. 1, divided in two books, contains 12 such sonatas, published first by E. Roger in Amsterdam in 1722,[142] and about 8 years later by Walsh in London.[143] A set of six "trio" sonatas by him is now lost.[144] The sonatas in Op. 1 are almost all in five contrasting movements. Often the final movements are an allemande and/or a gigue, thus combining the church and court types. Clearly phrased, attractive tunes, well-organized forms, a fairly advanced use of the violin's resources, relatively simple texture, and no distinct originality characterize this music.[145]

Among these lesser known composers in our third group, **Johann Friedrich Fasch** (1688-1758) stands out as a creator of somewhat greater force. This man was "rediscovered" in modern times by Riemann, who saw in him the most important forerunner of Johann Stamitz as regards style "reforms."[146] Fasch is also linked rather closely with Kuhnau and Graupner in Leipzig, who were among his teachers; with Telemann, whose overtures he took as models;[147] with J. S. Bach, who had copied in score a few overtures by Fasch;[148] and with others like J. P. Krieger, Heinichen, and Stöltzel, whom Fasch came to know during the years of wandering around central Germany that preceded his ultimate post as Kapellmeister in Zerbst (from 1722). Along with much church music, Fasch wrote in all the main Baroque forms of instrumental music, including sinfonias, concertos, overtures, and sonatas.

His known sonatas (or "Quadro" or "Trio" as they are called without apparent distinction) were all left in undated MSS, chiefly from around 1730.[149] They consist of about 20 of the "trio" type (SS/-, SSB/-, or SSBB/bass), only two of the "solo" type (S/bass), and about four in miscellaneous ensemble settings.[150] The instrumentation varies in the

---

142. Cf. KOOLE, p. 11.

143. Among mod. eds.: Son. 2, NAGELSm, no. 25 (Woehl); cf. also, ALTMANN, pp. 234 and 267.

144. MGG, I, 1859 (Redlich).

145. MOSER-VIOLINSPIEL, p. 304 ff., expresses stronger enthusiasm for Birckenstock's sonatas than has seemed justified in the present survey.

146. Cf. MGG, III, 1861 (Adrio), and SCHNEIDER-FASCH, p. 50.

147. Cf. Fasch's autobiography in MARPURG-BEYTRÄGE, III, 125.

148. MGG, III, 1853; but cf. the primary biographic study, ENGELKE-FASCH, p. 277 ff.

149. SCHNEIDER-FASCH, p. 25.

150. Thematic index, with liberal incipits from each movement, SCHNEIDER-FASCH (a dissertation on the sonatas), supplemented by MGG, III, 1852. Among

usual manner between violins, oboes, and flutes for the upper parts and cello or bassoon for the bass. One SSA/bass sonata is scored for violin, "oboe d'amour," "cornu du chasse," and *b. c.* In the majority of the sonatas the number of movements is either four in the older church plan or three in the newer S-F-F plan, with the transitional second slow movement left out. Three of the sonatas are of the strictly canonic type in the upper parts and most of the others contain at least one more-or-less concentrated fugal movement. The separate movements are headed by tempo inscriptions or an occasional "Affettuoso" or "Cantabile," but not dance titles. Some of the movements have a preludial quality and some tend to be sectional and homophonic.

Fasch's slow movements are generally expressive and sustained, but not introspective in the richly ornamented, subtly harmonized manner of Bach's. It is in his faster movements that the most strength and originality appear. There, characteristically, the ideas are wide-ranged and rhythmically vigorous (Ex. 59). Their reiterations occur as bold entries within forms that depend on convincing tonal organization. This organization often seems especially purposeful at the return to the home key. However, in the light of all the other Baroque instrumental music that has been "rediscovered" in the past half century or more, Riemann's

Ex. 59. From the opening of Sonata in G by Johann Friedrich Fasch (after Dresden 2423/Q 2 in the "Thematischer Katalog" of SCHNEIDER-FASCH).

---

mod. eds.: COLLEGIUMm, nos. 8-13 (all Riemann); NAGELSm, nos. 56 (Schäffler), 148 (Dancker-Lagner), and 169 (Hausswald); HORTUSm, no. 26 (Woehl), which is the same work as NAGELSm, no. 148.

special claims for Fasch as a pre-Classicist seem to be another example of misplaced enthusiasm. These claims are echoed in C. A. Schneider's dissertation on the sonatas, where a special point is made of the individuality of their themes and of a supposed thematic dualism, not only between one idea and the next but within a single idea or "theme."[151] In the experience of this study Fasch was a distinguished composer in the mature Baroque styles, but with no conspicuous foretastes of subsequent developments—not in the themes, textures, or structures.

Johann Christoph Graupner (1683-1760), in Darmstadt from 1709, was close to Kuhnau, Telemann, and Bach, among others and in various capacities. Graupner left some 2,000 works, mostly cantatas, operas, and orchestral music. Unfortunately, it has been difficult in many instances to know which are his own compositions and which are among the many works by other composers that he made a special point of copying during his lifetime, often without the composer's name. Thus, the *Sei Sonate per il cembalo,* dated 1718-26 and cited for "remarkably developed structure,"[152] turn out merely to be copies of the six sonatas by Quantz for flute and *b. c.,* Op. 1, published in 1734.[153] For that matter, no other keyboard sonata attributed to Graupner seems actually to be his.[154] The sonatas that do appear to be his are about three dozen in various ensemble categories—20 SS/- or SSB/bass types and one in quartet setting for strings; 5 for flute, trumpet, viola d'amore, and *b. c.;* 2 for viola d'amore or bassoon, chalumeau, and *b. c.;* one for flute, violin, and *b. c.;* 3 for 2 horns, 2 violins, viola, and cembalo; and 4 for violin or flute with realized clavier.[155]

Of all these only two sonatas in the last-named group and the one in string-quartet setting have been made available.[156] These three all have the S-F-S-F plan of movements, with tempo titles except for one "Menuet" finale. In the absence of concentrated or recherché polyphony and introspective or unusual harmony, this music seems relatively light. It is still well founded in the Baroque language, with the concise motives that constitute its melodic material and fairly consistent reiterations and imitations of these motives. But there is a slowing of the harmonic rhythm, apparent in some of the *b. c.* passages that are more chordal

151. Cf. SCHNEIDER-FASCH, pp. 47 ff., 50 ff., 54, 61; also, MENNICKE, p. 63 ff.; HOFFMANN-TRIOSONATE, p. 55 ff.; MOSER-DEUTSCHEN, II, 257 ff.

152. MENNICKE, p. 83.

153. HOFFMANN/ERBRECHT-GRAUPNER, p. 142 ff.

154. The Sonatina in D is accepted as his by the Graupner authority Noack (MGG, V, 723) but is not so accepted in HOFFMANN/ERBRECHT-GRAUPNER, p. 143.

155. Cf. MGG, V, 723.

156. HORTUSm, nos. 121 and 120 (both Hoffmann). Another mod. ed., cited in ALTMANN, p. 184, may not be an authentic work by Graupner.

than linear, and a grouping of the motives, sometimes into clearly balanced phrases, that bespeak the newer *galant* style, too.

High praise is bestowed on **Christoph Förster** (1693-1745) by Riemann and Mennicke, especially for his contributions to the French overture.[157] A resident of several central German towns and of Prague while Fux, Caldara, and other Imperial musicians were present, Förster left in MS six sonatas for violin with realized keyboard. But none of these is among the few instrumental works by him that have appeared in modern editions.

Finally, in central Germany, two Bach pupils who composed sonatas may be mentioned. **Johann Ludwig Krebs** (1713-80), who held several posts in Thuringia and Saxony, published six SS/bass sonatas with flutes or violins as the solo instruments (Nürnberg, 1738).[158] He also published six lighter sonatas "da camera" for flute or violin with realized keyboard (1760-62)[159] and a keyboard solo sonata by him appeared in ANTH. MAGAZINm (1763, not 1765). Sonata 1 in the SS/bass set is a suite, starting with a French overture and continuing with four French dances—"Rejouissance," "Menuet," "Bourée," and "Gigue." But the remaining sonatas in this set are all closer to the S-F-S-F church type, although in each of them there is at least one dance movement, too. In their adherence to motivic writing, Krebs' sonatas, at least in this early set, are still Baroque in style. But they have little of the harmonic, melodic, and polyphonic richness that might recall his great teacher.

Another Bach pupil, **Johann Christoph Altnikol** (1719-59), left two keyboard sonatas in holographs not yet explored but presumably still preserved in one of the main Berlin libraries.[160]

North Germany (Telemann, Mattheson, Handel)

The seven sonata composers to be noted in north Germany from our third group represent an even smaller number than those from the second group. But all except Schickhard are of more than passing significance, to the sonata as well as to other music. Those six include Telemann, Mattheson, Handel, the Graun brothers, and Frederick the Great. Again the main center was Hamburg, where the first three of these wrote most of their sonatas. The best known in his day and one of history's most

157. Cf. MGG, IV, 452 ff. (Adrio), including further sources; also, RIEMANN-LEXIKON, p. 522.
158. Mod. eds.: Son. 1, COLLEGIUMm, no. 31; Son. 6, NAGELSm, no. 109 (Werner, with preface).
159. Cf. EITNER-QL, V, 434; CAT. BRUXELLES, II, item 6757.
160. Cf. MGG, I, 398 (Blume); EITNER-QL, I, 120.

prolific and versatile composers was **Georg Philipp Telemann** (1681-1767), a composer, largely self-taught, who matured in the musical circles of Leipzig.

Only certain portions of Telemann's varied output have been explored systematically enough to permit an accurate bibliographic summary. Unfortunately, in spite of generous representations in modern reprints, the sonatas have been explored only in part.[161] Telemann himself, among several autobiographic remarks that are pertinent here, asks how he could possibly recall all (of some 600 instrumental works alone) that he had written for strings and winds, yet he felt, for example, that he had done some of his best composing in the trio setting (a view seconded by both Scheibe and Quantz among his contemporaries).[162] Telemann did list most of his main sonata publications.[163] From those titles and supplementary bits of information in later sources[164] at least the nucleus of a list can be assembled here.

Among SS/bass settings there are 12 *Trii a diversi stromenti* (separately called "Sonata"?), out of the 24 items in his collection *Essercizii musici* (Hamburg, 1724) ;[165] at least two *Sonates polonoise* (SA/- and SS/bass) ;[166] and there is a sonata for two block or transverse flutes, or violins, and *b. c.* in Telemann's unprecedented but short-lived music periodical known as *Der getreue Music-Meister* (founded in Hamburg, 1728).[167] Telemann also lists two published collections of SS/bass sonatas that are no longer known, at least not under his titles. Both offer the usual choice of violins or flutes. The set he calls *3. methodische Trii und 3. schertzende Sonaten* seems to imply a distinction in the use of the term "sonata" as the lighter type. *Corellisirende Sonaten,* the other set, must have been another of the numerous homages to the Italian master that we have met. Among the instrumental composers of various nationalities whom Telemann acknowledges as models

161. FUNK is a recent dissertation on 64 of the "trio" sonatas, including a complete English translation of VALENTIN (2d ed.) and a thematic index of every movement. Hans Gräser's earlier, unpublished doctoral dissertation on the chamber music (Munich, 1925), reported to contain a thematic index, was not available to me. Bärenreiter's new "complete" edition came too late for use here.

162. Cf. KAHL-SELBSTBIOGRAPHIEN, pp. 207, 213, 222, and 302 ; ROLLAND-ESSAYS, p. 143 ff.

163. KAHL-SELBSTBIOGRAPHIEN, pp. 210, 213 ff., 222, and 225 ; cf. also, DDTm, XXVIII (Schneider), liii, for a list of Telemann's works sold at auction in 1769.

164. EITNER-QL, IX, 375 ff., is still a main help. Cf. also, CAT. BRUXELLES, II.

165. Cf. HOFFMANN-TRIOSONATE, p. 27 ff. Among mod. eds.: Son. 9 in E, NAGELSm, no. 47 (Päsler). Partial summaries of mod. eds. of Telemann's instrumental music may be found in SCHENK-NEUAUSGABEN, p. 249 ff.; ALTMANN; VALENTIN, p. 79 ff.

166. Mod. eds.: NAGELSm, nos. 50 and 51 (both Simon).

167. Mod. ed.: No. 10 in HORTUSm, nos. 6-13 (Degen, with prefaces), which volumes contain most of the extant pieces from this periodical.

—including Kuhnau, Caldara, Rosenmüller, Lully, and Handel (younger than Telemann by four years)—the Italians, especially Corelli, are placed first.[168]

Telemann's sonatas in S/bass settings include *6 Sonates a violon seul, acc. par le clavecin* (*b. c.*), followed by *Sei Suonatine per violino e cembalo* (Frankfurt/M, 1715 and 1718; reprinted together as a set of 12 sonatas, with the option of violin or flute, by Walsh as Op. 1 in 1733, and by an unidentified publisher) ;[169] two more sets of six sonatas each, described by the composer as "methodische Sonaten mit Manieren für Viol. oder Travers. und GB" (Hamburg, 1728, 1732) ;[170] the 12 "Soli . . . à diversi stromenti" that comprise the other half of *Essercizii musici,* mentioned earlier; and at least 7 more sonatas in *Der getreue Music-Meister* (four for block flute; two for violin, flute, or oboe; and one for cello).[171]

Among Telemann's settings for two flutes or violins without accompaniment there is a set of six sonatas published in Hamburg in 1727,[172] and another that he described as "6. Sonaten, in 18. melodischen Canons [that is, three canonic movements, F-S-F, in each sonata], für 2. Trav. oder Viol. ohne Bass," originally published in Paris in 1738.[173] The latter set exists in a contemporary MS copy with "Duo pour le Clavessin" specified, suggesting the not very practical possibility that the pieces could be played at one or two keyboards in the manner of Couperin's *Pièces croisées.*[174] Otherwise, Telemann appears to have left no keyboard sonatas that are extant.[175] However, aside from his "three dozen" *Fantaisies pour le clavessin* (after 1737), very close in style to keyboard sonatas by his contemporaries, he did publish about 1736 a set, now lost, of *VI neue Sonatinen* of that sort "that can be played on the keyboard, or by a violin or flute and thorough-bass."[176]

The foregoing titles omit, of course, not only the many "Trios," "Quators," and allied pieces, in such collections as his *Tafelmusik,* that Telemann might well have called "sonatas," but numerous collections and single pieces, mostly in MSS, that await further exploration.   For

168. Cf. KAHL-SELBSTBIOGRAPHIEN, pp. 202, 205, and 228.
169. Mod. ed. of 1715 set: FRIEDRICH-TELEMANNm; Son. 5 in A minor is reprinted in MOFFAT-VIOLINm II, no. 8, only under Telemann's anagrammatic pseudonym "Georgio Melande" (or "Melante").
170. KAHL-SELBSTBIOGRAPHIEN, p. 213; cf. EITNER-QL, IX, 376.
171. Mod. eds.: HORTUSm, nos. 6, 7, and 13; NAGELSm, no. 23 (Upmeyer).
172. Mod. ed.: RIKKO-TELEMANNm.
173. KAHL-SELBSTBIOGRAPHIEN, p. 124. Mod. ed.: HERRMANN-TELEMANNm.
174. Cf. SEIFFERT-KLAVIERMUSIK, p. 356 ff.
175. Cf. SCHAEFER/SCHMUCK, pp. 2 and 27 ff.
176. Cf. SEIFFERT-KLAVIERMUSIK, p. 351, and SCHAEFER/SCHMUCK, p. 2 (including the correction of a faulty reference in EITNER-QL and mention of a sonata for a two-keyboard instrument).

example, a single Darmstadt MS is merely listed by Eitner as containing 83 sonatas for various instruments.[177] Some of the MSS may reveal more unusual sides of the composer, such as a late example of an SSS/bass setting, which was published recently, or a single piece in Rostock with the intriguing title of "Sonata discortato à 4," which has not been published.[178]

An appreciable majority of the available sonatas by Telemann have four movements in the S-F-S-F plan, while most of the others leave out the first slow movement. In half of the S/bass sonatas of the 1715 set it is interesting to note the convergence of the S-F-S-F plan with the core of four dances—allemande, courante, saraband, and gigue—that underlay the standard Baroque suite. His frequent use of both tempo and dance titles confirms this exceptionally complete fusion of the old church and court types. To achieve it, of course, he had to treat the allemande as a slow piece and admit the triple-metered, relatively homophonic courante in place of the usual quadruple-metered, fugal allegro.

The customary historical evaluation of Telemann as a fluent, popular, highly prolific, but not very original composer seems to require no special qualification after a review of the sonatas. If originality means, among other things, boldness of concept, there is boldness in some wide melodic leaps and some out-of-the-way harmonics. On the other hand, the dissonance treatment is both conservative and unimaginative. If originality means introspective fantasy, there is virtually none, notwithstanding such affective titles over certain slower movements as "Triste," "Spirituoso," "Soave," "Distrait," or "Affettuoso." Like the internationalisms suggested in other titles and inscriptions, these titles are often only "skin-deep" in their significance.

The strengths of Telemann's sonatas seem to lie in their fluent craftsmanship, clear lines, compelling harmony (sometimes strongly chromatic by dominants), effective writing for the instruments, and satisfactory structural organization. The chief weaknesses seem to lie in neutral ideas that stick too close to the scale or chord to achieve individuality, in similarly neutral rhythmic patterns, in a somewhat indifferent rhythmic organization at the phrase or period level, and in a lack of any special textural interest. Naturally, no one example would make a fair illustration, but it may be well to quote what seems like an average rather than an exceptional passage (Ex. 60). Actually, the most interesting rhythmic patterns are the borrowed ones, such as the

177. EITNER-QL, IX, 376.
178. Among mod. eds. of various MS sonatas: HORTUSM, nos. 25 and 36 (both Ruëtz), 97 (Hoffman).

Ex. 60. From the third movement of a MS "trio" Sonata in
E minor by Georg Philipp Telemann (after HORTUSM, no. 25,
but with editing deleted and minor corrections; by kind permission of Bärenreiter-Verlag).

mazurka and polonaise elements in the finales of the two *Sonates
polonoises*. As for the texture, most of the interest is found in relatively
simple imitations, with the bass participating only occasionally. Fugal
allegros are infrequent and fairly loose in structure, while the canonic
sonatas represent no great inventiveness or skill. Virtuosity for its own
sake seems not to have occupied Telemann.

Johann Mattheson (1681-1764) has been quoted here on several
occasions, for it is as an erudite author on music, of course, that he is
best known. But this versatile musician, scholar, linguist, lawyer, and
government official in Hamburg also composed extensively, including
four items of interest in sonata literature.[179] The earliest was a *Sonate
à due cembali* composed about 1705.[180] Here was the first example now
known of a "sonata" for two keyboard instruments, excepting Pasquini's
incipient pieces, with only the figured basses, as noted earlier. Mattheson's next contribution to the sonata was a set of 12 sonatas for 2 or 3
(block) flutes without *b. c.*, Op. 1, published by E. Roger of Amsterdam
in 1708.[181] In 1713 he himself engraved a *Sonate pour le clavecin* in G,
"dedicated to the one who can play it best."[182] The engraving, run off

180᠎

179. CANNON-MATTHESON includes a valuable introductory biography and a full
"Critical Bibliography" of his works.
180. CANNON-MATTHESON, p. 149. Dr. Beekman Cannon, who kindly provided
photostatic copies of this work and the solo keyboard sonata to be mentioned, has
projected a mod. ed. of both.
181. Mod. ed., complete: GIESBERT-MATTHESONm.
182. Cf. CANNON-MATTHESON, p. 157.

again in 1723, appears all on one side of a large sheet, "in the manner of a map," as he later described it. Lastly, in Hamburg in 1720 he published a set of *Zwölf neue Kammer-Sonaten* for flute or violin and *b. c.* under the title *Der Brauchbare Virtuoso*.[183] This title refers to his defense of the "good musician" as against the "unbrauchbare Virtuoso" in his lengthy preface to the set.

As noted in Chapter 2, Mattheson's conservative concepts of the sonata in his books included the introductory type as falling within the province of sacred choral works,[184] and other types mainly as vehicles for changing moods and fantasy.[185] Although his own sets of 1708 and 1720 combine elements of the church and court sonata in several movements, his reference to such cycles is limited to "violin pieces that consist of alternating adagio and allegro."[186] But in 1713 he was already writing that the violin sonata had begun to give way to a renewed interest in the realized solo keyboard sonata (cf. p. 25 ff.).[187] As we have seen, probably the "renewed interest" pertained to his own solo keyboard sonata of that year as compared with the sonatas of Kuhnau first published more than 20 years earlier.

Actually both his one- and his two-keyboard sonatas are virtuoso fantasias in only a single movement. They are full of runs, sequences, and even some motivic play in the few polyphonic passages, but have less harmonic, melodic, or rhythmic interest, and no tempo indications. Although Mattheson does speak of two-part form with reprise,[188] and his keyboard solo sonata does fall into three sections, of which the third is a "da capo" of the first, the attempt of Faisst and subsequent authors to make of this piece an evolutionary link between Kuhnau and men like Emanuel Bach seems labored, to say the least.[189] Mattheson himself mentioned the work specifically,[190] but only to assert that he could not play it, despite those who thought he meant himself when he dedicated it "to the one who can play it the best."

In the nature of the scoring the 1708 set has somewhat more contrapuntal interest than the 1720 set. Otherwise both sets have three to five movements, combining dances with freer types in no fixed order. Clear thematic relationships between the movements are frequent. Also worth noting is the title "Alla Corelli" over the first movement in Sonata 12 of the 1720 set. Mattheson's writing is much like that of

183. Cf. CANNON-MATTHESON, pp. 65 and 173. Mod. ed., complete: LEEUWENm.
184. -ORCHESTRE, p. 171 ff.
185. -KERN, p. 124 (repeated almost verbatim in -CAPELLMEISTER, p. 233).
186. -ORCHESTRE, p. 175.   187. *Ibid.*
188. *Ibid.*, p. 171.
189. FAISST, p. 29 ff.; cf. also, SEIFFERT-KLAVIERMUSIK, p. 343 ff.
190. -ORGANISTEN, p. 239.

Telemann—fluent, effective, intelligible, and classically restrained, with somewhat more distinctive melodic ideas. But it, too, is not outstanding, neither for melodic originality nor for expressive force.

Georg Friedrich Handel (1685-1759), the Baroque genius towering alongside Bach, lived in his birthplace of Halle until 1703, in Hamburg until 1706, in important Italian centers until 1710, in Hannover until 1712 (except for the visit to London in 1710), and in England thereafter.[191] Since his sonata publications and MSS date from about 1696 to as late as 1750, he cannot accurately be identified with any one city in the present study. Against the fact that all of the sonata publications appeared well after he reached London (*ca.* 1730-39) is the evidence that some if not most of the sonatas were actually composed or anticipated in earlier versions during his first years of writing.[192] If one environment must be singled out for its influence on his sonata writing it probably should be Hamburg, where he spent several formative years, working in close touch with Keiser and Mattheson, among others. At the same time, Handel's training under Zachau in Halle, his knowledge of Kuhnau's and Telemann's music in Leipzig, and especially his intercourse with such men as Steffani, Corelli, and both Scarlattis in Italy would certainly have to be given full credit in any study into the background of his sonatas. Such a study, or one on the sonatas themselves, has yet to be done in any substantial detail!   192a

As with Bach's, Handel's sonatas represent only a small fraction of his output—the equivalent of about 2 of the 93 volumes of original works and their adaptations in Chrysander's Händelgesellschaft edition[193]—yet at least today they, too, have assumed a proportionately greater importance, as evidenced in concerts, record catalogs, and reprints. Thanks to the patient bibliographic researches of William C. Smith, Jacob Coopersmith, and others,[194] the details of Handel's sonata production have been made fairly clear, more so than with Telemann's large output, though the record is not as complete as that for Bach's approximately 45 sonatas. Handel left a total of at least 76 pieces called   194a
"Sonata," including some 50 melo/bass types, 13 for keyboard, 12 in sacred choral works, one for orchestra, and one "Sonata by Mr. Handel For a Musical Clock." This total does not include the seven volumes

191. Biographic information primarily from MGG, V, 1229 ff. (Müller-Blatteau), and DEUTSCH-HANDEL.
192. Cf. CHRYSANDER-HÄNDEL, III, 145 ff.
193. HANDEL-WERKEM, XXVII, and portions of II, XXI, XXIV, XXXIV-XXXVI, and XLVIII.
194. A "Catalogue of Works" by Smith appears in ABRAHAM-HANDEL, p. 275 ff., and in abbreviated form in GROVE, IV, 50 ff. A copy of Coopersmith's unpublished "Thematic Index of the Collected Works" is in the Widener Library at Harvard University (cf. COOPERSMITH-PROJECT).

of arrangements for flute or violin and harpsichord that Walsh issued about 1739 under the title *Sonatas, or Chamber Aires,*[195] prepared, apparently at Walsh's direction, from "the most Celebrated Songs or Ariets Collected out of all the late Operas compos'd by Mr. Handel." Except for the clock sonata, seven keyboard sonatas, and about nine melo/bass sonatas, all discovered more recently,[196] Handel's sonatas can be found in the Händelgesellschaft edition (HANDEL-WERKEM). Many have also appeared in separate performing editions[197] and presumably all the genuine sonatas will be included in the excellent new Hallische Händel-Ausgabe that has been in progress only since 1955.[198]

To dispose of the lesser categories of Handel's sonatas first, we may note that these largely employ the term in the older, more general senses. Thus, the clock sonata, a novelty of little musical interest, is merely a single movement of 28 measures.[199] The orchestral "Sonata a 5"[200] clearly belongs with several works otherwise called "Concerto" or "Concerto grosso" by the composer. The first and last of its three movements (M-S-F) consist of brilliant solo violin passages supported or opposed by "tutti" strings with optional oboe parts. Two sonatas that occur in one of the earliest oratorios, *Il Trionfo del Tempo* (1708),[201] one an introductory "Sonata del Overtura" and the other an interludial "Sonata," are themselves miniature, one-movement concertos. The first of these, for example, opposes and combines a "concerto grosso" of strings and oboes and a "concertino" of two solo violins. Thereafter, and away from Italy, Handel preferred to call such movements in his operas and oratorios "Overture" or "Sinfonia." However, he did apply the title "Sonata" to 10 of the typical French overtures that introduce 11 of the 16 "Chandos Anthems."[202]

The 13 keyboard sonatas or sonatinas include an apparently early "Sonatina" in D minor, of which the first movement seems to be original yet weak, the second contains but nine measures of an incomplete "Bourée," and the third is an arrangement of a finale in a Corelli solo
203a sonata (which?).[203] Another apparently early Sonatina in D minor, a

195. Cf. BRITISH PRINTED, I, 565 ff., and CAT. WALSH, items 269-274.
196. Further details and mod. eds. in ABRAHAM-HANDEL, p. 301, and MGG, V, 1282 ff.
197. Cf. MGG, V, 1282 ff., and ALTMANN.
198. HANDEL-AUSGABEM, including 11 sons. for flute and *b. c.* (IV, Part 3) and 6 sons. for violin and *b. c.* (IV, Part 4) at the time of this writing.
199. Cf. SQUIRE-CLOCK, p. 539 ff., with mod. ed., p. 549.
200. HANDEL-WERKEM, XXI, 108.
201. HANDEL-WERKEM, XXIV, 3 and 33.
202. HANDEL-WERKEM, XXXIV-XXXVI.
203. Mod. ed. of the first movement only: NAGELSM, no. 3 (Werner, with preface); cf. also, WERNER-HANNOVER, p. 452 ff. The work is not included in HANDEL-WERKEM or Smith's catalog (ABRAHAM-HANDEL).

one-movement quasi gigue, was evidently intended to be part of Suite 4 in Handel's second collection of *Suites de pièces* (both Walsh and Le Cène, *ca.* 1733).[204] Five more relatively early keyboard sonatas or sonatinas, all single movements but one, occur as items 31-35 and 44 among the 76 harpsichord pieces in the four MS volumes of the rediscovered Aylesford collection.[205] One of these, with two movements in G (nos. 33 and 34), has the title "Concerto" in that collection, but "Sonata" in two other MSS.[206] Another, in G minor (no. 31), also appears as the "Allegro" in "Preludio ed Allegro" (1732 and later), item 9 of Handel's *Third Set of Lessons*. And another, an ingratiating, sizable piece in G (no. 35), requires a two-manual instrument. Two further keyboard sonatas, in B flat and G, appear never to have been published,[207] and three others appear in the Händelgesellschaft edition as items 10 to 12 in *A Third Set of Lessons*.[208] The last of these, dating from about 1750, is a three-movement Sonata in C. Finally, the fact should be noted that a slightly different version of "The Harmonious Blacksmith" variations exists in a MS with the title "Sonata per Cembalo."[209]

Most important among Handel's sonatas, of course, are the "trio" and "solo" ensemble types.[210] The three main sets must be mentioned first, Opp. 1, 2, and 5, originally published about 1722, 1731, and 1739, respectively. Op. 1 probably dates back, at least in part, to the composer's Hannover days. In the fullest of its various editions it contains 15 "solos" with *b. c.*, 7 for flute, 6 for violin, and 2 for oboe.[211] The violin sonatas, perhaps written for the then Prince of Wales or his teacher and Geminiani's pupil Matthew (not John) Dubourg,[212] comprise the set often published separately. The last two of them at least may not be by Handel, and the last may have been intended for viola da gamba.[213] Three others for violin—Sonatas 3 in A, 12 in F, and especially 13 in D—are the most played of all Handel's sonatas. Op. 2 contains six SS/bass sonatas with the option of violins, oboes, or

210a

204. HANDEL-WERKEm, XLVIII, 150; cf. p. v.   Cf. also, ABRAHAM-HANDEL, pp. 307 and 309; BRITISH MS, III, 150.
205. Mod. ed. of the harpsichord pieces: SQUIRE & FULLER/MAITLANDm (with preface).
206. Cf. J. M. Coopersmith's information as cited in NEWMAN-EARLIEST, p. 210.
207. Cf. NEWMAN-EARLIEST, p. 210.
208. HANDEL-WERKEm, II, 150 ff.
209. SEIFFERT-HÄNDEL, p. 135.
210. Broadly discussed by John Horton in ABRAHAM-HANDEL, p. 248 ff.
211. HANDEL-WERKEm, XXVII, 2 ff.; nos. 1 (2 versions), 2, 4, 5, 7, 9, and 10, all for flute, in HANDEL-AUSGABEm, IV, Part 3 (Schmitz, with preface and further bibliography); and nos. 3, 10, and 12-15, all for violin, in HANDEL-AUSGABEm, IV, Part 4 (Hinnenthal, with preface).
212. Cf. CHRYSANDER-HÄNDEL, III, 148.   Further discussions, among others, in MOSER-VIOLINSPIEL, p. 406 ff., and SCOTT-VIOLIN, p. 190 ff.
213. Cf. ABRAHAM-HANDEL, pp. 300 and 252.

transverse flutes,[214] and Op. 5 contains seven more, with only violins and
215a flutes named.[215]

Besides these three sets there is the MS set of six SS/bass sonatas,
with oboes specified.[216]   This earliest known music by an obviously
precocious lad, dating probably from his 11th year, is what Handel
referred to when he made his well-known remark, "I used to write like
the devil in those days, and chiefly for the oboe, which was my favorite
instrument."[217]   There are three more SS/bass sonatas left in MS,
wrongly included with Op. 2 in the Händelgesellschaft edition,[218] and
three others apparently never published.[219]   Furthermore, there are three
more "solo" flute sonatas in ANTH. HANDELm (1730),[220] perhaps dating
back to the Halle period (before 1703).   And there are the possibly
spurious Sonata in C for viola da gamba and realized keyboard,[221] at
least seven more "solo" sonatas, including one for cello in MS, and
another SS/bass sonata.[222]   But Handel is shown not to be the author
of six sonatas for two flutes without *b. c.* that are credited to him.[223]

Whereas the keyboard examples and other subordinate categories of
Handel's sonatas are primarily in one movement, the majority of his
melo/bass types have four movements in the standard church sequence.
However, Handel was no hidebound composer.   He changed the order
of movements when he pleased, as already in the second of the early
"trio" sonatas, where the compound-metered quasi gigue is placed second
and the quadruple-metered, polyphonic allegro last.   He added to the
number of movements, as in Op. 1, No. 9 (S-F-F-S-F-S-M).   And he
incorporated numerous French dances, especially in Op. 5, including the
gavotte, minuet, bourrée, musette, rondeau, and "Marche."   The forms
of the separate movements show no hidebound composer, either.   As is
well known, one of Handel's great strengths lies in the imaginative
freedom with which he treats and organizes his material.   He can leave
it and return to it, vary it, and oppose it in ways that might be described
paradoxically as premeditated caprice, whether the piece is a sonata

214. HANDEL-WERKEm, XXVII, 92-108 and 115-141.   Brief discussion of Opp. 2
and 5 in HOFFMANN-TRIOSONATE, p. 22 ff.
215. HANDEL-WERKEm, XXVII, 156 ff.
216. HANDEL-WERKEm, XXVII, 57 ff.
217. BURNEY-ACCOUNT, p. 3; cf. ABRAHAM-HANDEL, p. 250.
218. HANDEL-WERKEm, XXVII, 109-114 and 142-154.
219. Cf. ABRAHAM-HANDEL, p. 301.
220. HANDEL-WERKEm, XLVIII, 130 ff., and HANDEL-AUSGABEm, IV, Part 3, nos.
9-11.
221. HANDEL-WERKEm, XLVIII, 112 ff.   Cf. EINSTEIN-HÄNDEL, in which the
work is tentatively accepted as authentic.
222. Cf. ABRAHAM-HANDEL, p. 301.   The authenticity of a flute sonata in D
(HORTUSm, no. 3 [Hinnenthal]) is questioned in HANDEL-AUSGABEm, IV, Part 3, v.
223. MEYER-HANDEL.

allegro or a big choral number like "For Unto Us a Child Is Born" in *Messiah*. An exceptional and bold example of such caprice is found in much of Sonata 4 of Op. 5. But it is not unusual to find distinct elements of the rondo, the variation form, and the invention all in a single movement, an instance being the Sonata in G for a two-manual harpsichord that was mentioned earlier.

Largely because of this imaginative treatment and other strengths— particularly the varied syntax, transparent texture, fresh (often dotted) rhythms, and songful melody—a comparative reading of Handel's and Telemann's or Mattheson's sonatas leaves little doubt as to which works are the stereotypes and which the products of a truly creative genius. This is not to say that Handel does not follow certain patterns himself. Especially with regard to melodic ideas, several types have been noted that recur often throughout his music.[224]   To go very far into this point would open up the whole question, still not sufficiently investigated for the sonatas, of the many arrangements and adaptations Handel made of his own, not to mention others', music. Thus, Sonata 8, Op. 1, is an arrangement of Organ Concerto 5, Op. 4; the "Largo" of Sonata 1, Op. 1, recurs approximately as the "Affettuoso" (opening movement) of Sonata 13 in the same set; the "Allegro" from the latter can be found as an orchestral piece in *Jephtha;* the third movement of Sonata 1, Op. 2, appears in various forms in at least five choral works, including one by Keiser and "Comfort Ye My People" in *Messiah,*[225] etc., etc. But the melodic types are also evident in similar, not necessarily derived, incipits. The opening of Sonata 13, Op. 1, is suggested in several other move- ments, for instance the "Largo" of Sonata 2, Op. 2; the familiar "Largo" from *Serse* is hinted in numerous instrumental movements, such as the "Adagio" from Sonata 6, Op. 2; "I Know That My Redeemer Liveth" from *Messiah* is similarly hinted in such movements as the "Arioso" of the first sonata in ANTH. HANDELm; and a bass progression like that from the expressive opening movement of "trio" Sonata 1 (second version), Op. 2, is almost a mannerism of the times (Ex. 61).

Perhaps the least commanding aspect of Handel's sonatas is to be found in the harmony and tonality. Although there is some chromatic harmony, as in that that accompanies the unusually tortuous, Bach-like line in the opening movement of Sonata 1, Op. 1, Handel generally seemed to need the excitement of a text to bring forth his more daring chords and chord relationships.[226]   In slow, minor movements he made his chief use of altered chords (Ex. 62). As for tonality, the relatively

224. Cf. Abraham's own chapter in ABRAHAM-HANDEL, especially p. 266 ff.
225. Cf. ABRAHAM-HANDEL, pp. 265 ff. and 256 ff.
226. Cf. LEICHTENTRITT-HARMONIC, p. 219.

Ex. 61. From Georg Friedrich Handel's Sonata 1 (second version), Op. 2 (after HANDEL-WERKEm, XXVII, 99).

narrow range of modulations and their infrequency tend to keep key contrast from being quite the structural support and attraction that it might be, especially in the longer movements—for example, the two fast movements in the second sonata of ANTH. HANDELm.

One other composer to be mentioned in Hamburg, now all but forgotten, was **Johann Christian Schickhard** (?-1745). Between about 1705 and 1735 this prolific composer (flutist?) published concertos, a flute method, and some 20 sets of S/- and SS/bass sonatas with flutes, violins, or oboes usually as optional high instruments.[227] Enough of these were published in Amsterdam and London to suggest that he may have been in either or both of those places, too.[228] The last known opus of Schickhard, "XXX. Ouvrage," is called *L'Alphabet de la musique, contenant XXIV. sonates-solos* for flute or violin with *b. c.* His sonatas

227. Cf. EITNER-QL, IX 18 ff. Among mod. eds.: "Trio" Son. in C minor, MOFFAT-TRIOm, no. 18; 6 "trio" sons., GIESBERT-SCHICKHARDTm I; 6 sons. for violin [flute] and *b. c.*, GIESBERT-SCHICKHARDTm II (actually by J. E. Galliard—cf. MGG, IV, 1285 [Westrup]) ; Son. for violin and *b. c.* in D minor, MOFFAT-VIOLINm II, no. 31.
228. Cf. BRITISH PRINTED, II, 468; SMITH-WALSH, items 467, 571, and 616; HAAS-CAT. 20, nos. 579-583.

Ex. 62. From Sonata 3, Op. 2, by Georg Friedrich Handel (after HANDEL-WERKEm, XXVII, 112).

mix church and dance movements. These movements are short, graceful, and very light in content.

The once famous brothers, **Johann Gottlieb Graun** (or Giovanni Amadeo, *ca.* 1703-71) and **Carl Heinrich Graun** (*ca.* 1704-59), must be considered together,[229] both because they lived in such close touch with each other and because the larger, MS portion of their extant music and even some of the publications carry only the name Graun, without forename or other sufficient basis for deciding between them. Even Mennicke's painstaking thematic index, in which all the sinfonias and other independent orchestral works are credited to J. G. Graun,[230] and Schenk's assignment of 142 MS trio sonatas to J. G. and 31 to C. H. Graun[231] leaves much that is unanswered, not only because the scope of their studies is limited but because these raise serious questions of method and validity.[232] Both brothers were important figures in the musical sphere of Frederick the Great in Berlin. J. G. Graun trained in Dresden and Leipzig, studied violin with both Pisendel and Tartini (in Prague), taught Friedemann Bach and Franz Benda, among others, and served chiefly in Merseburg and Berlin. First of all he was an outstanding violinist. One would expect him to have been the more productive of the two brothers in instrumental composition, quite apart from

229. The oldest of the three brothers, August Friedrich, is not known for any sonatas.
230. MENNICKE, p. 536 ff.
231. SCHENK-GRAUN. The 35 more "trios" credited to J. G. Graun in CAT. HAUSBIBLIOTHEK, p. 85 ff., are at least in part duplicates of the 142 sonatas (cf. MGG, V, 707) ; no sonatas are definitely credited to C. H. Graun in this source.
232. Cf. MGG, V, 705 ff. (Freytag).

the fact that he lived at least a dozen years longer. Mennicke concludes that it was J. G. Graun who made the noteworthy advances in the sinfonia, whereas Hasse and C. H. Graun were mainly important, then and since, as opera and oratorio composers.[233]　However, C. H. Graun, who served chiefly in Braunschweig, Rheinsberg, and Berlin, did study cembalo as well as voice, and it seems probable that the few keyboard sonatas ascribed merely to "Sig.r. Graun" were his.

J. G. Graun published at least two collections of sonatas in his lifetime. One was a set of *Sei Sonate per il violino e cembalo,* which appeared in Merseburg in 1726 or 1727. The other was a set of *Eight Sonatas for two German Flutes or Violins with a Bass for the Violoncello or Harpsicord,* published by Walsh of London in 1759.[234]　Besides these evidences of J. G. Graun's success as an instrumental composer there is the fact that some of his 142 or more "trio" sonatas and 26 further "solo" sonatas in MS exist also in copies to be found in several other north German libraries, including two "trio" sonatas in J. S. Bach's handwriting.[235]　In some of these copies the same work may be found in a variety of settings (including one in a simple *scordatura*). These shed light on performance practices of the time as well as on the ancestry of the accompanied clavier sonata, which was so significant to the sonata of the Classic Era.[236]　The usual "trio" setting, of course, was that for two high instruments—flutes, or violins, or oboes, or any mixed pairing—and *b. c.* and/or cembalo. However, Mersmann finds,[237] for example, two sonatas that exist not only in that setting but in another in which the second violin part is replaced by a viola, and in still another that allots the second violin part to the cembalist's right hand, resulting in a "solo" sonata with realized keyboard. J. G. Graun's sonatas available for this survey are predominantly in three movements in the order S-F-F. They are earnest, expressive works, with polyphonic interest, full but not extravagant harmony, and purposeful tonal movement. The lines are somewhat fragmented by rests and rhythmic or ornamental minutiae in the manner that marked the breakdown of the sustained Corellian style and the onset of the *galant* style.

233. MENNICKE, p. 327 ff.
234. Listed in BRITISH HIRSCH, p. 36. No mod. eds. appear to have been made from this set.
235. Cf. MGG, V, 707 ff. Among mod. eds.: "Trio" Sons. in F, G, and C minor, COLLEGIUMm, nos. 24-26 (discussed in MERSMANN-KAMMERMUSIK, I, 157 ff., the last being one that Bach had copied) ; Sons. in B-flat and F for viola and *b. c.,* BREITKOPF KAMMERSON'ATENm, nos. 10 and 11 (Wolff).
236. Cf. NEWMAN-ACCOMPANIED. The facsimile of a passage from a "solo" sonata by J. G. Graun in simplified and ornamented versions appears in MGG, III, 499 (Engel).
237. -AUFFÜHRUNGSPRAXIS, p. 102 ff.

No examples of C. H. Graun's sonatas have been made available in modern editions. The third harpsichord sonata in ANTH. WELCKERm is presumably his, although this set of "Six Lessons" was not published until about 1770, with a re-edition "for the Piano Forte" in 1799.[238] Also, he is assumed to be the Graun who wrote "The Battle of Rosbach, A Favourite Sonata" and similar programmatic pieces for keyboard[239] that anticipate hardy best-sellers of the earlier 19th century like Kotzwara's "Battle of Prague" sonata, although the earliest publication dates of around 1780 and the constant "Alberti-bass" texture are suspiciously late for a man who died in 1759.   Perhaps an acquaintance with like pieces attributed to C. H. Graun has been a factor in the usual depreciation of his instrumental style.[240]   But his well-known "Gigue" in B-flat minor that still appears in many keyboard anthologies invites no such depreciation and, pertinently, is in a distinctly earlier, Baroque idiom.

The last Baroque composer to name in north Germany is **Frederick II** ("the Great," 1712-86), King of Prussia from 1740 to 1786.   This royal dilettante par excellence was not only "le protecteur des muses" and cultivator of music in particular at his Berlin court,[241] where we have already noted considerable interest in the sonata, but was himself the composer of at least 121 sonatas for flute and cembalo, as well as other music.[242]   He was a student of Quantz on his favorite instrument, the flute, of S. L. Weiss on the lute, of C. H. Graun in composition, and of others.   Between about 1728 and 1756 he wrote his sonatas, purely for his own use and private hearings, not for publication (unlike his literary efforts).   Each sonata he required to be copied in quadruplicate so that there would be separate scores for the two (or three?) performers in both Potsdam (at the Sans-Souci Palace) and Berlin.[243]   These sonatas plus the sonatas and concertos of Quantz he played for many years according to a fixed plan of rotation and an amusingly rigid method of procedure made well known by Burney and other select observers.[244]

In view of this formalism and the fact that Frederick played nothing but his own music or that which Quantz composed "by command," one would hardly expect anything daring and new from him.   The sonatas are consistently in the S-F-F plan we have noted in Tartini, Quantz,

241a

238. Cf. BRITISH PRINTED, II, 39 and 1st Supp. (in the same vol.), p. 16.
239. Cf. BRITISH PRINTED, I, 541, and II, 1st Supp., 16; MAYER/REINACH, p. 478.
240. Cf. MGG, V, 716 and 717.   A piece of this sort is reprinted in MAYER/REINACH, p. 479 ff.; and again, with variants, in ENSCHEDÉ.
241. Cf. BRENET-CLASSIQUES, p. 1017 ff.
242. Listed in full in CAT. HAUSBIBLIOTHEK, p. 64 ff.   Among mod. eds. (cf. MGG, IV, 960 ff. [Becker]) : 25 sons., SPITTA-FRIEDRICHm, I and II (with a valuable preface, which is largely repeated in SPITTA-FRIEDRICH).
243. Cf. SPITTA-FRIEDRICH, V, 354 ff.
244. Cf. BURNEY-GERMANY, II, 151 ff.; BOURKE-FREDERICK, p. 71 ff.

and numerous other sonata composers. All the movements are melodious and fluent. But the most distinctive are the slow movements, which are genuinely expressive and sensitive. One can understand the evidently sincere praise of Burney, C. F. C. Fasch, Reichardt, and others, especially with reference to Frederick's playing of adagios and free passages.[245] The best known sonata is one in C minor,[246] because it is linked, even in its musical material, with J. S. Bach's important visit to Potsdam in 1747 and the improvisation on the "Royal Theme" that followed.

245. Cf. SPITTA-FRIEDRICH, V, 357 ff.; BOURKE-FREDERICK, p. 71 ff.; MOSER-DEUTSCHEN, II, 269; and, for a single example, SCHERING-BEISPIELEm, no. 307.
246. SPITTA-FRIEDRICHm, I, no. 2 (cf. SPITTA-FRIEDRICH, V, 357).

Chapter 13

England from about 1660 to 1710

We are concerned in this chapter with that century of England's general history that began in 1660 with the Restoration and the return of the Stuart dynasty under Charles II. It is the period that soon saw the ultimate triumph of Parliament over the monarchy (upon the accession of William of Orange, 1688), followed by such other epochal landmarks as the union of England, Scotland, and Wales into Great Britain, in 1707; the introduction of the Hanoverian line with the accession of the first of the four Georges in 1714; considerable industrial, colonial, and material progress; and the growing rivalry with France under Louis XIV and his successors, culminating in the Seven Years' War, 1756-63. From the standpoint of England's music history this century divides into two periods. One, from about 1660 to 1710, takes us from the first composers of sonatas in England to a first peak under Purcell and his contemporaries. The other period, from about 1710 to 1775, is that largely dominated by Handel in England. It allows for a slightly later end to the Baroque style in England than in Italy and Germany.

The question of locale is relatively simple in this century of English music. Although we do include one resident each in Edinburgh, Aberdeen, and Dedham, nearly all activities here of concern were centered in London. On the other hand, the question of nationality is more complex than in any other region under discussion. Out of some 50 composers to be noted in England and Scotland, of which less than a third are in the first group, about half were foreigners. These last came mainly from Italy, especially in the later group. But they also came from four other countries, as is shown in the chart on the next page.

Predecessors of Purcell

The logical and actual consequence of so much internationalism was the production of many sets of sonatas that exhibit both imported and—

The Nationalities of Sonata Composers in
England During the Baroque Era

	England	Scotland	Italy	Germany	France	Belgium	Bohemia
First Group (1660-1710)	10	-	3	2	-	1	1
Second Group (1710-75)	15	1	16	2	1	1	-

especially in the music of the native Englishmen—indigenous traits.
The indigenous traits were chiefly those growing out of the immediate
instrumental background of the sonata in England.[1] Most pertinent were
the polyphonic instrumental fantasias (or fancies) and In Nomines,
and the dances, all in ensemble settings by men like William Lawes and
John Jenkins.[2] Other factors that paved the way for the sonata, most of
them already anticipated during the Commonwealth, were the development of public concerts; the growth of popular-minded publishers, culminating above all, from 1695, in the rich catalogs of the first John
Walsh and his successors;[3] an increased interest in solo rather than in
group music; an increased knowledge of Italian and French music and
related culture; and a gradual change-over from the various members of
the viol family to the violin, viola, and cello. The violin was made
popular by virtuosos in London like the Italian Nicola Matteis[4] and the
German or Swedish Thomas Baltzar (only the former of whom seems
to have written sonatas himself[5]) and by the "Twenty-four Violins" hired
at court by Charles II in direct imitation of Louis XIV's "Vingt-quatre
violons du roi."

Writing more than a century after the fact, the historian Hawkins
was the first to discuss the origins of the sonata in England. He
credited Robert Cambert with introducing "into concerts the violins,
and those other instruments of that species, the tenor violin and
violoncello. . . . To these were adapted compositions of a new structure,
namely Sonatas, the invention of some of the most eminent performers

1. For general discussions of this subject as well as the Baroque century under
discussion cf. WALKER & WESTRUP, p. 166 ff. and chaps. 6-8; MGG, III, 1378 ff. and
1382 ff. (Dart), 1383 ff. (Westrup), and 1389 ff. (Cudworth).
2. Cf. MEYER-ENGLISH, pp. 179 ff. and 216 ff. For recent findings on the In
Nomine cf. REESE-RENAISSANCE, pp. 779 ff. and 845 ff.
3. Cf. p. v ff. in SMITH-WALSH, a fundamental contribution to music bibliography
in this period, including much incidental information on other publishers, too.
4. Cf. NORTH-GRAMARIAN, p. 34, for a valuable early account.
5. Cf. EVANS-DURHAM, p. 223; BRIDGE-PURCELL, p. 4.

on the violin among the Italians. . . ."[6] Hawkins might have added that with the sonata came a greatly increased use of thorough-bass in England. Elsewhere he writes, "Notwithstanding that Jenkins [**John Jenkins, 1592-1678, in the service of Charles II**]

was so excellent a master, and so skillful a composer for the viol, he seems to have contributed in some degree to the banishment of that instrument from concerts, and to the introduction of the violin in its stead. To say the truth, the Italian style in music had been making its way into this kingdom even from the beginning of the seventeenth century. . . . In compliance therefore with this general prepossession in favor of the Italian style, Jenkins composed twelve Sonatas for two violins and a bass, with a thorough-bass for the organ, printed at London about the year 1660, and at Amsterdam in 1664; and these were the first compositions of the kind by an Englishman.[7]

Actually, as we have seen (p. 212), the sonatas by William Young that were published in 1653 in Innsbruck while he was in service there and before he himself returned to England are the earliest yet known by an Englishman. Furthermore, neither publication of Jenkins' set has ever been found, in spite of much interest on the part of recent scholars. However, a MS that may relate to them, although the title "Sonata" does not appear, is known in the British Museum (not the Bodleian Library at Oxford).[8]

Jenkins did use the title "Sonata" in at least five other of some 150 pieces that he left, including two for three bass viols and three for violin, viola da gamba, and *b. c.*[9] Though no sonatas by him or others in 9a England around 1660 exist in published form, old or modern, apparently there was no little interest in the sonata at the time. Peter Evans has surveyed some 80 different MS pieces in the Durham Cathedral Library.[10] Nearly half are anonymous. Three composers we met in 10a Germany or Austria are included, D. Becker, J. M. Nicolai, and J. H. Schmelzer. The rest of the pieces are by Jenkins and such obscure names as Henry Butler and the Italian (Giuseppe?) Zamponi. Out of the 80 pieces at least half are called "Sonata" or "Fantasia." The titles are used without distinction, Evans says, for the music seems to mark a transition phase between the old fantasia and the newly imported sonata.

6. HAWKINS, IV, 386.
7. HAWKINS, IV, 62; cf. his similar statement in IV, 393. Cf. also, Playford's negative view, quoted on p. 40 in the present study.
8. Cf. BRITISH MS, III, 188 (items 17-28 in Add. 31430); PULVER-ENGLISH, pp. 267 and 268 (could not the set of dances "voor twee Violes en Bass" cited from Goovaerts as an Amsterdam publication of 1664 be related?); MEYER-ENGLISH, p. 216.
9. Cf. MEYER-ENGLISH, p. 222 (with ex.); BRITISH MS, III, 44; and EVANS-DURHAM, p. 216. A charming account of Jenkins and his music is in NORTH-GRAMARIAN, p. 21 ff.
10. -DURHAM.

Of the "sonatas" (or "fantasias"?) the largest number (22) are in that characteristic setting for violin, viola da gamba, and *b. c.* that we met several times in 17th-century Germany and Italy; 16 are for 3 violas da gamba or 2 with *b. c.;* 9 are the regular "trio" setting for two violins and *b. c.;* and only one (anonymous?) is for the "solo" setting of violin and *b. c.* Of course, the last type is not far from that of violin with viola da gamba and *b. c.* when the viola da gamba is no more than a *concertante* version of the *b. c.* Among the structural methods or types are imitative movements suggesting the canzona; free, almost rhapsodic movements; dances; and divisions, especially on extended basses in two sections.

When we come to the successful composer and organist **John Blow** (1649-1708) we meet the most important of the Restoration composers aside from Purcell himself, who was the pupil of Blow. However, Blow's two little-known sonatas, which have been found in two MS copies each, are not regarded as the equal of his other music—his masque *Venus and Adonis,* his anthems, and other vocal music.[11] Both sonatas, in A and G, are in SSB/bass scoring, with violins on top and viola da gamba as the *concertante* bass when it is not actually independent of the *b. c.*[12] The second sonata, in G, is credited to Blow only on presumptive evidence. Each sonata has three movements, the first in what seems to be the order S-S-F, and the second F-S-S. The only tempo mark is "Larghetto" over a quasi saraband in each sonata. Both fast movements have the rhythmic and melodic angularity and the imitations of the canzona. The slow movements are more homophonic. In its larger rhythmic and tonal organization this music does seem to be somewhat at a loss for want of a text, notwithstanding some distinctive melodic ideas and the sure craftsmanship displayed in the part writing.

Henry Purcell

Henry Purcell (*ca.* 1659-95), great English composer of the Baroque Era, became composer to Charles II's Twenty-four Violins upon Matthew Locke's death in 1677, and replaced his teacher John Blow as 13a   organist at Westminster Abbey from 1679.[13] As a youth he had sung under Captain Cooke and then under the talented but short-lived Pelham Humfrey, who may well have passed on his presumed devotion to Lully. Besides his important opera and other dramatic music, his welcome songs, his odes, and his anthems, Purcell wrote important instrumental music. The latter includes the 15 fantasias *a 3-5* and two In Nomines

11. E.g., cf. WALKER & WESTRUP, p. 215.
12. Mod. ed. of both sons.: WHITTAKER-BLOWM (with preface).
13. WESTRUP-PURCELL is the chief over-all source.

a 6 and *7* in the older polyphonic style, harpsichord suites, organ voluntaries, and the 24 known sonatas.[14]   14a

Except for an (early?) orchestral sonata for trumpet, four string parts, and *b. c.*, which has never been published,[15] all of Purcell's sonatas are in the class of chamber music. He did not apply the term to any of the broad orchestral introductions in his vocal works such as the "Symphony" that precedes each of the three odes for St. Cecilia's Day. Only one of the sonatas is a "solo" setting, the mature and too little known Sonata in G minor for violin and *b. c.*[16] No earlier "solo" sonata definitely attributable to an Englishman has been found in the present survey. The remaining 22 sonatas are all in SSB/bass "trio" settings, there being no difference in this respect between the first set "of III Parts," in which Purcell tells us he had not originally planned to have the separate thorough-bass line engraved, and the second set "in Four Parts."[17] Following two years after the expert, unpublished fantasias that Purcell had composed at 21, there appeared in 1683 the first set of these sonatas, 12 *Sonata's of III Parts: Two Viollins And Basse: To the Organ or Harpsecord.*[18] The publisher (with John Carr) was old John Playford, the original author of *A Brief Introduction to the Skill of Musik* (1654). (It is in the thirteenth and subsequent six editions [1697-1730] of Playford's text, standard for nearly a century, that Purcell's contribution appears, as the third part, "The Art of Discant,"[19] including remarks to be noted presently.) The second set, *Ten Sonata's in Four Parts,* "composed by the late Mr. Henry Purcell," was published posthumously in 1697 by successors of John Playford.[20] Although further Italianisms and other stylistic advances have been noted, especially in the last three sonatas,[21] this set could have been composed about the same time as the first. At any rate, the preface by the widow, Frances

14. Full lists of his works may be found in WESTRUP-PURCELL, p. 271 ff., and GROVE, VI, 1010 ff. (Fuller Maitland, Squire, Colles). FAVRE/LINGOROW is a recent, somewhat circumscribed doctoral study of all the instrumental works, including the sonatas p. 15 ff.

15. Cf. GROVE, VI, 1018.

16. Mod. ed., among others (cf. ALTMANN, p. 242; MEYER-ENGLISH, p. 241) COLLEGIUMm, no. 102 (Schroeder); also, by Oxford University Press (A. Goldsbrough), 1959.

17. KLENZ-PURCELL, a master's thesis, is a valuable style study of both sets. For a shorter, more general discussion, among others, cf. WESTRUP-PURCELL, p. 229 ff.; also Michael Tilmouth, "The Technique and Forms of Purcell's Sonatas," ML, XL (1959), 109-21.

18. Among mod. eds. (cf. ALTMANN), entire set: PURCELL-WORKSm, V (Fuller Maitland, with preface and reproductions; cf. criticisms of accuracy in BRIDGEPURCELL, p. 8 ff., especially as regards the *b. c.*); WHITTAKER-PURCELLm (with preface and reproductions).

19. Reprinted in SQUIRE-PURCELL I.

20. Among mod. eds. (cf. ALTMANN), entire set: PURCELL-WORKSm, VII (Stanford, with preface); this set has not yet been issued in conjunction with WHITTAKERPURCELLm, although it is so announced in that edition; Sonatas 6 and 9 were published by Novello of London in 1959 (Donington and Emery).

21. E.g., cf. WESTRUP-PURCELL, p. 234 ff.

Purcell, speaks of the second set as "having already found many Friends."
In this set is one of Purcell's best known works, Sonata 9 in F, which has
often been singled out and reprinted, apparently for no special reason
other than the title of "The Golden Sonata" that it acquired very early.

Purcell's "trio" sonatas vary between four and seven movements,
with the exception being Sonata 6, 1697, a strong work consisting entirely
of variations on a five-measure ground. The second set is somewhat
more regularized at five movements. In both sets the general character
and the typical alternation of the contrasted movements suggest the
sonata da chiesa. However, the standard S-F-S-F plan itself is infrequent (so far as the tempo or title can be decided when these are lacking).
It does serve as the plan, however, in the "solo" violin sonata. The
focal movement in nearly all the "trio" sonatas is the fugal movement,
which is usually in second place, as would be expected of the church
sonata. Most often this movement is called "Canzona," the title that by
now had been reduced in all countries to this more limited sense except
in keyboard music.[22] Outstanding in the fugal movements are the fresh
ideas used as subjects (Ex. 63). No movements have dance titles, but
dances are certainly present in abundance in both style and spirit,
especially the gigue (e.g., Son. 2, 1683), the saraband (Son. 1, 1683),
and the old galliard.[23] With regard to the last type Fuller Maitland
laughs at an undeniably strained attempt to trace "God Save the King"

Ex. 63. From Sonata 10 in the 1697 set by Henry Purcell
(after PURCELL-WORKSm, VII, 107, but without the editorial
additions).

22. An extended discussion of Purcell's canzona movements occurs in FAVRE/
LINGOROW, p. 23 ff.
23. Cf. the illuminating discussions in KLENZ-PURCELL, chaps. 6, 7, and 9.

to the "Largo" (a "middle" tempo, says Purcell in his 1683 preface) of Sonata 6, 1683 (see Ex. 65 below).[24] But there is no denying the frequent hints of this tune in Purcell's triple-metered movements, and the even more frequent occurrences of its basic rhythmic pattern. Other types of movements include serious adagios in quadruple meter and some relatively free, expressive movements with tempo changes indicated or implied. Purcell was apparently little interested in relating the incipits of the separate movements of a sonata. However, in the 1683 set the successive keys of the 12 sonatas reveal a typically Baroque key plan, alternating between minor and major and progressing by thirds with but one exception (perhaps so as to stay within the meantone tuning system that then prevailed[25]).

One of the most intriguing problems related to Purcell's sonatas has been that of identifying the models intended when he said in his important note "To the Reader" in 1683 that he

faithfully endeavour'd a just imitation of the most fam'd Italian Masters; principally, to bring the seriousness and gravity of that sort of Musick into vogue, and reputation among our Country-men, whose humor, 'tis time now, should begin to loath the levity, and balladry of our neighbours . . . . he thinks he may warrantably affirm, that he is not mistaken in the power of the Italian Notes, or elegancy of their Compositions, which he would recommend to the English Artists.

Squire[26] calls attention to one **Lelio Calista** whom Purcell himself (in Playford's *Introduction*) cited as "famous" and quoted to illustrate fugal movements in sonatas. Squire reports up to 30 "trio" sonatas in MS in three English (but no foreign) libraries and a reference to "Lelius Colista" by Kircher[27] that probably pertains to this man. In the ten sonatas by Calista that Squire could examine, two contained fugal movements called "Canzona" (which cannot be said for any other Italian sonatas that have been suggested as models for Purcell). Further information about Calista is wanting. Unfortunately for our present knowledge of such forgotten men, one negative consequence of so much internationalism in England has been an absence at times of that nationalistic zeal for research such as has brought much obscure material in German libraries to view.

Another Italian in England (from about 1672), the violinist **Nicola Matteis** senior,[28] is suggested as Purcell's model by Bridge,[29] who may

26a

27a

24. PURCELL-WORKSm, V, iii.   25. Cf. ARUNDELL-PURCELL, p. 129.
26. -PURCELL I, 557, and -PURCELL II.
27. KIRCHER-MUSURGIA, I, 480. The Lelio Colista in SCHMIDL, II, 205, could be a descendant.
28. Cf. GROVE, V, 631 ff. (Husk and Kidson) ; SCHMIDL, II, 63.
29. BRIDGE-PURCELL, p. 4 ff.

have read too much into a remark he quotes from Purcell's contemporary Roger North:

He [Matteis] was the means of settling Italian music in England, and after him the French was wholly laid aside and nothing in town had relish without a spice of Italy. The masters began to imitate them—witness Mr. Purcell in his noble set of Sonatas.

Matteis left two S/bass sonatas in his four books of violin *Ayrs*,[30] and Bridge cites two "trio" sonatas in MS. Other Italians suggested as models include Bassani (doubtful both in style and date), G. M. Bononcini, and G. B. Vitali.[31] Corelli himself is almost never considered, mainly because of the error that still persists of dating his Op. 1 as 1683 instead of 1681.[32] His influence was soon to dominate the sonata in England as completely as Handel's was the opera. Although none of his collections was published in London until Op. 5 first appeared there, five years after Purcell's death, Op. 1 may well have found its way to England in a year or so, or have been known in MSS that circulated before publication.[33] But in any case the harmonic drive-to-the-cadence through dominants, the special melodic pathos, the idiomatic use of the violin,[34] and the standardized plan are all somewhat more developed in Corelli's than in Purcell's sonatas.

For that matter, it would probably be wrong to settle on any one Italian as Purcell's model. Others seem just as possible from the standpoints of style and form—Legrenzi or Cazzati, for example. Evidently, Purcell had a rather good representation of Italian music that he could hear and examine.[35] Furthermore, contrary to his own statement, some older, English precedents might be suggested, at least for the style if not the title. For instance, a clear instrumental precedent for the SS/bass setting can often be found in certain three-part examples of the English In Nomine, with the *cantus firmus* in the bass.[36] In Playford's *Introduction* Purcell seems to identify the Italian style chiefly with this sort of SS/bass setting as against the equal three-part (or fuller) writing that he had still employed in his own, earlier fantasias.[37]

Perhaps a new approach to the question of Purcell's models would be to ask in which ways his sonatas are not Italian but English in style.

30. Cf. SARTORI-BIBLIOGRAFIA, pp. 526 and 530.
31. Cf. PURCELL-WORKSm, p. i ff.
32. Even in GROVE, VI, 1008, and MGG, II, 1676 (Paumgartner).
33. Cf. RINALDI-CORELLI, p. 187; HAWKINS, IV, 527 and 497; PINCHERLE-CORELLI, p. 125 ff.; SMITH-WALSH, items 31 and 181.
34. Cf. the reaction to Purcell on this account in BURNEY-HISTORY, II, 403.
35. Cf. WESTRUP-PURCELL, p. 230 ff.
36. E.g., cf. DAVISON & APELm, no. 176 (by Thomas Tomkins).
37. Cf. SQUIRE-PURCELL I, 552 ff., or PLAYFORD, p. 133 ff.

Ways in which they are not like Corelli's sonatas have already been suggested. To these one might add, first, Purcell's remarkably diverse, sometimes startling harmony, which seems to hark back at times to the Elizabethan madrigal. Included are rich chromaticism, false relations, vestigial modality, whole series of dissonances, and poignantly expressive chords (Ex. 64).[38] The prevalence of movements in the galliard rhythm noted earlier is another Anglicism in Purcell's sonatas. One

Ex. 64.   From Sonata 4 in the 1697 set by Henry Purcell (after PURCELL-WORKSm, VII, 34 ff., but without the editorial additions).

becomes especially conscious of ideas that are thetic rather than anacrustic in their beginnings and patterns, of gay, steady quarter-notes in the triple meter, and of relatively few suspensions that carry over the bar (Ex. 65). With regard to texture, Purcell's bass parts still participate in the motivic exchanges somewhat more than Corelli's do (although Purcell's viola da gamba part is but rarely independent of the b. c., e.g., "Largo" of Son. 5, 1683). In fact, the total texture recalls the density of Purcell's own fantasias more often than one would expect from his remark on the Italian style. Not infrequently there is real

38. Cf. WHITTAKER-PURCELL (with many exx.) ; also, ARNOLD, p. 169.

Ex. 65. From Sonata 6 in the 1683 set by Henry Purcell (after PURCELL-WORKSm, V, 47, but without the editorial additions).

contrapuntal virtuosity, as in the "Canon by twofold augmentation in the 5th and 8th above" that opens Sonata 6, 1683. All in all, one is tempted to conclude that Purcell's Anglicisms are at least as much responsible as his Italianisms for the high quality and appeal of his sonatas.

Contemporaries and Successors of Purcell (Ravenscroft, Loeillet)

Gottfried Finger (*ca.* 1660 to at least 1723), of Moravian descent, was active in London from about 1685 to at least 1701.[39] During that time he seems to have composed all of his sonatas as well as his earliest dramatic music. From 1688, in London and Amsterdam, appeared at least 10 collections of Finger's sonatas, several in reprints that attest their considerable success.[40] At least three of these collections were done in conjunction with other composers, chiefly John Banister, Gottfried Keller, Ralph Courteville, or Purcell's son Daniel. The sonatas are written for strings, or flutes or oboes in place of violins, in a variety of settings. Op. 1 of 1688 includes SB/-, SSB/-, and SSSB/ bass sonatas. Op. 2 is for two flutes alone. Still another set (lost?), "in five parts," was scored for 2 flutes, 2 oboes, and *b. c.* Few of these sonatas have been examined or made available.[41] These reveal the

39. MGG, IV, 220 ff. (Senn), is the chief source.
40. Cf. MGG, IV, 222 ff.; SMITH-WALSH, items 82a (with Plate 8; cf. p. xxi ff., which shows Walsh's first use of a favorite cover, used also as a frontispiece in this book), 99, 142a, 177, 277e, 277f, 329, 396, and 542; HAAS-CAT. 20, no. 244.
41. Mod. eds.: 4 Sons. for 2 flutes alone, GIESBERT-FINGERm; Son. for flute, oboe or violin, and *b. c.*, RUBARDT-FINGERm.

standardized church plan and a fluent but conventional and undistinguished use of the current Italian idiom.

There are three names that would be too obscure merely to list here except for their early position among English composers of the Italian type of sonata, contemporary or almost so with Purcell. No information has been found here about **Matthew Novell,** who published 12 *Sonate da camera* in SSB/bass setting about 1690.[42] Probably in the year 1702, **Ralph** (or Raphael) **Courteville** (?-*ca.* 1735) of the Chapel Royal, the second of three generations of composers by this name, published at least six sonatas for two block flutes alone (initiating this popular setting in England).[43] And **William Williams,** who flourished between 1677 and 1704, published a set of six SS/bass sonatas in 1703, plus a single sonata for flute and bass in 1704.[44]

Somewhat better known are the remaining three Englishmen to be mentioned in the first group. **John Ravenscroft** (? to not later than 1708) was given a doubtful niche in music history when Hawkins accused him of passing off a later edition of nine sonatas from his Op. 1 as Corelli's Op. 7.[45] He has already been mentioned in this connection (p. 157) and as the composer of two sonatas (from the same Op. 1) formerly attributed to Caldara (p. 168). Here is the place to clarify the record a bit and, at the same time, to consider Ravenscroft's sonatas on their own merits, for—as the late Alfred Einstein once remarked to the present author—"they are more like Corelli's than Corelli's own sonatas!"

Ravenscroft's 12 sonatas, Op. 1, in SSB/bass setting, were originally published in Rome in 1695,[46] while he may well have been studying with Corelli.[47] The edition of nine of these sonatas as Corelli's Op. 7 was published about forty years later by Michel Charles Le Cène in Amsterdam,[48] who added, "It is thought that these [sonatas] were composed by

42. Cf. BRITISH PRINTED, II, 202; a copy is also in the Library of Congress.
43. Cf. GROVE, II, 502 (Fuller Maitland) ; also, SMITH-WALSH, items 50, 77, 98, and 155.
44. Cf. GROVE, IX, 308 (Dart) ; also, SMITH-WALSH, items 126 and 153.
45. HAWKINS, IV, 311 and 318. The present discussion is slightly expanded in NEWMAN-RAVENSCROFT.
46. Cf. SARTORI-BIBLIOGRAFIA, 1695c, and STEVENS-BODLEIAN, p. 72; also, HAAS-CAT. 20, no. 544, and SMITH-WALSH, item 277, for the early Roger edition (1696) of Op. 1, correctly attributed to Ravenscroft. Thematic index of MS copy in HAAS-ESTENSISCHEN, p. 155 ff. (where the sonatas are not yet confirmed as Ravenscroft's). Among mod. eds. (all three originally misattributed to Caldara) : Son. 2 in B minor, COLLEGIUMm, no. 44 (Riemann), and EINSTEIN-HISTORYm, no. 29; Son. 3 in G minor, RIEMANN-BEISPIELEm, no. 124.
47. The title of the MS copy in HAAS-ESTENSISCHEN, p. 155, includes "L.D.I.M.S. Inglese allievo d'Arcangelo Corelli."
48. Plate no. 566; cf. PINCHERLE-PIRATERIE, p. 136 ff., and PINCHERLE-CORELLI, p. 180 ff.

Arcangelo Corelli before his other works." Obviously Le Cène was the true culprit, practicing a familiar 18th-century piracy in order to exploit the more famous man's name. Pincherle's assumption that Ravenscroft probably did not even know of the deception could hardly have been more nearly right, for, as it turns out, this Ravenscroft must have died at least 27 years earlier. In Walsh's edition, about 1708, of Ravenscroft's only other known sonata collection—six court sonatas, Op. 2—the title includes "Composed by the late Mr. Ravenscroft"; and another, not later edition of the same set has on the cover, "Vivit post Funera Virtus."[49] Heretofore, the few listings of John Ravenscroft have always taken the death date of "about the year 1745" from Hawkins,[50] but Hawkins was evidently referring to a different John Ravenscroft, hornpipe composer.[51]

Ravenscroft's 12 church sonatas are indeed much like Corelli's, and very skillful, too. All but Sonatas 11 and 12 are in the S-F-S-F plan. Ravenscroft concentrated somewhat more intensively on his ideas than Corelli did, wrote a rather more dense kind of polyphony in the second, fugal movements, and kept the rhythmic flow going a bit more regularly. The writing for violins is idiomatic but less virtuosic. His music already shows signs of a post-Corelli stereotype. As fine as it is, it does not have the melodic or harmonic flashes that mark Corelli's special genius. Ravenscroft's six court sonatas are lighter in both texture and character, and shorter. The first five begin with a slow "Preludia," followed by any two or three of five dances in no set order—"Allemanda," "Corrente," "Giga," "Gavotta," or "Sarabanda." The last sonata, in the manner of the times, is a "Ceccona," though the variations are neither very long nor elaborate.

The English organist **William Croft** (1678-1727), a follower of Blow known especially for his church music, published two sets of sonatas around the turn of the century, along with some harpsichord "Lessons." The first of the two sets consists of three "solo" sonatas for violin and b. c., which follow three "solo" flute sonatas by an unnamed "Italian Mr."[52] First issued by John Young in 1699,[53] these sonatas belong, with Purcell's "solo" violin sonata, among the rare 17th-century examples of this type by Englishmen. Croft's second set consists of *Six Sonatas of two Parts Purposely made and Contrived for*

49. Cf. SMITH-WALSH, items 277 and 282a; the (earlier?) "Roger" edition of Op. 2 to which SMITH-WALSH refers can be found at the Library of Congress (M312.4/R27, Op. 2/Case), but seems actually to have been printed, not merely sold, by Isaac Vaillant.

50. E.g., GROVE, VII, 63 (Husk).

51. Cf. HAWKINS, V, 366 ff., and HAAS-CAT. 20, nos. 544 and 545.

52. Mod. ed.: Violin Son. in G minor, MOFFAT-VIOLINm III, no. 11 (with preface); regarding editorial abuses in this much needed series, cf. GARDNER-MOFFAT.

53. Cf. SMITH-WALSH, item 28.

Two Flutes, also first published by John Young, this time in 1704.[54] Like Courteville's, here were some of the first unaccompanied duets to be produced in England, a type soon to win special favor there. Croft preferred the S-F-S-F and S-F-F movement plans. His writing shows a fine sense of cantilena and a clear sense of harmonic direction, but otherwise seems rather limited in its resources and hence somewhat dull.

The last Englishman to be named in our first group was the violinist **William Corbett** (?-1748).[55] Between 1705 and about 1709 this interesting collector of music and violins published at least four sets of sonatas—6 for 2 flutes and *b. c.* ("The Instrumental Musick for January, February, March") ; 6 for one flute and *b. c.;* 6 "with an Overture and Aires, in 4 Parts, for Violins and Hoboys, with a Trumpet, Flute de Almain, and a thorough Bass for the Bass Violon Passoon or Harpsicord"; and 6 for 2 violins and *b. c.* ("Opera Quarta, Libro Secondo").[56] Evidently light pieces, especially dances, were Corbett's forte. His violin tutors and his successes in comic opera make an exploration of these sonatas desirable.

Four foreigners remain to be mentioned among the first of our two groups active in England. One came from Italy, two from Germany, and one from Belgium. The Italian was **Gasparo Visconti** (1683-?), dilettante from a noble Cremonese family and one of the many violinists reported to have studied with Corelli.[57] Known also as Mr. Gasperini or Gasparini (not to be confused with Francesco Gasparini), Visconti made himself popular as a violinist in London, especially as the performer and editor of other composers' sonatas.[58] He himself published "Solos" (called "Sonate" in the original Roger edition of the same year[59]) for violin and *b. c.,* Op. 1 (Walsh, 1703[60]), "Containing Preludes Allemands Sarabands &c."

One of the two Germans was **Nicholas Francis Haym** (*ca.* 1679-1729), a talented, versatile cellist born of German parents in Rome, where he was "very well acquainted with Corelli."[61] Except for some unethical commercial activities,[62] Haym moved in much the same circles as Visconti. Hawkins says he published two sets of "trio" sonatas, but only one set of 12 can be located,[63] published by E. Roger in Amsterdam

54. Cf. SMITH-WALSH, item 144. Among mod. eds.: entire set, RUBARDT-CROFTm.
55. Cf. GROVE, II, 435 ff. (Husk and Loewenberg).
56. Cf. SMITH-WALSH, items 172, 244, 285, and 324; BRITISH PRINTED, I, 304.
57. Cf. MGG, II, 1778 (Monterosso) ; SCHMIDL, II, 669 ff.; and SMITH-WALSH, p.
58 ("I . . . having been 5 year's Corelli's Scholar.").
58. Cf. SMITH-WALSH, items 143, 181, and 198.
59. Cf. EITNER-QL, X, 106.   60. Cf. SMITH-WALSH, item 125.
61. Cf. SMITH-WALSH, p. 57.
62. Cf. HAWKINS, V, 163 ff.; GROVE, 3d ed., II, 592 (Marshall).
63. EITNER-QL, V, 78.

the same year, 1704, that Haym came to England. Between that same year and 1712 the other German, **Johann Christoph Pepusch** (1667-1752), published at least ten sets of "solo" and "trio" sonatas, with flute or violin as the preferred instruments.[64]   A learned musician, organist, and violist, now remembered chiefly for his share in *The Beggar's Opera,* Pepusch had come to London four years earlier.[65] Presumably he had already composed a considerable number of his sonatas, some of which must never have reached publication.[66]   All but one of his sets of sonatas are of the "solo" type, including one edition of 24 for violin and *b. c.,* published by Walsh about 1708.[67]   A few sonatas of both types have appeared in modern editions.[68]   These reveal a preference for the S-F-S-F plan, a fine sense of line if not great melodic originality (cf. Burney's cruel censure, p. 326 below), and a superior command of both the part writing and the forms.   Again, Corelli must have been an influential model, although the style is somewhat more intensive in its concentration on single ideas.

66a

The Belgian with whom this section closes was **Jean Baptiste Loeillet** (1680-1730), best known for a harpsichord Suite in G Minor that has often been reprinted.   An expert harpsichordist, flutist, and oboist, Loeillet was in London by 1705, probably after spending some time in France.   He soon won substantial success for his playing and teaching.[69] His sonata publications numbered at least eight, most of them followed by reprints.   Both E. Roger and Walsh published his four sets of 12 sonatas each for flute and *b. c.,* as Opp. 1-4 (*ca.* 1712, 1715, 1718, and 1720).[70]   Op. 5 was assigned by E. Roger to a set of 6 more "solo" sonatas for flute (or oboe) with *b. c.,* plus 6 "trio" sonatas for flutes or oboes with *b. c.* (*ca.* 1717).   At least the second half of this last set was also published by Walsh as another Op. 2, about 1726.[71]   Finally, Walsh issued three further sets, two of "trio" and one of "solo" sonatas,

68a

64. Cf. SMITH-WALSH, items 144, 150a, 157, 232, 257, 264a, 335, 350, and 423; BRITISH PRINTED, II, 253 ff., and 2d Supp., p. 55.   One of the "trio" sonatas is also in ANTH. HARMONIAm, I, and 3 sets of sons. are listed in CAT. SCHWERIN, II, 112, with dedications on pp. 388-89.

65. General information in HUGHES-PEPUSCH, including a brief discussion of the sonatas (p. 68 ff.) with examples.

66. Cf. EITNER-QL, VII, 359 ff.   A doctoral dissertation by Mr. Herbert Fred on Pepusch's instrumental music—including MSS in Brussels, Rostock, and Uppsala—was in progress at the time of this writing, at the University of North Carolina.

67. SMITH-WALSH, item 264a.

68. Among them, 6 Sons. for block flute and *b. c.,* GIESBERT-PEPUSCHm; Son. in C for flute, violin, and *b. c.* (from a Rostock MS), HAUSSWALD-PEPUSCHm.   Cf. also, ALTMANN, pp. 186 and 241.

69. BERGMANS-LOEILLETS is the chief biographic source, including clarification of the confusions in name and origin that have been inherited from HAWKINS, V, 173; see also, GROVE, V, 359 ff. (Rendall).

70. Cf. SMITH-WALSH, items 429, 476, and 556; HAAS-CAT. 20, nos. 411-414.

71. Cf. HAAS-CAT. 20, no. 417; SMITH-WALSH, item 612; and BRITISH PRINTED, II, 58 (the two Loeillets being one and the same, of course).

as Opp. 1-3 (*ca.* 1722, 1725, and 1729).[72] Their distinction was a wider choice of instruments, including both the block and transverse types of flute, oboes, and/or violins above cello and harpsichord. Loeillet is credited with being among the first to introduce the transverse flute in England, where the block flute (recorder) had been so popular.

Loeillet is unusually well represented in modern editions for a composer who has been but little known.[73] In these examples may be heard a kind of average of the Baroque sonata in its "classic" phase, before an increased virtuosity, intimacy, and solo projection began to change its complexion. The sonatas are all centered around the standard church plan, sometimes with an actual dance finale or an added dance. Like the harpsichord Suite in G Minor, the music is attractive and thoroughly intelligible in its phrase syntax and tonal directions. But nowhere does it rise above the melodic and harmonic formulas that were becoming so commonplace. The originality and the force of a Handel, Bach, Corelli, or Vivaldi are hardly to be found here.

72. Cf. BRITISH PRINTED, II, 58.
73. Among mod. eds. (cf. ALTMANN) : 6 SS/bass sons. from the last Op. 2 mentioned in the preceding paragraph, RIKKO-LOEILLETm; 3 flute sons. from the first Op. 1, HORTUSm, no. 43 (Hinnenthal).

Chapter 14

England from about 1710 to 1760

In Handel's Circle (Babell, Ariosti)

The last few composers of our first group active in England were already coming into contact with the young Handel (in London permanently from 1712). Although it has seemed more appropriate here to relate Handel as a sonata composer to his earlier, Hamburg years, his fast-growing sphere of influence in England becomes more and more evident alongside Corelli's as we advance among the composers of our second group. The chief names in this group are those of Geminiani, Arne, and Boyce.

The obscure flutist **Robert Valentine** (or Roberto Valentino) published at least 13 sets of instrumental music between 1708 (or earlier) and 1735, of which 12 can be identified and 10 consist of sonatas.[1] In all the Walsh editions he is described as being "at Rome," while in the Rome and Amsterdam publications the word "Inglese" appears after the Italian form of his name. It seems likely that he was born in England and composed at least some of the sonatas before he left for Rome. Only one of the collections is in SS/bass scoring, the majority being for flute solo and *b. c.*, except for two collections for two flutes without bass. Several "solo" sonatas have been made available,[2] nearly all in the standard S-F-S-F plan. Their appeal is easy to understand, for the lines are songful, the passages fluent and facile, and the phrases clearly defined and balanced. However, no marked individuality of style is to be heard in them.

James (or Giacomo) **Sherard** (still living *ca.* 1735) was an English

---

1. Cf. SMITH-WALSH, items 419, 443, 458, 468, 554, 572, and 575; HAAS-CAT. 20, nos. 657-661; BRITISH PRINTED, II, 614 ff. and 2d Supp., p. 79; EITNER-QL, X, 25 ff. (including some MS sonatas in Rostock and Wolfenbüttel).

2. Among mod. eds.: Viola (actually flute?) Son. in A minor, MOFFAT-VIOLINm II, no. 17; 6 flute sons., NAGELSm, nos. 121 and 149 (Rodemann); 2 flute sons., GIESBERT-VALENTINOm (with preface).

apothecary and excellent amateur violinist, "very intimate with Handel and other Masters."[3] Two sets of "trio" sonatas by him, Opp. 1 and 2, were published by E. Roger about 1715 (not 1680) and 1725. These are described as having distinct merit by E. D. J. van der Straeten,[4] but are not otherwise known. Another Englishman who is only a little better   4a known was the short-lived harpsichordist, organist, and violinist **William Babell** (*ca.* 1690-1723).[5] Babell was the pupil of his father and of Pepusch. Besides some early examples of favorite opera arias in harpsichord arrangements (including some from Handel's *Rinaldo*), Babell left two sets of 12 sonatas each for violin, flute, or oboe. These were published shortly after his death as "Part the First . . ." and "Part the Second of his Posthumous Works."[6] The high praises with which the original editions are prefaced seem not unjustified. Here is music that does rise somewhat above the average and stand out from the stereotyped "classic" sonata of the Baroque Era. The movement plan departs frequently from the S-F-S-F order. It includes some dances, an "Air," and a "Round O" that are English in character by virtue of their well-defined, strongly thetic metric patterns. The adagios, interesting as well for the fact that they are notated "with proper Graces adapted to each," are broadly conceived and harmonically compelling. The quick movements have much rhythmic vigor (Ex. 66). Curiously, except for one sonata in G, all the sonatas in both books are in five keys of two to four flats (not including A flat). This is music that deserves further study and some modern reprints.

John Humphries was born about 1707, according to his own statement in the first (1726) edition of his six sonatas for violin and *b. c.* In the typically apologetic preface of the novitiate he begins, "These Compositions are the first fruits of a young Gentleman now not above **19.** . . ."[7] He was a "good performer on the violin," but died when he was only about 23, or in "about 1730," added Hawkins.[8] Hawkins also attributed to this Humphries a set of 12 SS/bass sonatas, the publication of which he placed in 1728. But since this latter set is marked "Opera prima" and is published in the name of "J. S. Humphries,"[9]

3. Cf. SHEDLOCK-SONATA, p. 223.
4. GROVE, 3d ed., IV, 742 (but with no details to help locate Straeten's report in *The Strad*).
5. Cf. GROVE, I, 281 (Rimbault); HAWKINS, V, 180.
6. Listed in HAAS-CAT. 20, item 32. Mod. ed.: Son. in B flat (pieced together from 5 separate movements in both sets, without acknowledgment), MOFFAT-VIOLINm III, no. 3.
7. Quoted in full in the preface to MOFFAT-VIOLINm III, no. 13, which is a mod. ed. of a son. in D minor presumably from this set.
8. V, 365 ff.; cf. SHEDLOCK-SONATA, p. 224 ff.
9. Cf. BRITISH PRINTED, I, 679, and HAAS-CAT. 20, no. 359.

Ex. 66. From the second movement of Sonata 1 in B flat,
Part II, by William Babell (after the original Walsh edition).

Moffat has preferred more recently to regard it as the product of a
different Humphries.[10]   Although original MSS or other evidences
sufficient to argue either way are lacking, one is tempted to go back to
Hawkins' original assumption.   The opus numbering means little, for,
as we have seen, it often varied with the publisher.   There is even an
earlier set of six SS/bass sonatas by "J. S." Humphries, also marked
"Opera prima," to confuse the issue.[11]   But in any case, the S/bass
sonatas carry no opus numbering, so that the 12 SS/bass sonatas could
be the "Opera prima" that preceded "John" Humphries' two successful
sets of concertos, Opp. 2 and 3.   There are also to be considered the
similarly flowery prefaces in the "solo" and "trio" sets,[12] the similar
order of church followed by dance movements, and Hawkins' statement
that the concertos were "precisely in the same cast with his sonatas"
(with special reference, apparently, to the SS/bass set).   Hawkins, by
the way, was mainly concerned that the SS/bass sonatas, being

of a very original cast . . . are in a style somewhat above that of the common popular airs and country-dance tunes, the delight of the vulgar, and
greatly beneath what might be expected from the studies of a person at all
acquainted with the graces and elegancies of the Italians in their compositions
for instruments.   To this it must be attributed that the sonatas of Humphries
were the common practice of such small proficients in harmony, as in his
time were used to recreate themselves with music at alehouse clubs and places
of vulgar resort in the village adjacent to London: Of these there were

10. Preface in MOFFAT-VIOLINm III, no. 13.
11. HAAS-CAT. 20, no. 358.
12. Reference is made here to the Cobb rather than the Walsh edition (HAAS-
CAT. 20, no. 359) of the 12 SS/bass sonatas.

formerly many, in which six-pence at most was the price of admission [with further details in a footnote].[13]

At this point several Italians active in London may be noted. One was **Pietro Giuseppe Sandoni** (*ca.* 1680-*ca.* 1750), an excellent harpsichordist from Bologna, remembered in London chiefly as the eccentric husband of Handel's homely but vocally sensational prima donna Francesca Cuzzoni.[14] Three keyboard sonatas by Sandoni were issued in London (publisher unknown) between 1726 and 1728 at the end of his six *Cantate da camera,* while the first of these plus eight more sonata movements exist in a MS for organ or cembalo in Bologna.[15]   15a
There is also a trio sonata by this Sandoni in ANTH. CORONAm. The three printed keyboard sonatas are in two or three movements, including dances and freer types. Their chief distinction is that of being the earliest keyboard sonatas known that were published in England and among the earliest by a composer resident in England, allowing for some of the undated keyboard sonatas of Handel that were noted (p. 293). In texture as well as character Sandoni's music is thin and fluent, without special distinction.

At about the same time (1728?) the dramatic composer and violist **Attilio Ariosti** (1666-?) published six "Lessons" for viola d'amore and *b. c.,* also in conjunction with some cantatas.[16] Like Sandoni, Ariosti   16a
came from Bologna and found himself in the thick of the Handel-Bononcini rivalry in London, where he lived from 1716 to 1717 and from 1722 to about 1728.[17] However, the similarity goes no further. Besides being for a less usual instrument, Ariosti's pieces (generally called "sonatas" except by the composer himself) are harmonically richer, structurally more extended, and melodically more distinguished.[18] The phrases, often completed by sequences, proceed with great dignity and a fine sense of balance. Most of the "Lessons" have four movements in the S-F-S-F sequence, with tempo and/or dance titles (both Italian and French). Special interest has centered in Ariosti's unique system of "accordatura" rather than *scordatura.* By this system the violinist reads in his accustomed manner as if on his normally tuned violin. But the notation that he reads has no conventional pitch significance, for it

13. HAWKINS, V, 365 ff.
14. Cf. FLOWER-HANDEL, p. 161 ff.
15. Cf. PRATELLA; SHEDLOCK-SONATA, p. 23 ff. Mod. ed.: the 3 published sons. and 5 of the MS movements, CLASSICIm I, no. 29 (Pratella).
16. Among mod. eds.: all six "Lessons," MARCHETm (transcribed for violin and piano); SCHOTT CELLOm, nos. 7-12 (Piatti; for cello and piano); SAINT/GEORGEm (violin and piano).
17. Cf. BURNEY-HISTORY, II, 724 ff.; HAWKINS, V, 277 ff. and 290 ff.; but cf. also, GROVE, I, 130 and 200 ff. (both Loewenberg).
18. BOYDEN-ARIOSTI is a rounded study of the Lessons.

leads him instead to the desired positions and fingering on the four strings of the viola d'amore to which Ariosti restricts his writing. Transcribed into normal notation and played on the violin the pieces suffer a loss in their original color and technical brilliance.[19]

Pietro Castrucci (1679-1752), the elder and better known of the two Castrucci brothers, came to London in 1715 from Rome, where he had developed into an outstanding violinist under Corelli's instruction. Among other assignments he played in opera orchestras directed by Handel. At least two sets of 12 "solo" violin sonatas each by this Castrucci can be confirmed, both published originally by Walsh (ca. 1725 and 1734).[20]   Probably, too, he was the Castrucci who composed the first six in a set of 12 "Solos" for flute and b. c. (1720 or earlier?), of which the other six are by Geminiani.[21]   One "solo" violin sonata by Pietro Castrucci has been made available, in two scarce Italian reprints,[22] but is obviously too much altered to permit any evaluation of this composer's sonatas, "which, though hardly known," says Hawkins, "have great merit."[23]   At the same time, Hawkins found less merit in the six S/bass sonatas published by the younger brother, **Prospero Castrucci** (?-1760), in London in 1739.[24]

Geminiani and Others (Festing)

Our mention of **Francesco Geminiani** (1687-1762[25]) brings us to the most important of the Italians in London and one of the chief names in 18th-century violin playing. Along with Castrucci and another excellent violinist, Giovanni Stefano Carbonelli (who published 12 S/bass court sonatas in London about 1722[26]), Geminiani was one of the three main students of Corelli active in Great Britain. Born in Lucca, he had started violin with C. A. Lonati in Milan (who had himself been in England earlier[27]) and reportedly went to A. Scarlatti for counterpoint training. But it was Corelli to whom he was chiefly indebted.[28]   Among obvious

27a

19. Cf. BOYDEN-ARIOSTI, pp. 545 ff. and 552 ff.
20. Cf. SCHMIDL, Supp., p. 174; BRITISH PRINTED, I, 236 ff.
21. Cf. SMITH-WALSH, item 611, and HAAS-CAT. 20, no. 136.
22. Cf. ALTMANN, p. 235. Another mod. ed.: Op. 1 in g (Rome: De Santis, 1952).
23. V, 361.
24. Mod. ed.: Son. in D, MOFFAT-VIOLINm II, no. 35.
25. In MGG, IV, 1690, Giegling still prefers (without source) the birth year 1679 or 1680, although noting the baptism date of Dec. 5, 1687 (reported by A. Betti in 1934; cf. BOYDEN-GEMINIANI, p. vii). There does still seem to be some justification for seeking an earlier birth year in view of contemporary reports of Geminiani's great age when he died—for example, Mrs. Delaney's statement that he was 86 in 1760 (FLOOD-GEMINIANI, p. 111). The middle name of Saverio in the MGG article may not be that of this Geminiani.
26. Mod. ed. of 3 sons. listed in ALTMANN, p. 235.
27. Cf. HAWKINS, V, 131.
28. Contrary to MOSER-VIOLINSPIEL, p. 139.

evidences are his well-known transcriptions from Corelli's Opp. 1, 3, and 5 as concerti grossi;[29] his close imitation of Corelli's Op. 5 in his own Op. 1 (including, in Sonata 1, one more of the many sonatas that begin as Corelli's Sonata 1 does); his own, early performances of Corelli's music;[30] and the fact that aside from his valuable pioneer essays on violin performance practices, his tutors, and his keyboard arrangements, he limited his output almost as exclusively as Corelli did to sonatas and concertos. When Geminiani arrived in London in 1714 he and F. M. Veracini, who began a three-year visit there in the same year, brought a new stimulus to violin playing in England. No other than Handel was among the first to accompany Geminiani in London.[31]

Geminiani's original sonatas that are known total at least 45, nearly all for strings and all originally cast in S/- or SS/bass settings except for one unaccompanied solo sonata.[32] Op. 1, first published in 1716,[33] soon after he came to London, contains 12 S/bass sonatas (not SB/bass in spite of "Violino, violone, e cembalo" in the original title).[34] Besides several reprints, which suggest that this inaugural set was an immediate and substantial success, there was a revision of Op. 1 (London, 1739) to which Geminiani carefully added ornaments, bowings, and other signs such, presumably, as he would have wanted added or improvised in actual performance.[35] Whether he was changing to the more explicit notation practices of contemporary French composers is not certain, but a comparison of the two editions permits an exceptional firsthand study of 18th-century performance practices. There are also new refinements in the harmony, and in a 1740 re-edition of this revision two movements are added to Sonata 10.[36] Of further bearing on performance practices and on the popularity of this set are Geminiani's arrangements of Sonatas 1 to 6 and 7 to 12 in Op. 1 as two sets of SS/bass sonatas, first published in London about 1740 and 1750.[37]

29. Cf. HAWKINS, V, 242.

30. Cf. BURNEY-HISTORY, II, 990; HAWKINS, V, 393 ff. (including the printing of Corelli's entire Son. 9, Op. 5, with the exquisite ornamentation added by Geminiani); and GROVE, III, 591 (David).

31. Cf. BURNEY-HISTORY, II, 990 ff.; HAWKINS, V, 239.

32. On the subject of Geminiani MCARTOR is an exceptionally helpful and thorough Ph.D. dissertation, including the man, his music, his writings, a full thematic index (p. 313 ff.) and full critical bibliography (p. 325 ff.).

33. The listing in MGG, IV, 1692, of a set (earlier?) of *Sonate a Violino solo* ("senza Basso"!), Op. 1, as published in Bologna in 1705 may well be an error derived by way of MOSER-VIOLINSPIEL, p. 139, from EITNER-QL, X, 383; no confirmation of the set has been found here in either old or recent sources.

34. Mod. ed., entire (but without the ornaments added in the revision of 1739): FINNEY-GEMINIANIm.

35. The two editions are compared in MCARTOR, chap. 4, including plates 9 and 10.

36. MCARTOR, p. 311.

37. Cf. BRITISH PRINTED, I, 506; MCARTOR, p. 327 ff.

Perhaps he had been prompted to make these arrangements by similar ones from the same set that had already been published by another composer. Around 1735 Walsh issued Sonatas 7 to 12 (not 1 to 6) as arranged by Geminiani's fellow townsman and associate in London, Francesco Barsanti (ca. 1690-?), himself the composer of concertos and of at least two sets each of six S/- and six SS/bass sonatas (published, ca. 1735-65, but not explored in modern times).[38] In his own arrangements Geminiani variously used both the original and the revised editions of Op. 1. He arranged "up," so to speak—that is, from a smaller to a larger group—by any means from merely dividing the soloist's multiple stops between the two violinists to inserting new lines, altering the forms, or even substituting or adding new movements (Ex. 67).

In the same year that his revision of Op. 1 appeared, or possibly as early as 1735, 12 more S/bass sonatas by Geminiani were published, as Op. 4.[39] This set exists in at least five editions or altered reprints (one with an added movement in Sonata 10[40]). It, too, underwent further arrangements by Geminiani to the extent of six concerti grossi made out of sonatas 1, 11, 2, 5, 7, and 9, respectively.[41] The changes are minimal, considering the difference of settings, but again of much bearing on problems of performance practices, including ornamentation and figured bass.

Six sonatas for cello and b. c. make up Geminiani's Op. 5. Originally published by Le Clerc in Paris in 1746, this set also appeared in two editions arranged for violin and b. c., one done the same year in The Hague and the other the next year in London.[42] All three editions contain detailed ornamentation and articulation. Other sonatas by Geminiani include the last six for flute and b. c. in the joint collection of about 1720 with (Pietro?) Castrucci, mentioned earlier, and another sonata for violin and b. c., in ANTH. HANDELm (no. 5). There is also a three-movement Sonata a violino solo senza basso in B flat by Geminiani, left without date in Dresden among other of his MSS. It is the only complete sonata of this sort by an Italian up to Geminiani's

---

38. Cf. EITNER-QL, I, 349 ff.; BRITISH PRINTED, I, 124; SCHMIDL, I, 119; HAWKINS, V, 371 ff.

39. Cf. MCARTOR, p. 333 ff. In BRITISH PRINTED, I, 506, an edition from Witvogel in Amsterdam is dated "1735?". Among mod. eds., separate sons. only (cf. ALTMANN): Sons. 8, 10, and 11, JENSEN-VIOLINm, nos. 7411, 7401, and 7402, respectively.

40. MCARTOR, p. 311.

41. Ibid., p. 335.

42. Cf. GROVE, III, 592; MCARTOR, p. 336 ff. For only one mod. ed., of Son. in C minor, see ALTMANN, p. 268.

Ex. 67. From the second movement of Sonata 10, Op. 1, by Francesco Geminiani, as found in the original "solo" edition of 1716 (after FINNEY-GEMINIANIm, p. 84, but without editorial additions; by kind permission of Smith College Music Archives) and in his "trio" transcription of about 1740 (after "Sonata IV" [i.e., 10] in the Walsh edition).

time that is now known.[43]   Furthermore, there are three so-called sonatas in Geminiani's essay published in 1749, *Treatise of Good Taste in the Art of Musick* (usually referred to as "Taste II").[44]   These are three "Airs made into SONATAS for two Violins and a Bass," in which a familiar tune and/or its variation makes up each of the two to four movements except for two called "Interlude."   Mention should be made,

43. Not mentioned in MCARTOR, but cf. GATES-SOLO, pp. 85 ff. and 276 ff. (with photograph of the Studeny edition published by Wunderhornverlag in 1911, including preface).   Among at least 3 mod. eds.: BETTI-GEMINIANIm.
44. Cf. MCARTOR, pp. 341 ff. and 246 ff.

too, of Geminiani's two collections of harpsichord pieces (1743 and 1762), which recombine many of his string sonata movements into other sonatas, usually involving no other transcription than that of assigning the "solo" to the right hand and the *b. c.* to the left.[45] Finally, the little known MSS in Dresden may reveal still other sonatas by Geminiani, perhaps including four transcribed for clarinet and piano by A. Perier.[46]

45a

Although Geminiani ranks with such late Baroque masters as Tartini, Veracini, and Locatelli in his knowledge and use of the violin, his sonatas seem somewhat more conservative and less inspired than those of his important contemporaries. The contrapuntal writing, multiple stops, wide shifts, embellishments, and passagework (especially Op. 4) offered a very real challenge to the violinist of his day, especially when Op. 1 appeared, and to the cellist (Ex. 68). But these problems are far less than in the sonatas of Tartini, Veracini, and Locatelli. And the musical innovations are fewer, although tendencies toward slower harmonic rhythm, more sectionalized designs, and simpler, more homophonic texture are evident in a comparison of Opp. 1 and 4.[47] Out of the 30 sonatas in the original versions of Opp. 1, 4, and 5, only five are not in the S-F-S-F plan, and only two of these last employ the newer S-F-F plan, preferred by Tartini, Quantz, and others. Although dance elements are naturally present, no dance titles occur in any of these sonatas, not even in the latter six of Opp. 1 and 4, which are apparently intended to be lighter in character, in the court sonata style, and lack the fugal treatment to be found especially in the first fast movements of the first six sonatas of Op. 1. Nor is there any title more intimate, in the newer manner, than the common one of "Affettuoso." The harmony, resourceful and occasionally even eccentric in its rapid modulations, seems to have been the chief factor that evoked some disapproval from both Burney and Hawkins.[48] Today it seems to be one of the chief strengths. Melodies that are undistinguished although well laid out, insufficient dissonance interest, and a tendency to let the passages straggle to the point where the forms become too loose-jointed may be among the reasons violinists show little interest in playing Geminiani's sonatas today, or why these sonatas have enjoyed relatively few reprints in modern editions. Above all, this musician influenced styles of violin playing, both through such writings as his celebrated *Art of Playing on*

45. Detailed clarification in MCARTOR, p. 349 ff.
46. Cf. MCARTOR, p. 324.
47. Cf. MCARTOR, chap. 5.
48. BURNEY-HISTORY, II, 993; HAWKINS, V, 389 ff. (with an interesting explanation for harmonic differences between Geminiani's and Corelli's music).

Ex. 68. From the opening of Francesco Geminiani's Sonata 4, Op. 5, for cello and *b. c.* as he transcribed it for violin and *b. c.* (after the London edition of 1747).

the Violin (1751) and through such notable pupils as Dubourg, Festing, and Avison.

Before we return to several native Englishmen of a little later period than the last group, mention may be made of another foreigner, this one a German of French descent. **John Ernest Galliard** (*ca.* 1680[49]-1749) was an oboist and flutist who came from Celle to London about 1706 after some study under Steffani and the violinist G. B. Farinelli.[50] Besides some playing in Handel's opera orchestra,[51] a few dramatic ventures of his own, a few cantatas and songs, the English translation (1742) of Tosi's *Opinioni,* and other musical activities, he left at least six sonatas for flute and *b. c.* (London, 1711),[52] six sonatas for bassoon or cello and *b. c.* (London, 1732; presumably the same as the six cello sonatas in the set of 12 published jointly with Andrea Caporale in 1746),[53] and—in a MS collection now in Manchester—up to 24 other sonatas for flute and *b. c.*[54] plus another sonata for oboe and two bassoons (1704).[55]   52a

Galliard's bassoon sonatas are among the infrequent examples we have met in the Baroque Era and the first that are known to have been

49. Cf. MGG, IV, 1283 (Westrup).
50. Cf. HAWKINS, V, 187 ff.; BURNEY-HISTORY, II, 989 ff.
51. GROVE, III, 553 (Husk).
52. Cf. HAAS-CAT. 20, no. 259; SMITH-WALSH, item 610. Mod. ed., entire: GIESBERT-SCHICKHARDTm II (misattributed to Schickhardt; cf. MGG, IV, 1285).
53. Cf. HAWKINS, V, 189; CAT. WALSH, item 226; HAAS-CAT. 20, no. 262. Mod. ed., entire: MARX & WEISS/MANNm.
54. GROVE, III, 553.
55. HAWKINS, V, 187.

composed in England. He cast his sonatas in four or five movements, not always centering around the S-F-S-F plan. Dances are included, among them a "Hornpipe a l'Inglese" in the first bassoon sonata. These are tuneful, the lines are otherwise songful and well contrived, and the forms are nicely proportioned. But the style is generally made more serious and weighty by imitations between the bass and solo, active harmony, and breadth of phrase structure. Even so, the music seems light and attractive enough to disqualify Burney's frequently quoted comment,[56] made with his typical opposition to recent art that was not innovative, "I must say, that I never saw more correctness nor less originality in any author that I have examined, of the present century, Dr. Pepusch always excepted." One might recall that Burney was himself the composer of six correct but academic "trio" sonatas (Op. 1, London, *ca.* 1747) before he turned to somewhat freer and more modern (pre-Classic) styles.

Richard Jones, a supposedly fine native violinist, traceable only around the 1730's in London, published two sets of pieces for violin and *b. c.,* Opp. 2 and 3, during that time.[57] These pieces relate to our subject, but our concern here with the actual use of the word "sonata" must not be forgotten. As with Ariosti's "Lessons" the composer did not employ this word but rather one of its several equivalents that were also in current use. In Op. 3 the term is "Suites of Lessons," while in Op. 2 it is "Chamber Airs." From the latter, Moffat edited two cycles that he chose to call by the title "Sonata,"[58] which certainly is the title modern editors have preferred for such "exhumations," regardless of what the original preference may have been. The quaint, full title of Op. 2 provides clues to the music: *Chamber Airs for a Violin (and Through Bass) Consisting Both of Double, and, Single Stops. The Preludes being Written (chiefly) in the Grace manner &c. Being a Work very Improveing for that Instrument . . . Opera (or work) the Second, etc.* As that title suggests, this is music of considerable technical advancement. It is also music of considerable vigor. The two "sonatas" made available show only a virtuoso rather than a songful side to Jones.

A pupil of Jones, then of Geminiani, was the capable violinist, opera director, and charter member of the important Royal Society of Musicians, **Michael Christian Festing** (?-1752), who is supposed to have been a native of English or perhaps of Austrian descent.[59]   In his

56. -HISTORY, II, 990.
57. Cf. GROVE, IV, 659 (Kidson); MOFFAT-VIOLINm III, no. 7, preface; HUMPHRIES & SMITH, p. 297.
58. -VIOLINm II, no. 12 (in A minor); -VIOLINm III, no. 7 (in D).
59. Cf. MGG, IV, 128 (Cudworth).

melo/bass string music, he made the distinction, prevalent in England around the mid century, between the term "solo" for the S/bass and "sonata" for the "trio" setting. Four sets of "solos" by him are known— Opp. 1 (1730), 4 (1736), 7 (*ca.* 1747), and 8 (*ca.* 1750). Two sets of "sonatas in three parts" are known—Opp. 2 (1731) and 6 (1742). Hawkins' high praise for Festing's "solo" writing, more than for his playing,[60] ought to encourage further modern editions of his music than the two "sonatas," one each from Opp. 4 and 7, that have been made available (in publications almost as scarce as the originals).[61] An examination of Opp. 4 and 6 by Festing does reveal a distinctive talent, with results similar in many ways to Geminiani's, but with frequent individualities of his own. The number and order of movements is variable, tending more toward five than three. Occasionally the final movement is an out-and-out dance. Technical difficulties—especially in the "solos," of course—are on a par with Geminiani's, both in kind and degree. The full and precise details of articulation and ornamentation also show the latter's influence. In fact, the rhythmic details, expressive leaps, and other niceties of the lines themselves, now begin to suggest the *galant* style. In addition, a growing taste for ternary designs is to be noted, such as was also evident at this time in Italy. However, Baroque traits still predominate, including persistent imitations, rich harmony, and the fast harmonic rhythm that is dictated by an active *b. c.*   61a
Such traits can be found even in the dance movements (Ex. 69).

The blind English composer, organist, and violinist **John Stanley** (1713-86) similarly preferred the term "solo" to "sonata." He left *Eight Solos for a German Flute, Violin, or Harpsicord* [alone?], Op. 1 (London, 1740[62]), and four more, Op. 4 (London, 1745), that he had reduced from his *Six Concertos in Seven Parts,* Op. 2. The available reprints show S-F-S-F cycles and competent writing of a somewhat routine character, with no exceptional technical requirements. As implied by G. Finzi, the shadow of Handel is not more marked here than in other English music of the time.[63]

Arne, Boyce, and Others (Gluck)

Thomas Augustine Arne (1710-78) ranks with Boyce among the chief English composers of the 18th century. A violinist trained by

60. HAWKINS, V, 364.
61. Cf. ALTMANN, p. 236.
62. Dates from p. 69 of FINZI, the chief general discussion of Stanley. Among mod. eds.: Son. 2 in G minor, MOFFAT-VIOLINm III, no. 4; Son. in A minor, MOFFAT-VIOLINm I, no. 29; cf. ALTMANN, pp. 242 and 277.
63. Cf. FINZI, pp. 63, 65, 66 ff., and 71.

Ex. 69. Two excerpts from the finale of Sonata 7 in F, Op. 4, by Michael Christian Festing (after the original William Smith edition of 1736).

Festing, a flutist, and a harpsichordist, he made his main reputation, of course, as a dramatic composer.[64]   Though they do have special interest, his two sets of sonatas were but a small part of his total output, which also included keyboard concertos and orchestral overtures among instrumental works.   No detailed study of the sonatas has been found here.   One set was that of *VIII Sonatas or Lessons for the Harpsichord,* published by Walsh in 1756.[65]   These first known keyboard sonatas by an English composer came about the same time as the first real flowering of the sonata on the Continent—as, for example, the publications of Bach's two oldest sons, of Galuppi, of Platti (senior or junior), of Barrière, of Martini, of Domenico Scarlatti, and of Pescetti.   Arne's use of "sonata" and "lesson" in the title as synonyms merely bears out an English equivalence that we have already noted (but scarcely war-

64. Two general surveys are CUMMINGS-ARNE and LANGLEY-ARNE.
65. Briefly described in GROVE, VII, 897 (Parry) ; SHEDLOCK-SONATA, p. 226 ff.; LANGLEY-ARNE, p. 102.   Among mod. eds.: entire set, PAUER-ARNEM.   A Sonata in B flat "for Violin or Cello and Piano," originally published in 1931 by Oxford University Press and republished by this firm as a clarinet sonata, is actually Harold Craxton's arrangement of Sonata 5 in this set.

rants Shedlock's curiously contemptuous remark, "With this double title it is, of course, impossible to regard them as serious sonatas").[66]

Arne's other set was that of *VII Sonatas for two Violins with a Thorough Bass for the Harpsichord or Violoncello,* Op. 3, originally published by Walsh in 1757, or about one year after the harpsichord set.[67] That neither set achieved a reprint or second edition must be taken as a sign of relatively little public success. Burney, whose high regard for the contemporary sonatas by Boyce is shortly to be noted, does not even mention either set by Arne in his several references to the latter.[68] Perhaps some of those very techniques that help to explain the quick success of such a song as his "Rule, Britannia" from *The Masque of Alfred* (also 1740) are the same whose consistent application in chamber music was more likely to detract than attract. The "trio" sonatas are not without melodic originality or charm but seem to go around in little circles that prevent broader views of the forms. Both the harmony and the tonality (key schemes) are somewhat sterile and fail to provide strong direction at either the local or over-all levels of these forms, which are not seldom ternary in plan. Even in the slow movements the ideas are short-breathed, almost invariably being repeated at once at the same or a different pitch level. The instrumental writing is of a modest sort. Such techniques lend themselves better to polyphonic forms, but polyphony was not Arne's chief forte. His chief forte was the charming melody, refined—as, indeed, in these sonatas—by slurs, ornaments, and careful dynamic gradations. In the matter of movements, by the way, his preference was for three to five in the general S-F-S-F order, and with a tendency (as with Festing) toward five, including an occasional out-and-out dance. Similar incipits relate some movements in several of the sonatas.

Arne's keyboard sonatas are at once freer and more convincing as instrumental music. They vary from one to four movements in no set

67a

66. SHEDLOCK-SONATA, p. 227.

67. Briefly described in LANGLEY-ARNE, p. 103. The date is suggested in the preface to MOFFAT-VIOLINm III, no. 6, and in MGG, I, 658 (Westrup). Perhaps the research that continues on Walsh publications of the 18th century has already turned up a more exact date for this set. At any rate, if the spelling of "Catharine" rather than "Catherine" Street on the title page is actually a clue (cf. DEUTSCH-NUMBERS, p. 25; but it is apparently not a clue recognized in either SMITH-WALSH or HUMPHRIES & SMITH), then the set must have been published before 1745 and not *ca.* 1750 as in BRITISH PRINTED, I, 72, and HAAS-CAT. 20, no. 23. Mod. eds.: Son. 1 in A, COLLEGIUMm, no. 57 (Seiffert); Sons. 2 in G and 3 in E flat, MURRILL-ARNEm; Son. 7 in E minor, MOFFAT-VIOLINm III, no. 6 (with the last movement omitted and many other unacknowledged licenses). Too recently for further use here, the new *British Union-Catalogue of Early Music* contradicts the foregoing information with dates of 1756 for the keyboard sons. and 1757 for the "trio" sons.

68. Mentions in -HISTORY are conspicuously absent on such pages as 1002, 1003, 1008, and 1015 ff. (Neither man is given a separate discussion in HAWKINS.)

plan, with two being the average. The one-movement sonata is the last, a set of four variations on a "plain Minuet . . . not Mr. Arne's."[69] Of all eight sonatas the fourth, with four movements, of which all but the second are in D minor, is the most sustained and expressive. An opening "Andante," of exceptional harmonic interest for Arne, is followed by a tender "Siciliano, Largo" in F, then an effective if contrapuntally limited "Fuga, Allegro," and finally a robust, gigue-like "Allegro," Arne being a real master of the "jigg." Except in the freest, preludial or interludial movements, ternary design becomes almost the rule rather than the exception in this set. That fact and the songful, *galant* keyboard writing (by which Arne was reportedly reacting against Handel's weightier keyboard style[70]) place at least this set on the border between the Baroque and Classic Eras in the present survey. Yet Arne probably would still have to remain on the Baroque side where a choice must be made and where Alberti, G. B. Platti, D. Scarlatti, all of Bach's sons, or even the Englishman James Nares (who began publishing his remarkable "Setts of Lessons" only about four years later) have been assigned to the next division for the same or similar reasons. Even so, Arne certainly knew Scarlatti's earlier music[71] and shows its influence, at least on a modest scale and in his faster keyboard movements—in the triplets, leaps, short trills, hand crossing, reiteration of short figures, and clean two-part texture (Ex. 70).

William Boyce (*ca.* 1710-79), organist and composer of church, dramatic, and instrumental music, evidently won much more success in his own day with his sonatas than Arne did, yet has drawn but little 72a   more attention from modern scholars.[72] Scarcely ten years after Boyce had died Burney wrote,

His next publication was *Twelve Sonatas or Trios for Two Violins and a Base,* which were longer and more generally purchased, and performed, and admired, than any productions of the kind in this kingdom except those of Corelli. They were not only in constant use, as chamber Music, in private concerts, for which they were originally designed, but in our theatres, as act-tunes, and public gardens, as favourite pieces, during many years.[73]

But today the almost total neglect of such a capable composer can only be

69. Attributed to Rameau in LANGLEY-ARNE, p. 102, without further identification.
70. Cf. PILKINGTON, p. 91.
71. Scarlatti's *Essercizi* are now known to have been published in London around the start of 1739 (cf. KIRKPATRICK-SCARLATTI, pp. 101 ff. and 402). Moreover, Arne was one of the "several Subscribers" (including Avison, Boyce, Pepusch, Stanley, and Geminiani) to the 2-volume edition of Scarlatti appearing later that year under Thomas Roseingrave's sponsorship (cf. NEWTON-SCARLATTI, p. 138 ff.).
72. The chief recent source is GROVE, I, 860 ff. (Shaw). He was overlooked in MGG!
73. -HISTORY, II, 493.

Ex. 70.   From the second movement of Sonata 3 for harpsichord by Thomas Augustine Arne (after PAUER-ARNEm, p. 177, but without the acknowledged editorial additions).

a matter of astonishment,[74] for Boyce's posthumous recognition can be summed up in an occasional article, the usual "passing mentions," a few single reprints, and a very few recordings.   Boyce's only sonatas are the 12 SS/bass examples in the set Burney named, published in 1747 by Walsh and in another Walsh edition (made from the same plates) that followed some three years later.[75]   It is interesting to find   75a
Pepusch (one of Boyce's teachers), Handel, and Arne among the impressive "List of [nearly 600] Subscribers" to the 1747 edition.   In spite of Burney's comments, no further editions of Boyce's sonatas are known from the 18th or 19th century.

74. Cf. FINZI, p. 64 ff., on this neglect.
75. Cf. BRITISH PRINTED, I, 185.   Again, as with Arne, the spelling "Catharine" rather than "Catherine" Street may be some evidence for a date before 1745, although it must be said to occur on the 1747 title page, too.   The sonatas are briefly discussed in COBBETT, I, 157.   They are the subject of a master's thesis by Mr. R. Lee Bostian, in process at the time of this writing at the University of North Carolina.   Mod. eds.: Son. 3 in A, JENSEN-VIOLINm, no. 32; Son. 7 in D minor, MOFFAT-VIOLINm III, no. 8; Son. 11 in C minor, MOFFAT-TRIOm, no. 24.   Contrary to the foregoing, the new *British Union-Catalogue of Early Music* gives 1750 for the "other" edition.

Boyce is conservative in his adherence to the S-F-S-F plan in the majority of his sonatas; in the slight predominance of major keys; in his preference for rich harmony, almost constant polyphonic activity, and the older forms, including strict fugue; and in his generally serious approach to the sonata. From the start his superior craftsmanship is manifest. But his writing is more than skillful. It is strong, fresh, and original—often in a Handelian manner, for it has nobility of line (Ex. 71), continual rhythmic vitality, and a fertile imagination

Ex. 71. From the opening of Sonata 12 by William Boyce (after score of the Walsh edition *ca.* 1745 prepared by R. Lee Bostian).

in the repetition of the primary idea (which is usually maintained with somewhat more persistence than in Handel's sonatas). Moreover, Boyce's sonatas are among the last important examples of that "classic" Baroque type that seems to proceed at its steady, majestic pace, whether fast or slow, excited or calm. Essential to that type are the broadly conceived lines, the well-spaced entries, the long-range climactic goals, and the sure but slow tonal movement (slow in spite of the characteristically rapid harmonic rhythm). Thus, it could be added, one might go right down the line in finding points of contrast rather than similarity between the "trio" sonatas of Boyce and Arne.

A particular and delightful trait in Boyce's sonatas is the return to a more antiphonal treatment of the upper parts. In most sonatas of the time these parts were gradually falling more and more into the homophonic, chordal texture of a melody with a filler part. Rapid exchanges between the parts, usually with finely graded dynamic markings, are to be found in various non-fugal movements of all tempos, whether

Ex. 72. From the "Allegro" of Sonata 2 by William Boyce (after score of the Walsh edition *ca.* 1745 prepared by R. Lee Bostian).

fast (Ex. 72), slow (e.g., "Adagio" of Son. 3), or moderate (e.g., "Gratioso" of Son. 4). The last-named type of movement is also a special contribution of this composer, with something of the expressive, gentle lilt one might expect in a Brahms "Allegretto grazioso." Further delights in Boyce's sonatas can be found in the large, driving fugues, the rollicking gigues (in spirit when not in title), and those occasional other dance movements, energetic and tuneful as they are, including the march, the minuet, and the gavotte.

Four other, more obscure British composers can only be treated briefly here, although their sonatas, all first works dating between about 1737 and 1750, have in each instance real distinction and musical worth, within the generally traditional outlines of the melo/bass types. Two of the composers were active in centers other than London. All four are among those brought to light in Moffat's sadly corrupt yet still indispensable editions of *Old English Violin Music.*[76] The earliest to publish was the Scotch violinist **Charles Macklean** (?-*ca.* 1772), who was in Aberdeen at the time.[77] It is his "Opera Primo," dated 1737 in Edin-

76. -VIOLINm III; reference is made again to GARDNER-MOFFAT.
77. Cf. GROVE, V, 479 (Farmer).

burgh, with which we are concerned—*Twelve Solo's or Sonata's for a Violin and Violoncello with a Thorough Bass for the Harpsichord. . . . The four last Solo's are adapted for the German flute.*[78] The music in the available editions has much rhythmic sparkle and its passagework bespeaks a capable performer in the composer himself.

The organist **Joseph Gibbs** (*ca.* 1699-1788) was in "Dedham in Essex" at the time he published his only work that is completely extant, eight "Solos" for violin and *b. c.* (*ca.* 1746).[79] The ornate style, the rich harmony, the expressive, involute lines, and the advanced use of the instrument make this music remarkable not merely as a "first work" but among other such works of the time. **Thomas Vincent** junior (*ca.* 1720-83) was an oboist in London who is represented in our subject by six "Solos" for oboe, flute, violin, "or" harpsichord and *b. c.*, Op. 1 (1748),[80] and a set of harpsichord "Lessons," Op. 2 (also 1748). In the available reprint, the solo part is outstanding for its songful quality, there being little of the chromaticism, jagged leaps, or decorative style that characterize Gibbs' writing. The last British composer to mention in this chapter is **John Collett,** who is known in no other way than by two copies of his *Six Solos For the Violin With a Thorough Bass for ye. Harpsicord,* Op. 1 (London, *ca.* 1755). The three sonatas that Moffat has made available from this set[81] show an advanced command of the instrument and an ability to write both themes and forms that are well conceived.

Christoph Willibald Gluck (1714-87), the German-born but internationally active composer and "reformer" of opera, comes at this point in English sonata history because one result of his visit to London in 1745 and 1746 seems to have been his only sonata publication. In 1746 Simpson of London published *Six Sonatas for two Violins & a Thorough Bass* "by Sig.r Gluck Composer to the Opera."[82] Three further, undated sonatas of this type by Gluck, in E, E-flat, and F, are known only in MS.[83] The published set may have been collected from works composed even before 1741 and while Gluck was still studying under

82a

78. Mod. eds.: Son. 5 in E, MOFFAT-VIOLINm III, no. 10 (with preface) ; Son. 9, BULLOCKm.
79. Cf. GROVE, III, 636 (Mellers) ; MGG, V, 94 ff. (Cudworth). Mod. ed.: Son. 1 in D minor, MOFFAT-VIOLINm III, no. 12 (with preface).
80. Mod. ed.: Son. in A minor, MOFFAT-VIOLINm III, no. 14 (with preface).
81. Son. 2 in A, MOFFAT-VIOLINm III, no. 5 (with preface) ; Son. in B-flat, MOFFAT-VIOLINm II, no. 34; Son. 5 in C, MOFFAT-VIOLINm I, no. 27.
82. Among mod. eds.: COLLEGIUMm, nos. 32-37 (Riemann) ; cf. also, MGG, V, 378 (Abert), but add Son. 2 in G minor, EINSTEIN-GLUCKm; Son. 6 in F, MOFFAT-TRIOm, no. 11. Gluck's "trio" sonatas are briefly discussed in GERBER-GLUCK, p. 68 ff., and EINSTEIN-GLUCK, p. 25 ff.
83. Cf. GERBER-UNBEKANNTE, p. 305 ff. Only the *b. c.* of the E-flat sonata is preserved. Mod. ed.: Son. in E, COLLEGIUMm, no. 38 (Riemann).

G. B. Sammartini in Milan. If so, perhaps Sammartini's own, first collection of six "trio" sonatas, issued two years earlier by the same publisher in London, was a model and incentive for Gluck's (although in this survey Sammartini's later works qualify him as a pre-Classic rather than a late Baroque composer). As in Sammartini's first two sonatas all six of Gluck's published sonatas and the E-flat MS sonata have three movements in the order of S-F-F, the final movement being a minuet in style and usually in name. On the other hand, one of Gluck's two other MS sonatas, the one in E, is like the other four of Sammartini's sonatas in having the Italian opera sinfonia plan of F-S-F. The MS sonata in F has only two movements, slow and quasi minuet, a plan used later by Sammartini.

There are minute rhythmic refinements, short ideas separated by rests, unison passages, the minuets, the chromaticism of various dominant embellishments, and a lightness in Gluck's sonatas that point to the *galant* style and to *opera buffa*,[84] especially in the MS sonatas. But there are also the fast harmonic rhythm and the prevailingly imitative relationship of the upper parts to confirm that his sonatas are still products of the Baroque Era. There is even a strict canon between the upper parts in the finale of Sonata 1 (1746). Contrary to Handel's oft-cited remark, supposedly made while Gluck was in London, the latter did seem to know more of counterpoint than Handel's cook is thought to have known.[85] However, the trios seem less significant as inspired, original music than as examples of good training in composition techniques. Neither the ideas nor their development suggests any of the imagination that was to enhance Gluck's later, dramatic works. Perhaps, as Abert suggests,[86] he (like Wagner a century later) needed the stimulus of the dramatic situation to draw him beyond the pale of mere correctness; significantly, he showed little interest in independent instrumental music in his middle or late period. He must be regarded as another of the many composers who made their entrance by way of an "Opera prima" of sonatas, only to continue in quite another direction.

During Gluck's visit to London an Italian associate of his was **Giovanni Battista Lampugnani** (1706-81[87]), a Milanese cembalist and opera composer. In London from 1743 to about 1746 and again in 1755,[88] this composer, too, made his debut with "trio" sonatas. One set of six, Op. 1, was first published as his alone by Walsh in 1745 and again as a joint collection with Sammartini about five years later.[89] And at the time the latter edition appeared, a further set of six "trio"

83a

84. Cf. EINSTEIN-GLUCK, p. 15.
85. Cf. SMITH-HANDEL, p. 167 ff.
86. MGG, V, 376.
87. SCHMIDL, I, 806.
88. GROVE, V, 39 (Loewenberg).
89. Cf. BRITISH PRINTED, II, 11.

sonatas, listed as the Op. 2 of the same two men, appeared in another joint edition from Walsh. Here, then, were further examples of the bibliographic confusion perpetrated by Walsh, and here was one more reason why Sammartini's enormous output has yet to be clarified.[90] No modern editions of Lampugnani's sonatas have been published. All six sonatas in the joint set marked Op. 2 (the only set examined in this survey) have three movements in the order F-S-F. Burney has only qualified praise for Lampugnani.[91] Lampugnani's tunes are fetching, chordal in outline, and square in cut. His rhythms are sprightly, including frequent syncopations. Both aspects of his writing sound modern for the time and may explain at least one further edition of the sonatas by Thompson of London about 1765.[92] It is interesting to note that Thomas Jefferson included in his rich and up-to-date library of sonatas and other music from abroad both sets by Lampugnani in the Walsh editions. These two sets stand along with some by Corelli, Geminiani, and Vivaldi among the relatively few sets of sonatas by Baroque composers that Jefferson bought.[93]

By way of concluding our survey of composers active in Great Britain, nine Italians resident in London for shorter or longer periods may be noted, although in not more than the briefest manner. Remembered only through occasional modern editions, they all published sonatas of considerable charm and technical interest, dating on into the later 18th century. These sonatas are classified here among Baroque products largely because they are still in the older melo/bass settings rather than the newer settings of J. C. Bach and others, for keyboard with optional violin or flute "accompaniment." Yet all of their composers were writing in a changing language, one characterized by more symmetrical phrases, clearer tunes that stand out in more elementary passagework of straight scales or arpeggios, extended tonal plateaus in which the *b. c.* becomes more a slow succession of primary-chord roots than a fast line, and a lighter homophonic texture enriched by only an occasional imitation. A distinguishing feature of these composers is the fact that nearly all were cellists of some importance—among the first, moreover, to introduce and compose for their instrument in England (along with G. B. Bononcini, who was mentioned earlier with Modenese composers).[94]

One such composer was the outstanding Neapolitan cellist **Salvatore**

---

90. Cf. GROVE, VII, 396 (Stevens).   91. -HISTORY, II, 842 ff.
92. Cf. BRITISH PRINTED, II, 11.
93. Information supplied, along with photostats of pages from Jefferson's MS catalog of his library, by Mrs. Helen Bullock, now at the National Trust for Historic Presentation, Washington, D. C.
94. Cf. STRAETEN-VIOLONCELLO, p. 160 ff.

Lanzetti (*ca.* 1710-*ca.* 1780), in London from about 1739-54. Lanzetti left a cello tutor and at least one set of twelve sonatas in three movements (F-S-F) for cello and *b. c.*[95] This set was first published in Amsterdam, perhaps in 1736,[96] followed by reprints done in Paris[97] and others done in London as two sets of six "Solos" each.[98] The first of the two London sets has in its title, "after an Easy and Elegant Taste." The second offers the choice of "two Violoncellos or a German Flute and a Bass."

Carlo Zuccari (*ca.* 1704 to at least 1786[99]), a violinist from Casalmaggiore, had already published two volumes containing 12 virtuosic S/bass sonatas, Op. 1 (Milan, *ca.* 1730), before coming to London about 1750. Here he also published a set of six SS/bass sonatas about 1764 and another of three SS/bass "Trios" soon after.

Giacomo Bassevi "Cervetto," "the Elder," reported to have lived more than 100 years (1682-1783), is thought to have been an Italian cellist of German descent.[100] In London from 1728 to at least 1760, he left among other instrumental works a set of 6 SS/bass "Trios"; a set of sonatas for 3 cellos, or 2 violins and *b. c.;* 2 sets of 12 and 6 "Solos" for cello and *b. c.;* and a set of 8 "Solos" for flute and *b. c.*[101] These sets, in which there seems to be some duplication, were first published between about 1740 and 1755.

Niccolò Pasquali (?-1757), a violinist in Edinburgh, Dublin, and London from 1740, left a set of six S/bass sonatas published by Walsh about 1745 and two sets of six SS/bass sonatas published by J. Johnson of London about 1750.[102] He is not to be confused, as by Eitner,[103] [102a] with **Pasqualini** "de Marzis," a cellist in London who left two sets, Opp. 1 and 2, of six "Solos" each for two cellos (that is, cello with bass), published about 1745 and 1748 in London.[104] The latter also left another such "Solo" in ANTH. BONONCINIm (London, *ca.* 1740) and six sonatas for "Cetra or Kitara" and *b. c.* (London, *ca.* 1740).[105]

95. Among mod. eds. (cf. ALTMANN, p. 269) : Sons. 1 in A and 2 in G, SCHROEDER-CELLOm, nos. 5521 and 5522.

96. Cf. EITNER-QL, VI, 48 ; SCHMIDL, I, 811.

97. Cf. BIBLIOTHÈQUE NATIONALE, VI, 90.

98. Cf. BRITISH PRINTED, II, 14 ; HAAS-CAT. 20, nos. 394 and 395.

99. Cf. SCHMIDL, II, 737 ff. and Supp., p. 787 ; MGG, II, 1778 (Monterosso).

100. Cf. SCHMIDL, I, 323 ; GROVE, II, 143 (Straeten) ; the 1969 dissertation by W. G. Conable, Jr. as listed in NOTES, XXVIII (1971), 244.

101. Cf. BRITISH PRINTED, I, 244 ; HAAS-CAT. 20, nos. 138-141. Among mod. eds. : 6 "trio" sons., RUYSSEN & GRUSSARDm ; 2 "solo" cello sons., SCHROEDER-CELLOm, no. 5504 ; also, cf. ALTMANN.

102. Cf. GROVE, VI, 574 (Fuller Maitland) ; SCHMIDL, II, 237 ; BRITISH PRINTED, II, 246.

103. -QL, VII, 327 ; cf. HAAS-CAT. 20, nos. 491 and 492.

104. Among 4 mod. eds. of same work : Son. "2" in A, SCHROEDER-CELLOm, no. 5508 ; cf. ALTMANN.

105. Cf. BRITISH PRINTED, I, 173, and II, 247.

The Brussels-born cellist **Joseph dall'Abaco** (1710-1805) was a pupil of his better-known, Italian-born father E. F. dall'Abaco before going to Bonn and elsewhere.[106] Of at least 34 sonatas for cello and bass that are known by him, all left only in MS, at least 31 are in two sets of 12 and 17 plus other items in the British Museum.[107] Most of these three-to six-movement sonatas may well have been written while he was in London about 1740 and where he was cited by Burney for his playing.[108] Unfortunately, the only sonata by him that has been made available in a modern edition is a well-known one in G for cello and bass that has been wrongly credited to G. B. Sammartini.[109]

Finally, among this group of Italians in London there were four who published numerous sets of sonatas as late as the period between 1765 and 1780. One was the cellist **Stefano Galeotti** from Valletri, whose several sets of SS/bass and "solo" cello sonatas were issued in London, Amsterdam, and Paris,[110] in all of which cities he may have lived, too. There is duplication among these publications and confusion with the music of the violinist **Salvatore Galeotti** (a brother?), who is also known to have been in London and to have published six SS/bass sonatas around 1768.[111] The cellist **Giovanni Battista Cirri** (*ca.* 1740-?), born in Forlì, published among at least 18 sets of instrumental music about 6 of "trio" sonatas (both SS/- and SSB/bass), 4 of "solo" sonatas for cello and *b. c.,* and one of organ sonatas (Op. 1).[112] The violinist **Giovanni Battista Noferi** (*ca.* 1730-?), reported in London in 1770,[113] was similarly prolific and similarly well represented by publications (in London, Berlin, and Amsterdam), chiefly "trio" and "solo" violin sonatas. So far, neither Cirri nor Noferi has been brought to light in modern editions.[114]

114a

106. Cf. GROVE, II, 581 (Straeten).
107. Cf. BRITISH MS, III, 171 and 179 ff.
108. -HISTORY, II, 1005.
109. Mod. ed.: SALMON-CELLom, no. 101; cf. GROVE, VII, 396 (Stevens).
110. Cf. EITNER-QL, IV, 127; BRITISH PRINTED, I, 494; CAT. BRUXELLES, II, 377; HAAS-CAT. 20, no. 258. Among mod. eds.: Sons. in C minor and D minor, MOFFAT-CELLom, nos. 6 and 15; Son. in D, SCHROEDER-CELLom, no. 5530.
111. Cf. BRITISH PRINTED, I, 494.
112. Cf. EITNER-QL, II, 451; GROVE, II, 311 (Blom); BRITISH PRINTED, I, 271; HAAS-CAT. 20, no. 162.
113. EITNER-QL, VII, 209.
114. But EITNER-QL, VII, 209, does cite two older, partial reprints of Noferi violin pieces.

Chapter 15

Other Northern Countries

Holland from 1688 to about 1700 (Schenk, Noordt, Albicastro)

Following the two chapters on English composers, a chapter is needed in which we may take note of several sonata composers active chiefly in three other northern countries—namely, Holland, Denmark, and Sweden. Most of these composers were in Holland, a country closely allied with England after the middle of the 17th century through royal ties and a common opposition to the France of Louis XIV. There also existed close relationships of immediate concern to the sonata, especially between the very active publishers of Amsterdam and London. In particular, from 1696 or soon after, the highly skilled Amsterdam engraver Estienne Roger kept pace with John Walsh—in fact, was often ahead of him in the issuing of new publications.[1] Only the cream of the music about to be discussed has been studied or reprinted in modern times. Of all the names, the most important is that of Pietro Locatelli. His name recalls the fact that, as in England, about half the composers were foreigners, chiefly Italians again. But again, except for Locatelli, the foreigners have had least appeal for modern scholars, even for scholars of either the native or the adopted country.

Before the sonata composers about to be mentioned—in fact, before the middle of the 17th century—a Florentine composer, **Nicolaus a Kempis,** was active in Brussels, where he served as organist from 1628. Although he did not use the term "sonata" Kempis published three sets of some 120 *Symphoniae a 1-5* in Antwerp (1644, 1647, and 1649) that would certainly belong in any more general survey of the instrumental music in this area and period. Riemann has been the chief investigator into Kempis' music,[2] which is notable variously for its cantabile lines, chromaticism, and fantasia treatment of the forms.

---

1. Cf. SMITH-WALSH, p. xvi ff.; PINCHERLE-VIVALDI, p. 294 ff.
2. Cf. RIEMANN-TRIOSONATEN, p. 145 ff., and RIEMANN-MUSIKGESCHICHTE, II, Part 2, 155 ff.; also, MEYER, p. 46, and MEYER-NIEDERLÄNDISCHEN, pp. 77 and 271 ff.

In 17th-century Holland the chief musical center, and one rapidly growing in importance, was Amsterdam.[3] Earliest among composers in Holland to name is the virtuoso on the viola da gamba, **Johann Schenk** (1656-*ca.* 1700?).[4] Born in Elberfeld, near Düsseldorf, where he saw some preliminary years of service, Schenk presumably arrived in Amsterdam before his Op. 1 was published there in 1687 (a group of songs from an opera). Out of 11 known publications of collections in Amsterdam by him, six contain works called "sonatas" (sometimes equated with "suites"). Opp. 2 (*Konst Oeffeningen,* 1688) and 10 (*Les Fantaisies bisarres de la goutte,* 1715 or later[5]) contain 15 and 12 sonatas for viola da gamba and *b. c.; Op.* 9 (*L'Echo du Danube, ca.* 1694?) contains 6 more sonatas for solo viola da gamba, of which two have *b. c.,* two have optional *b. c.,* and two (Sons. 5 and 6) are specifically assigned to that distinguished and more exclusive category of unaccompanied string solos.[6] Op. 3 (*Il Giardino armonico,* 1692) contains 12 SSB/bass sonatas; Op. 7 (1693) contains *XVIII Suonati, caprice e fantasie a violino o violine e cimbalo;*[7] and Op. 8 (*Le Nymphe di Rheno, ca.* 1694?) contains 12 sonatas for two violas da gamba alone.

Unfortunately, Schenk's publications, although they seem to have achieved re-editions at the time, are now very scarce (resting chiefly in the Durham and Bodleian libraries[8] and in the Library of Congress). Furthermore, none of the sonatas has been made available in a modern edition. An edition of Op. 9 is especially to be sought.[9] From Schenk's one publication that does exist in a complete modern edition (and separate excerpts)—*Scherzi musicali,* Op. 6 (*ca.* 1692) for viola da gamba with generally optional *b. c.*[10]—one can see how desirable a

---

Mod. eds.: "Son." for violin, viola, and *b. c.* (1644), RIEMANN-BEISPIELEM, no. 99; "Son." for violin and *b. c.* (1644), RIEMANN-CHAMBERm, IV, 142.

3. MGG, I, 431 ff. (Bottenheim).

4. MOES-SCHENK is the main biographic source (with birth information still not incorporated in the standard dictionaries), including a list of works (based partly on a fuller list in BOUWSTEENEN, III, 20). The list of works in MEYER-NIEDERLÄNDISCHEN, p. 277 ff., includes descriptive comments. The approximate time of Schenk's death is hinted by the year when his service in Amsterdam seems to have ended (cf. MEYER-NIEDERLÄNDISCHEN, p. 72).

5. Cf. EITNER-MISCELLANEA, p. 158; but if the E. Roger edition is a first edition, the date seems late in view of the fact that no other first edition of Schenk is known to date later than 1696. The beautifully engraved title page of an E. Roger reprint of Op. 2 is reproduced in MEYER-NIEDERLÄNDISCHEN, facing p. 73.

6. Cf. HUGHES-VIOL, p. 159; GATES-SOLO, p. 15 ff. (with example).

7. Perhaps it is one of these pieces that appears in BRITISH MS, III, 245 (item 65 of Add. 31466).

8. Cf. GROVE, VII, 476 ff. (Antcliffe & Newton); MEYER-NIEDERLÄNDISCHEN, p. 278 ff.

9. Cf. STRAETEN-VIOLONCELLO, p. 70 ff.

10. Cf. EINSTEIN-GAMBA, p. 132 ff.; STRAETEN-VIOLONCELLO, p. 65 ff.; HUGHES-VIOL, p. 157 ff. Mod. ed., entire: VNMm, XXVIII (Leichtentritt, with brief

study and edition of the sonatas would be. This set, in which 101 dances and freer pieces are grouped into 14 suites, reveals a serious, able composer with a sure control of harmony, a large view of form (including massive sets of variations), and a flare for virtuosity (including scarcely surpassed uses of multiple stops, especially in polyphonic writing) that could well discourage all but the most advanced players.

A native Dutch composer, presumably acquainted with Schenk,[11] was the organist and cembalist **Sybrandus van Noordt** (?-1702?[12]), who was active in Amsterdam from 1679 through 1691, and in Haarlem from the start (January 8) of 1692 to 1695.[13] Noordt's "Opera prima" and only known collection includes what might be called another incunabulum of the keyboard sonata—that is, one more instance (and our last to mention here) of an example published before 1700.[14] In an E. Roger reprint of this collection[15] the title is given, in French, as *Mélange italien, ou sonates à 1 flute et 1 basse continue, à 1 violon et basse continue, à 2 violons sans basse, et à un clavessin seul.* But the title of the original edition, published without date in Amsterdam ("con . . . spece di Henrico Anders . . . in casa di Sebastian Petzold"), reads in Italian *Sonate per il Cimbalo appropriate al Flauto & Violino.* There are just those four sonatas specified in the French title and in the order given. Of the fourth, separately entitled "Sonata à Cimbalo Solo," E. H. Meyer writes somewhat categorically, "This last must be the first of its sort in music history, since it evidently originated before Pasquini and Kuhnau."[16] If Meyer's definite but undocumented date of 1690 can be confirmed,[17] and if one disregards the borderline types by Schmelzer and Ritter that were noted in an earlier chapter, then Noordt's sonata may at least be called the earliest known keyboard sonata to be found outside of Italy.

Noordt's sonatas are characterized by long, expressive, climactic lines; compelling harmonies; virtuosity in the passagework; endless sequences of idiomatic figures based on recurring harmonic formulas;

14a

---

preface). The 1703 edition listed in SMITH-WALSH, item 136, may well have come from Schenk's Op. 6.

11. His portrait was painted by Schenk's brother Peter (EITNER-QL, VII, 211).

12. The eulogistic poem by A. Alewyn in praise of Noordt, dated 1702 (reproduced in BOUWSTEENEN, I, 97), may well have been intended as an elegy.

13. BOUWSTEENEN, I, 65.

14. Cf. NEWMAN-EARLIEST, pp. 205 ff. and 209.

15. Cf. BIBLIOTHÈQUE NATIONALE, VIII, 32 (under "Sibrando").

16. MEYER-NIEDERLÄNDISCHEN, p. 274 (with engraving from title page on p. 69) ; cf. also, MEYER-ENGLISH, p. 85.

17. It may merely have come from the conjectural date in BRITISH PRINTED, II, 200; but there is at least the fact that Noordt left Amsterdam by 1692, although, with the usual delays of publication and Haarlem less than 15 miles away, that fact is hardly conclusive in itself.

elements of the fantasia in the rather frequent tempo and dynamic changes, although the underlying plan of the S-F-S-F church sonata is apparent; and both a free and extensive use of dissonance. All of these traits are to be found in the solo keyboard sonata as well as the other sonatas. This piece seems mainly to recall the fact that keyboard sonatas could be, and were, made simply by giving the solo line of an S/bass sonata to the right hand and the *b. c.* to the left. Although most of the figuration is well enough suited to the keyboard idiom, the bass is figured (perhaps only so that the texture can be filled out?) and the writing is not chordal but strictly two-part throughout (Ex. 73).

Ex. 73. From Sonata 4 "à Cimbalo Solo" by Sybrandus van Noordt (after the original Dutch edition).

Among his valuable surveys of earlier Baroque instrumental music, E. H. Meyer has done one on composers active in the Netherlands from about 1650 to 1710, to which several references have already been made. In this survey[18] he speaks of *Harmonia parnassia sonatarium,* Op. 2 (Utrecht, 1686), by a Belgian-born violist da gamba **Carolus Hacquart** (*ca.* 1640-*ca.* 1730) as "one of the most significant instrumental works

18. MEYER-NIEDERLÄNDISCHEN, pp. 269 ff. and 77.

that the 17th century as a whole produced"[19] (a statement that we also
quoted from him about another obscure composer, G. Diessener; cf. p.
226). Hacquart's set contains 10 sonatas in SSB/-, SAB/-, SSAB/-,
and SSSB/bass settings. A resident first of Amsterdam and then of   19a
The Hague, Hacquart has also been credited with two sets of suites and
one set containing 10 sonatas for two violas da gamba and *b. c.* that
E. Roger issued about 1710 under the name "Carolo."[20] However,
Meyer argues, on stylistic grounds, that the last-mentioned set must come
from another composer.[21] No sonatas by Hacquart are to be found in
modern editions. Meyer reports that those in Op. 2 are all in five
movements, which follow the general though flexible plan of an adagio
introduction, a fugal movement (often called "Canzona"), a free or
virtuosic transitional movement, a "Bizarria," and a concluding instrumental aria. He calls special attention to the mastery of forms, bold
harmony, rich polyphony, and certain expressive slow movements.

Meyer[22] lists works by several other, contemporary composers of
sonatas in the Netherlands who, for want of music examples and further
information, can only be named here. Among them are the organist
Hendrik Anders (in Amsterdam from 1696-1719); Elias Broennemuller
(Amsterdam around 1700); the opera composer Servaes van Koninck
(1637-1716, chiefly in Amsterdam); Charles Rosier (Amsterdam and
Köln; cf. p. 363); Benedictus a San Josepho (1642-1706, Carmelite monk
in Nijmegen and Boxmeer, North Brabant, Holland), whose *Orpheus
elianus,* Op. 8 (13 SS/bass sonatas) Meyer calls "one of the most
interesting collections of the south-Dutch group," with bold harmony,
rich motivic play, unusual melody, and driving rhythm;[23] and Philipp
van Wicchel (instrumentalist in Brussels around 1678; also Antwerp?).

Henrico Albicastro (from not later than *ca.* 1670 to no sooner than
ca. 1738[24]) is said to have been a Swiss-born composer on military duty
in Holland around the last part of the 17th century.[25] Under his supposedly real name of Heinrich Weissenburg von Biswang rather than his
Italianized name he was apparently enrolled at the University of Leiden
in 1686.[26] Obviously an experienced violinist, Albicastro left nine in-

---

19. But neither WALTHER-LEXIKON, p. 298, nor GERBER-LEXIKON, II, 486 (both
under "Hakart") supports this view, as implied by Meyer, or opposes it, for that
matter.
20. E.g., cf. STRAETEN-VIOLONCELLO, p. 94.
21. -NIEDERLÄNDISCHEN, p. 267.
22. *Ibid.,* p. 264 ff.
23. *Ibid.,* p. 277.
24. Dates based on BOUWSTEENEN, III, 2, II, 4 and 255; ZWART.
25. WALTHER-LEXIKON, p. 23, is still the primary source.
26. Cf. BOUWSTEENEN, III, 2; MGG, I, 295 ff. (Beckmann, with other sources,
but without incorporating further information assembled in ZWART).

strumental collections, all published around 1700 in Rotterdam[27] and especially Amsterdam (both E. Roger and Witvogel). Except for Opp. 6 and 9, long lost, most of these collections were preserved in Hamburg prior to the devastations of World War II.[28] All contain sonatas except Op. 7, a set of 12 *Concerti a 4*. Opp. 1, 4, and 8 contain 12 SSB/bass sonatas each;[29] Opp. 3 and 9 contain 12 SB/bass sonatas each; and Opp. 2, 5, and 6 contain 15, 6, and ? S/bass sonatas.[30] The S-F-S-F plan predominates throughout Albicastro's known sonatas. The movement types and the purposeful, cantabile style also suggest Italian influences.[31] But the technical advances in the "solo" sonatas, particularly the multiple stops, arpeggios, and bowing techniques, suggest German influences.[32] In this regard it is worth noting that Quantz linked Albicastro with Biber and Walther as three composers whose music he had practiced before being won over by Corelli and other Italians.[33] Albicastro, too, may have known Corelli's Op. 5, for he ends his own Op. 5 with a set of variations (18 in all) on the Folia.[34]

Holland from about 1700 to 1750 (Fesch, Locatelli)

By the time of the next generation of composers Amsterdam had become one of the liveliest music centers in all Europe[35] and not merely a city of chimes as Burney later seemed to think.[36] One member of that generation, the concert violinist **Willem de Fesch** (1687-*ca.* 1757), lived in Amsterdam until 1725, in Antwerp to 1731, and in London thereafter (another in the shadow of Handel).[37] Fesch was a successful composer of songs and instrumental music, with many publications and re-editions to his credit.[38] He left some ten collections of sonatas, in more than the usual variety of settings. Confused by opus numbers that are often the same as those given to his several sets of concerti grossi, the sonata collections were originally issued, between 1716 and 1750, variously in Amsterdam, Paris, London, and Brussels. They include three sets for

27. Cf. LAND-CATALOGUS, p. 44.
28. Cf. EITNER-QL, I, 89; BIBLIOTHÈQUE NATIONALE, II, 227.
29. Cf. NEF-DEUTSCHEN, p. 33 ff. Mod. ed.: Son. 3, Op. 1, MOSER-ALBICASTROm (with preface).
30. Among mod. eds.: Son. 4, Op. 5, BECKMANNm, V, no. 12; Sons. 2 and 3, Op. 5, MARTINm.
31. Cf. BECKMANN, p. 74.
32. Cf. MOSER-VIOLINSPIEL, p. 124 ff.; NEF-ALBICASTRO, p. 432.
33. KAHL-SELBSTBIOGRAPHIEN, p. 108.
34. Cf. MOSER-FOLIES, p. 369 ff. (with examples).
35. Cf. KOOLE, chap. 1.
36. -GERMANY, II, 282 ff. (especially 289).
37. BREMT is the main source, including life, style studies, thematic index, and full bibliographies. A summary and detailed bibliographies by the same author are in MGG, IV, 85 ff.
38. Cf. BRITISH PRINTED, I, 356 ff. (under Defesch).

two cellos alone, two for two flutes alone, one in SB/bass setting, two in S/bass setting, one in SS/bass setting, and one for cello and *b. c.*[39] These sets are exceptionally well represented in modern editions.[40] Their popularity both then and now is not hard to understand.

Fesch was a kind of Dutch Mendelssohn in his day, a century before the German master flourished. In his music prevail clarity, directness, fluency, and accuracy of both the harmonic and the contrapuntal writing.[41] Nor is the music without originality, although hearing much at one setting tends to focus attention on lines that depart only seldom from stepwise or diatonic movement and on harmonies that depend too often on chains of dominants. The four or five movements in nearly all of the sonatas center, traditionally, around the S-F-S-F plan, with tempo inscriptions and standard dance titles freely intermixed. Burney found Fesch a skilled contrapuntist but dry.[42] The modern biographer F. van den Bremt finds three style periods in Fesch's sonatas—the Amsterdam period, characterized by virtuosity and the styles prevalent around the turn of the century; the Antwerp period, in which the virtuosity gave way to simplicity; and the London period (best represented by the six "solo" and six duet sonatas of Op. 8), in which traces of the *galant* style are present, along with greater depth and skill.[43]

If Fesch was an 18th-century Mendelssohn, then, as we shall see, the renowned violin virtuoso **Pietro Antonio Locatelli** (1695-1764) might be regarded as an 18th-century Paganini. Thanks to several Dutch and Italian discoveries in recent decades, and especially to the thorough, still newer book by Arend Koole, which summarizes and augments these discoveries, the haze that long obscured Locatelli's career has been penetrated at many points.[44] Born in Bergamo, Locatelli studied with Corelli in Rome, then concertized widely, eventually settling in Amsterdam in 1729.[45] There he spent his remaining 35 years, including those later years when he sold his own publications and his own special brand of violin, viola, and cello strings. He reached Amsterdam too late to know Fesch, although he could have met him when he played there in 1721.[46] But he did know many other of the important musicians of his time—among them, for example, Leclair and G. B. Martini.[47]

44a

39. Cf. BREMT, pp. 111 ff., 184 ff., 196 ff., 235 and *passim* for lists, thematic index, dedications, etc.
40. Cf. MGG, IV, 88, including all of the 6 "solo" (WOEHL-FESCHm, with extended preface) and 6 duet sons. that make up Op. 8.
41. The sonatas are discussed in detail, with examples, in BREMT, p. 111 ff.
42. -HISTORY, II, 1015.   43. BREMT, p. 173 ff.; MGG, IV, 87.
44. Cf. KOOLE, pp. 40 ff. and 284 ff.; also, BERG-LOCATELLI (among previous biographic researches).
45. KOOLE, p. 48 ff.   46. *Ibid.,* p. 43.
47. *Ibid.,* pp. 47 ff. and 66 ff.

The astonishing library that he left[48]—astonishing for its rich holdings in many diverse fields of learning—included among its music scores sonatas by Corelli, Tartini, Handel, Tessarini, Martini, Leclair, Geminiani, D. Scarlatti, and many lesser names.

Locatelli's output consisted of nine collections originally published in Amsterdam (about half by himself) between 1721 and 1762, followed by various re-editions chiefly in Leiden, London, and Paris.[49] These, like Corelli's six opera, included no vocal music but concentrated on the concerto (Opp. 1, 3, 4, 7, and 9) and sonata (Opp. 2, 5, 6, and 8, all published in the 12 years between 1732 and 1744).[50] Op. 9 is now lost, while several mentions of 6 SB/bass sonatas Op. 10 are based on an error.[51] Of the four sonata collections, typical of the scoring preferences in the late Baroque Era, three contain S/bass settings, whereas only one and part of another contain SS/bass settings. As solo instrument, the flute is designated in Op. 2, the violin or flute in Op. 5, and the violin only in both Opp. 6 and 8. There are 40 sonatas in all—12 sonatas for flute and *b. c.* in Op. 2 (1732),[52] 6 sonatas for two violins and *b. c.* in Op. 5 (1736),[53] 12 sonatas for violin and *b. c.* in Op. 6 (1737),[54] and six more "solo" violin sonatas plus four more "trio" sonatas in Op. 8 (1744).[55] The selection from these sets to be found in modern editions is spotty both in scope and editing[56]—not, certainly, what is to be desired for so important a figure and much less than that for Fesch.

The comparison of Locatelli with Paganini a century later, often made by writers on violin music,[57] rightly suggests that the former ranked with Tartini, Veracini, and Leclair among the great violin virtuosos of the later Baroque Era. Unfortunately, the interest in this side of his music, especially in the "XXIV Capricci" that are scattered among the movements of the 12 solo violin concertos of his Op. 3, has tended to

54a

55a

---

48. Full list in KOOLE, p. 91 ff.

49. Cf. KOOLE, chap. 2 *passim;* BRITISH PRINTED, II, 56; HAAS-CAT. 20, nos. 408-410 (with errors).

50. Detailed thematic index in KOOLE, p. 240 ff.; partial thematic index in BACHMANN-VIOLINISTES, p. 166 ff.

51. Cf. KOOLE, pp. 73 ff., 127 ff., and 232 ff.

52. Cf. KOOLE, pp. 49 ff., 160 ff. (with examples), and 245 ff. Among mod. eds.: Sons. 4-6, HORTUSM, no. 35 (Scheck & Upmeyer); Son. 6 (arranged for violin), DAVID-VIOLINSPIELM, II, 76.

53. Cf. KOOLE, pp. 55 ff., 190 ff. (with examples), and 261 ff. Among mod. eds.: Sons. 1 and 5, MOFFAT-TRIOM, nos. 22 and 2.

54. Cf. KOOLE, pp. 57 ff., 202 ff. (with examples), and 263 ff. Among mod. eds.: Son. 1, MOFFAT-VIOLINM I, no. 18; Son. 7 (not from Op. 4), VNMm, XXXI, 15 (Scheurleer, with preface).

55. Cf. KOOLE, pp. 63 ff., 227 ff. (with examples), and 270 ff. Among mod. eds. (S/bass only): Son. 5 (but with "Andante" from Son. 12, Op. 6, substituted), VNMm, XXXI, 3.

56. Cf. KOOLE, p. 279 ff. (up to 1949), and ALTMANN.

57. Cf. MOSER-VIOLINSPIEL, p. 225; WASIELEWSKI-VIOLINE, p. 202.

discourage interest in, or even to reflect negatively on, his sonatas.[58]
Already in his *History*[59] Burney wrote that Locatelli "had more hand,
caprice, and fancy, than any violinist of his time. He was a voluminous
composer of Music that excites more surprise than pleasure." (Burney
had written more tolerantly following a visit to Amsterdam eight years
after Locatelli's death.[60]) Not 20 years later Dittersdorf further expressed the Classic composer's attitude when he wrote that the sonatas
of Locatelli "may sound old-fashioned nowadays, but I would earnestly
recommend them to every beginner on the violin—for practice, not for
show pieces. Once master of them, he will make great progress in
fingering, bowing, arpeggios, double-stopping, etc."[61]

To be sure, Locatelli's sonatas as well as his concertos—especially
the sonatas in his most mature set, Op. 6—abound in technical problems
and display (Ex. 74). But there is certainly much else of interest in

Ex. 74. From the finale of Sonata 10, Op. 6, by Pietro
Antonio Locatelli (after the composer's own first edition of
1737).

them. For one thing, the order and plan of movements was brought to
an individual solution by Locatelli. Whereas in Opp. 2 and 5 Locatelli
wavered between the traditional S-F-S-F sequence and a variety of
three-movement plans, in Op. 6 he settled almost invariably on a particular three-movement plan. Thus, a lyrical, often florid opening move-

58. For a sampling of contrasting historical views cf. WASIELEWSKI-VIOLINE, p.
103 ff. (especially from TORCHI, p. 181 ff.).
59. II, 454.
60. -GERMANY, II, 289 ff.
61. DITTERSDORF, p. 28 ; cf. also, p. 40.

ment in slow to moderate tempos is followed by a polyphonic, often fugal movement in a fast tempo, and finally by an "Aria," "Cantabile," "Minuetto," or similarly titled piece, usually in the style and meter of the minuet, which becomes the theme for from one to seven brilliant variations. The exception is Sonata 12, with its five movements culminating in a "Capriccio, Prova del Intonatione" that does present a new world of pyrotechnics.

Within the separate movements Locatelli's treatment of form again reveals distinctions important to note. Quite apart from the accident of hitting upon "sonata form" now and then (e.g., "Andante" of Son. 2, Op. 6), he shares with Tartini and Veracini a propensity for writing lucid A-B-A designs[62] based not on motivic play and its associated traits but on more progressive principles, including full-fledged, tuneful "themes," balanced groupings of phrases, a homophonic texture, a relatively slow harmonic rhythm, and broad tonal plateaus (Ex. 75, first half of the "A" section in a *da capo* A-B-A design). With regard to the

Ex. 75. From the finale of Sonata 1, Op. 5, by Pietro Antonio Locatelli (after the Walsh re-edition, *ca.* 1745).

62. Cf. KOOLE, p. 198 ff.

homophonic texture, there are occasions when Locatelli created figures that anticipate the "Alberti bass." In one such, the "Allegro" from Sonata 3 of Op. 8, he explains that the figure or diminution of the *b. c.* is to be played by the bass, then, during the repetition of the section, by the cembalist ("Ia. Sminuisce il Basso, la rep. il Cemb."[63]). Locatelli also shows himself to be an expressive if not unusual melodist and harmonist, as in the "Andante" in Siciliano style that opens Sonata 5 from Op. 6, and a skilled polyphonist, as in some canonic movements—for instance, the "Largo" that opens Sonata 12 of Op. 2 and the "Vivace" from Sonata 5 of Op. 5.[64] The "Largo" is unusual in being an S/bass setting in which both parts can be imitated in strict canon at the discretion of the performers, thus resulting in an SS/BB setting. If the parts are added, Locatelli cautions that two cembalos on the bass part would overpower the two flutes, so that at least one of them should be a cello.[65]

Denmark (K. Förster) and Sweden (Roman)

Two composers, one each in Denmark and Sweden, remain to be mentioned in this chapter. The singer **Kaspar Förster** (1616-73), native of Danzig and product of Italian training, headed the impressive, cosmopolitan musical activities at the court of Frederick III in Copenhagen from 1652 to 1655 and 1661 to 1668.[66] It was apparently during these years that he wrote at least six SS/bass sonatas and an orchestral sonata *a 7* (2 *cornettini,* 2 violins, viola, bassoon, bass viol, and *b. c.*), now to be found among MSS in Uppsala.[67] E. H. Meyer finds Förster to be a cross between Weckmann and Rosenmüller, with reference to the opposite styles that he attributes to those two composers (cf. p. 244).[68] Förster has the over-all structural logic of Rosenmüller, he says, but his polyphonic writing in particular has the melodic style of Weckmann, characterized by short mechanical figures rather than long cantabile lines.

The violinist and conductor **Johann Helmich Roman** (1694-1758), active in Stockholm from 1720 to his retirement in 1745, is remembered as "the father of Swedish music."[69] He published 12 sonatas for flute   69a

63. Cf. KOOLE, p. 228.
64. Cf. KOOLE, pp. 166 ff. and 199 ff.
65. Cf. KOOLE, p. 249; also, p. 228, where Locatelli is stated to have owned a pianoforte and to have indicated dynamic changes that imply the use of one.
66. MGG, IV, 458 ff. (Fock). Cf. HAMMERICH-DANSK, p. 198 ff.
67. Cf. MEYER, pp. 204, 91, and 100 ff. (with examples). Mod. ed.: first movement SS/bass Son. 6, FOCK-TRIOSONATENm, p. 5 (with mention, in "Inhalt," of projected edition of entire set).
68. MEYER, p. 101 ff.
69. GROVE, VII, 213 ff. (Dale). The chief studies are VRETBLAD 1914, and VRETBLAD 1945.

and *b. c.* (Stockholm, 1727),[70] and left at least 22 more of this type, 17 "trio" sonatas, and 12 harpsichord sonatas in MSS preserved largely in Uppsala and Stockholm.[71] No modern publication of the MSS has been available for this survey, although a short study of the "trio" sonatas has appeared.[72] An opportunity to know the harpsichord sonatas should be

73a   especially interesting at this time.[73] In both his S/- and SS/bass sonatas Roman used from four to seven movements that centered around the S-F-S-F plan. No single feature—no unusual harmony, technical treatment, programmatic content, or other one aspect—distinguishes his music. But the music does confirm both the fine grounding he is said to have received from Ariosti and Pepusch in London and the lifelong admiration he is said to have had for Handel. In the available examples the long cantabile lines, the imaginative repetition and emphasis of ideas, the purposeful harmonic progressions and tonal plans, the excellent rhythmic organization, and the cogent ideas themselves all point to a mastery of composition well above average. In short, here again was the noble Baroque sonata at its Corellian peak and before it was transformed through preoccupation with details and other auspices of newer styles.

70. WALIN (in Swedish) is a detailed style study of this set (with examples). Among mod. eds.: entire, VRETBLADm; Sons. 1 in G and 6 in B minor, HORTUSm, no. 101 (Senn).
71. Full bibliography and thematic index in VRETBLAD 1914, I, 81 ff., and II, 28 ff., respectively.
72. LELLKY (in Swedish).
73. SOHLMANS, IV, 442, cites an edition of "XI" by H. Rosenberg, but without further details.

Chapter 16

France: Couperin and Other Pioneers

The Background

France, the last main country that is taken up in the present survey, saw the production of sonatas by some 40 Baroque composers to be noted here, including, above all, Couperin and Leclair. That country is not last in importance to the sonata but it did come last in chronology, being markedly slower than Italy, Germany, or England to cultivate this musical type. To be sure, still other countries, among them Spain, scarcely employed the term "sonata" until the first tangible signs of the Classic Era were appearing. As was observed in an earlier chapter, the progress of the sonata in each country depended, at least in a negative sense, on how great the resistance was to foreign—that is, Italian—importations. France's unequalled national unity and her pre-eminence as a European power during the long reign of Louis XIV (1643-1715) were more conducive than not to this resistance. As she deteriorated in unity and power during the Regency and the reign (1715-74) of Louis XV her letters and other arts, significantly enough, became more progressive and international in both form and character.

In the 17th century there were far fewer Italian musicians active in France than in Germany or England.[1] There would have been less opportunity for them, in any case, since France even more than England was not another loose geographical aggregate of many independent cities and other political divisions, but rather an absolute monarchy with its one main cultural center in Paris and its environs. Hence, the history of the French Baroque sonata is confined primarily to the "Privilège du Roy" and the musical activities at the brilliant court in Versailles.[2] As we shall see, when Couperin introduced the melo/bass sonata to France in 1692 he was doing something quite as consciously innovational as was Kuhnau, that same year in Leipzig, when he introduced what he

1. Cf. the helpful map and statistics in LANG-WESTERN, after p. 464.
2. Cf. BRENET-CONCERTS, chap. 7 and *passim*.

supposed to be the first keyboard sonata. Furthermore, the instrumental heritage of France that greeted Couperin, much as that of England that greeted Purcell scarcely a decade earlier, was largely an autochthonous art. It had consisted mainly of the important lute and clavecin music that was brought to a peak by the Gaultier, Chambonnières, d'Anglebert, and older Couperin families, of rather severe church organ music such as Titelouze wrote, and of the overtures, ballet settings, and other independent instrumental music to be found in early French opera.[3] It is no wonder that Mattheson regarded the sonata as an unnatural innovation in France.[4]

It is true that the first opera in France, just before the mid 17th century, was that imported by Cardinal Mazarin from his native country of Italy. But anti-Italian reaction came quickly and violently, especially after Mazarin's death in 1661, there being no opera composer who subscribed more ardently to the clarity and order of classic French art than the Italian-born Lully himself.[5] With Lully's *tragédie lyrique* as the dominant force in later 17th-century music, Italian influence was limited to certain church and chamber music. The chamber music became, of course, the gateway by which the sonata entered France. It also became the gateway by which the violin—hitherto in less good repute in France than the viol, lute, or clavecin—won full acceptance, though now in solo uses quite beyond the King's "Grande bande" of Twenty-four Violins or the "Petits violons" that had topped this group under Lully's jealous guidance.[6] Furthermore, the one Italian most responsible for opening this gate was certainly none other than Corelli again.[7] Although nothing of Corelli was published in Paris until about 1701,[8] his music had been played there, according to Couperin's own words (cf. p. 356), before the latter composed his first sonatas in 1692. Prior to such performances one of the chief introductions of the sonata in France must have been that in 1682 when the Dresden violinist J. P. Westhoff played his own sonata and a suite for the delighted Louis XIV, and the *Mercure galant* of Paris forthwith published the two works (cf. p. 235).

A strong conscious interest in such new importations is revealed time

3. Cf. MGG, IV, 756 ff. (Girardon), for a concise summary of French music in the Baroque Era.
4. -CAPELLMEISTER, p. 233 ff.
5. Cf. LANG-WESTERN, p. 379 ff.
6. Cf. BRENET-CONCERTS, p. 50 ff.; LAURENCIE, I, 17 ff., 21 and 23; MELLERS-COUPERIN, pp. 61 ff. and 102 ff.; CUDWORTH-VEIN, p. 29 ff.
7. Cf. BROSSARD, p. 139 ff.; LAURENCIE, I, 59 ff. and 103; PINCHERLE-CORELLI, p. 130 ff.
8. Cf. PINCHERLE-CORELLI, pp. 136, 165, 166, and 168. The date of 1708 given in LAURENCIE, I, 191, is too late.

and again in the remarkable, well-known polemics that Frenchmen began writing after the turn of the 18th century to prove the superiority of French or Italian opera (as but one facet of the much broader polemics between the ancients and the moderns in all the arts).   How early was it that the French author Fontenelle disparaged all instrumental music by implication with his famous, if flippant, remark, "Sonate, que me veux-tu?"[9]—a remark thereafter cited to support a variety of doctrines as late as the mid 19th century?[10]   François Raguenet, in his *Parallèle des Italiens et des Français* (1702), already found much to value in instrumental music, especially the violin playing and trio settings that he had just heard in Rome as against the French styles.[11]   By the time Freneuse (Le Cerf) could oppose this tract in his widely read *Comparaison* (1705), the sonata had become firmly established in France.[12] Parisian publishers were quick to issue the early French sonatas (as were the ever-alert Roger in Amsterdam and Walsh in London).   In fact, in 1713 an unknown writer remarked that "Cantatas and sonatas spring right out of the ground here [in Paris]; no musician arrives without a sonata or cantata in his pocket; there isn't a soul who doesn't want to compose his own set to be engraved and so outsmart the Italians on their own ground."[13]   One might add that Laurencie has even found an orchestral sonata by Marc-Antoine Charpentier.[14]

The composers in this chapter divide into only two groups, since there was no cultivation of the sonata in France before Corelli's music was imported.   There is the first group of some ten composers led by Couperin under the immediate influence of Corelli, and there is the

9. Tracing this remark to its source to date it might be significant, but all efforts have so far been unsuccessful (including a search of two works by him vaguely cited in this connection, *Pluralité des mondes* and *Digression*).   The remark is very characteristic of Fontenelle and could well have been made in a conversation, since its source seems nowhere to be cited.   If so, who first reported it and when?   The earliest references found, not dating from before the end of his century-long life (1657-1757), already speak of it as a famous remark.   They were made by Algarotti in 1755 (cf. OLIVER-ENCYCLOPEDISTS, p. 129) and thereafter by Rousseau, Grimm, D'Alembert, La Borde, Grétry, Burney, Fétis, etc. The remark is not yet cited in the highly pertinent chapter 12 of BOURDELOT & BONNET 1715 or in any of the three parts of Freneuse's *Comparaison* (1705; in BOURDELOT & BONNET 1725, II-IV).   Cf. ECORCHEVILLE-ESTHÉTIQUE, p. 24; WECKERLIN-NOUVEAU, p. 318; STRIFFLING, p. 82; LAURENCIE, III, 192 and 201.

10. E.g., ESCUDIER, II, 88.

11. Cf. STRUNK-READINGS, pp. 486 ff. and 480.

12. Cf. STRUNK-READINGS, p. 502; also, the reprint of all 3 parts of Freneuse's *Comparaison* in BOURDELOT & BONNET 1725, II-IV, especially III, 105 ff., 173 ff., 208 ff.   BOURDELOT & BONNET 1715 (428 ff., 433, and 438 ff.) is generally favorable to the Italian sonata.   Valuable studies of music aesthetics in the *ancien regime* are provided in ECORCHEVILLE-ESTHÉTIQUE, STRIFFLING, and, with particular reference to the sonata and other violin music, LAURENCIE, III, chap. 19.

13. Quoted in POUGIN, p. 159.

14. LAURENCIE, I, 98.

second group, culminating in Leclair, which fell in the late Baroque Era and began to publish from about 1710. Factual information about the violinists and violin music of both groups has been made available—in fact, offered on a silver platter—by not one but several French scholars of the 20th century, most notably by Lionel de la Laurencie, whose monumental, thorough, and systematic study of *L'École française de violon de Lully a Viotti* (Paris, 1922-24) is one of the major contributions to French biography, to the history of the sonata, and to instrumental music in general. Pioneer work in the dating of French publications from 1654 to 1789, based on royal privileges rather than the publishers' catalogs used more recently by Miss Johansson for the later 18th century, had already been done by Brenet.[15] Other recent authorities on French violin music include Marc Pincherle and Arthur Pougin. But we are distinctly less well off when we come to studies on flute, cello, keyboard, or other categories of French sonatas. Moreover, the availability of the sonatas themselves, in whatever category, is generally less than that of the studies, being about on a par with that of the Baroque sonatas in England.

Couperin "le Grand"

François Couperin "le Grand" (1668-1733), one of the chief names in all French music, came from a family almost as productive musically as that of J. S. Bach, whom he preceded both in birth and death by 17 years.[16] The relatively little that can be confirmed about Couperin's life amounts largely to a story of his increasing success and renown as organist, clavecinist, and composer at the court of Louis XIV (from 1693) and of the young Louis XV. He left a total of nine different sonatas that are now known. These fill the equivalent of about one volume in the excellent, modern, complete Lyrebird edition of 12 volumes,[17] as against three other volumes of chamber music, the four volumes of the four *livres de clavecin,* the one volume of two organ Masses, the two volumes of sacred and secular vocal music, and the one volume containing the two theoretical treatises.

15. BRENET-LIBRAIRIE, supplemented by CUCÜEL-DOCUMENTS; cf. JOHANSSON, I, 4 ff. HOPKINSON has supplied clues for dates from 1700 that have been helpful in the present survey, too.

16. BOUVET and TIERSOT-COUPERIN concern at least several members of the family, while TESSIER-COUPERIN, BRUNOLD-COUPERIN, and MELLERS-COUPERIN concentrate on Couperin le Grand, the last study including comprehensive and enlightening discussions of his aesthetic and social environment and of all his works. Further bibliography in MGG, II, 1737 and 1729 (Reimann).

17. COUPERINm, the sonatas all being in vols. IX and X (both Gastoué). CAUCHIE is a thematic index to this edition. MELLERS-COUPERIN, pp. 374 ff. and 377 ff., provides useful but not bibliographically detailed title indices and a list of other, partial editions. A new, practical, performing edition is much to be desired.

Four of Couperin's sonatas exist in a MS in Paris dating from about 1692,[18] and these plus two others exist in a MS in Lyon that may date from about the same time.[19] *La Pucelle, La Visionnaire,* and *L'Astrée* were published some 34 years later with few revisions other than new titles appropriate to their collective title of *Les Nations, Sonades et suites de simphonies en trio* (1726)—*La Françoise, L'Espagnole,* and *La Piemontaise,* respectively.[20] These three and one other, much later and more mature sonata, *L'Impériale,*[21] "merely serve," in Couperin's own words,[22] "as preludes or kinds of introductions" to the four suites that comprise *Les Nations,* although they are quite as developed and extended as his other sonatas. The remaining three sonatas to be found in the two early MSS—*La Steinquerque, La Sultane,* and *La Superbe*—were not published until modern times.[23] Two other, very different, programmatic sonatas were published in Couperin's later years. *Le Parnasse ou l'apothéose de Corelli, grande sonade en trio*[24] follows the ten "Nouveaux Concerts" in the collection of 1724 known as *Les Goûts-réünis. Concert instrumental sous le titre d'Apothéose, composé à la mémoire de l'incomparable Monsieur de Lully,*[25] in which the title "Sonade" actually appears only over the group of four concluding movements in church sequence (*La Paix du Parnasse . . . Sonade en trio*), was published separately in 1725. All of Couperin's published sonatas appeared "A Paris, Chés l'Auteur." None seems to have appeared in contemporary reprints, local or foreign.

It is hard to think of another front-rank composer so mindful of and articulate about his historical position as was Couperin, whether on the subject of his priority as a French sonata composer, his justification of the spelling "sonade," his performance practices, the disputes over national styles, the programmatic content of his music, or many another topic. Certain of his prefaces that bear particularly on the sonata are too significant not to be quoted at least in part here, as they have often been quoted elsewhere. In his "Aveu de l'Auteur au Public" in *Les Nations* (1726) he wrote,[26]

---

18. Cf. BIBLIOTHÈQUE NATIONALE, IV, 157.
19. MELLERS-COUPERIN, p. 375 ff., offers conjectural composition dates for each of the sonatas, but the only tangible evidence lies in *La Steinquerque,* last in the MS of 4 sonatas, which was apparently written to commemorate a victory by the Field-Marshall of Luxembourg on August 4, 1692 (cf. LAURENCIE, I, 63, and LAURENCIE-INCONNUES; COUPERINm, IX, 1 ff., and X, 3 ff.).
20. Cf. TIERSOT-NATIONS.
21. All in COUPERINm, IX, 9, 65, 140, and 225.
22. COUPERINm, IX, 7 ff.
23. *Ibid.,* X, 161, 186, and 211.
24. In COUPERINm, X, 7.
25. COUPERINm, X, 53.
26. *Ibid.,* IX, 7 ff.

It has already been several years since some of these trios were composed. Several of those manuscripts have circulated, which I distrust because of the negligence of copyists. From time to time I have added to their number, and I believe that the lovers of truth will be pleased with them. The first sonata in this collection was also the first that I composed and the first that was composed in France. The story of it is curious in itself.

Charmed by those [sonatas] of Signor Corelli, whose works I shall love as long as I live, much as [I shall love] the French works of Monsieur de Lully, I attempted to compose one, which I [then] had performed in the concert-hall where I had heard those of Corelli. Knowing the greediness of the French for foreign novelties above all else, and lacking confidence in myself, I did me a very neat service by means of a convenient little ruse. I pretended that a kinsman of mine [Marc-Roger Normand, grandson of the first Charles Couperin[27]]—in the service of the King of Sardinia, to be exact —had sent me a sonata by a recent Italian composer. I rearranged the letters of my name so that it became an Italian name, which I used instead ["Coperuni" and "Pernucio" are possible anagrams suggested by Tessier[28]]. The sonata was devoured eagerly and I felt vindicated by it. Meanwhile, that [success] gave me [further] courage. I wrote others; and my Italian-ized name brought much applause to me, under the disguise. Fortunately, my sonatas won enough favor that the deception did not embarrass me at all. I have compared these sonatas with those that I wrote since, and have neither changed nor added much of importance. I have only added some big suites of pieces to which the sonatas serve merely as preludes or kinds of intro-ductions.

Apropos of and prior to this statement Couperin had expressed himself on the subject of contrasting national styles in *Les Goûts-réünis* (among several instances),[29] much as had the cosmopolitans Telemann in Hamburg, Georg Muffat in Salzburg, and even G. B. Vitali (through his later dances) in Modena. His words add up to a veritable composer's credo.

The Italian style and the French style have divided the Republic of Music (in France) for a long time. For my part, I have always judged things on their merits without regard either to authors or nations; and the first Italian sonatas, which appeared in Paris more than thirty years ago [i.e., before 1694] and aroused me to compose some like them, did not dampen my spirits nor discredit either the works of Lully or those of my [own] ancestors, which will always be more admirable than imitable. Thus, by earning the right to my neutrality I move steadily ahead under the fortunate guidance that has helped me up to now. . . .

But in the title of the movement that concludes *Apothéose de Lulli*[30] Couperin made this etymological distinction:

The Peace of Parnassus, based on the conditions, argued by the French Muses, that when one speaks their [the French] language there, he shall

27. TIERSOT-COUPERIN, p. 74.   28. TESSIER-COUPERIN, p. 26.
29. COUPERINm, VIII (Schaeffner), 5.   30. *Ibid.*, X, 88.

henceforth say *Sonade* [and] *Cantade* just as he [now] says Ballade, Sérénade, etc. Sonade en Trio.

Although Couperin did finally use the setting of "solo" and *b. c.* in his *Pieces de violes avec la basse chifrée* (1728), his nine sonatas are all in SSB/bass settings except for *La Sultane, Sonade en quator,* which is an SSBB/bass setting.[31]   In *La Sultane* the "1re. Basse de viole" is an independent part more often than not.   But the "2e. Basse" and the *concertante* bass parts "d'Archet" in the eight sonatas "en trio" only rarely depart from the *b. c.* (as in the opening of *Apothéose de Lulli*). The clavecin was probably the preferred instrument for the realization of the *b. c.,* since Couperin himself played that part.[32]   Two violins are usually assumed to be his intention for the upper parts, the more so as he was deliberately introducing Italian styles.   But, especially in the sonatas, when there are any indications at all the two upper parts are simply marked first and second upper part ("1er. dessus" and "2e. dessus").   And in another of his noteworthy prefaces, his "Avis" to *Apothéose de Lulli,*[33] Couperin makes very clear his practical interest in a variety of combinations, violins being but one of these:

This trio, like *Apothéose de Corelli* and the completed book of trios that I hope to issue next July [*Les Nations*], can be played on two clavecins quite as on all other instruments. I perform them with my family and with my students with excellent results—that is, by playing the first upper part and the bass on one of the clavecins, and the second [upper part] with the same bass in unison on the other [clavecin]. The fact is that that [method] calls for two copies instead of one, and two clavecins as well. But I find in addition that it is often easier to bring together these two instruments than four persons who make their profession out of music [etc., including ways of compensating for the lesser sustaining power of the clavecin as against the bowed instruments].

In short, Couperin's trios might also be regarded as being among the earliest examples of the sonata for two keyboard instruments, along with the unrealized ones by Pasquini and the piece of about 1705 by Mattheson.   Further, more skeptical remarks by Couperin on the transfer of the Italian violin sonata to the clavecin occur in his celebrated treatise, *L'Art de toucher le clavecin* (1716-17).[34]   And one may note such an instruction as "Badinage pour le Clavecin, si l'on veut," in the finale of *L'Espagnole.*[35]

Couperin's sonatas average 6 to 8 movements, whereas his chamber suites average 7 to 9.   *Apothéose de Lulli* is exceptional in having 16

31. The sonatas are discussed in MELLERS-COUPERIN, chap. 6.
32. Cf. MELLERS-COUPERIN, p. 234 ff.   33. COUPERINm, X, 51 (and cf. p. 1 ff.).
34. COUPERIN-L'ART, pp. 22 and 23.   35. COUPERINm, IX, 83.

movements, although, as noted earlier, only the last four make up its
final church sonata proper (*La Paix du Parnasse*). Except in this and
the other two programmatic sonatas (*L'Apothéose de Corelli* and *La
Steinquerque*) the S-F-S-F core of the church sonata is present among
the movements, much as the standard core of four dances is present in
the suites. These core movements adhere to the usual metric and structural characteristics, too. Couperin used no dance titles in his sonatas,
no binary designs with repeats except in *Apothéose de Lulli,* and none
of the rondeaux or chaconnes that crown some of the ensemble suites so
effectively. The nonprogrammatic titles are such as "Gravement,"
"Gayement," "Lentement," "Vivement," and so on, with no further
descriptive terms than perhaps a "Tendrement," "Gracieusement," or
"Affectueusement." Dance traits do appear, of course—for instance,
those of the saraband (e.g., *L'Impériale,* third movement), gigue (e.g.,
finale of *La Piemontoise*), or minuet (Ex. 76). The master of the
French dance and follower of Lully could do no less. However,

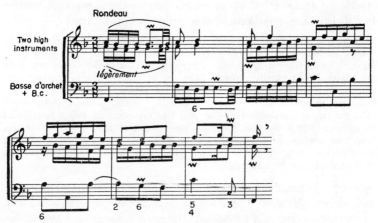

Ex. 76. From the fourth movement of *L'Impériale* by
François Couperin (after the original edition).

Couperin's sonatas are generally serious pieces, with considerable use of
polyphony, as in several complete fugues (e.g., the finale of *L'Espagnole*), and with numerous movements that reveal expressive depth and
broad lines. *Apothéose de Lulli* is exceptional for being almost entirely
homophonic and for using as many as six different, nearly related keys
in the 16 movements. The virtuosity of Couperin's clavecin music or of
the foremost violinists of his day is only rarely to be found in

Couperin's sonatas, although the ornamentation naturally makes significant demands on the performer's technical equipment.

In *La Steinquerque* the rather shallow programmatic content is chiefly that of the battle fanfare in the first and fifth movements ("Bruit de guerre" and "Movement de fanfares"). In *L'Apothéose de Corelli* the successive movements describe, according to their charming inscriptions, the ceremony of elevating Corelli to the heights of Parnassus —his request to be received, his joy at being received, his drinking at the fountain of Hippocrene (a wonderfully flowing, gentle piece), his resulting enthusiasm (with bold runs unusual in the sonatas), the sleep that follows, Corelli's awakening as the muses place him next to Apollo, and finally the thanks he offers.

But the 16 movements of *Apothéose de Lulli* have a much more developed and specific programme, one that clarifies in several ways Couperin's dedication to an artful blending of the contested national styles. First, Lully joins with the lyric shades in the Elysian fields ("Gravement," G minor, 2/2, steady falling quarter-notes), followed by an "Air for the same" (Gracieusement," G minor, 3/4, minuet style, binary with repeats). Next, Mercury flies in to announce the coming of Apollo ("Tres viste," B flat, 6/8, rapid passages). Apollo arrives to offer his violin to Lully and place him on Parnassus ("Noblement," B flat, 2/2, binary with repeats). What we have had so far, as Mellers suggests,[36] are French operatic devices transferred to chamber music. Now suppressed mutterings are heard from Lully's contemporaries ("Viste," E flat, 2/4, agitated 16th-note passages), followed by expressive "complaints from the same" played by flutes or very subdued violins ("Dolemment," C minor, 3/4, binary with repeats, in the style of a slow minuet), and then the elevation of Lully to Parnassus ("Tres légérement," G, 6/8, imitative for the first time in this work). From here on, Corelli is present, too, giving the occasion for frequent juxtapositions and alternations of Italian and French styles. A gentle, deferential reception is extended to Lully by Corelli and the Italian muses ("Largo," G minor, 4/4, dotted and tied notes, poignant suspensions and resolutions in the Italian manner). Lully gives thanks to Apollo in "a symmetrical opera aria which illustrates the absorption of the Lullian air into the tonally more developed Italian arias of Handel"[37] ("Gracieusement," G, 3/4, binary with repeats). Apollo persuades Lully and Corelli that the reconciliation of French and Italian styles should lead to ideal music ("Essai en forme d'Ouverture, Élégamment, sans lenteur," G, 2/2, French overture in the sequence S-F-S, with Lully and the French muses

36. -COUPERIN, p. 123.   37. MELLERS-COUPERIN, p. 124.

Ex. 77.   From the opening of *La Paix du Parnasse* . . .
Sonade en trio in *Apothéose de Lulli* by François Couperin
(after the original edition).

playing one upper part, Corelli and the Italian muses the other).   There
follow two airs for two (unaccompanied) violins, the first with Lully
playing the theme and Corelli accompanying, and the second vice versa,
each according to his native styles of melody, ornamentation, and
harmony (G and G minor, 3/4, binary with repeats; as always in this
work, with the old French G clef on the first line for Lully and the
modern G clef for Corelli).   Finally comes the four-movement, church-
type "Sonade en trio," a strong work in itself and one showing distinct
mixtures of the two national styles[38] (Ex. 77).

Rebel, Duval, and Others

Another early sonata composer in France was the violinist **Jean-Fery
Rebel** (1666-1747).   One of the many octogenarians throughout French
music history, Rebel was also a member of a long line of French mu-
sicians.[39]   As a young prodigy, he studied violin and composition with
Lully and became a member and ultimately a director of the King's
Twenty-four Violins.   His compositions include dramatic, dance, and
chamber music.   Among ten items in the last two categories, three
published between 1712 and 1720 have a total of 25 pieces entitled
"Sonata."   Earliest of the sonata items is *Recueil de douze sonates à
II et III parties,* published in 1712-13 but evidently composed in 1695.[40]
Containing 7 SS/bass followed by 5 S/bass sonatas, this set thus
contains some of the earliest "solo" violin sonatas from France (along
with those to be mentioned by Brossard and La Guerre).   Each of
these sonatas has a literary or mythological title such as Couperin used—
"la Vénus," "le Tombeau de M. de Lully," "la Toute-Belle," and so on.
The sonatas have 5 to 8 movements in no set order, with tempo or

---

38. Cf. MELLERS-COUPERIN, p. 125.
39. LAURENCIE-DYNASTIE and LAURENCIE, I, 71 ff., are the chief studies (both
with examples).
40. Cf. LAURENCIE, I, 77.

character titles, but not dance titles except for a "Grande Chaconne" in Sonata 11.

Rebel's second sonata collection, 12 *Sonates à violon seul mellées de plusieurs récits pour la viole,* was also published in 1713.[41] The violin solo part is now in the Italian rather than the French G clef of the first set. The first 6 sonatas have 4 or 5 movements in which tempo or descriptive titles predominate over dance titles. These sonatas have several movements with those typically 17th-century *concertante* parts for the viola da gamba (the "récits" in the title), varying from elaboration of the *b. c.* to an independent part. No doubt, Rebel knew the several books of suites (*Pièces*) that Marin Marais had published from 1686 for one or more violas da gamba and *b. c.*[42] The last 6 sonatas are more consistently court types, with nothing but dances except for 3 slow introductory movements. They all have S/- rather than some SB/bass settings. In other words, these 6 "Sonates" differ little from Rebel's *Pièces pour le violon* that he published in 1705.

La Terpsichore, Sonate by Rebel (1720) is an orchestral work for violins, flutes, and *b. c.*[43] Apparently it was not actually used for the dance but does contain numerous scoring and programmatic instructions.

The few available examples of Rebel's sonatas reveal a good sense of line, relatively simple harmonic and rhythmic structure, more than average sharing of material by the bass, somewhat excessive use of sequence, and modest technical requirements. The dances in particular show Rebel's heavy debt to Lully. Freneuse's estimate of Rebel seems not unjust today. After making his oft-quoted remark, "What joy, what good opinion of himself has not the man who knows something from Corelli's Op. 5, gradually making everything French look bad by comparison," Freneuse begrudgingly allows some beauties in the Italian sonata.[44] But turning to Rebel, he says,

We [the French] claim Rebel and do not do him the injustice of supposing that his sonatas would make a hit in Italy. Rebel has indeed caught some of the flare and fire of the Italians; but he has had the good taste and sense to temper these by the wisdom and gentleness of the French, and he has abstained from those frightening and monstrous cadenzas ["chûtes"] that are the delight of the Italians.

Mademoiselle Élisabeth-Claude Jacquet de La Guerre

another prodigy and a talented clavecinist, was a favorite composer of

41. GATES-REBEL is a helpful study of this set, with examples. Mod. ed.: Son. in D minor from second collection, JONGEN & DEBROUX-REBELm (with title page reproduced).

42. Cf. EINSTEIN-GAMBA, pp. 37 ff., 47 ff., and 79 ff. (2 complete examples).

43. Cf. LAURENCIE-DYNASTIE, p. 277.

44. BOURDELOT & BONNET 1725, II, 95-96.

Louis XIV.[45] Besides sacred and dramatic music and *Pièces de clavecin qui peuvent se joüer sur le Viollon* (1707), she left two sets of six sonatas each, or a total of 4 SSB/- and 8 S/- or SB/bass sonatas. Her first set, containing the 4 SSB/- and 2 of the SB/bass sonatas, was left in MSS dating back at least to 1695, for Brossard says he copied them in that year and that "they are delicious."[46] Thus, La Guerre was another of the first composers of the "solo" violin sonata in France. Her second set, published with the clavecin-violin pieces of 1707, contains 6 *Sonates bour le viollon et pour le clavecin* (*b. c.*). Four to 9 movements are found in her sonatas, with no fixed plan. There are both dance and tempo or descriptive titles. Sonata 4 of the published set begins with an "Ouverture à la française" that leaves no doubt of Lully's influence in spite of some obviously intentional Italianisms, including imitations of Corelli. Laurencie quotes strong contemporary endorsements of La Guerre's sonatas but himself finds a certain dryness in the lines and harmonies, in spite of some ingenious modulations.[47] Tessier, on the other hand, calls La Guerre's sonatas "among the best of those which the imitation of Corelli produced in France quite at the end of the 17th century."[48] No modern editions are available as a basis for further comment here.

Sébastien de Brossard (1655-1730) lived primarily in Strasbourg, which was then under French control.[49] A lutist, he can be mentioned only briefly here, although several of his varied activities are pertinent to the sonata. First of all, he left two SSB/- and two incomplete S/bass sonatas in MSS.[50] The SSB/bass sonatas are dated 1695. If the "solo" sonatas actually date from the same year, Brossard would be the third among our earliest composers of this type in France. These four sonatas have not been made available, but are described by Laurencie as very close to Lully in style and technical limitations. The two complete SSB/bass sonatas are in five and four movements of no set plan. Second, as author of one of the earliest music dictionaries, Brossard wrote one of the first important accounts of the sonata.[51] As we have seen (p. 24 ff.), this account, first published in Paris in 1701, shows him to have been remarkably aware of earlier and current trends, including a clear

45. Cf. LAURENCIE, I, 121 ff. (with biographic data derived from the researches of Brenet).
46. LAURENCIE, I, 124. VIOLLIER begins with a brief discussion of this set. Thematic index in BIBLIOTHÈQUE NATIONALE, VI, 58 ff.
47. LAURENCIE, I, 125 ff.
48. GROVE, V, 15.
49. Cf. LAURENCIE, I, 68 ff. (with biographic information based on the researches of Brenet).
50. Thematic index in BIBLIOTHÈQUE NATIONALE, III, 144.
51. BROSSARD, p. 139 ff.

distinction between the church and court types. However, his suggestion that Corelli's sonatas be examined for proper models did not appear until the third edition, published by Roger of Amsterdam about seven years later. It is also worth recalling that Brossard still identified the word "canzone" with "sonata," but chiefly as a title for the second, fugal movement.[52]

Lastly, Brossard must be recalled here in connection with the fine library he collected. It was he who preserved the important SS/bass collection listed here as ANTH. ROSTm.[53] He bought it in 1698 from the estate of the Strasbourg curate François Rost, adding these remarks in the *b. c.* part some 20 years later:[54]

A most curious collection of at least 151 sonatas, allemandes, fantasias, and other pieces composed by the most illustrious authors who flourished around the middle of the past century—that is, from about 1640 to 1688. Of the authors 27 are named at the beginnings of 63 pieces undoubtedly composed by them. . . . As for the 88 other pieces without a name at the beginning, most could be credited to some of these 27, as may be judged by the style. . . . This excellent collection, which is a veritable treasure of its sort, as extensive as it is unique. . . .

Interestingly, ANTH. ROSTm does contain two sonatas[55] by one composer who was probably French, **Charles Rosier.** Rosier must have anticipated even Couperin in the writing of sonatas, but was apparently in Köln at the time he left some 26 sonatas *a 3* and *a 6*.[56] On the other hand, a co-citizen of Brossard in Strasbourg, the supposedly German-born organist **Georgio Rauch** (?-1710), is not represented in ANTH. ROSTm but did leave a set of 11 SSB/- and one SSAAB/bass sonatas, *Cithera orphei,* published in Strasbourg in 1697.[57] These are well-developed pieces that have two to five movements based mainly on the church plan.

56a

"All the Parisian composers, especially the organists, at that time [turn of the 18th century] had the fever, so to speak, of writing sonatas in the Italian manner," wrote Brossard.[58] One such organist-composer was **Louis-Nicolas Clérambault** (1676-1749), who left six sonatas and

52. BROSSARD, p. 16. Cf. CROCKER, p. 16 ff.
53. Cf. BIBLIOTHÈQUE NATIONALE, VIII (Vm⁷ 1099), 35 ff.; also, H. J. Moser, "Eine pariser Quelle zur Wiener Triosonate des ausgehenden 17. Jahrhunderts: Der Codex Rost," in *Festschrift Wilhelm Fischer* (Universität Innsbruck, 1956), pp. 75-81.
54. From a MS copy made by Professor Ross Lee Finney.
55. Thematic index in BIBLIOTHÈQUE NATIONALE, VIII, 178.
56. Cf. EITNER-QL, VIII, 318; MGG, IV, 777 (Girardon); MEYER-NIEDERLÄNDISCHEN, p. 264 ff. See p. 343 above. NIEMÖLLER-ROSIERm, which appeared too recently for use here, includes mod. eds. of one SS/bass son. (1691) and one orchestral (trumpet) son. (*ca.* 1700), and a preface with reference to a new study; Rosier's dates are given as 1640?-1725 and his probable nationality as Dutch (contrary to the foregoing statement).
57. Cf. EITNER-QL, VIII, 136; NEF-DEUTSCHEN, p. 31 ff.; PIRRO-ALLEMAGNE, p. 1007.
58. Quoted in LAURENCIE, I, 143.

a one-movement "Simphonia" *a 5* (No. 4) in MS about the first decade of the 18th century.[59]   Recalling the similar equation of terms in Italy at this time, the six sonatas all actually have the compound title "Simphonia, Sonata."   Four of them also have individual literary titles such as "L'Abondance" in Sonata 3.   Sonatas 1, 2, and 7 are in SS/bass settings,[60] whereas 3, 5, and 6 are in S/bass settings.   Four to six movements are used in each sonata, with some tempo and some dance titles.   Typical is the polyphonic outlook of the organist, with the second movements being decidedly fugal and the others more imitative than usual.   The technical requirements are modest and the ideas somewhat conservative and plain.   But the flow is convincing both rhythmically and tonally, and the forms are the broadest we have seen thus far in France.   In view of these traits and Clérambault's importance to church and keyboard music, a fuller representation of his sonatas in modern editions is certainly in order.

Together with Clérambault, the organist **Jean-François Dandrieu** (1682-1738) should be noted here.[61]   Best known for his *Pièces de clavecin,* Dandrieu published a *Livre de sonates en trio,* Op. 1 (1705), 62a   and a *Livre de sonates a violon seul,* Op. 2 (1733 or later).[62]   The six sonatas of Op. 1 have four or five movements of the church type and order.   Their setting is often SSB/- rather than SS/bass, with an almost independent *concertante* bass.   In either setting the writing, like Clérambault's, is more polyphonic than average.   The six sonatas of Op. 2 are actually six suites of six dances each, with all the dance titles and other terms in Italian spellings.   Dandrieu's writing in the sonatas is distinctive—light, precise, and sensitive, with original turns of melody and interesting harmony.

Another member of the Twenty-four Violins and one of the few Frenchmen skilled enough to play Corelli's "solo" sonatas while the latter were first being introduced in France was **François Duval** (*ca.* 1673-1728).[63]   In the matter of priority in France, Duval may also be cited as the first Frenchman actually to receive and utilize a "Privilège du Roy" (1704) for the purpose of having his sonatas published,[64] although we have already noted five French composers who

59. Cf. LAURENCIE, I, 143 ff. (with biographic information based on Pirro's researches).   Thematic index in BIBLIOTHÈQUE NATIONALE, IV, 135 ff.   No detailed study has been done; cf. MGG, II, 1496 ff. (Girardon).

60. Mod. eds.: Son. 7 in E minor ("La Magnifique"), PEYROT & REBUFAT-CLÉRAMBAULTm; Son. 2 in G ("La Felicité") DEBROUX & WAGNER-CLÉRAMBAULTm.

61. Cf. LAURENCIE, I, 151 ff., with biographic information derived from Pirro's researches.

62. Mod. eds. of 2 full sons. are cited in LAURENCIE, III, 248, one from each set.

63. Cf. LAURENCIE, I, 102 ff.

64. Cf. BRENET-LIBRAIRIE, p. 419.

had left sonatas in MS by 1695. The publication of Duval's *Premier Livre de sonates et autres pièces pour le violon et la basse* in Paris in 1704 was, in effect, the first officially sanctioned acknowledgment of the French taste for such Italianisms. As we shall see, the year was the same as that in which the Italian Mascitti first had sonatas published in Paris. Furthermore, Duval may be recognized as the most prolific among the early sonata composers in France, with no fewer than six collections being published after Book 1 in the next 16 years (1706, 1707, 1708, 1715, 1718, and 1720).

All seven sets by Duval are in S/bass setting except Book 2, in SS/bass setting.[65] The composer mixed suites and sonatas in some of his sets, with a tendency to equate the terms as titles in Book 1. The average number of movements is four, most often in the church sequence of S-F-S-F, although dance and related titles occur at least as often as tempo and descriptive titles. The old French G clef is used in the first four sets for the solo instrument(s), and the newer Italian G clef in the last three sets. In spite of the composer's interest in the Italian sonata, he adhered in all the sets to French terms, generally similar to those Couperin used. The piquancy of these terms increases with the later sets, the last two having the collective titles *Amusemens pour la chambre* and *Les Idées musiciennes* respectively. Laurencie calls attention to the headings "Démocrite" and "Heraclite" over two sonatas in Book 6, titles which he says were often used in the 18th century to express contrasts.[66] The standard dances, rondeaux, and variations on recurring basses are among the lighter movements to be found in Duval's sonatas, including "Variations dans le goût de la trompette" (Son. 8, Bk. 4).

Both Duval's contemporaries and some later writers have pointed to a certain mediocrity and dullness in his sonatas.[67] But Laurencie does call attention to the suppleness and variety of his rhythms and to technical advances notable for France at the time, if not for Italy or Germany. Among these advances are new bowing styles, double-stops, and numerous passages in the third or extended third position. The few available examples by Duval reveal charming tunes, simple but effective harmony, fluent rhythm, and a generally light yet dignified style that is not without individuality for all the lack of any unusual or exceptional traits.

Another member of the Twenty-four Violins and of a whole family

65. Among mod. eds.: Sons. 1 & 2, Bk. 6, SCHOTT ANTIQUAm, no. 4168 (Ruf, with preface) ; for 1 son. each from Bks. 3 and 5 cf. LAURENCIE, III, 248.
66. LAURENCIE, I, 109.
67. Cf. LAURENCIE, I, 107 ff. and 110; VIDAL, II, 272; MOSER-VIOLINSPIEL, p. 173 ff.

of musicians identified by his surname, **Joseph Marchand** "le fils" (*ca.* 1673-1747) left but one publication that is known, *Suites de pièces, mêlées de sonatas, pour le violon et la basse, qui ont exécutez plusieurs fois devant Sa Majesté* (Paris, 1707).[68] This set has a semantic interest, for it seems to equate suite and sonata even more than Duval's Book 1, published three years earlier. However, one can detect a tendency this time to use "suite" in its literal sense to mean a series (of pieces) and "sonata" to mean, once more, the introductory movement. There is much variety in the number of movements (six to nine) and their types (dance, free, variation, and fugal). The technical requirements are generally slight. No modern edition is known here.

68. Cf. LAURENCIE, I, 159 ff.

Chapter 17

France from about 1710 to 1750

Composers Mostly under Italian Influences
(Mascitti, Senallié, F. Francoeur)

In the later Baroque Era the sheer quantity of French sonatas is greatly increased, no doubt reflecting a heightened interest in chamber music and such new activities as the Concerts spirituels (founded in 1725). Nearly 35 sonata composers active in France make up our other, second group. Culminating in the pre-eminent violinist Leclair, they show the Italian influence now in full force. Some of them actually studied in Italy, among them pupils of Corelli and pupils of his pupils. Others show the increasing influence of Vivaldi. During this period the violin and cello came into such full sway and such brilliant technical development that the amusing and informative essay of Hubert Le Blanc (Amsterdam, 1740),[1] intended to stem the tide in favor of the more venerable viola da gamba, must be regarded as a hopeless failure. Furthermore, the "solo" sonata soon attained a preponderance over the "trio" type quite as it did in Italy. On the other hand, marked French influences continued to show, too, in this period first of the aged Louis XIV, then the Regency, and then Louis XV. One direction these took is that of the keyboard sonata "with violin accompaniment," which derived at least as much from the important literature of *pièces de clavecin* as from the imported or adapted violin sonata. But this genre was to become one of the main roads to the sonata of the Classic Era. For that reason, although nearly all if not all of their sonatas were composed before the middle of the 18th century, the discussions of the important violinists Mondonville and Guillemain, two of the pioneers in the genre, are deferred until we get to pre-Classic composers.[2] To be sure, Rameau, the best known of all French musicians in this period,

1. LE BLANC. Cf. BRENET-CONCERTS, p. 154 ff.
2. Cf. NEWMAN-ACCOMPANIED.

belongs in that category, too, so far as he relates to the sonata at all. But it happens, in any case, that he wrote no actual sonatas, his nearest work to such being his *Pièces de clavecin en concerts* of 1741.[3]

We may begin in this second group with the first among the surprisingly few Italians of the Baroque Era who produced sonatas while resident in France. He was the excellent violinist **Michel Mascitti** (*ca.* 1664-1760; called simply Michel, Miquel, or Michelly by his contemporaries). Born in Naples and taught by Corelli in Rome, Mascitti arrived in Paris about 1704 and remained there until he died, almost a centenarian.[4] His Op. 1 was published in Paris that year, the same that Duval's first publication of sonatas by a Frenchman took place. But the eight further sonata publications by Mascitti were spread over the next 34 years (1706, 1707, 1711, 1714, 1722, 1727, 1731, and 1738), which fact explains why he is listed here among our second group.

4a

All of Mascitti's sonatas are scored for violin and *b. c.* except three in SSB/bass setting and three with an optional second violin part in the latter half of Op. 1 and the four sonatas *a 6* that conclude Op. 7, equated with "concerti" in the title and in a remark inserted by the composer.[5] Throughout the sonatas the number of movements averages four.[6] The church plan of S-F-S-F predominates. However, dance titles are intermixed with tempo or descriptive titles or even combined as in "Sarabanda andante." The twelfth and final sonata of Op. 5 is a "Divertissement" in nine sections, each with a descriptive title ("Grand air," "Les Vents," and so on). Occasionally the movements of a sonata are thematically related (e.g., Son. 1, Op. 1). Corelli is obviously the direct model for Mascitti. Besides several more instances of themes and movements that recall Sonata 1 in Corelli's Op. 5, there are some persistent melodic similarities[7] (Ex. 78). Furthermore, it was no coincidence that Mascitti dedicated his Op. 5 to the Cardinal "Pierre" Ottoboni who was one of Corelli's chief patrons in Rome.[8] But he makes a special point (in his preface to Op. 2) of fusing the Italian style with "si belles choses" that he found in French music.[9] The success of his sonatas in his own day is evidenced by their several reprints throughout the century,[10] their existence in numerous libraries today, and the high praise for them to be found in the writings of Daquin, Le Blanc, and La

---

3. Cf. Rameau's own words on this matter, quoted in LAURENCIE, II, 160.
4. Cf. LAURENCIE, I, 132 ff.; PINCHERLE-CORELLI, pp. 113 and 135.
5. Cf. LAURENCIE, I, 132, 136, and 139.
6. Thematic index of Opp. 2 and 5 in HAAS-ESTENSISCHEN, p. 95 ff. Mod eds. of 4 sons. are listed in ALTMANN, p. 241 (including MOFFAT-VIOLINM I, no. 7, and II, no. 24).
7. Cf. LAURENCIE, I, 139 ff.   8. Cf. PINCHERLE-CORELLI, p. 153.
9. Cf. LAURENCIE, I, 137.   10. Cf. BRITISH PRINTED, II, 108 ff.

Ex. 78. From the opening of Sonata 4, Op. 3, by Michel Mascitti (after the Walsh edition, *ca.* 1712 [SMITH-WALSH, no. 432]).

Borde, among others.[11]   Today these sonatas seem to depart from Corelli's only in certain slight Gallicisms and "modernizations" in the melodic lines and harmony.   The technical demands are about equal to those in Duval's sonatas but no greater.

Another excellent Italian violinist who was born in Naples and came to France in the early 1700's was **Giovanni Antonio Piani** "dit Des Planes napolitano" (? to at least 1760).[12]   In the service of the Bourbon family in Toulouse, Piani departed to join the Imperial court in Vienna in 1721.   Piani left at least one set of sonatas for violin and *b. c.,* published in 1712.[13]   In these the four-movement S-F-S-F plan predominates, with some tempo and some dance titles.   The solo lines, especially in the improvisatory "Preludio" movements, are unusually ornate, by virtue both of copious *agréments* and frequent decorative passages.   But most interest has centered on the attention to performance practices of the time.   Piani's preface refers to bowings, swell and diminish signs, articulation, and fingering.   Furthermore, his music contains frequent and precise dynamic instructions.   None of his sonatas has appeared in a modern edition.

The capable violinist **Jean-Baptiste Senallié** (1687?-1730) was the son and successor of a member of the Twenty-four Violins.[14]   Among

14a

11. Cf. LE BLANC, i, 45, 47, and 48; LA BORDE, III, 522; LAURENCIE, I, 136 ff.
12. Cf. EITNER-QL, VII, 428; MOSER-VIOLINSPIEL, p. 169 ff.; SCHMIDL, II, 272; LAURENCIE, I, 191 ff. (with biographic errors).
13. Cf. BIBLIOTHÈQUE NATIONALE, VII, 129.
14. Cf. LAURENCIE, I, 165 ff.

his teachers were Corelli's pupil Anet and T. A. Vitali in Modena, where, as Laurencie has confirmed,[15] Senallié served at court from about 1717-19. Apparently Senallié won praise for both his playing and his sonatas not only in France but on the home ground of the Italians themselves. Yet the fact that he was another proponent of "les goûts réünis" is already hinted in two of his royal privileges for music (1710 and 1722) that specify "sonates françaises." These must have been so called with reference to the "cantates françaises" that were currently appearing as counteraction to the new craze for Italian music.[16] Although the second of these privileges specifies pieces "à deux et trois parties," only sonatas for violin and *b. c.* by Senallié are known. He was another of those composers who limited his production so neatly to one category, leaving exactly 50 S/bass sonatas in 5 published sets of 10 each (1710, 1712, 1716, 1721, and 1727). At least a dozen of these sonatas have been made available in modern editions.[17]

Nearly 80 per cent of Senallié's sonatas are in 4 movements, the others being in 5. The S-F-S-F scheme predominates. Dance titles are mixed with descriptive or tempo titles in the same sonata, all terms being in Italian. Frequently the movements of a sonata are related by similar incipits. Corelli's influence is not so pronounced here as in Mascitti's sonatas. But it is present in the bittersweet pathos of the slow melodic lines, which is probably the chief appeal of Senallié's sonatas, and in the chordal figuration of more rapid passages. One difference is a more distinct tunefulness, even in Book 1 (Ex. 79). Perhaps the most pronounced French trait is the minuet-like air ("Aria") that occurs in so many of the sonatas. Senallié uses double-stops which are about equal in difficulty to those of Duval and Mascitti. But his use of the positions soon surpasses theirs, attaining the seventh position by Book 3 ("Allegro assai" of Son. 10). Cadenza-like passages over a "tasto solo," frequent trills, and up to 24 notes in a single bow are other technical applications to be found in his sonatas. Furthermore, the *b. c.* part, intended for the viola da gamba, was often very elaborate, to the point of distressing the contemporary opponents of this instrument and the *b. c.* in general.[18]

Louis-Antoine Dornel (*ca.* 1685-1765?[19]) is mainly remembered,

---

15. LAURENCIE, I, 167 ff.
16. Cf. BRENET-LIBRAIRIE, pp. 422 and 427; LAURENCIE, I, 166.
17. Cf. LAURENCIE, III, 252; ALTMANN, p. 242 (including 4 sons. in D'INDY-SENAILLÉm; MOFFAT-VIOLINm I, nos. 11 and 25, and II, nos. 20, 26, and 30; JENSEN-VIOLINm, no. 7405).
18. Cf. the views quoted in ROWEN, p. 74.
19. The dates are uncertain at best, but those in MGG, III, 639 ff. (Raugel), are preferred here to the obviously unlikely birth year of 1695 given in LAURENCIE,

Ex. 79.   From the finale of Sonata 8, Bk. 1, by Jean-Baptiste Senallié (after the original Paris edition of 1710).

if at all, as the man who won against Rameau in a contest for an organ post in 1706.[20]   Of three instrumental collections published by or for him in 1709, 1711, and 1713, the first contains six SS/bass "Suittes" and a "Sonate en Quattor" under the collective title *Livre de simphonies;* the second contains eight sonatas for violin and *b. c.* plus four suites for flute and *b. c.;* and the third, dedicated to the organist Chauvet in return for instruction, contains at least seven *Sonates en trio* for flutes, violins, oboes, "etc.," of which Sonata 7 is for three high instruments unaccompanied.   The "solo" sonatas of 1711 are named for composers—including "La Marais," "La Couprin," "La Clérembault," and "La Senallié."   Four to six movements are found in the sonatas, with the S-F-S-F plan as the core in most of them.   Anticipating his championship of the "tons naturels" in his treatise of 1745 (*Tour du clavier*), Dornel rarely exceeded keys of two sharps or flats in his sonatas.[21] Like the organists Clérambault and Dandrieu he tended toward a polyphonic style.   His harmony is often somewhat recherché, too, with expressive dissonances.   Unfortunately neither these facts nor such titles as "Fugue gay" and "Allemande comique" can cover the banality of Dornel's ideas and their mechanical treatment, as evaluated by Laurencie. No modern editions have been published.

Two brothers among the several members of the Francoeur family

I, 180, and to the statement "died about 25 years ago at the age of about 75" in LA BORDE, III, 414 (1780).
    20. LAURENCIE, I, 180 ff.
    21. Cf. LAURENCIE, I, 189 ff.

who served Louis XIV or XV as highly esteemed violinists[22] each left
two sets of "solo" violin sonatas in this period. The elder and less renowned was **Louis Francoeur** "l'aîné" (*ca.* 1692-1745), who had a turn
as leader of the Twenty-four Violins.[23] His lesser renown is still
reflected in the absence of modern editions such as have helped to keep
his brother's works alive. His two books of 8 and 12 sonatas, respectively, appeared in 1715 and 1726. Most of these sonatas follow the general five-movement church plan that prevails in the first half of Corelli's
Op. 5 (usually S-F-F-S-F). The ideas are based, according to
Laurencie, on the usual scales, arpeggios, and chromaticism of the time.
More exceptional are the leaps up to two octaves, the active and somewhat complex harmony, the extensive use of the second and third positions, the arpeggiations that require the left-hand thumb on the fingerboard, and the varieties of bowing.

The younger brother, **François Francoeur** "le cadet" (1698-1787),
achieved his greater and chief renown through opera, mostly in collaboration with Jean-François Rebel, son of the Rebel we met earlier.[24] These
friends had attended the spectacular coronation of Emperor Karl VI

22. Cf. MGG, IV, 698 ff. (Girardon).   23. Cf. LAURENCIE, I, 195 ff.
     24. Cf. LAURENCIE, I, 236 ff. (including the full account of a notorious, extra-
musical *affaire scandaleuse* that involved François Francoeur).

Ex. 80. Incipits in the 4 movements of Sonata 3, Bk. 2, by
François Francoeur (after the original edition).

in Prague (1723), where they met Tartini, Fux, Quantz, and Marpurg,
among other important musicians. François Francoeur was a pupil of
his father in violin, a "dessus de violon" in the "Grand choeur" of the
"orchestre de l'Opéra" from the age of 15, and a successor to Senallié
in the Twenty-four Violins. His two sets of 10 and 12 "solo" sonatas,
respectively, were published in 1720 and some time in the 1730's.[25]
Sonata 12 in Book 2 is a veritable trio, for it has an independent,
"obligée" part for cello or viola. Except for Sonata 8 in Book 2, these
sonatas have four or five movements in S-F-S-F, S-F-S-S-F, S-F-F-S-F,
or similar sequences. Tempo, dance, and descriptive titles are mixed

25. Cf. LAURENCIE, I, 249. For mod. eds. of 6 separate sons. cf. ALTMANN,
p. 236 ff. (including MOFFAT-VIOLINm I, nos. 14 and 26, and II, no. 6; ALARD-VIOLINm,
no. 33).

freely in single sonatas.   More often than not the several movements of
a sonata are interrelated by subtly similar incipits (Ex. 80).

Laurencie finds the influence of Vivaldi's style as well as Corelli's in
the sonatas of François Francoeur.[26]   As the accompanying example
suggests, the latter's writing is light, refined, melodically embellished by
both passages and *agréments,* accurately harmonized, yet not especially
original.   Other examples from his sonatas would show the developing
techniques of the violin in France, including free use of the first 5
positions, ingenious double-stop passages, and an increasing diversity of
bowings.

The violinist **Jacques Aubert** (1689-1753), another member of a
supposedly large family of musicians, was a pupil of the Italophile
Senallié, and both a member and son of a member of the Twenty-four
Violins.[27]   Most active during the Regency and the next two decades,
Aubert made a modest but not outstanding success through his activities
in opera and the Concerts spirituels,[28] the modern scoring of his
orchestral symphonies, his composition of the first concerto grosso by a
Frenchman to be performed (1735), and no fewer than 28 publications
of violin music (1719-*ca.* 1750), not to mention reprints and other
publications.[29]   Aubert started with a royal privilege in 1719 that
specified "*Sonates,* sans paroles,"[30] a qualification that still harks back to
the origins of "sonata" as a musical title.   The Opp. 1-4 that followed
(1719-31) contain 10 sonatas each for violin and *b. c.*[31]   One more set
of six such sonatas, Op. 25, appeared about 1739.   Furthermore, in
1738 Aubert published a set of sonatas for two violins unaccompanied,
Op. 24, the type that became increasingly popular in the later Baroque
Era.   Perhaps it was already one of these sonatas that he had played
with Senallié at a Concert spirituel 8 years earlier.[32]   Incidentally,
Aubert was the teacher of his son Louis (1720-*ca.* 1800), who published
6 sonatas for violin and *b. c.* in 1750 that are suites of dances.

Aubert was another who generally followed the S-F-S-F plan, who
mixed tempo and dance titles, all in Italian, and who related the movements through similar incipits.   Along with some striking, almost
suspicious resemblances to Corelli's melodies,[33] there is that tendency

26. LAURENCIE, I, 258.
27. The detailed account in LAURENCIE, I, 201 ff., is supplemented by a corrected
birth date and a few other facts in MGG, I, 776 ff. (Borrel).
28. Cf. BRENET-CONCERTS, p. 152; LAURENCIE, I, 215.
29. Cf. LAURENCIE, I, 216 and 210 ff.
30. Cf. BRENET-LIBRAIRIE, p. 426; LAURENCIE, I, 202.
31. Mod. eds. of 2 sons. are listed in LAURENCIE, III, 217.
32. Cf. LAURENCIE, I, 212 and 208.
33. Cf. LAURENCIE, I, 218 ff.

in his lines toward fragmentation through frequent rests and other minutiae, or toward overnice embellishments such as we have seen already impending in the French sonata and such as we noted, in a previous chapter, among Italian sonatas of the late Baroque Era. Aubert frequently achieves an A-B-A plan by writing movements in pairs—two rondeaux, gavottes, arias, prestos, and so on—followed by a *da capo* of the first one. Occasionally ternary design is anticipated within a single continuous movement, too. The only technical problems of real consequence are found in the polyphonic use of double-stops. From the scoring standpoint it is interesting to see how Aubert transcribed Sonata 10 of Book 3, which has an energetic "Carillon" movement and an added *concertante* part for cello or bassoon, into No. 4 in his Book 2 of concerti grossi.[34] The opinion that Aubert's music was generally facile, often to the point of superficiality, was expressed by his contemporaries, is held here, and is indicated by other recent writers who have troubled to look into his music.[35] However, we should note Laurencie's enthusiasm for certain melodic, rhythmic, and harmonic subtleties that he finds in Aubert's sonatas.[36]

At this point, seven other, more obscure contributors to the sonata in France may be mentioned, although only briefly. These include three violinists, Besson, Bouvard, and Denis; three popular introducers of the transverse flute in France, Boismortier, Naudot, and Blavet; and a popular musette player, Chédeville. **Michel-Gabriel Besson** (*ca.* 1689-1765), member of a family of musicians and successor to Duval in the Twenty-four Violins, left a set of 10 sonatas for violin and *b. c.*, published in 1720.[37] These pieces are all cast in four movements in no fixed order, with Italian dance or tempo titles. The ideas have a capricious quality, one favorite device being dotted repeated notes. The technical demands are moderate, but some programmatic effects are designated, such as "tromba" for quasi fanfares or "musette" for some characteristic doubling with the bass.

The violinist **François Bouvard** (*ca.* 1683-1760) turned to composition in Paris after some success as a boy soprano in opera and a period of study in Rome.[38] Although he also wrote operas, his only published work is his *Premier Livre de sonates à violon seul et la basse continue* (Paris, 1723).[39] The 8 sonatas in this set are in 4 to 6 movements

34. Cf. LAURENCIE, I, 217 and 227 ff.
35. Cf. PINCHERLE-VIOLINISTES, p. 23; MGG, I, 777 ff.
36. LAURENCIE, I, 219 ff. (cf. p. 215).
37. Cf. LAURENCIE, I, 230 ff.
38. Cf. LAURENCIE, I, 261 ff.
39. For a mod. ed. of Son. 8 in F, cf. ALTMANN, p. 234, and MGG, II, 170 (Raugel).

with no strict plan but with the usual mixture of dances and freer types. They show competence and careful attention to rather fussy melodic and dynamic details, but no special originality of style or form.

Martin Denis, who left almost no traces of his career, published 2 sets of 12 sonatas each for violin and *b. c.,* in 1723 and 1727.[40] Although the royal privilege of 1722 specifies "sonates allemandes"[41]—the earliest such implication of German influence on the French sonata—there is no question in this music but that the real influence was still Italian and, in particular, Corellian. Mostly in 4 movements that are thematically related, Denis' sonatas are distinguished, according to Laurencie, by gracious, elegant lines, by some use of what Laurencie calls "the famous *tremolo* of Mannheim," and by much use of sequence based on simple harmonies and extended in one instance (Son. 12, Bk. 1) to the eighth position.

The four other instrumentalists in France have had no Laurencie of the flute or musette to bring them and their sonatas out of their obscurity (except as Laurencie himself has had occasion to notice them in references to be mentioned shortly). **Joseph Bodin de Boismortier** (*ca.* 1691-1755) himself published in Paris more than 100 opera between 1721 and about 1747.[42] In so doing he competed with his contemporaries in virtually every main category of composition and amassed a considerable fortune. Out of some 35 opera that are extant are more than 22 sets of sonatas.[43] These last include all the popular flute scorings of the day and two of the most popular violin settings. Including Op. 1, there are 9 sets of sonatas for 2 high instruments unaccompanied, with some sets for flutes and some for violins. These are the earliest French examples that are known here of this popular setting in the later Baroque Era. There are also one set for 3 flutes alone, a set for 3 flutes and *b. c.,*[44] 2 sets for 2 bassoons alone, and 4 sets for 2 flutes or 2 violins and *b. c.* The sonatas average 4 to 5 movements, with short light dances predominating. The few available examples confirm the fluency and tuneful appeal to be expected of so prolific and successful a composer. Technically simple and not without a certain elegance, they are interesting as reflecting the popular taste. In a delightful account of Boismortier, written in 1780,[45] La Borde concluded, "Although they

41a

44a

---

40. Cf. LAURENCIE, I, 264 ff. A mod. ed. of one son. in A minor is listed in ALTMANN, p. 236.

41. Cf. BRENET-LIBRAIRIE, p. 427.

42. Cf. MGG, II, 71 ff. (Raugel, with errors) ; BIBLIOTHÈQUE NATIONALE, III, 100 ff.

43. Among mod. eds. (cf. MGG, II, 73, and ALTMANN) : Son. for 2 flutes alone, Op. 6, No. 6, HORTUSM, no. 85 (Raugel, with preface).

44. Cf. LAURENCIE & SAINT/FOIX, p. 18.

45. LA BORDE, III, 392 ff.

[his works] have long been forgotten, anyone who desires to excavate this abandoned mine will be able to find enough grains of gold dust there to make an ingot."

The flutist **Jean-Jacques Naudot** (?-1762) was another very prolific composer, although he confined himself largely to light sonatas and other still lighter instrumental pieces.[46] He wrote primarily for his main instrument and for both the vielle or hurdy-gurdy and the musette or bagpipe, two fashionable instruments of the time. In the Bibliothèque nationale alone, 13 sets of his sonatas, published between 1726 and 1740, are reported.[47] Among these sets, generally of 6 sonatas each, are 5 for flute or violin and *b. c.*;[48] 4 for 2 flutes, violins, or oboes and *b. c.*; 2 for 2 unaccompanied flutes of either type, and other options; one for vielle and *b. c.* "dont trois sont mêlées d'accord"; and one "en quatre parties" for 3 vielles or 5 other options and *b. c.*

Perhaps the finest of the French flutists at this time was the self-taught **Michel Blavet** (1700-68), who excelled at the Concerts spirituels along with Leclair, Guignon, and Mondonville. He transferred to royal service about 1738, and spent some time in Germany.[49] No less an authority than Quantz had warm praise for Blavet.[50] Besides his contributions to the "opéra bouffon," Blavet left at least three sets of sonatas between 1728 and 1740—Op. 1 (1728) for two flutes and *b. c.* and Opp. 2 and 3 (1731 or 1732 and 1740) for solo flute and *b. c.*[51] The sonatas are more accurately suites of character or programmatic pieces. Their technical difficulties reveal an extraordinary virtuoso in the composer, especially in the variation treatments that Blavet used so often.

Nicolas Chédeville "le cadet" (1705-82), one of three brothers in music from the renowned Hotteterre family, was the French master of the musette,[52] both as player and maker.[53] His taste for Italian music was strong, as evidenced by the lengthy royal privilege granted him in 1739 to transcribe for musette or vielle virtually all music by Vivaldi, Albinoni, Valentini, Corelli, Veracini, Tessarini, Locatelli, Brevio, Tartini, and D. Scarlatti (among composers of other nationalities)![54]

46. Cf. EITNER-QL, VII, 151. He is not discussed in LA BORDE.
47. Cf. BIBLIOTHÈQUE NATIONALE, VII, 86 ff.; 5 sets are listed in CAT. SCHWERIN, II, 84-85, with dedications in full on p. 387.
48. ALTMANN, pp. 276 and 111, lists one S/bass and one SS sonata in mod. eds.; cf. also, GIRARD, p. 93.
49. LAURENCIE-BOUFFONS includes biographic findings but no discussion of the sonatas.
50. Cf. KÖLBEL, pp. 148, 174, and 176; also, GIRARD, p. 50 ff., and LA BORDE, III, 497 ff.
51. Cf. BIBLIOTHÈQUE NATIONALE, III, 80; MGG, I, 1925 ff. Among mod. eds.: 6 S/bass sons., FLEURYM (cf. KÖLBEL, p. 192, for full listing).
52. Cf. LA BORDE, III, 501.   53. Cf. MGG, II, 1152 ff. (Wallon).
54. Cf. BRENET-LIBRAIRIE, p. 440; PINCHERLE-VIVALDI, I, 223 ff.

Out of 14 published opera and some other publications without opus number, Chédeville left at least one set of *Sonates amusantes pour les muzettes,* Op. 5 (*ca.* 1734); one set of six sonatas for flute or oboe or violin and *b. c.,* Op. 7 (*ca.* 1737); and *Les Galanteries amusantes, Sonates a deux musettes,* vielles, flutes, or violins, Op. 8 (1739).[55] These sonatas, like Blavet's, are suites of programme or character pieces clearly designed to meet the popular taste. They reveal melodious tunes in symmetrically balanced phrases and simple but purposeful harmony (Ex. 81). Light and elementary as they often are, they do have some

Ex. 81. From the second movement of Sonata 3, Op. 8, by Nicolas Chédeville "le cadet" (after NAGELSm, no. 263).

sizable fugues and variation forms here and there and are certainly considerably more advanced, original, and interesting than the positively rudimentary sonatas by the older brother Esprit Philippe Chédeville, who was equally celebrated as a musette player and maker, if not as a composer.[56]

Along with William Young in Innsbruck and John Ravenscroft in Rome, the violinist **Henry Eccles** (*ca.* 1652-1742) was one of the few Englishmen to compose sonatas abroad during the Baroque Era. A member of a London family of musicians, he moved from royal service in London to that in Paris about 1710, remaining in Paris until his death about the age of 90.[57] However, the statement that Eccles actually "composed" sonatas in Paris needs to be severely qualified.

55. Cf. BIBLIOTHÈQUE NATIONALE, IV, 76 ff. Mod. ed.: Sons. 3 and 6, Op. 8, NAGELSm, no. 26 (Upmeyer, with preface).
56. Cf. MGG, II, 1151 ff. (Wallon); HORTUSm, no. 81 (Arx).
57. Cf. JEFFREYS, especially p. 30 ff.; MGG, III, 1074 ff. (Percival).

Two sets of 12 sonatas each for violin and *b. c.* were published under his name in Paris, Book 1 in 1720 and Book 2 in 1723. In 1923 Andreas Moser reported his discovery[58] that at least 18 movements from Book 1 (including Sons. 1, 4, 8, 9, and 12) had been stolen, note for note, from Giuseppe Valentini's *Allettamenti per camera,* Op. 8 (cf. p. 183), with only the key or relative position changed now and then. Presumably the other 12 movements in Book 1 were stolen, too, perhaps from Nicola Matteis.[59] Eccles may have known the original edition of Valentini's Op. 8, published in Rome in 1714, or the Roger edition (no. 412) that followed in about 1716, but hardly the Walsh edition, which did not appear until the same year that Eccles' Book 1 appeared.[60]

The three modern editions attributed to Eccles are apparently all plagiarisms.[61] The one in D minor, with suspiciously extraordinary harmony on the second page of the score, is a mixture of movements from Sonatas 1 and 12 in Valentini's Op. 8.[62] Thus far no plagiarisms have been proved among the sonatas of Eccles' Book 2, which include two flute sonatas and are described as being in a very different, French style.[63]

Leclair and Others

The Frenchman **Jean-Marie Leclair** "l'aîné" (1697-1764), one of the greatest violinists and sonata composers of the Baroque Era, was born among a family of musicians in Lyon.[64] Called to Torino in 1722 and again in 1726 in the capacity of operatic dancer and choreographer, he was evidently persuaded by G. B. Somis to concentrate on violin instead.[65] It was no doubt through the teaching of this Piedmontese master that Leclair came to know the music of both Corelli and Vivaldi. Perhaps it was his meeting with Quantz during the second trip to Torino[66] that helped to spread his fame to Germany, for J. G. Walther

58. Cf. -CRIMINALIA, p. 424 ff.
59. Cf. REV. DE MUS., VIII (1924), 147 (Borrel).
60. Cf. EITNER-QL, X, 24; BRITISH PRINTED, II, 615; SMITH-WALSH, no. 577.
61. Listed only under Eccles' name in ALTMANN, p. 236. Moffat, who had a copy of Eccles' Bk. 1 in his library (HAAS-CAT. 20, no. 226), "edited" Son. in D minor and "La Guitare" in E minor in -VIOLINm III, no. 2, and I, no. 28, repectively.
62. Cf. SQUIRE-ECCLES.
63. SQUIRE-ECCLES; JEFFREYS, p. 30 ff.
64. Extended basic researches, including earlier studies, are brought together in LAURENCIE, I, 269 ff. (cf. III, 267 ff.). PINCHERLE-LECLAIR summarizes this research along with a little new information (cf. pp. 7 ff. and 127) and gives a valuable view of Leclair in his environment. Both men discuss the music in detail, too, although differently. The full discussion of Leclair's life in POUGIN, p. 188 ff., appears often to be another, although almost unacknowledged, summary of Laurencie's findings (cf. PINCHERLE-LECLAIR, p. 129).
65. Cf. MARPURG-BEYTRÄGE, I, 466 ff.
66. Cf. KAHL-SELBSTBIOGRAPHIEN, p. 143.

already listed him in 1732.[67]   Leclair moved to Paris in 1728, where he entered the royal service and won acclaim at the Concerts spirituels. In 1730 he married his young music engraver Mademoiselle Louise Roussell (his second wife), who engraved all of his publications but the first (1723).[68]   About then, too, he received training in theory from the composer André Chéron, which he warmly acknowledged later, although the early claim that Chéron actually harmonized Leclair's first sets of sonatas[69] is now regarded as highly unlikely.[70]   About 1736 Leclair quit the royal service after an evidently bitter rivalry with the Torino-born violinist J.-P. Guignon, another Somis pupil.[71]   From then to the time of the cultured, misanthropic old man's unsolved assassination in 1764[72] he seems to have devoted himself primarily to composition and teaching.   The chief interruptions occurred during a period of about five years (*ca.* 1738-42) in Amsterdam and The Hague, where Leclair apparently went twice, primarily to hear the celebrated Locatelli and perhaps even to study with him.[73]

Except for one opera done in his later years and a few other pieces for the theater, Leclair wrote only instrumental music, all with the violin as the primary instrument.   We do not need to recognize the *Sonates pour le clavecin* that Leclair seems to have plagiarized, under the name of J. W. Lustig, from the works of D. Scarlatti, L. Giustini, and others.[74]   Between 1723 and 1753, 12 sets of instrumental music were published, followed by numerous reprints.   Included are 7 1/2 sets of sonatas in S/-, SS/bass, and SS settings, 2 1/2 of lighter "trios," and 2 of solo violin concertos.[75]   A "trio" and an S/bass sonata were also published posthumously by Madame Leclair in 1766 and 1767, respectively.   In all, Leclair left a total of 70 pieces called "sonata," of which the three that alternate with the three "Overtures" (suites) in Op. 13 (1753) are actually transcriptions of "solo" Sonata 8 in Op. 2, Sonata 12

67. -LEXIKON, p. 172, under "Clerc (le) oder Claire."
68. Cf. LAURENCIE, I, 277 ff.; HOPKINSON, pp. 70 ff. and 128.
69. LA BORDE, III, 405.
70. Cf. PINCHERLE-LECLAIR, p. 26 ff.
71. Cf. LAURENCIE, I, 282 ff.
72. In the intriguing accounts, suspicion has centered variously on the gardener, the nephew, and Madame Leclair herself (cf. LAURENCIE, I, 298 ff.; SLONIMSKY-THING, p. 86 ff.).
73. Cf. SCHEURLEER-LECLAIR; POUGIN, p. 197 ff.; PINCHERLE-LECLAIR, p. 31 ff., including new information from KOOLE.
74. Cf. PINCHERLE-LECLAIR, p. 35 ff.
75. Unfortunately, the "Complete Edition" of Leclair's works that was projected by Heugel & Cie in 1952, under Pincherle's editorship, has not materialized.   A thematic index of one S/bass (Op. 1) and 3 (!) SS sets of sonatas, plus some miscellaneous sonatas, trios, and concertos, all inadequately identified, may be found in BACHMANN-VIOLINISTES, p. 140 ff.   The contents and keys of each of Leclair's sets may be seen in MUSIC & PHONORECORDS, 1954, p. 88, and 1955, p. 45 ff.

in Op. 1, and Sonata 12 in Op. 2.[76] Typical of the times, some 70 per cent of these sonatas are S/bass, 17 are SS alone, and 13 are SS/bass settings. There are 4 "Livres" of 12 "solo" sonatas each—Opp. 1 (1723), 2 (ca. 1728), 5 (1734), and 9 (1738).[77] In 8 of these sonatas the transverse flute is made optional to the violin, and in about 8 movements the viola or cello is given a *concertante* part quite independent of the *b. c.*[78] Best known of the "solo" sonatas is the one in C minor known as "Le Tombeau." It was played "en grande symphonie" at commemorative services for Leclair in 1765[79] and has been kept alive primarily through Ferdinand David's enterprising though unbridled anthology of the 19th century.[80] There are 2 "Livres" of 6 sonatas each for 2 violins unaccompanied—Opp. 3 (1730) and 12 (ca. 1747).[81] And 8oa besides the 3 transcribed "trio" sonatas already noted in Op. 13 there are 6 SS/bass sonatas in Op. 4 (ca. 1730).[82] In this last set 2 viols are made optional to the two violins, a fact that must have pleased Le Blanc.[83]

The S-F-S-F plan prevails in or underlies the majority of Leclair's sonatas. But in many titles—for example, "Allegro ma non troppo" or "Un poco Andante"—there is a tendency characteristic at the time toward more moderate tempos, which fact ties in with Leclair's own request to avoid excessive speeds (preface to Op. 13).[84] Exceptions to the S-F-S-F plan are more likely to occur in the unaccompanied, SS settings, which sometimes have 3 movements in the more modern F-S-F plan or even in the order of F-F-F. Otherwise, the most distinguished, advanced, and virtuosic writing is certainly to be found in the "solo" rather than in the more purely diversional, duo or "trio" sonatas. The use of similar incipits to interrelate the movements is frequent. Leclair's titles and other terms are Italian, as is the G clef almost invariably placed on the second line by now. But French dances are frequent, including a musette, airs, and rondeaux, the gavotte as a frequent penultimate movement, or the tambourin and minuet among finales. Also French was the

76. Cf. LAURENCIE, I, 338.
77. Among mod. eds.: Op. 1, entire, GUILMANT & DEBROUXm (wrongly called "Oeuvre III") ; Op. 2, entire, EITNER-LECLAIRm (with preface) ; Sons. 8 in Op. 1, 1 and 12 in Op. 2, 1 and 4 in Op. 5, and 4 in Op. 9, PINCHERLE-LECLAIRm II (with preface) ; for many other single eds. cf. ALTMANN, p. 239 ff.
78. Cf. PINCHERLE-LECLAIR, pp. 55 ff. and 83 ff.
79. Cf. LAURENCIE, I, 306.
80. DAVID-VIOLINSPIELm, I, no. 5; also in ALARD-VIOLINm, no. 4; JENSEN-VIOLINm, vol. 7428, etc. (cf. MUSIC & PHONORECORDS, 1955, p. 45).
81. Among mod. eds.: Op. 3, entire, PINCHERLE-LECLAIRm I ; cf. ALTMANN, p. 93.
82. Among mod. eds.: Sons. in D minor and B-flat, MOFFAT-LECLAIRm ; cf. LAURENCIE, III, 249 ff.
83. Cf. LE BLANC, iii, 189 ; LAURENCIE, I, 277.
84. Cf. PINCHERLE-LECLAIR, p. 60.

addition of a variation or an "Altro" to most of the gavottes and many o
the other dances, with an A-B-A or rondeau design resulting (Ex. 82)
As the finale of Sonata 4 in Op. 5 there is a resourceful "Ciaccona" or

Ex. 82. From two sections in the third movement of Sonata
12, Op. 2, by Jean-Marie Leclair l'aîné (after EITNER-LECLAIRm,
p. 112 ff.).

a simple descending tetrachord of four dotted half-notes. Aside from
these forms the typically Baroque binary design with repeats is often
employed. Leclair showed a fine command and variety of current forms
but was not ahead of his time in their treatment.

Leclair's melodies evince a high degree of creative force, whether
short or long, plain or ornamental.[85] International influences are often
clearly present—traits of his immediate French predecessors, of Bach

85. Cf. the illuminating discussion in PINCHERLE-LECLAIR, p. 71 ff.

and Handel, of Vivaldi. There are even references to the opening of Tartini's "Devil's Trill" sonata ("Largo" of Son. 7, Op. 5, and Son. 10, Op. 9) and another instance of a movement that resembles Corelli's celebrated, ever-present "Gavotte" in F ("Allegro" in duple meter in Son. 3, Op. 1). But more important are the freer, distinctly original melodies (Ex. 83). These, as Pincherle suggests,[86] are ornamental

Ex. 83. Opening of Sonata 4, Op. 5, by Jean-Marie Leclair l'aîné (after the original edition).

in a less exuberant but more French, meticulous way than those of Leclair's chief Italian contemporaries. One might add that his slow melodies are generally less introspective but often more stately and classic in character (as in Ex. 71, again) than those of Bach. Except for the limited interpretations ad libitum of the frequent cross sign (+),[87] these melodies do not invite the improvised embellishment that was assumed in the slower Italian melodies.[88]

Leclair's fine, careful craftsmanship is also apparent in the sensitive, varied harmony, both diatonic and chromatic; in some nicely planned dynamic markings; and in the polyphonic writing. Marpurg ranked   88a

86. -LECLAIR, pp. 57 and 76 ff. Leclair's "Avertissement" to Op. 9 actually prohibits such embellishment.
87. Cf. DOLMETSCH, p. 91 ff.
88. Cf. PINCHERLE-LECLAIR, p. 67 ff.

him with Handel, Telemann, the Graun brothers, and the Bachs among
the most renowned fugue writers of the time and reproduced in full the
first "Allegro" of "trio" Sonata 3, Op. 4, which is a double fugue (two
subjects).[89] Of course, Leclair must also be signalized for the outstanding, natural virtuosity in his "solo" sonatas (and concertos).[90] He himself was fully aware of the formidable difficulties, as suggested (along
with other interesting advices) in the preface to his Op. 2.[91] The scope
of Leclair's technical devices increased with each set of "solo" sonatas,
Op. 9 seeming to come under Locatelli's influence. He did not show
Locatelli's interest in bizarre stunts or in the use of the highest positions,
his use of the eighth position in "Allegro assai" of Sonata 8, Op. 9,
being an exception. But in skips across the strings, long bows, bariolage,
variety of articulations, and extended passages in double-stops (up to
whole movements, as in the opening of "Le Tombeau") his technical
requirements were hardly surpassed in his day (Ex. 84).

Ex. 84. From the second movement of Sonata 4, Op. 9, by
Jean-Marie Leclair l'aîné (after the original edition).

Along with Mondonville, one of the chief contemporaries of Leclair
was the brilliant and highly applauded violinist **Jean-Baptiste Anet**
(*ca.* 1661-1755; known in his time as "Baptiste").[92] This nonagenarian

---

89. According to PINCHERLE-LECLAIR, p. 82, with reference to *Abhandlung von
der Fuge* in the French translation (Berlin, 1756).
90. LEMOINE is a topical study of Leclair's technical treatments, with numerous
examples and references.
91. Cf. LAURENCIE, I, 316.
92. Cf. LAURENCIE, I, 350 ff., where this Anet is shown not to be the son of an
older violinist with the same name (*ca.* 1651-1710) although he might have been
his younger brother.

apparently had studied with Corelli in Rome,[93] then served both Louis XIV and Louis XV, and performed often with much success[94] (especially during his own period of rivalry with the Italian J.-P. Guignon). Although he was old enough to have antedated Leclair in several of his styles, Anet did not publish the first of at least 5 instrumental opera until 1724. Among these were at least 2 sets of 12 and 10 sonatas, respectively, for violin and b. c.—Opp. 1 (1724) and 3 (1729). The sonatas of both these sets are in the nature of suites, averaging 5 movements. The first set shows Corelli's influence. The second shows it, too, but prefers picturesque French titles above the movements, such as "Boutade," "Gigue en cor du chasse," or the rare term "Allaigre" for "allegro."[95] In spite of Anet's reputation as a great virtuoso his technical demands in these pieces are comparatively modest. The lesser significance of Anet's sonatas must be the main reason for no known re-editions, either early or modern.

The sonata composers of the Baroque Era who came after Leclair in France (based on the chronology of first sonata publications) were generally of only minor significance. **Jean-Baptiste Quentin** "le jeune" was the younger of two brothers who were violinists in the Paris opera orchestra.[96] Whereas his brother Bertin published one set of 10 S/bass sonatas (1730), Jean-Baptiste published at least 18 sets, between 1724 and some time after 1738.[97] These include 4 sets of 36 sonatas in S/bass and 14 sets of over 80 sonatas in SS/- or SSB/bass settings, with frequent choices of violins or flutes. Laurencie reports cycles of three to five movements, often in the S-F-S-F plan; moderate technical difficulties; fluent melodies, artfully decorated; supple if somewhat monotonous rhythms; and the increasing use of *doubles* (that is, single variations, often in minor) and *da capo* indications that result in ternary designs.

The only extant sonatas of **Antoine Favre,** another violinist in the Paris opera orchestra, are the six for violin and bass in his *Second Livre de sonates,* published in 1731.[98] These are suites, mostly in five movements, with such precise French titles as "Gayement et point trop viste." **André Chéron** (1695-1766), who was mentioned here as a theory teacher of Leclair, became one of the directors of the Paris opera. He left two sets of six and four SS/bass sonatas, published in 1727 and 1729. These sonatas are described as four- or five-movement suites of dances.[99] The violinist **de Tremais** was a pupil of Tartini and left seven sets of sonatas (four in S/-, one in SS/bass, and two in SS settings), of which

93. Cf. PINCHERLE-CORELLI, p. 113 ff.   94. Cf. LAURENCIE, I, 360 ff.
95. Cf. LAURENCIE, I, 362 ff.   96. Cf. LAURENCIE, I, 365 ff.
97. Cf. CUCÜEL-DOCUMENTS, p. 387.   98. Cf. LAURENCIE, I, 374 ff.
99. MGG, II, 1169 (Barthélmy).

only two S/bass sets (1726 and *ca.* 1740) and the one SS set (*ca.* 1737) are extant.[100]   Beyond those facts scarcely a thing is known about him (not even his Christian name) except as revealed by his music.   The 16 "solo" sonatas are reported to be generally in four movements, the six "trio" sonatas in three.   Simple Italian titles are used.   The melodies are a bit angular and hard, yet rather fully figurated, especially with triplet runs and arpeggios.   The technical demands that de Tremais makes are, in fact, the most interesting aspects of his sonatas.   For, obviously by way of his teacher, he was one of the first Frenchmen (if he really was French) to introduce *scordatura,* complete with the explanatory signatures at the start of each such movement, and perhaps the first to call for *pizzicato.*   Both of these techniques are well advanced in his writing, as are the difficult runs and passages far into the violin's upper range.

Jean-Pierre Guignon (1702-74) was born Giovanni Pietro Ghigone in Torino, where he reportedly changed from cello to violin, studied with Somis,[101] and, like Leclair, came to know the music of Corelli and Vivaldi well through this master.   We have already met him here as the rival of both Leclair and Anet at the Concerts spirituels and during many years of royal service.   In Paris and in the course of international travels as one of the more successful violin virtuosos of the 18th century, he was also associated with Blavet, Mondonville, Guillemain, the aging Geminiani, and the young Gaviniès, among others.   And he knew Rameau during a short period as concert master in the orchestra of that dilettante *fermier général* and wealthy patron of new music, La Pouplinière.[102]   Guignon's lively episodes as rascal and mercenary political schemer (leading to his title in 1742 of "Roy des violons") must remain beyond the scope of this survey.[103]

Out of 8 extant publications left by Guignon between 1737 and 1746, 5 contain sonatas.   Opp. 1 (1737) and 6 (after 1742) contain 12 and 6 sonatas, respectively, for violin and *b. c.*[104]   There are also two MS sonatas in this setting.[105]   Op. 2 (1737) contains six sonatas for two cellos alone, an infrequent setting in any case, and one of the earliest of its sort in France.   Op. 3 (*ca.* 1739) contains six sonatas for two violins alone, sonatas that Guignon is supposed to have played with both

100. Cf. LAURENCIE, II, 34 ff.
101. Cf. LAURENCIE, II, 40 ff.; MGG, V, 1081 ff. (Briquet).
102. Cf. CUCÜEL, p. 329 ff.
103. Cf. LAURENCIE, II, 41 ff., 49 ff., 53 ff., and 59 ff.; PINCHERLE-FEUILLETS, p. 40 ff.
104. A mod. ed. of Son. 4, Op. 6, is listed in ALTMANN, p. 237.
105. LAURENCIE, II, 64.

Mondonville and Gaviniès.[106] And Op. 4 (before 1742) contains six sonatas "en trio"—that is, in SS/bass setting. Throughout these 38 [106a] sonatas the newer F-S-F plan of movements, usually identified with the Italian concerto and opera sinfonia, appears in the ratio of about one to two of the older, S-F-S-F plan. Other modernisms can be seen in the more developed rondeaux and the occasional use of two opposing themes within a movement. Thematic interrelations of incipits are frequent between the movements of a sonata. The themes themselves are often songful and graceful, but without any great depth in the slow movements. Scale and chord outlines characteristically furnish the melodic material. The technique is advanced but still well short of that required by Leclair and Guillemain. As usual, the chief advances of all sorts are to be found in the "solo" rather than the relatively simple duo and "trio" pieces.

Four more French violinists may now be noted, none of more than minor importance. All began to publish sonatas in 1739. One was **Antoine Dauvergne**(1713-97), orchestra member and eventually the last director of *l'Opera royal*.[107] From this composer are extant 6 "trio" sonatas in 3 movements, Op. 1, and 12 "solo" sonatas in 4 or 3 movements, Op. 2,[108] both published in 1739. The influence of Locatelli's music (first published in Paris from 1738) is evident in numerous melodic and advanced technical traits.[109]

The highly eccentric violinist **Louis-Antoine Travenol** (1698?-1783) was a pupil of Clérambault and Senallié and something of a poet. He was active in the Concerts spirituels and experienced interesting conflicts with Francoeur, Mondonville, Voltaire, Rousseau, and others during his long life.[110] His only set of sonatas—6 for violin and *b. c.* (1739) —is conservative in style and scope, mainly interesting for his longish, odd preface on Leclair's manner of indicating the minor 6th in the figured bass.[111]

Another one-and-only set of six sonatas for violin and *b. c.* was published in 1739 by the violinist **Jean Lemaire,** about whom virtually nothing definite is known.[112] These sonatas are all in four movements, with frequent doubles. Highly ornamented lines in long sustained phrases are characteristic of the slow movements. Besides other technical advances, *scordatura* is used, qualifying Lemaire as another early

106. LAURENCIE, II, 73.
107. Cf. LAURENCIE, II, 97 ff.
108. Cf. ALTMANN for mod. eds. of S/bass sons. in C-minor and G.
109. Cf. LAURENCIE, II, 125 ff.
110. Cf. LAURENCIE, II, 131 ff.
111. Cf. LAURENCIE, II, 145 ff.
112. Cf. LAURENCIE, II, 147 ff. The mod. ed. of a Son. in G minor is listed in ALTMANN, p. 321.

composer to use this device in France along with de Tremais and Corrette.

Mention may be made, too, of Leclair's younger brother with the same name, **Jean-Marie Leclair** "le second" or "le cadet" (1703-77).[113] Himself an excellent violinist, he remained in his native city of Lyon, achieving substantial respect and success as performer and teacher. Two sets of 12 and 6 sonatas, respectively, are known by him, the first for violin and *b. c.* (1739) and the second for two violins or soprano viols alone (before 1751). Leclair "le second" mixed Italian tempo and dance titles, preferring the newer three-movement, F-S-F plan in the second set. His sonatas reveal a certain breadth, elegance, and technical mastery, but are lacking in originality, according to Laurencie.

113a

Some Cellists

114a

In the 1730's and '40's a school of cello playing was established in France, notably by J. Barrière and M. Berteau.[114] Four composers of early cello sonatas should be noted here. The cellist **Jean Barrière** (?-1751 ?[115]) may have studied under one of the Saint Sévin brothers, two pioneer French cellists active in Agen and then in Paris.[116] In 1736 he went to Rome to study with the celebrated cellist Franciscello,[117] returning to Paris and the royal service in 1739.[118] Out of at least 11 publications by Barrière, 7 contain sonatas.[119] A first set of sonatas for cello and *b. c.,* Op. 1, had been published in 1733.[120] Probably Barrière brought the other sets back from Rome, since all were published under the same royal privilege in 1740 (in the beautiful engraving of Madame Leclair) and all show advances in techniques and Italianisms over the first set. Besides Op. 1, Books 1-4 of the 1740 sets are for cello and *b. c.* with occasional duo and "trio" settings mixed in;[121] Book 5 is for "pardessus de viole" (treble viol?) and *b. c.;* and Book 6 is a set of *Sonates et pièces pour le clavecin.*[122] As will be noted, Barrière had the double honor of introducing both the "solo" cello sonata and the keyboard sonata in France.

The available cello sonatas by Barrière are in three or four move-

113. Cf. LAURENCIE, I, 340 ff.
114. Cf. STRAETEN-VIOLONCELLO, p. 260 ff.
115. Not 1753; cf. BRENET-LIBRAIRIE, p. 447.
116. Cf. STRAETEN-VIOLONCELLO, p. 261 ff.
117. Cf. SCHMIDL, I, 561.
118. Cf. BRENET-LIBRAIRIE, pp. 435 and 440.
119. Cf. BIBLIOTHÈQUE NATIONALE, III, 35.
120. Cf. WEIGL, p. 56, including listing of a mod. ed. of Son. in D (Moffat).
121. Mod. ed.: 12 Sons., CHAIGNEAU & RUMMELm II.
122. Mod. ed.: Son. 1 in B minor, NEWMAN-THIRTEENm, no. 1, with preface, p. 3 ff.

ments, with a mixture of Italian tempo and dance titles, a tendency toward the S-F-S-F plan, and similar incipits. The melodies proceed in nicely balanced phrases and in the noble, elegant, dignified manner that we found in Marcello's cello sonatas. The ornamentation, range, and technical requirements are greater, however, than Marcello's. The harmony, on the other hand, is somewhat more circumscribed. As for the similarly planned keyboard sonatas, the style is mostly that right out of the contemporary sonata for solo violin and *b. c.* The right hand, often suggesting bowing techniques in its figurations, has nearly all the melodic and technical interest, while the left hand, in the manner of an unrealized *b. c.,* provides a simple succession of bass tones (without figures) by way of harmonic support. Yet there are also specific techniques shared by the left hand that belong unquestionably to the keyboard idiom—for example, crossing, overlapping, or rapid alternation of the hands (Ex. 85). Although not great music, Barrière's sonatas are well conceived, effective, and expressive. They deserve more than the little recognition they have had.

Another musician in the royal service was **Jean-Baptiste Joseph Masse,** a member of the Twenty-four Violins. Masse published four sets of sonatas for two cellos alone ("dédiées à Messieurs les Comédians François," to which he also belonged), between 1736 and no later than 1744.[123] In each set, bassoons or viols or violins, even, are named as optional instruments. Straeten says that these sonatas "have distinct merit and testify to their author's technical ability" (as cellist?).[124]

François Martin (?-1773), a cellist who served in the chapel of the Duke of Grammont,[125] published six sonatas, Op. 2, in 1746.[126] The available example reveals the traditional S-F-S-F plan, with related incipits. The lines are songful and less ornate than those in Barrière's sonatas. Double-stops present the chief technical challenge.

Most important of the early French cellists was **Martin Berteau** (?-1756), born in Valenciennes. Berteau is said to have started on the viola da gamba, studying with a Bohemian teacher Kozecz, then changing to cello when he heard a piece by Barrière's Italian teacher Franciscello.[127] A teacher of several important cellists in the later 18th century, Berteau made his debut at the Concerts spirituels in 1739, followed by numerous other successes. Three sets of sonatas are

123. Cf. EITNER-QL, VI, 372; BRENET-LIBRAIRIE, p. 437; LAURENCIE, II, 7.
124. -VIOLONCELLO, p. 262 ff.
125. Cf. STRAETEN-VIOLONCELLO, p. 306; EITNER-QL, VI, 348; BRENET-LIBRAIRIE, pp. 447 and 448.
126. Mod. ed.: Son. in E minor, STRAUWENm.
127. Cf. STRAETEN-VIOLONCELLO, p. 263 ff.

Ex. 85. From the first movement of Sonata 1 for clavecin (Bk. 6) by Jean Barrière (after the original edition of 1740).

credited to him by Straeten,[128] but unfortunately only two single sonatas for cello and *b. c.* are extant, both made available in modern reprints.[129] What then reduces the whole matter to a purely historical comment is the fact that both sonatas, so far as one can judge from these reprints, are in a distinctly later style, with the homophonic texture, slow harmonic rhythm, tonal plateaus, and thematic organization generally ascribed to Classic music. In short, did Martin Berteau actually leave any cello sonatas at all?

There remain to be mentioned three other minor composers who published sonatas in France just prior to the middle of the 18th century. Especially noticeable is the increased use of the 3-movement, F-S-F plan

128a

128. -VIOLONCELLO, p. 263; but the Op. 2 he cites appears not to have been issued before about 1767 (cf. JOHANSSON, facs. 1 ff.; also, facs. 15 for Op. 3, 1767) and no earlier references have been found here. If Martin's death date of 1756 is correct, perhaps the son Corneille (born 1736; cf. EITNER-QL, II, 2) was the composer of these sets. Curiously, the only royal privilege that has been found here for any Berteau was one for "Martineau Bertheau," dated April 22, 1751, for "Sonates de violin dédiées à l'ambassadeur de Hollande" (CUCÜEL-DOCUMENTS, p. 388).

129. Cf. WEIGL, p. 58 (including Son. in F, SCHROEDER-CELLOm, no. 28).

and a tendency toward more chordal writing in slower harmonic rhythm. The excellent violinist **Etienne Mangean** (?-*ca.* 1756), active in the Concerts spirituels from 1742-55, left two sets of "Concertos de Symphonie," a set of six *Sonates a deux violons égaux sans basse,* Op. 3 (1744), and a set of six sonatas for violin and *b. c.,* Op. 4 (1744).[130] Mangean preferred the three-movement F-S-F plan. The available "solo" sonata in F has considerable melodic appeal, revealing much chordal figuration and a fine technical command of the violin as it was then played. As usual, the "trio" sonatas are less imposing in melodic range and instrumental technique, although they do reach the sixth position and include trills in double-stops.

One of several Pagins in music, the outstanding violinist **André-Noël Pagin** (1721 to after 1785) played at the Concerts spirituels from 1747 to 1750, stopping apparently after criticism that he played nothing but the music of his teacher Tartini and after implications that his playing was too refined for the public taste.[131] However, he played at least one of his own sonatas when he made his debut there, presumably one from his six *Sonates à violon seule et basse continue,* published the following year (1748).[132] These sonatas have three or four movements, generally with two allegro movements together in the order S-F-F or, unconventionally, S-F-F-S. The figuration, frequent trills, "pedal" tones in double-stops, bold leaps, varied bowing, and difficult chordal passages all suggest the influence of Tartini, as does the modern cantabile style, *à la* romance, in certain movements.

Charles-Antoine Branche (1722 to at least 1779), member of a family of musicians, was the leading violinist in the *Comédie française* around the mid century.[133] His sonatas consist of one published set of 12 for violin and *b. c.*[134] All but Sonata 10, with an S-F-S-F plan, have 3 movements, the order being F-S-F or S-F-F. The final movement is often a minuet with variations or a rondeau. In the slow movements the melodic lines achieve introspective depth and undergo extreme ornamentation. The ideas in the quick movements are often bold, even abrupt. Sonata 2 contains a fine fugue in F.[135]

With the mention of these last, relatively obscure Frenchmen our survey of the sonata in the Baroque Era is completed. Contemporary

130. Cf. LAURENCIE, II, 30 ff. For Op. 4, cf. EITNER-QL, VI, 299; 2 mod. eds. of Son. in F are listed in ALTMANN, p. 240.
131. Cf. LAURENCIE, II, 178 ff.; MARPURG-BEYTRÄGE, I, 471; FÉTIS-BU, VI, 419.
132. For mod. eds. of Sons. 1 in D and 5 in A (ALARD-VIOLINm, no. 47) cf. ALTMANN, p. 241.
133. Cf. LAURENCIE, II, 185 ff.
134. For a mod. ed. of Son. in G minor, cf. ALTMANN, p. 234.
135. Reprinted in CARTIERm.

with the trends, styles, and names that were met in the later phases of this era were others that could be noted here only for the fact that they must be deferred to a succeeding volume. They have to do especially with the development of the accompanied and the solo keyboard sonata. As suggested at the start of this chapter and elsewhere in the present book, these were the trends, styles, and names that first pointed to the sonata in the Classic Era.

Addenda 1966 and 1972

P. 6.   12a. Riccardo Allorto follows up this discussion and related questions in "La Sonata a uno o più strumenti in Italia: spunti critici," CHIGIANA, XIX (1962), 45-57.

P. 12.   17a. For new over-all encyclopedia accounts, cf. NEWMAN-MGG and -RICORDI.

P. 18.   5a. Dr. Robert Linker at the University of North Carolina reports examples more than 2 centuries earlier, as in the hagiographic account from 13th-century Provençal literature, *Vida de Santa Douce*: "Mens que sonavan la rediera sonada de matinas."

P. 18.   7a. But "Soneto" or "Soneto a sonado" can be found over more than 20 short Spanish lute tablatures in 1547 in Enriquez de Valderavano's *Silva de Sirenas*, chiefly in the "sexto libro" (according to a communication from Mr. P. G. Strassler at the University of North Carolina).

P. 20.   15a. KUNZE is a further study of the canzona and related instrumental music in the early Baroque Era, including a volume of complete examples in score (6 by G. Gabrieli and 5 by Gussago, among others). Floyd Sumner explores possible distinctions between *canzone, canzona francese,* and *canzona alla francese,* in JAMS, XXII (1969), 529-530.

P. 21.   17a. A further helpful study is Arthur Hutchings, *The Baroque Concerto* (New York: W. W. Norton, 1961); for pertinent reviews, cf. W. S. Newman in JAMS, XV (1962), 228-31, T. Warner in NOTES, XIX (1962), 608-609, and W. Kolneder in DMF, XVII (1964), 190-91.

P. 21.   19a. We shall see, interestingly enough, that it was chiefly the French writers, especially from Brossard in 1701 through Rousseau in 1755, and not the Germans who made a point of the *chiesa-camera* distinction.

P. 23.   28a. Further consideration of this distinction will be found in KUNZE, Ch. VI, and by E. F. Kenton in MQ, XVIII (1962), 430-31.

P. 24.   32a. The year 1701 rather than 1703 for the first edition of Brossard comes from James B. Coover, *Music Lexicography* (Denver: Denver Public Library, 1958), p. 13.

P. 27. 46a. From the same period, Leonard Ratner, in "Eighteenth-Century Theories of Musical Period Structure," MQ, XII (1956), 48, reports specific comments on tonal and cadential aspects of sonata movements, by Christian Gottlieb Ziegler, to be found in an incomplete MS treatise dated 1739, "Anleitung zur musikalischen Composition."

P. 31. 59a. In BRENET-LIBRAIRIE, p. 421 ff., royal privileges are also cited for "Sonates italiennes" and "Sonates allemandes."

P. 31. 61a. But in his definition quoted earlier, Mattheson had ended by deploring the French style, too (an early sample of the German attitude that the Mozarts were to evince later), finding it too much like the Italian style in sonatas as well as cantatas, with the results being little more than patchworks or *"pièces de rapport."*

P. 36. 13a. William Klenz supplies further evidences of this sort and some speculations (cf. John G. Suess's review in JAMS, XVII [1964], pp. 124-32). He also cites brief mentions of the problem by Peter Wagner in the *Festschrift Hermann Kretzschmar* (Leipzig: C. F. Peters, 1918), p. 165, and by Otto Ursprung in *Die katholische Kirchenmusik* (Potsdam: Akademische Verlagsgesellschaft Athenaion, 1931), p. 300. A new, significant investigation into "The Uses of the *Sonata da Chiesa*" has been made by Stephen Bonta, in JAMS, XXII (1969), 54-84.

P. 43. 18a. Typical is the collection of Paolo Benedetto Bellinzani, "Dodici sonate da Chiesa a 3, con due Violini e Basso ad imitazione di quelle di Arcangelo Corelli" (MS, *ca.* 1725; cf. CAT. BOLOGNA, IV, 83).

P. 44. 25a. New help with dating and editions is offered by François Lesure in *Bibliographie des Éditions musicales publiées par Estienne Roger et Michel-Charles Le Cène, Amsterdam, 1696-1743* (Paris: Heugel, 1969).

P. 46. 32a. Further illustrations of attractive engraving in important Baroque sonata editions may be seen in Gottfried S. Fraenkel, *Decorative Music Title Pages* (New York: Dover, 1968), plates 105-9 (Purcell and Corelli), 124-25 (Dandrieu), 138-39 (Kuhnau), 150 (D. Scarlatti), and 200-201 (J. S. Bach).

P. 47. 35a. The descriptive thematic index, with valuable historical and biographical notes, in DUCKLES & ELMER brings to light another major collection of manuscript sonatas, acquired in 1958 by the University of California in Berkeley. It includes some 1200 works, many called "Sonata," by 82 Italians, chiefly in Tartini's sphere. Besides Tartini (234 works!) certain other composers (a few not hitherto known) are especially well represented, but all of these were active chiefly in the later 18th century.

P. 50. 1a. Since 1946, with this distinction in mind, Henry Clarke at the

University .of Washington in Seattle has proposed the interesting term "Amphonic Period" for the Baroque Era (cf., especially, "Toward a Musical Periodization of Music," JAMS, IX [1955], 25-30).

P. 54.   10a. Cf. the important new study by David Boyden, *The History of Violin Playing from Its Origins to 1761* (London: Oxford, 1965), including demonstration recording.

P. 54.   11a. Information on this subject was substantially enriched in 1967 by two similarly purposed dissertations: Ute Zingler, *Studien zur Entwicklung der italienischen Violoncellsonate von den Anfängen bis zur Mitte des 18. Jahrhunderts* (Frankfurt/M: Johann Wolfgang Goethe-Universität); and Elizabeth Cowling, "The Italian Sonata Literature for the Violoncello in the Baroque Era" (Chicago: Northwestern University, unpublished). Zingler has also contributed an article, "Über die Rolle zusätzlicher Noten im Basso continuo bei Violoncellsonaten," in the *Festschrift* for *Helmuth Osthoff zu seinem siebzigsten Geburtstag* (Tutzing: Hans Schneider, 1969), 135-138.

P. 55.   12a. The latter size refers to the earlier 17th-century "Violone, Gross Viol-de-Gamba Bass" as illustrated and measured on Plates V and VI in PRAETORIUS-SYNTAGMA, II (contrary to Westrup in MR, XX [1959], 317-18); it was later in the century, of course, that the "violone" was equated with the cello.

P. 56.   18a. For a further region of cultivation, with other early sonatas, cf. Don Smithers, "Seventeenth-Century English Trumpet Music," in ML, XLVIII (1967), 358-365.

P. 56.   19a. Valuable information on the instrument's history as well as its French cultivation is included in the new dissertation by Dr. J. M. Bowers cited below in footnote 41a to p. 376.

P. 56.   20a. A recent, unpublished dissertation is that of Brian Kent Klitz, "Solo Sonatas, Trio Sonatas, and Duos for Bassoon Before 1750" (University of North Carolina, 1961). Chiefly a style study of the music, this helpful dissertation lists (on pp. 6-8) sonatas by B. Marini, G. A. Bertoli, P. F. Buchner, "G. A. S." (Modena), "Mr. Carolo" (Durham), J.-B. Boismortier, J. E. Galliard, G. F. Suggione, L. Merci, J. B. Masse, J. P. Guignon, M. Corrette, J. D. Braun, B. Guillemant, J. F. Fasch, F. Karl, G. Chabrano, S. Lapis, G. P. Telemann, (?) Dard, and W. de Fesch.

P. 56.   20b. For a discussion of the keyboard in its triple capacities as accompanying, chamber, and solo instrument, cf. Hans Hering, "Das Klavier in der Kammermusik des 18. Jahrhunderts," in DMF, XXIII (1970), 22-37.

P. 57.   22a. As of Dec., 1965, Mr. Tharald Borgir was working at the University of California in Berkeley on the dissertation topic "Basso Continuo in Italy During the 17th Century," including the question of supporting instruments.

P. 57.   23a. In 1753, in *Le Maître de clavecin pour l'accompagnement* (Paris: L'Auteur), p. B of the preface, Michel Corrette recalled that when no violinists were present to play Corelli's trio sonatas the parts were sung!

P. 58.   25a. But *Mercure* for Nov., 1713 (p. 23), suggests that the Italian S/bass sonatas ought to be played by only one person on the violin part so as to avoid confusion in the improvising of diminutions (as quoted by La Laurencie and Saint-Foix in *L'Année musicale*, I [1911], 11).

P. 58.   25b. As to when or whether "e" or "ó" in titles meant these instruments were alternatives or adjuncts, cf. ARNOLD, pp. 328-30; also, footnote 22a, above.

P. 59.   27a. Cf., also, Caraffa's ineptness in *Der musikalische Quacksalber* (1700), Kuhnau's satire on Italian music, in the excerpt translated by Paul Nettl, *The Book of Musical Documents* (New York: Philosophical Library, 1948), pp. 71-72. A rare surviving example of a realization written out for a complete set of sonatas is the full-voiced realization left in 1725 by one Antonio Tonelli for Corelli's Op. 5, as reported by Imogene Horsley in JAMS, XXIII (1970), 545-556.

P. 63.   39a. 16th-century vocal precedents are argued by Ernst Apfel, "Zur Vorgeschichte der Triosonate," in DMF, XVIII (1965), 33-36, with further reference to Edith Kiwi, "Die Triosonate von ihren Anfängen bis zu Haydn und Mozart," in *Zeitschrift für Hausmusik*, III (1934), 37 ff.

P. 65.   45a. The rich, comprehensive dissertation by Gordon J. Kinney, "The Musical Literature for Unaccompanied Violoncello" (Florida State University, unpublished, 3 vols., 1962) turns up only one collection of pieces called "Sonata" prior to the 20th century (Vol. I, p. 273). These last are twelve naïve, inept little cycles in a MS dated 1691, "Trattenimento musicale," by the obscure Parmesan composer Domenico Galli. (All 12 are discussed and analyzed by Kinney in Vol. I, pp. 269-314, and the first 7 are copied in Vol. III, pp. 66-93).

P. 65.   45b. On the importance of the unaccompanied duet, cf. Quantz's extended remarks as translated by Edward R. Reilly in "Further Musical Examples for Quantz's *Versuch*," JAMS, XVII (1964), 157-69, with exx.

P. 76.   17a. More immediate in effect and hence of less over-all influence on the forms are the imitations of actual sounds, such as the animal calls and noises approximated in the sonatas of Farina (pp. 207-208) and of the Venetian Stefano Pasino (Op. 8; SARTORI-BIBLIOGRAFIA, item 1679b).

P. 80.   19a. Cf. the important insight by Jan LaRue, "Bifocal Tonality: An Explanation for Ambiguous Baroque Cadences," in *Essays on*

Music in Honor of Archibald Thompson Davison by his Associates (Cambridge: Department of Music, Harvard University, 1957). pp. 173-84.

P. 97. 2a. To this list should be added Foriano Pico (Naples. 1608. guitar tablature; cf. Wolffheim, I, item 1206 and Tafel 31).

P. 98. 2b. Insert Francesco Fiamengo (Messina, 1637, multivoice; cf. SARTORI-BIBLIOGRAFIA, item 1637c).

P. 99. 3a. The discovery of a MS "Sonata con voce" in 20 parts, in the Kassel Landesbibliothek, attributed to G. Gabrieli, is reported by Christiane Engelbrecht in KONGRESS 1956 (Hamburg), pp. 88-89. and in *Die Kasseler Hofkapelle im 17. Jahrhundert* (Kassel: Bärenreiter, 1958), pp. 67-70; she regards it as an immediate ancestor of Monteverdi's similar work (p. 110 below). KUNZE is an important new study of G. Gabrieli's instrumental music. including its background and environment, although the sonatas get relatively little attention, especially the late ones; his supplementary volume of 20 complete examples in score, 14 by contemporaries, includes no G. Gabrieli sonatas. A major study recently published (though evidently written by 1955) is Egon Kenton's *Life and Works of Giovanni Gabrieli* (Rome [?]: American Institute of Musicology, 1967), complete with examples, tables, illustrations, documents, and a chapter on the instrumental works (pp. 437-522).

P. 101. 4a. Cf. Egon F. Kenton, "Lo Stile tardo di Giovanni Gabrieli" (an expanded translation of "The Late Style of Giovanni Gabrieli" in MQ, XVIII [1962], 427-43), in CHIGIANA, XIX (1962), 9-34. The five volumes received to date (Aug., 1971) of G. Gabrieli's *Opera omnia* edited by Denis Arnold (Rome: American Institute of Musicology, 1956—) have not yet reached the instrumental works.

P. 101. 6a. The dissertation projected by Mr. L. F. Brown in 1956 was not pursued.

P. 102. 9a. Not yet received here (as of Aug., 1971) is CHIGIANA, XXII/2 (1968), reportedly containing an article by Fabio Fano, "Biagio Marini violinista in Italia e all'estero (suoi contributi all'evoluzione dell'arte violinistica)."

P. 108. 20a. Further mod. eds.: No. 10, GIEGLING-SOLOm, no. 3; Friedrich Cerha (ed.), *G. B. Fontana: Six Sonatas* (London: Universal Ed., 1962; cf. ML, XLIII [1962], 313).

P. 110. 26a. More on the nature, use, and derivations of this work may be found in Denis Arnold, "Notes on Two Movements of the Monteverdi 'Vespers,'" MMR, LXXXIV (1954), 59-66 (including the discovery of the Crotti work); Arnold, "Monteverdi's Church Music: Some Venetian Traits," MMR, LXXXVIII (1958), 83-91 (with an earlier precedent in A. Gabrieli's motet "Judica Me" [before 1587]); Denis Stevens, "What are the Vespers of Yesteryear?" MQ, XLVII (1961), 315-30 (especially pp. 321-22, with a successor in 1613, a "Concerto *a* 5 by Amante Franzoni); plus

mod. ed. of "La Zambecari" *a 5*, in C (W. Prizer). Cf. William F. Prizer, "Some Bolognese Sonate con tromba," 2 vols., unpublished M.M. thesis, Yale University, 1969 (including scores of three sonatas each by Cazzati, D. Gabrielli, and Torelli).

P. 135. 24a. An important recent Ph.D. dissertation (unpublished) is that of John G. Suess, "Giovanni Battista Vitali and the Sonata da Chiesa," Yale University, 1962; while exploring background, environment, and functions, this study includes a full chapter (VI) on Cazzati and the *sonata da chiesa*.

P. 136. 28a. New mod. ed.: Op. 13 in full, in open score, Louise Rood and G. P. Smith (eds.), *Giovanni Battista Vitali: Artifici musicali, Opus XIII* (Northampton: Smith College Music Archives No. 14, 1959).

P. 141. 36a. Mod. ed.: Son. in D for 2 solo trumpets, strings, and *b.c.*, by P. Franceschini (London: Musica Rara, 1968).

P. 141. 38a. In 1967 at Northwestern University was completed the unpublished dissertation of Richard E. Norton, "The Chamber Music of Giuseppe Torelli," which treats primarily of the printed works and includes numerous examples, a list of works, and a bibliography.

P. 142. 41a. In press (as of Aug., 1971; New York: Mentor Music) is a mod. ed. of a MS "Sonata a 5" in D (W. Prizer).

P. 143. 48a. Mod. ed., with preface: *Zehn Sonaten für Orgel* (A. Reichling; Berlin: Merseburger, 1966), including two pieces by Arresti.

P. 144. 50a. An over-all view has been provided by Gino Roncaglia in *La Cappella musicale del Duomo di Modena* (Florence: Olschki. 1957). Schenk's article cited in footnote 50 above is translated unaltered into German in szmw, XXVI (1964), 25-46.

P. 144. 51a. Klenz's dissertation, cited in footnote 51 above, has been completed at the University of North Carolina (1958) and has been published with revisions as *Giovanni Maria Bononcini of Modena: A Chapter in Baroque Instrumental Music* (Durham: Duke University Press, 1962), including valuable orientations, especially on the environment and current dance forms. The "Supplement" consists of 89 examples in score (in 312 pages), including 30 full sonatas from Opp. 1, 3, 6, 9, and the Silvani collection by Bononcini, and from Opp. 8, 18, and 35 by Cazzati.

P. 147. 57a. In spite of considerable further investigation, based on the MS of the *Ciaccona* found in Dresden, no known composer can be identified with it as yet (Nov., 1965; cf. *Beiträge zur Musikwissenschaft*, VII [1965], 149-54 and the article on T. Vitali bv J. G. Suess scheduled to appear in mgg).

P. 156. 87a. For Rameau's objection to this same passage cf. W. J. Mitchell in jams, XVI (1963), 230. Cf., also arnold, pp. 901-3.

P. 157. 91a. The same may be said for "Corelli's Trumpet Sonata," as described by Michael Tilmouth in mmr, XC (1960), 217-21, and by Norman Cherry, "A Corelli Sonata for Trumpet, Violins, and Basso continuo," in *Brass Quarterly,* IV (1960-61), 103-12 (with exx., and with "A Postscript" on pp. 156-58; mod. eds.: Mentor Music in New York City (R. Nagel, 1967) and Musica Rara in London (1968).

P. 157. 93a. Mario Fabbri argues for the authenticity of the twelve so-called "Sonate di Assisi" (S/bass) in "Tredici ignote composizioni attribuite a Corelli in due manoscritti di Firenze e di Assisi," in CHIGIANA, XX (1963), 23-42 (with a facsimile opposite p. 32 and a thematic listing of all movements, pp. 34-38). But in "Some Corelli Attributions Assessed" (MQ, LVI [1970], pp. 88-98), Hans Joachim Marx (ed. of a new complete ed. of Corelli's works to be published by the Musicological Institute of the University of Basel) questions this and numerous other attributions, at the same time accepting as authentic one further "trio" sonata and nine further "solo" sonatas. On this last and other new Corelli research cf. Sven Hansell in JAMS, XX (1967), 310, and Pierluigi Petrobelli in DMF, XXII (1969), 212-15. The only autograph MS by Corelli that has been confirmed comes from Op. 6 and not from any opus of sonatas, according to H. J. Marx in AM, XLI (1969), 116-118.

P. 157. 93b. Mod. ed.: *Arcangelo Corelli: 24 Pieces* [movements] *for the Piano* [*sic*] (New York: E. F. Kalmus, [*ca.* 1960]).

P. 159. 98a. The dissertation by Haynes cited in footnote 98 was completed in 1960 in 4 vols. with the title "The Keyboard Works of Bernardo Pasquini (1637-1710)." The same author has edited Pasquini's *Collected Works for Keyboard* in 7 vols. as item 5 in the American Institute of Musicology *Corpus of Early Keyboard Music* (Rome, 1964-68), including two solo sonatas each in Vols. I and VI, the 14 sonatas "a due cembali" in Vol. VII, and 14 so-called "sonatas" represented by a single *b.c.* line in Vol. VII.

P. 161. 105a. Further discussion of Strozzi's contribution, by W. Apel and M. Reimann, occurs in the articles cited on p. 127 above, footnote 65a. New discussion and analysis are provided by Barton Hudson in "Notes on Gregario Strozzi and his *Capricci,*" in JAMS, XX (1967), 209-221, with exx.

P. 162. 106a. Further mod. ed.: *Concerto (Sonata nona)* in A minor for flute, 2 violins, and *b. c.,* no. 35 in *Kammermusik* series (Celle: Hermann Moeck, 1957; information from Professor Dale Higbee of Catawba College in Salisbury, N. C.). According to Professor William Klenz at Duke University, three 4-movement sons. for solo cello and *b.c.* exist in MS. Reported to be in CHIGIANA, XXV/5 (1968) but not seen here is an article by Luciano Bettarini, "Appunti critici sulle 'Sette Sonate' per flauto e archi di Alessandro Scarlatti."

P. 165. 8a. Further mod. eds.: R. Giazotto (ed.), *Tomaso Albinoni: Sonata in la, Op. II n. 3* (Milan: Ricordi, 1959); Op. 2, No. 6, NAGELSm, no. 189 (Giegling): W. Reinhart (ed.), *Tomaso Albinoni: Tre Sonate*, Op. 6, Nos. 4, 5, and 7 (Zürich: Hug, 1959).

P. 168.   13a. A recent study is that of Marysue Barnes, "The Trio Sonatas of Antonio Caldara," 2 vols., unpublished Ph.D. dissertation, Florida State University, 1960. Besides the orientation and style analysis in Vol. I, 15 sonatas are scored in full from Opp. 1 and 2 in Vol. II.

P. 168.   16a. Mod. ed.: Sonata III in Bb, SSA/bass, ed. from a Vienna MS by F. F. Polnauer (Mainz: B. Schott, 1968).

P. 169.   18a. Among the valuable writings of Walter Kolneder on the master is an excellent new book, *Antonio Vivaldi—His Life and Work*, translated by Bill Hopkins (from the original German of 1965) and slightly updated (Berkeley: University of California Press, 1970); cf. M. Tilmouth's review in ML, LII (1971), 314-316. The most recent research is summarized on pp. 207-209 and the sonatas are surveyed on pp. 36-44.

P. 169.   19a. Cf., also, Kathi Meyer-Baer in JAMS, XXIV (1971), 139-41.

P. 169.   20a. Cf. H. R. Rarig, "The Instrumental Sonatas of Antonio Vivaldi," unpublished Ph.D. dissertation, University of Michigan, 1958, including detailed style analyses and a full list of works with concordance (pp. 410-19). In connection with the "complete" Ricordi edition reported in footnote 20 above (400 works in 91 vols. as of Nov., 1965), the Library of Recorded Masterpieces in New York is issuing a "Complete Works of Antonio Vivaldi" that includes the scores with the phonograph recordings (73 works on 17 LP discs as of Nov., 1965). As of Feb., 1971, the "complete" Ricordi ed. had reached 500 works in 114 vols. With further regard to thematic indices, cf. W. Kolneder in DMF, XIX (1966), 186-188, and the copious, newly inaugurated periodical *Vivaldiana* I (Brussels, 1969), with new evaluations, corrections, and documents.

P. 170.   22a. Mod. ed. of all 4 S/bass sonatas "fatto per il Maestro Pisendel," ed. by W. H. Bernstein: VEB Deutscher Verlag für Musik (Leipzig, 1965).

P. 176.   46a. The need for a reliable mod. ed. of the 12 MS Sons. in the Bibliothèque nationale has been met by Lorenzo Bianconi and Luciano Sgrizzi (Paris: Heugel, 1971; No. 28 in the series "Le Pupitre"), with a helpful Preface that includes additions to the thematic index in NEWMAN-MARCELLO.

P. 182.   69a. A new, thoroughgoing study has been completed: Howard Brofsky, "The Instrumental Music of Padre Martini," unpublished Ph.D. dissertation, New York University, 1963, including a detailed biographic chapter (I), a style-and-form analysis of the keyboard sonatas (Chap. V), and a thematic *catalogue raisonné* that shows 78 MS keyboard sonatas (pp. 268-97: mostly liturgical organ pieces and harpsichord sons.) in addition to those in the two printed collections.

P. 182. 70a. A mod. facs. ed. of the 1742 set has been published by Broude Brothers (New York, 1967).

P. 183. 71a. On Martini's lighter style cf. TORREFRANCA 735-36.

P. 184. 76a. Although the Paumgartner biography was not achieved, the aforementioned neglect has been lessened considerably by the unpublished Ph.D. dissertation of Mary Gray (Clarke) White, "The Violin Sonatas of F. M. Veracini: Some Aspects of Italian Late Baroque Instrumental Style Exemplified" (The University of North Carolina, 1967) and by Walter Kolneder's fully completed mod. ed. of Veracini's sonatas (as noted below).

P. 184. 80a. Mod. ed. of entire set: Edition Peters 4965a-d, 4 vols. (W. Kolneder).

P. 184. 81a. Mod. ed. of entire set: Edition Peters 4937a-d, 4 vols. (W. Kolneder).

P. 185. 82a. Mod. ed. of entire set: Edition Peters 9011a-m, in 12 separate vols. (W. Kolneder). Reported but not seen here is an article by Guido Salvetti, "Le 'Sonate Accademiche' di Francesco M. Veracini," in CHIGIANA, XXV/5 (1968).

P. 186. 85a. Mod. ed. of entire set: B. Schott, 4 vols. (W. Kolneder). Cf. M. G. White, "F. M. Veracini's 'Dissertazioni sopra l'Opera Quinta del Corelli'" (revision of Chap. VIII from the dissertation cited above), in MR, XXXII (1971), 1-26.

P. 187. 86a. Cf., also, Bianca Becherini, "Un Musicista italiano del XVIII secolo: Giovan Battista Somis," in CHIGIANA, XVI (1959), 7-15; and Federico Ghisi, "Giovanbattista e Lorenzo Somis musicisti piemontesi," CHIGIANA, XX (1963), 16-22.

P. 187. 90a. But Ghisi (note 86a above) and Boris Schwarz (MGG, XII, col. 865), both assign this Op. 1 to Lorenzo rather than G. B. Somis.

P. 189. 102a. A basic new study of the man and the sources and styles of his sonatas is that of Paul Brainard, "Die Violinsonaten Giuseppe Tartinis," unpublished Ph.D. dissertation, Georg August-Universität zu Göttingen, 1959, including a full catalogue raisonné (pp. 238-337) of some 215 sonatas, arranged mostly by keys. A new documentary biographical study, which also throws light on numerous contemporaries, is that of Pierluigi Petrobelli, Giuseppe Tartini —Le Fonti biografiche (Vienna: Universal, 1968); cf. F. Giegling in DMF, XXIV (1971), 226-227.

P. 190. 106a. Cf., also, Paul Brainard, "Tartini and the Sonata for Unaccompanied Violin" (concerning about 30 "piccole sonate"), in JAMS, XIV (1961), 383-93, with facs.; NOTES, XXVIII (1971), 299-301.

P. 192. 120a. Burney includes this story in his enthusiastic report of Tartini, who had "died a few months before my arrival here" in Padua

(BURNEY-FRANCE, pp. 120-28).

P. 195.   134a. In *Annuario,* IV (1968), 3-6, Robert Stevenson shows that Giovanni de Seixas was actually the Brazilian-born João Seyxas da Fonseca.

P. 197.   144a. Further consideration of authentic and spurious instrumental works occurs in MGG, cols. 1054-55, 1058, 1062 (Hucke). Cf., also, Edwin L. Stover, "The Instrumental Chamber Music of G. B. Pergolesi," unpublished Ph.D. dissertation, Florida State University, 1964. Cf., also, C. V. Palisca in NOTES, XXIII (1967), 510.

P. 199.   146a. In PUBBLICAZIONI-NAPOLI 623 a "Sonata per Organo" in a collection of 1764 and 4 other MS sonatas for cembalo or organ are all attributed to Pergolesi. Cf. NOTES, XXVII (1970), 282 regarding attributions of five of the "trio" sonatas to one Domenico Gallo (probably a Venetian who flourished in the mid-18th century and not the Domenico Galli cited above in footnote 45a to p. 65); cf., also, DUCKLES & ELMER, 102-104.

P. 204.   2a. To the over-all sources cited in footnote 2 above should be added the unpublished Ph.D. dissertation by Albert Biales, "The Sonatas and Canzonas for Larger Ensembles of the Seventeenth Century in Austria," University of California in Los Angeles, 1962.

P. 214.   4a. F. W. Riedel has contributed new information in MGG, X, cols. 1368-72; in AFMW, XIX-XX (1962-63), 124-135 (biographic); and in *Quellenkundliche Beiträge zur Geschichte der Musik für Tasteninstrumente in der 2. Hälfte des 17. Jahrhunderts* (Kassel: Bärenreiter, 1960), pp. 142-63 (on the keyboard music, including the "Sonata und Fuga Do Re Mi Fa Sol La" falsely ascribed to Poglietti, of which the first movement "could hardly have originated before the middle of the 18th century" and the second movement on the hexachord is by Doctor Bull [No. 51 in *The Fitzwilliam Virginal Book*]).

P. 215.   11a. For new biographic information cf. Adolph Koczirz, "Zur Lebensgeschichte Johann Heinrich Schmelzers." SZMW, XXVI (1964), pp. 47-66.

P. 215.   11b. Complete mod. ed.: DTÖm, CV (Schenk), 3 ff.

P. 215.   12a. Mod. ed. in full of this set: DTÖ, XCIII (Schenk), 3 ff.

P. 215.   13a. Mod. eds. (Schenk) of 3 "solo" and 4 "trio" sons.: respectively, DTÖm, XCIII, 61 ff. (including a "Sonate 'Cucù,'" p. 82), and CV, 81 ff. (including "Sonata 'Lanterly' a tre," p. 111, on which cf. Rudolf Flotzinger in SZMW, XXVI [1964], 67-78, regarding Italian melodic origins).

P. 218.   23a. New, mod. ed. in full: DTÖm, CVI-CVII, 3 ff. (Schenk).

P. 218.   25a. From an unrevealed MS comes the mod. ed. of a "Sonata à 6 for B♭ Trumpet Solo and Strings" published by Musica Rara (London, 1958), edited by K. Janetzky.

P. 220. 33a. New information is offered in MGG, IX, cols. 915-19 (H. Feder-hofer).

P. 222. 43a. On another interesting, but neglected, composer in this same milieu, cf. Helene Wessely-Kropik, "**Romanus Weichlein**, ein vergessener österreichischer Instrumentalkomponist des 17. Jahr-hunderts." in KONGRESS 1956 (Vienna), pp. 689-707, including an Op. 1 (1695) of 12 SSAA/bass sonatas.

P. 227. 70a. For a thematic index and discussion of 6 church sonatas for small orchestra by **Clemens Thieme** (1631-68; another Schütz protégé in Zeist), cf. Hans-Joachim Buch in DMF, XVI (1963), 368-71.

P. 231. 85a. Another German organ sonata from about the same period—"Sonata â 2 Clavir Pedal" in French organ tablature—is listed on p. 109 in F. W. Riedel's *Quellenkundliche Beiträge zur Geschichte der Musik für Tasteninstrumente in der 2. Hälfte des 17. Jahrhunderts* (Kassel: Bärenreiter, 1960); cf., also, pp. 103 and 104. It appears anonymously in a mixed collection of MSS.

P. 239. 113a. For a MS source of what appears to be an earlier version of most of the *Biblische Historien*, cf. John R. Shannon, "The Mylau Tabulaturbuch" (unpublished Ph.D. dissertation, 2 vols., the University of North Carolina, 1961), I, pp. 69-72 and 135-36.

P. 242. 126a. This relationship, also noted by Arnold Schering in his *Geschichte des Oratoriums* (Leipzig: Breitkopf & Härtel, 1911, p. 350), gets further confirmation in Kuhnau's own title—*Music-alische Vorstellung einiger biblischer Historien in 6 Sonaten auff dem Claviere zu spielen* (on the meaning of *Historia* cf. Blanken-burg in MGG, VI, especially cols. 469-70)—as well as in several remarks in his preface, such as his reference to programmatic models, among them "so wohl ein Geistliche als prophan Historie" (third paragraph).

P. 249. 158a. A recent (unpublished?) dissertation is that of Arno Lehmann, "Die Instrumentalwerke von Johann Rosenmüller" (University of Liepzig, 1965); cf. the abstract in DMF, XIX (1966), 59-60.

P. 265. 61a. SCE, pp. 265-73; cf., also, W. S. Newman in MQ, L (1964), 526-35.

P. 268. 70a. Mod. ed. of the "Urtext" by Hermann Keller: Edition Peters 9066 (1966), with "Revisionsbericht und Bemerkungen. . . ."

P. 269. 76a. Cf., also, Hans Hering, "Bachs Klavierübertragungen, ein Beitrag zur Klavieristik," in BJ, XLV (1958), 94-113, with exx.

P. 272. 87a. Cf., also, Karl-Heinz Köhler, "Zur Problematik der Violin-sonaten mit obligatem Cembalo [by J. S. Bach]," in BJ, XLV (1958), 114-22. A major new study is the Ph.D. dissertation (Uni-versity of Uppsala, 1966) by Hans Eppstein, *Studien über J. S. Bachs Sonaten für ein Melodieinstrument und obligates Cembalo* (Stockholm: Almqvist & Wiksells, 1966); cf. the abstract in DMF, XX (1967), 198-199, the discussion by Alfred Dürr in DMF, XXI

(1968), 332-340, Eppstein's defense in DMF, XXII (1969), 206-208, and Dürr's further comment in DMF, XXII (1969), 209.

P. 273.　91a. Cf. Hans Eppstein, "J. S. Bachs Triosonate G-Dur (BWV 1039) und ihre Beziehungen zur Sonate für Gambe und Cembalo G-Dur (BWV 1027)," DMF, XVIII (1965), 126-37.

P. 273.　93a. Further views on origins, sources, and plans are offered by the editor of this collection for the *Neue* [Bach] *Ausgabe,* Christoph Wolff, in "New Research on Bach's *Musical Offering,*" MQ, LVII (1971), 379-408.

P. 275.　102a. For more about the HORTUSM ed., cf. DMF, XXII (1969), 209-12 (Schoenbaum refuting charges by H. Unverricht). Among increasing studies, cf. Camillo Schoenbaum, "Die Kammermusik-werke des Jan Dismas Zelenka," in KONGRESS 1956 (Vienna), pp. 552-562, with exx. and reference to a dissertation on this music (Jena, 1956) by Karl-Heinz Köhler; also, Hubert Unverricht, "Einige Bemerkungen zur 4. Sonate von Johann Dismas Zelenka," DMF, XIII (1960), pp. 329-333 (reporting recovered parts), and "Zur Datierung der Bläsersonaten von Johann Dismas Zelenka," DMF, XV (1962), 265-268 (with the composition year placed early, perhaps around 1714-15). On the state of Zelenka MSS in Dresden, cf. D. Plamenac in NOTES, XIX (1962), 589-90. New Bohemian sonatas are being brought to light in the *Musica antiqua bohemica* series (Prague: Artia, from about 1948)—e.g., the 17th-century orchestral sonatas of **P. J. Vejvanovský** (vols. 36, 47-49) and **Jan Křtitel Tolar** (vol. 40), and the 18th-century ensemble Sonata in a, of **František Ignác Antonín Tuma** (1704-74; a pupil of Fux in Vienna; vol. 69).

P. 276.　108a. A recent unpublished Ph.D. dissertation is that of Hans Rudolf Jung, "Johann Georg Pisendel (1687-1755), Leben und Werke" Friedrich-Schiller-Universität: Jena, 1956), with discussions of the two sonatas (pp. 255-64), with conjectured dates that would put Pisendel's sonatas before Bach's (p. 266: "before 1716" for the unaccompanied sonata, and "shortly after 1717" for the other sonata), and with a thematic index (sons. on p. XXXIV of the "Anhang").

P. 277.　116a. The first extended discussion of Quantz's sons., including MSS, eds., and structures, is provided by Edward R. Reilly in the companion vol. to his translation of Quantz's *Versuch* (see QUANTZ-FACSIMILE in the Bibliography): *Quantz and his Versuch* (New York: Galaxy [for the American Musicological Society], 1971), 1-39 and 134-163.

P. 278.　118a. QUANTZ-FACSIMILE, p. 327.

P. 279.　123a. Cf., also, CAT. SCHWERIN, I, p. 352.

P. 285.　159a. Mod. ed.: Sonata in E minor (Kassel: Bärenreiter, 1958), edited by Ermeler.

P. 285. 159b. A recent unpublished Ph.D. dissertation is that of Jean Horstman, "The Instrumental Music of Johann Ludwig Krebs" (Boston University, 1959), including a discussion of the chamber music (pp. 274-85), with exx., and a thematic index (pp. 90-144, with some 20 sons.).

P. 287. 170a. Cf. the facs. of the cover page in SUBIRÁ-ALBA, opposite p. 118.

P. 289. 180a. The projected mod. ed. of the *Sonata à due cembali*, cited in footnote 180, above, was published by Hinrichsen in London in 1960.

P. 291. 192a. The monumental but incomplete study by the late Walter Serauky—*Händel, sein Leben, sein Werk*, vols. 3-5 (Kassel: Bärenreiter, 1956-58)—includes a discussion only of the "trio" sons. Op. 5. But an unpublished Ph.D. dissertation has been completed by Albert Oran Gould on "The Flute Sonatas of George Fredrich Handel" (University of Illinois, 1961), including background, editions, structure, performance, and a thematic index (pp. 190-96). The only article directly devoted to the sonatas in the *Händel-Jahrbuch* through 1968 (Leipzig: VEB Deutscher Verlag für Musik, 1955—) is that by Robert Gottlieb (Vol. XII [1966], 93-108), "Französischer, italienischer und vermischter Stil in den Solosonaten Georg Friedrich Händels," including numerous exx.

P. 291. 194a. Among the steadily continuing additions to the literature on Handel may be noted the comprehensive *Händel Bibliographie* by Konrad Sasse (Leipzig: VEB Deutscher Verlag für Musik, 1967 [2d ed.]), with son. literature on pp. 212-214 and 399, and son. recordings on pp. 252-253 and 408; and the important new treatment of the man and his works by Paul Henry Lang, *George Frideric Handel* (New York: W. W. Norton, 1966), in which the discussion of the chamber music (pp. 640-647) emphasizes Italian influences, especially Corelli's. Cf., also, A. Mann and J. M. Knapp, "The Present State of Handel Research," in AM, XLI (1969), 4-26 (including editions of the violin and flute sonatas on pp. 24-25).

P. 292. 203a. Five of the keyboard sonatas have appeared (1970) in HANDEL-AUSGABEM IV/6.

P. 293. 210a. The presumably better, earliest known dates are given as 1773, *ca.* 1722, and 1739, respectively, in BRITISH UNION, I, p. 442.

P. 294. 215a. In A. Craig Bell's *Chronological Catalogue of Handel's Works* (Greenock [Scotland]: The Grain-Aig Press, 1969), p. 60, Op. 5 is found to be but "a series of Suites strung together from earlier works such as the Chandos Anthems, Oboe Concertos, Te Deums, [and] Operas," whether made by Handel or some other.

P. 299. 241a. For a general survey, cf. Ernest Eugene Helm, *Music at the Court of Frederick the Great* (Norman: University of Oklahoma Press, 1960).

P. 302.   2a. In *William Lawes* (London: Routledge and Kegan Paul, 1960), Murray Lefkowitz sees the pre-Commonwealth "fantasia-suites" or "setts" (to which he freely applies the term "sonata") as ancestors of Purcell's sonatas and as "counterparts" (but not in style!) of the Italian *sonata da camera* (cf., especially, pp. 106-125, with exx., and pp. 293-316, with a completely scored "Fantazia" by William Lawes for violin, bass viol, and organ). Cf. the reviews of Lefkowitz's edition of Lawes's "Consort Music" (*Musica Britannica*, XXI) by David Boyden in NOTES, XXII (1965-66), 804-6, and Franklin Zimmerman in JAMS, XVIII (1965), 414-16.

P. 303.   9a. Cf., also, the facs. in MGG, VI, cols. 1877-78.

P. 303.   10a. Recall, also, the article cited in footnote 18a to p. 56.

P. 304.   13a. The second of 3 Purcell studies projected by Franklin B. Zimmerman is *Henry Purcell, 1659-1695—His Life and Times* (New York: St. Martin's Press, 1967). The first of these studies is the *Analytic Catalogue* cited below in footnote 14a to p. 305; the third is to consist of "Analytical Essays on His Musical Forms."

P. 305.   14a. Cf. the important new bibliographic study by Franklin B. Zimmerman (initiated as an appendix to "Purcell's Musical Heritage, A Study of Musical Styles in Seventeenth-Century England," unpublished Ph.D. dissertation, University of Southern California, 1958), *Henry Purcell, 1659-1695, An Analytic Catalogue of His Music* (New York: St Martin's Press, 1963), with "Sonatas and Related Forms" on pp. 383-99, an additional "Sonata While the Sun Rises" or "Symphony" to Act IV of *The Fairy Queen* (item 629/27), and two "Sonata" fragments (p. 427). Cf., also, Helene Wessely-Kropik, "Henry Purcell als Instrumentalkomponist," SZMW, XXII (1955), 85-141.

P. 307.   26a. A new study is that of Helene Wessely-Kropik, *Lelio Colista* [preferred spelling], *ein römischer Meister vor Corelli: Leben und Umwelt* (Vienna: Hermann Böhlaus, 1961), including a partially thematic index but no separate discussion of the music; cf. Owen H. Jander's review in JAMS, XVI (1963), 401-3. Cf., also, Tilmouth's article cited in footnote 17 above.

P. 307.   27a. Mod. eds.: Son. 3, HAUSMUSIKm, no. 139; Son. in A, HORTUSm, no. 172. Anonymous Son. 10 (by "N. N. Romano") in Anth. SILVANIm is actually by Colista (according to Wessely-Kropik as cited in footnote 14a above).

P. 308.   30a. Two recent studies are those of George Alfred Proctor, "The Works of Nicola Matteis, Sr." (unpublished Ph.D. dissertation, Eastman School of Music, 1960), and Michael Tilmouth, "Nicola Matteis," MQ, XLVI (1960), 22-40. The latter edited a "trio" son. in G in 1963 (London: Stainer & Bell).

P. 314.   66a. The dissertation cited in footnote 66 above was completed in 1961 and includes both a "Source Index" of the works (pp. 94-101) and a complete "Thematic Index" (Supplement).

P. 314.   68a. The Loeillet and his works described above largely conforms to the brother known as "John of London" but must be distinguished further from Jacques L. Loeillet, and from the Jean-Baptiste Loeillet born in 1688, as he has been in the valuable article by Alec Skempton, "The Instrumental Sonatas of the Loeillets," ML, XLIII (1962), 206-17, including a full music bibliography and further references to mod. eds. The distinctions had not yet been clarified when the similarly valuable thematic index of Loeillet compositions (overlooked above) appeared in *Revue belge de musicologie*, VI (1952), 219-74.

P. 317.   4a. They have now been discussed by Michael Tilmouth, in "James Sherard: An English Amateur Composer," in ML, XLVII (1966), 313-322, including an ex. from Op. 1, No. 6, and a facs. (opposite p. 299) of the title page of Op. 1 in print.

P. 319.   15a. BRITISH UNION, II, p. 919, also lists *Six Setts of Lessons for the Harpsichord* (*ca.* 1745), which may or may not derive from the sonatas listed above.

P. 319.   16a. The discovery of more music for the same instruments (but in normal notation) is reported by Günther Weiss in "57 unbekannte Instrumentalstücke (15 Sonaten) von Attilio Ariosti in einer Abschrift von Johan Helmich Roman," in DMF, XXIII (1970), 127-138, with exx. and tables.

P. 320.   27a. Mod. ed.: Son. 5, GIEGLING-SOLOM, no. 8. A high tribute to Lonati from F. M. Veracini is quoted (pp. 38-39) by G. Barblan in "Un ignoto Omaggio di Francesco Geminiani ad Arcangelo Corelli," CHIGIANA, XIX (1962), 35-41.

P. 324.   45a. Cf., also, Franz Giegling, "Geminiani's Harpsichord Transcriptions," ML, XL (1959), 350-52. Geminiani's transcription of his own S/bass Son. Op. IV/8,3 is reproduced in GIEGLING-SOLOM, no. 10.

P. 325.   52a. They are not the same according to Westrup in MR, XX (1959), 317-18. The "1732" set is dated 1733 in BRITISH UNION, I, 358; it is reproduced in facs. in Klitz's dissertation (see p. 56n above).

P. 327.   61a. Interesting harmonic problems created by the *b. c.* are analyzed in ARNOLD, pp. 609, 612, 661, 820, 823, and 827, with 8 exx.

P. 328.   64a. Cf., also, Charles Cudworth, "Boyce and Arne: 'The Generation of 1710,'" ML, XLI (1960), 136-45; and footnote 72a below.

P. 328.   65a. Cf., also, A. E. Dickinson, "Arne and the Keyboard Sonata," MMR, LXXXV (1955), 88-95.

P. 329.   67a. All 7 of these sons. have now been issued by Hinrichsen (Murrill). A facs. of the first ed. has been published by Stainer & Bell (London, 1969), with preface by Gwilyn Beechey and Thurston Dart.

P. 330.   72a. Cf. footnote 64a above and Stanley Sadie, "The Chamber Music of Boyce and Arne," MQ, XLVI (1960), 425-36.

P. 331. 75a. Mod. ed. of complete set: Hinrichsen (Sadie and Murrill).

P. 334. 82a. The new edition of Gluck's *Werke* contains the complete set in Vol. V/1, with preface.

P. 335. 83a. For more detailed comparisons of the two sets cf. Fausto Torrefranca, "Le Sinfonie dell'imbrattacarte (G. B. Sanmartini)," RMI, XXII (1915), p. 439, and Robert Sondheimer, "Giovanni Battista Sammartini," ZFMW, III (1920-21), 95-97.

P. 337. 102a. Mod. ed. of a "Sonate en la mineur" (S/bass; ed. by E. Ysaÿe) : Schott Frères (Brussels, 1966).

P. 338. 114a. Stanley Sadie singles out another composer of this period as obscure, yet "among the finest of their time"—**F. E. Fisher** (MT, CIV [1963], 864-66) with discussion of 2 sets of his sons. and 5 exx.

P. 340. 7a. Mod. ed. complete: *Das Erbe deutscher Musik*, vol. 44 (Kassel: Nagels, 1956).

P. 341. 14a. Mod. ed. from this set: *Oud-Nederlandsche Speelmusik* (1948).

P. 343. 19a. Mod. ed.: 3 SSB/bass sons., Broekmans & van Poppel (Amsterdam; C. F. Peters in U. S. A.), 1960 (Brandts-Buys); cf. NOTES, XVIII (1961), 648-49.

P. 345. 44a. New information on the life and works, including a new index of authentic and questioned works (with incipits as needed), may be found in Albert Dunning and Arend Koole, "Pietro Antonio Locatelli," TVNM, XX (1964-65), 52-96. In 1961 a complete edition of Locatelli was being projected by Dr. Koole (cf. the review of Vol. IV, containing the six *introduttioni teatrali* in Op. 4, in NOTES, XXI [1963-64], 233-235 [Ringer]). A further extended study to report, greatly augmenting the available information in English, is the unpublished Ph.D. dissertation by John Hendrik Calmeyer, "The Life, Times and Works of Pietro Antonio Locatelli" (The University of North Carolina, 1969), including exx., illustrations, and documents.

P. 346. 54a. Further mod. eds.: 6 sons., CLASSICIm II, vol. 14 (Polo) ; Son. 2, GIEGLING-SOLom, no. 9.

P. 346. 55a. The cover of the original edition appears in SUBIRA-ALBA, p. 117. Another mod. ed.: Son. 2, Op. 8, ed. by E. Koch and B. Weigart (Mainz: B. Schott, 1968).

P. 349. 69a. An extended, outstanding study of this important composer appeared while the present book was being written: Ingmar Bengtsson, *J. H. Roman och hans Instrumentalmusik, käll- och stilkritiska studier* (Uppsala: Almqvist & Wiksells, 1955), including style analyses, full indices and catalogues, an especially rich investigation into the problem of authenticity (supplemented by an appendix volume, same year and publisher), and an English "Summary" (pp. 423-43) : cf. Jan LaRue's review in MQ, XLV (1959), 397-99.

P. 350. 73a. Roman's complete works are to be included in the new *Monumenta Musicae Svecicae* (cf. MQ, XLV [1959], 395-97 [La-Rue]), starting with Vol. I, *Assaggi à violino solo*. The 12 "Sviter" for harpsichord (surprisingly *galant* pieces in 3 to 6 movements, which might well have been called "sonatas" at that time) were published in 2 vols. by Nordiska in Stockholm in 1947 and 1948 (O. Vretblad).

P. 352. 8a. A charming account of the early performances of Corelli in Paris is given by Michel Corrette in *Le Mâitre de clavecin pour l'accompagnement* (Paris: L'Auteur, 1753), pp. A and B.

P. 363. 56a. For a mod. ed. of a son. for trumpet, oboe, and strings, cf. NOTES, XXII (1965-66), 833.

P. 364. 62a. A further mod. ed. from Op. 1· is reviewed in NOTES, XXII (1965-66), 810-11.

P. 368. 4a. All nine sets are listed in CAT. SCHWERIN, II, 41-42, with dedications in full, pp. 385-387. Mod. ed.: 6 Sons., Op. 2, 2 vols., ed. by W. Kolneder (Edition Peters WM 44 and WM 80); cf. NOTES, XXIII (1967), 615-616.

P. 369. 14a. A recent unpublished Ph.D. dissertation is that of Anne L. Kish, "The Life and Works of J. B. Senaillé," Bryn Mawr College, 1964.

P. 376. 41a. But cf. the outstanding new, unpublished Ph.D. diss. by Jane Meredith Bowers, "The French Flute School from 1700 to 1760" (University of California at Berkeley, 1971), including substantial discussions and full lists of works for Boismortier, Naudot, and Blavet (SBE, pp. 376-377), among others. Cited in Dr. Bowers' preface (p. iv) are two other recent, unpublished doctoral dissertations that pertain here, both completed in 1970—that of Jervis Underwood on Naudot (North Texas State University) and that of Walter J. Jones on French duets for transverse flutes (University of Iowa).

P. 376. 44a. Add 3 sets of sons. for 2 cellos, violes, or bassoons, Opp. 14, 40, and 46; and 2 sets for cello and *b.c.*, Opp. 26 and 50. Mod. ed.: *Sonates pour flûte et* [realized!] *clavecin*, Op. 91, ed. by Marc λincherle (Paris: Heugel [No. 20 in the series "Le Pupitre"], 1970); cf. J. Caldwell in ML, LII (1971), 209.

P. 380. 74a. Cf. further in SCE, p. 783, footnote 44.

P. 380. 75a. A recent, important, unpublished dissertation is that of Robert Elwyn Preston, "The Forty-Eight Sonatas for Violin and Figured Bass of Jean-Marie Leclair," University of Michigan, 1959, with extended sections on the background, styles and forms, performance practices, and sources. Cf., also, Preston's article, "Leclair's Posthumous Solo Sonata [Op. 15]; An Enigma," in *Recherches sur la Musique française classique*, VII (1967), 154-163; and his mod. ed. (to date) of the 12 sons. in Op. 5 and Sons. 1-6 from Op. 9, 3 vols., with extended Preface and facs. of original eds. (Madison: A-R Editions, 1968-70; Op. 5 is reviewed in NOTES, XXVI [1970], 609-610 [E. Borroff]).

P. 381.   80a. Mod. ed., complete set: Music Press, 2 vols. (New York, 1946-47; Sydney Beck). A further mod. ed. of Op. 3 was edited by W. Rost in 1963 (New York: C. F. Peters).

P. 383.   88a. Leclair's use of *b. c.* raises exceptional harmonic problems, often requiring 5-part realizations, as discussed in ARNOLD, pp. 353-59, 404-5, 556-57, 589, 598, 606-9, 622-25, 636, 671, 723, 809, 817, 821, 833, 844, 851, 853, 859, 863, 865, 868-72, 885-86, with 66 (!) exx.

P. 387.   106a. In SUBIRÁ-ALBA, opposite pp. 113-15, are facs. of the covers of Opp. 4 and 5, and a *b. c.* part.

P. 388.   113a. Another violinist who might have been included here for 3 sets of "solo" and "trio" sons. is **André Joseph Exaudet** (*ca.* 1710-62). Cf. LAURENCIE, II, 164-73; SUBIRÁ-ALBA, opposite p. 112 (for a facs. of the cover of Op. 1); MGG, III, cols. 1648-51. **Barthélemy De Caix** (1716-?), violinist from Lyon under the influence of Corelli and Vivaldi, should also be mentioned, for his *VI Sonates pour deux pardessus de viole à cinq cordes, violons ou basses de viole,* Op. 1 (ca. 1750?, cf. MGG, III, cols. 77-79, with facs. of title page).

P. 388.   114a. Cf., also, the valuable, recent unpublished Ph.D. dissertation by G. Jean Shaw, "The Violoncello Sonata Literature in France During the Eighteenth Century," The Catholic University of America, 1963.

P. 390.   128a. Shaw (note 114a, above), p. 75, concludes that he did not.

Bibliography

Note: All the short-title references in the present book, including initials used only in this Bibliography to represent the most cited periodicals, will be found in the one approximately alphabetical listing that follows. References with a lower-case "m" at the end indicate sources made up primarily of music. Articles in GROVE and MGG and single volumes in the various "Denkmäler" series do not have separate entries in the Bibliography, but their authors or editors are cited where the first references occur in the text.

ABERT-LEOPOLDm   Hermann Abert (ed.), *Leopold Mozart's Little Music Book.* New York: Edwin F. Kalmus, 1950.

ABRAHAM-HANDEL   Gerald Abraham (ed.), *Handel, A Symposium.* London: Oxford University Press, 1954.

AFMW   *Archiv für Musikwissenschaft.* 1918-27, 1952—.

ALARD-VIOLINm   Delphin Alard (ed.), *Les Maîtres classiques du violon.* Leipzig: B. Schott's Söhne (from *ca.* 1868).

ALBINI-GABRIELLI   Eugenio Albini, "Domenico Gabrielli, il Corelli del Violoncello," RMI, XLI (1937), 71-75.

ALDEN-MOTIVE   Edgar Hiester Alden, "The Role of the Motive in Musical Structure," unpublished Ph.D. dissertation, The University of North Carolina (Chapel Hill), 1956.

ALLEN-PHILOSOPHIES   Warren Dwight Allen, *Philosophies of Music History.* New York: American Book Co., 1939.

ALTMANN   Wilhelm Altmann, *Kammermusik-Katalog.* 6th ed. (to Aug., 1944). Leipzig: Friedrich Hofmeister, 1945; Suppl., 1944-58, ed. by J. F. Richter (1960).

ALTMANN-BACH   ————, "Zur Verbreitung von Bachs Sonaten und Suiten für Violine bzw. Violoncell allein," DM, XV, Part I (1922-23), 206-207.

AM   *Acta musicologica.* 1928—.

AMZ   *Allgemeine musikalische Zeitung.* 3 series: 1798-1848, 1863-65, 1866-82.

ANTH. ARRESTIm

Sonate da organo di varii autori. Bologna (ca. 1700). Cf. SARTORI-BIBLIOGRAFIA, 1700K; NEWMAN-EARLIEST, pp. 207 and 57. See footnote 48a, p. 143.

ANTH. BOLOGNAm I

Sonate per camera a violino e violoncello di vari autori C. B. F. Bologna? (*ca.* 1700). Cf. SARTORI-BIBLIOGRAFIA, 1690 or 1700?; HAAS-ESTENSISCHEN, pp. 115 ff.

ANTH. BOLOGNAm II

Sonate a tre di vari autori. Bologna? (*ca.* 1700). Cf. SARTORI-BIBLIOGRAFIA, 17001.

ANTH. BOLOGNAm III

Sonate à violino e violoncello di vari autori. Bologna? (*ca.* 1700). Cf. CAT. BOLOGNA, IV, 76; PINCHERLE-CORELLI, p. 177.

ANTH. BONONCINIm

Six Solos for Two Violoncellos, composed by Sigr. Bononcini and other eminent Authors. London: J. Simpson (*ca.* 1740). Cf. BRITISH PRINTED, I, 173.

ANTH. CORONAm

Corona di dodici fiori armonici tessuta da altretanti ingegni sonori a trè strumenti. Bologna, 1706. Cf. CAT. BOLOGNA, IV, 76.

ANTH. HAFFNERm

Johann Ulrich Haffner (ed.), *Oeuvres mêlées . . . pour le clavessin,* 12 vols. Nürnberg: J. U. Haffner (1755-65). Cf. HOFFMANN/ERBRECHT-HAFFNER.

ANTH. HANDELm

Six Solos, Four for a German Flute and a Bass and Two for a Violin with a Thorough Bass for the Harpsicord or Bass Violin. London: I. Walsh (*ca.* 1730). Cf. BRITISH PRINTED, I, 580.

ANTH. HARMONIAm

Harmonia mundi: Consisting of Six Favorite Sonata's [SS/bass]. . . . London: I. Walsh (1707). Cf. SMITH-WALSH, item 257.

ANTH. MAGAZINm

Musikalisches Magazin, in Sonaten, Sinfonien, Trios und andern Stücken für das Clavier bestehend. Leipzig: Breitkopf und Sohn, 1765. Cf. CAT. BRUX-ELLES, II, item 6316.

ANTH. MARPURGm

Friedrich Wilhelm Marpurg (ed.), *Musikalisches Allerley von verschiedenen Tonkünstlern,* 40 pieces in 9 collections. Berlin: Birnsteil, 1761-63. Cf. WOLFFHEIM, I, item 1223.

ANTH. ROSTm

A collection of 150 instrumental pieces in MS, mostly German and Italian "trio" sonatas; formed by Canon Rost of Strasbourg and acquired by Brossard in 1688. Cf. p. 363; BIBLIOTHÈQUE NATIONALE, VIII, 35 ff.

ANTH. SILVANIm

Scielta delle suonate a due violini, con il basso continuo per l'organo, raccolte da diversi eccelenti autori. Bologna: Giacomo Monti, 1680. Cf. p. 138 and SARTORI-BIBLIOGRAFIA, p. 495.

BIBLIOGRAPHY 415

ANTH. VENIERm   *XX Sonate per cembalo di varri autorri . . . Opera prima.* Paris: Venier (*ca.* 1758). Cf. BIBLIOTHÈQUE NATIONALE, VIII, 34.

ANTH. WELCKERm   *Six Lessons for the Harpsichord. . . .* London: Welcker (*ca.* 1770). Cf. BRITISH PRINTED, II, 39, and 1st Supp., p. 16.

ANTIPHONALEm   *Antiphonale sacrosanctae romanae ecclesiae.* Rome: The Vatican, 1912.

APEL-DICTIONARY   Willi Apel, *Harvard Dictionary of Music.* Cambridge, Mass.: Harvard University Press, 1944.

APEL-NEAPOLITAN   ———, "Neapolitan Links Between Cabezon and Frescobaldi," MQ, XXIV (1938), 418-437.

ARNOLD   Frank Thomas Arnold, *The Art of Accompaniment From a Thorough-Bass,* 2 vols. New York: Dover Publications, 1965 (reprint of Oxford ed. of 1931).

ARNOLD-CORELLI   Frank Thomas Arnold, "A Corelli Forgery?" PMA, XLVII (1920-21), 93-99.

ARUNDELL-PURCELL   Dennis Arundell, *Purcell.* London: Oxford University Press, 1928.

BABITZ-TARTINI   Giuseppe Tartini, "Treatise on Ornamentation," translated and edited by Sol Babitz, JRME (Fall, 1956), 75-102.

BACH-FACSIMILEm   Johann Sebastian Bach, *Sei Solo a violino senza basso accompagnato, libro primo . . . 1720.* Facsimile, with preface by William Martin Luther. Kassel: Bärenreiter-Verlag, 1950.

BACH-WERKEm   *Johann Sebastian Bachs Werke.* 47 vols. Leipzig: Bach-Gesellschaft (Breitkopf & Härtel), 1851-99 and 1926.

BACHMANN-VIOLINISTES   Alberto Bachmann, *Les grands violinistes du passé.* Paris: Librairie Fischbacher, 1913.

BÄR-VERACINIm   Franz Bär (ed.), *Francesco Maria Veracini,* [3] *Sonaten für Violine (Flöte) und Generalbass* (1716 [before Op. 1], Nos. 1-3). Kassel: Bärenreiter-Verlag, 1950.

BAGGE   Selmar Bagge, "Die geschichtliche Entwickelung der Sonate," in Paul Graf Waldersee, *Sammlung Musikalischer Vorträge* (Leipzig: Breitkopf & Härtel, 1880), II, 201-224.

BAINES   Anthony Baines, *Woodwind Instruments and their History.* New York: W. W. Norton, 1957.

BARBLAN-BONPORTI   Guglielmo Barblan, *Un musicista trentino: Francesco A. Bonporti.* Florence: Felice le Monnier, 1940.

416 BIBLIOGRAPHY

BARISON-STRADELLAm   Cesare Barison (ed.), Alessandro Stradella: Two "solo" violin "sonatas" in D and G. Trieste: Schmidl, 1912. Cf. SCHMIDL, II, 554; ALTMANN, p. 223; RMI, XLV (1941), 9 and 11.

BECHLER & RAHM   Leo Bechler and Bernhardt Rahm, *Die Oboe und die ihr verwandten Instrumente*. Leipzig: Carl Merseburger, 1914.

BECKER-HAUSMUSIK   Carl Ferdinand Becker, *Die Hausmusik in Deutschland in dem 16., 17. und 18. Jahrhunderte*. Leipzig: Fest'sche Verlagsbuchhandlung, 1840.

BECKER-KLAVIERSONATE   ———, "Die Klaviersonate in Deutschland," NZM, VII (1837), 25, 29, and 33.

BECKER-TONWERKE   ———, *Die Tonwerke des 16. und 17. Jahrhunderts*. Leipzig: Ernst Fleischer, 1855.

BECKMANN   Gustav Beckmann, *Das Violinspiel in Deutschland vor 1700*. Leipzig: N. Simrock, 1918.

BECKMANNm   ——— (ed.), *Das Violinspiel in Deutschland vor 1700: 12 Sonaten für Violine und Klavier . . .*, 4 vols. Leipzig: N. Simrock, 1921.

BECKMANN-PACHELBEL   ———, "Johann Pachelbel als Kammerkomponist," AFMW, I (1918-19), 267-274.

BERG-LOCATELLI   J. Berg, "Pietro Locatelli da Bergamo," TVNM, X (1915), 185-194.

BERGMANS-LOIELLETS   Paul Bergmans, *Une Famille de musiciens belges du XVIIIᵉ siècle: les Loiellets*. Brussels, 1927.

BESWICK   Delbert Meacham Beswick, "The Problem of Tonality in Seventeenth-Century Music," unpublished Ph.D. dissertation, The University of North Carolina (Chapel Hill), 1950.

BETTI-GEMINIANIm   Adolfo Betti (ed.), *Francesco Geminiani: Sonata a violino solo senza basso*. New York: Music Press, 1949.

BIBLIOTHÈQUE NATIONALE   Jules Ecorcheville, *Catalogue du fonds de musique ancienne de la Bibliothèque nationale*, 8 vols. Paris: Terquem, 1910-14.

BIE   Oscar Bie, *A History of the Pianoforte and Pianoforte Players*, translated by Kullak and Mayer. New York: E. P. Dutton, 1899.

BJ   *Bach-Jahrbuch*. 1904—.

BLUME-VIOLINSONATE   Friedrich Blume, "Eine unbekannte Violinsonate von J. S. Bach," BJ, XXV (1928), 96-118.

BODLEIAN MSS   *Summary Catalogue of Western Manuscripts in the Bodleian Library at Oxford*, 7 vols. Oxford: Clarendon Press, 1897-1953.

BÖHME-STÖLTZELm   Erdmann Werner Böhme (ed.), *Enharmonische Claviersonate von Herrn Capellmeister Stoelzel zu Gotha*. Kassel: Bärenreiter-Ausgabe 959, 1935.

BOGHEN-PASQUINIm   Felice Boghen (ed.), *Bernardo Pasquini: Due Sonate per 2 pianoforte*, realizzate e pubblicate da. . . . Paris: Durand, 1924.

BOHN-MUSIKDRUCKWERKE   Emil Bohn, *Bibliographie der Musik-Druckwerke bis 1700 welche . . . zu Breslau aufbewahrt werden.* Berlin: Albert Cohn, 1883.

BONAVENTURA-PASQUINI   Arnaldo Bonaventura, *Bernardo Pasquini.* Rome: Ascoli Piceno, 1923.

BORREL   Eugène Borrel, *La Sonate.* Paris: Larousse, 1951.

BOSQUET-ORIGINE   Emile Bosquet, "Origine et formation de la sonate allemande pour clavecin de 1698 a 1742," RIM, I (1939), Nos. 5 and 6 ("Le Piano"), 853-862.

BOURDELOT & BONNET 1715   Abbé Bourdelot, Pierre Bonnet, and Jacques Bonnet, *Histoire de la musique.* Paris: J. Chochart, 1715.

BOURDELOT & BONNET 1725   ———, *Histoire de la musique,* 4 vols. (vols. 2-4 being Freneuse's *Comparaison* in 3 parts). Amsterdam: Le Cène, 1726.

BOURKE-FREDERICK   John Bourke, "Frederick the Great as Music-Lover and Musician," ML, XXVIII (1947), 71-77.

BOUVET   Charles Bouvet, *Une Dynastie de musiciens français: les Couperin.* Paris: Delagrave, 1919.

BOUWSTEENEN   *Bouwsteenen, Jaarboek der Vereeniging voor noord-nederlands Musiekgeschiedenis.* 1869—.

BOYDEN-ARIOSTI   David D. Boyden, "Ariosti's Lessons for Viola d'Amore," MQ, XXXII (1946), 545-563.

BOYDEN-GEMINIANI   ——— (ed.), *Francesco Geminiani: The Art of Playing on the Violin, 1751.* London: Oxford University Press (1952). Cf. D. D. Boyden, "Geminiani and the First Violin Tutor," AM, XXXI (1959), 161 ff., and XXXII (1960), 40-47 ("Postscript").

BOYDEN-TARTINI   ———, Review of recording of 4 S/bass sonatas by Giuseppe Tartini, MQ, XXXIX (1953), 151-153.

BOYDEN-TECHNIQUE   ———, "The Violin and its Technique in the 18th Century," MQ, XXXVI (1950), 9-38.

BREITKOPF KAMMERSONATENm   *Kammersonaten ausgewählte Werke alter Musik für ein Soloinstrument mit Begleitung.* Leipzig: Breitkopf & Härtel, from 1928.

BREMT   F. van den Bremt, *Willem de Fesch (1687-1757?) Nederlands Componist en Virtuoos, Leven en Werk.* Leuven: Universiteitsbibliotheek, 1949.

BRENET-CLASSIQUES   Michel Brenet (Marie Bobillier), "Les grands Classiques," ENCYCLOPÉDIE, I, Part 2, 1014-1060.

BRENET-CONCERTS   ———, *Les Concerts sous l'ancien régime.* Paris: Librairie Fischbacher, 1900.

BRENET-LIBRAIRIE   ———, "La Librairie musicale en France de 1653
                        à 1790, d'aprés les Registres de privilèges," SIMG,
                        VIII (1906-07), 401-466.

BRENZONI-ABACO   Raffaello Brenzoni, "Un grande Musicista veronese,
                        Evaristo Felice dall'Abbaco," NA, XII (1935), 154-
                        164.

BRENZONI-TORELLI   ———, "Giuseppe Torelli, musicista veronese . . . ,"
                        NA, XIII (1936), 22-37.

BRIDGE-PURCELL   J. Frederick Bridge, "Purcell's Fantazias and
                        Sonatas," PMA, XLII (1915-16), 4-13.

BRITISH HIRSCH   *Music in the Hirsch Library* (*Catalogue of Printed
                        Music in the British Museum:* Accessions, Part 53).
                        London: The Trustees of the British Museum, 1951.

BRITISH MS   Augustus Hughes-Hughes, *Catalogue of Manuscript
                        Music in the British Museum,* 3 vols. London,
                        1906-09.

BRITISH PRINTED   W. Barclay Squire, *Catalogue of Printed Music . . .
                        in the British Museum,* 2 vols. (incl. First Supple-
                        ment). London, 1912. Second Supplement, 1940.

BRITISH UNION   Edith B. Schnapper (ed.), *The British Union-
                        Catalogue of Early Music, Printed Before the Year
                        1801,* 2 vols. London: Butterworths Scientific Pub-
                        lications, 1957.

BROSSARD   Sébastien de Brossard, *Dictionaire de musique,* 3d
                        ed. Amsterdam: E. Roger (*ca.* 1710).

BROWN-BACH   Virginia Hare Brown, "The Use of the Term
                        'Sonata' by J. S. Bach," unpublished master's thesis,
                        The University of North Carolina (Chapel Hill),
                        1952.

BRUNOLD-COUPERIN   Paul Brunold, *François Couperin,* translated by J. B.
                        Hanson. Monaco: Lyrebird Press, 1949.

BUCHMAYER-RITTER   Richard Buchmayer, "Christian Ritter, ein verges-
                        sener deutscher Meister des 17. Jahrhunderts," in
                        Riemann-Festschrift (Leipzig: Max Hesses Verlag,
                        1909), pp. 354-380 (plus 16 pps. of exs., incl.
                        "Sonatina für Orgel" 9-16).

BUKOFZER-BAROQUE   Manfred Bukofzer, *Music in the Baroque Era.*
                        New York: W. W. Norton, 1947.

BULLOCKm   Ernest Bullock (ed.), *Charles Macklean: Sonata for
                        Flute and Bass.* London: Oxford University Press,
                        1948.

BUONAMICI-DELLA   Giuseppe Buonamici (ed.), *3 Sonate per cembalo.*
CIAJAm   Florence: C. Bratti, 1912.

BURNEY-ACCOUNT   Charles Burney, *An Account of the Musical Per-
                        formances in Westminster Abbey, and the Pantheon.*
                        London: T. Payne, 1785.

BURNEY-FRANCE ———, *The Present State of Music in France and Italy*. London: T. Becket, 1771.

BURNEY-GERMANY ———, *The Present State of Music in Germany, the Netherlands, and United Provinces*, 2 vols. London: T. Becket, 1773.

BURNEY-HISTORY ———, *A General History of Music* (1776-89), with critical and historical notes by Charles Mercer, 2 vols. New York: Harcourt, Brace, 1935.

BUSI-MARTINI Leonida Busi, *Il Padre G. B. Martini*. Bologna: Nicola Zanichelli, 1891.

CANNON-MATTHESON Beekman C. Cannon, *Johann Mattheson, Spectator in Music*. New Haven: Yale University Press, 1947.

CAPRI Antonio Capri, *Giuseppe Tartini*. Milan: Garzanti, 1945.

CARSE-XVII Adam Carse, "XVII Century Orchestral Instruments," ML, I (1920), 334-342.

CARSE-XVIII ———, *The Orchestra in the XVIIIth Century*. Cambridge, Eng.: W. Heffer, 1940.

CARTIERm Jean-Baptiste Cartier (ed.), *L'Art du violon ou collection choisie dans les sonates des ecoles itallienne, françoise et allemande*, 2d ed. Paris: Decombe, 1798.

CAT. BOLOGNA *Catalogo della Biblioteca del Liceo musicale in Bologna*, 5 vols. Bologna: Federico Parisini, 1890-1905, 1943.

CAT. BRUXELLES Alfred Wotquenne, *Catalogue de la Bibliothèque du Conservatoire royal de musique de Bruxelles*, 2 vols. Brussels: J. J. Coosemans, 1898 and 1902.

CAT. CHRIST CHURCH G. E. P. Arkwright, *Catalogue of Music in the Library of Christ Church*, Oxford, vol. I. London: Oxford University Press, 1915.

CAT. CORELLIANA *Catalogo della Mostra Corelliana*. Rome (Palazzo Braschi), 1954.

CAT. HAUSBIBLIOTHEK Georg Thouret, *Katalog der Musiksammlung auf der Königlichen Hausbibliothek im Schlosse zu Berlin*. Leipzig: Breitkopf & Härtel, 1895.

CAT. SCHWERIN Otto Kade, *Die Musikalien-Sammlung des Grossherzoglich Mecklenburg-Schweriner Fürstenhauses aus den letzten zwei Jahrhunderten*, 2 vols. Schwerin: Sandmeyer, 1893.

CAT. UPSALA Åke Davidsson, *Catalogue critique et descriptif des imprimés de musique des xvie et xviie siècles conservés a la Bibliothèque de l'Université royale d'Upsala*, vol. II. Uppsala: Almqvist & Wiksells, 1951.

CAT. WALSH — *A Catalogue of Vocal & Instrumental Musick Published by John Walsh and his successors, 1706-90,* with a preface by William C. Smith. London: The First Edition Bookshop, 1953.

CAUCHIE — Maurice Cauchie, *Thematic Index of the Works of François Couperin.* Paris: The Lyrebird Press, 1949.

CHAIGNEAU & RUMMELm I — Marguerite Chaigneau and Walter Morse Rummel (eds.), *Vivaldi: 6 Sonates originales pour violoncelle et piano* (Op. 14?). Paris: Salabert, 1916.

CHAIGNEAU & RUMMELm II — ———, *J. Barrière: . . . Douze Sonates pour violoncelle solo avec basse,* 2 vols. Paris: M. Senart, 1918 and 1924.

CHIGIANA — Guido Chigi Saracini (ed.), *Accademia musicale chigiana: Ente autonomo per le settimane musicale senesi. Ca.* 1943—.

CHILESOTTI-MELODIAm — Oscar Chilesotti (ed.), *Sulla Melodia popolare del cinquecento.* Milan: G. Ricordi (1899).

CHRYSANDER-HÄNDEL — Friedrich Chrysander, *G. F. Händel,* 3 vols. Leipzig: Breitkopf & Härtel, 1858, 1860, and 1867.

CHRYSANDER-MUSIKVERLAG — ———, "Der italienische Musikverlag um 1700," AMZ, 3d Folge, IV (1869), 137-140.

CLASSICIm I — *I Classici della musica italiana,* 36 vols. Milan: Raccolta nazionale delle musiche italiane, 1919-20.

CLASSICIm II — *I Classici musicali italiani,* 15 vols. Milan, 1941-43.

CLEMENTI-HARMONYm — [*Muzio*] *Clementi's Selection of Practical Harmony for the Organ or Pianoforte,* 4 vols. London: W. C. Bates (1803-15).

CLERCX-BAROQUE — Suzanne Clercx, *Le Baroque et la musique.* Brussels: Librairie Encyclopédique, 1948.

CLERCX-KUHNAU — ———, "Johann Kuhnau et la Sonate," RM, XVI (1935), 89-110.

COBBETT — [*Walter Willson*] *Cobbett's Cyclopedic Survey of Chamber Music,* 2 vols. London: Oxford University Press, 1929 and 1930.

COLLEGIUMm — *Collegium Musicum, A Collection of Old Chamber Music . . .* adapted for general use by H. Riemann, M. Seiffert, P. Klengel, and others. Leipzig: Breitkopf & Härtel, from 1903.

COMBARIEU-SYMPHONIE — Jules Combarieu, "Les Origines de la symphonie," RMC (1903), pp. 355-358, 459-464, 539-542.

CONTINUOm — *Continuo, A Collection of Old Ensemble Music.* Vienna: Universal Edition, from 1936.

COOPERSMITH-PROJECT — Jacob Maurice Coopersmith, "Handelian Lacunae: A Project," MQ, XXI (1935), 224-229.

COUPERINm — Maurice Cauchie (general ed.), *Oeuvres complètes de François Couperin,* 12 vols. Paris: Éditions de L'Oiseau Lyre, 1932-33.

COUPERIN-L'ART — François Couperin, *L'Art de toucher le clavecin* (1716-17), in French, German, and English. Leipzig: Breitkopf & Härtel, 1933.

CROCKER — Eunice C. Crocker, "An Introductory Study of the Italian Canzona for Instrumental Ensembles and Its Influence Upon the Baroque Sonata," unpublished Ph.D. dissertation, Radcliffe College (Cambridge, Mass.), 1943.

CUCÜEL — Georges Cucüel, *La Pouplinière et la musique de chambre au XVIIIe siècle.* Paris: Librairie Fischbacher, 1913.

CUCÜEL-DOCUMENTS — ———, "Quelques documents sur la librairie musicale au XVIIIe siècle," SIMG, XIII (1911-12), 385-392.

CUDWORTH-PERGOLESI — Charles L. Cudworth, "Notes on the Instrumental Works Attributed to Pergolesi," ML, XXX (1949), 321-328.

CUDWORTH-RICCIOTTI — ———, "Pergolesi, Ricciotti, and the Count of Bentinck," IMS, 5th Congress (Utrecht, 1952), pp. 127-131.

CUDWORTH-SPURIOSITY — ———, "Ye Olde Spuriosity Shoppe, or Put It in the Anhang," NOTES, XII (1955), 25-40 and 533-553.

CUDWORTH-VEIN — ———, " 'Baptist's Vein'—French Orchestral Music and Its Influence, from 1650 to 1750," PMA, LXXXIII (1956-57), 29-47.

CUMMINGS-ARNE — William H. Cummings, "Dr. Arne," PMA, XXXVI (1909-10), 75-91.

DADDER — Ernst Dadder, "Johann Gottlieb Goldberg," BJ, XX (1923), 57-71.

DANCKERT-GIGUE — Werner Danckert, *Geschichte der Gigue.* Leipzig: Fr. Kistner & C. F. W. Siegel, 1924.

D'ANGELI — Andrea D'Angeli, *Benedetto Marcello, Vita e opere.* Milan: Fratelli Bocca, 1940.

DAVID-OFFERING — Hans Theodore David, *J. S. Bach's Musical Offering.* New York: G. Schirmer, 1945.

DAVID-OFFERINGm — ——— (ed.), *Musical Offering by J. S. Bach.* New York: G. Schirmer, 1944.

DAVID-SCARLATTIm — ——— (ed.), *Alessandro Scarlatti: Sonata a quattro in D Minor.* New York: Music Press, 1940.

DAVID-VIOLINSPIELm — Ferdinand David (ed.), *Die Hohe Schule des Violinspiels,* 3 vols. Leipzig: Breitkopf & Härtel, 1867.

DAVISON & APELm

Archibald Thompson Davison and Willi Apel (eds.), *Historical Anthology of Music,* 2 vols. Cambridge, Mass.: Harvard University Press, 1946 and 1950.

DDTm

Denkmäler deutscher Tonkunst, erste Folge, 65 vols., 1892-1931.

DEBROUX & WAGNER-CLERAMBAULTm

J. Debroux and E. Wagner (eds.), *Clérambault: Sonate [2] en G (La Felicité) pour 2 violons et piano.* Paris: Henri Lemoine, 1914.

DELLA CORTEm

Andrea Della Corte (ed.), *Scelta di musiche per lo studio della storia.* Milan: G. Ricordi, 1928.

DENT-ENSEMBLES

Edward J. Dent, "Ensembles and Finales in 18th Century Italian Opera," 'SIMG, XII (1910-11), 112-138.

DENT-QUARTETS

———, "The Earliest String Quartets," *Monthly Musical Record,* XXXIII (1903), 202-204.

DENT-SCARLATTI

———, *Alessandro Scarlatti: His Life and Works.* London: Edward Arnold, 1905.

DEUTSCH-HANDEL

Otto Erich Deutsch, *Handel, A Documentary Biography.* New York: W. W. Norton (1955).

DEUTSCH-NUMBERS

———, "Music Publisher's Numbers" (reprint from *The Journal of Documentation,* I and II [1946]). London: Association of Special Libraries and Information Bureaux, 1946.

DITTERSDORF

The Autobiography of Karl von Dittersdorf, translated from the German by A. D. Coleridge. London: Richard Bentley, 1896.

DM

Die Musik. 1901—.

DMF

Die Musikforschung. 1948—.

DOLMETSCH

Arnold Dolmetsch, *The Interpretation of the Music of the XVIIth and XVIIIth Centuries.* London: Novello (1915).

DORING-DUBOURG

Ernest N. Doring (ed.), "Dubourg's 'The Violin'" (1836 and later), vv, VII-XI (1946-50), serially.

DOUNIAS

Minos Dounias, *Die Violinkonzerte Giuseppe Tartinis.* Berlin: Georg Kallmeyer-Verlag, 1935.

DTBm

Denkmäler der Tonkunst in Bayern (DDTm, zweite Folge), 36 vols., 1900-31.

DTÖm

Denkmäler der Tonkunst in Österreich. 1894—.

DUCKLES & ELMER

Thematic Catalogue of a Manuscript Collection of Eighteenth-Century Italian Instrumental Music. Berkeley: University of California Press, 1963

DÜRR-GOLDBERG

Alfred Dürr, "Johann Gottlieb Goldberg und die Trionsonate BWV 1037," BJ, XL (1953), 51-80.

ECORCHEVILLE-
ESTHETIQUE
Jules Ecorcheville, *De Lulli à Rameau, 1690-1730, L'Esthétique musicale.* Paris: Marcel Fortin, 1906.

EDMLm
Das Erbe deutscher Musik, Landschaftsdenkmale (2d series). 1936—.

EDMRm
Das Erbe deutscher Musik, Reichsdenkmale (1st series). 1935—.

EICHBORN-FANTINI
H. Eichborn, "Girolamo Fantini, ein Virtuos des siebzehnten Jahrhunderts und seine Trompeten-Schule," MFMG, XXII (1890), 112-138.

EINSTEIN-ANCORA
Alfred Einstein, "Ancora sull' 'Aria di Ruggiero,' " RMI, XLI (1937), 163-169.

EINSTEIN-CHORAL
———, Correspondence "Zur deutschen Literatur für Viola da Gamba," ZIMG, VI (1904-05), 272.

EINSTEIN-CONCERTO
———, "Ein Concerto grosso von 1619," in *Festschrift Hermann Kretzschmar* (Leipzig, 1918), pp. 26-28.

EINSTEIN-GAMBA
———, "Zur deutschen Literatur für Viola da Gamba im 16. und 17. Jahrhundert," PIMG, II, Part 1 (1905).

EINSTEIN-GLUCK
———, *Gluck,* translated by Eric Blom. London: J. M. Dent, 1936.

EINSTEIN-GLUCKm
——— (ed.), *Christoph Willibald Gluck: Trio Sonata No. 2 in G Minor.* New York: Music Press, 1942.

EINSTEIN-HÄNDEL
——— "Zum 48. Bande der Händel-Ausgabe," SIMG, IV (1902-03), 170-172.

EINSTEIN-HISTORY
———, *A Short History of Music,* 2d American ed. New York: Alfred A. Knopf, 1938.

EINSTEIN-HISTORYm
——— (ed.), 39 Musical Examples added to 2d Amer. ed. of EINSTEIN-HISTORY, q. v.

EINSTEIN-RUGGIERO
——— "Die Aria di Ruggiero," SIMG, XIII (1911-12), 444-454.

EINSTEIN-SCORESm
A MS collection of Italian and German instrumental music of the 16th-18th centuries prepared in score by Alfred Einstein (*ca.* 1899-1903) and presented to Smith College Library. Vol. nos. are assigned for the present listing as follows: I includes sonatas by Gussago, Riccio, F. & G. Usper, S. Bernardi, Vivarino; II, Buonamente; III, Rossi, B. Marini, Merula, Legrenzi; IV, Schmelzer, Loewe, D. Becker, J. J. Walter, D. Buxtehude.

EITNER-BÖDDECKER
Robert Eitner, "Philipp Friedrich Böddecker," MFMG, XXV (1893), 116-118.

EITNER-KRIEGERm ——, "Johann Philipp Krieger" (a cross-section of his music), MFMG, Beilage XXX (1897-98).

EITNER-LECLAIRm —— (ed.), *Jean-Marie Leclair l'aîné: Zwölf* [actually *Elf*] *Sonaten für Violine und Generalbass nebst einem Trio für Violine, Violoncell und Generalbass, 2. Buch der Sonaten.* PAPTM, XXVII (1903).

EITNER-MARCELLO ——, "Benedetto Marcello," MFMG, XXIII (1891), 187-194 and 197-211.

EITNER-MISCELLANEA Hermann Springer, Max Schneider, and Werner Wolffheim, *Miscellanea musicae bio-bibliographica* [1904-13] . . . als Nachträge und Verbesserungen zu Eitners Quellenlexikon, 2d ed. New York: Musurgia, 1947.

EITNER-QL ——, *Biographisch-bibliographisches Quellenlexikon der Musiker und Musikgelehrten* . . . , 10 vols. Leipzig: Breitkopf & Härtel, 1899-1904.

EITNER-SONATE ——, "Die Sonate, Vorstudien zur Entstehung der Form," MFMG, XX (1888), 163-170 and 179-185.

EITNER-VINCENTI —— (ed.), *Indice di tutte le opere di musica che si trovano nella stampa della Pigna: di Alessandro Vincenti* (1618 [actually 1621?] and 1649). MFMG, Beilage XIV-XV (1883).

ENCYCLOPEDIE *Encyclopédie de la musique et dictionnaire du conservatoire*, 11 vols. Paris: Delagrave, 1913-31.

ENGELKE-FASCH Bernhard Engelke, "Johann Friedrich Fasch," SIMG, X (1908-09), 263-283.

ENGELKE-GRAF ——, "Die Rudolstädter Hofkapelle unter Lyra und Joh. Graf," AFMW, I (1918-19), 594-606.

ENSCHEDÉ J. W. Enschedé, "Zur Battaglia del Re di Prussia," SIMG, IV (1902-03), 677-685.

ESCUDIER Marie and Leon Escudier, *Dictionnaire de musique,* 2 vols. Paris: Bureau central de musique, 1844.

EVANS-DURHAM Peter Evans, "Seventeenth-Century Chamber Music Manuscripts at Durham," ML, XXXVI (1955), 205-223.

FAISST Imanuel Faisst, "Beiträge zur Geschichte der Claviersonate von ihrem ersten Auftreten bis auf C. P. Emanuel Bach" (Berlin, 1845), reprinted from Dehn's *Cäcilia* (Mainz, 1846/7) in *Neues Beethoven-Jahrbuch*, I (1924), 7-85.

FANTINI-FACSIMILEm Girolamo Fantini, *Modo per imparare a sonare di tromba* (Francofort, 1638), facsimile. Milan: Bollettino Bibliografico Musicale, 1934.

FAVRE/LINGOROW — Stella Lingorow (Favre), *Der Instrumentalstil von Purcell.* Bern: Eicher, 1949.

FÉTIS-BU — François-Joseph Fétis, *Biographie universelle des musiciens . . .* , 2d ed., 8 vols.; supplement, 2 vols. Paris: Firman Didot, 1860-65; 1878-80.

FINNEY-CAZZATIm — Ross Lee Finney (ed.), *Two [S/- or SB/bass] Sonatas [by] Mauritio Cazzatti.* New York: M. Witmark, 1935.

FINNEY-GEMINIANIm — ———, *Geminiani: Twelve Sonatas for Violin and Piano* (Op. 1). Northampton, Mass.: Smith College, 1935.

FINO — Don Giocondo Fino, "Una grande violinista torinese ed una famiglia di violinisti G. B. Somis," in *Il Momento,* Torino, Oct. 25-26, 1927.

FINZI — Gerald Finzi, "John Stanley," PMA, LXXVII (1950-51), 63-75.

FISCHER-BODINUSm — Hans Fischer (ed.), *Sebastian Bodinus: Sonate für 2 Violinen oder Oboen mit Continuo.* Berlin-Lichterfelde: Chr. Friedrich Vieweg, 1939.

FISCHER-WIENER — Wilhelm Fischer, "Zur Entwicklungsgeschichte des Wiener klassichen Stils," SZMW, III (1915), 24-84.

FISCHER-1750/1828 — ———, "Instrumentalmusik von 1750-1828," in Guido Adler, *Handbuch der Musikgeschichte,* 2d ed. (Berlin, 1930), pp. 795-833.

FISCHER & WITTENBECHERm — Oskar Fischer and Otto Wittenbecher (eds.), *Johann Joachim Quantz: 8 Ausgewählten Sonaten* (S/bass). Robert Forberg, 1924.

FLEURYm — Louis Fleury (ed.), *Michel Blavet: 6 sonatas for flute and bass,* 6 vols. London: Rudall, Carte, 1908-11.

FLOOD-GEMINIANI — W. H. Grattan Flood, "Geminiani in England and Ireland," SIMG, XII (1910-11), 108-112.

FLOWER-HANDEL — Newman Flower, *George Frideric Handel.* New York: Charles Scribner's Sons, 1948.

FOCK-TRIOSONATENm — Gustav Fock (ed.), *Hanseatische Meister des Barock Triosonaten und Stücke.* New York: Edition Peters 4539, 1945.

FOGACCIA — Piero Fogaccia, *Giovanni Legrenzi.* Bergamo: Edizioni Orobiche (1954).

FORKEL-ALMANACH — Johann Nikolaus Forkel, *Musikalischer Almanach für Deutschland,* 4 vols. Leipzig: Schwickertschen Verlag, 1782, 1783, 1784, and 1789.

FORTUNE-CONTINUO — Nigel Fortune, "Continuo Instruments in Italian Monodies," *The Galpin Society Journal,* VI (1953), 10-13.

FRIEDRICH-TELEMANNnI   Wilhelm Friedrich (ed.), *Georg Philipp Telemann: Sechs Sonaten für Violine und Generalbass*. Mainz: B. Schott's Söhne, 1954.

FROTSCHER   Gotthold Frotscher, *Geschichte des Orgelspiels und der Orgelkomposition*, 2 vols. Berlin-Schöneberg: Max Hesses Verlag, 1935-36.

FÜRSTENAU   Moritz Fürstenau, *Zur Geschichte der Musik und des Theaters am Hofe der Kurfürsten von Sachsen und Könige von Polen*, 2 vols. Dresden: Rudolf Kuntze, 1861 and 1862.

FUNK   Floyd Donald Funk, "The Trio Sonatas of Georg Philipp Telemann (1681-1767)," unpublished Ph.D. dissertation, George Peabody College for Teachers (Nashville, Tenn.), 1954.

GANZER & KUSCHE   Karl Ganzer and Ludwig Kusche, *Vierhändig*. Munich: Ernst Heimeran Verlag, 1937.

GARDNER-MOFFAT   Hugh Gardner, Letter to the Editor, MT, LXII (1921), 718.

GÁSCUE   Francisco Gáscue, *Historia de la Sonata*. San Sebastian: Palacio de Bellas Artes, 1910.

GATES-CORELLI   Willis C. Gates, "The Works of Arcangelo Corelli," unpublished master's thesis, The University of North Carolina (Chapel Hill), 1948.

GATES-REBEL   ————, "Jean-Fery Rebel's 'Sonates a violon seul mellées de plusieurs recits pour la viole' (1713)," unpublished paper read in Portland, Oregon, May 23, 1954 (abstract in JAMS, VII [1954], 251-252).

GATES-SOLO   ————, "The Literature for Unaccompanied Solo Violin," unpublished Ph.D. dissertation, The University of North Carolina (Chapel Hill), 1949.

GAZZETTA ANTOLOGIAm   *Antologia classica musicale*, special number of *Gazzetta musicale di Milano*, V (1846). Cf CAT. BOLOGNA, IV, 54.

GEIRINGER-BACH   Karl Geiringer, *The Bach Family*. London: George Allen & Unwin, 1954.

GENTILI   Alberto Gentili, "La raccolta Mauro Foà nella Biblioteca Nazionale di Torino," RMI, XXXIV (1927), 356-368.

GEORGII-KLAVIERMUSIK   Walter Georgii, *Klaviermusik*, 2d ed. Zürich: Atlantis-Verlag, 1950.

GERBER-GLUCK   Rudolf Gerber, *Christoph-Willibald Gluck*. Potsdam: Akademische Verlagsgesellschaft Athenaion, 1950.

GERBER-LEXIKON   Ernst Ludwig Gerber, *Neues historisch-biographisches Lexikon der Tonkünstler*, 4 vols. Leipzig: A. Kühnel, 1812-14.

GERBER-UNBEKANNTE   Rudolf Gerber, "Unbekannte Instrumentalwerke von Christoph Willibald Gluck," DMF, IV (1951), 305-318.

GIAZOTTO-ALBINONI   Remo Giazotto, *Tomaso Albinoni*. Milan: Fratelli Bocca, 1945.

GIEGLING-SOLOm   Franz Giegling (ed.), *The Solo Sonata* (in *Das Musikwerk* series). Köln: Arno Volk Verlag, 1960. Cf. the review in NOTES, XIX (1962), 685-87 (Newman).

GIEGLING-TORELLI   ———, *Giuseppe Torelli, ein Beitrag zur Entwicklungsgeschichte des italienischen Konzerts*. Kassel und Basel: Bärenreiter-Verlag, 1949.

GIESBERT-FINGERm   Franz Julius Giesbert (ed.), *Gottfried Finger: Vier Duette für zwei Altblockflöten*. Kassel: Nagels Verlag (after 1953).

GIESBERT-MATTHESONm   ———, *Johann Mattheson: Vier Sonaten für zwei Altblockflöten* and *Acht Sonaten für drei Altblockflöten*, 2 vols. Kassel: Nagels Verlag, Nos. 505 and 506, 1932 and 1940.

GIESBERT-PEPUSCHm   ———, *Joh. Chr. Pepusch: Sechs Sonaten für Altblockflöte in f . . . und Cembalo*, 2 vols. London: Schott & Co., 1939.

GIESBERT-SCHICKHARDTm I   ———, *Joh. Chr. Schickhardt: Sechs Trio-Sonaten für zwei Blockflöten und Bc.* Kassel: Nagels Verlag, n. d.

GIESBERT-SCHICKHARDTm II   ———, *Joh. Chr. Schickhardt: Sechs leichte Sonaten für Violine und Generalbass*. Mainz: B. Schott's Söhne, 1936. (Actually flute sons. by J. E. Galliard! Cf. MGG, IV, 1285 [Westrup].)

GIESBERT-VALENTINOm   ———, *Roberto Valentino: Sonate IX und X* [from] *"Zwölf Sonaten für Altblockflöte in f."* Mainz: B. Schott's Söhne, 1938.

GIRARD   Adrien Girard, *Histoire et richesses de la flûte*. Paris: Gründ, 1953.

GIUSTINI-FACSIMILEm   Lodovico Giustini, *Sonate Da Cimbalo di piano, e forte* (Florence, 1732), facsimile, with preface by Rosamond E. M. Harding. Cambridge, Eng.: The University Press, 1933.

GÖHLER   Albert Göhler, *Verzeichnis der in den Frankfurter und Leipziger Messkatalogen der Jahre 1564 bis 1759 angezeigten Musikalien*, 4 vols. in one. Leipzig: C. F. Kahnt, 1902.

GOLDSCHMIDT   Hugo Goldschmidt, "Die Entwicklung der Sonatenform," *Allgemeine Musik-Zeitung*, XXIX (1902), 93-95, 109-111, 129-132.

GOMBOSI-OSTINATO — Otto Gombosi, "Italia: patria del basso ostinato," RAM, VII (1934), 14-25.

GROVE — *Grove's Dictionary of Music and Musicians*, 5th ed., 9 vols. London: Macmillan, 1954. References are to this edition unless an earlier edition is specified.

GUILMANT & DEBROUXm — Alexandre Guilmant and Joseph Debroux (eds.), *J.-M. Leclair: Premier Livre de Sonates, Oeuvre III* (actually Op. 1). Paris: Max Eschig, 1907.

GUILMANT & PIRROm — Alexandre Guilmant and Andre Pirro, *Sebastian Anton Scherer: Oeuvres d'orgue* (vol. 8, *Archives des maîtres de l'orgue* [Paris: Durand, 1898-1914]).

GUTMANN-KUHNAU — Rudolf Gutmann, "Johann Kuhnau (1660-1722)," *Zeitschrift für Hausmusik*, VIII (1939), 25-30.

HAAS-AUFFÜHRUNGSPRAXIS — Robert Haas, *Aufführungspraxis der Musik*. Potsdam: Akademische Verlagsgesellschaft Athenaion, 1931.

HAAS-BAROCK — ———, *Die Musik des Barocks*. Potsdam: Akademische Verlagsgesellschaft Athenaion, 1928.

HAAS-CAT. 20 — Otto Haas, *Catalogue 20: The Valuable Music Library Formed by Alfred Moffat, Esq.* London (*ca.* 1945).

HAAS-ESTENSISCHEN — Robert Haas, *Die estensischen Musikalien*. Regensburg: Gustav Bosse Verlag, 1927.

HAMMERICH-DANSK — Angul Hammerich, *Dansk Musikhistorie indtil ca. 1700*. Copenhagen: G. E. C. Gads Forlag, 1921.

HANDEL-AUSGABEm — Max Schneider and Rudolf Steglich (eds.), *Hallische Händel-Ausgabe*, im Auftrag der Georg-Friedrich-Händel-Gesellschaft. Kassel & Basel: Bärenreiter-Verlag, begun in 1955.

HANDEL-WERKEm — *Georg Friedrich Händel's Werke*, 93 vols. (vol. 49 never appeared) plus 6 vols. by other composers. Leipzig: Ausgabe der deutschen Händelgesellschaft, 1858—.

HANDSCHIN-PEDALKLAVIER — Jacques Handschin, "Das Pedalklavier," ZFMW, XVII (1935), 418-425.

HARDING-EARLIEST — Rosamond E. M. Harding, "The Earliest Pianoforte Music," ML, XIII (1932), 194-199.

HARDING-ORIGINS — ———, *Origins of Musical Time and Expression*. London: Oxford University Press, 1938.

HARICH/SCHNEIDER — Eta Harich-Schneider, *The Harpsichord*. St. Louis: Concordia, 1954.

HASELBACH — Richard Haselbach, *Giovanni Battista Bassani*. Kassel und Basel: Bärenreiter-Verlag, 1955.

HAUSMUSIKm   Erich Schenk (ed.), *Hausmusik.* Vienna: Oster-reichischer Bundesverlag, from *ca.* 1948.

HAUSSWALD-BACHZEIT   Günter Hausswald, "Zur Sonatenkunst der Bach-zeit," in *Bericht über die Wissenschaftliche Bach-tagung . . . 1950* (Leipzig: C. F. Peters, 1951), pp. 340-348.

HAUSSWALD-HEINICHEN   ———, *Johann David Heinichen's Instrumental-werke.* Berlin: Georg Kallmeyer, 1937.

HAUSSWALD-PEPUSCHm   ——— (ed.), *Johann Christof Pepusch: Sonate* (for flute or other soprano instrument, violin, and cembalo). Mainz: B. Schott's Söhne, 1951.

HAUSSWALD-STILISTIK   ———, "Zur Stilistik von Johann Sebastian Bachs Sonaten und Partiten für Violine allein," AFMW, XIV (1957), 304-323.

HAUSSWALD-ZELENKA   ———, "Johann Dismas Zelenka als Instrumental-komponist," AFMW, XIII (1956), 243-262.

HAWKINS   John Hawkins, *A General History of the Science and Practice of Music,* 5 vols. London: T. Payne, 1776.

HAYDON-EXPRESSION   Glen Haydon, "On the Problem of Expression in Baroque Music," JAMS, III, Part 2 (Summer, 1950), 113-119.

HENDERSON   Hubert Henderson, "A Study of the Trumpet in the 17th Century: Its History, Resources, and Use," unpublished master's thesis, The University of North Carolina (Chapel Hill), 1949.

HERRMANN-TELEMANNm   Carl Herrmann (ed.), *Telemann: Sechs kanonische Sonaten.* New York: Peters (*ca.* 1950).

HEUSS-ORFEO   Alfred Heuss, "Die Instrumental-Stücke des Orfeo" (including Appendix 1, "Ein Beitrag zur Klärung der Kanzonen- und Sonaten-Form"), SIMG, IV (1902-03), 175-224.

HEUSS-SINFONIEN   ———, "Die venetianischen Opern-Sinfonien," SIMG, IV (1902-03), 404-477.

HILLEMANNm   Willi Hillemann (ed.), *Antonio Vivaldi: Zwölf Sonaten für Violine & Generalbass,* Op. 2, 2 vols. Mainz: B. Schott's Söhne, 1953.

HILLER-LEBENS-BESCHREIBUNGEN   Johann Adam Hiller, *Lebensbeschreibungen be-rühmter Musikgelehrten und Tonkünstler neuerer Zeit.* Leipzig: Dykische buchhandlung, 1784.

HITCHCOCK   H. Wiley Hitchcock, review of *Giovanni Legrenzi* by Piero Fogaccia, MQ, XLII (1956), 109-112.

HOFFMANN-TRIOSONATE   Hans Joseph Karl Hoffmann, *Die norddeutsche Triosonate des Kreises um Johann Gottlieb Graun und Carl Philipp Emanuel Bach.* Kiel: Walter G. Mühlau, 1927.

HOFFMANN/ERBRECHT-GRAUPNER — Lothar Hoffmann-Erbrecht, "Johann Christoph Graupner als Klavierkomponist," AFMW, X (1953), 140-152.

HOFFMANN/ERBRECHT-HAFFNER — ———, "Der Nürnberger Musikverleger Johann Ulrich Haffner" and "Nachträge," AM, XXVI (1954), 114-126, and XXVII (1955), 141-143.

HOFFMANN/ERBRECHT-KLAVIERMUSIK — ———, *Deutsche und italienische Klaviermusik zur Bachzeit.* Leipzig: Breitkopf & Härtel, 1954.

HOFMEISTER — *Hofmeisters Jahresverzeichnis.* Leipzig: Friedrich Hofmeister, from 1828.

HOPKINSON — Cecil Hopkinson, *A Dictionary of Parisian Music Publishers,* 1700-1950. London: Printed for the author, 1954.

HORTUSm — *Hortus musicus.* Kassel: Bärenreiter-Verlag, from 1948.

HUGHES-PEPUSCH — Charles W. Hughes, "John Christopher Pepusch," MQ, XXXI (1945), 54-70.

HUGHES-VIOL — ———, "The Music for Unaccompanied Bass Viol," ML, XXV (1944), 149-163.

HULL-QUARTET — Arthur Eaglefield Hull, "The Earliest Known String Quartet," MQ, XV (1929), 72-76.

HUMPHRIES & SMITH — Charles Humphries and William C. Smith, *Music Publishing in the British Isles.* London: Cassell, 1954.

ILGNER — Gerhard Ilgner, *Mathias Weckmann, sein Leben und seine Werke.* Wolfenbüttel-Berlin: Georg Kallmeyer, 1939.

IMS — *International Musicology Society,* including various congresses at irregular intervals from 1904.

D'INDY-COURS — Vincent d'Indy, *Cours de composition musicale,* with collaboration of A. Sérieyx and De Lyoncourt, 3 vols. Paris: Durand, 1909-50.

D'INDY-SENAILLÉm — ——— (ed.), *Senaillé: Sonates, piano et violon* (Sons. 8, Bk. II; 8, III; 9, IV; 7, V). Paris: Durand, 1915.

IP — *Il Pianoforte.* 1920-27. Superseded by RAM in 1928.

ISELIN — Dora J. Iselin, *Biagio Marini, sein Leben und seine Instrumentalwerke.* Hildburghausen: F. W. Gadow, 1930.

ISTITUZIONIm — *Istituzioni e monumenti dell' arte musicale italiana,* 7 vols. (up to 1941). 1931—.

JAMS — *Journal of the American Musicological Society.* 1948—.

JANOVKA-THESAURUM Tomas Baltazar Janovka, *Clavis ad thesaurum.* Prague: Georgij Labaun, 1701.

JEFFREYS John Jeffreys, *The Eccles Family.* Enfield (England): J. W. Hatch, 1951.

JENSEN-VIOLINm Gustav Jensen (ed.), *Classical Violin Music.* . . . London: Augener (*ca.* 1890), reprinted by Schott (*ca.* 1911).

JEPPESEN-ORGELMUSIK Knud Jeppesen, *Die italienische Orgelmusik am Anfang des Cinquecento.* Copenhagen: Einar Munksgaard, 1943.

JMP *Jahrbuch der Musikbibliothek Peters.* 1894—.

JOACHIM & CHRYSANDERm Joseph Joachim and Friedrich Chrysander (eds.), *Les Oeuvres de Arcangelo Corelli,* 5 vols. London: Augener (*ca.* 1890).

JOHANSSON Cari Johansson, *French Music Publishers' Catalogues of the Second Half of the Eighteenth Century,* 2 vols. Stockholm: Publications of the Royal Swedish Academy of Music, II, 1955.

JONGEN & DEBROUX-REBELm J. Jongen and Joseph Debroux (eds.), *Jean Ferry Rebel: Sonate en re mineur* (Bk. 2, second part). Paris: B. Roudanez, 1905.

JONGEN & DEBROUX-SOMISm ———(eds.), *Giovanni Battista Somis: Sonate en sol majeur* (Op. 6, No. 10). Paris: Henry Lemoine, 1910.

JRME *Journal of Research in Music Education.* 1953—.

KAHL-SELBSTBIOGRAPHIEN Willi Kahl, *Selbstbiographien deutscher Musiker des XVIII. Jahrhunderts.* Köln: Staufen-Verlag, 1948.

KASTNER-SEIXAS Santiago Kastner, *Carlos de Seixas.* Coimbra, Portugal: Coimbra Editora, 1947.

KELLER-BACH Hermann Keller, *Die Klavierwerke Bachs.* Leipzig: C. F. Peters, 1950.

KELLER-REINKEN ———, "Über Bachs Bearbeitungen aus dem 'Hortus musicus' von Reinken," IMS, 4th Congress (Basel, 1949), pp. 160-161.

KENTON Egon F. Kenton, "The Instrumental Works of Giovanni Gabrieli's Late Period," abstract in JAMS, IX (Fall, 1956), 234-236.

KENYON Max Kenyon, *Harpsichord Music.* London: Cassell, 1949.

KING-PIANO A. Hyatt King, "Mozart's Piano Music," MR, V (1944), 163-191.

KINKELDEY — Otto Kinkeldey, *Orgel und Klavier in der Musik des 16. Jahrhunderts.* Leipzig: Breitkopf & Härtel, 1910.

KINSKY-PICTURES — Georg Kinsky, *A History of Music in Pictures.* New York: E. P. Dutton, 1937.

KIRCHER-MUSURGIA — Athanasius Kircher, *Musurgia universalis,* 2 vols. Rome: F. Corbelletti, 1650.

KIRKPATRICK-SCARLATTI — Ralph Kirkpatrick, *Domenico Scarlatti.* Princeton: The University Press, 1953.

KLAUWELL — Otto Klauwell, *Geschichte der Sonate.* Leipzig: H. vom Ende's Verlag (1899).

KLENZ-PURCELL — William Klenz, "The Church Sonatas of Henry Purcell," unpublished master's thesis, The University of North Carolina (Chapel Hill), 1948.

KNAPP — John Merrill Knapp, "The Canzon francese and Its Vocal Models," unpublished master's thesis, Columbia University, 1941.

KOCZIRZ — Adolf Koczirz, "Zur Lebensgeschichte Alexander de Pogliettis," SZMW, IV (1916), 116-127.

KÖCHEL & EINSTEIN — Ludwig Ritter von Köchel, *Chronologisch-thematisches Verzeichnis sämtlicher Tonwerke Wolfgang Amade Mozarts,* 3d ed., revised by Alfred Einstein. Leipzig: Breitkopf & Härtel, 1937.

KÖCHEL-FUX — ———, *Johann Joseph Fux.* Vienna: Alfred Hölder, 1872.

KÖLBEL — Herbert Kölbel, *Von der Flöte.* Köln: Staufen-Verlag, 1951.

KOLETSCHKA — Karl Koletschka, "Esaias Reussner de Jüngere und seine Bedeutung für die deutsche Lautenmusik," SZMW, XV (1928), 3-45.

KOLNEDER-FRAGE — Walter Kolneder, "Zur Frage der Vivaldi-Kataloge," AFMW, XI (1954), 323-331.

KOLNEDER-FRÜHSCHAFFEN — ———, "Das Frühschaffen Antonio Vivaldis," IMS, 5th Congress (Utrecht, 1952), pp. 254-262.

KOLNEDER-PÄDAGOGISCHE — ———, "Vivaldis pädagogische Tätigkeit in Venedig," DMF, V (1952), 341-345.

KONGRESS 1956 (Hamburg) — *Bericht über den internationalen musikwissenschaftlichen Kongress Hamburg 1956.* Kassel: Bärenreiter-Verlag, 1957.

KONGRESS 1956 (Vienna) — *Bericht über den internationalen musikwissenschaftlichen Kongress Wien Mozartjahr 1956.* Graz-Köln: Hermann Böhlaus, 1958.

KOOLE

Arend Koole, *Leven en Werken van Pietro Antonio Locatelli da Bergamo*. Amsterdam: Jasonpers Universiteitspers, 1949.

KRETZSCHMAR-WEITERE

Hermann Kretzschmar, "Weitere Beiträge zur Geschichte der venetianischen Oper," JMP, XVII (1910), 61-71.

KUNZE

Stefan Kunze, *Die Instrumentalmusik Giovanni Gabrielis*, 2 vols. Tutzing: H. Schneider, 1963.

LA BORDE

(Jean Benjamin de La Borde), *Essai sur la musique ancienne et moderne*, 4 vols. Paris: P.-D. Pierres, 1780.

LACCETTIm

Guido Laccetti (ed.), *Nicola Porpora: Sonate a tre istrumenti* (Op. 2, Nos. 1-4). Naples: Curci fratelli, 1925.

LAFONTAINE

Henry Cart de Lafontaine, *The King's Musick, A Transcript of Records Relating to Music and Musicians* (1460-1700). London: Novello (1909).

LAND-CATALOGUS

J. P. N. Land, "Catalogus van allerley musijk, met hare pryse, 't welk te Rotterdam by Pieter van der Veer, Boekverkooper, te bekome is (1701)," TVNM, IV (1891-94), 36-48.

LANG-WESTERN

Paul Henry Lang, *Music in Western Civilization*. New York: W. W. Norton, 1941.

LANGLEY-ARNE

Hubert Langley, *Dr. Arne*. Cambridge, Eng.: Cambridge University Press, 1938.

LAURENCIE

Lionel de la Laurencie, *L'École française de violon de Lully a Viotti*, 3 vols. Paris: Delagrave, 1922-24.

LAURENCIE-BOUFFONS

———, "Deux Imitateurs français des bouffons, Blavet et Dauvergne," *L'Année musicale*, II (1912), 65-125.

LAURENCIE-DYNASTIE

———, "Une Dynastie de musiciens aux XVIIe et XVIIIe siècles: Les Rebel," SIMG, VII (1905-06), 253-307.

LAURENCIE-INCONNUES

———, "Deux Sonates inconnues de François II Couperin," REV. DE MUS., VI (1922), 59-61.

LAURENCIE & SAINT/FOIX

Lionel de la Laurencie and Georges de Saint-Foix, "Contribution a l'histoire de la symphonie française," *L'Année musicale*, I (1911), 1-123.

LE BLANC

Hubert Le Blanc, *Défense de la basse de viole contre les enterprises du violon et les prétentions du violoncel* (Amsterdam: Pierre Mortier, 1740), reprinted in RM, IX (1927-28), no. i, 43-56, 136-142; 247-251; no. ii, 21-25, 138-142; no iii, 187-192.

LEEUWENm   Ary van Leeuwen (ed.), *Joannes Mattheson: zwölf Kammer-Sonaten für Flöte und Klavier,* 2 vols. Frankfurt/M: Wilhelm Zimmerman, 1923.

LEICHTENTRITT- HARMONIC   Hugo Leichtentritt, "Handel's Harmonic Art," MQ, XXI (1935), 208-219.

LELLKY   Åke Lellky, "Ett Bidrag till Kännedomen om J. H. Romans Trio-Sonater," *Svensk Tidskrift för Musikforskning,* XVIII (1936), 133-137.

LEMOINE   Micheline Lemoine, "La Technique violinistique de Jean-Marie Leclair," RM, XXV (1953-54), 117-143.

LEONARDm   Hubert Léonard (ed.), *Giuseppe Tartini: Six Sonates pour violon et pianoforte* (from Op. 2). Mainz: B. Schott's Söhne, 1865.

LEYDEN   Rolf van Leyden, "Die Violinsonate BWV 1024," BJ, XLII (1955), 73-102.

LIESS-FUX   Andreas Liess, *Johann Joseph Fux, ein steirischer Meister des Barock.* Vienna: Ludwig Doblinger, 1948.

LIESS-TRIO   ———, *Die Trio-Sonaten von J. J. Fux.* Berlin: Junker und Dünnhaupt, 1940.

LIESS-WIENER   ———, *Wiener Barockmusik.* Vienna: Ludwig Doblinger, 1946.

LIVINGSTON   Herbert Stanton Livingston, "The Italian Overture from A. Scarlatti to Mozart," 2 vols., unpublished Ph.D. dissertation, The University of North Carolina (Chapel Hill), 1952.

LOTHAR-GOLDBERGm   Friedrich Wilhelm Lothar (ed.), *Johann Gottlieb Goldberg: Sonata (C moll) für zwei violinen, viola und violoncello mit continuo.* Copenhagen: Wilhelm Hansen, 1932.

LUCIANI-VIVALDIm   Sebastiano Arturo Luciani (ed.), *Antonio Vivaldi: XII Sonate per violino e basso* (Op. 2), facsimile of the John Walsh ed. (*ca.* 1720). Milan: Istituto di Alta Cultura (*ca.* 1942).

LUIN   Dott. E. I. Luin, "Sulla vita e sulle opere di Antonio Caldara," in *La Scuola veneziana* (secoli XVI-XVIII) *note e documenti,* issued by Accademia musicale chigiana. Siena: Ticci, 1941.

MCARTOR   Marion E. McArtor, "Francesco Geminiani Composer and Theorist," unpublished Ph.D. dissertation, The University of Michigan (Ann Arbor), 1951.

MACHABEY- FRESCOBALDI   Armand Machabey, *Gerolamo Frescobaldi Ferrarensis.* Paris: La Colombe, 1952.

MACKERNESS   E. D. Mackerness, "Bach's F Major Violin Sonata," MR, XI (1950), 175-179.

MARCELLO — Benedetto Marcello, "Il Teatro alla moda," translated and annotated by Reinhard G. Pauly, MQ, XXXIV (1948), 371-403, and XXXV (1949), 85-105.

MARCHETm — Gaston Marchet (ed.), *Ariosti: 6 Sonates pour violon et piano.* Paris: M. Senart, 1920.

MARPURG-BEYTRÄGE — Friedrich Wilhelm Marpurg, *Historisch-kritische Beyträge zur Aufnahme der Musik,* 5 vols. Berlin: G. A. Lange, 1754-78.

MARPURG-CLAVIERSTÜCKE — ———, *Clavierstücke mit einem practischen Unterricht für Anfänger.* Berlin: Haude und Spener, 1762-63.

MARTINm — Frank Martin (ed.), *Henrico Albicastro: Zwei Violinsonaten aus Op. 5* (Nos. 2 and 3). Geneva: Henn, 1931.

MARTUCCI-MARCELLOm — Giuseppe Martucci (ed.), *Benedetto Marcello, Quattro Sonate . . . Flauto o Oboe* (Op. 2, Nos, 1, 5, 8, and 11). Rome: De Santis, 1948.

MARX & BODKYm — Josef Marx and Erwin Bodky (eds.), *Antonio Vivaldi: Sonata in G Minor* (Op. 13, No. 6). New York: McGinnis & Marx, 1946.

MARX & WEISS/MANNm — Josef Marx and Edith Weiss-Mann (eds.), *Johann Ernst Galliard: Six Sonatas for Bassoon or Cello and Piano.* New York: McGinnis & Marx, 1946.

MASON-WEISS — Wilton Elman Mason, "The Lute Music of Sylvius Leopold Weiss," 2 vols., unpublished Ph.D. dissertation, The University of North Carolina (Chapel Hill), 1949.

MATTHESON-BESCHÜTZTE — Johann Mattheson, *Das beschützte Orchestre.* Hamburg: Schillerische buchladen, 1717.

MATTHESON-CAPELLMEISTER — ———, *Der vollkommene Capellmeister* (Hamburg: Christian Herold, 1739), facsimile. Kassel: Bärenreiter-Verlag, 1954.

MATTHESON-EHRENPFORTE — ———, *Grundlage einer Ehren-Pforte* (Hamburg: In Verlegung des Verfassers, 1740), edited by Max Schneider. Berlin: Leo Liepmannsohn, 1910.

MATTHESON-KERN — ———, *Kern melodischer Wissenschafft.* Hamburg: Christian Herold, 1737.

MATTHESON-ORCHESTRE — ———, *Das Neu-Eröffnete Orchestre.* Hamburg: Benjamin Schiller, 1713.

MATTHESON-ORGANISTEN — ———, *Exemplarische Organisten-Probe.* Hamburg: Schiller-und-Kissnerischen, 1719.

MAYER/REINACH — Albert Mayer-Reinach, "C. H. Graun, La battaglia del Re di Prussia," SIMG, IV (1902-03), 478-484.

MELLERS-COUPERIN — Wilfrid Mellers, *François Couperin and the French Classical Tradition.* London: Dennis Dobson (1950).

MENKE — Werner Menke, *History of the Trumpet of Bach and Handel*, translated by Gerald Abraham. London: William Reeves (1934).

MENNICKE — Carl Mennicke, *Hasse und die Brüder Graun als Symphoniker*. Leipzig: Breitkopf & Härtel, 1906.

MERSMANN-AUFFÜHRUNGSPRAXIS — Hans Mersmann, "Beiträge zur Aufführungspraxis der vorklassichen Kammermusik in Deutschland," AFMW, II (1919-20), 99-143.

MERSMANN-KAMMERMUSIK — ———, *Die Kammermusik*, 4 vols. (in Hermann Kretzschmar, *Führer durch den Konzertsaal*). Leipzig: Breitkopf & Härtel, 1930.

MEYER — Ernst Hermann Meyer, *Die mehrstimmige Spielmusik des 17. Jahrhunderts in Nord- und Mitteleuropa*. Kassel: Bärenreiter-Verlag, 1934.

MEYER-DIESSENER — ———, "Gerhard Diessener," ZFMW, XVI (1934), 405-413.

MEYER-ENGLISH — ———, *English Chamber Music*. London: Lawrence & Wishart, 1946.

MEYER-HANDEL — ———, "Has Handel Written Works for Two Flutes Without a Bass?" ML, XVI (1935), 293-295.

MEYER-KREMSIER — ———, "Die Bedeutung der Instrumentalmusik am Fürstbischöflichen Hofe zu Olomouc (Olmütz) in Kroměřiž (Kremsier)," DMF, IX (1956), 388-411.

MEYER-NIEDERLÄNDISCHEN — ———, "Die Vorherrschaft der Instrumentalmusik im niederländischen Barock," TVNM, XV (1936-39), 56-83 and 264-281.

MEYER & HIRSCH — Kathi Meyer and Paul Hirsch, *Katalog der Musikbibliothek Paul Hirsch*, 4 vols. Frankfurt am Main, 1936; Cambridge, Eng.: The University Press, 1947.

MFMG — *Monatshefte für Musikgeschichte*. 1869-1905.

MGG — *Die Musik in Geschichte und Gegenwart*, 5 vols. up to this writing (through HA-). Kassel: Bärenreiter-Verlag, 1949—.

MICHEL — Henri Michel, *La Sonate pour clavier avant Beethoven*. Amiens: Yvert & Tellier, 1907.

MISHKIN — Henry G. Mishkin, "The Solo Violin Sonata of the Bologna School," MQ, XXIX (1943), 92-112.

MISHKIN-SEQUENCE — ———, "The Function of the Episodic Sequence in Baroque Instrumental Music," unpublished Ph.D. dissertation, Harvard University, 1938.

MITTELDEUTSCHESm — *Mitteldeutsches Musikarchiv* (Leipzig: Breitkopf & Härtel). 1953—.

ML — *Music and Letters*. 1920—.

MMR — *Monthly Musical Record*. 1871—.

BIBLIOGRAPHY

MOES-SCHENK — E. W. Moes, "Iets over Joan Schenk," TVNM, VIII (1908), 21-24.

MOFFAT-CELLOm — Alfred Moffat (ed.), *Sammlung klassischer Violoncello-Sonaten berühmter Komponisten des 17. und 18. Jahrhundert.* Berlin: N. Simrock, from 1904.

MOFFAT-LECLAIRm — ———, *Leclair: Trio Sonatas in D Minor and B-flat for 2 violins, violoncello (ad. lib.) & piano.* London: Alfred Lengnick, 1934.

MOFFAT-TRIOm — ———, *Trio-Sonaten alter Meister für zwei Violinen und Piano.* Berlin: N. Simrock, from 1902.

MOFFAT-VIOLINm I — ———, *Kammer-Sonaten des 17ten und 18ten Jahrhunderts* nach den Original-Ausgaben für Violine mit bezifferten Bass bearbeitet für Violine und Piano. Mainz-Leipzig: B. Schott's Söhne (*ca.* 1912).

MOFFAT-VIOLINm II — ———, *Sammlung klassischer Violin-Sonaten berühmter Komponisten des 17. und 18. Jahrhunderts.* Berlin and Leipzig: N. Simrock, from *ca.* 1920.

MOFFAT-VIOLINm III — ———, *Old English Violin Music.* London: Novello, from 1906.

MONTEVERDIm — G. Francesco Malipiero (ed.), *Tutta le opere di Claudio Monteverdi,* 16 vols. to date. Asolo: Enrico Venturi, 1926-42.

MORINI — Nestore Morini, *La R. Accademia filarmonica di Bologna.* Bologna: L. Cappelli, 1930.

MORONI — Gaetano Moroni, *Dizionario di erudizione storio-ecclesiastica di S. Pietro sino ai nostri giorni, ca.* 100 vols. Venice: Emiliana, 1851.

MOSER-ALBICASTROm — Rudolf Moser (ed.), *Henrico Albicastro: Dritte Sonate für 2 Violinen und Violoncello mit Cembalo.* Berlin-Lichterfelde: Chr. Friedrich Vieweg (1927).

MOSER-BACH — Andreas Moser, "Zu Joh. Seb. Bachs Sonaten und Partiten für Violine allein," BJ, XVII (1920), 30-65.

MOSER-CRIMINALIA — ———, "Musikalische Criminalia," DM, XV (Mar., 1923), 423-425.

MOSER-DEUTSCHEN — Hans Joachim Moser, *Geschichte der deutschen Musik,* 5th ed., 3 vols. Stuttgart and Berlin: J. G. Cotta, 1930.

MOSER-FOLIES — Andreas Moser, "Zur Genesis der *Folies d'Espagne,*" AFMW, I (1918-19), 358-371.

MOSER-LEXIKON — Hans Joachim Moser, *Musik Lexikon,* 4th ed., 2 vols. Hamburg: Hans Sikorski, 1955.

MOSER-SKORDATUR — Andreas Moser, "Die Violin-Skordatur," AFMW, I (1918-19), 573-589.

MOSER-VIOLINSPIEL ————, *Geschichte des Violinspiels*. Berlin: Max Hesses Verlag, 1923.

MQ *The Musical Quarterly*. 1915—.

MR *The Music Review*. 1940—.

MT *The Musical Times*. 1844—.

MÜLLER-PEZELIUSm Adolf Müller (ed.), *Johannes Pezelius: Hora decima, 2. Teil, 21.-40. Sonate*. Kassel: Bärenreiter-Verlag, n. d.

MÜLLER-REICHEm ————, *Gottfried Reiche, 24 neue Quatricinia*. Kassel: Bärenreiter-Verlag, 1927.

MÜNNICH Richard Münnich, "Kuhnau's Leben," SIMG, III (1901-02), 473-527.

MURRILL-ARNEm Herbert Murrill (ed.), *T. A. Arne: Trio-Sonata No. 2 in G; . . . No. 3 in E-flat*. London: Hinrichsen Edition Nos. 64 and 78, 1939 and (*ca.* 1952).

MUSIC & PHONORECORDS *Music and Phonorecords*, a cumulative list of works represented by Library of Congress printed cards. Washington: The Library of Congress, from 1953.

NA *Note d'archivio*. 1924—.

NAGELSm *Nagels Musik-Archiv*. 1929—.

NALDO A. R. Naldo, "Un Trattato inedito e ignoto di F. M. Veracini," RMI, XLV (1938), 617-635.

NBGm *Neue Bachgesellschaft* (Leipzig: Breitkopf & Härtel). 1900—.

NEEMANN-WEISS I Hans Neemann, "Die Lautenschriften von Silvius Leopold Weiss in der Bibliothek Dr. Werner Wolffheim, Berlin," ZFMW, X (1927-28), 396-414.

NEEMANN-WEISS II ————, "Die Lautenistenfamilie Weiss," AFMW, IV (1939), 157-189.

NEF-ALBICASTRO Karl Nef, "Een Zwitsersch toonkunstenaar uit de 18de eeuw in Nederland," *De Muziek*, I (1926-27), 429-432.

NEF-DEUTSCHEN ————, "Zur Geschichte der deutschen Instrumentalmusik in der zweiten Hälfte des 17. Jahrhunderts," PIMG, V (1902).

NEF-INSTRUMENTATION ————, "Zur Instrumentation im 17. Jahrhundert," JMP, XXXV (1928), 33-42.

NEF-SUITE ————, *Geschichte der Sinfonie und Suite*. Leipzig: Breitkopf & Härtel, 1921.

NETTL-BERGAMASKA Paul Nettl, "Die Bergamaska," ZFMW, V (1922-23), 291-295.

NETTL-BUONAMENTE ————, "Giovanni Battista Buonamente," ZFMW, IX (1926-27), 528-542.

NETTL-FORGOTTEN ———, *Forgotten Musicians.* New York: Philosophical Library, 1951.

NETTL-WIENER ———, "Die Wiener Tanzkomposition in der zweiten Hälfte des siebzehnten Jahrhunderts," szmw, VIII (1921), 45-175.

NEWMAN-ACCOMPANIED William S. Newman, "Concerning the Accompanied Clavier Sonata," mq, XXXIII (1947), 327-349.

NEWMAN-ALBINONI ———, "The Sonatas of Albinoni and Vivaldi," jams, V, Part 2 (Summer, 1952), 99-113.

NEWMAN-BACH ———, "The Keyboard Sonatas of Bach's Sons and Their Relation to the Classic Sonata Concept," *Proceedings for 1949* of the Music Teachers National Association, pp. 236-248.

NEWMAN-BACHm ——— (ed.), *Sons of Bach* [W. F., C. P. E., and J. C. Bach]: *Three Sonatas for Keyboard.* New York: Music Press (succeeded by Mercury Music), 1947.

NEWMAN-CLIMAX ———, "The Climax of Music," *The University of North Carolina Extension Bulletin,* XXXI, Part 3 (Jan., 1952), 22-40. Abridged in mr, XIII (1952), 283-293.

NEWMAN-COLLECTOR ———, "A Private Collector Takes Inventory," notes, I (1944), 24-32.

NEWMAN-DEL BUONO ———, "The *XIIII Sonate di cimbalo* by Giovanni Pietro Del Buono, 'Palermitano' (1641)" in *Collectanea historiae musicae* (Florence: Leo S. Olschki, 1956), II, 297-310.

NEWMAN-DURANTE ———, Review of Bernard Paumgartner's edition of *Francesco Durante, Sei Studii e sei divertimenti,* jams, III (Fall, 1950), 270-271.

NEWMAN-EARLIEST ———, "A Checklist of the Earliest Keyboard 'Sonatas' (1641-1738)," notes, XI (1954), 201-212, with "Correction," XII (1954), 57.

NEWMAN-GENERATIVE ———, "Musical Form as a Generative Process," *The Journal of Aesthetics and Art Criticism,* XII (1954), 301-309.

NEWMAN-MARCELLO ———, "The Keyboard Sonatas of Benedetto Marcello," am, XXIX (1957), 28-41, and XXXI (1959), 192-196.

NEWMAN-MGG ———, "Sonate," in mgg, XII, cols. 868-910.

NEWMAN-ORIGINS ———, "The Origins and First Use of the Word Sonata," *The Journal of Musicology,* V (Sept., 1947, as of May, 1943), 31-39.

NEWMAN-RAVENSCROFT ———, "Ravenscroft and Corelli," ml, XXXVIII (1957), 369-370.

NEWMAN-RICORDI ———, "Sonata," in RICORDI, IV, 243-49.

NEWMAN-THEORISTS ———, "The Recognition of Sonata Form by Theorists of the 18th and 19th Centuries," *Papers of the American Musicological Society,* 1941 (printed 1946), pp. 21-29.

NEWMAN-THIRTEENm ——— (ed.), *Thirteen Keyboard Sonatas of the 18th and 19th Centuries.* Chapel Hill: The University of North Carolina Press, 1947.

NEWMAN-TREND ———, "The Present Trend of the Sonata Idea," unpublished Ph.D. dissertation, Western Reserve University, 1939.

NEWMAN-UNDERSTANDING ———, *Understanding Music.* New York: Harper & Brothers, 1953.

NEWTON-SCARLATTI Richard Newton, "The English Cult of Domenico Scarlatti," ML, XX (1939), 138-156.

NIEDT Friedrich Erhardt Niedt, *Musicalische Handleitung,* 3 vols. Hamburg: B. Schiller, 1706, 1721 (3d ed.), and 1717, respectively.

NIEMÖLLER-ROSIERm Ursel Niemöller (ed.), *Carl Rosier: Ausgewählte Instrumentalwerke.* Düsseldorf: Schwann, 1957.

NORTH-GRAMARIAN Roger North, *The Musicall Gramarian (ca. 1728),* edited by Hilda Andrews. London: Oxford University Press, 1925.

NOTES *Music Library Association Notes,* Second Series. 1943—.

NZM *Neue Zeitschrift für Musik.* 1834—.

OESTERLEm Louis Oesterle (ed.), *The Golden Treasury of Piano Music,* 5 vols. New York: G. Schirmer, 1904-09.

OLIVER-ENCYCLOPEDISTS Alfred Richard Oliver, *The Encyclopedists as Critics of Music.* New York: Columbia University Press, 1947.

ORGANUMm Max Seiffert (ed.), *Organum: Ausgewählte ältere vokale und instrumentale Meisterwerke.* Leipzig: Fr. Kistner & C. F. W. Siegel (later, London: Novello), 1923—.

PANCALDI & RONCAGLIA Evaristo Pancaldi and Gino Roncaglia, "Maestri di Capella del Duomo di Modena," Nos. V, VII, and VIII of the series, in *R. Deputazione di storia patria per l'Emilia e la Romagna, Studi e documenti, Sezione di Modena,* III-V (1939-41).

PANNAIN-PIANISTICA Guido Pannain, *Le Origini e lo sviluppo dell' arte pianistica in Italia.* Naples: Raffaele Izzo, 1917.

PAPTM *Publikation älterer praktischer und theoretischer Musikwerke,* 29 vols. 1873-1905.

PARIBENI Giulio Cesare Paribeni, "Francesco Durante cembalista," IP, II (1921), 303-307.

PASINI Francesco Pasini, "Notes sur la Vie de Giovanni Battista Bassani," SIMG, VII (1905-06), 581-607.

PAUER-ARNEm Ernst Pauer (ed.), *Arne: Popular Pieces, 8 Sonatas.* London: Augener (*ca.* 1895).

PAUER-MEISTERm ———, *Alte Meister, Sammlung wertvoller Klavierstücke des 17. und 18. Jahrhunderts,* 6 vols. Leipzig: Breitkopf & Härtel (1868-85).

PAUMGARTNER-DEGLI Bernhard Paumgartner (ed.), *Pietro Degli Antoni:* ANTONIm *Tre Sonate,* Op. 5 (Nos. 1, 4, and 6). Zurich: Hug, 1947.

PAUMGARTNER- ———(ed.), *Francesco Durante, Sei Studii e sei* DURANTEm *divertimenti.* Kassel und Basel: Bärenreiter-Verlag, 1949.

PENTE & ZANONm Emilio Pente and Maffeo Zanon (eds.), *Giuseppe Tartini: Undici Sonate e un Minuetto variato per violino con pianforte.* Trieste: C. Schmidl, 1911.

PERGOLESIm Giovanni Battista Pergolesi, *Opera omnia,* 5 vols., edited by Duke Filippo Caffarelli. Rome: Gli Amici della Musica da Camera, 1940-42.

PERRACHIO-VITALI Luigi Perrachio, "Dodici sonate di Tomaso Antonio Vitali trovate a Torino," IP, VI (1925), 344-346.

PEYROT & REBUFAT- J. Peyrot and J. Rebufat (eds.), *Clérambault: 7me* CLÉRAMBAULTm *Sonate en mi mineur (La Magnifique) pour 2 violons et piano.* Paris: M. Senart (1910).

PILKINGTON C. Vere Pilkington, "A Collection of English 18th Century Harpsichord Music," PMA, LXXXIII (1956-57), 89-107.

PIMG *Publikationen der Internationalen Musikgesellschaft,* Beihefte. 1901-02, 1905-14.

PINCHERLE-CORELLI Marc Pincherle, *Corelli et son temps.* Paris: Plon, 1954. The English translations of PINCHERLE-CORELLI and -VIVALDI/1955 (New York: W. W. Norton, 1956 and 1957), which have the advantage of indexes, appeared too recently for reference in this study.

PINCHERLE-EDIZIONE ———, "L'Edizione delle opere di Antonio Vivaldi," RAM, XXI (1951), 134-138.

PINCHERLE-FEUILLETS ———, *Feuillets d'histoire du violon.* Paris: G. Legouix, 1927.

PINCHERLE-LECLAIR ———, *Jean-Marie Leclair l'aîné.* Paris: La Colombe, 1952.

PINCHERLE-LECLAIRm I ——— (ed.), *Jean-Marie Leclair l'aîné: Six sonates pour deux violons sans basse,* Op. 3. Paris: Maurice Sénart, 1924-25.

PINCHERLE-LECLAIRm II ——— (ed.), *Jean-Marie Leclair l'aîné: Six Sonates pour violon et clavecin ou piano* (Sons. 8 in Op. 1, 1 and 12 in Op. 2, 1 and 4 in Op. 5, 4 in Op. 9). Monaco: Oiseau-Lyre, 1952.

PINCHERLE-OSPITALI ———, "Vivaldi and the *Ospitali* of Venice," MQ, XXIV (1938), 300-312.

PINCHERLE-PIRATERIE ———, "De la piraterie dans l'édition musicale aux environs de 1700," REV. DE MUS., XIV (1933), 136-140.

PINCHERLE-QUARTET ———, "On the Origins of the String-Quartet," MQ, XV (1929), 77-87.

PINCHERLE-RINALDI ———, Review of Mario Rinaldi's *Arcangelo Corelli* (Milan, 1953), REV. DE MUS., XXXV (1953), 92 ff.

PINCHERLE-VIOLINISTES ———, *Les Violinistes.* Paris: Renouard, 1922.

PINCHERLE-VIVALDI ———, *Antonio Vivaldi et la musique instrumentale,* 2 vols. Paris: Floury, 1948.

PINCHERLE-VIVALDI/ ———, *Vivaldi.* Paris: Plon, 1955.
1955

PIRRO-ALLEMAGNE André Pirro, "La Musique en Allemagne pendant le XVIIe siècle et la première moitié du XVIIIe," ENCYCLOPÉDIE, I, Part 2, 971-1013.

PIRRO-BUXTEHUDE ———, *Dietrich Buxtehude.* Paris: Librairie Fischbacher, 1913.

PIRRO-CLAVECINISTES ———, *Les Clavecinistes.* Paris: Renouard (1925).

PIRRO-ORGANISTES ———, "L'Art des organistes," ENCYCLOPÉDIE, II, 1181-1374.

PIRRO-REINKEN ———, "Notes pour servir, eventuellement, à la biographie de Reincken," in *Gedenboek aangeboden aan Dr. D. F. Scheurleer op zijn 70sten verjaardog* (The Hague: Martinus Nijhoff, 1925), pp. 251-266.

PLAYFORD John Playford, *An Introduction to the Skill of Musick,* 16th ed. London: William Pearson, 1713.

PMA *Proceedings of the (Royal) Musical Association.* 1874—.

POLO-TARTINIm Enrico Polo (ed.), *Sei Sonate per Violino di Giuseppe Tartini* (Op. 1, Nos. 1, 3, 4, 5, 10 and Op. 2, No. 12). Milan: G. Ricordi, 1921.

POSCH Franz Posch, *Stefano Bernardi's weltliche Vokal- und Instrumental-Werke.* Salzburg, 1935.

POUGIN Arthur Pougin, *Le Violon: Les Violinistes et la musique de violon du XVIe au XVIIIe siècle.* Paris: Fischbacher, 1924.

PRAETORIUS-SYNTAGMA Michael Praetorius, *Syntagma musicum,* 3 vols. Wolffenbüttel: E. Holwein, 1615-20.

PRALLm   Margaret Prall (ed.), *Alessandro Scarlatti: Third String Quartet* (with preface, "The String Quartets of A. Scarlatti"), *The Musical Mercury,* III, Part 1 (March, 1936).

PRATELLA   F. Balilla Pratella, "Le Sonate per Clavicembalo di Pier Giuseppe Sandoni," IP, I (1920), 7-9.

PUBBLICAZIONI   *Bollettino dell'Associazione dei musicologi italiani.* 1909—.

PUBBLICAZIONI-MODENA   Biblioteca Estense di Modena (Series VII).

PUBBLICAZIONI-NAPOLI   Biblioteca del R. Conserv. di Musica di Napoli (in Series X).

PUBBLICAZIONI-PETRONIO   Archivio di S. Petronio di Bologna (in Series II).

PUBBLICAZIONI-TORINO   Biblioteca nazionale di Torino (in Series XII).

PUBBLICAZIONI-VENEZIA   Biblioteca di S. Marco di Venezia (in Series VI).

PULVER-BACH   Jeffrey Pulver, "Bach's Solo Sonatas and Partitas for the Violin," serially in *The Strad,* XXXVII-XL (1926-29).

PULVER-ENGLISH   ———, *A Biographical Dictionary of Old English Music.* London: Kegan Paul, Trench, Trubner, 1927.

PURCELL-WORKSm   W. H. Cummings (ed.), *The Works of Henry Purcell.* London: Novello, Ewer (for the Purcell Society), from 1889.

QUANTZ-FACSIMILE   Johann Joachim Quantz, *Versuch einer Anweisung die flute traversière zu spielen,* 3d ed. (Berlin, 1789). Facsimile. Kassel: Bärenreiter-Verlag, 1953. Translated by Edward R. Reilly, unpublished Ph.D. dissertation, University of Michigan, 1958; published as *On Playing the Flute* (New York: The Free Press, 1966). See Addenda 116a to p. 277.

RABSCHm   Edgar Rabsch (ed.), *Diedrich Becker:* Sonatas à 3-5 from *Musikalische Frühlingsfrüchte,* in *D. Rahter's Kammer-Orchester,* Nos. 5-7. Leipzig: D. Rahter (1932).

RADICIOTTI   Giuseppe Radiciotti, *Pergolesi.* Milan: S. A. Fratelli Treves, 1935.

RAM   *Rassegna musicale.* 1928—.

RATZ-FORMENLEHRE   Erwin Ratz, *Einfürhung in die musikalische Formenlehre.* Vienna: Österreichischer Bundesverlag, 1951.

REEDm — Phyllis Reed (ed.), "XVII Sonate da organo o cembalo del Sig Ziani Polaroli Bassani e altre famosi autori" (score with preface, after 2d ed., Amsterdam, 1716), unpublished master's thesis, Smith College, 1937.

REESE-RENAISSANCE — Gustave Reese, *Music in the Renaissance.* New York: W. W. Norton, 1954.

REFOULÉ — Robert Refoulé, *La Sonate pour piano.* Orleans: Paul Pigelet, 1922.

REIMANN-FANTASIA — Margarete Reimann, "Zur Deutung des Begriffs Fantasia," AFMW, X (1953), 253-274.

REITZm — Robert Reitz (ed.), *Heinrich Franz Biber: Fünfzehn Mysterien.* Vienna: Universal Edition, 1923.

REV. DE MUS. — *Revue de musicologie,* founded in 1917 as *Bulletin de la société française de musicologie.*

RICORDI — Claudio Sartori (ed.), *Enciclopedia della musica,* 4 vols. Milan: G. Ricordi, 1963-64.

RICORDI ARTEIn — *Arte antica e moderna,* 21 vols. Milan: G. Ricordi, from *ca.* 1890.

RIEMANN-ABACOm — Hugo Riemann (ed.), *Sonata da camera [SS/bass] ... Op. 3, No. 7 ... by Evaristo Felice dall'Abaco.* London: Augener (1898).

RIEMANN-BEISPIELEM — ———, *Musikgeschichte in Beispielen,* 2d ed., with annotations by Arnold Schering. Leipzig: Breitkopf & Härtel, 1921.

RIEMANN-CHAMBERm — ———, *Old Chamber Music,* a selection of canzonas, sonatas, etc., 4 vols. London: Augener (1898).

RIEMANN-KOMPOSITIONSLEHRE — ———, *Grosse Kompositionslehre,* 3 vols. Berlin: W. Spemann, 1902-13.

RIEMANN-LEXIKON — *Hugo Riemanns Musik Lexikon,* 11th ed., edited by Alfred Einstein, 2 vols. Berlin: Max Hesses Verlag, 1929.

RIEMANN-MUSIKGESCHICHTE — ———, *Handbuch der Musikgeschichte,* vol. II, Parts 1-3, 2d ed., edited by Alfred Einstein. Leipzig: Breitkopf & Härtel, 1920-22.

RIEMANN-SUITE — ———, "Zur Geschichte der deutschen Suite," SIMG, VI (1904-05), 501-520.

RIEMANN-TRIOSONATEN — ———, "Die Triosonaten der Generalbass-Epoche," in *Präludien und Studien* (Munich: Aula, 1901), III, 129-156.

RIETSCH-FUX — Heinrich Rietsch, "Der 'Concentus' von Johann Josef Fux," SZMW, IV (1916), 46-57.

RIKKO-LOEILLETm — Fritz Rikko (ed.), *Loeillet: Six Sonatas for Two Violins and Figured Bass,* 2 vols. New York: Weaner-Levant, 1945.

RIKKO-TELEMANNm ——, *Telemann: Six Sonatas for Two Violins, Flutes or Recorders*, 2 vols. New York: Weaner-Levant, 1944.

RIM *La Revue internationale de musique.* 1939—.

RINALDI-CORELLI Mario Rinaldi, *Arcangelo Corelli.* Milan: Edizioni Curci, 1953.

RINALDI-VIVALDI ——, *Antonio Vivaldi.* Milan: Istituto d'alta cultura, 1943.

RINALDI-VIVALDI/1945 ——, *Catalogo numerico tematico delle composizioni di Antonio Vivaldi.* Rome: Editrice Cultura moderna (1945?).

RM *La Revue musicale* (founded by Prunières). 1920—.

RMC *La Revue musicale* (founded by Combarieu). 1901-1910.

RMI *Rivista musicale italiana.* 1894—.

ROLLAND-ESSAYS *Romain Rolland's Essays on Music.* New York: Allen, Towne & Heath, 1948.

RONCAGLIA-COLOMBI Gino Roncaglia, "Giuseppe Colombi e la vita musicale modenese durante il regno di Francesco II d'Este," in *Accademia di scienze lettere e arti di Modena, Atti e memorie*, Series 5, X (1952), 31-52.

RONCAGLIA-STRADELLA ——, "Le composizioni strumentali di Alessandro Stradella esistenti presso la R. Biblioteca Estense di Modena," RMI, XLIV (1940), 81-105 and 337-350.

RONGA Luigi Ronga, *Gerolamo Frescobaldi.* Torino: Fratelli Bocca, 1930.

ROSENTHAL-BACH Karl August Rosenthal, "Über Sonatenformen in den Instrumentalwerken Joh. Seb. Bachs," BJ, XXIII (1926), 68-89.

ROUSSEAU-DICTIONNAIRE Jean Jacques Rousseau, *Dictionnaire de musique*, 2 vols. Amsterdam: M. M. Rey, 1768.

ROWEN Ruth Halle Rowen, *Early Chamber Music.* New York: King's Crown Press, 1949.

RUBARDT-CROFTm Paul Rubardt (ed.), *William Croft: Sechs Sonaten für zwei Blockflöten oder andere Melodieinstrumente.* Kassel: Nagels Verlag (1932).

RUBARDT-FINGERm ——, *Gottfried Finger: Sonata für Flöte, Oboe oder Violine und Bass.* Kassel: Nagels Verlag (1932).

RUDGE Olga Rudge, "Antonio Vivaldi," in *Grove's Supplementary Volume* (New York: The Macmillan Co., 1940), pp. 653-657.

RUYSSEN & GRUSSARDm C. A. P. Ruyssen and Cl. G. Grussard (eds.), *Giacomo Cervetto: Six Sonates* (SS/bass). Paris: P. Schneider, 1926.

SACHS-INSTRUMENTS Curt Sachs, *The History of Musical Instruments.* New York: W. W. Norton, 1940.

SAINT/FOIX Theodore de Wyzewa (vols. I and II only) and Georges de Saint-Foix, *Mozart,* 5 vols. Paris: Desclée de Brouwer, 1912-46.

SAINT/FOIX-PERGOLESI Georges de Saint-Foix, "Pergolesi (1710-36)," RMI, XLI (1937), 24-30.

SAINT/GEORGEm G. Saint-George (ed.), *Attilio Ariosti: Sei Lezioni,* transcribed for violin and piano. London: Augener, 1901.

SALMON-CELLOm Joseph Salmon (ed.), *Oeuvres d'auteurs anciens harmonisée pour violoncelle avec accompagnement de piano.* Paris: Société anonyme des Éditions Ricordi (founded *ca.* 1914).

SALTER Lewis S. Salter, "An Index to Ricordi's Edition of Vivaldi," NOTES, XI (1954), 366-374.

SANDBERGER-KLAVIERMUSIK Adolf Sandberger, "Zur älteren italienischen Klaviermusik," JMP, XXV (1918), 17-25.

SARACINI Guido Chigi Saracini, "Azzolino Bernardino Della Ciaia," Bulletino dell'Accademia musicale chigiana, III, Part 1 (March, 1950), 1-11. (The promised continuation had not appeared by the end of 1957.)

SARTORI-BIBLIOGRAFIA Claudio Sartori, *Bibliografia della musica strumentale italiana stampata in Italia fino al 1700; Volume secondo di aggiunte e correzioni con nuovi indici* (cf. NOTES, XXVI [1970], 738-739 [O. Jander]). Florence: Leo S. Olschki, 1952; 1968.

SARTORI-SCARLATTI ———, "Appendice" in CLASSICIm II, No. 13, 131-134.

SARTORI-"44" ———, "Le quarantaquattro edizioni italiane delle sei opere di Corelli" (raised to 46 in a postscript), RMI, LV (1953), 29-53.

SARTORI-"51" ———, "Sono 51 (fino ad ora) le edizioni italiane delle opere di Corelli e 135 gli esemplari noti," in *Collectanea historiae musicae II* (Florence: Leo S. Olschki, 1956), pp. 379-389.

SCE William S. Newman, *The Sonata in the Classic Era.* Chapel Hill: The University of North Carolina Press, 1963.

SCHAEFER/SCHMUCK Käte Schaefer-Schmuck, *Georg Philipp Telemann als Klavierkomponist.* Leipzig: Robert Noske, 1934.

SCHÄFKE Rudolf Schäfke, "Quantz als Asthetiker," AFMW, VI (1924), 213-242.

SCHEIBE-CRITISCHER Johann Adolph Scheibe, *Critischer Musikus.* Leipzig: Bernhard Christoph Breitkopf, 1745.

SCHENK-GRAUN Erich Schenk, "Zur Bibliographie der Triosonaten von Joh. Gottl. und Carl Heinr. Graun," ZFMW, XI (1928-29), 420-422.

SCHENK-MODENESE ———, "Osservazioni sulla scuola istrumental modenese nel seicento," in *Accademia di scienze lettere e arti di Modena, Atti e memorie*, Series 5, X (1952), 3-30.

SCHENK-NEUAUSGABEN ———, "Neuausgaben alter Musikwerke," ZFMW, XII (1929-30), 247-252.

SCHENK-TRIOSONATEm ——— (ed.), *Die italienische Triosonate* (in *Das Musikwerk* series). Köln: Arno Volk-Verlag (1954?).

SCHERING-BEISPIELEm Arnold Schering (ed.), *Geschichte der Musik in Beispielen*. Leipzig: Breitkopf & Härtel, 1931.

SCHERING-INSTRU- ———, *Geschichte des Instrumentalkonzerts*, 2d ed.
MENTALKONZERT Leipzig: Breitkopf & Härtel, 1927.

SCHERING-LEIPZIG ———, *Musikgeschichte Leipzigs*, vol. II. Leipzig: Fr. Kistner & C. F. W. Siegel, 1926.

SCHERING-REICHE ———, "Zu Gottfried Reiches Leben und Kunst," BJ, XV (1918), 133-140.

SCHERING-SOLOSONATE ———, "Zur Geschichte der Solosonate in der ersten Hälfte des 17. Jahrhunderts," in *Riemann-Festschrift* (Leipzig: Max Hesses Verlag, 1909), pp. 309-324.

SCHEURLEER-LECLAIR Daniel François Scheurleer, "Jean Marie Leclair L'aîné in Holland," SIMG, X (1908-09), 259-262.

SCHLOSSBERG Artur Schlossberg, *Die italienische Sonata für mehrere Instrumente im 17. Jahrhundert*. Heidelberg: Heidelberger (University) Studien, 1932 (actually, 1936?).

SCHMID-SÄCHSISCHENm Otto Schmid (ed.), *Musik am sächsischen Hofe VI*. Leipzig, 1904.

SCHMIDL Carlo Schmidl, *Dizionario universale dei musicisti*, 2 vols. and "Supplemento." Milan: Sonzogno, 1926 and 1938.

SCHMIEDER-BWV Wolfgang Schmieder, *Thematisch-Systematisches Verzeichnis der musikalischen Werke von Johann Sebastian Bach*. Leipzig: Breitkopf & Härtel, 1950.

SCHMITZ-BIBER Eugen Schmitz, "Bibers Rosenkranzsonaten," *Musica*, V (1951), 235-236.

SCHNEIDER-BESETZUNG Max Schneider, "Die Besetzung der vielstimmigen Musik des 17. und 16. Jahrhunderts," AFMW, I (1918-19), 205-234.

SCHNEIDER-BIBER ———, "Zu Biber's Violinsonaten," ZIMG, VIII (1906-07), 471-474.

SCHNEIDER-FASCH Clemens August Schneider, *Johann Friedrich Fasch als Sonatenkomponist*. Münster: Westfälischen Wilhelms-Universität (1932).

448 BIBLIOGRAPHY

SCHNEIDER-SALZBURG — Constantin Schneider, *Geschichte der Musik in Salzburg von der ältesten Zeit bis zur Gegenwart.* Salzburg: Verlag R. Kiesel, 1935.

SCHÖKEL — Heinrich Peter Schökel, *Johann Christian Bach und die Instrumentalmusik seiner Zeit.* Wolfenbüttel: Georg Kallmeyer Verlag, 1926.

SCHOTT ANTIQUAm — *Antiqua, eine Sammlung alter Musik Meisterwerke des 13.-18. Jahrhunderts.* Mainz: B. Schott's Söhne, from 1933.

SCHOTT CELLOm — *Cello-Bibliothek klassischer Sonaten.* Mainz: B. Schott's Söhne (*ca.* 1930).

SCHRADE-MILANm — Leo Schrade (ed.), *Luys Milan: Libro de musica de vihuele de mano intitulado El Maestro.* Leipzig: Breitkopf & Härtel, 1927.

SCHRADE-MONTEVERDI — Leo Schrade, *Monteverdi, Creator of Modern Music.* New York: W. W. Norton, 1950.

SCHRAMMEK — Winfried Schrammek, "Die Musikgeschichtliche Stellung der Orgeltriosonaten von Joh. Seb. Bach," BJ, XLI (1954), 7-28.

SCHREITER-QUANTZm — Heinz Schreiter (ed.), *Johann Joachim Quantz: Sonate in E moll* (S/bass). Leipzig: Breitkopf & Härtel, 1934.

SCHROEDER-BACH — Ralph Schroeder, "Über das Problem des mehrstimmigen Spiels in J. S. Bachs Violinsolosonaten," in *Bach-Probleme* (Leipzig: C. F. Peters, 1950), pp. 74-80.

SCHROEDER-CELLOm — Carl Schroeder (ed.), *Classical Violoncello Music* by celebrated masters of the 17th and 18th centuries. London: Augener (1895).

SCHUBART — Christian Friedrich Daniel Schubart, *Ideen zu einer Ästhetik der Tonkunst.* Vienna: Degen, 1806.

SCHÜZ — A. Schüz, "Die Sonate: Ihre geschichtliche Entwickelung," serially in *Neue Musik-Zeitung,* XXIII and XXIV (1902-03).

SCHWEITZER-BACH — Albert Schweitzer, *J. S. Bach,* translated by Ernest Newman, 2 vols. London: Adam and Charles Black, 1935.

SCHWEITZER-GEIGENBOGEN — ——, "Der für Bachs Werke für Violine solo erforderte Geigenbogen," in *Bach-Gedenkschrift 1950* (Zürich: Atlantis Verlag, 1950), pp. 75-83.

SCOTT-VIOLIN — Marion M. Scott, "The Violin Music of Handel and Bach," ML, XVI (1935), 188-199.

SEIBEL — Gustav Adolph Seibel, *Das Leben des Königl. Polnischen und Kurfürstl. Sachs. Hofkapellmeisters Johann David Heinichen.* Leipzig: Breitkopf & Härtel, 1913.

SEIFFERT-HÄNDEL — Max Seiffert, "Zu Händel's Klavierwerken," SIMG, I (1899-1900), 131-141.

SEIFFERT-KLAVIERMUSIK — ———, *Geschichte der Klaviermusik* (completed only to 1750 but published as 3d ed. of WEITZMANN). Leipzig: Breitkopf & Härtel, 1899.

SEIFFERT-WECKMANN — ———, "Matthias Weckmann und das Collegium Musicum in Hamburg," SIMG, II (1900-01), 76-132.

SELVA — Blanche Selva, *La Sonate*. Paris: Rouart, Lerolle, 1913.

SENN-INNSBRUCK — Walter Senn, *Musik und Theater am Hof zu Innsbruck*. Innsbruck: Österreichische Verlagsanstalt, 1954.

SHANET-BACH — Howard Shanet, "Why Did J. S. Bach Transpose his Arrangements?" MQ, XXXVI (1950), 180-203.

SHEDLOCK-PASQUINIm — John South Shedlock (ed.), *Selection of Pieces Composed for the Harpsichord*. London: Novello & Ewer (1895?).

SHEDLOCK-SCARLATTI — ———, "The Harpsichord Music of Alessandro Scarlatti," SIMG, VI (1904-05), 160-178.

SHEDLOCK-SONATA — ———, *The Pianoforte Sonata*. London: Methuen, 1895. Reprint by Da Capo Press of New York, 1964, with Foreword by W. S. Newman.

SIEGELE — Ulrich Siegele, "Noch einmal: Die Violinsonate BWV 1024," BJ, XLIII (1956), 124-139.

SILBERT & PARKER & ROODm — Doris Silbert, Gertrude Parker, Louise Rood (eds.), *Tommaso Antonio Vitali: Concerto di Sonate, Op. 4; for violin, violoncello, and continuo*. Northampton: Smith College Music Archives, 1954.

SIMG — *Sammelbände der Internationalen Musikgesellschaft*. 1900-14.

SITTARD — Josef Sittard, "Samuel Capricornus Contra Philipp Friedrich Böddecker," SIMG, III (1901-02), 87-128.

SLONIMSKY-THING — Nicolas Slonimsky, *A Thing or Two About Music*. New York: Crown Publishers, 1949.

SMITH-HANDEL — William C. Smith, *Concerning Handel*. London: Cassell, 1948.

SMITH-WALSH — ———, *A Bibliography of the Musical Works Published by John Walsh during the years 1695-1720*. London: Printed for the Bibliographical Society at the University Press, Oxford, 1948. In 1968 a 2d vol. appeared, 1721-66 (co-authored by Charles Humphries).

SOHLMANS — *Sohlmans Musiklexikon*, 4 vols. Stockholm: Sohlmans Förlag, 1951-52.

SOLERTI-ORIGINI — Angelo Solerti, *Le Origini del melodramma*. Torino: Fratelli Bocca, 1903.

SONNECK
Oscar George Sonneck, *Early Concert-Life in America* (1731-1800). Leipzig: Breitkopf & Härtel, 1907.

SONNECK & UPTON
———, *A Bibliography of Early Secular American Music,* revised and enlarged by William Treat Upton. Washington: The Library of Congress, 1945.

SPEER-KLEEBLATT
Daniel Speer, *Vierfaches musicalisches Kleeblatt.* Ulm: G. W. Kühnen, 1697.

SPITTA-AUFSÄTZE
Philipp Spitta, *Musikgeschichtliche Aufsätze.* Berlin: Gebruder Paetel, 1894.

SPITTA-BACH
———, *Johann Sebastian Bach,* trans. from the German by Clara Bell and J. A. Fuller Maitland, 3 vols. London: Novello, 1899.

SPITTA-FRIEDRICH
———, "Musikalische Werke Friedrichs des Grossen," VFMW, V (1889), 350-362, and VI (1890), 430-436.

SPITTA-FRIEDRICHm
——— (ed.), *Friedrich des Grossen musikalischen Werke,* 4 vols. Leipzig: Breitkopf & Härtel, 1899.

SQUIRE-CLOCK
William Barclay Squire, "Handel's Clock Music," MQ, V (1919), 538-552.

SQUIRE-CORELLI
———, " 'A Corelli Forgery,' " MT, LXII (1921), 720.

SQUIRE-ECCLES
———, "Henry Eccles's Borrowings," MT, LXIV (1923), 790.

SQUIRE-PURCELL I
———, "Purcell as Theorist," SIMG, VI (1904-05), 521-567.

SQUIRE-PURCELL II
———, "Purcell and Italian Music," MT, LVIII (1917), 157.

SQUIRE & FULLER/ MAITLANDm
W. Barclay Squire and J. A. Fuller Maitland (eds.), *Pieces for Harpsichord by G. F. Händel,* 2 vols. Mainz and Leipzig: B. Schott's Söhne, 1928.

STAHL-BUXTEHUDE
Wilhelm Stahl, *Dietrich Buxtehude,* 2d ed. Kassel: Bärenreiter-Verlag, 1952.

STAHL-REINKEN
———, "Zur Biographie Johann Adam Reinken's," AFMW, III (1921), 232-236.

STEVENS-BODLEIAN
Denis Stevens, "Seventeenth-Century Italian Instrumental Music in the Bodleian Library," AM, XXVI (1954), 67-74.

STEVENS-UNIQUE
———, "Unique Italian Instrumental Music in the Bodleian Library," in *Collectanea historiae musicae II* (Florence: Leo S. Olschki, 1956), pp. 401-412.

STILLINGS
Frank S. Stillings, "Arcangelo Corelli," unpublished Ph.D. dissertation, The University of Michigan (Ann Arbor), 1955.

STILZ — Ernst Stilz, *Die Berliner Klaviersonate zur Zeit Friedrichs der Grossen.* Saarbrücken: Friedrich-Wilhelms Universität, 1930.

STONE-ITALIAN — David Stone, "The Italian Sonata for Harpsichord and Pianoforte in the Eighteenth Century (1730-90)," 3 vols., unpublished Ph.D. dissertation, Harvard University, 1952.

STONE-KUHNAUm — Kurt Stone (ed.), *Johann Kuhnau: Six Biblical Sonatas,* with English translation of Kuhnau's preface. New York: Broude Brothers, 1953.

STRAETEN-FIDDLE — Edmund S. J. van der Straeten, *The Romance of the Fiddle.* London: Rebman, 1911.

STRAETEN-VIOLONCELLO — ———, *History of the Violoncello, the Viol da gamba.* . . . London: William Reeves, 1915.

STRAUWENm — Jean Strauwen (ed.), *François Martin: Sonate en mi mineur, violoncelle et piano.* Paris: Maurice Senart, 1923.

STRIFFLING — Louis Striffling, *Esquisse d'une histoire du goût musical en France au xviiie siècle.* Paris: Delagrave, 1912.

STRUNK-READINGS — Oliver Strunk, *Source Readings in Music History.* New York: W. W. Norton, 1950.

STUDENY — Bruno Studeny, *Beiträge zur Geschichte der Violinsonate im 18. Jahrhundert.* Munich: Wunderhorn-Verlag, 1911.

STUDENY-PISENDELm — ——— (ed.), *Johann Georg Pisendel: Sonate für Violine allein ohne Bass.* Munich: Wunderhorn-Verlag, 1911.

SUBIRA-ALBA — José Subirá, *La Música en la casa de Alba.* Madrid: Sucesores de Rivadeneyra, 1927.

SULZER-ALLGEMEINE — Johann George Sulzer, *Allgemeine Theorie der Schönen Künste,* 2d printing, 4 vols. Leipzig: M. G. Weidmanns Erben und Reich, 1773-75.

SZMW — *Studien zur Musikwissenschaft,* Beihefte of DTÖm, 1913-34.

TAGLIAPIETRAm — Gino Tagliapietra (ed.), *Antologia di musica antica e moderna,* 18 vols. Milan: G. Ricordi, 1931.

TANGEMAN-MOZART — Robert S. Tangeman, "Mozart's Seventeen Epistle Sonatas," MQ, XXXII (1946), 588-601.

TESSIER-COUPERIN — André Tessier, *Couperin.* Paris: Renouard, 1926.

TIERSOT-COUPERIN — Julien Tiersot, *Les Couperin.* Paris: Félix Alcan, 1926.

TIERSOT-NATIONS — ———, "Les Nations, Sonates en trio de François Couperin," REV. DE MUS., VI (1922), 50-58.

452 BIBLIOGRAPHY

TORCHI Luigi Torchi, *La musica istrumentale in Italia nei secoli XVI, XVII e XVIII.* Torino: Fratelli Bocca, 1901.

TORCHIm —— (ed.), *L'Arte musicale in Italia,* 7 vols. Milan: G. Ricordi, 1897-1907.

TORREFRANCA Fausto Torrefranca, *Le Origini italiane del romanticismo musicale: i primitivi della sonata moderna.* Torino: Fratelli Bocca, 1930.

TORREFRANCA-DELLA CIAJA ——, "L'impressionismo ritmico e le Sonate del cavalier della Ciaja," *Vita musicale* (Milan), June and July, 1913.

TORREFRANCA-RICOGNIZIONI ——, "Prime Ricognizioni dello stile violoncellistico Plattiano," IMS, 4th Congress (Basel, 1949), pp. 203-211.

TOVEY-BACHm Donald Francis Tovey (ed.), *J. S. Bach: Forty-Eight Preludes and Fugues,* 4 vols. New York: Oxford University Press, 1924.

TRÉSORm *Le Trésor des Pianistes,* 20 vols. Paris: Aristide and Louise Farrenc, 1861-1872.

TVNM *Tijdschrift der Vereeniging voor nederlandsche Musiekgeschiedenis.* 1882—.

UPMEYER-JACCHINIm Walter Upmeyer (ed.), *Giuseppe Jacchini: Op. 5, Nr. 3, Triosonate G-Dur für 2 Violinen, Violoncello und Cembalo.* Berlin-Lichterfelde: Chr. Friedrich Vieweg, 1936.

UPMEYER-VIVALDIm ——, *Antonio Vivaldi, Op. 1, Sonata da camera a tre.* Kassel: Bärenreiter-Ausgabe 351/2, 1949.

VALENTIN Erich Valentin, *Georg Philipp Telemann,* 3d ed. Kassel: Bärenreiter-Verlag, 1952.

VATIELLI-BOLOGNA Francesco Vatielli, *Arte e vita musicale a Bologna.* Bologna: Nicola Zanichelli, 1927.

VATIELLI-CORELLI ——, "Il Corelli e i maestri bolognesi del suo tempo," RMI, XXIII (1916), 173-200 and 390-412.

VATIELLI-MAESTRIm —— (ed.), *Antichi maestri Bolognesi,* Musica strumentale (vol. II). Bologna: C. Venturi (1914).

VFMW *Vierteljahrsschrift für Musikwissenschaft.* 1884-94.

VIDAL Antoine Vidal, *Les Instruments à archet,* 3 vols. Paris: J. Claye, 1876-78.

VILLANIS-CLAVECINISTES Luigi Alberto Villanis, "Les clavecinistes," ENCYCLOPÉDIE, I, Part 2, 798-814.

VIOLLIER Renée Viollier, "Les sonates pour violon et les sonates en trio d'Elisabeth Jacquet de La Guerre et de Jean-François d'Andrieu," *Schweizerische Musikzeitung,* IX (1951), 349-351.

BIBLIOGRAPHY

453

VITALI-MARTINImi — Mario Vitali (ed.), *Padre Giambattista Martini: Dodici Sonate per cembalo od organo.* Milan: G. Ricordi, n. d.

VIVALDImi — *Istituto italiano Antonio Vivaldi,* fondato da Antonio Fauna, direzione artistica di Gian Francesco Malipiero. Milan: Ricordi, from 1947 (index, 1955).

VNMm — *Vereeniging voor Nederlands Muziekgeschiedenis,* Uitgaven. Amsterdam: G. Alsbach, from 1869.

VOIGT — F. A. Voigt, "Reinhard Keiser," vfMW, VI (1890), 151-203.

VOLKMANN — Hans Volkmann, "Sylvius Leopold Weiss, der letzte grosse Lautenist," DM, VI, Part 3 (1906-07), 273-289.

VRETBLADm — Petrik Vretblad (ed.), *Johann Helmich Roman: 12 Sonate da camera* (S/bass). Stockholm: Elkan & Schildknecht, 1937.

VRETBLAD 1914 — ———, *Johann Helmich Roman,* 2 vols. Stockholm: A.-B. Nordiska, 1914.

VRETBLAD 1945 — ———, *J. H. Roman: Minnesteckning.* Stockholm, 1945.

VV — *Violins and Violinists Magazine.* 1938—.

WAGNER-KRIEGER — Rudolf Wagner, "Beiträge zur Lebensgeschichte Johann Philipp Kriegers und seines Schülers Nikolaus Deinl," zFMW, VIII (1925-26), 146-160.

WALIN — Stig Walin, " 'Sonate a flauto traverso, violone e cembalo da Roman, svedese,' en Stilstudie," *Svensk Tidskrift för Musikforskning,* XXVII (1945), 5-60.

WALKER-PERGOLESI — Frank Walker, "Two Centuries of Pergolesi Forgeries and Misattributions," ML, XXX (1949), 297-320.

WALKER & WESTRUP — Ernest Walker, *A History of Music in England,* 3d ed., revised and enlarged by Jack Allan Westrup. Oxford: Clarendon Press, 1952.

WALTHER-LEXIKON — Johann Gottfried Walther, *Musikalisches Lexikon* (Leipzig: Wolffgang Deer, 1732). Facsimile. Kassel: Bärenreiter-Verlag, 1953.

WASIELEWSKI-XVI — Joseph Wilhelm von Wasielewski, *Geschichte der Instrumentalmusik im XVI. Jahrhundert.* Berlin: J. Guttentag, 1878.

WASIELEWSKI-XVII — ———, *Die Violine im XVII. Jahrhundert und die Anfänge der Instrumentalcomposition.* Bonn: Max Cohen, 1874.

WASIELEWSKI-XVIIm ———— (ed.), *Instrumentalsätze vom Ende des XVI. bis Ende des XVII. Jahrhunderts* (ex. vol. to WASIELEWSKI-XVII). Bonn: Max Cohen, 1874.

WASIELEWSKI-VIOLINE ————, *Die Violine und ihre Meister,* 5th ed., revised and enlarged by Waldemar von Wasielewski. Leipzig: Breitkopf & Härtel, 1910.

WECKERLIN-NOUVEAU Jean Baptiste Théodore Weckerlin, *Nouveau musiciana, extraits d'ouvrages rares ou bizarres.* Paris: Garnier Frères, 1890.

WEIGL Bruno Weigl, *Handbuch der Violoncell-Literatur,* 3d ed. Vienna: Universal-Edition, 1929.

WEITZMANN Karl Friedrich Weitzmann, *A History of Pianoforte Playing,* translated from the 2d German edition of 1879 by Theodore Baker. New York: G. Schirmer. 1897.

WERNER-HANNOVER Theodor Georg Wilhelm Werner, "Die Musikhandschriften des Kestnerschen Nachlasses im Stadtarchiv zu Hannover," ZFMW, I (1918-19), 441-466.

WESTRUP-PURCELL Jack Allan Westrup, *Purcell,* 3d ed. London: J. M. Dent, 1947.

WHITTAKER-BLOWm W. Gillies Whittaker (ed.), *John Blow: Deux Sonates pour deux violons, viole de gamba, et basse.* Paris: L'Oiseau Lyre, 1933.

WHITTAKER-PURCELL ————, "Some Observations on Purcell's Harmony," MT, LXXV (1934), 887-894.

WHITTAKER-PURCELLm ———— (ed.), *Henry Purcell: The First Set of Twelve Sonatas.* Paris: L'Oiseau Lyre, 1936.

WHITTAKER-YOUNG ————, "William Young," in *Collected Essays* (London: Oxford University Press, 1940), pp. 90-98.

WHITTAKER-YOUNGm ———— (ed.), *William Young: Sonata[s] 1-11,* 11 vols. London: Oxford University Press, 1930.

WINTERFELD Carl von Winterfeld, *Johannes Gabrieli und sein Zeitalter,* 3 vols. Berlin: Schlesinger'schen Buch- und Musikhandlung, 1834.

WOEHLm Waldemar Woehl (ed.), *Arcangelo Corelli: 48 Trio-Sonaten* (Opp. 1-4) and *Sonaten für Violine und Generalbass, Op. 5,* 19 vols. Kassel: Bärenreiter-Verlag, 1934-35 and 1944.

WOEHL-FESCHm ————, *Willem de Fesch: Sechs Sonaten für Violine . . . mit Bass,* 2 vols. Kassel: Bärenreiter-Verlag, 1949.

WÖRMANN-ALBERTI Wilhelm Wörmann, "Die Klaviersonate Domenico Albertis," AM, XXVII (1955), 84-112.

WOLF-
NOTATIONSKUNDE

Johannes Wolf, *Handbuch der Notationskunde*, 2 vols. Leipzig: Breitkopf & Härtel, 1913 and 1919.

WOLFFHEIM

Versteigerung der Musikbibliothek des Herrn Dr. Werner Wolffheim, 2 vols. Berlin: Martin Breslauer & Leo Liepmannsohn, 1928.

WOLFFHEIM-BACHIANA

Werner Wolffheim, "Bachiana," BJ, VIII (1911), 37-49.

ZFMW

Zeitschrift für Musikwissenschaft. 1918-35.

ZIMG

Zeitschrift der Internationalen Musikgesellschaft. 1899-1914.

ZWART

Jan Zwart, "Henricus Albicastro in Nederland," *De Muziek*, II (1927-28), 270-271.

Index